HANDBOOK OF

Language &
Ethnic Identity

HANDBOOK OF

Language &
Ethnic Identity

Edited by
JOSHUA A. FISHMAN

New York • Oxford

Oxford University Press

1999

Oxford University Press

Oxford   New York
Athens   Auckland   Bangkok   Bogotá   Buenos Aires   Calcutta
Cape Town   Chennai   Dar es Salaam   Delhi   Florence   Hong Kong   Istanbul
Karachi   Kuala Lumpur   Madrid   Melbourne   Mexico City   Mumbai
Nairobi   Paris   São Paulo   Singapore   Taipei   Tokyo   Toronto   Warsaw

and associated companies in
Berlin   Ibadan

Published by Oxford University Press, Inc.
198 Madison Avenue, New York, New York 10016

Oxford is a registered trademark of Oxford University Press

Library of Congress Cataloging-in-Publication Data
Handbook of language and ethnic identity / edited by
Joshua A. Fishman.
p.   cm.
Includes index.
ISBN-13: 978-0-19-512429-3
1. Language and culture—Handbooks, manuals, etc.
2. Ethnicity—Handbooks, manuals, etc.
3. Areal linguistics—Handbooks, manuals, etc.
I. Fishman, Joshua A.
P35.H34   1999
306.44'089—dc21   98-34984

9 8 7 6 5 4 3 2 1

Printed in the United States of America
on acid-free paper

אַ מתּנה פֿאַר מײַן ייִנגסטן אייניקל,
יעקבֿ-לײב. לאַנג לעבן זאָל ער:
עד-מאה-ועשׂרים, אַ ייִדישער ייִד!

Contents

Contributors

Efurosibina Adegbija, department of modern European languages, University of Ilorin (Nigeria), is the author of *Language Attitudes in Sub-Saharan Africa: A Sociolinguistic Perspective* (1994) and has contributed to the issue on "Sociolinguistic Research in West Africa," a thematic issue of the *International Journal of the Sociology of Language* (1999).

Colin Baker, professor of education, University of Wales, Bangor, is coeditor of *Policy and Practice in Bilingual Education: A Reader Extending the Foundations* (1995) and of the *Encyclopedia of Bilingualism and Bilingual Education* (1998). His *Foundations of Bilingual Education and Bilingualism* (2nd ed., 1996) has been translated into Japanese (1996) and Spanish (1997).

Richard Y. Bourhis, professor of psychology, University of Quebec (Montreal, Canada), is director of the Concordia-UQAM Chair in Ethnic Studies. Among his publications are *Conflict and Language Planning in Quebec* (1984), *Stereotypes, Discrimination et Relations Intergroupes* (1994), and *French-English Language Issues in Canada* (1994).

Florian Coulmas, professor of sociolinguistics, Chuo University (Tokyo, Japan), is associate editor of the *International Journal of the Sociology of Language*. He has edited *Language Adaptation* (1989), *Language and Economy* (1992), *The Handbook of Sociolinguistics* (1997), and *The Blackwell Encyclopedia of Writing Systems* (1996).

Nancy C. Dorian, professor of linguistics in the German and anthropology departments of Bryn Mawr College (Pennsylvania), is the editor of the rubric "Small Languages and Small Language Communities" of the *International Journal of the Sociology of Language*. She is the author of an oral history of the Gaelic-speaking fisherfolk of East Sutherland, Scotland, *The Tyranny of Tide* (1985).

James R. Dow is professor of German and former chair of the department of foreign languages and literatures at Iowa State University (Ames). His most recent publications include *Language and Lives; Essays in Honor of Werner Enninger* (1997) and *Old and New World Anabaptists: Studies on the Language, Culture, Society and Health of the Amish and Mennonites* (1994).

Moha Ennaji, professor of language and linguistics at Sidi Mohamed Ben-Abdellah University (Fez, Morocco), is a coauthor of *Introduction to Applied Linguistics* (1996) and the editor of thematic issues on "Berber Sociolinguistics (1997)," "Sociolinguistics in Morocco (1995)," and "Sociolinguistics of the Maghreb (1991)" in the *International Journal of the Sociology of Language.*

Joshua A. Fishman, Emeritus Distinguished University Research Professor of Social Sciences, Yeshiva University (New York) and visiting professor of linguistics and education, Stanford University (California), is a coeditor of *Post-Imperial English: The Status of English in Former British and American Colonies, 1940–1990* and author of *In Praise of the Beloved Language* (1997).

Ofelia García is dean of the School of Education at Long Island University, Brooklyn Campus (New York). She is a coauthor of *The Rise and Fall of the Ethnic Revival* (1985), editor of *Bilingual Education* (1991), and a coeditor of *English across Cultures, Cultures across English* (1989) and *The Multilingual Apple: Languages in New York City* (1997).

François Grin is assistant professor in the departments of economics at the University of Geneva (Switzerland), senior analyst for Western Europe, and deputy director of the European Center for Minority Issue (Flensburg, Germany). He is the editor of "Economic Approaches to Language and Language Planning" (1996), a thematic issue of the *International Journal of the Sociology of Language.*

Harald Haarmann, Helsinki, has been a professor of linguistics in Germany and Japan. He is the author of some 40 books, among them *Symbolic Values of Foreign Language Use* (1989), *Die Sprachenwelt Europas* (1993), and *Early Civilization and Literacy in Europe* (1995), and the editor of *European Identity and Linguistic Diversity* (1995).

Miroslav Hroch, professor of general history at the Institute of World History, Charles University (Prague, Czech Republic), is the author of *V Zajmu Narodna* [In the Nation's Interest] (1996), *Social Interpretation of the Linguistic Demands in National Movements* (1994), and *Social Preconditions of National Revival in Europe* (1985).

Leena Huss is research fellow at the Center for Multiethnic Research and lecturer in the department of Finno-Ugric languages, Uppsala University (Sweden). She is the editor of *Many Roads to Bilingualism* (in Swedish; 1996).

Sonja L. Lanehart, assistant professor of English and linguistics at the University of Georgia (Athens), has published "The Language of Identity" (*Journal of English Linguistics,* 1996) and "Our Language, Our Selves" (*Journal of Commonwealth and Postcolonial Studies,* 1996).

Karmela Liebkind is professor in the department of social psychology, University of Helsinki (Finland). She is the author of *Minority Identity and Identifica-*

tion Processes (1984) and *New Identities in Europe* (1989). The Council of Europe (Strasbourg) published her "Bilingual Identity" in *European Education* (1995).

Anna-Riitta Lindgren is professor of Finnish in the Faculty of Humanities at the University of Tromsø (Norway). She is the author of *Samis in Helsinki and Their Own Language* (in Finnish; 1999) and of a large number of research papers on Sami and Finnish speakers in Norway.

Teresa L. McCarty, associate professor of language, reading, and culture at the University of Arizona (Tucson), is also codirector of the American Indian Language Development Institute there. She is coauthor of *Mother Earth and Father Sun* (1989) and *Indigenous Language Education and Literacy* (1995) and author of *A Place to Be Navajo* (in press).

David F. Marshall, professor of English at the University of North Dakota (Grand Forks), is editor of *Language Planning* (1991) and author of "The Question of an Official Language: Language Rights and the English Language Amendment" (1986, a focus issue of the *International Journal of the Sociology of Language*).

Samuel Gyasi Obeng, assistant professor of linguistics at Indiana University (Bloomington), is the author of "An Analysis of the Linguistic Situation in Ghana," *African Languages and Cultures* (1997). His other research and publications dealing with ethnicity also focus on the Ghanaian context.

Tope Omoniyi, doctoral tutor-supervisor at Thames Valley Open University, London, has taught and engaged in research in Nigeria and Singapore. He has focused on the language and identity of minority, borderland, immigrant, and island communities.

Amado M. Padilla, professor of psychological studies in education and chair of the language, literacy, and culture program, Stanford University, is editor of *The Hispanic Journal of Behavioral Sciences*. He has prepared a video recording, *Cultural Factors in Behavior* (1994), and has edited *Hispanic Psychology* (1995).

Robert Phillipson, associate professor in the department of languages and culture at the University of Roskilde (Denmark), is the author of the widely translated *Linguistic Imperialism* (1992) and coeditor of *Linguistic Human Rights: Overcoming Linguistic Discrimination* (1994).

William Safran, professor of political science, University of Colorado (Boulder), is editor-in-chief of the journal *Nationalism and Ethnic Politics*. He is coauthor of *Ethnicity and Citizenship: The Canadian Case* (1996) and author of *The French Polity* (5th ed., 1998).

Harold F. Schiffman, professor in the department of South Asian regional studies, University of Pennsylvania (Philadelphia), is also academic director of the "Penn Language Center." His most recent book related to language and ethnicity is *Linguistic Culture and Language Policy* (1996).

Tove Skutnabb-Kangas, University of Roskilde (Denmark), is coeditor of *Linguistic Human Rights: Overcoming Linguistic Discrimination* (1994), editor of *Multi-*

lingualism for All (1995), and coeditor of *Approaching Linguistic Human Rights* (1999).

Bernard Spolsky, professor of English and director, Language Policy Research Center, Bar-Ilan University (Israel), is coauthor of *The Languages of Jerusalem* (1991), coeditor of *The Influence of Language on Culture and Thought* (1991), and author of *Measured Words* (1995) and *Sociolinguistics* (1998).

Andrée Tabouret-Keller, Professor Emeritus, Louis Pasteur University (Strasbourg, France), is coeditor of *The Fergusonian Impact* (2 vols., 1986), coauthor of *Vernacular Literacy: A Re-Evaluation* (1997), and author of *La Maison du Langage* (1997) and *Le Nom des Langues* (1997).

Colin H. Williams, research professor, department of Welsh, University of Wales (Cardiff), is author of *Called unto Liberty: On Language and Nationalism* (1994) and coauthor of *The Community Research Project on Regenerating Welsh as a Community Language* (1997).

Glyn Williams, director of the Research Center Wales and University Reader in Sociology, University of Wales (Bangor), is the author of *Sociolinguistics: A Sociological Critique* (1992) and *French Discourse Analysis: The Method of Poststructuralism* (1998).

Ofelia Zepeda, assistant professor of linguistics, University of Arizona (Tucson), is codirector of the American Indian Language Development Institute, editor of *When It Rains* (1982), coeditor of *Home Places* (1995), and author of *Ocean Power: Poems from the Desert* (1995) and *Earth Movement* (1997).

HANDBOOK OF

Language & Ethnic Identity

Introduction

JOSHUA A. FISHMAN

The literature on ethnicity is already huge and is constantly being added to. It is also international and, therefore, multilingual, large parts of it being regrettably inaccessible to readers who depend on English (or any other single language) for their familiarity with this topic. Finally, it is interdisciplinary and, therefore, highly diversified as to its underlying theories and assumptions. It is the goal of this handbook to bring to the nonspecialized reader a substantial selection that reflects the above-mentioned regional and disciplinary variations in views toward and experiences with ethnicity.

The differences between regions and disciplines begin with the very definitions of the terms *ethnicity* and [*ethnic*] *identity*, extending to all the ramifications of these terms for the social, psychological, economic, political, and cultural interactions within and between groups of human beings. Although this virtually built-in variety of views and experiences cannot help but influence individual researchers and observers of ethnicity, such influences are rarely taken into account in any systematic manner when either local case studies or comparative and theoretical inquiries are undertaken or reported. It is my hope and the hope of the participants in this volume, all of whom have published extensively on the topic, that the overall effect of the selections we are bringing to our readers will be to foster greater awareness of some of the overlooked sources of disagreement (and also of concurrence) that have characterized thinking with respect to this topic for so many, many decades. The variety of views within Western European thought itself and between Eastern and Western European views, European and non-European views, humanistic and social science views, theoretical and applied perspectives, are all sampled in this volume and, therefore, can be subjected to comparative analysis.

Admittedly, sampling may still be subject to error. It may result in presenting atypical views, or it may inadvertently skip over important instances (whether disciplines or regions) and report on discrepant ones. The number of disciplinary areas of specialization and the number of geographic and cultural regions are legion, and it was impossible to include all of them in one volume, both for reasons of space and of time. Given the artificiality of many boundaries between disciplines and polities, some of the apparently missing disciplines and areas of specialization are implied by or associated with others that have been included (e.g., much of anthropology is implied within fieldwork), whereas certain regional distinctions that might not necessarily be made under other circumstances are considered important in this case (e.g., Germany might not be separated from Western Europe were it not for its very great impact on the topic under consideration). Ultimately, perhaps another volume will be called for to supplement this one. Be that as it may, this volume represents a beginning, whether it is exhaustive or not (and can a topic such as this ever be fully exhausted?), of a kind of exploration of the complex realm of ethnicity-related behaviors that has long been overdue.

However, ethnicity per se is not the only (or, in most cases, not even the main) focus of this volume. Its cofocus, at the very least, is language. The language and ethnicity link itself has also been subjected to a good deal of scrutiny and speculation, some of it going back (and still ongoing) across millennia of philosophical and scientific inquiry. Although language has rarely been equated with the totality of ethnicity, it has, in certain historical, regional and disciplinary contexts, been accorded priority within that totality. The last third of the twentieth century—often referred to as a time of "ethnic revival"—has often been witness to a renewed stress on language in various mobilizations of ethnicity throughout the world. How and when the link between language and ethnicity comes about, its saliency and potency, its waxing and waning, its inevitability and the possibility of its sundering, all need to be examined. And, as with ethnicity and ethnic identity, so too in the case of language and its manifold links with ethnicity: a varied regional and disciplinary perspective over time would be highly desirable and is undoubtedly long overdue. This is not a task that the established language sciences and areas of specialization can accomplish by themselves, even though they have focused so much of their energies on this issue. As we approach the twenty-first century, it would be intellectually gratifying (and, perhaps, even welcome in everyday practical terms) to shed more light on the diversity of language and ethnic identity links by viewing them in a fuller panoply of comparative regional and disciplinary perspectives (all of them also being viewed over time) than that which they have, thus far, been accorded.

This volume is intended for the nonspecialized reader, whether student or layperson. Although it is not easy for specialists to write for such an audience, considerable effort has been expended in an attempt to do so. Quite predictably, this too is a variable, some writers undoubtedly having succeeded better than others in the onerous task of communicating complex concepts and findings simply. The short lists of references following each chapter are intended to steer readers to the most crucial further readings. Similarly, the "Questions for Further Thought and Discussion" at the end of every chapter are intended to be of help in carrying the impact of the chapters themselves one step further, into the realm of the further reflection and inquiry which "language and ethnic identity" doubtlessly deserve. This has been a topic that has generally been associated more with heat than with light in the world at large. While we hope not to have rendered lifeless the strong emotions and deeply held values with which language and ethnicity have long been associated far and wide (and with which they have been and still are obviously approached even by some academics) nor to have doubted the sincerity with which such emotions and values are held and implemented, the authors themselves will, nevertheless, be most pleased if they can join the readers in further efforts along the lines of thought and discussion about language and ethnic identity during the years ahead.

DISCIPLINE &
TOPIC PERSPECTIVES

Economics

FRANÇOIS GRIN

Although there are distinct schools in economic theory, it is certainly one of the most integrated of the social sciences, and the overwhelming majority of researchers in the discipline operate within the framework of mainstream, also called *orthodox* or *neoclassical*, economics. In what follows, *economics* will therefore refer to this numerically and ideologically dominant school and the paradigm it adheres to—not out of ideological preference or oversight of other streams but simply because alternative paradigms (for example, Marxian economics) have never paid much attention to these dimensions of human experience.

Although mainstream economics has been slow to develop an interest in matters of language and ethnic identity, economic work on these topics had begun in the mid 1960s within the mainstream tradition; it has since produced a significant body of contributions that cover a wide range of issues. The goal of this chapter is to introduce the reader to these materials.

The Economic Paradigm

Economics as a Social Science

Economics as a discipline encompasses a much broader range of issues than is often assumed. This reflects Lionel Robbins's 1935 definition of economics as "a science which studies human behavior as a relationship between ends and scarce means that have alternative uses" (pp. 16–17). By virtue of this definition, a problem is an economic one as soon as actors (or, as economists call them, "agents") must make decisions about how to use their limited resources. Because the resources available are limited, choices must be made about how to allocate them to various objectives, knowing that not all objectives can be achieved. In other words, economics studies how people deal with scarcity, but there is no a priori restriction on the nature of the ends pursued nor on the resources used to achieve them.

The Rationality Hypothesis

Economic theory, however, introduces one important restriction at the outset: actors are assumed to behave rationally. What this assumption comes down to is, quite simply, that actors will generally use their limited resources in the most efficient way to achieve their goals, whatever the latter might be—or, in plainer terms, that actors will make the most of what they have. This is assumed to hold for all actors, whether they are consumers buying goods or services, workers selling their time and skills, or entrepreneurs using capital and labor to produce goods and services. This process is known as efficient resource allocation, where individuals maximize their well-being (or, in economic jargon, "utility"), and firms maximize their profits. The state is a third type of actor, which can be more or less important depending on the precise issue considered; we shall, however, forgo any discussion of its role until the section on "Language policy and planning."

Nonmaterial Variables in Economics

For the most part, economics studies efficient resource allocation and its outcomes in relation with the production, exchange, and consumption of goods and services. As a consequence, most of economics deals with prices, earnings, and costs—in short, material or financial variables with a clear quantitative interpretation. However, the problem of scarcity turns up in just about any sphere of human activity, and the economic approach can be applied to many problems where material or financial aspects are not central. On the one side, the ends pursued are not necessarily confined to maximum consumption or profit and can comprise complex nonmaterial "goods" like environmental quality or psychological well-being. On the other side, the constraints on resources are not just financial or technological; they can include one's social network, mental and physical health, time, and, of course, just about any political, social, or cultural parameters that affect what actors can actually do. The breadth of scope implicit in the definition of economics as a discipline is what has allowed economic approaches to the family, fertility, religion, education, the environment, culture, crime, and language to emerge.

Including nonmaterial or nonfinancial variables in economic analysis can be difficult, because their qualitative aspects are very important in relation with their quantitative dimension, and economic methodology is mainly designed to handle relatively simple, unidimensional variables. However, an economic approach to areas of human endeavor that traditionally fall within the purview of disciplines like sociology, political science, or linguistics can raise questions and yield insights that these disciplines do not necessarily provide.

Essential Caveats

Defining economics by its approach rather than by its subject matter significantly broadens its usefulness as a social science. This, however, calls for some clarifications. First, although it follows from the preceding discussion that just about *any* aspect of human behavior could be approached from an economic perspective, it must be clear that *no* aspect of human behavior can be adequately understood using economics *alone*. The combined contribution of several disciplines remains the best way to take stock of its complexity, and depending on the aspect of behavior being studied, the relative importance of the contributions from economics, sociology, political science, linguistics, and so forth will vary. It is important never to lose sight of this warning, lest the economic approach become somewhat imperialistic. Second, although economics is, at heart, a theory of individual behavior, it does not follow that economists must always assume individuals to be only and selfishly concerned with their own well-being or that society does not matter. For example, it is perfectly possible to make room for altruism among an individual's objectives or "ends." Third, the rationality hypothesis does not imply that actors actually enter an explicit calculus of the costs and benefits of every possible course of action, but that, by and large, actors behave *as if* they did.

Techniques and Methods

Economics favors the use of certain methods, and a grasp of the main features of these methods helps to understand economists' work on language and ethnic identity. At the outset, a distinction must be made between *theoretical* and *empirical* research.

Formal Modeling

Theoretical research relies heavily on formal model building. *Models* are abstract, simplified representations of the problem to be studied. In economics, a model is normally not confined to description but requires the specification of a causal structure, where the key ingredients are *variables* and the explicit *relationships* between the variables. In its elementary form, a model will connect two variables, a and b, in the following way. Suppose that b represents an individual's language skills and that a stands for the individual's labor income, or "earnings". A simple model could be of the form $a = f(b)$, where variables a and b are connected by the relationship f, which takes the form of a mathematical function. In the above example, the *gradient* of the relationship between a and b is assumed to be positive. This means that if b is higher, a will, as a consequence, tend to be higher, too. In other words, the model assumes that people who have more language skills (for example, because they are bi- or trilingual) earn a higher salary. This, in turn, can be explained by the fact that they qualify for more demanding positions or reflect the higher productivity made possible by the possession of language skills. Technically, function f will then have to be chosen in such a way that the first derivative of a with respect to b, written $\partial a/\partial b$, is positive. For example, we could suppose that $a = \gamma b$, where γ is a positive parameter.

Of course, formal theoretical models often are much more elaborate and contain more than one equation, but if a model is broken down into smaller units, each of them is ultimately of the $a = f(b)$ form and is conceptually very simple. It is important to remember, however, that the point of a model is much less to provide a reflection of reality than to be an *instrument to help us think about reality*. Their chief usefulness is that they force researchers to be very precise and rigorous in their definition of the *relationships* connecting variables and to provide demanding internal consistency checks. This can help avoid logical leaps and forces researchers to go beyond metaphor. In an illuminating comment, the sociologist Richard Brown once observed that "models are metaphors whose implications have been spelled out."

Formal modeling's weak point, by contrast, often is the definition of variables. Precisely because it requires all variables, even essentially qualitative ones, to lend themselves to a quantitative interpretation (that is, it must be possible to distinguish "more" from "less" for all the variables in a model), much of the phenomenological depth is squeezed out of them. The result is that some sides of modeling (particularly the logical conditions under which some cause-and-effect relationships actually hold) are highly refined, whereas others (the meaning of variables) can be somewhat simplistic. This is not a problem when simple, unidimensional variables are used (for example, a price is a price); it is not always adequate, however, in the case of more complex variables (for example, it is never fully satisfactory to represent "education" as an individual's number of years of schooling). In economic approaches to language and ethnicity, these limitations must never be forgotten, and, as much as possible, economic researchers working on language and ethnicity must integrate variables and concepts developed by practitioners from other disciplines, particularly the sociology of language.

Empirical Testing

A formal model is an abstract representation of reality whose bricks are relationships and variables. However, if data are available, it becomes possible to *test* the model. More precisely, this means checking whether the *actual* relationship between variables, such as variables a and b introduced above, matches the *theoretical* relationship put forward in the model. The techniques used then are common to all the social sciences. In the economic approach to language and ethnicity, a popular method is that of *ordinary least squares*, called OLS for short. Because it is used so frequently, it deserves a few words of explanation. If we wish to use OLS to check the link between a (individual earnings) and b (individual language skills), we need a data set (ideally, census returns, or, failing that, a random sample of adequate size) containing information about individuals' earnings and language skills. But we also need information about other variables, such as the economic sector in which an individual works, his or her age, education, previous work experience, and so forth. These are called *control* variables. They are used to standardize the sample and to estimate statistically the relationship between language skills and earnings, *all other things being equal.* In other words, the OLS technique will estimate the degree to which higher language skills are really associated with higher earnings for people of comparable age, education, and experience working in similar occupations. Taking account of these control variables, which obviously do have an influence on people's earnings, prevents us from unduly crediting the entirety of observed earnings differentials to language skills alone.

The Development of Economic Approaches to Language and Ethnicity

A Definition

It is always a difficult task to define a research field because the apparent rigidity of a definition cannot do justice to the evolutive nature of research in terms of practice, methods, or results. Nevertheless, it remains helpful to agree, if not on the limits of a research field, at least on what constitutes its core. In our case, reference must be made to the economic paradigm, but language and ethnicity must be explicitly mentioned, too. The following definition, slightly extended from some already proposed in the recent literature, meets these specifications while attempting to remain open enough:

> The economics of language and ethnicity refers to the paradigm of mainstream theoretical economics and uses the concepts and tools of economics in the study of relationships featuring linguistic or ethnic variables; it focuses principally, but not exclusively, on those relationships in which economic variables also play a part.

This definition is illustrated in the rest of this section, in which the emergence of economic approaches to language and ethnic identity is reviewed.

Main Orientations

The economics of language and ethnicity has developed in several rather scattered directions, probably because there was no obvious starting point in economic theory. If we start out from the basic economic paradigm, in which people are assumed to act rationally in order to maximize their well-being (or, if they act on behalf of a firm, the latter's profits), then it makes little difference what language(s) they speak, or what their ethnic identity is. Economists are quite happy to concede that actors's values, needs, and tastes (and, by way of consequence, their objectives) will differ considerably depending on culture and that constraints (including culturally determined ones) will vary; within any *given* context defined by specific constraints and culturally determined objectives, however, actors are still assumed to make the most of what they have—that is, to maximize utility. Distinctions are made between actors as consumers or producers of goods and services and as buyers or suppliers of labor force, or, in the case of international trade theory, distinctions are between country A and country B, but language and ethnicity play no part in these distinctions.

In the mid-1960s, however, economists observed that traditionally economic variables, such as labor income, appeared to be related to linguistic or ethnic variables. Some work from the late fifties had already examined, theoretically and empirically, earnings differentials between blacks and whites in the United States; a similar approach was then applied to explain why French Canadians earned less than English Canadians. In other words, people's language and/or ethnic identity was seen as an *explanatory factor* of a centrally important economic variable, that is, labor income.

In this early line of work, no analytical difference was made between language and ethnic identity, which implied an oversight of the role of language as a communication tool. In the 1970s, more attention was paid to this dimension of language. This allowed researchers to tie economic research on language to an increasingly important body of economics, namely, *human capital theory*. Language attributes, particularly second-language skills, could then be viewed as assets, comparable to education in general or to specific skills such as computer literacy. This line of research, however, tended to neglect precisely what the preceding one had stressed—namely, that language is an essential marker of ethnic identity, both for individuals and for groups. Since the early 1980s, however, the two approaches have been increasingly combined, particularly in empirical work, and linguistic attributes are now viewed as applying to both people's ethnic identity (usually represented by their mother tongue) and their linguistic human capital (usually, their competence in additional languages).

Following an entirely different line of reasoning, in the 1970s and 1980s some authors have attempted to develop the language-as-currency analogy by defining language as a medium of (international) trade. It yields some interesting results on the rationale of second-language learning. It must be pointed out, however, that the relevant analogy is not between language and currency proper but between *differences between languages* on the one hand and *differences between (national) currencies* on the other. Furthermore, *conversational* exchange has analytically nothing to do with *market* exchange, and several analogies (apparently quite popular in other disciplines) between the circulation of words and the circulation of goods and services, which are normally delivered against payment of a certain price, can be misleading.

Apart from a few isolated papers, most of the economic research up until the late 1980s looked at linguistic or ethnic variables as explanatory factors in the determination of standard economic variables such as labor income. In recent years, there has been increasing interest in the opposite causal direction—namely, the way in which economic variables could affect linguistic ones. Economists have been modeling or studying empirically issues such as language use in the workplace, language use in advertising, and language dynamics (acquisition, maintenance, and shift), particularly in the case of minority languages like Irish or Welsh, as they are influenced by economic variables such as prices, incomes, or the structure of production costs.

Since the late 1960s, economists and rational-choice theorists who hail from the field of political science (and whose work is often hardly distinguishable from that of mainstream economists) have taken an interest in language policy and planning. (For the purposes of this chapter, no distinction is made between these two terms; but the reader is cautioned that the specialist literature does not treat them as synonyms.) Much of the research in this field was carried out in connection with actual language planning issues, such as language legislation, or the problem of choosing official languages in supranational entities like the European Union. This line of work, which stresses the operationality of results, is one of the most exciting in current research; it is discussed in a subsequent section.

The Economics of Language and Ethnicity Today

Economic research on language and ethnic identity is now beginning to take shape as a full-fledged area of specialization. This evolution reflects the increased frequency of linguistic and ethnic diversity in modern societies and explains current developments in policy implications. Apart from the latter, which will be discussed in the next section, the main directions of contemporary research are the following.

Empirical Analysis of the Relationship between Language and Labor Income

Research on the relationship between language and labor income remains numerically the most important in the economics of language and ethnic identity. Its focus has already been briefly described in the preceding section on techniques and methods. Much of the work in this field is empirical rather than theoretical and has originated in the United States and Canada as explorations of earnings differentials between immigrants and native-born workers or between anglophones and francophones. Similar work is now beginning to appear on European issues. These include the case of *Gastarbeiter* ("guest workers," e.g., in Germany) or speakers of autochthonous minority languages (e.g., members of the Italian-speaking minority in Switzerland). European research also places more emphasis on the returns of competence in foreign languages, such as English in continental Europe. A few theoretical models have been put forward to explain (instead of just measuring statistically) these earnings differentials; the main explanatory factors considered are within-firm communication costs or downright discrimination.

Let us consider, for example, the earnings differentials between linguistic groups in the Canadian province of Quebec, where some 90% of the resident population speaks French as a first language. After controlling for the effects of other determinants of earnings, notably people's education, experience (both measured in number of years), number of weeks worked, marital status, industry, and occupation, their linguistic attributes are still associated with earnings differentials. In 1985 (using unilingual francophones as a basis for comparison), unilingual anglophones earned 9.71% *less*, whereas bilingual francophones earned

5.14% *more*; otherwise comparable individuals whose mother tongue is neither English nor French (called "allophones" in the Canadian literature) earned *less* (the earnings difference was a fairly modest 5.14% for those allophones who had mastered both English and French, but was a substantial 17.77% less for those who had learned only English, and even 24.47% less for those who had learned only French). Figures for 1990 indicate that in the United States, Hispanic immigrants in high-proportion Hispanic regions (Arizona, California, Colorado, New Mexico, Texas, and the metropolitan areas of the states of Florida and New York) earned some 14% less than whites if they knew English and 24% less if they did not, although they would be otherwise comparable in terms of standard determinants of earnings, including education and experience. Penalties were lower in low-proportion Hispanic areas—that is, in the rest of the country.[1]

Spread, Survival, and Decline of Languages

Research on the spread, survival, and decline of languages is mainly concerned with minority languages, but it taps into the more general question of the long-term dynamics of languages, including "languages of wider communication" such as English. So far, most of the work in this area has been theoretical rather than empirical. This question can be approached on two different, but obviously interrelated, levels: why people learn certain languages and why, if they have the choice of using more than one, they prefer to use one or the other—a choice which eventually affects patterns of language maintenance and shift. The first type of issue can be analyzed in terms of human capital theory (mentioned earlier in this chapter) or in terms of *network externalities*, which hark back to a very interesting feature of languages: The higher the number of people who speak language Y, the more interesting it becomes for additional people to learn Y as well, creating what could be called a snowball effect. Exploring the necessary circumstances for this snowball effect to occur, what factors reinforce it, what factors keep it in check, and what long-term consequences it can have on diversity are obviously very important questions. The second type of issue focuses on bilinguals, who can a priori carry out the various activities of everyday life in either one of two languages. They will use one or the other depending on their preferences, values, and needs on the one hand, and on the other on various constraints that are reflected in the "shadow price"—that is, the implicit material and nonmaterial costs of performing various activities in the two languages they speak.

For instance, it can be shown that an increase in the income of bilinguals (native speakers of Irish who also speak English as one example) may have a positive or a negative effect on minority language use and that the outcome will result from the interplay of a variety of factors. The latter include people's preferences for carrying out their activities (say, spending leisure time with their children) in one language or another, the cost of the goods needed to do so (for example, the relative price of children's books in Irish and English), and the degree to which people can substitute goods for time when performing such activities (for example, spending leisure time with children can require a large expense on time and a small expense on goods when parents play ball in the yard with their children or take them on bicycle rides in the countryside; by contrast, leisure time can be "goods-intensive," as opposed to "time-intensive," if parents take their children to theme parks with pricey attractions). Theoretical modeling allows us to examine precisely how these various aspects interact.

Language and Economic Activity

A wide, somewhat heterogeneous body of research on language and economic activity examines two questions about families of causal links: first, whether linguistic features have an influence on the level of economic activity; and second, what the factors are that determine patterns of language use in economic activity. The former line of work explores regional economic development in minority language areas: Traditional views, according to which holding on to a minority language was a cause (or even a proof) of economic backwardness in remote and peripheral areas, are progressively being reconsidered, and current research shows that local language characteristics (or, more broadly, linguistic diversity) can actually be used to economic advantage. The latter body of work documents language use in the workplace, in advertising and labeling, in international trade, and so forth; its goal is to ascertain what factors will prompt agents, whether as consumers, workers, business owners, managers, or tradesmen, to use one language or another in economic activity. Existing research is a mix of empirical and theoretical work, with a strong but not exclusive orientation to minority languages; some recent research on "ethnic business," however, ignores the linguistic aspects altogether and emphasizes other aspects of cultural identity. One original aspect of this research work is that it sometimes addresses these issues at the macroeconomic level, on which economic activity is viewed as an integrated whole, whereas most of the research in the economics of language and ethnicity has a clear microeconomic orientation.

Generally, the absence of hard data makes it difficult to test these relationships empirically, and it has been comparatively easier to use survey data to investigate the language in which people work. For example, in the case of Quebec, language of work appears to be directly related to the main language of the owners of the business.

Communication between Language Groups

The study of communication between members of different language groups is a numerically smaller, and also more recent, area of research. Economists and rational-choice scientists, sometimes using game theory, have tried to cast light on the conditions under which people with different linguistic repertoires (some unilingual, some bi- or even trilingual) will end up using language X, Y, or Z when they get together. Is it simply a matter of efficient communication, or do social norms play a major role? What could explain continuing adherence to norms if it results in apparently inefficient communication patterns? Studies in this area, which are still relatively few, are mostly of a theoretical nature, and they tie into highly interesting questions about the relative efficiency of a broad distribution of second language skills in the population as opposed to widely available translation and interpretation services as alternative ways to guarantee intergroup communication.

This research often serves to guard against drawing hasty conclusions. For example, it can be shown that depending on the priorities chosen, the European Union (which actually recognizes eleven official languages: Danish, Dutch, English, Finnish, French, German, Greek, Italian, Portuguese, Spanish, and Swedish) should either stick to its current model *or* officialize only the languages of the three largest language groups *or* use only one of its languages for all official business *or* pick an artificial language such as Esperanto for this task.[2]

Language Policy and Planning

Some Definitions

It follows from the definition presented earlier that economics does not just offer a theoretical perspective on human behavior in general; it is also largely a theory of choice and an instrument in decision making. This goes to show the relevance of economics in language policy and/or planning, which is essentially concerned with making appropriate decisions: The latter bear upon the selection, design, and implementation of measures that will modify what we shall call a *linguistic environment*. At this point, a few definitions are in order.

A linguistic environment is a theoretical construct used for analytical purposes. It subsumes in an extensive—but clearly not exhaustive—fashion all the relevant information about the relative position of the languages present in a given polity at a certain time. This includes the number of speakers; speakers' proficiency levels in the various languages; the status, domains, and frequency of use of each language by different categories of actors; and the latter's attitudes toward the languages present. On the one hand, a linguistic environment is a *given* at a certain point in time; on the other hand, it also the *object* of language policy, because language policy seeks to influence one or many aspects of the linguistic environment. For example, a language policy that aims at restoring a self-priming mechanism for the production and reproduction of a minority language community may include measures such as giving legal status to the language in question in the administration or in courts; making its use compulsory (usually alongside a majority language) in public signs, expanding the offer of language courses in the education system, and so forth. In line with the recent language planning literature, we can therefore define language policy as follows:

> Language policy (or planning) is a systematic, rational, theory-based effort at the societal level to modify the linguistic environment with a view to increasing aggregate welfare. It is typically conducted by official bodies or their surrogates and aimed at part or all of the population living under their jurisdiction.

This definition must not be interpreted as giving a free rein to purely technical approaches to policy choices; language policy is only a tool to assist in democratic decision making pertaining to language issues.

Policy Analysis and the Rationale
for Government Intervention

In the preceding definition, "increasing aggregate welfare" is the goal of language policy. It follows that from an economic perspective it also constitutes the chief *justification* of language policy. It would make no sense to engage in policy at all if its result were to *reduce* welfare. This apparently straightforward rationale, which lies at the heart of mainstream *policy analysis*, hides several difficulties that we cannot discuss at length but that must be pointed out.

First, this approach contains an implicit ideological choice: It requires a translation of all the aspects of the problem into costs and benefits. We have seen that the latter are *not* confined to material and financial dimensions, but the fact remains that defining welfare increases as the ultima ratio of state intervention automatically relegates some arguments widely used in language and ethnic policy to secondary rank. In this perspective, a policy cannot be adequately justified with purely moral arguments such as "this is a matter of human rights" or "this is a simple question of justice"; human rights and justice need to be reinterpreted as factors concurring to aggregate welfare. More generally, the invocation of "values" is treated with skepticism in policy analysis because values are diverse and sometimes irreconcilable; the underlying principle is that nobody has legitimacy to dictate morality and values. The appeal to values can be suspected of reflecting special interests rather than selfless virtue. One-person, one-vote democracy is then the only solution that mainstream policy analysis considers appropriate. The concept of aggregate welfare, however, offers the advantage of pushing back the frontier beyond which differences between policy alternatives will simply reflect opposite values and expands the range of questions in which the objectivized (which does not mean "objective") comparison of alternatives is a relevant strategy.

Second, it would be naive to suppose that the weighing of the costs and benefits of various policy alternatives eschews issues of power. The very definition of what constitutes a cost and a benefit, let alone their measurement, is in itself a prerogative of power. This confirms the importance of the distributive consequences of policy options (see the following subsection on "Efficiency and fairness"), and hence the necessity of systematically assessing them with the questions: Who gains? And who loses?

Measurement Problems
and the Quest for Optimality

On what basis is it possible to say that one linguistic environment is "better" than another and that spending resources to bring about change in a given direction (for example, greater recognition and use of minority languages) would increase welfare? Dealing with this question requires some instruments to measure the costs and benefits of language policies. Cost measurement is comparatively less difficult, because departing from an existing situation requires identifiable money outlays (and can induce actual savings, too) that can be budgeted with some degree of accuracy, although some nonfinancial costs may be present as well.

Measuring benefits raises trickier conceptual problems. There is little empirical research on benefit estimation in language policy, but useful parallels can be drawn with the evaluation of the benefits of environmental improvement. Linguistic environments share crucial features with the natural environment, particularly because every person is exposed to both environments and also because neither environment has an observable market price (for example, it is not possible to buy the cleanness of a lake in the same way as one can buy, in return for paying a certain price, a restaurant meal or a seat at the opera house). There are roundabout ways of estimating the value that people assign to a clean lake, whether they actually "use" the lake or not—for example, for swimming or fishing. The development of similar instruments for the measurement of the relative value of different linguistic environments is likely to become an important task of language policy research in future years, because it sooner or later becomes indispensable in the weighing of various policy alternatives.

Assuming that the difficulties associated with the identification and measurement of costs and benefits have been solved—at least on the theoretical plane—a net value can be assigned to linguistic environments by subtracting costs from benefits for each. It bears repeating once again that the costs and benefits talked about here are *not* confined to material or financial aspects and that nonmarket dimensions are of primary importance in the evaluation of both. The question of estimating whether a particular language policy is worth engaging into can then be extended to the broader one of identifying what appears to be the *optimal* linguistic environment—that is, the one which promises to bring about the highest degree of aggregate welfare—and then selecting the corresponding set of policy measures. Research on specific issues, such as the choice of official languages for the European Union discussed in the preceding section, raises precisely this type of question.

Efficiency and Fairness

The relationship between *distributive justice* and *aggregate welfare* needs to be clarified. The conceptually simplest way to deal with this question is to assume that distributive justice is an explicit component of welfare; hence, the policy option that maximizes aggregate welfare constitutes a "package" in which fairness is taken into account. However, it is often the case that welfare is defined only in terms of efficient resource allocation (see the earlier subsection on "The rationality hypothesis"). Societal resources may then be used in the best possible way, but this still tells us nothing about how welfare is distributed among society's members. Hence, an allocatively optimal solution can be distributively unjust. It follows that it can be perfectly rational for society not to adopt a policy that maximizes aggregate (allocative) welfare but instead to select an alternative whose allocative performance is merely adequate, if it also promises to be more just.

Consider, for example, the problem of the granting of linguistic human rights to different language communities in a multilingual polity. It may well be the case that allocative welfare will be maximized if *no resources* are devoted to the provision of minority language schooling for very small language communities but are spent instead on health programs for the poor (irrespective of their language group). However, this places the full weight of linguistic adaptation, not to mention eventual deprivation of cultural identity, on minority language communities; therefore, the choice to provide schooling only in the dominant language has distributive consequences which can be considered unfair, strikingly so in the case of indigenous minorities with no home nation-state to turn to. In such a case, a concern for fairness can rationally justify the adoption of allocatively suboptimal policies.

Summary, Limitations, and Extensions

The preceding sections have only roughed out the essential traits of economic research on language and ethnic identity. Nevertheless, I have established the following points.

After presenting the paradigm of mainstream economics and describing some of the essentials of its theoretical and empirical methodology, I examined how an economic analysis of language and ethnicity issues has developed and what its main orientations are. I reviewed current research and provided examples of key results in four major areas. Turning first to language-based earnings differentials, I showed that linguistic attributes *do* have an impact on people's labor income. I then described how microeconomic modeling can help researchers to understand the complex interplay of variables (including standard economic ones like "preferences," "income," and "prices") that influence people's language use, particularly in the case of bilinguals. The paragraph on language and economic activity lists several aspects of economic life (for example, advertising or international trade) whose linguistic dimensions are beginning to be investigated. Finally, I discussed research on communication between language groups, using the problem of the choice of official languages in supranational entities as an illustration.

Language policy probably is the area in which an economic approach has most to contribute, and it has therefore been allotted an entire section of this chapter. I have shown why, from an economic standpoint, language policy is a perfectly legitimate endeavor, and I have established parallels with other forms of public intervention, such as environmental, education, or health policy. Just like any public policy, it also raises the problem of a possible conflict between objectives, notably *efficiency* and *fairness*, and I have shown what precise implications can be derived in the case of language.

Lack of space precludes the discussion of other substantive or methodological issues; however, it is important to be aware of some of these issues. Among the areas of research not discussed here, the following deserve mention.

First, there is a growing literature on what is somewhat vaguely referred to as "ethnic business"—that is, (usually) small- to medium-size enterprises owned and run by migrants from "southern," sometimes third-world, countries to OECD (Organization for Economic Cooperation and Development) countries. These firms typically specialize in importing, producing, or distributing goods and services with ethnically specific features. A typical example is ethnic restaurants. So far, linguistic aspects have been all but omitted from this line of research, but at the time of writing, some analytically and empirically promising links are being established between cultural and linguistic dimensions in the context of international trade.

Second, contrary to what one might expect, the market for language-related goods and services (language schools, textbooks, translation services, etc.), is *not* a major area of work in the economics of language. The reason for this is that this market, though significant in business terms, raises quite common microeconomic questions. Treating the latter does not require significant analytical elaboration over and above the standard instruments for the study of markets for generic goods and services.

Third, what matters in economic approaches to language is language status—that is, the position of languages with respect to one another—or, more to the point, the respective socioeconomic positions of speakers of different languages. However, language corpus, that is, the internal features of a language, is generally taken as given and not subjected to economic analysis. For example, there is no economic perspective on whether economic value attaches to spelling reform or lexical development. Although future work on this category of questions is possible, it is unlikely to become a major area of research, if only because the socioeconomic implications for language corpus are instrumental in comparison with those of language status.

Fourth, the existence of an interesting body of research on the language of economics must be pointed out. This literature, however, analyzes the discourse of economists and hence addresses questions that are entirely different from those studied in the economic approaches to language and ethnic identity.

Fifth, it should be noted that existing economic work makes little, if any, distinction between *language* and *ethnicity*, either as a cause or as a consequence of economic processes. One reason is that in the causal relationships previously discussed, "language" and "ethnicity" often are interchangeable; for example, earnings differentials between language groups or between ethnic groups raise analytically similar problems, even if they constitute two distinct issues in real life. Of course, this is not always the case, and many research questions in the economics of language (for example, language use in multinational corporations) have no obvious counterpart in terms of ethnicity. A focus on language rather than on ethnicity in economic analysis opens the door to the study of a wider range of issues, as well as providing a crisper set of variables to work with. Another reason, already mentioned at the beginning of this chapter, is that because economic research is mainly concerned with variables that have a clear quantitative interpretation, it tends to pay relatively less attention to variables that are mostly qualitative. Hence, economic research has little to say about the link between language and ethnicity. Both objects tend to be minimally, somewhat sketchily, "constructed," and economics as a discipline does not have much in the way of the hermeneutic tradition that is used in other social sciences or in the humanities to discuss the links between concepts or between the aspects of human experience that these concepts are intended to describe.

This last point must be viewed in connection with an epistemological question that is frequently overlooked. We have so far stressed the instrumental contribution of the economic perspective: It helps understand reality with a view to altering it in a positive direction. But do economic approaches to language have a contribution to make in the same way as the humanities do, that is, to study and provide meaning to human experience? This, admittedly, is not their chief aim. However, they are of assistance, albeit indirectly, in this endeavor as well, in that their demanding analytical standards can provide ways to lend some necessary rigor to the essentially noneconomic discussion of why some states of affairs may be said to be better than others. For this contribution to be genuinely helpful, however, economic work on language and ethnic identity must be combined with analytical tools developed in other disciplines, particularly the sociology of language. In this enterprise, interdisciplinarity is not just a virtue or an exciting broadening of horizons but an intellectual necessity.

Questions for Further Thought and Discussion

1. Why does Lionel Robbins's definition of economics broaden the relevance and applicability of economic analysis?

2. What are some of the key features and objectives of a "model" in the sense in which economic theory uses this concept?

3. What can be given as the chief reasons why language matters were ignored by mainstream economic theory until the recent past?

4. Discuss the language-as-currency analogy and present reasons why it can be misleading.

5. Should language decline and language spread be seen as necessarily self-reinforcing processes? Identify some factors that can strengthen or dampen such a self-reinforcing character.

6. Discuss the political implications of viewing increases in welfare as the overarching goal of language policy.

Notes

1. For a survey of results for Quebec and the United States, respectively, see François Vaillancourt, "Language and socioeconomic status in Quebec: Measurement, findings, determinants, and policy costs" and David Bloom and Gilles Grenier, "Language, employment and earnings in the United States: Spanish-English differentials from 1970 to 1990," both in the *International Journal of the Sociology of Language*, vol. 121, 1996.

2. On this question, see, for example, François Grin, 1997, "Gérer le plurilinguisme européen: approche économique au problème de choix," in U. Ammon, K. Mattheier, and P. Nelde (eds.), *Monolingualism is curable* (*Sociolinguistica*, vol. 11). Tübingen: Niemeyer, 1–15.

Selected Bibliography

This bibliography includes only contributions in English; however, a significant share of the literature is published in other languages, particularly French, occasionally German or Catalan. More extensive references can be found in survey papers, for example, in Grin 1996.

Bloom, David, and Gilles Grenier (1992). Economic perspectives on language: The relative value of bilingualism in Canada and the United States. In *A Source Book on the Official Language Controversy*, J. Crawford (ed.), 445–451. Chicago: University of Chicago Press.

Ministry of Canadian Heritage (1997). *Official Languages and the Economy*. Ottawa: Minister of Public Works and Government Services Canada (Cat. no. CH3-2/5-1996E).

Chiswick, Barry (1991). Speaking, reading and earnings among low-skilled immigrants. *Journal of Labor Economics* 9(2): 149–170.

Church, Jeffrey, and Ian King (1993). Bilingualism and network externalities. *Canadian Journal of Economics* 26:337–345.

Elster, John (1989). *Nuts and Bolts for the Social Sciences*. Cambridge: Cambridge University Press.

Grin, François (ed.) (1996). Economic approaches to language and language planning. Special issue. *International Journal of the Sociology of Language*, 121.

Grin, François, and François Vaillancourt (1997). The economics of bilingualism. *Annual Review of Applied Linguistics*, 17:43–65.

Lang, Kevin (1996). A language theory of discrimination. *Quarterly Journal of Economics* 101:363–382.

Lewis-Beck, Michael (ed.) (1993). *Regression Analysis* (International Handbooks of Quantitative Applications in the Social Sciences, Vol. 2). London: Sage.

Pool, Jonathan (1991). The official language problem. *American Political Science Review* 85:495–514.

Robbins, Lionel (1935). *An Essay on the Nature and Significance of Economic Science*, 2nd ed. London: Macmillan.

Linguistic and Ethnographic Fieldwork

NANCY C. DORIAN

The Language and Ethnicity Link: Ideal and Actual

A people and their language—what could be more straightforward? In the ideal case, it really is straightforward. There is a particular place where a certain group of people live, and in that particular place they speak a certain language. They have a name for themselves and their language, and no other people goes by that name or claims to speak that language as a mother tongue. If you seek them out, they will tell you who they are and what language they speak; and if they see that you are really interested in them, they will teach you about themselves and their language, perhaps even help you learn to speak their language if you desire.

But things are rarely so straightforward in actual fact. Nearly everything in this little picture of the ideal fieldwork situation is potentially full of problems. For one thing, ethnic labels are not always good guides to the actual situation where language is concerned (or customs, for that matter). Two groups that call themselves by different names may speak (and behave) very much alike, yet elsewhere a single ethnic name may be applied to clusters of people who speak (or behave) quite differently from one another. It can be surprisingly hard to decide just how many ethnic groups should be recognized in a study area and on just what basis the distinctions can reasonably be made. Ethnicity can feel very primal, but it rests fundamentally on social rather than on biological underpinnings—and socially constructed categories are subject to change. People will redefine themselves when circumstances make it desirable or when circumstances force it on them. Warfare and conquest, voluntary or involuntary migration, resource scarcity or resource abundance, intense trade contacts—all these can lead to great changes. Populations that were once cohesive can separate into distinct groups, decline to a remnant and be absorbed, or gradually develop into a subgroup of some larger population in the same or a neighboring region. They may themselves absorb other groups and rename themselves in the process. History is long, and for every group its sweep will include some calamitous events such as war, famine, pestilence, and natural disasters. Over a long period of time, a people that was once distinct and cohesive can easily lose the memory of places in which their ancestors used to live, of lifeways their ancestors once followed, and of identities their ancestors formerly claimed.

For another thing, most of the world's languages are not confined to their own exclusive areas. There are only about two hundred countries in the world, but there are over five thousand languages. This means that the majority of all the world's languages are spoken in places in which another language is officially recognized and favored over any exclusively local languages. Because the resources of the state chiefly support the official language, any other languages that happen to be spoken within the same country get less support and less respect. This has consequences for all the unofficial languages, because the social standing of a group of people carries over to the language they speak. If the more powerful, more prestigious, and wealthier people in a country or a region speak one or two languages, those languages will become the desirable languages, the ones people who were not born to them want to learn to speak. Social and economic opportunity go mainly to speakers of the state-sponsored language; people who grew up speaking less favored languages at home, then learned an official language through schooling, military service, or work experience may not want to admit knowing their original home language. Groups whose languages have no official standing may be actively trying to blur the lines between themselves and certain other groups slightly above them in the social hierarchy by shifting to the use of other languages and by marrying into other groups if they can. Wherever such a process is underway, some people in a particular district may call themselves by one ethnic name while their neighbors call them by another. The people trying to switch groups may claim not to speak their original ancestral language, or they actually may no longer speak it with normal proficiency because they have distanced themselves from it so completely.

In other cases, especially since the ethnic consciousness-raising of the 1960s and 1970s, groups that speak a language that has no official standing may be very clear about their identity and about maintaining that identity and may be all the more opposed to sharing any knowledge about themselves or their language for that very reason. Because of their weak position in the social and linguistic hierarchy, it is very likely that they have been taken advantage of in the past, politically or economically or both. The more subjugation they have experienced, the more determined they may be to keep to themselves what is left of their own culture, including their language. Outsiders are often unwelcome among peoples with this sort of history, and outside researchers, even if interested and sympathetic, will more or less automatically be seen as just the latest wave of exploiters to arrive in the area.

What Field Researchers Have Found
When They Reached the Field

A South Asian Case: Garo in India

In spite of all these potential problems, some field researchers really are lucky enough to find a perfectly clear-cut, one-to-one connection between a people, a place, and a language. Anthropologist and linguist Robbins Burling found such a connection in the Garo Hills of Assam, in northern India, when he went there to study the lifeways and language of the Garo people in 1954 (Burling 1963). The Garos, who numbered in the hundreds of thousands, were a minority group in India as a whole but were the majority population in the Garo Hills. They were farmers who cultivated rice for their own consumption and produced cotton and some other crops for the market. Apart from the Garo farming folk, only a small population of dairy-farming Nepali immigrants was present in the central part of the Garo Hills district. The people called Garos were mother-tongue speakers of Garo (a Tibeto-Burman language), and the whole Garo population was quite homogeneous in its general culture except for some differences in religious adherence that were introduced by missionary groups. It was a simple matter for Burling to identify the population he was looking for when he went there as a fieldworker, because the Garo clearly and unambiguously identified themselves as Garo. With his wife and infant son, Burling settled down for a two-year stay in the village of Rengsanggri, where he worked productively and successfully. He faced his share of fieldwork problems, especially where the health of his family was concerned, but identifying the people he was interested in and distinguishing them from other peoples was not problematic at all in the Garo context.

A Southeast Asian Case: Ugong in Thailand

Things were very different for David Bradley, who went in search of a minority language called Ugong (belonging to the Burmic division of the Tibeto-Burman language family) in a part of western Thailand where Ugong, a language not related to Thai, was known to have been spoken in the early part of the twentieth century. Bradley located a number of villages where Ugong people lived, but he found that they did not always admit to being Ugong. Descent lines might make it clear that certain individuals were Ugong, yet they claimed Thai identities and had come to be seen as Thai. Thai identity is the mainstream identity in Thailand, of course, and moving into the ethnic mainstream brought social and political advantages that some people of Ugong descent were eager to have. An individual in one village would sometimes deny that he was Ugong or could speak Ugong but would direct Bradley to an individual in another village who, said the original man, was Ugong and did speak the language. When Bradley reached the second village and located the individual in question, this second person also denied that he was Ugong or spoke the language, but he said he knew someone who was and did. And at that point the second individual directed Bradley to the very person in the first village who had sent him to this second individual (Bradley 1989: 38). Bradley found just two villages in which Ugong was still regularly spoken. When he had learned to speak some Ugong himself, by working with the more willing speakers in those two villages, he went back to two other villages and, by using his own Ugong, persuaded some people there to speak Ugong with him.

A North American Case: Cayuga in Oklahoma

Changes of ethnic name and identity can take place even when people are not trying to conceal an earlier ethnic identity and to slip into a socially more favorable ethnic category. North America had a great variety of distinct tribal populations with cultural traditions stretching back to immemorial times before Europeans entered the picture, but most of them suffered dislocation and contraction after European contact. The disastrous conditions that overtook Native American tribes included huge death rates from newly introduced infectious diseases, loss of traditional livelihoods through sharp drops in game populations, defeat in warfare, and forced relocations under the reservation system. Some tribes relocated repeatedly, first to avoid incoming settlers and find new game herds, and later under government inducement or coercion.

The severe discontinuities in tribal life, brought about by the losses and dislocations of the eighteenth, nineteenth, and early twentieth centuries, had a lethal effect on many Native American languages. A considerable number became extinct, and nearly all of the ones which now remain are in danger of the same fate. Even when a tribal group managed to maintain some use of its ancestral language, the upheavals that it passed through could obscure the group's history, sometimes even to its own members. So it was that a fieldworker investigating an Iroquoian population in Oklahoma (a major site for involuntary relocations, as the former "Indian Territory") found a Native American group speaking one Iroquoian language (Cayuga) but calling themselves by the name of another (Seneca).

It might seem surprising that one group of people could take on another group's name when they still spoke their own ancestral language, but it is not particularly unusual once the history of the two tribes is taken into account. The Cayuga were living around Cayuga Lake in what is now north-central New York State when they were drawn into the American Revolution on the British side. Unfortunately for the Cayuga, this was the losing side. Their villages were destroyed by an American expedition in 1779, and after this disaster the tribe scattered. A small number of Cayuga remained in the ancestral territory, some joined other Iroquoian peoples in Ontario, and some went to live with the Seneca a little to their west. Some residents from the various Seneca settlements in New York soon moved to the Lower Sandusky River in Ohio, and although nearly half of the Ohio settlers were Cayuga, according to an 1829 count, the whole group became known collectively as the "Sandusky Seneca." These Sandusky Seneca then became the "Seneca" of present-day northeastern Oklahoma. Originally, both Seneca and Cayuga, two quite distinct Iroquoian languages, were spoken by members of the Oklahoma population, but in the course of the twentieth century Seneca died out completely. Marianne Mithun, a linguist specializing in Iroquoian languages, made a visit to Oklahoma in 1978 and found a half-dozen or so people descended from the Sandusky Seneca who were still able to speak their ancestral language. But what they spoke was not in line with what they called themselves: "Although the Oklahoma speakers consider themselves 'Seneca,' their language is pure Cayuga, with little observable influence from the other Iroquoian languages" (Mithun 1989: 243–244). Considering the multistage migration that brought the Cayuga to Oklahoma, it is not surprising that the ethnic label the group used had changed. What *is* surprising is that the ethnic language they used had survived for so long and had even kept its original very clear Cayuga character.

An African Case: The Elmolo of Kenya

Even if a distinctive group has managed to stay on in their ancestral territory, local conditions around the group may change and cause unexpected changes in their lives. In the 1880s and '90s, a rinderpest epidemic carried off most of the cattle in East Africa, a part of the world where a man's wealth and social status were directly related to the size of his cattle herd. The Samburu of what is now Kenya were among the high-status cattle-herding peoples, but when their cattle died of the rinderpest they moved in among the low-status Elmolo people, who lived on the southeast shores of Lake Turkana and fished for a meager living. The Samburu survived by fishing and hunting until the rinderpest passed and they could rebuild their cattle herds and return to their former higher-status way of life. But the Elmolo had been changed by the period of close contact. They were not a strong enough people to build up herds of their own and to hold those herds against the cattle-raiding habits of stronger peoples in their vicinity, so they remained fishermen. Many of their customs became those of the Samburu, however, and over a period of fifty or sixty years they also became speakers of Samburu (a Nilotic language), no longer transmitting Elmolo (a Cushitic language) to their children.

The Samburu, as cattle-herding pastoralists, had a language rich in terms relating to their cattle-based culture but seriously lacking in terms for a livelihood based on fishing. Although they shifted to speaking Samburu, the Elmolo-turned-Samburu retained their own Elmolo vocabulary to refer to fishing and to everything related to the marine life of the lake they lived beside. In fact, when the Elmolo-Samburu talk about matters related to fishing, non-Elmolo Samburu speakers cannot understand them. Fieldworker Bernd Heine, trying to untangle the ethnic and linguistic histories of the region and to document as many as possible of Kenya's remaining languages, came among the Elmolo-Samburu in 1971 and again in 1976 and found a few elderly individuals who could remember the process of changing over from speaking Elmolo to speaking Samburu. But even if no such individuals had still been alive, Heine might have guessed the linguistic history of the subgroup of Samburu who fished for a living, thanks to their specialized Cushitic-origin fishing vocabulary (Brenzinger 1992: 236–249).

The Effect of Modern Conditions
on the Language and Ethnicity Link

In recent times, real isolation has become a rarity, even in what seem like very remote spots, and modern conditions are making it rarer all the time. Enormous changes in transportation and communications have made contacts between peoples more common than they once were. With better transportation, individuals and groups are more likely to move, seasonally or permanently, to locations where wage labor is available or where resources are more abundant. Distant central governments are a much more intrusive presence in outlying regions than they were half a century ago. Government officials and administrators carry into outlying regions a state-sponsored language that the local people may have been unaware of previously, and the state's long arm draws young men away to military service far from home. The more geographically mobile members of the community may now bring home wives or husbands who belong to different ethnic groups.

Field researchers, whether they happen to be in search of languages or of specialized lore about local plants, come in for some surprises nowadays. A fieldworker who has made his way with great difficulty to a remote location in which he has been assured that a small population lives, speaking a little-known language and practicing traditional lifeways, may find that nearly all the men under fifty have been traveling far downriver for the past half-dozen years to take seasonal jobs in a timber or mining operation. Instead of a largely monolingual population living by traditional methods, he might find a partly bilingual population eager to use what they know of the official language and more interested in canned foods brought in from outside than in the traditional resources that local plants represent. A large part of a group's traditional knowledge can disappear in a surprisingly short time under these conditions, as people stop collecting local plants for food or medicine and begin to forget not just the uses the plants were once put to but even the names for the plants.

Many of the surprises and disappointments that field researchers meet with today arise from the fundamental fact, mentioned earlier, that the great majority of all human languages are spoken by relatively small numbers of people and have no official standing or state support. Even when a country declares itself multilingual and recognizes two or more official languages, that does not necessarily eliminate the problems. Whatever the number of officially recognized languages, in most countries a number of unofficial languages are also spoken. Canada recognizes both English and French, but that leaves unrecognized all the many Native American languages of the country. Nigeria officially recognizes three languages (Yoruba, Hausa, and Igbo), but with more than 400 languages actually spoken in the country, those three official languages do not begin to accommodate the speakers of smaller languages spoken in particular districts. Even in India, where more than a dozen languages are recognized officially, upwards of 150 other languages go without state recognition. Lack of official standing for a language always puts its speakers at a disadvantage in purely practical terms. Few outsiders are likely to learn their language if it has little to offer in the way of economic or social advantages, and they themselves will need to be at least bilingual, possibly multilingual, if they want to participate fully in national life. The schools will use some other language, for example, and so will other state institutions such as the police, the military, and all the administrative bureaucracies. National politics will typically be conducted in some other language or languages, and regional politics may be as well.

In the last century or so, with growing momentum, languages with a small population base and without official standing have been facing the possibility of extinction. A few languages have been gaining speakers at a rapid rate—namely, those of certain countries with past or present expansionist policies. This accounts for the fact that English, Spanish, French, Portuguese, Russian, Mandarin Chinese, Indonesian, and a few others have grown steadily in number of speakers. When outlying regions or overseas territories come under some form of centralized state control, the strictly local languages typically contract, declining to small numbers of speakers or passing out of use altogether. Many of the languages of the Americas have shrunk or disappeared in this fashion, and the same is true in Australia and in parts of the Pacific Island region. The linguist or ethnographer who hopes to work with any of the indigenous peoples in these vast parts of the world today can expect to find a linguistic situation in flux, with a larger or smaller degree of language shift under way and often with some weakening of what many people think of as the intimate link between an ethnic group and an ethnic language.

Identity-Marking Links and Culture-carrying Links

In reality there are two different kinds of links between an ethnic group and its language. They are not always clearly separated in the minds of observers or even in the minds of the speakers themselves, but one is a much deeper link than the other.

In its simpler, less far-reaching function, an ethnic language serves its speakers as an identity marker. Like a traditional costume or a special cuisine, it identifies the people who belong to a certain group. Because it is only one of an almost infinite variety of potential identity markers, it is easily replaced by other markers that are just as effective. At this level of connection to the group, then, the ancestral ethnic language is functionally expendable.

The second and deeper connection between an ethnic language and the people who speak it is not so easily replaced. Although many behaviors can mark identity, language is the only one that actually carries extensive cultural content. The distinctive sounds uttered in speaking a particular language encode meaning, and the link between ethnic group and ethnic language becomes much more important at this level. Many people suppose that some languages are so "primitive"— so lacking in structural complexity or in vocabulary—that nothing much would be lost if they disappeared forever. But apart from some pidgin languages that arise in conditions of socially superficial contact between peoples with very different mother tongues, there are no such languages. Even peoples with very simple material culture speak highly complex and rich languages (often extraordinarily complex and rich, in fact), and associated with each language is a large body of special cultural lore and almost always an impressive oral literature as well.

The link between an ethnic language and the history of the ethnic group is usually a close one. For example, if the group still occupies its traditional land, geographical features will have indigenous-language names that reflect the group's profound connection to the region: Places where important events took place have names that reflect those events, and places with mythological or supernatural associations also have names rich in meaning for the group. The plants and animals of the native region, too, may have indigenous names that suggest their local use (just as, for example, the name *milk vetch* in English reflects an old belief that the plant increased the milk yield of goats). Traditional stories that relate high points in the group's history usually abound, and traditional tales that convey spiritual beliefs and mythological lore will probably be even more plentiful. These stories, so fundamental to a people's sense of themselves, will be unavoidably stripped of a good deal of their original character if the language in which they were originally told is replaced by a different language. Other sorts of material with major cultural significance face the same stripping process: sacred chants, hero tales, rhetorical performances, genealogical recitations. In fact, loss of resonance, tone, and some degree of inferential meaning will affect every verbal art form that depends for part of its beauty, significance, and uniqueness on properties specific to the language in question, such as syllabic structure, rhythmic patterns, sentence melodies, and repetitions of certain sounds or sound sequences, not to mention nuances deeply embedded in the grammar of the indigenous language but not easily expressible in other languages. Core spiritual concepts framed in the heritage language of the group can be difficult or impossible to express with equal clarity or depth of meaning in another tongue. Much of this clarity or depth is inescapably diminished or lost when a people replaces its ancestral language with another.

The structural distinctiveness of each language is part of what makes the cultural content of a heritage language untransferable if the language is lost, and it is also part of what makes the language special to the field researcher who comes to know and appreciate it. Each of the world's languages encodes human experience in its own fashion, and each can be said to have its own flair or genius created by the particular way its structure organizes whatever it encodes. Vocabulary and grammar organize human experience in unique ways, as anyone who has ever attempted a faithful translation from one language to another knows. Culture-specific abstract concepts are notoriously difficult to express adequately in another language. And grammatical categories or discourse-marking devices that do not have a match can make what is supposed to be identical text seem very different in two different languages. This mismatch problem can crop up even when languages are quite closely related to each other. German and English belong to the same western branch of the Germanic language family, for example, but German has a distinctively marked verbal form (the subjunctive of indirect discourse) that can be used to indicate that the speaker or writer disclaims personal knowledge of the subject and is merely repeating second-hand knowledge. Because that grammatical device has no counterpart in English, it seems impossible that any translator could reproduce in English the tone and atmosphere of the dazzling 1962 German political novel *Bericht über Bruno* (*Report about Bruno*) by Joseph Breitbach. The novel concerns Bruno's evil political career and uses the subjunctive of indirect discourse to render what Bruno and all the other characters except the first-person narrator say. An English translation might resort to a variety of clumsy devices ("I understood him/her/them to say," "purportedly," etc.) to convey the general idea, but the original effect could not be achieved.

If a language as closely related to English as German can create so unreproduceable a tone by means of a single grammatical device that English does not share, then differences in tone, nuance, implication, and the like will be very much greater when languages with much less similar structures are involved. Translations can always be contrived, of course—I have contrived them myself. But we should not expect them to convey what the original conveyed. Nor should ethnic group members who have not learned the heritage language expect to receive their heritage in its fullest and most meaning-rich form if they come to it through translations.

The Fieldworker's Dilemma in a Language-shift Setting

By the very nature of the work, the field researcher soon becomes acutely aware of all that will be lost if an ethnic heritage language is allowed to die out. If he or she has been able to gain some real appreciation for the verbal skills of gifted speakers and of storytellers, singers, and other tradition-bearers, the sense of loss will be still greater. Linguistic fieldworkers are also well aware of how difficult it is to learn a language that has not been transmitted in childhood to the point of full fluency, and linguists who have taken pains to analyze or maybe even to learn the language of a group they were not born to have an especially keen appreciation of the structural properties of the language in question and of their special potency and intricacy. The group itself is seldom consciously aware of that potency and intricacy; ordinary people, even if they are literate in their own language, usually lack both the techniques and the specialized metalanguage (that is, a language for talking about language) that make it possible to compare the properties of languages and so to recognize the particular distinctiveness of a language, even one's own. Apart from not recognizing the unique opportunity that childhood offers for acquiring natural fluency, group members may even imagine that anyone who belongs by heritage to their group will somehow have an easier time acquiring the ancestral language after the childhood years than complete outsiders would (a very common folk belief that leads American college students of, say, French or German descent to expect—unrealistically—that they will learn French or German more easily than classmates of Welsh or Polish descent will).

Once some part of the ethnic population has been allowed to reach adulthood without acquiring the heritage language, the group faces a thorny problem. Unless they are willing to marginalize some of their own young people by insisting that knowing the heritage language is essential to "real" membership, they are forced to attach less importance to language as a component of ethnicity and more to other aspects. This is no particular blow to ethnic identity, because other identity markers easily substitute for the ancestral language. But an ethnic language once lost is far less easily recovered than other identity markers, and the cultural content that the ethnic language carried is never fully recoverable. Fieldworkers confronted with this sort of situation can either bow to what seems to be the inevitable, taking the loss of the ethnic language to represent "the will of the people," or they can resist and become advocates for the ethnic language, a tricky stance for an outsider to take. Anthropologist Morris Foster was interested in the process of language shift among the Comanches in southwestern Oklahoma as they changed from speaking the ancestral Comanche language among themselves to speaking English instead. But when he tried to pursue that topic with Comanches he met, he found it was not a subject they cared to talk about. The subject dear to their hearts was how a person remained a Comanche by performing various deeply Comanche behaviors regardless of the language being spoken. Foster opted to research that topic (Foster 1991), a wise choice for rapid success in his fieldwork—it is more sensible to study topics that the people under study are themselves interested in. But when he abandoned his original topic, Foster also gave up the small but sometimes significant opportunity that outside scholars have of helping to create a more favorable climate for the ancestral language by showing their own interest in it and expressing their appreciation for the subtleties of its grammar and vocabulary.

Many linguistic fieldworkers have been inclined to take the same tack that Foster did. They claim that scholars cannot dictate what should be important to the people they study; the people would not pay attention and would most likely resent the intrusion into their affairs. Some linguistic fieldworkers disagree, however. R. M. W. Dixon, who has worked extensively with a number of Australian Aboriginal languages and more recently with an indigenous language in Brazil, points out that communities often do not realize that their traditional language is in danger of extinction until only a few elderly speakers remain; by then it is too late to change the situation (Dixon 1991: 230). He advocates intervening by encouraging a community "to take pride in its own language and develop a positive desire to pass it on to future generations" and by helping to start a bilingual education program, with the linguist-outsider producing the grammars and dictionaries that can pave the way for school primers and storybooks. Dixon urges this course of action even in the absence of local enthusiasm or requests for help: "In the matter of language maintenance, help must be given where it is needed (even if it is not presently being asked for), not solely where it is asked for (since in most such cases it is really too late to do anything)" (Dixon 1991: 231).

It is not easy to find ways to support a language unless there are at least a few potential local leaders who share the fieldworker's concern for the heritage language and something of the linguist's appreciation for the singular genius of that language. It may even be offensive to the local community if the timing is bad or the fieldworker clumsy. And yet Dixon has a point. Odd as it may seem, speech communities can in fact dwindle down to a handful of elderly speakers before they recognize that they are facing the extinction of their heritage language. In my own fieldwork in the northeast Scottish Highlands, I found that in one village fluent Gaelic speakers moving into and then past middle age were buffered from linguistic reality by their vivid personal sense of the universally Gaelic-speaking village they had grown up in and by the surviving elders among them who continued to use Gaelic regularly. The middle-aged scarcely noticed that young people were growing up without knowing Gaelic until they suddenly recognized that *they themselves* had become the Gaelic-speaking elderly in a population that was otherwise almost entirely English-speaking. It was a shock they were not really prepared for, even though they had helped to make it inevitable by not speaking Gaelic regularly to their own children and to younger kinsfolk and by not requiring Gaelic replies when they did use Gaelic.

When the Ebb Tide Begins to Turn: Two Cases

Gaelic in Scotland

Arguing in favor of Dixon's position is the possibility that a real change of attitude will emerge, either locally or more generally, if only the language can hold on a little longer. This does happen even when the outlook has seemed bleak, as recent changes in Scotland show. Scottish Gaelic had long been undervalued in Scotland, looked upon as a language typical of backward, countrified people. English was considered to be the language of enterprising, progressive people to whom the future would belong. With these attitudes prevailing, Gaelic was fading slowly away, generation by generation. In the Highland fishing villages of East Sutherland, on the far northeast coast, I watched a population of about 200 speakers decline to perhaps twenty, most of whom do not speak with full fluency, in a period of a little more than thirty years. As I write this, just one speaker, a woman in her nineties, remains who can still draw on a rich store of proverbs to make a telling point, can still name some of the landmarks the fisherfolk used to avoid quicksand when gathering shellfish for bait on the shore, can recall the names for traditional local fishing grounds and most of the terms for gear used at the local fishery and at herring curing stations, can name a rich variety of marine life, and can recite a number of local children's rhymes. Just one octogenarian man survives who can do some (not all) of these same things and can also "precent" the Gaelic metrical psalms in religious services (line them out as a soloist, in a lead that is followed by the rest of the congregation).

What will disappear with these last two individuals and a few others close to them in age represents a real loss, not just for the local community but for the whole regional culture. This has suddenly become clear to everyone, and in recent years folklorists, linguists, and interviewers from the Gaelic broadcasting media have been beating a path to the doors of the last speakers, scrambling to record a vivid and unique local culture that is on the verge of disappearing. The painful irony in this is that there has been a real turnaround in Scottish attitudes toward Gaelic in the last decade or two, with both national and local appreciation for the Gaelic language increasing dramatically. Immersion schooling in Gaelic is now available in many parts of the country, and money has been found for a major increase in television and radio programming in Gaelic. In East Sutherland, too, people are viewing Gaelic much more positively than they did just twenty or thirty years ago, and some families of fisherfolk descent are now sending their children to special Gaelic classes, hoping to make Gaelic speakers of them after all. Some of these children may learn a good deal of Gaelic, and if they do they will gain access to a rich Highland cultural tradition they would not otherwise have experienced. But, sad to say, even if they achieve that highly worthwhile goal, they will not be able to recover their own local Gaelic heritage, because too little of it remains now, and only a small part is preserved in any form. For other varieties of Gaelic, time is not quite so crucial, and possibly the long, slow fade of the Gaelic language may yet be halted, at least in some locations.

Greenlandic in Greenland

Just as national and local attitudes have recently changed dramatically for Gaelic in Scotland, language attitudes can change in other regions, too, as well as within families. This is especially likely to happen in the course of an ethnic awakening that precedes or accompanies a movement toward political autonomy or toward greater prosperity. In Greenland, a country with an indigenous population closely akin to the Inuit (Eskimo) of Canada and Alaska, political rule by Denmark had made a Danish identity seem socially desirable and had led some Greenlandic parents to decline to teach Greenlandic to their children. But in the 1970s, during a period of increasing ethnic feeling in many parts of the world, debate about Greenlandic identity led to a rise in ethnic consciousness and a reevaluation of the Greenlandic language. A good many individuals, discouraged from speaking Greenlandic by their parents, set about learning the language on their own as adults. Those who did not do so have had problems being accepted as Greenlanders, because the ability to speak Greenlandic is one of the most important criteria for "being Greenlandic" (Petersen 1985: 297). Home rule was achieved in Greenland in 1979, and ethnic consciousness has remained high. The Greenlandic language is used more today and used for more functions than it was in the mid-twentieth century.

What Role for the Fieldworker?

Certainly rising ethnic feeling can be favorable to the survival of a language, as it has been for Greenlandic and seems likely to be for other languages—for example, Basque, spoken in northern Spain and southern France, and Maori, spoken in New Zealand. For the fieldworker, rising ethnic feeling can create great opportunities or great difficulties, depending on local conditions and on the fieldworker. In the best of all possible cases, the fieldworker will be a birthright member of the ethnic population, someone who has a keen appreciation of the ethnic heritage, including the language, and has the determination and dedication to acquire special training that can be used in analyzing and describing the ancestral language, in collecting traditional oral literature, in preparing teaching materials, and in training more language specialists to carry forward the work. If the indigenous community has not produced specialists of this sort, an outside fieldworker can sometimes encourage the development of such individuals by providing start-up training or by helping to arrange funding to provide a local speaker with specialized training. A fieldworker who is committed to the local community as well as to its language may be able to play a useful role in activities such as providing a basic descriptive grammar, developing an orthography, producing a dictionary, helping with the preparation of oral or written teaching texts, starting an indigenous-language archive, or even helping in legal matters such as land claims by drawing on traditional material (evidence drawn from placenames or traditional stories, for example). At the other extreme, fieldworkers who have exclusively professional goals, from the advancement of their discipline's database to the advancement of their scholarly careers, may find communities in which ethnic consciousness is rising very uncomfortable places to work or may find themselves unwelcome to the point of being excluded altogether.

In today's world, with many small languages still scattered about the globe, a very large number of small language communities show no sign of rising ethnic consciousness, and purely documentary fieldwork is probably the best that can be hoped for. This is likely to be the case if there is no apparent prospect of either local leadership or state support, and all the more so if there are indications that the state is indifferent (or worse) and sees small peoples as standing in the way of "development" or "progress." There will continue to be plenty of scope for fieldwork of the more traditional and less involved sort for half a century, perhaps even for a century, in ever-dwindling pockets of linguistic diversity. But by the end of that period, the very dispassion for which academic scholarship is famous will quite possibly be reckoned as one more small factor that contributed to the loss, already fully foreseeable now, of most of the world's smaller languages and so also of most of its rich linguistic diversity.

A North American Case: Native Languages of California

In the lucky cases where local leadership and outside expertise both happen to be available, courage and determination can bring about some modest miracles. One of the most inspiring cases I know of is the brave initiative in California known as the Master-Apprentice Language Learning Program. Before Euroamericans arrived on the scene, the region that is now California was exceptional in the number of distinct Indian languages to be found there. There were more than 100 of them, and they represented an unusually large number of different language families as well. Even now about fifty Indian languages are still spoken in the state, but none of them has a large number of speakers and most have been reduced to a small number of elderly fluent speakers. At this very final-looking hour, the Native California Network was formed, allowing Indians from around the state to pool their experience and their creative ideas to devise strategies that could prevent the ultimate loss of their heritage languages. Mere documentation was not an acceptable goal. By the late 1900s, Native Americans had had 500 years of experience with cultural loss, stretching back to the arrival of Columbus in 1492. Those who cared passionately enough to come together in an attempt to stem the tide of loss had a lively sense of the cultural disinheritance that typically accompanies the disappearance of a heritage language. Their aim was to keep what still remained to them of their ethnolinguistic heritage and return it to more vigorous everyday use.

Schoolbooks and dictionaries were not available for most of the languages, and in any case Western classroom teaching methods, which encourage a competitive and self-assertive student response, are not compatible with Indian ways of learning and teaching. Instead, the Native California Network called on the experience and expertise of Native teachers who had become involved in efforts to support what survived of the indigenous languages and of university scholars who had studied, described, and documented many of the indigenous languages in the course of long-term research projects. Putting these two resources together and drawing on the incalculably precious knowledge of elders who were still fluent, they created the Master-Apprentice Language Learning Program. Under the program, dedicated volunteer learners apprentice themselves to equally dedicated fluent elders (the "masters"), often older kinsfolk from their own extended family circle, agreeing to spend ten to twenty hours a week in their company, using no language except the ancestral one that the apprentice is trying to learn. Before beginning, both partners participate in a two-day training workshop in which they learn some fundamental techniques for teaching and acquiring a language without resorting to any other language. Some follow-up supervision is available by phone and through visits from coordinators and trainers associated with the workshop. Candidates apply for the program, which operates officially during the summer months and offers a modest stipend that frees some time for each of the partners. In some cases, the language work continues on an informal basis during the rest of the year, if the master and the apprentice are near enough at hand and have the opportunity. Not all of the two-partner teams that begin the program prove successful. It takes enormous determination, plus a bit of creativity and some of the mysterious chemistry that goes into an effective partnership, to carry it off. Successful teams can be very effective, however, and some of these teams continue their work together for the full three summers that the program supports.

The program began in 1993 with just six teams. By the summer of 1996 there were twenty-six teams undertaking the program, and six apprentices working under the program had reached real conversational proficiency—two each for the Karuk, Yowlumne, and Hupa languages. Two new conversationally fluent speakers may not seem like much, but for languages that may have had just half a dozen or even fewer speakers, two new speakers is a huge advance. The apprentices, with all the enthusiasm of successful learners, tend to become teachers in their turn. Occasionally a new team is formed with the original learner's children as the apprentices, drawing another generation into the circle of people who can now tap directly into their own cultural heritage. It's easy to see what this means to an ethnic group that has trembled on the brink of losing direct access to that heritage altogether.

Reclaiming a Heritage by Reclaiming a Language

There are other creative initiatives under way in other parts of the world—among the Äyiwo of the Solomon Islands, the Maori of New Zealand, the Sámi of Norway, and the Basques of Spain, to mention just a few. The people who take up the hard, long-term work that goes into restoring an ancestral language to the descendants of its original speakers are testifying to a fundamental truth that everyone already knows deep down: the ancestral language connects a people to its heritage in ways that there is simply no substitute for. (Awareness of this is what inspires so many third-generation grandchildren of immigrants to learn a language their grandparents deliberately abandoned.) In indigenous communities, revitalizing the language necessarily involves giving new attention and respect to ancestral knowledge and ancestral lifeways, and this is a reconnection that ethnic populations are often in search of. The language-learning programs typically have a major cultural component, and in fact they seem to work best when they are linked to a more general cultural revitalization effort.

The heart of the matter is this: Most people feel a degree of attachment to their ancestral language, and many feel a very strong attachment. If conditions are reasonably favorable, people identify with their own language and do not seek a preferable substitute. In cases in which people have changed to another language and given up their own entirely, it has nearly always been due to a local history of political suppression, social discrimination, or economic deprivation. More often than not, all three have been present. Recognition of this underlies Joshua Fishman's strongly stated position: "Uniformation [i.e., everyone speaking the same language] is never an optimal *human* solution. It necessarily involves subjugation of the weak by the strong, of the few by the many: in short, the law of the jungle" (Fishman 1991:31).

As a linguist, I have made a special study of the linguistic changes that appear when a language is passing out of use. It is fascinating to observe what does and what does not remain intact in the grammar of a language as the fully fluent speakers give way to a final group of "semi-speakers," younger speakers who have not acquired their ancestral language to the point of full fluency and who make easily detected errors as a result. As a fieldworker, though, my experience has been quite different. There is something inexpressibly sad about watching the disappearance of a unique local language that will never again be heard flowing in its full magnificence from the tongue of a verbally gifted speaker. I conversed with a number of speakers of East Sutherland Gaelic who had just such exceptional verbal gifts and listened to others. It was a privilege I will not forget. The sadness lies in the realization that the great-grandchildren of those magnificent speakers will never have the chance to hear the like of what I heard.

Questions for Further Thought and Discussion

1. Can distinct ethnic groups exist within a population that speaks only one language? What criteria might favor distinguishing more than one?

2. If you were the first person to discover the descendants of the mutineer sailors from HMS *Bounty* and the Polynesian women who accompanied them to Pitcairn Island, how much difference would it make to your designation of their ethnic identity, when you wrote your report on the discovery, if you found them speaking English or, alternatively, a Polynesian language?

3. Nearly every country in Europe and the Americas includes within its population some people who are recognized as Gypsies in origin; that is, people who migrated from India centuries ago. Because they all derive from the same population of Indian migrants, should they be considered a single ethnic group?

4. In a certain neighborhood, one family has a name that begins with *Mac-*. Two of the children play the bagpipes, and the whole family enjoys wearing clothing in a distinctive tartan, but they speak only English. Another family in the same neighborhood has a name that ends in *-lini*. One of the children plays the mandolin, and the family enjoys frequent meals of pasta with various sauces. All of the family speak English, but they also speak Italian. Is one of these families more "ethnic" than the other? What do we mean by "ethnic" in this sense?

5. An elderly woman who left her German homeland for Australia fifty years ago but still speaks German tells her Australian grandson that he will never really comprehend the works of Goethe, Schiller, or even the Brothers Grimm (of fairy-tale fame) unless he reads them in German. Does she have a point? Would you expect a Portuguese who had read Charles Dickens' novels in Portuguese to have essentially the same sense of the works as a Pole who had read them in Polish?

6. Languages have been dying out for thousands of years. Gothic became extinct, and so did Etruscan and Cornish in Europe, as well as many east-coast indigenous languages of North America after the Europeans arrived. Why might people feel more concern about language extinctions today than their ancestors did four or five hundred years ago?

Selected Bibliography

Bradley, David (1989). The disappearance of the Ugong in Thailand. In *Investigating Obsolescence: Studies in* *Language Contraction and Death*, N. C. Dorian, (ed.), 33–40. Cambridge: Cambridge University Press.

Brenzinger, Matthias (1992). Lexical retention in language shift: Yaaku/Mukogodo-Maasai and Elmolo/Elmolo-Samburu. In *Language Death: Factual and Theoretical Explorations with Special Reference to East Africa*, Matthias Brenzinger (ed.), 213–254. Berlin: Mouton de Gruyter.

Burling, Robbins (1963). *Rengsanggri: Family and Kinship in a Garo Village*. Philadelphia: University of Pennsylvania Press.

Dixon, R. M. W. (1991). The endangered languages of Australia, Indonesia, and Oceania. In *Endangered Languages*, R. H. Robins and E. M. Uhlenbeck (eds.), 229–255. Oxford: Berg.

Fishman, Joshua A. (1991). *Reversing Language Shift*. Clevedon, England: Multilingual Matters.

Foster, Morris W. (1991). *Being Comanche: A Social History of an American Indian Community*. Tucson: University of Arizona Press.

Hinton, Leanne (1997). Survival of endangered languages: The California Master-Apprentice Program. *International Journal of the Sociology of Language* 123:177–191.

Mithun, Marianne (1989). The incipient obsolescence of polysynthesis: Cayuga in Ontario and Oklahoma. In *Investigating Obsolescence: Studies in Language Contraction and Death*, Nancy C. Dorian (ed.), 243–257. Cambridge: Cambridge University Press.

Petersen, Robert (1985). The use of certain symbols in connection with Greenlandic identity. In *Native Power: The Quest for Autonomy and Nationhood of Indigenous Peoples*, Jens Brøsted, Jens Dahl, Andrew Gray, Hans Christian Gulløv, Georg Henriksen, Jørgen Brøchner Jørgensen, and Inge Kleivan (eds.), 294–300. Oslo: Universitetsforlaget.

Education of Minorities

TOVE SKUTNABB-KANGAS

If social integration is taken to be a psychological state characterized by positive self/ingroup identity along with positive other/
outgroup identification, then bilingualism, both at the individual
and at the social levels, seems to promote social integration.

(Ajit Mohanty)

Goals in the Education of Minority and Majority Children

Accomplishments

A good educational program accomplishes the following goals from a language(s)
and identity point of view: (1) high levels of multilingualism; (2) a fair chance of
achieving academically at school; and (3) strong, positive multilingual and multicultural identity and positive attitudes toward self and others.

Of course, the education of ethnic minorities also must fulfill the further demands that can be made of good education in general. This article looks at some
of the prototypes for education from the point of view of the role language(s),
especially the medium of education, plays in achieving the three goals above. I
see them as positive for *all* children, both minority and majority. The prototypes
can be discussed in terms of nonmodels, weak models, and strong models of
bilingual/multilingual education. The *nonmodels* do not attain the three goals
but instead often lead to monolingualism or to very strong dominance in the
majority language and a negation of goals 2 and 3. The *weak models*, even when
assimilationist, are not quite as harsh for the child. They may often lead to somewhat better chances of school achievement. But in general they do not reach the
goals, either, especially goals 1 (where they may reach limited bilingualism) and
3. *Strong models* are the only ones that may fulfill the goals at a group level.

Their linguistic aim is to promote multilingualism (or, minimally, bilingualism) and multiliteracy.

The nonmodels and weak models—models which are insufficient in reaching the goals and which violate linguistic and cultural human rights and participate in committing linguistic genocide—are, regrettably, still the most common models for educating indigenous and minority children. At a group level, the bulk of minority children still "fail" in school. Many are pushed out early, and the school achievement of many is below that of majority children as a group. Later on, they are overrepresented in unemployment and youth criminality statistics and in other statistics that show results of an unequal society.

This is the general picture. However, there are both individuals and groups who are exceptions and who are managing well, sometimes even better than majority children. Mostly they do it despite the way their education is organized, not because of it.

My contention, one shared by many researchers, is that the education of minorities in most countries, especially in the West, is organized in ways that counteract sound scientific evidence. We know approximately how education should be organized, but it is not organized in this way. Likewise, I claim that the wrong choice of medium of education is the main pedagogical reason for "illiteracy" in the world. Still, the right medium is not chosen, and most "development aid" supports the wrong languages.

How Have Ethnic Minorities Been Educated?

The Earliest Phases

The development of education for many indigenous peoples and for ethnic minorities (hereafter referred to as minority education) has followed a similar line in many countries, both in the West and in other parts of the world. It often started with indifference. Minorities were not formally educated. If they attended school at all, no concessions were made in terms of language or culture. They were taught as if they were majority children and as if the majority language was their mother tongue.   *Noble Savage*

Next, especially for indigenous children, came romantic-racist segregation, the "Noble Savage" idea of separate development, which was later perfected in the apartheid system. Some early missionaries knew (some of) the languages of the minorities. Literacy in the minority mother tongue was sometimes attempted because some believed that the way to the soul was through the mother tongue.

The nationalist-romantic nation-state ideology spread together with early industrialization. Both led to a growing need for some formal education, because national unity and a better qualified workforce were thought to demand linguistic and educational homogenization. This rapidly made the official language the sole medium of education in the West (Europe and neo-Europes, e.g., Australia, Canada, New Zealand, the United States), starting from the early 1860s and continuing for more than a century. For instance, in Swedish state schools, between

1888 and 1957 it was officially forbidden to use the indigenous minority languages Finnish and Sámi, not only as a medium of education but also even during breaks. "Civilization" and sometimes defense arguments legitimized these assimilation policies.

Some Asian countries had more multilingual education systems, especially before and again after colonization. In most African and Latin American colonies, the colonial language was used in the education of all those who had access to formal schooling. This was true at least after the first years of primary school but often from the very beginning, regardless of what the children's mother tongues were and regardless of their minority or majority status. Autobiographical fiction from all over the world describes punishments for using the mother tongue, both physical and psychological, and the resulting colonization of the mind.

Pragmatic ad hoc solutions have been and are common. To this very day, there are few areas in which the wheel has been reinvented as often as in minority education.

Deficiency-Based Theorizing and Assimilation

In the West, the ideology of the nation state has to a large extent prevailed until now. In this linguistically, culturally, and socially homogenous community of an integrated population, national and linguistic identities are supposed to coincide. Most states in the world are of course *not* nation-states in this sense. Because there are between 7,000 and 10,000 oral languages (and probably equally many sign languages) but only some 200 states, there are necessarily many "nations" and speakers of many languages in all but a few states. Therefore this assimilatory "integration" and homogenization has to be achieved through social engineering and state-initiated reforms. Formal education has always played a decisive part in trying to achieve it. The nationalistic, racist (and classist and sexist) tendencies in this ideology were directed toward all those who had to be forcefully "uplifted" from their "otherness": linguistic minorities, the working class, women, and so forth.

This static and ethnocentric view still prevails in many countries: The whole burden of integration is on the dominated groups and individuals alone; they are the ones who have to change. The dominant group is presented as nonethnic. Its values are presented as the norm or as standard and as somehow shared and universal, rather than particularistic and changing, as all values are. When the majority population is presented in this way as an integrated mainstream, homogenously sharing universal cultural values, this characteristic legitimates its access to most of the power and resources. The latter are, of course, shared unevenly on a class and gender basis within the majority population, but this is often not mentioned when integration is discussed.

For a few national minorities (e.g., Swedish speakers in Finland, English and Afrikaans speakers in South Africa), the right to exist, to define independently who they are (to endocategorize), and to reproduce themselves as minorities and, accordingly, to have mother-tongue-medium education, have been more or less self-evident. For most minorities who have some of these rights today, achieving these rights has been a result of a long struggle. Most minorities do not have these rights. Most minorities are still exocategorized, that is, defined by others. The problems they may face in the educational system are misdiagnosed by representatives of the dominant group(s).

Typically, the minorities themselves have been and are blamed for any failures. Reasons for problems in school have been said to stem from several deficiencies or handicaps in the minorities themselves. The minority child or his or her parents and group have been seen as causing the problems. The most often used diagnoses of these problems have been, according to Stacy Churchill, linguistic (related to either first or second language), social, or cultural. The child is seen as suffering from handicaps that are

Second-language-related: the minority child (and his or her parents) do not know the dominant language—for example, English—well enough;

Social: the children's parents represent the lowest social groups, with little formal education, high rates of unemployment, and so forth; the children do not get enough school-related support at home;

Cultural: the minority culture—family patterns, gender roles, relations between the generations, and so forth—is different from the dominant group's culture; there is a cultural clash that prevents the child from achieving; and, in a later phase,

First-language-related: the child does not know his or her mother tongue well enough and is therefore left without a solid basis for second-language-learning as well.

In deficiency theory, the minorities themselves and their characteristics (including bilingualism) are seen as the problem. Measures to cure the problems have typically included more second-language teaching, social support, some forms of multicultural or intercultural education, and some first-language teaching, respectively. Quick assimilation, linguistically and culturally, and acceptance of the dominant group's linguistic, social, and cultural norms have been official or unofficial goals.

The educational models used in these early phases of deficiency theorizing can be called nonmodels or, at best, weak models of bilingual education. I shall discuss more positive alternatives later.

Nonmodels and Weak Models for the Education of Ethnic Minority (and Majority) Children

A submersion, or sink-or-swim, program is a program in which linguistic minority children with a low-status mother tongue are forced to accept instruction through the medium of a foreign majority language with high status. They are placed in classes in which some children are native speakers of the language of instruction. Usually the teacher does not understand the mother tongue of the minority children. The majority language constitutes a threat to the minority children's mother tongue. It runs the risk of being displaced or replaced—a *subtractive* language learning situation. The mother tongue is not being learned properly or at all; it is forgotten or does not develop because the children are forbidden to use it or are made to feel ashamed of it. This is the most common—and most disastrous—method in the present world for educating minority children.

In another variant of a submersion program, powerless majority children (or groups of minority children in a country with no decisive numerical and/or power majorities) are forced to accept instruction through the medium of a foreign (often former colonial) high-status language (because mother-tongue-medium education does not exist). This happens in mixed-mother-tongue classes, mostly without native speakers of the language of instruction. But it also happens in linguistically homogenous classes, sometimes because mother-tongue-medium education does not exist and sometimes because the school or the teachers hesitate to implement a mother-tongue medium program. The teacher may or may not understand the mother tongue of some of the children. The foreign language of instruction is not learned properly. At the same time, the children's mother tongues are being displaced and not learned properly in formal domains (for instance, literacy is not achieved). Often the children are made to feel ashamed of their mother tongues, or at least to believe in the superiority of the language of instruction. Many African, Latin American, and Asian countries use these programs.

A transitional program is a program in which linguistic minority children with a low-status mother tongue are initially instructed through the medium of their mother tongue for a few years. But their mother tongue has no intrinsic value, only an instrumental value. Teaching through the medium of the mother tongue is not seen as a right to which the child is entitled. The mother tongue is seen as useful only so far as its auxiliary use enhances the knowledge of the dominant language. Using the mother tongue also gives the children some subject matter knowledge while they are learning the majority language. As soon as they can function orally, at least to some extent, in the majority language (early exit) or at the latest around grade 6 (late exit), they are transferred to a majority language medium program.

A transitional program is a more sophisticated version of submersion programs, a more "humane" way of assimilating. Transitional bilingual education encourages shift to, first, dominance and, later on, monolingualism in the majority language. These programs are common in the education of migrant children in some of the more progressive settings (for example, some programs in Sweden, Holland, and the United States). They are also used in parts of Anglophone Africa.

In a segregation program, linguistic minority children with a low-status mother tongue are forced to accept instruction through the medium of their own mother tongue or the national language of their country of origin: for example, Kurdish children from Turkey in Bavaria, Germany, are taught through the medium of Turkish, not Kurdish. The children are in classes only with minority children with the same mother tongue. The teacher may be monolingual or bilingual but is often poorly trained. Often the class or school has poorer facilities and fewer resources

than classes and schools for dominant group children. The teaching of the dominant language as a second or foreign language is mostly poor or nonexistent.

Majority children also have nonmodels: mainstream monolingual programs,
perhaps with some foreign language teaching. In the worst case (as in many North
American or Russian classrooms), no foreign languages are taught at all, leading
to what we call monolingual stupidity or monolingual reductionism. In other
countries, one or several foreign languages are taught as subjects for a few hours
per week. This is still the preferred mode of foreign language instruction in the
world. The best foreign-language-as-a-subject teaching, for instance, in the Netherlands or in the Nordic countries, can give a solid basis for bi- or multilingualism
if it is combined with travel or use of the language in daily intercourse.

Assessing the Nonmodels and Weak Models

Minority struggle often starts when parents can see that their children are not doing
well at school, despite trying to do whatever the majority society and school demand. In addition, the parents often feel that they are losing their children, who
no longer know the mother tongue, who may feel ashamed of their parents, language, and culture, and who assimilate rapidly but without the benefits that were
promised with assimilation. Many minorities start the struggle by demanding the
teaching of the minority's own culture and instruction in the mother tongue, first
as a voluntary subject and later as a required medium. In the initial phases of
mother-tongue-medium education, the legitimation has often been that it leads
to greater second-language competence and helps school achievement because
the children do not lose content while learning the second language. This is still
the only (grudgingly accepted) general legitimation for bilingual education in most
Western countries. It leads in the best cases to transitional early-exit programs.
These programs are still based on seeing the minority child as deficient and education as trying to compensate for the deficiencies.

Transitional early-exit programs are a more humane way to assimilate minority children than direct submersion (i.e., placing the children in majority-language-
medium classes). Still, they are language shift programs. They do not normally
lead to high-level bilingualism.

All nonmodels and weak models for minority children fit the United Nations'
definition of linguistic genocide. When the United Nations did preparatory work
for what later became the International Convention for the Prevention and Punishment of the Crime of Genocide (E 793, 1948), linguistic and cultural genocide
were discussed alongside physical genocide and were seen as serious crimes
against humanity (see Capotorti 1979).

When the convention was accepted, Article 3 covering linguistic and cultural
genocide was voted down in the General Assembly, and it is not part of the final
convention of 1948. What remains, however, is a definition of linguistic genocide,
which most states then in the United Nations were prepared to accept. Linguistic
genocide is defined as "prohibiting the use of the language of the group in daily
intercourse or in schools, or the printing and circulation of publications in the
language of the group" (Art. 3, 1). Prohibition can, of course, be overt and direct

(e.g., killing or torture for using the mother tongue, as in Turkey vis-à-vis Kurds) or covert and indirect, accomplished via ideological and structural means. If the minority language is not used as the main medium of education and child care, the use of the minority language is indirectly prohibited in daily intercourse or in schools, that is, it is an issue of linguistic genocide. This is the situation for most immigrant and refugee minority children in all Western European countries and in the United States, Canada, and Australia, for many "national" minorities, and for most indigenous first nations.

How Should Minority Education Be Organized?

In the next phase, enrichment-oriented theorizing may emerge. Bi- or multilingualism is increasingly seen as something positive, not only for minorities (for whom it is necessary) but also for majorities. For majorities, immersion programs are begun (see the next section), initially mainly for instrumental reasons. Minorities start demanding the right to positive endocategorization. This is often a part of a revitalization process, especially for indigenous peoples and old national minorities. In addition, they and those few immigrant minorities who are arguing from an enrichment-oriented point of view often use human rights arguments.

These can be individually oriented ("it is a linguistic human right to learn one's mother tongue fully and also to learn an official language fully"). They can also be more collectively oriented ("it is a human right for a minority to exist, and this presupposes learning both first and second languages fully"). A combination of both argument types may be used to express the viewpoint that linguistic and cultural diversity are not only necessary for the planet but also are positive resources in any society.

With more sympathy toward the right of minorities to endocategorize, initially transitional late-exit programs may be accepted. This was happening in the United States in the early 1990s, until a strong backlash arose in the last year or two of the millennium. At the same time, the more human-rights-oriented demands often expose the power struggles involved in minority education as a part of the more general polarization that is happening throughout the world. Some educators and parents with foresight, from both the minority and the majority populations, start relating the groups to each other. They claim that high levels of bi- and multilingualism are beneficial for everybody; that majorities need to become bilingual, too; that for real integration to happen, both majorities and minorities need to change; and that granting educational language rights may prevent ethnic conflict and disintegration. It does no good to try to change the minority child to fit a majority school. It is not enough to try to give the minority child an emergency kit so that the child can manage in a racist society. It is not enough to enrich the majority child through a bit of exposure to other cultures. Instead, the whole school must change. Society must change.

Often people have discussed only the instrumental necessities for minorities (they must learn the majority language) or the instrumental benefits for majorities (bilinguals get better jobs) that a certain type of education can produce. Alternatively, people discuss only ethnically/linguistically motivated identity-oriented necessities that a certain type of education can give to minorities. But a less naive human-rights argument is also emerging that combines both instrumental and affective benefits. I discuss this issue at the end of the chapter. The new discussions have also led to the development of better educational models.

Strong Models for the Education of Ethnic Minority and Majority Children

Immersion Programs for Majorities

An immersion program is a program in which linguistic majority children with a high-status mother tongue voluntarily choose, among existing alternatives, to be instructed through the medium of a foreign (minority) language. The children are placed in classes that contain only majority children, all with the same mother tongue (the classical model); or, if minority children are in the class, the language of instruction is a foreign one for all the children. The teacher is bilingual so that the children, in the beginning, can use their own language, even if the teacher replies in the foreign language. The children's mother tongue is in no danger of not developing or of being replaced by the language of instruction—they are in an additive language learning situation. Canada has been the pioneer of immersion programs (see Lambert and Tucker 1972, Swain and Lapkin 1982). Most of the programs are in French (for mainly English speakers), but many other languages are also involved. Most European countries and the United States also have immersion programs in different languages.

Language Maintenance (Language Shelter) Programs for Minorities

In a maintenance program or language shelter program, linguistic minority children with a low-status mother tongue voluntary choose, among existing alternatives, to be instructed through the medium of their own mother tongue. The children are placed in classes with other minority children with the same mother tongue only. The teacher is bilingual. They receive high-quality teaching in the majority language as a second or foreign language, provided by a bilingual teacher. These programs are most often organized by an ethnolinguistic minority community itself. Initially, the students' native language is used for most education in content, especially in cognitively demanding, decontextualized subjects, whereas the majority language is taught as a subject only. Later, some, but by no means all, maintenance programs use the majority language as the medium of education for part of the time. But in proper maintenance programs, the minority language continues as a medium of education in many if not all subjects throughout the school.

For a few national minorities, maintenance programs are a self-evident, "normal" way of educating their children, a natural human right. It is significant that most minorities of this type—for example, Swedish speakers in Finland, Afrikaans and English speakers in South Africa, or Russian speakers in Estonia, Latvia and Lithuania—are groups that formerly held power and may be in a transitional phase in which the power they once held has been returned to the numerical majority. They still, however, have the power to organize their own children's education through the medium of their own language. Of course, it should be a fundamental, self-evident linguistic and educational human right for any ethnolinguistic minority to use its own language as the main medium of education. But, in fact, most minorities in the world do not have this basic right. Although a few indigenous peoples (who are numerically a minority in most of their own countries) have maintenance programs, most of them do not. Nor do most immigrant and refugee minority children have access to maintenance programs, even though such programs would result in high levels of bi- or multilingualism, enhanced school achievement, and greater social equity.

The purpose of this type of multilingual program is to ensure that language minority children continue to maintain and develop their mother tongue at a native-speaking (national minorities, indigenous peoples) or at least a near-native-speaking (immigrant minorities) level. They also learn the majority language at a native level and become biliterate. In European schools, they typically also learn other foreign languages. Many mother-tongue-medium programs in African countries (all but the segregation programs) could also be counted as maintenance programs. Birgit Brock-Utne (1993) observes that "in many of the African countries the majority language is treated in a way that minority languages are treated in the industrialized world."

This type of multilingual program enriches society at large by promoting pluralism and mutual understanding and by ensuring that minorities gain access to linguistic and educational prerequisites for social, economic, and political integration. The results are positive. A recent World Bank report by Nadine Dutcher gives a summary of some late-exit and maintenance programs, including the largest evaluation done in the United States, by David Ramirez and his colleagues. In my own study, Finnish working-class youngsters in Sweden who had had nine years of mostly Finnish-medium education were compared with mostly middle-class Swedish children in parallel classes in the same schools. In addition to doing almost as well as Finnish controls in Finland on a Finnish-language test, they performed slightly better than the Swedish controls on a Swedish-language test. Their overall school achievement was somewhat better than that of the Swedish speakers. They had a positive bilingual, bicultural, binational identity.

Two-Way Programs and the European Union Schools Model

A two-way program is one in which 50% minority (with the same mother tongue) and 50% majority children are taught together by a fully bilingual teacher. Initially, this happens through the medium of the minority language, later through both. Both languages are taught as subjects to both groups. A two-way program combines a language shelter program for minority children and an immersion program for majority children. There are two-way programs in more than two hundred schools in the United States. The results are positive.

A European Union schools model is a program in which each language group is taught separately in its own section. Initially, the teaching is completely through the medium of the group's own language. Later, they are taught partly, together with children from other sections, through the medium of one or two foreign languages that are first studied as subjects, then used as media of education in concrete contextually embedded subjects. Only after the eighth grade are these languages also used, according to a careful plan, as media of instruction in decontextualized, intellectually and linguistically demanding subjects. Both the mother tongue and the first foreign language are taught as subjects in the first through twelfth grades. The mother tongue continues to be the medium used for several subjects throughout the program. All staff are bi- or multilingual.

Admittedly, the strong forms of multilingual education outlined in the preceding discussion face different sociolinguistic realities with regard to the linguistic background of the students and the language(s) of the classroom and different sociopolitical realities with regard to the power relations between the attending groups and the rest of their society. However, they all share the aim of cultural and linguistic pluralism, with the bi- or multilingualism and bi- or multiliteracy of students as an avowed goal.

Assessing the Main Principles of Strong Models

The experiments described above have attained good results in terms of the goals we mentioned initially: high levels of bi- or multilingualism, a fair chance of success in school achievement, and positive multilingual/multicultural identities and attitudes. The principles which have to a large extent been followed in these programs can be formulated as the following eight recommendations. They form a possible baseline, which the reader can relate to or agree or disagree with.

1. Support by using as the main medium of education, at least during the first eight years, that language (of the two that the child is supposed to become bilingual in initially) which is least likely to develop to a high formal level. For all minority children, this is their own mother tongue. For majority children, it should be a minority language. (The European schools do not follow this principle completely, because they also teach majority children initially their own mother tongues; e.g., the Italian-speaking children in the European school in Italy are initially taught in Italian, instead of in a minority language.)

2. In most experiments, the children are initially grouped together according to their first language. Mixed groups do not show positive results in initial stages, certainly not in cognitively demanding decontextualized subjects. Spanish-English two-way programs in the United States are an exception. They have mixed classes of half minority and half majority children. All are initially taught in the minority language, later in both languages. This may be a relevant factor in accounting for the Spanish-speaking children's sometimes relatively less impressive gains in

both languages, compared to English-speaking children in the same programs. The mere presence of majority-language children in the same classroom may be too overwhelming for minority children, despite the minority language being the medium of education.

3. All children, not only minority children, are to become high-level bilinguals. This goal seems to be especially important in contexts in which majority and minority children are in the same classes.

4. All children have to be equalized vis-à-vis the status of their mother tongues and their knowledge of the language of instruction. Nice phrases about the worth of everybody's mother tongue, the value of interculturalism, and so forth, serve little purpose unless they are incorporated into the organization of the schools. There must be equality in the demands made on the children's and the teachers' competencies in the different languages involved so that the same demands are made on everybody. Both minority and majority children and teachers must be or become bi- or multilingual. There has to be equality in the roles that the languages are accorded in class schedules and in higher education, in testing and evaluation, in marks given for learning of the languages, in the physical environment (signs, forms, letters, the school's languages of administration, the languages of meetings and assemblies, and so forth), and in the status and salaries of the teachers and their working conditions, career patterns, and so forth.

It is possible to equalize the children vis-à-vis their knowledge of the language of instruction in several ways:

a. All children know the language of instruction (in maintenance programs and European schools initially).
b. No children know the language of instruction or everybody is in the process of learning it (in immersion programs and European schools in certain subjects in a later phase).
c. All children alternate between knowing and not knowing the language of instruction (in a late phase of two-way programs; in alternate-day programs (of half minority and half majority children in which the medium of education alternates daily).

5. All teachers must be bi- or multilingual. Thus they can be good models for the children and support them in language learning through comparing and contrasting and being metalinguistically aware. Every child in a school must be able to talk to an adult who speaks the same native language.

This principle is often experienced as extremely threatening by majority group teachers, many of whom are not bilingual. Of course, not all minority-group teachers are high-level bilinguals, either. But it is often less important that the teacher's competence in a majority language is at top level—for instance, in pronunciation—because all children have ample opportunities to hear and read native models of a majority language outside of school, whereas many of them do not have the same opportunities to hear or read native minority language models. A high level of competence in a minority language is thus more important for a teacher than a high level of competence in a majority language.

6. Foreign languages should be taught through the medium of the children's mother tongue and/or by teachers who know the children's mother tongue. No teaching in foreign languages as subjects should be done through the medium of other foreign languages (for instance, Turkish children in Germany should not be taught English through the medium of German but via Turkish).

7. All children must study both first and second languages as compulsory subjects from first through twelfth grades. Both languages have to be studied in ways that reflect their meaning to the children: as mother tongues or as second or foreign languages. Many minority children are forced to study a majority language, their second language, as though it were their first.

8. Both languages have to be used as media in some phase of the children's education, but how and how much each is used seems to vary for minority and majority children.

For majority children the mother tongue must function as the medium of education for some cognitively demanding, decontextualized subjects, at least in eighth through twelfth grades, if not earlier. But majority children can be taught through the medium of a second language in at least some if not all cognitively less demanding context-embedded subjects from the very beginning. The second language can also be the medium of education, at least partially, in cognitively demanding decontextualized subjects in eighth through twelfth grades.

For minority children the mother tongue must function as the medium of education in all subjects initially. At least some subjects must be taught in the first language through the twelfth grade, but the choice of subjects may vary. The following techniques seem to work well:

- transfer from the known to the unknown;
- transfer from teaching a language as a subject to teaching through the medium of that language;
- transfer from teaching through the medium of the second language in cognitively less demanding, context-embedded subjects to teaching through the second language in cognitively demanding decontextualized subjects.

The progression used for all children in the European Union schools seems close to ideal for minority children. The progression in relation to the (minority) *mother tongue* is as follows:

1. All subjects are taught through the medium of the mother tongue during the first two years.
2. All cognitively demanding decontextualized core subjects are taught through the medium of the mother tongue during the first seven years.
3. There is less teaching through the medium of the mother tongue in eighth through tenth grades and more teaching through the medium of the mother tongue in eleventh and twelfth grades, especially in the most demanding subjects, in order to ensure that the students have understood, can express, and can critically evaluate them thoroughly.
4. The mother tongue is taught as a subject throughout schooling, from first through twelfth grades.

The progression in relation to the *second language* is as follows:

1. The second language is taught as a subject throughout schooling, from first through twelfth grades.
2. The second language becomes a medium of education in third grade, but only in cognitively less demanding context-embedded subjects. Teaching can take place in mixed groups, but ideally together with other children for whom the language is also a second language.
3. Teaching of cognitively demanding decontextualized subjects through the medium of the second language begins only after the children have been taught that language as a subject for seven years (first through seventh grades) and have been taught through the medium of that language in cognitively less demanding context-embedded subjects for five years (third through seventh grades). Before the eighth grade, children should not be taught demanding decontextualized subjects through their second languages in the same classes with children for whom the language of instruction is their first language. European Union schools for the most part do this only in elective courses, not compulsory subjects, even in the highest grades.

When applying the principles to the strong models discussed above, it appears that the European Union schools model—which factually achieves the best results—gets more plus ratings than any of the other models. Even if many of these schools are elite schools, they seem to succeed because the model is scientifically sound, not because of their elitism.

Linking Ethnicity, Identity, and Language for Minorities and Majorities

Ethnicity, Identity, and Mother Tongue: Primordial Sources Shaped by Social Forces

Ethnicity has been proclaimed dead many times during this century, especially after the Second World War. Liberal researchers claimed (and many continue to claim) that it was a traditional, romantic characteristic which would disappear with modernization, urbanization, and global mobility. Ethnic identities would be replaced by other loyalties and identities: professional, social, gender, interest-group, state-related, global, and so on. Marxist researchers claimed that class-related solidarities that crossed national borders would replace ethnicity: International proletariat would unite against world capitalism. Postmodernist researchers now pronounce that we have, or should have, no lasting identities, only flexible temporary nomadic ones: All that is solid melts in the air.

Of course, all of us have multiple identities. We may identify ourselves simultaneously as, for instance, woman, socialist, ecological farmer, world citizen, mother, daughter, wife, researcher, Finnish, Scandinavian, European, witch, theosopher, lover of music and plants, and so on. This can be done without these identities necessarily being in conflict with each other. Of course, some identities will be more or less salient, focused, and emphasized than others at different times, and new identities will emerge or be added, with others fading or being rejected over time.

Still, ethnic identities and, especially, linguistically anchored ethnic identities seem to be remarkably resilient. Ethnicity is not dead at all; quite the opposite.

Both ethnicity and an attachment to one's language or mother tongue(s) as a central cultural core value seem to draw on primordial, ascribed sources: You are born into a specific ethnic group, and this circumstance decides what your mother tongue (or tongues, if your parents speak different languages) will initially be. But what happens later to your ethnicity, your identity, and your language(s) and how they are shaped and actualized is influenced by economic and political concerns and by your social circumstances and later life. These things also influence to what extent you are aware of the importance of your ethnicity and your mother tongue(s) and the connection between them.

I do not agree with those researchers who see both ethnicity and a mother tongue in an instrumentalist way, as something you can choose to have or not have, to use or not use, according to your own whims and wishes. Because of the primordial sources that reach back into infancy and personal history, neither ethnicity nor mother tongue nor even identities can be treated as things, commodities, that one can choose and discard like an old coat at will. This does not mean, however, that they are givens or impossible to influence or change.

What is important to study, then, is under what circumstances can ethnicity and language(s) become positive forces and strengths, sources of empowerment in people's lives?

Ethnicity, Language, and the Medium of Education

Education that leads to multilingualism has been used, fought for, and fought against with different motivations. Different strategies have been needed in different countries, even by different minorities in the same country at the same time, because the circumstances have differed. If forced segregation, with denial of access to the power language, was the worst enemy (as in apartheid South Africa or guest-worker Germany), a different model had to be chosen than in cases in which forced assimilation was the enemy, with the killing of the minority language as a concomitant. Here we shall relate the models described earlier to the roles that ethnicity and language have played in their development.

For majority groups, ethnicity often does not play any conscious role when choosing the medium of education. In most cases, choosing the majority mother tongue as the medium is done by individuals routinely, as something self-evident—even if the function of such education is to reproduce a majority ethnic identity.

When powerful majorities choose another language as a medium, instrumental reasons in most cases prevail: They have recognized the economic and career-oriented benefits of making their own children multilingual, thereby improving opportunities of doing business with and getting ahead in an increasingly interdependent world. Immersion programs, the European Union schools and international schools are examples of this approach that emphasizes enrichment and extra benefits. In most cases, there is no change of identity for students in these schools, and the connection between language and ethnic identity is hardly discussed.

In addition to these instrumental reasons, both immersion programs and, especially, two-way programs may contain an element of integrative motivation. In situations of potential conflict, multilingual education for majority children may represent a means of improving their understanding of other ethnolinguistic groups with which they are in contact. With revitalizing minority groups, different types of two-way programs may become more common—an optimistic reading.

For many oppressed and often segregated minorities, ethnic identity was not initially seen as important. Rather, they focused on school achievement, educational opportunity, and equality. Submersion programs initially gave them a hope of learning the dominant language and culture. These programs were rightly seen as possessing instrumental value which their own languages, cultures, and ethnicities could not promise. For most, the hope failed, and the promised results did not materialize. In addition, many lost their only linguistic resource, their own language, or at least lost the chance of developing it to a high formal level; and many children were made to feel ashamed of their ethnic background. When the first mother-tongue-as-a-subject programs and the transitional early-exit programs arrived, the justification was—and still is—instrumental and second-language-oriented: The minority mother tongues were accepted because mastering them led to greater competence in the second language. Schools should not train minority children for fatherland, folk dances, and ethnolore but for jobs, school authorities say. Often the authorities show a poor understanding of what mother tongue and ethnicity mean. They also see the world as either/or rather than both/and: either first *or* second language; either tradition *or* modernity; either parents *or* a job—all false polarizations. Many early-exit programs for indigenous peoples may also belong to the type of program that emphasizes educational achievement. In theory, many Latin American bilingual programs emphasize the language, culture, and ethnicity of the indigenous group. But the model chosen (early-exit) does not lead to the proclaimed goals.

Late-exit transitional, two-way, and even maintenance programs often concentrate on mother-tongue-medium education for minorities who have previously been excluded from equal educational opportunity and, especially, from equality of outcome. Even if the mother tongue is seen as important and if emphasis is placed on creating and supporting positive ethnicity, instrumental career-oriented concerns are at least equally important. These are usually both/and models rather than the either/or that are typical of submersion and segregation and also of early-exit transitional programs.

Many threatened ethnolinguistic groups have adopted multilingual education as a prerequisite or means of linguistic survival. Maintenance and language shelter programs or revitalization programs for minorities, for example, the Frisian schools in the Netherlands or Kōhanga Reo programs in New Zealand for the Maori, or Hawaiian immersion programs, are of this type. These programs often focus on cultural and ethnic identity, and the link between language and ethnicity is strong.

The reasons and goals for using two or more languages in the educational system thus vary greatly, ranging from increased knowledge and economic gain to increased mutual understanding to improved educational opportunity and outcome to ethnolinguistic survival. Many programs are multipurpose and combine several of the goals. Linguistic human rights and viewing minority languages and ethnicities as resources, not handicaps, are central to many of the most advanced programs.

Whereas earlier, biologically argued racism was used to legitimate unequal access to formal education and later to good jobs, housing, and so forth, today ethnically and linguistically argued racisms, ethnicism and linguicism, are used. These can be defined as ideologies, structures and practices which are used to legitimate, effectuate and reproduce an unequal division of power and (both material and non-material) resources between groups which are defined on the basis of

- "race" (biologically argued racism)
- ethnicity and culture (culturally argued racism: ethnicism)
- language (linguistically argued racism: linguicism) (Skutnabb-Kangas 1986)

Linguicism is a major factor in determining whether speakers of particular languages are allowed to enjoy their linguistic human rights. Ethnicism and linguicism are more sophisticated but equally efficient weapons as biological racism in committing ethnocide (ethnic genocide, the destruction of the ethnic sociocultural identity of a group) and linguistic genocide.

Linguistic and cultural human rights are prerequisite to preventing ethnic and linguistic genocide. Lack of these rights—for instance, the absence of these languages from school curricula—makes minority languages invisible. Alternatively, minority mother tongues are constructed as nonresources, as handicaps which are believed to prevent minority children from acquiring the majority language (the only valued linguistic resource), so that it becomes in the interest of minority children to abandon them. At the same time, many minorities, especially minority children, are in fact prevented from fully acquiring majority resources, and especially majority languages, by educational structures in which instruction is organized through the medium of the majority languages in disabling ways that contradict most scientific evidence.

Human rights, especially economic and social rights, must, according to human rights lawyer Katarina Tomaševski, act as correctives to the free market, overruling the law of supply and demand. In other words, they should guarantee that the basics needed for survival and for the sustenance of a dignified life have no price tags and are outside market forces. The necessities for survival include not only basic food and housing, but also basic civil, political, and cultural rights. Education, including basic educational linguistic rights, is one of the necessities from which price tags should be removed. According to human rights principles, it is the duty of each government to create conditions under which people can provide these necessities for themselves and to provide the necessities for those unable to do so themselves.

The fewer speakers a language has, the more necessary it is for the children to become high-level multilinguals, in order to be able to obtain the basic necessities needed for survival. The mother tongue is needed for psychological, cognitive, and spiritual survival—cultural rights. All the other languages, including an official language of the state in which the children live, are needed for social, economic, political, and civil rights. A child must be able to speak to parents, family, and relatives, to know who he or she is, to acquire skills in thinking, analyzing, and evaluating. The mother tongue(s) is (are) vital for this. Further education, job prospects, and the ability to participate in the wider society require other languages. Thus high levels of multilingualism must be one of the goals of proper education.

Everybody, not just privileged elites or poor minorities, needs to be fluent and literate in at least two languages, preferably more. Everybody, not just minorities, needs to become aware of and acknowledge the importance of their ethnic and linguistic roots, in order to be able to develop, analyze, criticize, create, and reflect. Language rights for all are part of human rights. Language rights are prerequisite to many other human rights. Linguistic human rights in education are a prerequisite for the maintenance of the diversity in the world that we are all responsible for.

Questions for Further Thought and Discussion

1. Discuss examples of the different models that you know.

2. Think of minority education as you know it. Does it fit the definition of linguistic genocide?

3. How could minority education be organized in your school/district/state if the recommendations in this article were to be followed?

4. What would the consequences be? For parents? Teachers? Other staff? Children?

5. Read the final chapter in Skutnabb-Kangas (ed.) (1995) by Skutnabb-Kangas and Ofelia García. Compare the "Characteristics in multilingual education" (Table 3, pp. 246–249) with the curriculum in a school of your choice. Discuss them with a teacher in that school. Compare results.

6. List possible causes of failing to organize minority education in a scientifically sound way. Discuss them. Do you know enough about power relations? Exchange suggestions for further reading, useful e-mail lists, and Web sites with other students or colleagues.

7. Find out which community organizations in your area try to change minority education. Invite some of them to your class. Exchange experiences.

Selected Bibliography

Baker, Colin (1993). *Foundations of Bilingual Education and Bilingualism.* Clevedon, Eng.: Multilingual Matters.

Brock-Utne, Birgit (1993). *Education in Africa: Education for Self-reliance or Recolonization?* Rapport No. 3. Oslo: University of Oslo, Institute for Educational Research.

Capotorti, Francesco (1979). *Study of the Rights of Persons Belonging to Ethnic, Religious and Linguistic Minorities.* New York: United Nations.

Crawford, James (1989). *Bilingual Education: History, Politics, Theory and Practice.* Trenton, N.J.: Crane.

Cummins, Jim, and David Corson (eds.) (1998). *The Encyclopedia of Language and Education.* Vol. *Bilingual Education.* Dordrecht: Kluwer.

García, Ofelia (ed.) (1991). *Bilingual Education: Focusschrift in Honor of Joshua A. Fishman.* Vol. I. Amsterdam: Benjamins.

International Journal on Minority and Group Rights 4(2): 1996/1997. Special Issue: Education rights of national minorities.

Lambert, Wallace E., and Richard G. Tucker (1972). *Bilingual Education of Children: The St. Lambert Experiment.* Rowley, Mass.: Newbury House.

Pattanayak, D. P. (1981). *Multilingualism and Mother-Tongue Education.* Delhi: Oxford University Press.

Rubagumya, Casmir M. (ed.) (1990). *Language in Education in Africa: A Tanzanian Perspective.*

Skutnabb-Kangas, Tove (ed.) (1995). *Multilingualism for All.* Lisse: Swets & Zeitlinger.

Skutnabb-Kangas, Tove, with assistance from Ilka Kangas and Kea Kangas (1986). *Minoritet, språk och rasism* (Minority, Language and Racism). Malmö: Liber.

Swain, Merrill, and Sharon Lapkin (1982). *Evaluating Bilingual Education: A Canadian Case Study.* Clevedon, Eng.: Multilingual Matters.

History

HARALD HAARMANN

Ethnic processes are as old as human history. Ever since the appearance of modern humans (*Homo sapiens sapiens*), cultural diversity and the variety of patterns of social behavior associated with it have been a part of the archeological record humans have left behind. Cultural diversity has been a major factor in the formation of local groups among humans from earliest times (Megarry 1995). Awareness of cultural boundary marking among local groups has been an element of a group's self-identification, of its orientation in a local cultural environment, and of its categorization of outsiders. These elements of awareness have contributed to the evolution of group cohesion and to the construction of in-group solidarity, the collective equivalent of the self contrasted with the collective other, that is, out-group members.

Cultural diversity is strikingly absent from the archeological record left by the archaic human communities formed by the Neanderthals and *Homo erectus*, the first hominids to walk upright. What survives of the material culture of these hominid subspecies (i.e., artifacts of stone and bone) indicates rather simple stages in human development which are characterized by cultural homogeneity rather than heterogeneity. The only element of variation is apparent in the pace of evolution, this being the difference between the rather primitive stage of the stone industry in the communities of *Homo erectus* and the more refined techniques of chipping stones or drilling bones used by Neanderthals.

The linguistic resources, that is to say, the structuring of the sound system, paradigmatic and syntactic patterns of grammar, and lexical structures, which were available to Neanderthals were evidently rather crude. Whether *Homo erectus* had a kind of primitive and very restricted language remains a matter of dispute. Although the possibility of some kind of linguistic diversity in the communities of Neanderthal man cannot be ruled out, this hominid subspecies can hardly be assumed to have had an awareness of linguistic and cultural boundary marking. Because there were no impulses to promote an awareness of cultural difference, the communities formed by *Homo erectus* and Neanderthals had little reason to think about the descent of their local group. In all traditional cultures of modern humans, evaluating descent is a major determinant of ethnic relations. The most widespread type of mythical narrative in the world's cultures is the myth of origin, which explains the descent of the local group with its individualizing language and its specific cultural patterns.

Accordingly, ethnicity as we understand it from our contemporary experience cannot be assumed to have existed as a constructive element in the communities of earlier hominids.

The Relationship of Identity and Ethnicity over Time

Various fields in the humanities, behavioral psychology, cultural anthropology, and the sociology of prehistoric societies have all reached conclusions that strongly support the assumption that identity, the mental capacity for both self-identification and categorization of the other, is the prime motor of human evolution, with language as the major signifier in human relations. Identity is not a simple matter of the social and cultural institutions that influence or dominate an individual's lifestyle. In order to understand the complexity of identity, and of ethnic identity in particular, one has to consider its anthropological infrastructure.

A person's identity evolves to the extent that he or she succeeds in establishing a reliable profile of the "self" in contrast to the "other." Thus identification is always a matter of finding a balance between consciousness both of the self as an individual and of the role played by the individual in group relations. Identity processes are naturally related to a person's individual kinship relations (identifying with one's relatives); to specific local conditions of community life (acculturation); to a related worldview, whether religious or political-ideological; and to a culturally specific value system (a phenomenology). Consequently, such processes are definitely subject to cultural diversity and ethnic boundary marking. Ethnicity can thus be regarded as the most elementary dimension of identity in the construction of human society, regardless of the degree to which ethnic relations play a role in the individual's behavior or are manipulated by outside factors. A community of Germans living in a small town in northern Germany, for example, may not be aware of what makes them German, and they may think of their lifestyle as being completely ordinary. Their habits, ideas about life, and values may seem very different or even outlandish to someone living in southern France, Greece, or Bulgaria. A German's lifestyle may actually seem exotic to an Afghan Muslim, an Indian Hindu, or a Maasai from Kenya. "Germanness" can thus be defined by contrasting it with features of non-German ethnicity. In the course of history, ethnic boundary marking, seemingly, has been more important for identification than an awareness of cultural specificity that comes from within a reference group (Jones 1997).

Regardless of whether ethnic identity is actively professed (along the lines of "I am proud to be a black American and behave like one") or internalized as an unconscious ingredient of a person's group membership (for instance, in the case of an ordinary Russian who is Russian simply because he or she is unfamiliar with any other culture), it can become the object of manipulation, often with the intention to use ethnic boundaries for creating cultural stereotypes and racial prejudices. Unfortunately, human history offers many cases of ethnic relations being manipulated as a vehicle of competing political interests. The record of Jewish-Arabic confrontation, for example, is long, and the convulsive struggle for a pattern of coexistence between the Israelis and the Palestinians is only the most recent offshoot of a persistent historical conflict.

The ethnic conflict in the former Yugoslavia, and in Bosnia-Hercegovina in particular, has sometimes—although inappropriately—been termed a culture conflict. This characterization is inaccurate because the conflict is not the reflection of a clash of civilizations. Features of Croat ethnicity (particularly descent and Catholic Christianity) that differ from Serbian identity have been manipulated by Serbian political circles as a vehicle for promoting hostility. A similar strategy of hostile ethnic boundary marking, focusing on descent and Islamic traditions, has been applied by the Serbs to negatively categorize Bosnians. Serbian descent and Orthodox Christianity have been turned into symbols of ethnic hatred among Croats and Bosnians, hatred directed toward the Serbs. Ethnic cleansing in Bosnia, which was practiced by all parties although to a greater extent by Serbs, became an instrument of politically instigated ethnic hatred.

The alliance of Croats and Bosnians against the Serbs that was forged during the war in Bosnia originated in the needs of the two weaker parties to resist the dominant group. This fragile alliance dissolved immediately after the war. Despite the peace accord among the competing ethnic groups, considerable covert hostility still remains, accumulated on all sides. Thus the impression of peaceful interethnic relations and community life conveyed by the accord is a deceptive one.

There are cases in which ethnic conflicts are so deeply rooted that all political efforts to solve the crisis fail. The war in Chechnya (1995–1996) illustrates that combining political interests with ethnic issues may produce an explosive mixture. Here is a true clash of worldviews. This war did not involve only two armies fighting each other. The desperate resistance of the Chechen rebels against the Russian high-tech war machine was inspired by an ethnic moral ethos. The high degree of motivation among the Chechen fighters was nourished by the Muslim interpretation of the war in terms of a jihad, "holy war," against an unworthy aggressor, a former colonial power. All elements of ethnicity differed on both sides, thus ethnic boundary marking was rich in contrasts and attracted considerable racial prejudice.

The Chechens are an indigenous people of the Caucasus, their mother tongue belongs to the northeastern group of Caucasian languages, they are Muslims, and they are educated in an Islamic worldview. They also retain the memory of a glorious and militant past. The conflict in Chechnya has a long tradition, having originated in the eighteenth century when the czarist army occupied the region. Throughout their modern history, Chechens have been in armed conflict with the Russians. They resisted Soviet rule during the first decades of Soviet power and were ready to join forces with the Germans when the invading Nazi army was approaching the Caucasus in the summer of 1942. The Chechen rebellions during the Soviet era were all crushed, but the flame of resistance has never been extinguished, nor has the struggle for national self-determination ever been abandoned.

The Historical Role of Language in Ethnicity

Mankind has devised many sign systems for constructing the cultural environment. These sign systems may be related to language, or they may function independently without the vehicle of language. Examples of the latter category range from the very elementary, such as elements of gestures and poses which form a gestural code, to the very specialized, such as the digital processing of information in computers. In human history, language is undoubtedly the sign system that has assumed the greatest variety of functions. It is related to many other sign systems, such as the written information on bank notes in the monetary system; or it interacts with nonverbal systems, for example, in its role in traffic signs: "through traffic," "slow down," "construction ahead."

The use of language to convey information is not the only major function of this sign system, nor, arguably, is it the most elementary one. If mankind constructs its world using language, then this means of communication necessarily covers every domain of human existence. In addition to constructing a network of knowledge about the world, language also serves for expressing feelings, attitudes, and values; for telling lies and making evasions; for cursing and insulting; for praising and scolding. Language is a vehicle which does things to people, causing positive and negative reactions. Language enables a person to experience joy, such as hearing a confession of love, or to have his or her mind put at ease, as through words of comfort or prayer. Words can have a devastating effect, as when a newspaper reveals a rumor of an alleged scandal, or they may even influence the existence of entire communities, as is the case with a declaration of war. Language is a vehicle of man's intentionality; its users' intentions may be positive, resulting in a harmony of interaction, or negative, resulting in the construction of cultural prejudices and stereotypes.

If ethnicity provides the most elementary framework of human relations on which identity can be constructed, then language provides the most elementary means for fulfilling this task. Language is always involved in ethnic relations as the most refined vehicle of interacting according to local behavioral traditions, of expressing attitudes and values, and of stereotyping culture. This elementary function of language in ethnicity, however, does not support the idea of language always being the major constructive element of ethnic boundaries or an exclusive marker of ethnicity (Haarmann 1986).

The most general marker of Jewish ethnicity, for instance, is Judaism, which actually is a combination of a religious pattern, Yahwism, with the element of descent. However, there are cases of both self-proclaimed Jewish atheism and the existence of Judaism among Turkic peoples, such as the Khazars in historic times and the Karaims today. Hebrew, the sacred language of Yahwism, is a symbolic marker of Judaism but not necessarily of Jewishness. It serves in this function only for those Jews who have adopted modern Hebrew (*Ivrit*), most of whom live in Israel. There are several other Jewish languages, such as Ladino (often referred to as "Jewish Spanish") and Yiddish ("Jewish German"), which are markers of a local proliferation of Jewry but not exclusive or overall features of it.

In the case of the populations in Bosnia-Hercegovina, language is not a major marker of ethnic identity. What makes Serbs Serbs, Croats Croats, and Bosnians Bosnians is their membership in different religious communities. They can all communicate in the same language (i.e., Serbo-Croatian), despite some specific local differences in pronunciation and vocabulary. Since the war, each group has been actively promoting a language policy of segregation by trying to emphasize local features and evaluate them as boundary markers to exclude other varieties. This development might ultimately result in the linguistic separation of the three varieties of Serbo-Croatian to become additional markers of ethnicity, and Serbo-Croatian would correspondingly devolve into distinct Croat, Serbian, and Bosnian languages.

Language is a major marker of ethnicity for many local groups around the world, and there have been historical periods when language was assigned an ideological role as the marker par excellence of ethnic identity. An example of this is the idea of the national language as the bond which unites individuals in what has been termed the "linguistic nation." This idea was developed in intellectual circles in the eighteenth century, that is, during the Age of Enlightenment, and it spread throughout Europe as an instrument of politics during the nineteenth century. The importance of the idea of a national language was foremost during the French Revolution of 1789, the activists in which established French as the exclusive means of education and of national self-awareness for all inhabitants of France, regardless of whether they were of French, Basque, Catalan, Breton, Occitan, German, or Flemish descent. The people in the first newly proclaimed nation-state in Europe, Greece, which was founded in 1822, constructed their self-identification primarily on the role of the Greek language in the shaping of Greek culture.

Since the beginning of recorded history, people have been aware of language as a marker of ethnicity. The marking of collective ethnic identity has always been linked to a name for the reference group (ethnonym) and to their language as the vehicle of the speech community (Smith 1986). The power struggle and cultural rivalry of Sumerians, Elamites, and Akkadians in the ancient Orient are reflected in the conflict of languages as distinctive markers of their local communities. Elam was subdued by the Sumerians, and language use was dominated by the conqueror's language. The Akkadians then conquered the Sumerian city-states. The primary explanation for the survival of Sumerian is that this language was also held in high esteem by non-Sumerians and thus continued to be used in learned literature. The self-contained ways of society in ancient Egypt were definitely related to the Egyptian language, which held the terminological key to understanding its mysteries. It was not until the successful decipherment of Egyptian hieroglyphics by Jean-François Champollion in 1824 that experts in the modern world could read ancient Egyptian and managed to gradually decode Egyptian civilization.

The best proof of the validity of language as a marker of ethnicity in antiquity is the concept of the "barbarian," which was invented by the ancient Greeks to raise the prestige of their own culture. The main criterion of a barbarian was his language, because the Greek word *barbaros* means "a person who speaks inarticulately" (that is, a person who does not know Greek and speaks an unintelligible language). All local cultures that surrounded the Greek territory were categorized as barbarian. It was a truism in Greek public opinion—which was reinforced by writers, historians, and politicians—to consider the Scythians, Celts, Illyrians, Thracians, and others barbarian. Only cultures with an acknowledged high standard of civilization and literary tradition were considered by the Greeks to be equal to their own (e.g. Roman, Etruscan, Egyptian).

With the spread of Hellenism in the third century B.C.E., a new functional element was introduced to the relationship of language in ethnicity: This was the significance of Greek for a cosmopolitan lifestyle. The Hellenistic idea of cosmopolitanism was still ethnic. People of Greek, Egyptian, Syrian, Phoenician, and Persian descent were accepted as members of equal status in Greek society, provided they professed a *Hellenistic* lifestyle and expressed their ideas in Greek. In many parts of the considerable area dominated by Greek, Hellenistic cosmopolitanism evolved in an atmosphere of bilingualism, with local ethnic languages as the mother tongue and Greek as the vehicle of universal civilization. So language also retained its role as an important marker of ethnicity during that period.

The peoples of Europe have experienced several periods during which language played a more significant role in the formation of ethnic groups than it did at other times. This development may be interpreted as indicative of fluctuations in ethnic relations. The principal periods in which language-related ethnicity functioned to promote cultural development are the following (Haarmann 1995).

1. *The transition from late antiquity to the early Middle Ages.* This age saw the flourishing of Irish, Anglo-Saxon, and continental Germanic cultures (in particular, Visigothic, Longobard, Frankish, and Saxon).

2. *The Middle Ages.* The formation of regional Romance (French, Occitan, Spanish, Galician, Italian), Slavonic (Old Bulgarian, Old Russian) and Nordic (Danish, Swedish, Norwegian, Icelandic) cultures was intrinsically interwoven with the rise of their vernaculars to literate status. One can argue that language-related ethnicity in Europe has since this time been explicitly associated with the development of a written standard language.

3. *The Protestant movement in the sixteenth and seventeenth centuries.* Although basically a religious movement, Protestantism had a long-term effect on the elaboration of literary languages, in particular for smaller speech communities (e.g., Finns, Estonians, Sorbs, Slovenes, Latvians, Romansh). The establishment of a literary standard supported in-group solidarity in a world in which literacy had become an instrument of religiously motivated political struggle.

4. *The Enlightenment and the Age of Nationalism.* During the eighteenth century, the idea of language as the prominent marker of a national culture spread as the product of intellectual reasoning. This development has for long been misunderstood as though European intellectuals had invented the notion of the linguistic nation. In fact, national language ideology meant elaborating earlier trends

of language-related ethnic identity to make it adaptable to political thought. The awareness of language as a means of ethnic boundary marking appeared as early as the early Middle Ages. Drawing on the differentiation of people's mother tongues after the destruction of the biblical Tower of Babel, Isidore of Seville (c. 560–636), the schoolmaster of medieval Europe, attributes to language a prime role in producing ethnic diversity. He stresses that "races arose from different languages, not languages from different races."

The idea of the national language was manipulated by politicians of the nineteenth century and used as a tool for nationalistic competitiveness. The "great" historical nations built up their states and consolidated their power at the cost of smaller nations. In the process of constructing nation-states and political spheres of interest, the Europeans experienced wars on all scales: the attempts to establish French hegemony in the Napoleonic wars, Hitler's disastrous plans to reorganize Europe's political landscape that led to the outbreak of the Second World War, the numerous wars of independence (e.g., Greece, 1822–1823; Serbia, 1882; Finland, 1917–1918); and the clash of the great powers in the Crimean War (1853–1856) and in the First World War. The ideology of the national language as the main marker of national culture and as an exclusive symbol of the nation-state has continued even into the era of integration in western Europe. The notion of "Frenchness" as defined in association with the concept of French, *la langue de civilisation par excellence*, is perhaps the most illustrative example in our days.

5. *The age of modern nationalism.* The repercussions of historical nationalism have been felt in recent history, and nationalism has continued to play the role of a "quasi-religion" (Smith 1994). The period of modern nationalism, of its most modern wave to be exact, commenced in the late 1980s, when national movements among the non-Russian population in the Soviet Union began to articulate their demands for greater political and cultural autonomy in an atmosphere of glasnost (clarity) and perestroika (reconstruction, reform). The new nationalism has flourished since the political changes of 1989–1990 which ultimately led to the dissolution of the former Soviet empire, to the emergence of new nation-states (the former "inner Soviet colonies"), and to a revival of national(istic) trends in the former satellite states of the Soviet Union in eastern Europe.

Three Reasons for Ethnic Revival in the 1990s

The recent ethnic revival which has been felt throughout the world is a still-evolving process, so one can only speculate about its future influence on worldview and world politics. The awareness that ethnic relations play an ever-increasing role in people's lives has grown, both in the positive sense of experiencing ethnic self-consciousness and in the more negative sense of having to confront the reality of ethnic frictions, conflicts, and cultural clashes. In theory, ethnicity may be assigned a neutral place in social interaction by the scholar of ethnic studies. However, in reality, this factor will always be intertwined with evaluations of all kinds and may readily be exploited to serve political interests. Where values and interests are polarized or in conflict, the effect on interethnic relations will be negative.

The reasons for the ethnic revival in our day are rooted much more deeply than is apparent in recent history. We have to deal with yet another, and this time very powerful, periodic fluctuation of ethnicity as an anthropological arbitrator of global interaction. In addition to impulses which have originated in recent years, the immanent role of ethnic identity is linked to ethnic processes in history which, in a continuous flow of impulses, are shaping trends of our time. Modern nationalism cannot reasonably be evaluated as a completely new development, and it came as a surprise only to those who underestimate the elementary role of ethnicity in human relations. The new nationalism reflects the working of older ideas of national culture and nation-state politics, modified according to modern living conditions.

Three major developments have provided impetus for a reevaluation of ethnic relations.

The Dissolution of Ideological Tensions and the Revitalization of Local National Cultures

The political changes of the 1990s owe much of their dynamics to the decline of ideological barriers. This major development was triggered unintentionally by the movement to attempt reform of the Communist system in the Soviet Union, starting in the mid-1980s, which fell short of its goal and had an outcome that was much different from that envisioned by Mikhail Gorbachev, the initiator of the reform. Instead of being reformed, Soviet power was deconstructed, eventually dissolving under the pressure of newly emerging democratic movements. Immediate reactions to the decaying of Soviet totalitarianism came from within the non-Russian communities in the Soviet Union. Starting in the Baltic region and rapidly spreading to Moldavia, the Ukraine, and the Caucasus, national movements claimed political and cultural rights to compensate for decades of Russian hegemony.

The awakening of nationalism in the non-Russian Soviet republics came as a surprise to Soviet Russian ideologists, who had declared the "national question" solved long ago and who had promoted an ideological course of "brotherly" intercommunication between Russians and non-Russians. The revitalizing of non-Russian ethnic interests was, however, expected by many Westerners who had never been persuaded by the interethnic harmony propagated by Soviet authorities. And yet the rapid pace of disintegration of the Soviet state and of national segregation was astounding to everybody.

The year 1991 brought a fragmentation of what had been the Soviet Union into a number of independent nation states such as Estonia, Latvia, Lithuania, Belarus, Ukraine, and Moldova, the only exception being Russia, which retained its official status as a federation (*Rossiyskaya Federatsiya*, "Russian Federation"). In the territory of Russia itself, Russians make up 81.5% of the population; the other 18.5% are non-Russians such as Tatars, Kalmyks, Buryats, Komi, and more than 100 other ethnicities. Repercussions of the rising nationalism in the decaying

Soviet empire were also felt in the states of the former Eastern bloc: Poland, East Germany, Czechoslovakia, Hungary, Romania, and Bulgaria. The Communist regimes were forced to resign and democratic governments were installed. In all of those countries, language and culture as symbols of national identity have experienced a renaissance as a counterweight to the Soviet ideology which had held the nation-states of eastern Europe in an iron grip of delimited sovereignty.

Secondary national movements resulted from the reestablishment of complete national self-determination. Slovakia separated from the Czech Republic, and the democratically elected new government of East Germany promoted the process of reunification with West Germany. Under the aegis of the four allied powers that had defeated Nazi Germany (i.e., the United States, France, Britain, and the Soviet Union), an international treaty was negotiated between the two Germanys. The German territory was united but not within the frontiers of 1937. Those formerly German areas east of the Neisse and Oder rivers which had been occupied by Soviet troops and later incorporated into Poland, Russia, or Lithuania have remained under foreign rule, and in a bilateral contract Germany and Poland have acknowledged the status quo. The idea of the German historical nation that included the Germans in both German states had never been given up in West Germany, although it was branded as imperialist by the Communist governments in the former German Democratic Republic. Political forces in the German Democratic Republic desperately tried to dissociate German identity in the East from that in the West, a project which failed because Germans in both states have kept alive the memory of common cultural roots and a shared history (until 1945 and again since 1990).

The dissolution of the Iron Curtain and the Eastern bloc, the Warsaw Pact, and the subsequent renewal of nationalism as a maxim of politics in many European states all contributed to the deconstruction of ideological barriers outside Europe as well. For example, the fall of the socialist regime in Ethiopia and the separation of northern Eritrea from the central parts of the country with its ethnically differing population is a reflection of similar processes in Europe. A direct comparison may be drawn with the dissolution of the former Yugoslavia through civil war, with the emergence of successor states such as (modern) Yugoslavia (i.e., a federation of Serbia and Montenegro), Slovenia, Croatia, Bosnia-Hercegovina, and the former Yugoslav Republic of Macedonia.

In many parts of Asia, the impact of communism on local politics has faded. The civil war in Afghanistan lost the motivation of ideological warfare after the Soviet army withdrew in 1989. The fragmentation of the currently warring factions in the country results from differences in religious worldview and the interpretation of how a modern Muslim society should be constructed. After many years of civil war and war with its neighbors (i.e., with Cambodia and China), Vietnam is reconstructing its society by gradually replacing older socialist ideals of lifestyle, and it is opening, economically and culturally, to the West.

However, remnants of the ideological struggle for a new world order still exist in some parts of Asia. An example of extreme political contrast is the two Koreas. North Korea still maintains its ideological barriers toward the south, although one can expect a narrowing of political and cultural interests once ideological stereotypes have been abandoned. The integrity of Korean ethnic identity has never been questioned by any government, even if the conditions for reunification have been conceived very differently in the north and south.

The ideological warfare between East and West is partly responsible for the strengthening of cultural self-awareness and the rise of nationalism in countries of the Third World. The poorer nations of Africa and Asia, situated in what were formerly colonial territories of European states, profited from the "international-istic" support provided by the Soviet Union, and local nationalism largely drew its vigor from the construction of a hostile image of the "imperialist" West and of "decadent bourgeois democracy." After the fading of ideological barriers in the late 1980s, national self-awareness has remained vigorous, and its vitality may be judged in terms of the flexibility with which it is adapting to the changing political climate.

Without the involvement of the superpowers as ideological enemies in the local conflict between North and South Vietnam, the war in Southeast Asia might not have blown out of proportion. North Vietnamese ethnic identity profited from its victory in 1975, which created the myth of invincibility and assured it the role of a guarantor of stability (at Vietnamese terms) in the whole region. The invasion and occupation of neighboring Cambodia by the Vietnamese army in the 1980s was a blunt demonstration of the working of the new national pride.

A similar influence for the strengthening of ethnic identity resulted from the support for the politically opposed liberation movements in the former Portuguese colonies of Africa, which were abandoned by Portugal in 1975. In the clashes between leftist and rightist guerrillas in Mozambique, as well as in Angola, the Soviet Union and the United States waged proxy wars that involved satellites such as Cuba, which mediated arms to the leftists in Angola and provided mercenaries who actively participated in the civil war. Other proxy wars, such as those in Afghanistan, Nicaragua, and El Salvador, brought conflict near the borders of the superpowers.

The Impact of Growing Ethnic Self-awareness on Political Affairs

The era of ideological rivalry created a political climate that has been termed the "cold war." Some aspects of this clash of worldviews, of its collateral and after-effects as a catalyst on ethnicity, have been highlighted in the foregoing discussion. Although a major political driving force, ideological warfare is, neverthe-less, not alone responsible for the ethnic revival in our time. Ethnicity being a highly complex phenomenon, its impulses and variables are manifold. Among the prominent factors in ethnicity in our world today is an ever-increasing self-awareness of cultural traditions and values among nations of all continents. This development was triggered by a growing consciousness that ethnicity is an important factor in group cohesion and a crystallizing focus of human rights and that it has been associated with economic growth and demands for political influence. Additional factors are also at work. Some illustrative cases will be discussed in the following.

Continental China has officially continued Communist maxims in its external and internal politics, despite changes in its economy since the early 1980s that may be termed a silent capitalist revolution. Economic growth and the raising of living standards have created an atmosphere in which Chinese can look to a prosperous future. This prospect is definitely a supportive factor in strengthening ethnic identity. In Chinese society, a new social class distinction has emerged. The living standards of the urban upper and middle classes differ considerably from those of Chinese who live in the countryside.

This distinction does not speak in favor of communist ideology; rather, it is a signal of flourishing capitalism. Those who participate in the economic development and profit from it are aware that economic competition in the world of the future will no longer reflect ideological positions. Rather, it will create conditions for a scenario in which competition is culture-oriented, in which Chinese skills compete with American, Russian, or German know-how. It was already observed years ago that world trade does not follow universal rules, operating rather on cultural terms. Consequently, modern conceptions of management acknowledge the importance of cultural diversity.

Ethnic revival has been linked to economic growth also in countries with mainly Muslim populations. For the most part, economic development has been dependent on ties with Western states but with former Eastern bloc countries as well. Against the background of an intermingling of Oriental and Western ideas, the encounter of West and East has created tensions in the Muslim societies and has resulted in the most diverse political developments in Arabic and other Islamic countries. Muslims in Asia and Africa have responded to Western influx in various ways, depending on local conditions of lifestyle and cultural traditions. Many choices were available: Marx, Western ideals of democracy, Oriental traditions of kingdom, or Mohammed.

Libya's Mu'ammar Gadhafi has chosen the affiliation with leftist ideology, and his country remains isolated after the decline of global communism. Turkey has continued its course toward Western-style democracy; yet its government adheres to the unitarian principle, which seems outdated in view of the conflicts with the Kurdish minority that have persisted for decades. Egypt's history of democratic government is colorful, with the authority of presidents oscillating between the democracy of Mubarak and the dictatorship of Nasser. Saudi Arabia, Jordan, and Morocco continue their tradition of kingship, with varying degrees of Western influx. Iran has experienced a history of contradictory developments. The regime of the Shah represented the essence of traditional kingship, but his way of opening the country to Western ideas was conceived of as controversial. The radical change after the Shiite revolution of 1979 brought about the institution of an Islamic state which, after years of ideological convulsion, has entered the stage at which it is ready for a moderate reexchange of ideas with the West.

The importance of the oil-producing countries for world economy has contributed to the consolidation of ethnicity, Arabic and other, in the postcolonial phase of history. As in the case of historical and recent nationalism elsewhere in the world, modern Muslim nationalism has also produced its specific kind of radicalism: Islamic fundamentalism. Fundamentalist movements—the Islamic offensive reaction to internationalization and Americanization—manipulate ethnic identity, the Islamic worldview in particular, and use it as a weapon against Western influence in Muslim society. Fundamentalists not only pose a serious threat to the progress of local democratic development, but they also construct impediments to communication with the West. The latter aspect is particularly severe, because an interruption of the dialogue between the Muslim world and the West may produce alienation on both sides and even result in terrorism—as it has in Algeria, where any Western foreigner is in potential danger of being murdered.

The spread of ideas associated with human rights issues has contributed to increased sensitivity to self-awareness in interethnic relations, in particular among ethnic groups that have traditionally been objects of discrimination The development in South Africa is an illustrative example of this. The issue of ethnic identity has been on the agenda ever since European settlers occupied territories inhabited by indigenous African populations in the seventeenth century. In the history of interethnic relations in southern Africa, the concept of ethnic identity has undergone many changes, many of them dramatic.

Populations in southern Africa were long categorized into larger groups for the convenience of the ruling whites. There were whites, blacks, and coloreds. Splitting the blacks up into local groups and tribes was not a matter of major concern for the white governments, and political provisions were made for the blacks in terms of a generic category. Experts have long known that the Khoisan people (e.g., Bushman and Hottentot) are not black, and modern human genetics has proven that genetically they differ considerably from the core of black Africans (Cavalli-Sforza et al. 1994: 174 ff.). Nevertheless, the Khoisan were treated as blacks during the times of apartheid. The colored people are of Asian descent, mainly immigrants from the former British colonies of India and Pakistan. The offspring of Asians and Europeans were also included in the category of colored people.

As a consequence of the shift of power in 1994, a flip-flop change occurred in the evaluation of ethnic relations. Ethnic identities have since been acknowledged according to criteria such as speech community, religion, and cultural traditions. Individual ethnic groups demanded their rights of cultural self-determination and their share of political power. A clear reflection of this change in attitude is apparent in the new organization of official language use. During the era of apartheid, the main languages of the whites, Afrikaans and English, were acknowledged in state affairs. Nowadays, there are eleven official languages. Alongside the languages of the whites (i.e., Afrikaans, English), there are several languages of the black people that have assumed official status: Ndebele, Pedi, Sotho, Swazi, Tsonga, Tswana, Venda, Xhosa, Zulu.

And yet racial distinctions are still relevant even in modern South Africa. Colored people have experienced a strong in-group cohesion, in contrast to whites and blacks, despite internal subdivisions on the basis of language (e.g., Tamil vs. Hindi) or religion (e.g., Hindu vs. Muslim). Government provisions are directed, as before, to the colored population as a whole. The same holds true for the whites, linguistic diversity (e.g., Afrikaans vs. English) or religious differences (e.g., Protestant vs. Catholic) notwithstanding.

In neighboring Namibia, racial conflicts during the imposed apartheid rule were not as severe as in South Africa. This is one of the reasons why, in the newly independent state, the former colonial language, English, has been adopted as the one and only official language. There are more native speakers of German than of English in Namibia. Nevertheless, it was felt that a neutral language such as English would provide the most favorable prospects for avoiding the cumbersome business of official multilingualism, with the participation of several European and indigenous African languages. Experts have noticed, however, that official monolingualism in Namibia is developing at the cost of local languages, which lack a tradition of standardization and its resulting language cultivation and maintenance.

Reactions to the Ethnic Mixing of Populations in Western Industrialized Countries

Recent years have seen the level of awareness of ethnicity rise in many communities of the Euro-American hemisphere as a reaction to population changes. A common source of change becomes apparent in the neighborhood that has become restructured with the introduction of migrants from abroad. Some decades ago, one could still find a local linguistically and culturally homogeneous population in many places where ethnic diversity predominates today. In Western Europe, traditional patterns of areal ethnicity have dissolved and are being transformed into settings of multiple ethnic identity. Most towns in Germany were still monolingual in the 1950s. With the constant influx of foreign migrant workers, emigrants from Eastern Europe, and political refugees from outside Europe, urban society in Germany has become a kaleidoscope of languages, cultures, and people of different ethnic stock (Cohen 1995).

Similarly, the populations in other countries of Western Europe, particularly in urban environments, have been transformed from ethnically homogeneous to heterogeneous and culturally multifaceted. This is true for France and Britain, for Denmark and Sweden, and for other states. In countries such as Belgium or Switzerland, the mosaic of traditional multiculturalism has proliferated, so that it now also includes a variety of nonindigenous ethnic patterns.

In the United States, the traditional picture of multiculturalism (e.g., as in Italian, German, Polish, Russian, Jewish communities) and ethnic diversity (as reflected in the autochthonous population of Indian descent, in white people of European descent, in American blacks, and in communities of Japanese, Korean, and/or Chinese descent) has become more varied with the first and second generations of modern immigrants (e.g., Cubans, Haitians, Puerto Ricans, Filipinos). In neighboring Canada, modern immigration has also changed the traditional patterns of multiculturalism. There are the English- and French-speaking Canadians who consider themselves the founding nations of the country, various Indian and Eskimo groups who have organized themselves for the purpose of safeguarding their rights as autochthonous people, and naturalized Canadians, the offspring of former Ukrainian, Polish, and other immigrants to the country.

The intermingling of languages, cultures, and races in an ever more accelerating pace has triggered the most divergent reactions among local populations and newcomers. On the one hand, the interaction of "old" and "new" citizens has widened many individuals' understanding of foreign cultures and has increased the amount of knowledge about ethnic boundary marking. In addition, intercommunication among people of different ethnic affiliation has enhanced the acceptance of foreignness. On the other hand, interethnic relations have produced various negative effects, such as an increase in cultural stereotyping and ethnic friction, conflicts of identity arising from situational pressure of dominant languages on minority languages, and the transformation of a fear of foreignness into either aggressiveness or seclusion (Fishman 1989).

In most societies, it has become apparent that neither the experience of positive intercommunication in an environment of modern multiple ethnicity nor the alienation that results from an "overdose" of foreignness in traditionally monoethnic surroundings is necessarily an alternative option. Instead, both become noticeable in individuals' behavior and attitudes, depending on each person's communicative flexibility and commitment to cultural exchange. In Germany, for instance, there are millions of Germans who get along well with millions of Turks, and in thousands of German-Turkish families, biculturalism and bilingualism are facets of people's lives which do not produce conflict.

In the same neighborhood, one may find peaceful coexistence of members of both ethnic groups on the one hand and German families sharply opposed to cultural pluralism on the other. Opposition based on cultural prejudice may develop into political radicalism, which attracts more attention than does the everyday functioning of multicultural community life in a democratic society. The neo-Nazi outrage against political refugees and the terrorist actions against Turks were broadly covered by the mass media in recent years. However, the fact that interethnicity and multiculturalism have been working fairly well in daily affairs in Germany for decades has not been noticed with equal interest abroad.

Rightist extremist groups with definite racist overtones in their ideology are a reality in other European countries, such as Belgium, Denmark, Sweden, and Finland. As is the case in Germany, the activities of neo-Nazi groups in these countries are handled as a police matter rather than as incidents that are allowed to find backing among the broader population. Neo-Nazism has also been a scourge in the United States, where we find today the largest organization of its kind in the world, as well as among some of German communities abroad whose members had no chance to participate in the process of democratization after the Second World War in West Germany. Nationalistic attitudes and even lingering traces of Hitlerite ideology may be found among individual Germans in Namibia, South Africa, or Argentina.

A failure of state authorities to respond to the demands of educational support and of cultural autonomy for immigrant groups may result in alienation and may cause ethnic frictions. In Europe, many immigrant languages have been included in educational programs, but provisions are still far from reaching the ideals of a completely balanced multicultural society in which the rights of each ethnic group are not only officially declared but also implemented in practice (Extra and Verhoeven 1993). In the educational sector, the teaching of immigrant languages requires trained personnel and teaching material. The selection of proper school facilities located in areas with concentrations of immigrants is another task which poses problems. Last but not least, the fate of the whole organization of education in immigrant languages depends on the financial resources that state authorities are willing to provide.

In several European countries, the increase in immigration and the pressures it exerts on local societies have been felt as too great a strain. In recent years, provisions for the acceptance of asylum-seekers and other refugees have been drastically tightened, and the annual quota of immigrants has been reduced. The fate of refugees is nowadays much more subject to the vicissitudes of political will than ever before (Miles and Thränhardt 1995). The country which accepts refugees is no longer a "safe" haven for everybody. Some governments have taken the option of sending certain refugees back to their land of origin after the local crisis is considered to have ended.

This is true, for instance, for the German government, which plans to repatriate all Vietnamese boat people and to send Bosnian refugees back to Bosnia, even against their will. Germany has accepted more Bosnian refugees than all other European Union countries together, so the transfer of hundreds of thousands of refugees back to southern Europe will cause much social unrest. The repatriation plans have also stirred up resentment among Germans, because many Bosnians have already become integrated into German communities.

Outlook

The current state of ethnic affairs indicates that ethnicity-related issues will remain on the agenda of private intercommunication, public intergroup management, and political decision making on a global scale. If we do not want ethnicity to become a strain on human relations, then we have to deal with it, as individuals, in terms of mutual intercommunication and, on the governmental level, by contriving solutions for interethnic community life with flexible pragmatism, not by creating bureaucratic barriers. It is vital to avoid tensions that are responsible for the activation of the ethnic mechanism of self-defense against foreignness, because this is equal to succumbing to treacherous boundary marking and negative stereotyping.

In a positive vision of the future, ethnic identity can be a source of cultural enrichment which can assume a significant role in balancing self-esteem plus the recognition of others in interethnic relations. This balancing process can readily function without the disturbing effects of raising ethnic boundaries for the purpose of stereotyping, of mobilizing destructive intentions to manipulate ethnicity as part of political power plays, or of denying other ethnic groups their acknowledged rights of linguistic and cultural self-identification. We all know, however, that keeping ethnic identity under control depends primarily on individual good will and less so on the measures taken by any government.

Questions for Further Thought and Discussion

1. Why is language always involved in processes of ethnic identity even if it is not necessarily its major marker?

2. Which do you consider the most important criterion for your own group membership: language, religion, descent, or something else?

3. Do you consider it important that your native language is used in your native environment, or would you also accept the use there of some other language?

4. What makes a black American different from a black African?

5. Does multiculturalism enhance the development of a multifaceted identity, or is it likely to produce pressures for alternative choices of ethnic identification?

6. Will self-identification always be associated with a local culture and language, or will a global cosmopolitan identity eventually prevail over ethnicity in the future?

7. Is the successful management of interethnic strife, such as the Jewish-Palestinian, Russian-Chechen, Turkish-Kurdish, Chinese-Tibetan conflicts, possible?

8. Can ethnic prejudices and cultural stereotypes be overcome through education?

Selected Bibliography

Cavalli-Sforza, L. Luca, Paolo Menozzi, and Alberto Piazza (1994). *The history and geography of Human Genes.* Princeton: Princeton University Press.

Cohen, Robin (ed.) (1995). *The Cambridge Survey of World Migration.* Cambridge: Cambridge University Press.

Extra, G., and L. Verhoeven (eds.) (1993). *Immigrant Languages in Europe.* Clevedon, England: Multilingual Matters.

Fishman, Joshua A. (1989). *Language and Ethnicity in Minority Socio-linguistic Perspective.* Clevedon, England: Multilingual Matters.

Greenfeld, Liah (1992). *Nationalism—Five Roads to Modernity.* Cambridge: Harvard University Press.

Haarmann, Harald (1986). *Language in Ethnicity. A View of Basic Ecological Relations.* Berlin: Mouton de Gruyter.

——— (1995). Europeanness, European identity and the role of language—giving profile to an anthropological infrastructure. *Sociolinguistica* 9: 1–55.

Jones, Sian (1997). *The Archaeology of Ethnicity. Constructing Identities in the Past and Present*. London: Routledge.

Megarry, Tim (1995). *Society in Prehistory. The Origins of Human Culture*. London: Macmillan.

Miles, Robert, and Dietrich Thränhardt (eds.) (1995). *Migration and European Integration. The Dynamics of Inclusion and Exclusion*. Madison/Teaneck, NJ: Fairleigh Dickinson University Press.

Smith, Anthony D. (1986). *The Ethnic Origins of Nations*. Oxford: Blackwell.

Smith, John E. (1994). *Quasi-Religions. Humanism, Marxism and Nationalism*. London: Macmillan.

Nationalism

WILLIAM SAFRAN

The relationship of language and nationalism has long been a matter of controversy. In the eyes of historians and students of culture, language has served as a major building block of nations. For them, national sentiment, based on a common cultural heritage, a common history or memory, and common descent (or a myth of such descent), is expressed in a distinct idiom, and it is in terms of that idiom that national sentiment is generalized to become a major factor in social cohesion. In the view of many historians and anthropologists, the enhancement of collective cultural consciousness may be institutionalized, but that process does not necessarily have a political dimension. To political scientists, however, language is important insofar as it plays a role in the "politicization" of a nationalism that culminates in the creation of a state.

In his writings, Hans Kohn, the prominent historian of nationalism (Kohn 1945) makes a strong argument for the connection between nationalism and language. He points out that in some cases, the emphasis on a common language led to collective national identity, especially in the nineteenth century; in others, the promotion of nationalism by intellectuals made it necessary to rediscover, legitimate, or restructure a "primordial" idiom (as was done by a number of Slavic-speaking intellectuals).

Language—Nationalism—Statehood

The connection between nationalism, statehood, and language is also made by a number of social scientists. To Ernest Gellner, nationalism is "primarily a principle which holds that the political and national unit should be congruent"; and the national unit is most commonly defined in terms of language (Gellner 1983: 1). Some twentieth-century scholars have gone even further; thus Fernand Braudel has insisted repeatedly that the French language *is* the French nation (Braudel 1990–1992).

In an article written during World War I Carl Darling Buck argued that there must be "a certain likemindedness as the fundamental characteristic of nationality," for example, in customs, institutions, and, most important, religion and language; and, although language "[was] no universal criterion," he quoted an Irishman as saying (at the time of the First World War) that "a people without a language of its own is only half a nation." Buck admitted that language is neither sufficient nor absolutely necessary for state building; yet "language is the one conspicuous banner of nationality, to be defended against encroachment, as it is the first object of attack on the part of a power aiming to crush out a distinction of nationality among its subject peoples . . . [and] that with few exceptions , the European nationalities are essentially language groups" (Buck 1916: 47–49).

After the First World War, the principle of self-determination was applied largely to communities defined in terms of language. The role of language has been crucial in explaining the transpolitical attraction of neighboring states, such as the attraction of Hungary to Rumanian and Slovak Magyars and of Hitler's Reich to German speakers in Czechoslovakia and, in more recent years, of Austria to German speakers in northern Italy and of Russia to Russian-speaking Ukrainians. As for the attraction of German-speaking Swiss to Nazi Germany during the Second World War, the ethnolinguistic factor was probably more important than the prospect of material gain, at least initially.

Languages and Nonpolitical Collective Identity

The preceding analysis is informed by the principle of self-determination of *European* communities, all of which had languages with long literary traditions and which were in process of being "politicized." Scholars were not yet concerned with the political development of newly independent Third World countries, where state-building generally implied "nation-building." The nations (to be created beginning in the 1960s) could not, however, be based on specific tribal languages (for there were too many tribes) but rather on underemphasizing the latter in favor of a superordinate transtribal language, which in most cases happened to be the language of the former colonial overlord.

According to Kohn,

> nationalities come into existence only when certain objective bonds delimit a social group. A nationality generally has several potentially unifying elements; very few have all of them. The most usual of them are common descent, language, territory, political entity, customs and traditions, and religion, [but] none of them is essential to the existence or definition of nationality. (1945: 13)

If language were the sufficient ingredient of nationalism (defined as a politically mobilizing and state-seeking ideology), there would be several thousand sovereign states, rather than the existing two hundred.

Some scholars argue that it was not the consciousness of having a common language that made for nationalism but the other way around. Although Kohn places considerable emphasis on language as a force shaping nationalism, he implies that it was the growth of nationalist sentiment that endowed language with political importance. "Before nationalism," he argues, "language was very rarely stressed as a fact on which the prestige and power of a group depended" (1945: 7). And to the extent that language was stressed, it was not the (spoken) language of the masses but that of the social and intellectual elite; that included leaders of minority communities, who often spoke the same language as the dominant elite of the state from which they wished to break away.

According to Kohn, three basic elements of nationalism originated with the Jews: the idea of the chosen people, consciousness of national history, and national messianism (1945: 36–37). None of these was necessarily connected with race or ethnicity, for foreigners could be admitted into membership in the community of the chosen people by signing a "covenant" (e.g., by marriage or conversion), thereby sharing both the historical consciousness and the messianic aspirations of the Jews—in the same way that, much later, Frenchmen who were naturalized (thus participating in a "social contract") would act *as if* their ancestors were the ancient Gauls and would come to share the belief in the French republican ideology. None of these elements was necessarily connected with language, although Hebrew was widely considered the most convenient medium for their expression, just as French was later considered to be the ideal language for articulating republican sentiments and fulfilling the *mission civilisatrice* (Safran 1992b).

Before the Revolution, the French language served not to promote national sentiment but to provide religious instruction, which was intended to foster Catholicism as a rival to secular nationalism. In Eastern Europe, religion was more important than language; nevertheless, linguistic diversity made it difficult to create a collective cultural consciousness based on religion. The multilingual city was the norm, but (due in part to religious and class diversity) municipal identity did not make for national identity (Armstrong 1982: 117–123). It was in the context of that diversity that languages were disseminated and "vulgarized." That process did not normally carry political overtones. Translations of the Bible (especially in Protestant countries) into various vernacular languages were undertaken "not from any motives of nationalism, but purely for the spreading of the true religion" (Kohn 1945:7). However, a collective religious consciousness developed into a national consciousness, and biblical texts in the common language were used as an important source of vocabulary for the development of a national culture. Dante, Cervantes, and Goethe made significant contributions to emphasizing the place of language as a secular cultural ingredient of their respective ethnonational communities, but they were not state-building nationalists.

Kohn asserts (1945:13) that two common concepts that have been used as the basis of nationality have been fictitious: blood and *Volksgeist* (the "spirit" inherent in a people). These two have often been related to language, in the belief that a common national consciousness and a common way of looking at reality can be shared only by people who share hereditary bloodlines, as the Nazis held. But the contract for the acquisition of membership in the Jewish nation could be made in any language; membership in the French nation, since the Revolution, had to do with accepting certain political values and not with a mastery of French; and many of the Germans who articulated the German national *Geist* in philosophy or poetry were of Slavic or other non-German descent.

This permeability is not confined to "advanced" nations; it applies to "primordial" ethnic communities as well. Among the Gypsies in Hungary, speaking the Romany language shapes one's identity and helps one to share collective activities and thus to define persons as Gypsies—regardless of their origins (Stewart 1997: 59). It does not, however, shape Gypsy nationalism, if by nationalism is meant a collective political consciousness or the will to achieve an independent state (Smith 1991: 72). Conversely, speaking Hebrew or Yiddish is neither sufficient nor necessary for defining individuals as Jews.

Adopting a language does not always mean adopting a particular political ideology; nor do language changes necessarily imply changes in collective consciousness. The replacement of Hebrew by Aramaic as the vernacular language of the Jews did not mean the decline of Jewish nationalism and its replacement by an Aramaic nationalism. In Europe and the Middle East, Jewish collective consciousness was associated with two languages: Hebrew for the religious aspect of that consciousness, and Yiddish, Ladino, or Judeo-Arabic for quotidian (and often transboundary) communication from which the aim of state building was absent, at least until the twentieth century (Harshav 1993).

Language serves as an important instrument for protecting collective identity and communal cohesion. It is important because it marks the "at-homeness" of a people threatened by cultural homogenization. It has helped to preserve the of identity of the Tamils in Sri Lanka; the Turks in Cyprus; the Québécois in Canada; the Ibos and Fulanis in Nigeria; and the Bamileke in Cameroon. However, language may not be sufficient, because linguistic differences do not always demarcate ethnic groups. In Greece and Norway, linguistic distinctions reflect rural-urban, parochial-cosmopolitan, and social class cleavages rather than ethnic ones. In Guyana and Trinidad, conflicts exist between groups that speak the same language (Horowitz 1985: 50–51). In Eastern Europe, assimilated middle-class Jews spoke the language of the country, whereas members of the "lower" classes, especially those who were Orthodox, spoke Yiddish. Language is sometimes associated with other markers of identity, such as religion, myth, kinship ties, and territoriality; at other times, it has served as a substitute for those markers, as in the case of Armenians, Bretons, and Jews, whose religious ties have weakened. The bases of collective identity vary according to history and context: thus, originally, the Bengalis broke away from India because of religion, but later seceded from Pakistan because of language and geographic distance. In Israel and Pakistan, religion, not language, was the main ingredient of nationalism, whereas Polish nationalism has been based on both religion and language. Croatian nationalism has been based on a combination of socioeconomic resentments and religious differences, and these have, in turn, led Croatians to put renewed stress on language differences.

It is unclear whether Arab nationalism is founded on Islam, on hostility to the West (or more particularly, to Israel), or on culture, history, and myths, which are expressed primarily in the Arabic language. There are many Arab nationalists who are Christian but who speak Arabic (in fact, one of the earliest proponents of modern Arab nationalism, George Antonius, was a Christian). Arabic is the classic vehicle in which Islam, a major ingredient of Arab nationalism, is expressed. However, language is obviously not enough, for if it were, there would be no specifically Syrian, Egyptian, or Palestinian nations, and there would be no inter-Arab conflicts.

The Pushtu speakers in Afghanistan, the speakers of Kurdish, Yiddish, or Sorbian, and the Berbers and the Catalans did not regard the languages that defined their respective ethnicities as sufficient grounds for seeking political independence. The reasons for that have varied: an underdeveloped sense of nationalism (in the case of the Berbers); the powerlessness of small size (Sorbians); internal cultural and other divisions resulting from physical dispersion across frontiers (Armenians, Jews, and Kurds); economic considerations (Catalans); external constraints (Tibetans); the lack of a committed ethnic elite (Bretons, Basques, and Gypsies); and linguistic weakness in the face of a dominant rival language (Irish Gaelic vis-à-vis English and Berber vis-à-vis Arabic). Conversely, the replacement of Irish Gaelic by English did not dampen Irish nationalist sentiment; and, although the loss of their native tongue may have added to the "cultural grief" of the Irish elite, it did not add measurably to that sentiment.

Similarly, the use of a common language may not lead to a common state based on pan-nationalism: There are no large commonwealths founded on English, Spanish, French, or Arabic that embrace all communities that speak these languages. The Spanish language is not sufficient to create a politically articulated pan-Hispanism; the English language is not sufficient for merging American, British, Irish, Australian, and Canadian nationalisms. Arabic, to be sure, is one of the elements defining the "Arab nation," but it can be argued that Islam is an even more decisive element. The Chinese language plays a major role in the cohesion of diaspora Chinese; at the same time, it is an important medium of expression of Taiwanese and Singaporean nationalisms that seek to differentiate themselves from Chinese nationalism. The Chinese-speaking Malays, Vietnamese, Singaporeans, and inhabitants of Hong Kong have not ipso facto become Chinese nationalists; and Irish, Swiss, Latin American, and Jewish nationalisms are not clearly dependent on language. It is money that holds multilingual states such as Switzerland and Singapore together; it is economic interest, as well as tradition, that holds the United Kingdom and Spain together; and it is religion and common historical experiences that hold Jews together. The nationalisms of Pakistan, Israel, and (in part) Ireland, Sri Lanka, and Poland are based not (or not only) on language but on religion. There are attempts in many newly independent countries of sub-Saharan Africa to build transethnic nations in which common political ambitions transcend linguistic diversities.

The connection of Hebrew to Jewish (or Israeli) nationalism is even more problematic. A Jewish subpolitical nationalism existed in late-nineteenth-, early-twentieth-century Eastern Europe that was based not on Hebrew but on Yiddish. Conversely, there still exists a Jewish nationalism that is expressed in Hebrew but that is eschatological rather than political; moreover, an American or French Jew may belong culturally and politically to the American or French nation but may identify as well with the Jewish (or even Israeli) nation.

Language and the Role of the Elite

It has been argued (Gellner, 1983) that intellectuals play a dominant role in the development of nationalism by manipulating language as an instrument for the expression of collective consciousness. But, as suggested above, their own language is not necessarily that of the peasants, who often speak a semiliterate dialect. The elite must legitimize, upgrade, and restructure that dialect in order to turn it into a proper vehicle for the expression of a national sentiment that is capable of being politicized. However, ethnic intellectuals may not always wish to do this. In the Middle Ages, intellectual elites were transpolitical or nonpolitical in their cultural orientations and spoke a transnational lingua franca (Latin); more recently, such elites have been co-opted by the majority and have adopted its language. Conversely, even if intellectuals were conscious purveyors of ethnic nationalism, they might be linguistically handicapped. In some cases, the important promoters of political nationalism, or "state builders," were not themselves masters of the respective "national" languages: Herzl knew no Hebrew; de Valera knew no Gaelic; Napoleon's French and Stalin's Russian were imperfect; and Nehru expressed himself better in English than in Hindi.

Language may be used by the elite to promote a specifically nationalist goal, as in the case of Palacky and Safarik, whose aims, respectively, were to recreate independent Czech and Slovak nation-states; but language may also be used to make a community aware of its culture and to instill a collective pride in it without encouraging political aspirations. Such a nonpolitical aim was promoted by Johann Gottfried Herder, who stressed the importance of language in *all* cultures, which he valued equally for their unique qualities. Sometimes, a language—for example, Latin, French, Hebrew, and Sanskrit—may be used by an elite for the purpose of demarcating itself from the masses and keeping its status. According to Armstrong (1982:194), the imperial elites before nationalism were expected to have a common language—not in order to develop nationalism but to facilitate communication and promote administrative efficiency and, later, modernization, including the creation of an industrial workforce. Such a language would have to have a uniform grammar, a literary tradition, and a degree of sophistication; that is, it should be a vehicle of "high culture." In much of central Europe, that language was Latin and later German; in France, it was Parisian French. Because all this took place before the age of nation-states, "low culture" idioms were permitted to exist for subpolitical or nonpolitical domains (Fishman 1970: 78). There are times, moreover, when the elite uses a language as an instrument to fight against particularist nationalism and to protect and strengthen transnational and transpolitical ties—for example, Chinese, Arabic, Yiddish, French, and English have been so used in modern times.

Language as an Artifact
of the Political System

Nationalism depends on a sense of place, kinship, and race, on common memories and experiences, common values, and economic conditions—all of which may cut across language barriers. The specific articulation of nationalist sentiments in terms of these factors is influenced by a particular idiom. But the idiom used for that articulation may be of recent date; it may be imposed from the outside, or it may be an old tribal vernacular reconstructed by an elite. At the time the nation-states of France, Italy, and Germany were created—the first by the Revolution and the other two by territorial mergers—only a small minority in each of these countries spoke the respective "national" language. Such a language was created in each case out of mutually unintelligible dialects. In short, "national languages are . . . almost always semi-artificial constructs" built by the same state and the same elite that constructed nationalist ideology (Hobsbawm 1990: 38, 54–63; Shafer 1955: 47–50, 77–81, 233–235).

Languages become standard, scientific, and national state idioms as a result of compulsory education and the spread of mass media, which are products of conscious public policy, and it is in that sense that national languages, like modern or "civic" nations, are artifacts of a politicized community. Nevertheless, the "primordial" languages that existed before the development of modern nationalism should not be dismissed out of hand. National languages are not created out of thin air; most of them are, after all, based on idioms spoken by a large number of people. The national languages of the majority of east-central European states are based on Slavic regional dialects. Irish Gaelic, although admittedly spoken by relatively few people, had been used by monks for several centuries. Similarly, the modern Hebrew language spoken in Israel was not, as Hobsbawm has argued, "virtually invented" (Hobsbawm 1990: 54); rather it was based on a language that, although largely used for religious purposes and not for secular ones, had never died out. It continued to be used by the elite in formal correspondence, exegesis, and poetry, to be widely understood by the masses, and to serve as a link for a dispersed ethnoreligious community.

Paul Brass has argued that language is important as an instrument for "mobilizing large numbers of people around symbols and values with a high emotional potential" (Brass 1991: 303). In theory, it can be any language, including the language of those against whom the people are being mobilized. In India and Ireland, the English language was used to articulate anti-English nationalisms. Translinguistic nationalism is also shown in the case of the Soviet Union, where a collective political consciousness was to be developed above and beyond the particular national cultures, languages, and sentiments of Latvians, Lithuanians, Tadjiks, and Georgians. Both in the Soviet Union and India, the various provincial and regional languages were to be recognized as legitimate and official. In the meantime, however, the medium for the expression of a transnational and ideologically based Soviet nationalism was the Russian language; in India, it was both Hindi and English. These choices, however, were not merely matters of happenstance and convenience; rather, they emerged from the fact that the languages in question were those of the politically dominant elite. The creation of modern Czech, Slovak, and Norwegian was the result of deliberate decisions by intellectual leaders who wished to create a lexicographical underpinning for claims to political independence. Similarly, changes in alphabets were decided upon by political leaders in order to demarcate their countries politically from their neighbors. In Turkey, the alphabet of the national language was Latinized in order to distinguish Turkish nationalism from transnational Islam; in Moldavia and Tadjikistan, the Soviet authorities imposed the Cyrillic alphabet on the local languages in order to differentiate them, respectively, from Rumanian and Persian; and the writing of Yiddish was phoneticized in order to eliminate traces of Hebrew (which was identified with religion and/or Zionism). In Yugoslavia, the differences in script determined, or reflected, the differences between Serb and Croat nationality (based in turn on differences in religious traditions). Under Tito's rule, efforts were made to understate these differences by cultivating the idea of a "Yugoslav" language in the interest of creating a transethnic nation based on a superordinate ideology that was enforced by political constraints and common political institutions presided over by a charismatic leader. The moment these institutions disappeared, Yugoslav nationalism began to disintegrate, and the differences between Serbian and Croatian began to be stressed anew.

The foregoing suggests that the relationship between a "civic" (or political) and an "ethnic" (or cultural) nation is reciprocal; it is a two-way process in which a preexistent language facilitates the creation of a state, and in which the state, once established, legitimates and develops a language and a culture laden with state-specific ingredients. There is no doubt that it is the state that makes an idiom respectable by politicizing it—by transforming a dialect into a language, as happened in the case of Czech, Slovak, Moldavian, and Afrikaans. As one particular language is officialized by the state in becoming the sole language of public administration and instruction, the development of other languages is arrested. This process is illustrated in the cases of Breton, Yiddish, Sorbian, Occitan, Wendish, Kashubian, and a host of tongues in India, all of which were "inferiorized"—on the one hand because they lacked legitimation, and on the other because speakers of these minority languages (in particular the elite) were co-opted by, and incorporated into, the host society by economic inducements or political improvements that caused them to prefer the language of the majority. In some cases, such as Breton, children were penalized by state authories for using their "ethnic" language on school grounds (Jakez-Hélias 1975). If, as has often happened, a smaller national community is absorbed by a larger one because the latter is more powerful, more efficacious, more democratic, more prosperous, and more capable of providing all sorts of benefits to its members—in short, more advanced—the language of the smaller community is devalued as well. If these languages survive, they will be confined to folk festivals and narrow household uses (Hobsbawm 1990: 36).

A state-controlling segment of a society may leave minorities alone and allow them to practice their languages in private if they do not threaten the dominant culture and its values; it may even permit the teaching of such languages on a selective basis. There may, however, be situations in which such permission is withheld: if, for example, its proponents are thought of as positing a value system that runs counter to that of the state. Thus the demands of members of the Breton and Basque communities in France for official language support were rejected because their cultures were equated with opposition to the Jacobin doctrine of a France "one and indivisible"; the demand of Yiddish-speaking immigrants to Israel for some sort of recognition of their language was discouraged because it was regarded as interfering with attempts of the new state to build a political culture distinct from that of the diaspora by means of Hebrew; and the demand for the dissemination and officialization of Arabic (rather than Wolof) in Mauritania was rejected because it came from the schools of Islamic studies.

To French Jacobins and American assimilationist liberals, the connection between language and nationalism is uncertain and not necessarily crucial. Cultural assimilationists, especially in democracies, tend to emphasize the idea of language not as a shaper of nationalism but as a consequence of it and to reject the notion of language as a preexistent reality that is politically determinant. Political scientists in the United States tend to deal with political phenomena according to one or the other of the dominant analytic paradigms—structuralist (institution-oriented), culturalist (focused on "national character"), or rational choice (emphasizing benefits or payoffs)—none of which makes much room for the factor of ethnic language.

For the structuralist, the institutions associated with the state define language in an essentially utilitarian fashion. The culturalist is concerned with political culture rather than culture in a larger sense; thus political culture, which refers to political orientations, expectations, and forms of behavior, has little reference to the prepolitical culture and the language associated with it. Rational-choice theorists explain political attitudes and behavior in terms of cost-benefit criteria, which are not much influenced by a linguistic tradition. The choice of language is purely instrumental in the sense that it serves as a convenient vehicle of communications; therefore, it does not matter which language happens to be at hand for the creation of a functioning community. The rational-choice theorists argue that French, Russian, and English are languages that are continually changing by incorporating terms from other languages and adapting to the needs of increasingly mixed populations. In short, the structuralists regard the activities of a variety of political institutions and the relations among them as being more important than the language they use.

Moreover, political scientists in the United States, especially those who are concerned with "nation-building" in newly independent countries of the Third World, tend to define "nation" according to the American ideal type. For example, Karl Deutsch (1953: 44–45, 49ff, 123ff) stresses the paramount role of the practical rather than the emotional element of nation-building and national identification, in such terms as transportation, economic exchanges, and professional relationships. In this view, the prevalence of a particular language may be accidental: It may simply be the language spoken by the active modernizing and nation-building elite. In any case, kinship-based language is thought to be quite unimportant. This, perhaps, accounts for the fact that those who tend to define nations (or even ethnic groups) functionally rather than culturally stress reactions to discrimination, political-institutional disadvantage, or perceptions of relative economic deprivation rather than language as such, and they have relatively little to say about language. It is not a coincidence that a major recent work on ethnic conflict (Gurr 1993) devotes virtually no attention to language as a factor of discontent among "ethnic contenders." To many American social scientists, language tends to be irrelevant; to the extent that it shapes or expresses a collective sentiment, culture is itself defined not in terms of a particular language or intellectual tradition but of attitudes and patterns of behavior determined by structural factors (such as access to decision-making institutions and participation in them), race, and economic status. This indifference to language explains why American political scientists (most of whom are unilingual assimilationists) and French intellectuals (most of whom are Jacobin) alike tend to ignore language rights when they discuss human rights (Safran 1992a). It is true that political scientists who have defined nationalism in civic rather than ethnic terms have increasingly come to admit that affective ties have not been replaced by functional (e.g., economic, professional, and political) relationships as reliable markers of collective consciousness. They have acknowledged the fact of an "ethnic revival," which has developed in reaction to the overweening claims of a centralized state, to the political domination by the ethnic majority, to the coldness of industrial relations, and to the boredom of an increasingly homogenized global culture. However, they insist that such a revival has not necessarily led to a revival of ethnic languages, despite a growing concern with "multiculturalism"—a term that is often used to refer to the legitimation of racial and lifestyle diversity rather than cultural-linguistic pluralism.

The economic (or cost-benefit) criterion can perhaps be illustrated by the case of Switzerland. In that country, national cohesion often seems to be challenged by the fact that there is no common language. But to at least one Swiss, that lack is precisely what makes such cohesion possible (Buhrer 1996). He argues that the Swiss get along *because* they do not really understand each other (*"Les Suisses s'entendent parce qu'ils ne se comprennent pas"*). A common Swiss nationalism exists because divisive elements are isolated and depoliticized by means of institutional arrangements and because certain political values and economic interests are translinguistic. Prosperity has certainly helped to permit the Swiss to live peaceably side by side, and the recent attacks by outsiders on the avarice of Swiss banks (and the massive looting of victims of the Second World War from which the Swiss people as a whole benefited) have fortified (often latent) Swiss national sentiments.

Nationalism and Language as Independent and Insufficiently Related Variables

Despite its flaws, the structural-functional argument, as outlined above, should not be entirely dismissed. In the nineteenth century, German nationalism was based largely on language; yet the unification of Germany was incomplete. Austria-Hungary maintained a separate identity, and today the German language is the medium of expression of three nationalisms: German, Austrian, and Swiss. Language has little to do with patriotism, for a feeling of closeness to the land depends on rootedness, love of the soil and familiar physical surroundings, and spatially defined kinship associations, which can be expressed in more than one language. When the Jews of Warsaw thought of their city, they thought of it in Yiddish, not Polish. For many inhabitants of Brussels, identification with the Belgian capital is expressed more comfortably in Flemish than in French terms; and for most Dubliners, life in their city is interpreted in English rather than Irish Gaelic.

According to Alfred Cobban, the nation is the result of a collective desire of people to live together. The common consciousness of being a nation "was derived far more from living in common and sharing common ideals than from any racial, linguistic, or cultural inheritance. A nation may therefore be built up by a monarchy in the course of time on the most diverse foundations, as were the British and French nations, or it may be constituted by a deliberate act, as was Belgium" (1970: 121–122). This is a clearly functionalist conception of the nation; it assumes that consciousness developed, not out of the inheritance of a common culture, a common language, and common myths, but rather out of quotidian transactions, and that these have little to do with inherited culture. It is no accident that, whereas most social scientists in the United States, Britain, and France acknowledge the primacy of culture and myth in the shaping of ethnic identity, the political scientists in these countries would argue that these elements apply to "primordial" ethnic communities but not to modern nations and that the former are transcended in the process of "nation-building." As modern nations ("nation-states") are built, ethnic languages are replaced by national languages, which are superior because they are idioms of "high culture," intercommunal transactional utility, global functional significance, and/or the best expressions of a political ideology or a "social compact" on which the nation is based. This process presumably explains why Russian, English, and French superseded various indigenous minority idioms. (Cobban's notion of monarchy as an instrument for building up a nation is a typically British conceit.)

In part, this view is a reflection both of an overreaction to German nation building and an overinterpretation of the organic nature of that process, which was equated with racism, and, in part, it is a reflection of the development theories of the 1960s, according to which nation building in newly independent states of the Third World would follow the pattern of the United States, which was regarded as the ideal type. Thus, in the nation-building experiments in sub-Saharan Africa, an external and superordinate language (English or French) has been used in attempts to overcome the divisive impact of numerous rival ethnic languages.

To some extent, Cobban's view is an echo of that of Ernest Renan, a nineteenth-century French historian. For Renan, language is less important than common experiences, common values, and the will to share a common fate (Renan 1947: 903–904). Renan was not at all disturbed by the fact that many residents of France did not speak French, and he had little doubt about their membership in the French political community. He was not even sure whether the French language might not be replaced some day by some other language. In the view of many French intellectuals, however, political values and commitments are easier to share with the possession of a common language.

Unfortunately, this classically Jacobin formulation represents an ideal, for neither common values nor a common language necessarily suffices for membership in a national community. The "barbarians" in Hellas spoke Greek but were not considered—and could not become—Athenian citizens. Jews in Vichy France were excluded from the national community although they spoke nothing but French; and English-speaking Hong Kong residents were technically British subjects but were for the most part not considered "belongers." Arabic-speaking Maronites born and raised in Lebanon have not been considered full members of the Arab nation. German-speaking (and German-born) children of Turkish "guest workers" could not easily become members of the German nation, or Polish-speaking Jews of the Polish nation.

Such exclusivist attitudes may be both responses to and causes of exclusivist or defensive attitudes on the part of ethnolinguistic minorities. For example, there is some doubt whether Russian-speaking inhabitants of Ukraine share Ukrainian national sentiment; whether Magyars (whom the Rumanian authorities regard as Hungarian-speaking Rumanians) share Rumanian rather than Hungarian national sentiment; and whether Hungarian-speaking Slovaks share Slovak national sentiment. Obviously, much depends on the nonlinguistic (e.g., economic and political) aspects of Slovak or Rumanian identity and their relative attractiveness—for example, the extent to which a minority community is put on an equal footing with the majority rather than being dominated by it.

Because "language is a symbol of domination" (Horowitz 1985: 219–224), the glorification of the idiom spoken by an indigenous population has been part of that population's cultural and national legitimation. In order to assert the legitimacy or priority of their national claims, specifically against the claims of minority communities, whether immigrant or native, ethnic communities claim a "rightful place" for their languages—for example, Assamese, Magyar, Malay, and Sinhalese—which means some sort of officially recognized status. As an indicator of political equality, a minority community may assert its own lingustic claims; it may demand the use of its language in parliament, government offices, and schools, even though most members of that community may actually prefer to speak another language, usually that which facilitates their professional advancement and upward mobility. Such a language, more often than not, is the language of the former colonial overlord; to choose that language as the interethnic link means "preserving the advantages of the advanced group, with its greater mastery of the language. . . . To choose an indigenous language is to make job recruitment more egalitarian classwise, but to discriminate ethnically" (Horowitz 1985: 220–223).

"Language issues are symbolically capable of weaving together claims to exclude others with claims to shore up uncertain group worth. Language is the quintessential entitlement issue. . . . Politics can be used not only to confirm status [of a language] but to enhance it" (Horowitz 1985: 220–221). The extent to which speakers of minority languages identify politically with the larger community (or state) in which they reside is heavily dependent on the degree of legitimation their language is accorded. This is seen in the case of Catalunya, which has expressed no desire to found a separate state. Yet such legitimation is no guarantee against the development of separatist nationalism on the part of the minority. For example, the granting of official status to the speakers of the Tamil language in Sri Lanka did not lead to the abatement of Tamil nationalist violence.

Linguistic-Cultural Values and Political Values: The Medium and the Message

There are those who have accepted the proposition that "the medium is the message" or, at least, that it has an important influence on the message. They have argued that there is an intimate connection between the values that define a nation politically and the language in which the definition is articulated. Thus some white Anglo-Saxon Protestant intellectuals of the eighteenth and nineteenth centuries argued that the spirit of liberty that gave rise to the American republic—and the individualist ethic of Protestantism that inspired it—could be expressed best in English; some French intellectuals have argued that French has been the ideal idiom for articulating the doctrines of the Enlightenment and later those of the Revolution; and Soviet intellectuals have argued that Russian was ideally suited to express the Bolshevik ideology. Such arguments are spurious and reflect a cultural conceit. English has been the language of several African dictators; French was the language of the Vichy regime; and Russian was the language of Czarist autocrats in the nineteenth century and of the administrators of the gulag in the twentieth century. Conversely, Marxism has been expressed also in languages other than Russian, and revolution and republicanism in languages other than French. The political values associated with constitutional democracy—liberty, equality, popular sovereignty, and *laïcité*—are now widely accepted and are expressed in various languages (Safran 1992b). Today, language is insufficient as a unique medium for the expression of political ideology on which "civic" nationalism is presumably based—either because political values have come to be shared by many nations or because the ideology has become tarnished, if not irrelevant. Given the experience of the Vichy regime and, conversely, the democratization of most of Western Europe after the Second World War, there no longer is a convincing congruence between the French language and republicanism; given the development of polycentrism during the cold war and the collapse of the Soviet Union thereafter, there is no congruence between Russian and communism. The Arabic language is not congruent with Islamic fundamentalism; there are Arabic-speaking Christians and Farsi- and Turkish-speaking Muslims. There are also Slavic-speaking Muslims, but there is doubt whether the Bosnian Muslims of Sarajevo were considered as practicing "normative" Islam. A similar question can be raised about the connection between the Hebrew language and Zionism: The early Zionists were Yiddish-speaking, although to the ultra-orthodox, Hebrew is more important as a holy tongue, which must not be used for the articulation of a secular ideology, including nationalism. There is no denying that an initial common culture and language, such as French, Russian, and English, facilitated a variety of transactions on which the collective identities of the respective nations were based. The globalization of the economy has led to the development of a transnational mass culture and a global technocratic medium, which, at the moment is one or another form of English. Conversely, the English language has become so universal that a variety of nationalisms can be comfortably expressed in it.

Those who define a nation in ethnic terms argue that it is possible to speak of multilingual states but not multilingual nations and that, as a corollary, there is not one nationalism found in those states but two or more. But that is an excessively narrow approach. In multilingual countries such as Switzerland, Belgium, Singapore, and (to a lesser extent) Italy, Canada, and Ukraine, it is not language but political and economic commonalities that help shape distinctive national orientations. Nevertheless, in all these countries there are "transpolitical " attractions between neighboring states based on language links. In some cases, these links are significant enough to generate irredentist sentiments; in others, there are ideological sympathies that are not shared by citizens who speak a different language, as, for example, in Switzerland, where widespread Nazi sentiments of German-speaking Swiss existed before and during the Second World War; and in post-Soviet Ukraine, with the Russian sentiments of many inhabitants of the Crimea and the eastern part of the country. The pan-Germanic nationalism of the Austrians in the interwar period and during the war and their enthusiastic cooperation with Nazi policies were based on a language shared with the German Reich. Conversely, after the end of the war, the Austrians began to insist on a purely Austrian national consciousness that had nothing do with German nationalism. Feelings of "Frenchness" were stimulated by fluency in French; nevertheless, the fact that many West African leaders were fluent in French (and were often graduates of prestigious French schools) did not prevent their fighting for the national independence of their countries. Similarly, many of the Latvian, Ukrainian, and Armenian nationalists and almost all Zionists in the Soviet Union spoke Russian as their primary, if not their only, language.

Conclusions

It is perhaps too early or perhaps impossible to "prove" that the distinct language-based ethnonationalisms of these communities can be contained in a nonpolitical sphere by consociational or various other mechanisms of elite management or functional autonomy. Indeed, the very existence of "multicultural" institutional arrangements—to the extent that they are designed to depoliticize the impact of language—shows that language remains an important factor of collective consciousness, one which might become politically explosive and lead to separatism or irredentism unless domesticated and depoliticized.

There are countries of linguistically mixed communities that contain significant populations who speak minority languages, as, for example, in Ukraine, where at least one-fourth of the population is Russian-speaking.. In order to prevent diglossia that might lead to the assertion of political claims by minorities, efforts must be made to emphasize nonlinguistic bases of nationalism. Nevertheless, a nation of purely "political" essence is a fantasy (Cahen 1994), despite Jacobin, Marxian, or American functionalist pretensions; for in order for the "political" to do its work, there must be an identitive readiness that is based on psychological and cultural foundations. These foundations are kinship, religious, or linguistic, in various combinations. Among them, language would seem to be the most important, for kinship lines are often difficult to substantiate; religious links are weakening in an age of growing secularization; and culture without language is a global mass culture that is ephemeral and implies little in the way of tradition or emotional commitment. There remains language; more specifically, an ethnonationally distinct language.

As mentioned, the sentiment of belonging to an ethnonational community is not necessarily connected with a language, although a specific language may be considered part of the cultural heritage of that community. The connection between national identity and language is equally ambiguous on an individual level. Some individuals have an instrumental view of their ethnonational language: They may believe that ethnonational culture and attitudes can be expressed only in that language, and they may undertake to learn the language of their community in order to reaffirm their identity. Others, on the contrary, may hold an expressive view about learning the language; they may argue that, in principle, such learning ought to be done; or they may believe that what is most important, and what may be sufficient, is that the ethnic language be legitimated by its "officialization" in the form of allowing its use in government dealings, in broadcasting, election ballots, street names, and the subsidization of cultural projects. Still others may be indifferent to any of these efforts, believing them to be irrelevant to the affirmation of a particularistic ethnonational identity. In this kind of identity—it is sometimes referred to as "neoethnicity"—language is more or less on par with family customs, cuisine, and dress patterns as an identitive marker.

Open Questions

The impact of officialization of an ethnic language on nationalism is far from clear. On the one hand, the public use of a language—in newspapers and the media—helps to make members of an ethnic community literate in their own tongue and to lend respectability to its national political aspirations. This was clearly the case among speakers of the Nuuk dialect in Greenland and among Yiddish speakers in Eastern Europe in the early twentieth century (Stenbaek 1992). On the other hand, the officialization of an ethnic language may go a long way toward satisfying the minority's cultural demands (which may be little more than symbolic) and may serve to dampen the nationalist sentiments of that minority.

Does the promotion of a mass idiom as a national language by the intellectual elite of an ethnonational community undermine the position of that elite, whose status was protected vis-à-vis the masses by the fact that it spoke a more classic or elegant idiom (e.g., Latin and later French)? Or, on the contrary, does it preserve the position of that elite as the sector that has the major responsibility for shaping, developing, and legitimating the "national" idiom? Are language claims asserted for political reasons or cultural ones? For instrumental reasons or expressive ones? For reasons of integration or autonomy? And does the legitimation of such claims strengthen a politically based nationalism and state loyalty or does it undermine them? There are no consistent answers to these questions.

Today, there is an emphasis on "national" language in order to preserve and assert a feeling of uniqueness in a time of cultural globalization, economic interdependence, and the weakening of traditional sovereignties. The nationalism fostered by those who make strong efforts to revive an ethnic language may be cultural rather than political: it may not aim at political independence but rather at a restructuring of the state along federal lines or at one or another form of functional cultural autonomy or even socioeconomic codetermination.

In sum, we conclude that if nationalism is defined in civic terms, language tends to be a product of state policy; if it is defined in ethnic terms, then language is an important element of an organic historical community that gives rise to a state. Civic nationalism may, however, exist in the context of multiglossia; conversely, ethnically based cultural nationalism (based on a particular language) may be a subpolitical component of a politically based nationalism in which the language of a dominant ethnic group becomes a superordinate medium.

Questions for Further Thought and Discussion

1. How do you evaluate the importance of language as compared to religion, race, or territory as a marker of collective identity?

2. Under what conditions does language assume greater or lesser importance to an ethnonational community?

3. What are the most effective institutional approaches that combine the maintenance of linguistic pluralism with the preservation of transethnic political unity?

4. Do languages influence political values or vice versa?

5. Are there substitutes for language as instruments of "nation-building"? What are they?

6. What is the place of language in Jacobin, or "civic," nationalism as contrasted with organic, or "ethnic," nationalism?

7. Under what conditions does economic status determine the importance attached to language?

8. Do members of the elite encourage or discourage the revival of the language of the ethnic minority to which they belong?

9. What is the relationship between "multiculturalism" and ethnocultural pluralism?

10. What are the criteria that should be used to determine whether a language should be preserved or protected?

Selected Bibliography

Armstrong, John A. (1982). *Nations before Nationalism*. Chapel Hill: University of North Carolina Press.

Brass, Paul R. (1991). *Ethnicity and Nationalism*. Newbury Park, CA: Sage.

Braudel, Fernand (1990–1992). *The Identity of France* (2 vols.). New York: Harper.

Buck, Carl Darling (1916). Language and the sentiment of nationality. *American Political Science Review* 10(1): 44–69.

Buhrer, Jean-Claude (1996). La Suisse à l'épreuve des langues. *Le Monde*, 7 December.

Cahen, Michel (1994). *Ethnicité politique*. Paris: L'Harmattan.

Cobban, Alfred (1970). *The Nation-State and National Self-Determination*. New York: Crowell.

Deutsch, Karl W. (1953). *Nationalism and Social Communication: An Inquiry into the Foundations of Nationality*. Cambridge: MIT Press.

Fishman, Joshua A. (1970). *Sociolinguistics*. Rowley, Mass.: Newbury House.

Gellner, Ernest (1983). *Nations and Nationalism*. Oxford: Blackwell.

Gurr, Ted R. (1993). *Minorities at Risk*. Washington, D.C.: U.S. Institute of Peace Press.

Harshav, Benjamin (1993). *Language in Time of Revolution*. Berkeley: University of California Press.

Hobsbawm, Eric (1990). *Nations and Nationalism since 1780*. Cambridge: Cambridge University Press.

Horowitz, Donald L. (1985). *Ethnic Groups in Conflict*. Berkeley: University of California Press.

Jakez-Hélias, Pierre (1975). *Le cheval d'Orgueuil*. Paris: Plon.

Kohn, Hans (1945). *The Idea of Nationalism*. New York: Macmillan.

Renan, Ernest (1947). Quest-ce qu'une nation? In *Oeuvres complètes* (vol. 1). Paris: Calmann-Lévy.

Safran, William (1992a). Pluralisme, démocratie, et droits linguistiques aux Etats-Unis. In *Les Minorités en Europe: Droits Linguistiques et Droits de l'Homme*, Henri Giordan (ed.), 537–568. Paris: Kimé.

Safran, William (1992b). Language, ideology, and state-building: A comparison of policies in France, Israel, and the Soviet Union. *International Political Science Review* 13(4): 397–414.

Shafer, Boyd C. (1955). *Nationalism: Myth and Reality*. New York: Harcourt, Brace & World.

Smith, Anthony D. (1991). *National Identity*. Reno: University of Nevada Press.

Stenbaek, Marianne (1992). Mass media in Greenland: The politics of survival. In *Ethnic Minority Media*, S. H. Riggins (ed.), 44–62. Newbury Park, Cal.: Sage.

Stewart, Michael (1997). *The Time of the Gypsies*. Boulder: Westview Press.

Political Science

ROBERT PHILLIPSON

In view of widespread agreement that linguistic identity is of central importance for the individual, the group, and the state and that language is a major defining characteristic of ethnicity, one might be forgiven for thinking that language policy must be of central concern to sociology and political science, the disciplines that are particularly concerned with societal power and institutions. That would be a misconception. Although there is no doubt about the importance of language in the functioning of such social institutions as education, the media, public administration, and civil society in general, this does not mean that language has been a major concern of most political scientists. Despite pleas for political scientists and linguists to collaborate and some signs of this having taken place (e.g., Weinstein 1990, Dua 1996), it is still widely felt that language policy and planning as undertaken by language specialists is inadequately grounded in political theory and that political scientists accord too little attention to language policy.

This is paradoxical, granted that virtually all states confront major challenges in the management of multilingualism. Political decisions are taken that aim to bring about or resist change in language policy, and language has been a salient issue in several of the major political upheavals of recent decades. This chapter presents key trends in the postcolonial, post-Communist, and postnational worlds, considers how linguistic dominance is approached in political science, and probes two topics that are connected to the increasing global dominance of English. The first is the validity of the assertion that English is now a postethnic or de-ethnicized language. The second is the handling of ethnicity in South African language-policy making and the efforts to counteract what language-policy makers there regard as the "blatant hegemony of English."

Descriptions of language in a given country typically take into account the history of the evolution and impact of particular languages; a demographic profile of language users; language use in education, particularly which language is

94

used as the medium of instruction; language in the public sphere; language in the mass media; language use in creative literature; language attitudes; and language and national consciousness.[1] Descriptions based on each of these variables can then serve as a springboard for analysis of key language policy issues. They can also lead to comparative study, for instance, analysis of language policy in Kenya, Tanzania, and Uganda, three former British colonies in East Africa. Policies differ considerably in the three states, but English remains at the top of the language hierarchy in each.

Postcolonial

Language policy has figured prominently in the political sphere in several states in Asia, but in Africa it has generally had a low profile, mostly because those in power do not wish to implement change that might challenge their power. The rich, diverse linguistic potential of many postcolonial states therefore remains largely untapped, most languages being deprived of resources and rights. The majority of citizens in Asia and Africa, some of them in fledgling "democracies," are governed in a language that they do not speak. Elites differ from the rest of the population in their lifestyles and their linguistic identities. Competence in the dominant language is a precondition for membership in the elite.

A primary concern of the leaders of newly independent former colonies has been to consolidate embryonic states. One means of forging unity has been to select one or more languages as "official" and/or "national." This choice has involved reconciling the claims of local languages, which connote authenticity and legitimacy, with those of the language of the former colonial power, typically English or French, which connote instrumentalism, modernization, and the status quo. Decolonization could involve replacing a European language with local languages, but in practice in virtually all former colonies the language hierarchies of the colonial period have been maintained. A European language remains as the dominant language of political and economic power internally and as the key link language externally.

English in Kenya and Nigeria is therefore a language of national (state) identification that sits at the peak of a multiplicity of languages and is known well by only a small elite. English is a foreign language in terms of its origins and its external functions, but it is a local language by virtue of its internal social stratification functions. Below English in the hierarchy are languages that may be associated with the privileging of one ethnic group (e.g., Hindi in India and Hausa or Yoruba in Nigeria, languages which may be perceived as involving internal linguistic imperialism) or a language of interethnic communication that is not the mother tongue of any group (e.g., Swahili in East Africa and many languages used for trading purposes). Other languages have regional or local currency. Some represent a reduced form of language, a pidgin. English serves to maintain a class in power, a group that often cuts across ethnic group boundaries.

Western concepts of language and ethnicity fail to capture the reality of complex, fluid, and plural cultural and linguistic identities in many postcolonial contexts, both in Asia and Africa. It is inappropriate to think in terms of "one language, one nation, one state," as is presumed to be the case with, for instance, German speakers in Germany and French speakers in France. Even here the notion of a straight fit between a monolingual ethnic identity and the language of the state is more of a myth than a reality. Nations have been produced by nationalism rather than the reverse. Postcolonial states have largely been fashioned by the colonial powers and the political elites who replaced them.

Post-Communist

Language was a major mobilizing force in the cultural revitalization processes that led to the collapse and fragmentation of the Soviet Union. In a changed world with different social, economic, and cultural goals, the new post-Communist states have often downgraded Russian and upgraded local languages so as to reassert ethnic identity while seeking to balance the claims of a linguistically diverse population.

As in many parts of the world, language policy must address not only the internal linguistic ecology but also external needs. Foreign languages therefore figure as a central component of obligatory education. Incorporation into the free market that Western interests dominate is facilitated by use of English, for which the demand is substantial. It has even been suggested by North American language experts that English could play a role as an interethnic language in such post-Communist states as Estonia and Latvia, though little evidence is offered to justify the suggestion.[2] It probably has less to do with local needs and language competence in these Baltic states than with the advance of Western products, values, and imagery, spearheaded by McDonalds and Hollywood. A range of types of aid, economic and scientific, are integral to the asymmetrical relationship between strong and weak states, interlocking with commercial, media, political, and military links. The global expansion of the capitalist system, whether seen as imperialist or liberal, has major cultural and linguistic dimensions.

The expansion of English in the postcolonial and post-Communist worlds has not been left to chance but has been deliberately promoted by the American and British governments (Phillipson 1992), which have been concerned with promoting corporate interests and investments. The teaching and learning of English is itself a multibillion-dollar business, the largest generator of income for the British economy after oil. English for business is business for English. The English-teaching business has even been considered as second only to drug trafficking in its importance in some countries, an analogy that is perhaps flippant but is also illuminating: Addiction to the drug of English is a widespread phenomenon.

Postnational

As a result of migrations from poorer countries to richer countries, literally hundreds of languages are now spoken in virtually all major cities in the West. This process has created new diasporas, new forms of language contact, and new types of hybrid ethnic identity (Appadurai 1993). This development, combined with re-vitalization processes among speakers of many marginalized indigenous minority languages (e.g., Catalan, Sámi, Welsh), has forced states that were fashioned through a myth of a linguistically uniform nation (e.g., Spain, Norway, Great Britain) to rec-ognize their manifest multilingualism. New forms of political and cultural devolu-tion and autonomy are being devised. Such reorientations, combined with technol-ogy, communication, and inexpensive air travel that erode national borders, are leading to new forms of postnational identity that reflect the diverse origins of those who make up the population of the contemporary state, as well as new alignments. New forms of postnational identity have evolved at individual, group, and state levels. In countries like Australia and Canada, this has led to a major rethinking of national identity and the role that languages play in its formation.

Another factor that promotes postnational identities is global consumption of the same cultural products: CNN, Hollywood, "fast" food, and so forth. The trend toward creating the impression of a global culture through production for global markets, so that products and information aim at creating "global customers that want global services by global suppliers" can be termed McDonaldization, which means "aggressive round-the-clock marketing, the controlled information flows that do not confront people with the long-term effects of an ecologically detri-mental lifestyle, the competitive advantage against local cultural providers, the obstruction of local initiative, all converge into a reduction of local cultural space" (Hamelink 1994, 112).

Globalization and localization pressures are thus competing influences on eth-nic identity. The English language has many features of a global language (e.g., links with finance, commerce, science, politics, and the media) that take on dis-tinctive local forms in each country (the diverse uses to which the language is put and the sounds and written forms in which this is expressed). Thus newspapers in India or Nairobi are written in a form of standard English but have a distinctly local feel and character.

Language policies also underpin the multifarious activities of the European Union (EU), in which fifteen member states[3] are moving gradually toward supra-national integration. The term *supranational* is used to refer to an alliance that brings a number of nation-states together.[4] There is a "European" Parliament, a deceptive label in that European countries that are not EU members (e.g., Hun-gary, Switzerland) are not represented. More decisions are taken at the EU admin-istrative headquarters in Brussels than in the capital cities of the member states. These legislative and policy measures can in principle be negotiated by the rep-resentatives of the fifteen countries in the eleven official languages and are re-quired to be promulgated in all the languages, but in practice there is a hierarchy of working languages, with French and English at the top.

Although the formal status of languages has been agreed on in intergovernmen-tal treaties, language policies in EU supranational bodies largely follow unwritten rules which consolidate hegemonic structures. Essentially, this means that the use of English is inexorably expanding. At the national level, some European states (particularly Norway, which is not a EU member, and France) are actively concerned with limiting the impact of McDonaldization on their cultures and languages.

The member states of the EU are engaged in intensive supranational policy making in all sociopolitical fields: There is a "common agricultural policy" and common policies for the economy, finance (a common currency, the euro), and, increasingly, for foreign policy. A British newspaper has advocated a "common language policy,"[5] which would make English the sole official language. Culture and education are by tradition regarded as national prerogatives, but a large number of EU schemes promote greater crossnational experience, exchange, and understanding. Many such schemes (LINGUA, SOCRATES, etc.) involve learning the languages of partner countries. There are therefore a number of policies in place in the field of language. There is also a language dimension that permeates all supranational negotiations and administration, but the underlying language policies are largely covert.

When additional states join the European Union, as seems certain to happen over the coming decade, it is likely that the logistics of operating in an increased number of languages (for instance, through the addition of Czech, Estonian, Hungarian, and Polish) will lead to a change in language policies. It is probable that translation of all key texts into the dominant language of each member state will remain a cardinal principle but that access to interpretation facilities will be constrained. This would necessitate a formalization of the regulations governing the use of working languages. At present, all the eleven official languages have in theory the same right to serve as working languages. There is evidence from a number of small empirical studies that EU bureaucrats are keen for the number of working languages to be restricted, whereas members of the European Parliament, particular those from "small" linguistic communities such as Greece and Portugal, do not endorse this, as it could lead to further marginalization of their languages.

It is arguable that there should be an explicit supranational EU language policy, since the EU's supranational institutions, in particular the Parliament and the Commission, are progressively taking on more features of a single state. The member states are voluntarily abandoning part of their political sovereignty. Such a language policy could represent an alternative to the laissez-faire free market that facilitates the expansion of international languages. The policy would address how McDonaldization affects internal national language ecologies in the current phase of increasing postnationalism and supranationalism. No such policy has been elaborated. The treaties that are the bible of European unification, the treaties of Maastricht (1992) and Amsterdam (1997), proclaim that cultural and linguistic diversity are central features of Europe and will be maintained. However, the schemes for promoting contact between citizens of EU countries, links at the school and university levels, and foreign-language learning do not provide a counterweight to the economic and political pressures of McDonaldization and Englishization.

Approaches to Linguistic Dominance

In each of these contexts, postcolonial, post-Communist, and postnational, specific languages compete for space and resources, or, to be more precise, the speakers of each language (whether as a first or second language) do. The resulting pecking order of languages, both within each polity and in supranational fora, is attributable to many factors, but the tendency is for languages that have the backing of the state and are used in official functions and education to expand and for others to contract. Different scientific traditions, in history, anthropology, sociology, and political science (all of which cover similar ground), stress different factors when accounting for language hierarchies and the management of multilingualism, but none ignore the role that language has played in the consolidation of nation-states over the past two centuries.

Although political theory in Western countries derives from Greek and Roman thought, political science can be considered "the only genuine made-in-America social science without obvious European counterparts or antecedents" (Appadurai 1993, 423). On the other hand, American social science has been energetically exported throughout this century, so that its influence is global.

Political scientists, anthropologists, geographers, and language planners have documented the complexity of the language scene in many different parts of the world. Many such scholars are based in North America, some of them of African or Asian origin. There are detailed national studies (e.g., McRae 1983on Switzerland). Some political scientists attempt to increase the rigor and predictive power of analyses of the dynamics of language through an algebraic formalization of relevant variables: For a survey of several traditions, including those inspired by functionalism and game theory, see Sonntag 1996.

Laitin (1992) proposes a detailed, flexible three-language formula for language rationalization in Africa but is criticized for assuming that language planning and language behavior can be captured by a framework drawn from economic planning, for a top-down approach that regards government as the sole source of language policies, and for regarding language outcomes as predictable (Akinnaso 1994). The dynamics of language in postcolonial countries such as Nigeria are much more complex, involving a tension between linguistic unification and the rights of speakers of a very diverse hierarchy of languages (Akinnaso 1994).

The concept "ethnic conflict" is journalistic shorthand for a confrontation in which ethnic group loyalty is seen as a mobilizing factor. Unfortunately, the term seems to imply that ethnic groups are inevitably in conflict with each other, which is manifestly untrue. Conflicts are largely the outcome of perceived or real injustice, and there is no simple correlation between ethnicity or language and conflict. Likewise, there is no straight correlation between a single language such as English and positive ascriptions such as progress, peace, international understanding, or the enjoyment of human rights.

Another concept that tends to be used loosely in popular speech is hegemony, referring to economic or political dominance and its acceptance by those affected by it. It is also a major concept in political theory in the Marxist tradition that is intended to address issues of cultural reproduction and, specifically, the ways in which class societies perpetuate inequalities. In the substantial scientific literature spawned by Gramsci's term, hegemony is invariably seen as noncoercive, as involving contestation and adaptation, a battle for hearts and minds. It is therefore a useful concept when seeking to understand how the dominant ideas in a given society are internalized in processes of political legitimation. Such ideas tend to saturate public discourse, the media, and public education to the point at which they are accepted as natural, normal, and uncontestable, despite the fact that the beliefs and values reflect a particular model of society and particular interests, especially those of dominant groups (see Phillipson 1992, 72–75).

A central aspect of linguistic reproduction in education systems is the role assigned to literacy skills, as a result of which a standard form of a language is privileged at the expense of dialectal and sociolectal variation. One of the consequences of the universalization of education in Western societies over the past century has been the reduction of linguistic variety, or polyglossia, and the marginalization both of other forms of the dominant language, that is, of dialects, and of other languages.

Similar hegemonic processes are at work in the legitimation of dominant international languages. Thus it tends to be regarded as "natural" at international conferences for English to be used as though the language were a neutral instrument. In fact, use of this language clearly puts most nonnative speakers of English at a disadvantage. There is a tendency for native speakers to dominate, without reflecting on the reasons for the situation or on whether a fairer, more symmetrical way of organizing the communication could be accomplished. This is a typical example of linguistic hegemony in operation.

Hegemonic processes are not merely a matter of attitudes, beliefs, and values. Such processes contribute to the maintenance and reproduction of a structure in which some groups have more power and resources than others and are able to use these to their advantage. Thus languages that figure prominently on schedules, languages for which there are trained teachers with teaching materials and software available, are the beneficiaries of investment. They have had resources allocated to them. Resource allocation, as well as hegemonic beliefs about the rights or superiority of certain languages, are essential for the maintenance of linguistic hierarchies. Such hierarchies are, in the contemporary world, national, supranational, and global.

There will be a need in the coming years to monitor the ways "world languages" are used in global bodies such as the United Nations and major trading and military alliances and the ways supranational languages influence each other and national language ecologies. De Swaan (1993) identifies a dozen or so supranational languages used globally,[6] and stresses the role of users for whom the language is not a first language, seeing them as key multilingual mediators. "In the political sociology of language the question arises whether the processes of language spread and language decline reveal a dynamics of their own, or rather are completely determined by other processes, such as military conquest, religious proselytization, and commercial expansion" (1993: 221). He tends towards the position that language is not merely an epiphenomenon with no explanatory value but that they have a "momentum of their own," which he attributes to the fact that "language learning is a long-term investment in linguistic capital" and that education systems suffer from "inertia" in that it takes time to train teachers and to replace one school foreign language by another (221). Users are also sensitive to the communication potential of languages. This sensitivity guides choice of language both at the level of the individual and of decision makers in education systems.

Analyses of the dynamics of language in East and West Africa, India, and eastern and western Europe lead de Swaan to conclude that

> the processes of language competition have a limited but distinct autonomy vis-à-vis other social processes in the spheres of politics, culture, and the economy, and that they do display some intrinsic dynamics that have to do with inertia, interactive expectations, jealous group relations, and the interfering presence of very central or numerous third languages. (de Swaan 1993: 222)

In his analysis, the political sociology of language needs insights from linguistics (e.g., the closeness or distance of particular languages) and education (e.g., ease of learning).

It needs to be recalled that there is a great deal of mythmaking about languages; for instance, a belief in the intrinsic superiority of a language (French was marketed as a uniquely clear, logical language for centuries) or a belief that English is easier to learn than other languages (whereas its irregular spelling, grammar, and vocabulary reflect its multiple origins, and it is pronounced very differently in different parts of the globe). Analysis of such mythology is needed when studying the power of competing languages, nationally and supranationally. It is important to go beyond individual choice, the freedom to shift to a particular language, or competition between languages to study the ways that dominant languages are structurally favored, how both beliefs about language and economic and political resources serve to strengthen some languages and weaken others. It is in political and academic discourse, some of which filters down into popular discourse, that powerful languages are construed and consolidated. In principle, any language can be used for any purpose; for instance, to promote human rights or to counteract them. What is important in any given context is to see what goals the users of particular languages are pursuing and to clarify whose interests are served by the existing policies.

English as a Postethnic Language?

The English language has been subjected to a great deal of analysis, including that of its role in the modern world. In a study of language policy in the supranational institutions of the European Union, the following conclusion is drawn:

> Whether by design or accident, English has taken on a truly pluricentric character which gives the language a de-ethnicized and culture-unbounded quality and allows its speakers to use it freely without identifying with one particular country. So it comes as no surprise that the use of English in the European Institutions has grown despite the fact that the British are among the most reluctant members of the EU. (Quell 1997: 71)

Quell studied the use that bureaucrats at the European Union Commission make of the various languages that are eligible as working languages at meetings, in drafting documents, and so forth. His rich empirical study of one context in which the use of English is increasing is valuable, but the comment extracted here is debatable on several counts.

First, to suggest that the spread of English may be due to "design or accident" obscures the fact that a substantial number of factors do account for the spread of English (Fishman, Conrad, and Rubal-Lopez 1996) and have direct and indirect impact on Western Europe. British imperial might, succeeded by American economic and military might, have been causal factors. The expansion of a language is not a matter of conspiracy or chance, and the spread of English in Europe was not left to chance. The British and French have promoted their languages in many ways (as have the Americans) and have also funded language learning in European Union institutions. In addition, the member states (France, Germany, etc.) invest heavily in the learning of English. The British regard an increased use of English as being to their advantage, irrespective of whether they feel committed to a more integrated or federal Europe.

Second, *pluricentricity* is a term mostly used in linguistics to refer to the fact that one language has several centers from which norms for correctness emanate and radiate, for instance, in the form of dictionaries and grammars. Thus German is a pluricentric language, with centers in Germany, Austria, and Switzerland. The citizens of each of these countries look to their own centers for guidance (endocentric norms). By contrast, people in neighboring countries who speak German as a mother tongue, minorities in Belgium, Denmark, France, and Italy, as well as those learning German as a foreign language, look to Germany for guidance (exocentric norms).

English is a polycentric language in the sense that there are centers in states to which Britons moved and became the dominant group, in North America, Australia, and New Zealand. Whether norms are endocentric or exocentric in states such as South Africa and India, where English is typically strongly influenced by other languages in the local cultural ecology, is more controversial and is a very significant issue when it comes to establishing norms, local or global, in education systems.

Pluricentric languages are pluriethnic. A speaker of English as a mother tongue may have one of several possible ethnic identities, Australian, British, Canadian, and so forth. But just as we all have multiple identities, ethnic dimensions may be more or less salient in language use, and it is false to regard language and ethnicity as coterminous. A language's original centre (England for English) or a transplanted center (the United States, with norms defined by the Webster dictionaries) may or may not be relevant when someone from Sweden or the Netherlands uses English in negotiations in Brussels, in commercial transactions, or when writing a scientific paper. In such contexts, whether English is polycentric or monocentric is irrelevant in that the user does not need in any way to identify or to be identified with any English-speaking center. For such users, Quell is right in considering that the language is de-ethnicized. In addition, the user's primary ethnic identity, as a Swede, Dutchwoman, or even a Briton, may or may not be salient.

The same individual can identify with both a national language (a state linguistic identity, e.g., English in Great Britain) and a regional dialect or an ethnic minority language (a subnational linguistic identity, e.g., Scottish English or Scots Gaelic). Users of an international language in a supranational organization such as the Council of Europe or the European Union can also identify with French or

English, irrespective of their primary ethnic identification. Indeed, one of the main goals of the European Union in its contemporary integrative phase is to establish "Europe" as an imagined community (in Benedict Anderson's sense) that people will identify with as strongly as they do with their own nations. This supranational political identification can probably be superimposed on other identities without detracting from them.

To assume that a language is necessarily associated with its native speakers is a Western way of looking at linguistic identity, one that is remote from the reality of many non-Westerners for whom multilingualism is the norm. It seems to be inspired by a primordialist notion that a language is intrinsically bonded with a specific culture and worldview. Primordialism tends to regard a culture, a language, or ethnicity as a given, a constant, whereas instrumentalism tends to see ethnicity and languages as social constructs that serve particular interests and are historically grounded, shifting, relational, and malleable. It looks at the purposes served by, for instance, linguistic or ethnic mobilization for consolidating a nation or for resisting oppression.

Primordialism can be seen in popular beliefs about languages—for instance, the notion that English is intrinsically associated with progress and modernity, whereas African languages are not fit for the task of "development."[7] Such arguments have been misused so as to perpetuate the hierarchy of languages of the colonial period in the postcolonial age. They still guide World Bank policy in education, particularly as regards choice of language as the medium of education. The arguments often focus on instrumental language functions (e.g., English as a language of unity, international cooperation, and technology) as a means of privileging this language vis-à-vis others.

It is important to identify the purposes and interests served by a given language. Thus a conclusion that particular functions of English may be de-ethnicized should not be taken as meaning that the language is neutral or has no cultural or ideological baggage. As English is often a language of power, not least in postcolonial and supranational contexts, the power relations exercised in and through English are decisive for the choice of this language rather than others. The discourses in which English is used, political, scientific, commercial, and so forth, serve to constitute and shape the reality that its users experience.

Although some uses of English may be regarded as postethnic or de-ethnicized, this is unlikely to be the case in postcolonial contexts in which it is a dominant language. In former colonies in which English has indigenized or "gone native," it may be more appropriate to regard English as "multiethnic," as in India, where English gives expression to an Indian identity, one that is invariably multilingual.[8]

For rather similar reasons, using the term *lingua franca* in such contexts may be unhelpful, if the term is understood in the historical sense of a reduced form of language, one serving limited functional purposes.[9] English has not only acquired local forms, pragmatics, and cultural resonance, but it also has significant social stratificational functions, bonding a class together horizontally, often across ethnic boundaries. Such functions have more to do with nation-state building than those associated with a restricted repertoire, as in a lingua franca for trade or international scientific or diplomatic contact.

If it appears to be "natural" to use English in many parts of the modern world, at international conferences, in supranational organizations, in entertainment, and so forth, this naturalness has been acquired through processes of hegemonic ordering. It is central to hegemony that what is taken for granted, what has been internalized as normal, is in fact the result of struggles for power that represent the triumph of some interests over others.

Postethnicity in South Africa

One place in which it might seem eminently "natural" for English to be used widely is South Africa. English has been the key language of the African National Congress. Afrikaans is discredited as the language of apartheid. African languages were also closely associated with the hierarchical ordering of the old regime, marginalization, and stigmatization. South Africa is linguistically diverse, but "South Africa does not have a 'national language,' nor has it ever had one," according to the Language Plan Task Group (LANGTAG 1996: 219). This statement clearly reflects the wish to make a break with the linguistic hierarchy of the apartheid system and bring in a new, more democratic order.

In the current draft constitution the number of official languages is eleven. South Africa is moving from a system of institutionalized injustice to one which recognizes diversity and attempts to build on it in order to achieve basic social justice. Language policy has a major role to play in this process. A key question when seeking to valorize the African languages is whether English can be "reduced to equality," a vivid expression used earlier in relation to Afrikaans by Neville Alexander, a key figure in South African language planning and chair of the group which produced the LANGTAG report.

The use of the term *ethnic* under apartheid in South Africa was a refinement of the way tribes and ethnic groups were manufactured during European colonialism in southern Africa. "We Blacks . . . execrate ethnicity with all our being," wrote Archbishop Desmond Tutu in 1984, when the apartheid system was consciously using "race" and ethnolinguistic diversity as tools for dividing and suppressing the non-European population of South Africa.[10] Tutu's reaction to one dimension of a vicious political system does not mean that the wellsprings of ethnic identification do not exist among South Africans. The protracted dormancy of ethnic loyalties in many parts of the world, Communist and capitalist, was misleading, and the closing years of the twentieth century showed that they could easily be reinvigorated for both constructive purposes (e.g., minorities being granted greater rights to govern their own affairs) and destructive ones (e.g., the "civil" wars in the former Yugoslavia).

In the new South Africa, the word *ethnic* is avoided. In the language policy report referred to earlier, the only use of ethnic is in a section devoted to "depoliticizing language": "Speakers of some languages, notably Afrikaans and Zulu, feel that their languages may receive inequitable treatment because of their association with ethnic politics which are unacceptable to the present government" (LANGTAG 1996: 57). Ethnicity is here seen as divisive, in conflict with goals of national reconciliation and unity. It is therefore an inappropriate term to use in a report that is mainly concerned with strategies for improving the status and use of all languages, including previously marginalized languages and sign languages.

If all eleven official languages are to be strengthened, policies have to be evolved that allocate resources to each of them, that elaborate strategies appropriate for each region, and that promote multilingualism and language rights in all spheres of public life, including education and the media. Campaigns are under way to raise consciousness about many aspects of language policy. The tendency for English to assert itself as a sole hegemonic language is being resisted, for which the experience of successful measures elsewhere in strengthening other languages (e.g., French in Canada, Swahili in Tanzania) is relevant, but the implementation of rights for all languages will need constant vigilance. Whether the political will to achieve this is present will be decisive. In the work of the Truth and Reconciliation Commission, which is a key body in the process of bringing together the various communities of South Africa and which is taking evidence from South Africans from all walks of life, interpretation facilities are being provided so as to ensure that those who happen not to be proficient in English or Afrikaans can exercise their democratic rights to participate in civil society.

The complexity of language-policy issues can be seen in relation to Afrikaans, which is generally associated with whites of Dutch origin, though it is in fact also the mother tongue of large numbers of people who, under apartheid, were classified as "Colored" and whose political and cultural rights were minimal. Groups with very different interests can therefore identify with Afrikaans, just as they can with English.

There are comparable but different problems in relation to African languages. The difficulties in assuring them greater status and influence relate to their marginal status in the past and inadequate teaching (often by nonnative speakers with little competence in the languages) and the fact that little use is made of them in public by influential politicians. This may be linked to a wish on the part of national leaders to avoid being perceived as identifying with or favoring any one ethnic group (for instance, speakers of Sotho or Xhosa).

Language policy should aim to ensure equity for all language groups. The power of English is such that all groups can see the value of proficiency in the language. The challenge of reducing English to equality involves ensuring that English is learned as an additional language, perhaps in much the same way as it is learned in countries such as Sweden or the Netherlands, where thus far the expansion of English has not been at the expense of Swedish or Dutch—although the forces of McDonaldization and cultural and linguistic imperialism are pushing in this direction. Speakers of African languages must be able to learn and use these languages for the full range of social, commercial, and political purposes. Education must necessarily involve consolidating the multilingualism that is a feature of social life for most South Africans.

Choice in education must attempt to ensure that use of a particular language as medium of instruction does not imply condemnation of other languages to low positions in a hierachical linguistic ordering or the exclusion of particular groups from access to power and resources. A first step might be to break with the pattern of schools being defined as educating children through the medium of language X or Y (Afrikaans, English, Zulu, etc.), when the goal for such learners must be high levels of competence in languages X, Y, and Z. A choice between X or Y is unfair when one language has much higher status than all others and when parents cannot be expected to know what consequences will follow from an uninformed assumption that greater use of English will necessarily bring success. The evidence from both the postcolonial world and immigrant education in the West is that this will only be the case for the few.

There is a tendency for both elite and marginal groups in many states worldwide to desire competence in English for the obvious reason that English is seen to open doors. The appeal of English should not obscure the fact that in Africa as a whole 90% of the population speak only African languages. In India, the number of English speakers ranges from 3 to 5%. If the citizens of countries worldwide are to contribute to the solution of local problems, to use the local environment for locally appropriate purposes, cultural, economic, and political, local languages must be involved. Language policy must reconcile these dimensions of language ecology with the pressures of globalization and supranationalization that are propelling English forward. Language policy must be made explicit and must embrace equitable conditions for all people and all languages. This is a challenge to politicians and other policy makers. There is enough scientific documentation of the issues to ensure that more visionary and democratic policies could be evolved globally and locally.

Questions for Further Thought and Discussion

1. Are there any states in the world that fit into the model of "one nation, one state, one language"? Relate your findings to the role of language in forming an ethnic group or a state.

2. Is there a more appropriate label than *postnational* for states that are at the receiving end of McDonaldization?

3. Are there supranational bodies like the European Union in other parts of the world? Does the North American Free Trade Agreement (NAFTA) have a language policy? If not, what are the implications for French, Spanish, and all other languages than English?

4. Is it possible to draw a clear line between uses of language which are ethnic, nonethnic, or postethnic?

5. English in South Africa is closely associated with political and economic power. Can a democratic language policy be implemented without a major change in the political-economic system?

6. What factors might cause political science to accord greater prominence to language policy?

Notes

1. These are the section headings in Mazrui and Mazrui 1996.

2. For instance, "English is beginning to play the role of a lingua franca between Estonia's two national communities" (Laitin, cited in Dua 1996: 60). See also the analysis of Sandra Mackay's description of Latvia in Phillipson and Skutnabb-Kangas 1997. There is no doubt that English is increasing in importance in the Baltic states for external functions but emphatically not as an internal lingua franca.

3. These are Austria, Belgium, Denmark, Finland, France, Germany, Greece, Ireland, Italy, Luxemburg, the Netherlands, Portugal, Spain, Sweden, and the United Kingdom. Many additional countries have applied for membership, and negotiations are under way with the Czech Republic, Estonia, Hungary, Malta, and Poland. Several other post-Communist states and Turkey have also applied for membership.

4. *International* tends to be used for relations between states (international affairs) and individuals of different national background (e.g., Danish as an international language when used, productively or receptively, by citizens of Greenland, Iceland, Norway, and Sweden). *Transnational* tends to be used for (multinational) corporations, an appropriate term for companies that know no nation-state boundaries.

5. The *Daily Mail* ran a campaign on this theme in 1991.

6. Arabic, Chinese, English, French, German, Hindi, Malay, Japanese, Portuguese, Russian, Spanish, and Swahili.

7. For analysis of such special pleading for English, particularly in the context of "aid" to postcolonial education systems, and classification of such discourse into intrinsic, extrinsic, and functional arguments for English, see chapter 9 of Phillipson 1992.

8. All forms of English are, in fact, hybrid: English English is a blend of elements from Anglo-Saxon, Norman, Nordic, and other cultures, draws substantially on Latin and Greek, and even has some elements from Arabia and Asia, although its diverse roots are often obscure to contemporary users of the language. Most Indians regard English as an Indian language and identify with it as such, due to the depth of penetration over several centuries of English in India. Whether English is seen as an African language in similar ways is a more open question, although there are probably some (Afro-Saxons, to use Ali Mazrui's term) who identify with English as a local language, and this is reflected in the creative writing of successful novelists from all parts of Africa.

9. On the history of the term, see Kachru 1996, and for varying uses of it, Phillipson 1992, 41–42.

10. A similar reaction might occur in other parts of the world. In Denmark, *ethnic* is mostly used to refer to cultures which diverge from that of the dominant group, the Danes. In this typical Western European, hybrid, Americanized country, it is a way of stigmatizing immigrants and refugees whose "ethnic" food, appearance, language, or behavior differs from an assumed norm. By implication, the Danes have no ethnicity.

Selected Bibliography

Akinnaso, F. Niyi (1994). Linguistic unification and language rights. *Applied Linguistics* 15(2): 139–168.

Appadurai, Arjun (1993). Patriotism and its futures. *Public Culture* 5: 411–429.

de Swaan, Abram (1993). The emergent world language system: An introduction. *International Political Science Review* 14(3): 219–226.

Dua, Hans (ed.) (1996). Language

planning and political theory. Special issue, *International Journal of the Sociology of Language* 118.

Fishman, Joshua A., Andrew W. Conrad, and Alma Rubal-Lopez (eds.) (1996). *Post-Imperial English: Status Change in Former British and American Colonies, 1940–1990*. Berlin: Mouton de Gruyter.

Hamelink, Cees (1994). *Trends in World Communication: On Disempowerment and Self-Empowerment*. Penang: Southbound and Third World Network.

Kachru, Braj B. (1996). English as a lingua franca. In *Kontaktlinguistik / Contact Linguistics / Linguistique de contact: An International Handbook of Contemporary Research*, H. Goebl, P. H. Nelde, Z. Starý, and W. Wölck (eds.), 906–913. Berlin: de Gruyter.

Laitin, David (1992). *Language Repertoires and State Construction in Africa*. Cambridge: Cambridge University Press.

LANGTAG (1996). *Towards a National Language Plan for South Africa*. Final Report of the Language Plan Task Group (LANGTAG) Pretoria: Ministry of Arts, Culture, Science and Technology.

Mazrui, Alamin M., and Ali A. Mazrui (1996). A tale of two Englishes: The imperial language in post-colonial Kenya and Uganda. In Fishman, Conrad & Rubal-Lopez (eds.), 271–302.

McRae, Kenneth (1983). *Conflict and Compromise in Multilingual Societies, Switzerland*. Waterloo, Ontario: Wilfred Laurier University Press.

Phillipson, Robert (1992). *Linguistic Imperialism*. Oxford: Oxford University Press.

Phillipson, Robert, and Tove Skutnabb-Kangas (1997). Linguistic human rights and English in Europe. Special issue. *World Englishes* 16(1): 27–43.

Quell, Carsten (1997). Language choice in multilingual institutions: A case study at the European Commission with particular reference to the role of English, French and German as working languages. *Multilingua* 16(1): 57–76.

Sonntag, Selma K. (1996). Political science and contact linguistics. In *Kontaktlinguistik/Contact Linguistics/ Linguistique de contact: An International Handbook of Contemporary Research*, H. Goebl, P. H. Nelde, Z. Starý, and W. Wölck (eds.), 75–80. Berlin: Mouton de Gruyter.

Weinstein, Brian (ed.) (1990). *Language Policy and Political Development*. Norwood, NJ: Ablex.

Psychology

AMADO M. PADILLA

Suppose an airline pilot and a psychologist arrive at a party at the same time. When the pilot is introduced to the other guests and his occupation is mentioned, no one is likely to be confused or apprehensive about what he does. Airline pilots fly airplanes. But when the psychologist is introduced and his profession is revealed, the reactions of the other guests may be quite varied. Psychologists hear things like, "Watch out, he'll analyze you," "Now I'll have to be careful or he'll know what I'm thinking," "Where is your practice and what kind of crazies do you see," and so on. Often these comments embarrass the psychologist, whose area of specialization may have very little to do with the direct assessment of people's mental health problems.

People outside the field of psychology often believe that every psychologist is an expert at figuring out people's emotional difficulties and detecting hidden personality quirks, but this is usually not the case. In fact, many psychologists do not see clients for mental health concerns. Psychology is an extremely diverse field of study, involving many different specialty areas. Some psychologists devote their entire careers to the study of human memory. These psychologists try to understand complex, unseen mental events that we normally call "thinking." Another group studies how children and adolescents develop emotionally, socially, and intellectually. Still others are interested in career counseling and helping people find occupations best suited to their skills and interests. Other psychologists are more interested in the physical basis of behavior and how the brain and nervous system connect to determine our behavior. These psychologists may also be interested in vision, hearing, sleep, abnormal behavior, and so on. Social psychology is still another area of specialization in which the focus is on how people behave in social groups. The important thing is that psychology is very diverse and made up of many specializations.

What is psychology then? In a sense, I have already taken a stab at defining psychology. I have done it, not with a single sentence, but by describing the many things that psychologists do. And yet it would be satisfying to provide a one-sentence definition of what we mean by psychology. Most definitions emphasize that psychology is the *science* of *behavior*. By emphasizing science and behavior, psychologists mean that they use the scientific method to study how people of any age, social group, or culture behave. At the base of psychology, as with any science, is the aim of understanding, predicting, and helping to improve the welfare of people. Now that we have an understanding of what psychology is, we can turn our attention to the study of language and some of the ways in which psychologists go about studying this most important form of human behavior.

The Study of Language

Language has been one of the most important behaviors studied by psychologists in different specialty areas. Let us look briefly at how psychologists from just three different branches of psychology make use of language in studying behavior. A developmental psychologist may be interested in how preschool-age children acquire and use language. These psychologists try to understand how children are able to become proficient speakers of their parents' language seemingly without much effort. Through the study of children and their language, we know much about the intellectual prowess that children are capable of when they learn language.

Cognitive psychologists, who represent another branch of psychology, study the relationship between language and thinking, often with the task of trying to understand how language is used to encode the tremendous amount of information that humans are exposed to. One of the central questions in cognitive psychology is how humans use language to efficiently process and code knowledge so that it can be used at later points in time. In still another specialization, clinical psychologists use language to assist clients to understand their thought processes and emotions. Often people have perceptions of reality that create difficulty for them in coping with their environment and with the people with whom they must interact on a daily basis. The clinical psychologist using language-based therapy enables clients to communicate more effectively in their personal and social life.

In essence, it is the use of language which sets humans apart from other members of the animal kingdom. As humans, we also have invented various writing systems to convey information to others. Writing is especially important because it allows us to communicate with people with whom we are not in direct contact and also to communicate with future generations long after the writer's lifetime. In short, we humans talk and write incessantly, expressing everything from our most basic survival needs to the most abstract intellectual concepts. Furthermore, we do this through a vast array of complicated oral and written systems. We use spoken and written language for many different purposes. Table 8-1 illustrates just a few of the ways in which spoken and written languages are used across many different languages and cultures that have been studied.

Written language enables humans to "stockpile" information. It is possible today for an individual to know more facts than did the greatest thinkers of the past.

Table 8-1. A Few Common Ways in Which Spoken and Written
Languages Are Used

Spoken Language	Written Language
Description of events and thoughts	Description of events, places, and objects
Information seeking and questions	Communicating current events
Teaching	Instructional materials
Expressing emotion	Storytelling, poetry
Greeting and thanking people	Invitations, announcements
Storytelling	Fiction and nonfiction narratives
Singing	Record keeping

Aristotle, Galileo, and Newton all seem relatively ignorant compared to a person who steeps him- or herself in the contents of the local library. In today's information-based society, computers and the Internet have even made it possible to access more information without stepping outside of one's home than could ever be housed in the greatest library in the world. With a computer, modem, and the Internet, even elementary-school-age children can communicate with people around the world or access information of almost any type for school projects or just to satisfy their curiosity.

Writing ensures that knowledge is cumulative and readily available. We need not rediscover everything for ourselves or repeat the mistakes of the past. In short, writing makes language far more useful and flexible. A very important and related point is that language is what we use to transmit information about our culture from one generation to another. In other words, language and culture are intimately bound together. It is language, spoken and written, which allows us to know about ourselves as members of a certain country, society, and social group. Thus language is in a very real sense the glue that holds together a single social group or a collectivity of groups that have enough in common to form complex social networks and to create and maintain a culture.

In sum, because of spoken and written language we are able: (1) to communicate with others in the present and into the future; (2) to store information beyond the capacity of our memory in an efficient manner that can be retrieved and used by ourselves or others; (3) to think more abstractly and creatively about a wide array of problems and situations, freeing us to move beyond our survival needs; and (4) to use the symbolic tools that language gives us to form meaningful social units such as families, communities, and cultures.

Language and Social Groupings

To better understand the importance of language in a social context, imagine that you have been appointed by the student body president of your campus to serve on a financial board to plan how student fees should be spent on speakers, entertainment groups, and other programs. You walk into the room for the first meeting and find yourself facing ten strangers who are diverse in ethnicity, gender, and age. You know you will have to work together for several months, so you are eager to get to know the others. What kind of information do you need about your fellow board members to form an opinion about them? Several students introduce themselves right away, smile, shake hands, and look you in the eye. Others stay seated and do not approach, or they merely glance in your direction without making eye contact with you. Most of the students are about your age, dressed in jeans or casual clothes; but you notice one older man wearing a suit with a vest and carrying a briefcase. There are other details you pick up as the meeting gets under way. Several of the board members speak English with an accent, and the older man speaks to another person in a language you do not understand. After a few meetings of the group, you have formed a definite impression of most of the student board members. You have drawn some firm conclusions about their personalities and entertainment preferences, and you can even predict who will be the first to speak, who will likely reject any idea that is proposed, and who will jump in to defend anyone whose ideas are attacked by another member of the group. All of these impressions are formed from the group discourse while trying to arrive at a consensus of how to spend the student fee money.

All of us in our social contacts are constantly forming impressions in this way. For instance, we interpret what we observe and draw conclusions about other people's personalities on the basis of what they say and how they say it. To take a term from social psychology, we *attribute* people's behavior either to enduring motives and qualities or to the demands of the situation. These attributions form the basis of our attitudes, which in turn influence how we behave toward members of our social group or of another social group. Social psychologists have long studied how the attributions that we make about others shape our attitudes toward them. This work forms the core of what is called *attribution theory* in social psychology (Weiner 1987).

Two basic human motives underlie attribution theory. The first is our need to understand the world around us. The second is our need to try to control as many as possible of the factors that influence our social interactions with others. I can illustrate these two motives by going back to our example involving the student financial board. The numerous impressions that you formed of your fellow board members are your attempts to understand the world around you. While you were forming your impressions of others, you may have also been trying both to control the impressions that others had of you and to persuade them that your views were worthy of serious consideration.

Obviously, we do not spend all of our time making attributions about every person we encounter or every situation in which we find ourselves. Rather, we form attributions only when necessary and when motivated to do so. Therefore, motivation is a critical component in attribution theory, and in order to understand attributions, we also need to know something about human motivation. Making attributions is both a perceptual and a cognitive process. Think back and ask yourself what aspects of other people's behavior you pay particular attention to. What perceptual information do you use to form impressions of others? And then how do you mentally assemble that information in your explanation of the person's behavior? Are you attracted or repelled by their behavior?

Because this chapter is about language and ethnicity, we return to the example of the members of the student financial board. Remember that several student board members spoke English with a distinct accent and that another two students spoke to each other in a language foreign to you. How important do you think a person's language is in the attributions that you make about him or her? Note that this is different from the question of the content of the person's statements; rather, the focus is on *how* the person speaks. Does a speaker's accent influence your attributions about his or her intelligence, trustworthiness, or temperament? Do you feel more comfortable with people who speak in exactly the same manner that you do? Do you judge some accents more positively than others? Do you find yourself ceasing to listen to someone with a heavy accent? Research shows that people generally form positive or negative attributions about speakers who have accents and that these attributions are dependent on the person's attitudes toward the region, the country, or the language group to which the speaker is perceived to belong (Giles and Coupland 1991).

Thus how we react to accents is important in understanding how we evaluate strangers, whether we interact with them personally or are indirectly exposed to them because of the mass media. For example, probably no one who is reading this chapter ever actually met former Secretary of State Henry Kissinger, who speaks English with a distinct accent that indicates that German was his first language. Despite his rather heavy accent, though, most Americans hold the opinion that Kissinger is a remarkably intelligent man (although we might question his trustworthiness). Do you have the same opinion about a person who speaks with an Appalachian accent from the mountains of North Carolina? What about a businessman from Taiwan for whom English may be a third language? Or what about an Indian woman with a strong British accent? And, finally, what is your feeling about a speaker of Ebonics from an American inner city? Although all four individuals are speaking English, our attributions and, consequently, our attitudes about each might be quite dissimilar.

In sum, we know from research findings that people often make positive attributions about people with high-status accents (e.g., French) and negative attributions about people with low-status accents (e.g., Ebonics) (Giles and Coupland 1991). Thus accents and the resulting attributions we make about people who speak differently may influence in powerful ways the attitudes and behaviors that we express toward these linguistically different speakers. In a similar way, how we behave toward someone who speaks with an accent or speaks a different dialect often influences how that person responds to the social situation. If the individual perceives that the listener is reacting positively to him or her, then the interaction will probably be very friendly and cordial. On the other hand, if the speaker believes that he or she is being evaluated negatively, the interaction is probably going to be tense and formal.

Similarly, people have different reactions when they hear two or more people around them speaking in a language other than English. Some people will actually jump immediately to the conclusion that these "foreigners" are talking about them. They may also openly express their outrage that English is not being used. These people hold very negative attitudes about people who do not speak English in public and frequently question why such individuals live in the United States at all (Crawford 1992). Often people make very negative attributions about immigrants who use their native language in public. A commonly held belief is that these speakers refuse to assimilate and that they are taking advantage of taxpayers by requesting social and health services in their native language. People who hold this belief find it hard to justify public services in any language other than English. These advocates for English are frequently heard to say that their own parents and/ or grandparents did not ask for or receive any assistance in their native language, so these newcomers should not expect to receive it.

In recent years, the issue of non-English public services has sparked considerable debate throughout the country and has resulted in state legislators or the electorate itself in various states passing some form of English-only legislation. For example, in 1987, voters in California overwhelmingly approved Proposition 63, which made English the official language of the state.

The English-only debate is highly politicized and has often resulted in direct conflict between members of different ethnic groups. At a public policy level, the debate has to do with whether the federal or state government should provide any type of service in a non-English language, whether public funds should be spent on printing government documents in languages other than English, and whether bilingual education is sound social and educational policy (Crawford 1992). Although much of the debate surrounding English-only legislation has little to do with psychology, psychological processes, such as the way in which people form attributions and attitudes toward others, become central in understanding intergroup relationships. Furthermore, it is these same psychological processes that lead us to support one side or the other on social issues such as English-only legislation or such programs as bilingual education. For example, Leonie Huddy and David Sears (1990), two psychologists who study political behavior, concluded, after analyzing the attitudes held by white Americans toward bilingual education, that opposition was greatest among respondents who had negative attitudes toward minority groups and immigrants in general. It was these respondents who were the most opposed to any type of instruction in a language other than English, regardless of whether they knew anything about bilingual education or not. Thus it was not language per se but the ethnicity and immigration status of recipients of bilingual education that was the underlying reason for opposition.

The English-only debate has created controversy even among members of the same ethnic group. For example, even though many Hispanics and Asian Americans opposed Proposition 63 (the English-only amendment) in California, there were also many individuals of these two ethnic groups who supported the proposition. Similarly, there are some ethnic group members who believe firmly that the critics of bilingual education are correct and that education should be conducted exclusively in English (Chavez 1991). There are also strong ethnic advocates for bilingual education who maintain that without bilingual education immigrant children will have even greater difficulty in achieving success in school and in eventually competing effectively with the majority group (Olsen 1997). Thus attitudes about home language maintenance and whether public services should be provided in languages other than English are varied and pervasive, both among members of the majority group and among some members of ethnic groups who may have an ancestral language that they wish to pass along to their children.

The controversy over English-only and bilingual education that has played such an important role in public policy debates in many states and in Congress over the past twenty years or so has been highlighted here to demonstrate how seriously Americans take the question of language and what some perceive to be threats to the English language by foreigners who refuse to learn it. Although these are matters generally discussed in political arenas, the bases of these debates rest in people's perceptions of and attributions about members of ethnic groups who are "different" from the mainstream. How these perceptions and attributions are formed is a psychological question and deserving of more attention by psychologists. We turn now to the question of ethnicity and how language plays such a crucial role in defining it.

Ethnicity and Language

Ethnicity is an important part of the human experience, but interestingly it has not been extensively studied by psychologists. Ethnicity refers to an individual's membership in a social group that shares a common ancestral heritage. This ancestral heritage is multidimensional in nature and involves the biological, cultural, social, and psychological domains of life. The psychological dimension of ethnicity is perhaps the most important because, regardless of variations in the biological, cultural, and social domains, if a person self-identifies as a member of a particular ethnic group, then he or she is willing to be perceived and treated as a member of that group. Thus self-ascribed and other-ascribed ethnic labels are the overt manifestations of individuals' identification with a particular ethnicity.

Most people come to identify with a particular ethnic group through their primary socialization with parents, other family members and friends, and, of course, with peers and teachers (Phinney and Rotheram 1987). Socialization refers to the practices through which children acquire social identities. Generally, socialization comes about through a combination of direct instruction, modeling, feedback, and other-generated experiences (Bandura 1977). Direct instruction consists of verbal exhortations that reflect the appropriateness of various behavioral alternatives. Modeling consists of observational learning through identification with and imitation of significant others, such as parents and teachers. Feedback consists of rewards and punishments that indicate the appropriateness of various behavioral alternatives. Other-generated experience consists of selective exposure to environments that guide behavior and that are determined by the socialization agent. Although each of these forms of socialization is distinct, together they provide the foundation on which ethnicity and ethnic self-identification rest. Importantly, these various forms of socialization practices all take place through the language of the home and community. This means that language becomes a crucial element of what constitutes ethnicity for many individuals. Furthermore, the language of socialization becomes part of the core of ethnicity and is highly valued as a critical element in the meaning of identifying oneself as a member of an ethnic group.

The language that a person speaks often takes on extralinguistic characteristics that go far beyond the need to communicate. For members of many ethnic groups with their own language, the language itself comes to be symbolic of the group's vitality and place in the world. For instance, we use the term "mother tongue" to signify the first language learned and/or the language of the home. There is perhaps no greater way to express the importance that language has to a group than to equate it to the affection that we give our mothers! In other words, language, like a mother, provides the nurturance and stability so necessary for healthy development and fulfillment. Language gives meaning to an ethnic group because it connects the present with the past through its oral traditions, literary forms, music, history, and customs. In essence, it is frequently language which gives an ethnic group its distinctiveness. So important is language that any threat to a group's language by means of colonization or legislation is a call to arms. By way of example, efforts to legislate English as the official language in the United States probably have the same effect on many members of ethnic groups who cherish their home language that can be seen in other parts of the world where home languages have been repressed (Edwards 1985). That is, when a person's language is threatened, rather than submit to the dominant and powerful group, the ethnic person forms unions of resistance with others of the same ethnicity who seek to undo the threat that they perceive to their ethnic group and language. This resistance may take several forms. It may be legalistic, through seeking remedies in the courts (Piatt 1990), or it may involve elements of warfare, as witnessed in Spain with certain Basque groups (Edwards 1985).

Although language is not the only glue which binds people together as members of an ethnic group, it does have qualities which make it especially important and deserving of attention from a psychological perspective. I mention a few of these qualities. First, the main medium of socialization for children is language. Through language the young child learns what his or her parents and community value by way of their cultural beliefs and practices. Thus language becomes associated with the emotional and behavioral texture of what it means to be a member of a certain group. This may be why we affectionately refer to our first language as our "mother" language and why we are generally willing to fight to preserve it. Second, a group's language provides the mantle of distinctiveness from nonspeakers of the language. Thus language not only serves as a means of interpersonal communication between members of the group but also it can be used to effectively establish boundaries between the in-group and the out-group. Third, the status given to the ethnic group's language by the larger society conveys to the child the status that the group as a whole has in society. If the language is given little status by the dominant social group, the child readily learns that he or she is a member of an ethnic minority group whose language and culture is not valued by the dominant and powerful social group.

Now the psychological perspective that I offer regarding ethnicity is based on an ecological and situational analysis of ethnicity and on interactional approaches to the role of language in the social construction of group identity. For me, ethnicity can be grounded in models of social organization and in the ways that members of social (i.e., ethnic) groups relate to one another as they carve out their lives. From this perspective, ethnicity is a product of social networks and of the shared experiences of members of those networks; networks, in turn, are subject to the external constraints of the social and physical ecology of their environment. The most notable external constraint between members of different ethnic groups that plays out daily in communities, regions, and countries has to do with economic and territorial competition. Heller summarizes this position well:

> Ethnicity is based on boundaries; it does not acquire meaning except as a func-
> tion of opposition to that which lies on the other side of the gap in social ties
> that differentiates one ethnic group from another. To be a member of an ethnic
> group is to participate in certain social networks, and therefore to have access
> to certain social roles and to the resources controlled by members of the ethnic
> group. (1987: 182–183)

To illustrate her position on ethnicity, Heller argues that social relationships between the French-speaking and English-speaking Canadians in the 1950s were not as strained as they are today because then the two groups maintained their separateness and each had its own social institutions that supported the separation. However, as the ecology changed and greater competition for resources and a blurring of boundaries arose, ethnicity issues between the two social groups began to take on the important political overtones that we see in Canada today. According to this view, language per se does not create the separation, but it often sharpens the distinction between ethnic groups. Some political analysts, however, look at the bifurcation of French- and English-speaking Canada and argue mistakenly that such separation would not occur if everyone in Canada spoke English.

Advocates for English-only legislation in the United States see parallels between Canada and this country and use this as a basis for claiming that English must be protected from the great masses of immigrants and their children who "refuse to assimilate and speak English." The fact of the matter is that ethnicity and language would not be an issue in the United States if groups such as Hispanics maintained their lowly status and did not challenge the status quo of prejudice and discrimination by calling for fair treatment in education, employment, and housing as mandated by civil rights legislation. It is when challenges to the status quo are presented to the dominant social (ethnic) group by lower status groups that ethnic competition and rivalry begin. It is this ecological constraint then that gives meaning to ethnicity (Edwards 1985).

Let us return briefly to the student financial board and the various students who make up that group. We may also assume that for the first time in the history of the student financial board a proposal has been made to fund a year-long multicultural series of speakers, artists, and musical groups. The planned activity is very exciting to some members of the financial board, but it is also very costly. If funded, the multicultural series would require about one-half of the entire student fee budget, and many activities that traditionally had been supported could no longer be funded. Furthermore, the primary advocates on the board for the multicultural series are members of ethnic groups who are quite vocal on campus. Thus we have now changed the dynamics of the financial board and created a competitive situation that involves the allocation of resources. Because of limited resources, it is clear that not all proposals from various student groups can be supported.

In this context of scarce resources and the need to allocate monies, what guesses would you make about the attributions that different members of the board would make about each other? There might be some common-interest coalition building between different student members, as well as some heated exchanges about what is fair and in the best interest of the student body in how monies are allocated. This situation most likely will also provoke some division between students along ethnic lines. If this occurs, the student financial board becomes a microcosm of the ways in which the competition for resources sharpens the division between social groups in accordance with Heller's (1987) conceptualization of ethnicity. For instance, some members of the student financial board may claim that the campus does not need a "special" multicultural program because the entertainment and speaker series already include speakers from various walks of life and the music is often international in flavor. However, the "multiculturalists" on the board argue firmly that the campus's commitment to ethnic and cultural diversity as represented in student-sponsored activities must reflect a broader and more diverse view of the American fabric than it has to date. They further argue that the speakers and entertainers they have in mind have never been invited to perform or speak on campus. This discussion could be marked by extreme negativity, with heavy overtones of ethnic prejudice on both sides. Remember that there was already some negativity toward members of the board who spoke with an accent and toward two members who conversed in a different language. If disagreements occur between the various members of the board, and if these run along ethnic lines, then the board will likely become dysfunctional, as often happens when members of different ethnic groups become embroiled in battles in which the participants can be identified by their ethnicity and language.

Another important feature of Heller's view of ethnicity has to do with how ethnic identification changes across social situations. According to Heller, ethnicity becomes important only when social groups come into contact with each other. In isolation, it means nothing to be English, Arab, French, or Mexican. Thus, ethnic identity is a direct function of intergroup contact and opposition and not necessarily an important part of all aspects of daily life. Ethnicity may be more meaningful in certain intergroup contexts than in other situations. Moreover, the ethnic label that an individual chooses to wear may differ according to social context. I know this well from first-hand experience. Typically, I do not think about myself within the narrow confines of an ethnic box; however, depending on the context, I have identified with all of the following ethnic labels—Mexican American, Chicano, Hispanic, Latino, and American.

Because neither I nor my parents or grandparents were born in Mexico, I cannot claim to be Mexican, although I am bilingual and have been all my life. I have also traveled extensively in Mexico and other parts of Latin America and feel very much at home wherever I am. So for me, how I identify really has much to do with who I am associating with and with my perception of their attributions about me. In Latin America, I have been identified as an American who speaks fairly good Spanish and who knows the culture better than most Americans. In that context, "American" suits me very well. However, when I visit my parents, who live in a barrio (neighborhood) in a southwestern city, I am very likely to self-identify as Chicano. This is a term which grew in popularity in the 1960s with the civil rights movement and which connotes social justice for a repressed ethnic group. In the San Francisco Bay area where I now reside, I am quite comfortable identifying as Latino, because this is the more common ethnic term used by the very diverse Latin population that comprises people from all the countries in Central and South America. In this context, Latino is a more unifying descriptor for ethnicity than are the other labels. Finally, in the mid-1970s, the label Hispanic as an ethnic descriptor appeared, which has roughly the same connotation as Latino but which appears to carry more acceptability in some contexts (e.g., political) than the other ethnic terms. Thus in the past this term has been attributed to me by colleagues; frequently, it is the only ethnic box on a questionnaire that is suitable for my ethnicity.

In sum, all the ethnic labels that I use have been learned through a series of complex social relationships between myself and individuals of the same or different ethnicity. Thus my ethnicity is a blend of my ancestry, my two cultures (both Mexican and American), my bilingualism, and my personal and professional associations with many individuals over many years in countless social contexts in which questions of ethnicity and language have arisen.

Although my personal story of ethnicity may appear complex, it is not unusually so. It is typical of many ethnic people in America. For example, under what circumstances does a second-generation woman of Korean ancestry describe herself as Korean, Korean American, Asian American, or simply American? Similarly, when does a man identify as African American, black, or American? Questions of ethnicity and the role of language are becoming even more complicated as our country diversifies through interracial marriage. What ethnic identification does the offspring of our Korean American woman and African American man give when asked, "Where are you from?"—a question that ethnic people hear all too frequently in this country. A few psychologists (Root 1992) have already begun to conduct research on questions of the psychological development and social functioning of racially mixed people. This research will be important in the coming years because, as the population of the United States becomes more diverse, so, too, will questions of ethnicity and language.

In summary, in this chapter I have tried to outline a few basic tenets of psychology and how the discipline has contributed to the study of ethnicity and language. I did mention earlier in this chapter that psychology has generally been rather silent on the question of ethnicity and the role played by ethnicity in a person's life. However, psychologists have much to offer in the study of ethnicity and language. It remains to be seen what the future will bring.

Questions for Further Thought and Discussion

1. Think of some ways in which psychologists might be interested in studying language beyond those discussed in the chapter. Why are these of interest to psychologists?

2. How does language contribute to the development of a culture? Give several examples to illustrate your answer.

3. Beginning with a concrete group situation that you were recently in, describe why and how you formed your different impressions of the members of the group. How did language influence or shape your impressions of other members of the group? Thinking back, do you think your attributions about some of the group members were accurate?

4. Think about how you personally react to others who speak with an accent. What experiences or information do you use to help you form a first impression of such people? Have your impressions changed (positively or negatively) over time as you have interacted with these people?

5. Do you have a family member or good friend whose first language is not English? What reactions have you observed from strangers who interact with your family member or friend?

6. Do you believe that public services and/or education should be offered in languages other than English? Explain your answer.

7. Describe the psychological process by which an individual acquires his or her identity. What role does language play in the process?

8. Why do you think people react so strongly when their language is threatened? Can you relate to an experience when you felt your home language was threatened in some way? What did you do? Do you feel like you were justified in your actions?

9. If a stranger were to ask you what your ethnic identity was, how would you reply? Would your answer be different if a good friend asked you?

10. Explain how and why intergroup competition for scare resources can sharpen ethnic differences among people.

Selected Bibliography

Bandura, Albert (1977). *Social Learning Theory*. Englewood Cliffs, N.J.: Prentice-Hall.

Chavez, Linda (1991). *Out of the Barrio: Toward a New Politics of Hispanic Assimilation*. New York: Basic Books.

Crawford, James (1992). *Hold your Tongue: Bilingualism and the Politics of "English Only"*. Menlo Park, Cal.: Addison-Wesley.

Edwards, John (1985). *Language, Society and Identity*. New York: Blackwell.

Giles, Howard, and Nikolas Coupland (1991). *Language: Contexts and Consequences*. Pacific Grove, Cal.: Brooks/Cole.

Heller, Monica (1987). The role of language in the formation of ethnic identity. In *Children's Ethnic Socialization: Pluralism and Development*, Jean S. Phinney and Mary J. Rotheram (eds.), 180–200. Newbury Park, Cal.: Sage.

Huddy, L., and David O. Sears (1990). Qualified public support for bilingual education: Some policy implications. *Annals of the American Academy of Political and Social Science* 508 (March): 119–134.

Olsen, Laurie (1997). *Made in America: Immigrant Students in Our Public Schools*. New York: The New Press.

Phinney, Jean S., and Mary J. Rotheram (eds.) (1987). *Children's Ethnic Socialization: Pluralism and Development*. Newbury Park, Cal.: Sage.

Piatt, B. (1990). *Only English? Law and Language Policy in the United States*. Albuquerque: University of New Mexico Press.

Root, Maria P. (ed.) (1992). *Racially Mixed People in America*. Newbury Park, Cal.: Sage.

Weiner, Bernard (1987). *An Attribution Theory of Motivation and Emotion*. New York: Springer-Verlag.

Sign Language and the Deaf Community

COLIN BAKER

The theme of this chapter is that there has been an ethnic awakening among the Deaf community no less than among other ethnic minority groups in the world. This chapter covers three major issues. First, I deal with the importance of understanding that Deaf people and Deaf communities are very varied and include different types of Deaf people. Second, I present the pre-1970s view of deafness. This is the medical model, which consists of an interlinked series of negative myths, false beliefs, assumptions, values, and popular hypotheses and convictions about the disabilities, deficiencies, and disadvantages of the Deaf community. Part of this view is that sign language is a mark of abnormality. Third, I examine different elements of the ethnic awakening among Deaf people. This section examines the reconstruction of deafness, the growth of status of sign language, new perspectives on Deaf people as bilinguals, modern progressive bilingual education for Deaf people, and some "ethnic revival" views of the nature, purpose, and identity of Deaf communities.

The theme of the chapter is symbolized in the spelling of "deaf" as preferred by Deaf groups. In the first paragraph, the word "deaf" has been spelled both with a lower case "d" and with a capital "D." Why? Just as it is accepted that we use a capital "J" for Jewish and a capital "W" for Welsh, so writing of a Deaf community or of someone who culturally identifies as a Deaf person requires a capital "D." A lower case "d" is reserved to refer to the audiological (nonhearing) condition. Also, rather than talking about "the deaf," the use of "Deaf people" is often preferred. This practice moves from using an audiological condition alone to define the person to accenting the humanity of Deaf people. These recent changes mirror a movement in the identity of Deaf people that derives from their "ethnic revival."

Who Are Deaf People?

There are not only different subgroupings of "Deaf people" but also differences of opinion about the appropriate language of Deaf people, the education of Deaf people, what constitutes the nature of a Deaf community, and the integration of Deaf people into mainstream speaking society or their separation from it. To begin, differences among Deaf people will be briefly considered.

Hagemeyer (1992) suggests that there are nine subpopulations among Deaf people in the United States. Such subdimensions refer to Deaf people's patterns of communication.

1. Those who use sign language (e.g., American Sign Language, often represented as ASL) as their primary language.
2. Those who can communicate in both ASL and English.
3. Those mostly from the hearing-impaired group who communicate primarily through speech (e.g., English, Spanish, Yiddish).
4. Adults who became deaf later in life. They were not born deaf and may have acquired speech before deafness. Such people have had the experience of hearing normally for either short or long periods, and may have had speech patterns relatively well embedded before deafness occurred.
5. The elderly who became hearing-impaired or deaf later in life as the result of the aging process.
6. Those who do not know either ASL or English but communicate through gestures, mime, and their own signing systems. Such people may have been denied access to a Deaf culture, to ASL, or even to education at an early age.
7. Those who have residual hearing, who perhaps describe themselves as hard of hearing, and who can hear with the use of various aids.
8. Those who are both deaf and blind (e.g., Helen Keller).
9. Those who have normal hearing, but because their parents, children, or other members of the family are deaf, they understand signing or are fully conversant with Deaf culture and integrate with a Deaf community.

Such a system of classification shows that Deaf people are not a single group. However, the classification mostly depends on language differences, an increasingly important but insufficient basis for grouping, as will be seen in the remainder of this chapter.

Are Deaf People a Minority Group?

Given that there are about one in one thousand people who are born each year with varying degrees of hearing loss, in numerical terms Deaf people form a distinct minority. Although Deaf people form a numerical minority of the total population, minority-group status actually refers to dimensions of power and status. Generally, Deaf people have much less power and prestige and lower recognition and leverage than majority groups in society. Deaf people have historically often been regarded as "problems" within the education and social welfare systems, among doctors and psychologists, and in the employment market. This situation is similar to those of most ethnic minority groups in the world.

However, whereas most ethnic minority groups live in geographically defined areas, Deaf people are scattered throughout most villages, towns, and cities in the world. Many Deaf people also are not born into a Deaf culture—the parents, for example, are usually hearing members of the majority community (about nine out of every ten Deaf people are born into hearing families). Can we therefore talk about the existence of a Deaf community, especially in rural areas? What about Deaf people who are also members of an ethnic minority? Do they identify with the ethnic minority, with other local Deaf people, with both groups, or are they ostracized from all communities? These questions are briefly explored later in this chapter.

The Centrality of Sign Language

There is a growing common denominator among Deaf people throughout the world—sign language. If Deaf people do not share a common specific geographical location, they share (potentially at least) a common language. Sign language can be a major marker in defining Deaf community membership. Through a common sign language, there is the possibility of establishing community culture, a sense of identity, shared meanings and understandings, and a way of life that is owned by the Deaf community:

> Anything can become symbolic of ethnicity (whether food, dress, shelter, land tenure, artifacts, work, patterns of worship), but since language is the prime symbol system to begin with and since it is commonly relied upon so heavily (even if not exclusively) to enact, celebrate and "call forth" all ethnic activity, the likelihood that it will be recognized and singled out as symbolic of ethnicity is great indeed. (Fishman 1989: 32)

Sign language, once a symbol of oppression, has become transformed into a symbol of unity. "Sign language became the distinction that gave dignity to the Deaf community and transformed the 'abnormal' into the 'distinguished' by creating a reversal of the hierarchy . . . and to define normality on their own terms" (Jankowski 1997: 44). Sign language has allowed Deaf people to match the skills and abilities of hearing people in communication and cognition and enabled them to build an empowering community. Sign language has enabled Deaf people to create their own sense of "normality."

George Veditz, the seventh president of the National Association of the Deaf, made a famous statement in 1913 that sign language is the noblest gift God gave to Deaf people. This implies that sign language is divinely bequeathed, that Deaf people should seek salvation in sign language, and that opponents of sign language are thus of the Devil.

What Is Sign Language?

Sign language is a fully developed, authentic language which allows its users to communicate the same complete meaning as does a spoken language. Sign language is not gesturing. Gesturing is relatively unsystematic and is used in an ad hoc way to express a small number of basic ideas (e.g., pointing to something that is wanted). We all use nonverbal communication to add emphasis to our speech.

In contrast, signing is a very extensive, structurally complex, rule-bound, complete means of communication. Sign language can perform the same range of functions as a spoken language and can be used to teach any aspect of the curriculum. As part of an ethnic awakening, sign language has increasingly been seen as the natural language of Deaf people. There are a wide variety of sign systems in existence—American Sign Language, British Sign Language, Chinese Sign Language, Danish Sign Language, French Sign Language, Russian Sign Language, and Thai Sign Language, to name but a few.

There have been various important political and public-relations breakthroughs for the acceptance of sign language as a language in its own right. William Stokoe's work on American Sign Language, followed by British research at Edinburgh and Bristol on British Sign Language, demonstrated that sign language has a complete grammar and full communicative possibilities. In 1965, William Stokoe, Carl Kronenberg, and Dorothy Casterline published a *Dictionary of American Sign Language*. The dictionary was based on linguistic principles that also included a description of the social and cultural characteristics of Deaf people who used American Sign Language.

However, many Deaf people in the United States do not use American Sign Language. Some have not learned ASL because their parents were hearing people. Others have been to schools which taught them oralist (speaking) approaches (discussed later in this chapter). Other Deaf people prefer to use speech rather than sign language in their communities.

Another breakthrough occurred in 1983, when the Swedish government officially recognized Swedish Sign Language as a native language of Sweden. This was a crucial global precedent and inspired Deaf communities in other countries to work toward the goal of achieving political recognition as a distinct social group rather than, as is sometimes the case, a scattering of individuals living on state charity.

Why Not Lipreading?

A "pre-ethnic revival" view about a language for Deaf people is that lipreading is preferable to sign language. From a hearing person's perspective, it has often been argued that Deaf people should understand what hearing people say by learning to lip-read. Lipreading is often cited as the "normal" way for Deaf people to communicate with each other and with hearing people and thus join (or become assimilated into) mainstream society.

From the hearing person's viewpoint, lipreading may seem superficially straight-forward. In reality, lipreading is very difficult and is often "hit or miss." Imagine trying to lip-read when the light is fading or with a person who has a bushy moustache and beard or in a group situation in which people are standing at different angles or when everyone is eating a meal and talking with food in their mouths. Imagine what degree of concentration is required for a Deaf person to watch the lips of someone who is speaking; the effort often leads to eyestrain and physical exhaustion. Many of the sounds of speech are produced inside the mouth and do not appear on the lips (e.g., H, S, T), and many sounds have similar lip patterns (e.g., man, pad, bat). Also, for people who are brought up in a Deaf community, successful lipreading assumes a knowledge of spoken language and a knowledge of the context of the conversation and inevitably requires much guessing of the meaning from the few words that can be decoded. Thus lipreading is an unsatisfactory answer for Deaf people.

Lipreading carries with it the perspective of hearing people rather than Deaf people themselves. It assumes that Deaf people must assimilate and accommodate themselves to the world of hearing people. Lipreading assumes that the hearing community is the one to which Deaf people must belong. In contrast, sign language gives Deaf people their own norms, values, expectations, and community culture. The imposition of lipreading is therefore similar to requiring minority language speakers (e.g., Spanish speakers in the United States) to operate in the majority language (e.g., as demanded by the "English only" movement in the United States).

Perspectives about Deaf People before the Ethnic Revival

Little is known about Deaf people in early history, as little was written about deafness in early chronicles. However, the dominant and typical historical view of Deaf people is as people who were retarded, incapable, disadvantaged, incomplete, and a medical problem. In Europe from the Middle Ages through the sixteenth century, Deaf people were generally deprived of the rights accorded to "normal" hearing people. For example, Deaf people could not inherit property from their parents, and they were forbidden to take part in the Catholic Mass because they could not engage in confession and absolution. Deaf Catholics were unable to marry without the permission of the Pope.

One popular historical conception of Deaf people is that they live in a silent, and therefore deprived, world. The following poem by William Wordsworth (1770–1850; extracted from *The Excursion*, Book 7) sums up how hearing people have often conceived of deafness: a world that is silent, tragic, and empty, devoid of the experience of the stimulating and wonderful sounds of nature.

> Almost at the root
> Of that tall pine, the shadow of whose bare
> And slender stem, while here I sit at eve,

Oft stretches toward me, like a long straight path
Traced faintly in the greensward; there, beneath
A plain blue stone, a gentle Dalesman lies,
From whom, in early childhood, was withdrawn
The precious gift of hearing. He grew up
From year to year in loneliness of soul;
And this deep mountain-valley was to him
Soundless, with all its streams. The bird of dawn
Did never rouse this Cottager from sleep
With startling summons; not for his delight
The vernal cuckoo shouted; not for him
Murmured the labouring bee. When stormy winds
Were working the broad bosom of the lake
Into a thousand, thousand sparkling waves,
Rocking the trees, or driving cloud on cloud
Along the sharp edge of yon lofty crags,
The agitated scene before his eye
Was silent as a picture: evermore
Were all things silent, wheresoe'er he moved.

This view is typical of opinions about Deaf people before the ethnic revival: the view that the world of Deaf people is lifeless and hollow. However, as considered in the next section, sound, or the lack of sound, is not an issue for Deaf people unless they are told by hearing people that it is a problem.

This popular misconception of deafness is also found in popular stereotypes. Following are some extracts from actual newspaper items (Open University 1991). What view of the Deaf people do they present and from whose perspective?

"Joy as deaf couple wed."
The headline suggests that it is remarkable that Deaf people should marry. The article indicates that "there were tears of joy as the happy pair exchanged vows—something they were determined to do in spite of their handicap."

"A love beyond words."
Part of this article says, "Sarah and Stewart both being locked in a world of silence since birth after they were born profoundly deaf." . . . That Deaf people should marry is posed as being exceptional and their deafness as an affliction.

"Parents who will never hear their baby cry."
This article commences by saying that the devoted couple had never heard each other say "I love you" and that they had "fought to overcome their handicap and now are adapting to the role of bringing up a baby."

The headline emphasizes that not hearing a baby cry was a major issue—a perspective of the hearing community, not of the Deaf community.

Headlines and articles in newspapers tend to present the Deaf person's world as one of sadness and sorrow. Typical and actual quotations include: "locked in a world of silence before birth" . . . "never able to hear Christmas bells or sing carols" . . . "handicapped from birth." When Deaf people do something that hearing people do regularly (e.g., marry, have children) it is considered newsworthy, conveying the assumption that Deaf people should not be expected to behave "normally" or to engage in tasks such as driving a car, becoming a teacher, owning a gun, enjoying nature, adopting children, becoming a Senator, or singing a psalm. When Deaf people do something newsworthy, their deafness rather than the action tends to be accented, as the following headlines illustrate:

Deaf Basketball Whizzkid . . .

Deaf Hero in Car Crash . . .

Deaf Student Receives Achievement Award . . .

Deaf Politician Wins Leadership Race . . .

Another "pre-ethnic revival" stereotype of deafness concerns their supposed vulnerability, as the following newspaper extracts suggest:

Deaf Children Face Risk of Sexual Abuse . . .

Deaf Parents Barred from Adopting Child . . .

Deaf Drivers at Risk in Heavy Traffic . . .

The preceding real quotations from newspapers reveal an uninformed and naive view of Deaf people rather than one that is deliberately malicious or abusive. Such views are those of the majority who look at Deaf people from a perspective of what they consider to be "normal," accepted, and publicly palatable. However, this is not the perspective of the Deaf community about itself. The "ethnic revival" view of Deaf people themselves is presented later in this chapter.

Popular conceptions of Deaf people can derive from meaner origins than ignorance and insensitivity. The portrayal of Deaf people in jokes often reveals the most negative, discriminatory view of the deaf to the point of mockery and ridicule. The image produced of Deaf people can be that of a despised and marginalized group. In a similar way, everyday talk reveals negative impressions of Deaf people in such expressions as deaf as a post, deaf as a door nail, deaf and dumb, deaf-mute. Take, for example, the "deaf and dumb" phrase. Although "dumb" originally meant "mute," the connotation has become that Deaf people are usually ignorant, dim-witted, and deficient. The fact that Deaf people can be as intelligent as anyone from the hearing community is overshadowed by the stereotype of Deaf people as locked in a world of ignorance and silent stupidity.

Unfortunately, when advertising reverses this view, for example, in attempting to raise charitable funds for Deaf people, the results are often patronizing. Actual advertisements have included statements such as:

It works perfectly well without ears . . . .

Just because we're deaf it doesn't mean we've nothing between our ears . . . .

There are 50,000 innocent prisoners of silence in Britain today. Isn't it time we helped them escape? . . . .

The problem for profoundly Deaf people is dealing with dummies all day . . . .

Despite benevolent intentions, such advertisements still portray a negative image of the deaf. Rather than accenting the positive, negative stereotypes remain. This "pre-ethnic revival" negative image of Deaf people accents popular misconceptions rather than focusing on the positive aspects, such as the pride Deaf communities have in themselves, the positive virtues of Deaf culture, the complete nature of sign language, and many other very positive images of Deaf people that could be conveyed. The advertisements convey an image of deaf people as different from "normal" and do not project an image or an awareness that Deaf people live their own "normal" lives that have great vitality.

New Perspectives of Deaf People

A New Construction of Identity

Deaf people do not necessarily identify with the hearing world and increasingly regard the hearing world as a different language community. Rather than allowing themselves to be defined by the majority hearing group, Deaf people are progressively expressing and valuing their own self-constructed identity.

As part of this growing move toward self-identification, the Deaf community does not define itself by audiological criteria, as do hearing people. That is, the Deaf community does not center upon its lack or loss of hearing as a main characteristic. Instead, the Deaf community defines itself as a cultural group in which membership is defined by attitude toward one's deafness rather than by measured hearing loss. Identification with the Deaf community is therefore about self-perception rather than physical characteristics.

However, not all Deaf people fit this pattern. Similar to the way that some minority ethnic language groups (e.g., Latinos in the United States) choose not to identify with their heritage language group but with the mainstream majority, so some Deaf people wish to belong solely to mainstream culture and not to the Deaf community. Thus, in the following discussion, there are numerous exceptions.

For Deaf people, one central distinguishing feature of belonging to a Deaf community is often the use of sign language as their first and preferred language. Use of sign language establishes a boundary or a marker, indicating a difference and distance from the hearing community. Use of sign language tends to lead to interactions with other Deaf people, socialization into Deaf culture, identification with Deaf people, and engagement in Deaf society's cultural activities and their shared values, meanings, and understandings.

This sense among Deaf people of inner understanding of who they are, the sense of their own defined identity and their own construction of their world, is illustrated by Groce (1985), who describes the life of people on Martha's Vineyard, an island off the coast of Massachusetts in the United States. Many Deaf people on this island community never thought or referred to themselves as Deaf people. For example, a ninety-year-old woman was asked, "Do you know anything similar about Isaiah and David?" "Oh, yes," she replied, "They were both good fishermen, very good indeed." "Weren't they both deaf?" asked the interviewer. "Yes, come to think of it, I guess they both were," she replied. "I'd forgotten about that."

The Deaf Vineyarders did not see themselves as disabled, deaf, or having a handicap. They grew up in a way they considered normal. They married, raised families, and worked and earned money in the same way as did their hearing relatives, friends, and many others. An elder on the Vineyard remarked, "I didn't think about the deaf any more than you would think about anybody with a different voice," and another elderly woman in her eighties said, "Oh, these people weren't handicapped. They were just deaf." To them, being deaf was not perceived as a problem or even an issue or concern. It was normal, therefore not worthy of any attention.

The key issues of, Whose viewpoint counts? and, Whose values and expectations are dominant? are prominent in an account given by Sam Supalla of one of his childhood friendships (cited in Padden & Humphries 1988). Sam was born into a deaf family and had deaf older brothers. He became friendly with the girl next door but found her rather odd and strange. He could not talk to her in sign language as he did with his parents and older brothers. She had extreme difficulty in understanding his most simple signs. After a few futile attempts to talk to her, he simply pointed at things he needed or held her hand when going somewhere. He wondered what was the peculiar problem or affliction his friend had. Since they enjoyed each other's company, he was content to accommodate her peculiar lack of communication.

One particular incident, forever vividly remembered by Sam, led to an understanding of why his friend was so peculiar. They were playing happily in her home when suddenly her mother walked up and began to move her mouth. As if by magic, the girl moved the toys to a more convenient place. Sam was mystified. When he went home, Sam asked his mother about the girl's disability. His mother explained that she was a hearing person and that because of this, neither she nor her mother knew how to sign. Instead of signing, his friend and her mother talked by moving their mouths to communicate with each other. Sam tried to understand but could not help wondering how curious and unusual hearing people were—at least until his mother explained that hearing people were in the majority.

What Sam had not learned at this stage was that hearing people's views of communication were dominant, considered by much of society to be "normal," and that what was natural to Sam was regarded by many in that majority group as unnatural. What Sam had not learned was that hearing people tended to define him and his family by the characteristics they lacked. This was not Sam's view of the world.

Deaf people, in their ethnic awakening, increasingly define themselves by the characteristics that lead to creation of relatively separate and autonomous communities of Deaf people.

A New Meaning of Deafness among Deaf People

The last section made clear that when deaf children grow up among deaf friends and family, they often do not know that they are deaf. For them, not hearing is normal and natural. Only when such children go to school and mix with the hearing people's community do they learn that they cannot hear. When children who are deaf first come across the word *deaf*, their initial reaction is that it refers to 'us.' The word has many positive connotations relating to parents, friends, and members of the Deaf community; it means people who behave like us, members of our normative, cultural Deaf group.

Children who are deaf and brought up in families in hearing people's communities also often initially regard themselves as normal and do not consider being unable to hear a concern or an issue. They usually accept the way they were born. It is only when other people's constructions of their deafness are relayed to them that deafness becomes a perceived problem. Only as such children grow older do they learn that deafness has another meaning, a meaning that is given to it by members of the majority hearing community. The hearing community often defines deafness as being deficient and not being able to communicate "properly." A child who has learned to sign from birth finds signing normal and natural and takes it for granted. Later on, that child may learn that signing is regarded by the majority community as being different, odd, a lower form of communication, and a symbol of an affliction.

Yet perceptions are changing both in Deaf people's and in hearing people's communities, with the ethnic awakening of Deaf communities. Deaf people are beginning to assert the naturalness and normality of sign language and their rights as a group and as individuals to have self-functioning communities of Deaf people. Hearing communities are slowly but progressively acknowledging sign language as the "native" language of Deaf people and their right, for example, to bilingual education (see the discussion later in this chapter).

Membership in the Deaf Community

Deaf people do not always belong to Deaf communities. For example, those in isolated rural regions may meet no other Deaf person regularly. Other Deaf people choose to belong to hearing communities. Being deaf does not make someone a member of a local or regional Deaf community. Nevertheless, there has been a growing interest in and development of the "Deaf community." For many Deaf people, this means belonging to Deaf groups, societies, and clubs, interacting with Deaf people in the evenings and during weekends. For other Deaf people, much of their day may be spent among other Deaf people—at jobs, at home, with the extended family, and among Deaf friends in the neighborhood.

Deafness is often regarded as a necessary but not a sufficient condition for membership in the Deaf community. Higgins (1980) suggests that membership in a Deaf community is achieved through three overlapping and interacting criteria: first, identification with the Deaf world; second, shared meanings and experiences that come from being a Deaf person; and third, participation in the Deaf community's activities.

There often comes a time in Deaf people's lives when they realize or feel that their natural identity lies not in being part of the hearing world but in being allied with other Deaf people. They feel a sense of identity, a feeling of oneness and involvement with other people who are deaf. For example, Deaf people in their teenage years and early twenties often sense that they belong to a world of similar Deaf people and not to the hearing world. Others go to schools for the Deaf when they are young and find that interaction with Deaf people is normal, customary, and fulfilling, often in ways that interaction with hearing people rarely is. Just as most Quechua speakers feel most at home with the Quechua community and Yiddish speakers with Yiddish-speaking Jews, so Deaf people often feel most comfortable with other Deaf people, with whom they have a sense of belonging and identity. Being deaf can instantly unite Deaf people who would otherwise be complete strangers.

However, it is important to reiterate that stereotyping and generalization is dangerous. Not all Deaf people wish to identify with Deaf communities. Just as some Quechua speakers prefer to identify with Spanish communities and some Jews with English-only communities, so some Deaf people prefer to identify with majority community groups. Some Deaf people feel they are stigmatized as members of Deaf communities and therefore wish to mix with hearing groups.

Membership in the Deaf community may come about through shared experiences and may be related to everyday problems of living in a world dominated by hearing people or to being educated in special programs for deaf. Friendship, sociability, and gregariousness among Deaf people is considerably aided when there is communality of language. Importantly, it is through sign language that the special and particular culture of Deaf people can be transmitted. When Deaf people use sign language, they are creating both distance from the hearing community and a marker of identity with the Deaf community. The inner understandings, wise sayings, stories and tales, ideas and ideals, expectations and understandings among Deaf people have become increasingly embedded in sign language. It is sign language that often most vibrantly encapsulates the historical traditions of Deaf people and their community life and subcultures. The thoughts and experiences of Deaf people are increasingly deeply embodied in sign languages, with Deaf people's culture and heritage stored and shared through such sign languages.

However, Deaf communities force a perpetual dilemma. The extent to which they either strive for separation from mainstream hearing society or prefer integration (e.g., for economic gain) is endlessly discussed and individually resolved. Such a basic dilemma has implications for choice and use of language. Separation favors sign language; integration favors other paths (e.g. cochlea implants, hearing aids, lipreading). Sometimes mainstream pressure is for social and cultural (but not necessarily economic) assimilation rather than integration.

Ethnic Awakening and Diglossia among Deaf People

Many Deaf people do not use sign language as their only language. Diglossia occurs when two languages exist together in a society in a relatively stable arrangement by attaching different uses to each language (see Fishman 1989). Deaf people are increasingly bilingual; for example, they may use sign language for conversation while being fully literate in the majority (or minority) language of the region. For example, in the United States, American Sign Language may be the means of communication between Deaf people, who learn literacy in English as well. In the United Kingdom, Deaf people are increasingly using British Sign Language as their natural means of communication while also learning to read and write fluently in English. Other Deaf people may use sign language with Deaf people and spoken language with hearing people.

Sign language does not have a written literary form. Those Deaf people who use sign language (and those who speak instead of or in addition to signing) often become literate in a majority (or minority) language. A Deaf person can access the Deaf community via sign language and also access the experiences of a majority (or minority) language community through its literature. This is a form of diglossia, where the uses of two languages have distinct and separate uses.

What does the lack of a written literary form of sign language mean for the ethnic awakening among the Deaf? From one viewpoint, it would seem to lower the status of sign language. A minority language without a written form has fewer functions, less status, and possibly little chance of long-term survival. Colonialists (e.g., English, French, Portuguese) often insisted on indigenous peoples' using the invaders' language for all literacy purposes, thereby relegating the indigenous language to a lower status among the "natives." A shift to the colonial language, in both written and oral forms, usually occurred.

Having both sign language and literacy in a majority language presents a danger of a perceived difference in status, with literacy—for example, in English—being seen as more prestigious than signing. However, this perception depends on where and how literacy is taught. If such literacy is taught by, for example, Deaf teachers in pro-signing schools, then literacy in a majority or minority language is likely to be broadening and empowering. However, if literacy is taught by those keen on the assimilation of Deaf people, then such literacy may work against the ethnic awakening of Deaf people.

A Symbol of the Awakening: Gallaudet University

Since the 1960s, the Deaf community's ethnic revival has drawn strength from and been part of other liberation movements (e.g., civil rights, language minority rights movements; Native American and African American ethnic revivals). One particular event in recent history has come to represent a new era in Deaf people's ethnic revival.

One of the best-known representations of an ethnic awakening among Deaf communities is the recent development and vitality of Gallaudet University, based in Washington, D.C. It is renowned as an undergraduate, graduate, and research center for Deaf and hard of hearing people from the United States and around the world. Gallaudet University has eight extension centers, including those in Hawaii,

Puerto Rico, and Costa Rica. There are currently more than 1600 full-time students, 300 part-time students, 1400 full-time Deaf students, and about 200 part-time Deaf students. Services provided on the campus include sign interpreters, volunteer note takers, amplified phones, group listening systems, and different technologies to help the Deaf (e.g., computer systems). Communication throughout the university in classrooms and meetings and between students is by signing (with or without voice). Gallaudet University also operates two national demonstration education programs. The Kendall Demonstration Elementary School and the Model Secondary School for the Deaf (both in Washington, D.C.) not only educate Deaf students but also conduct research and developmental activities, providing a living demonstration of excellence for other schools and programs for Deaf children throughout the world.

There is one particular event in the history of Deaf people in the United States that symbolizes the ethnic revival in the power and politics of this minority group. In 1988, the Board of Trustees announced the selection of Dr. Elisabeth Anne Zinser, a hearing person, as the seventh president of Gallaudet University. Students mounted a protest movement called "Deaf President Now," declaring that the appointment of a hearing person to the presidency of a college for Deaf students carried an apparent message about the lower status and capability of Deaf people.

A vigorous, assertive student-led movement united students, faculty, staff, alumni, and members of Deaf communities across the United States in support of the selection of a deaf President for the university. Sign-language students articulated a powerful political language. A smoldering and growing consciousness about Deaf rights and status burst into the flames of action and affirmation. Inflamed by the appointment, a communal mind and a sense of united purpose was generated. The movement closed the university for a week and captured worldwide media attention, creating considerable awareness about deafness, Deaf people and their languages and cultures. Two days after her appointment, under pressure from the student protest, Elisabeth Zinser resigned, and Gallaudet's eighth president— the first deaf president in its 124-year history, Dr. I. King Jordan—was selected. The election of a deaf president at Gallaudet came to mark a new era in the identity, power, and position of Deaf people. This new era is well demonstrated in the recent development of bilingual education for Deaf children.

Action from the Awakening: Deaf Students and Bilingual Education

There are differing approaches to the education of Deaf and hearing-impaired students. Current approaches range from minimal help to specially designed programs, and no unanimous agreement exists on preferred methods of approach: for example, whether to use a combination of signing and literacy in the spoken language, a total communication approach; whether to use sign-supported English; what kind of sign language to use; whether to develop oral and/or written skills in the spoken majority language; and whether to create policies to integrate with hearing children or to develop relatively segregated Deaf communities. At its worst, in mainstream "hearing" education, Deaf people may be regarded as having a serious mental, as well as an auditory, "defect" and may be classified as remedial. In the history of schooling in most countries, there are plentiful examples of such insensitive and uncivilized treatment.

One traditional approach, oralism, seeks to develop any residual hearing with the assistance of hearing aids and to develop speech reading skills and speech production among Deaf people and the hearing-impaired. For most of this century, until the 1970s, this was the approach that dominated the education of Deaf children in North America and Europe. Such an approach was based on beliefs that:

- Deaf children should integrate into mainstream society.
- The curriculum could not be taught through sign language but required majority language proficiency.
- Signing as a language was insufficient for full intellectual development.
- Sign language was only a temporary crutch for those for whom the majority spoken language was essential.
- Achievement in the curriculum requires both oral and written literacy in a majority language (e.g., English).

A second approach. developed since the 1970s, is based on the philosophy of "total communication." All modes of communication are regarded as appropriate for those who are deaf or partially hearing (e.g., speech, sign language, lipreading, writing, and reading). Simultaneous communication may be used that combines auditory input with visual information, for example, via the use of signed English. Such a total communication philosophy attempts to embrace both integrationists, who believe that Deaf people should be part of mainstream society, and separatists.

In contrast, there are special schools and units for Deaf people in which, for example, the children are first taught sign language, then are given a full curriculum—mostly through sign language—and finally develop written (and sometimes oral) skills in the majority spoken language. This bilingual approach can be considered as part of the ethnic revival movement that affects Deaf children.

This most recent approach has been developed in light of ten principles:

1. Sign language should be the first language of all Deaf children and should be regarded as their primary language.
2. Sign language should be used to teach curriculum subjects such as science, humanities, social studies, and mathematics.
3. Sign language can be used to teach English or another majority language as a second language. Usually reading and writing, rather than oral, skills in the second language will be taught.
4. The culture and language of the Deaf community are recognized and validated, with children learning that they belong to the culture of Deaf people. This approach tends to be favored by most of the Deaf community but has not been favored by many of the politicians and education professionals who formulate policy and provision.

5. Programs of bilingual education for Deaf people are partly based on the research and arguments for enrichment forms of bilingual education for hearing children, the tenets of which are:

- It is important to begin with and build on a child's existing linguistic and intellectual resources.
- Concepts and knowledge developed in the first language transfer easily to the second language.
- Use of children's ethnic language gives them pride and confidence in their culture and community.
- Children's self-esteem and self-identity are boosted and not threatened by use of their ethnic language.
- School performance and curriculum attainment is raised when the ethnic language is celebrated rather than devalued.
- The lower achievement of minority language students and Deaf students needs to be addressed by enrichment forms of bilingual education. (Baker 1996)

6. Deaf children cannot acquire a spoken language easily or quickly because they have limited hearing abilities. If the curriculum is transmitted in the spoken language, they are being expected to learn the content of the curriculum using a level of language not yet acquired. This is analogous to minority language children being expected to operate in mainstream education in the language of the majority that they have yet to master.

7. The acquisition of a sign language should begin as early as possible, ideally soon after birth. This gives the Deaf child the opportunity to develop age-appropriate competence in a first language, that is, sign language. Without the development of language, a child cannot form concepts or develop cognitive skills, nor can a child learn social and communicative skills through interaction with others.

   When a Deaf child has had the opportunity to develop adequate sign language during the preschool years, that child arrives in school ready to cope with the curriculum and able to socialize with others. Children who have had early access to sign language appear to progress better in school (Mashie 1995; Strong 1995). It is important to avoid language delay in Deaf children, such as has been found to occur with the use of auditory approaches and sometimes the total communication approach.

   When Deaf children arrive in school with very little grasp of either sign language or hearing language, the priority must be sign-language learning.

8. Approximately 90% of Deaf children are born to hearing parents. With the increasing willingness of such parents to learn signing, the first language of such Deaf children can be sign language. It is important that hearing parents receive adequate support from sign language teachers

and that there is good preschool provision for Deaf children. Parents of Deaf children need to be aware of Deaf communities and of bilingual education for Deaf children and, to enhance their child's curriculum achievement, to expect signing to be the medium of curriculum delivery as well as of literacy in the majority language.

The parents of Deaf children need considerable emotional support, information, and guidance to help their children become bilingual. In order for cognitive, linguistic, social, and emotional development to occur among Deaf children, there must be a partnership between school and parents and between school and community. Because there is considerable debate about integrating Deaf children into a hearing society and about whether their first loyalty should be to the Deaf community, hearing parents of Deaf children need to be given considerable support and treated with sensitivity.

9. The supply of trained personnel in Deaf bilingual education and the availability of staff preservice education programs, sign-language-teaching resources (e.g., signed stories on video), in-service education and certification, and funding are challenges that are currently being faced by Deaf educators. These are practical problems to be overcome, not insurmountable problems of principle.

10. Teaching in a bilingual Deaf education system may require team teaching. The Deaf teacher may serve as a natural model for the acquisition of sign language, with a hearing teacher acting as a model for the acquisition of proficiency in a majority language such as English or French. Ideally, both teachers should be bilingual models, able to communicate in both sign and the "hearing" language. Also, both teachers in the team should have a knowledge of Deaf culture, Deaf differences, and all the possibilities that exist for Deaf children and adults.

Concluding Remarks

Ethnic minorities are usually the poor, low-power, low-status relations of majority groups. This is just as true of Deaf people, even more so when they belong to other minority communities as well. A Deaf Latino person in the United States, a Deaf Turk in Germany, and a Deaf Bengali in the United Kingdom all represent individuals who are a minority within a minority. They are often the doubly underprivileged and the doubly despised. In cases in which being a member of an ethnic minority is compounded by being deaf, then disempowerment, low status, discrimination, and low self-esteem may be compounded as well.

As a mirror of the ethnic revival among language minority groups, the winds of change have begun to blow through Deaf communities and also to affect the hearing majority's attitudes toward Deaf people. Some lines from a poem by an ASL poet, Ella Mae Lentz, about Deaf people and sign language provide a counterpoint to Wordsworth:

Damn your chains!
We'll pronounce in our own deliverance
and articulate our message loud and clear.

And for the width of a breath we grant each other asylum
talking in our language of signs. . . .

Come out of your dark and silent world
and join us in our bright and lovely world.

Among Deaf people from both minority and majority groups, the ethnic revival has led to a redefinition of identity, a drive for empowerment, increasing recognition of the right to self-ownership of destinies, a distinctiveness in community life, and the generation of needed assertiveness, action, and ambition.

Questions for Further Thought and Discussion

1. Discuss the different ways sign language is important for Deaf people in terms of communication, culture, cognitive development, community building, and networking. Also discuss how sign language is a "boundary marker" between Deaf and hearing people. Then consider how answers to the above issues relate to an ethnic awakening for Deaf people.

2. Lipreading has been cited as the best way for Deaf people to integrate into mainstream society. Discuss different views of lipreading, considering the different perspectives of Deaf people and of "mainstream" hearing people. Discuss also the issues of identity, integration, assimilation, and community that such different perspectives raise, focusing on "pre-ethnic revival" and "postethnic revival" viewpoints.

3. What is the medical model of Deaf people? Historically, and before the ethnic revival, who may have perpetuated this viewpoint and why? Why is a postethnic revival critical of the medical model of Deaf people?

4. Examine the William Wordsworth poem. What experiences does it consider "normal" and essential and what characterization of Deaf people does it make? What does each line of Ella Lentz's poem convey? Analyze her images and use of particular phrases to portray another viewpoint of Deaf people. How does this viewpoint differ from Wordsworth's?

5. Outline how Deaf people may construct their deafness. How may such a construction begin? How early in life? Who plays a part in such constructions? Has the ethnic revival changed the origins, nature, and effects of Deaf people's constructions of themselves?

6. What does diglossia mean among Deaf people?

7. Search for more details about the Gallaudet University presidential election (e.g., Jankowski 1997) and the current nature of the university. The address is Gallaudet University, 800 Florida Ave, NE, Washington, DC 20002–3695, USA. The Internet address is http://www.gallaudet.edu/.

   Locate in your research and subsequent discussions the signs and symbols of an ethnic awakening of Deaf people. What advances still need to be made for a more comprehensive and deeper ethnic revival among Deaf people?

8. Examine the differences between the education of Deaf people before and after the ethnic revival. Discuss whether a "total communication" approach is justified. Examine this approach from the viewpoints of both the hearing community and the Deaf community. Do you support the full integration of Deaf people into mainstream society or separate Deaf communities, and what part should education play in this preference?

Selected Bibliography

Baker, C. (1996). *Foundations in Bilingual Education and Bilingualism.* Clevedon, England: Multilingual Matters.

Fishman, J. A. (1989). *Language and Ethnicity in Minority Sociolinguistic Perspective.* Clevedon, England: Multilingual Matters.

Groce, N. E. (1985). *Everyone Here Spoke Sign Language: Hereditary Deafness on Martha's Vineyard.* Cambridge: Harvard University Press.

Hagemeyer, A. (1992). *The Red Notebook.* Silver Spring, Md.: National Association of the Deaf.

Higgins, P. C. (1980). *Outsiders in a Hearing World: A Sociology of Deafness.* Beverly Hills, Calif.: Sage.

Jankowski, K. A. (1997). *Deaf Empowerment: Emergence, Struggle and Rhetoric.* Washington, D.C.: Gallaudet University Press.

Mashie, S. N. (1995). *Educating Deaf Children Bilingually.* Washington, D.C.: Gallaudet University Press.

Miller-Nomeland, M., and S. Gillespie (1993). *Kendall Demonstration Elementary School: Deaf Studies Curriculum Guide.* Washington, D.C.: Gallaudet University Press.

Open University (1991). *Issues in Deafness* (D251). Milton Keynes, U.K.: Open University Press.

Padden, C., and T. Humphries (1988). *Deaf in America: Voices from a Culture.* Cambridge: Harvard University Press.

Parasnis, I. (ed.) (1996). *Cultural and Language Diversity and the Deaf Experience.* Cambridge: Cambridge University Press.

Strong, M. (1995). A review of bilingual/bicultural programs for Deaf children in North America. *American Annals of the Deaf* 140(2): 84–94.

Wordsworth, William (1814). *The Excursion, Being a Portion of the Recluse, a Poem.* London: Longman et al.

Social Psychology

KARMELA LIEBKIND

What Is Ethnicity?

In dealing with language and ethnic identity, we touch upon two major concepts within the social sciences which have been given numerous different definitions: ethnicity and identity. Ethnicity is often seen as the focus of identity. All people are members of one ethnic group or another, but ethnic-group membership is more often associated with minority than with majority group status.

As a term, *ethnicity* has its roots primarily in anthropology and ethnology. Usually, an ethnic group is defined on the basis of so-called objective criteria, that is, biological, geographical, linguistic, cultural, or religious characteristics. However, cultures change, but the continuation of group boundaries themselves may be more long-standing. For example, third- and fourth-generation immigrants in the United States are generally quite unlike their first-generation forebears, even though they still often define themselves as members of their ancestral ethnic group. Subjective criteria seem to be more important than objective ones. An ethnic group could be defined simply as any group of people who identify themselves or are in any way identified as Italian, Polish, Indian, Greek, and so forth. One can consider oneself to be a Greek-American without understanding the Greek language, without practicing the Greek Orthodox religion, and even without liking Greek food.

Ethnicity is also a matter of subjective belief in common ancestry. Members of ethnic groups often have a subjective belief in their common descent. It does not matter whether or not an objective blood relationship really exists. Ethnic membership differs from the kinship group precisely by being a presumed identity.

Can Ethnicity Be Changed?

There are two polar positions to explain ethnic phenomena. One of these emphasizes the changeable aspects of ethnicity. According to this view, people are seen as acknowledging their ethnic identity only when they consider it to be useful for themselves. For example, if it is easier to get a job or an apartment by changing ethnic characteristics, people will do it, if possible. In other words, a language which hinders an individual's personal security and well-being will more easily be given up. In this perspective, modern man is (often exaggeratedly) viewed as "a shrewd calculator of membership benefits" (Fishman 1989: 37).

However, if we would acknowledge our ethnic identity only when that brings us clear benefits, why would members of some ethnic minorities rather starve to death or burn themselves than give up their ethnicity? The other perspective views ethnicity as comprising irrational, deep-seated allegiances, attachments to kin, territory, or religion. Ethnicity is seen as part of the herd instinct of human primates, ordinarily unquestioned and taken for granted but forcefully activated in times of stress or threat to group life.

In a sense, it is true that both of these positions are examples of the unnecessary polarization of inherently complementary aspects of human life. It seems clear by now that ethnicity can be manipulated, although it cannot be created situationally out of nothing. A person's ethnicity is ascribed in the sense that one cannot choose the ethnic group into which one is born, but it is achieved to the extent that the meaning it acquires for one's total identity can also be a matter of choice.

Ethnic Identity as Social Identity

One of the major cognitive tools individuals use to define themselves vis-à-vis the world in which they live is social categorization: ordering the social environment by grouping persons in a manner that makes sense to the individual. Individuals perceive themselves as belonging to social groups, and recognition of membership in these groups carries with it a knowledge of the values, positive or negative, that are attached to these groups. Within the social psychology of identity, a person's self-image is seen to have two components, personal identity and social identity. The latter derives from membership in various groups. Ethnic identity can be defined simply as the ethnic component of social identity. Social identity, in turn, is that part of an individual's self-concept which derives from his or her membership in social groups. We try to achieve a positive sense of social identity by trying to perceive our own group as favorably distinct from other collectivities on valued dimensions. This is called the need for positive distinctiveness (Tajfel 1978).

There are important psychological differences between the actions of individuals as individuals and their actions as group members. The transition from personal to social identity is a psychological process. As a consequence of this transition, the interpersonal interaction between two individuals changes into intergroup behavior, which implies interaction in terms of group identifications. The key feature of this intergroup behavior is depersonalization; the two individuals involved react both to themselves and to each other not as differentiated individual persons but as exemplars of the common characteristics of their groups.

Language Groups in Contact: Alternative Strategies of Individuals

Berry (1990) has identified four alternative acculturation strategies open to minorities in contact with majorities. Depending on whether or not the minority members wish to remain culturally as before (in terms of language, identity, etc.) and whether or not they wish to have day-to-day interaction and good relationships with mainstream society, the intergroup contact can result in integration, assimilation, separation, or marginalization. In integration, some degree of cultural integrity is maintained while one moves to participate as an integral part of the larger social network. In assimilation, original cultural features (language, religion, etc.) are given up totally in favor of those of the majority. In separation, the opposite is true; that is, no features of the majority culture are accepted, and only the original minority culture is valued. In marginalization neither the majority nor the minority can offer a satisfactory identity. In terms of language, it could mean loss of original language without simultaneous sufficient acquisition of the dominant language.

However, minority members may use different strategies in different areas of life. For example, one may seek economic assimilation (in work), linguistic integration (by way of bilingualism), and marital separation (by endogamy). This implies that the minority can share some values with the majority without sacrificing their minority culture.

The result of the integration strategy is a truly bicultural identity. Although this means that elements of the person's original identity are seen as negotiable and that identity loss does not hinge on any particular marker (such as language), it also means that, in true integration, the individual has accepted his or her ethnic and cultural heritage (i.e., maintained identification with the ethnic group), acquired necessary cultural skills (e.g., proficiency in the dominant language) in order to integrate into the larger society, and made a careful—and personally relevant—selection of the ethnic/cultural markers to be retained and those that can be altered. Language may or may not be among the markers to be preserved. If it is, the result of the integration is a bilingual person with a bicultural identity.

The Social Psychology of Language and Identity

What about language as an ethnic marker? What make people want to either maintain their language or give it up? Under which conditions are they ready to temporarily switch to another language, abandon their language completely, or stubbornly stick to their own language? These questions came more strongly into the focus of research with the general renaissance of ethnicity.

When the first textbook on the social psychology of language was written more than twenty years ago, it took somewhat fewer than 200 pages to present the field. Today, no single author could do justice to the whole field, as amply demonstrated by the first *Handbook of Language and Social Psychology* (Giles and Robinson 1990). The social psychology of language focuses on the roles of motives, beliefs, and identity in individual language behavior. It tries to link language and ethnic identity together and studies how this identity is formed, presented, and maintained. Ethnic or ethnolinguistic identity is involved in all social psychological research on language, even if the research deals with such diverse topics as ethnic language attitudes, second language learning, or communication breakdown (Liebkind 1996).

Credit for the birth of the social psychology of language goes primarily to Howard Giles and his colleagues (Giles and Johnson 1987). Giles introduced the so-called ethnolinguistic identity theory. This theory suggests that, when ethnic group identity becomes important for individuals, they may attempt to make themselves favorably distinct on dimensions such as language. Members of ethnolinguistic groups, like those of other social categories, strive for positive social identities to enhance their self-esteem. Thus members of such groups who value highly their own language may, in communicating with members from other groups, adopt various strategies of so-called psycholinguistic distinctiveness, such as accentuating their speech styles, switching to their in-group language, and so forth.

If, however, one's own language is a source of shame only, contributing primarily to a negative social identity, other strategies may be adopted. Some group members may use assimilation strategies and try to pass into and become members of the dominant group. "Passing" here means not only speaking the dominant group language but also assimilating linguistically, that is, identifying with the speakers of the dominant language.

Language and Ethnic Identity

It has been claimed that ethnic identity is intrinsically connected with language. Language interweaves the individual's personal identity with his or her collective ethnic identity. There are several conditions that promote this connection. First, language is very significant to the individual as an instrument for naming the self and the world. Second, the upbringing of a child is dependent on linguistic interaction. Third, spoken language is one of the most salient characteristics of ethnic groups.

Almost all contemporary nations are multicultural; that is, they contain two or more social groups which can be distinguished to varying degrees in terms of culture. Language is frequently a highly salient feature of such cultural differences and can become the most important symbol of ethnic identity. This is so even if that language is not actively used (e.g., Gaelic for the Irish). Although not all members of the ethnic group need to speak the ethnic language, the language is readily available and can act as a symbol of ethnic identity, especially if the language used within the family is ethnically distinctive.

People generally have a so-called integrative attitude toward their mother tongue—that is, they identify with the speakers of that language and want to maintain that identification. Much social psychological research has suggested that language and identity appear to be reciprocally related: Language use influences the formation of group identity, and group identity influences patterns of language attitudes and usage.

However, the role of language in ethnicity is far from unambiguous, and the language-ethnicity link has been subject to considerable debate. Many researchers claim that language is not an essential component of identity. They say that many groups manage to continue living as distinct groups even after communicative language shift. According to this view, the usefulness of a language is always emphasized above its symbolic or emotional value. Most scholars agree that language can be an important component of ethnic identity but that this identity can, and does, survive the loss of the original group language. For example, the rapid language shift from Irish to English in Ireland shows that people can use a language (English) for the socioeconomic and other advantages it offers even though they hold intrinsically unfavorable attitudes toward that language that contrast with the favorable attitudes maintained toward their ethnic language. Language use or language proficiency, consequently, should not be confused with linguistic identity.

Thus, although language has been considered by some as the single most important component of ethnic identity, its importance clearly varies with the particular situation and is minimal for some groups. The association between language and identity depends on the social context pertinent to the language groups in question. Although language can be the most significant criterion of social identification, it is not the only one, nor is it necessarily the most significant one for all social groups. Consequently, it is obvious that original-language maintenance is not a necessary feature of group identity but that language may be more central for some groups than for others.

Language Attitudes
and Ethnolinguistic Vitality

A basic feature of most multicultural societies is that the language of the dominant group is also the most important one; therefore, it is to the advantage of the subordinate ethnolinguistic group to be able to speak it. Failure to do so can have heavy social and economic consequences. Furthermore, the subordinate group's language is often considered to be of lesser value and as such is often the object of ridicule from the dominant group.

Given the evaluative connotations of language, it is important to know the conditions under which subordinate ethnic groups either lose their language, maintain it, or promote or revive it, and what the reactions are of the dominant group. Giles and his colleagues coined the term *ethnolinguistic vitality*—a concept that refers to a group's ability to survive as a distinctive collective entity in an intergroup setting. Ethnolinguistic vitality is dependent on three sets of factors:

Status (e.g., economic, political, and linguistic prestige)

Demographic strength (e.g., absolute numbers, concentration, birthrates, migration, etc.)

Institutional support and control factors (i.e., representation of one's own language in media, government, education, etc.)

All these factors combine to make up the vitality of ethnolinguistic groups. The language of an ethnolinguistic group with high vitality has a high status; the size and concentration of the group is sufficient for maintenance of the group as a collectivity; and the group has strong formal and informal institutional support in the society. Low ethnolinguistic vitality of a group is marked by the opposite characteristics.

It is the perceived or subjective, not the real or objective, vitality that counts. That is, vitality has its impact on language use in the same way as do other sociocultural factors, via subjective perceptions of, or beliefs concerning, the nature of things, rather than the objective reality of things. Members of groups with low vitality are more likely to use assimilation strategies; the group may even cease to exist as a distinctive collective entity. Conversely, groups with high vitality are most likely to survive as distinctive collectivities in multilingual settings. The basic assumption here is that speakers who perceive their own group vitality to be high have more positive attitudes about the use of their own group language than those who perceive it to be low.

But there are at least two other factors that may influence attitudes toward one's own language: perceived group boundaries and multiple group membership. If group boundaries are perceived as hard and impermeable, that is, almost impossible to cross, then the assimilation option is not available, and identification with one's own language group is probably strong. And if there are few alternative social categories except the linguistic one with which to identify, then one's identification with one's language group is probably very strong, too.

Evaluation of speakers of a particular language is dependent on many different factors. Some of these factors are related to the sociocultural context in question (i.e., the standardization and vitality of the language) and some to the immediate social situation (e.g., its degree of formality). Yet other factors are related to the language speakers themselves (i.e., their personal and social attributes and the content of their messages) and to those who judge or evaluate these speakers (especially their own personal and social attributes).

However, the survival of an ethnolinguistic minority in a particular social context ultimately depends on how the majority uses its power and dominance. The dominant group frequently imposes its own language as the only legitimate one and pursues a policy of minority assimilation. In this case, the minority language may be devalued and stigmatized. Analysis of the power of dominant groups is central to understanding the development and maintenance of favorable ethno-linguistic identities.

Language Identity and Speech Accommodation

A great deal of speech as communication occurs between individuals who are engaged in face-to-face interaction. Such encounters between two persons can be interpreted in various ways by those involved. The encounter can be seen as strictly interpersonal, and then individual characteristics of the participants are the only ones that matter. Alternatively, the encounter can be seen as intergroup in nature, and then the participants' different group memberships become very salient. It is partly the specific situation and context which determine the interpretations, but it is also partly a question of negotiation between the interlocutors; as the communication goes on, the participants negotiate their mutual roles and identities in the encounter taking place.

Sometimes language use is determined by long-term identity processes, but sometimes it is very much a matter of situational norms and has little to do with identity. The questions about how individuals use, evaluate, and alter their speech styles in face-to-face interactions have been more formally considered under the rubric of speech accommodation. Research in this area seeks to account for language use in terms of interlocutors' motives, attitudes, perceptions, and group loyalties. The nature and extent of speakers' multiple goals will have a strong bearing on linguistic outcomes. The speech or communication accommodation model developed by Giles and his colleagues attempts to predict and explain language use in terms of different social psychological processes.

People use different strategies in communication. In speech convergence, speakers try to become more like their listeners in the language/speech style they use. In speech maintenance, the speakers maintain their speech styles; and in speech divergence, they accentuate the linguistic differences between themselves and their listeners. Speakers are not always aware that they are modifying their speech, but levels of awareness appear to be higher for speech divergence than for speech convergence.

Generally speaking, convergence evokes positive reactions in the other and thus satisfies the converging individual's need for approval or liking. Clearly, the greater an individual's need for approval, the greater his or her tendency to converge. However, this need is not necessarily a permanent characteristic of an individual's personality but can be a function of the prestige and status of the interlocutors. Usually the low-status speaker converges (upward) more than the high-status speaker converges (downward). Divergence indicates that the individual does not need the approval of the other interlocutor. But if the interaction is intergroup rather than interpersonal in nature, divergence may fulfill an identity function.

People adapt their speech styles in order to satisfy a variety of motivations, but motivations to achieve or maintain a positive social/ethnic/ethnolinguistic identity have been most clearly implicated in studies that demonstrate language divergence and maintenance. Drawing together research on ethnolinguistic vitality, group boundaries, status, and identity, it can be argued that people tend to adopt positive linguistic distinctiveness strategies—that is, to diverge—in interaction with members of other groups when they

(a) See language as an important dimension of their group
(b) Are aware of possible alternatives to their group's present status position
(c) Perceive little overlap with the out-group person in terms of other social categories
(d) Do not identify strongly with many other social categories
(e) Consider their social identities that derive from other social category memberships to be relatively unsatisfactory
(f) Perceive their status within the ethnic group to be higher than their status within their other social category memberships
(g) See their group boundaries (especially linguistic boundaries) as hard and closed
(h) See their in-group as having high ethnolinguistic vitality. (Gudykunst & Gumbs 1989)

In reality, however, most of us belong simultaneously to many social groups. Most of us do identify (more or less) strongly with many social categories simultaneously and derive a (more or less) strong social identity from many social category memberships. The greater the number of our membership groups, the greater the likelihood that conflict, ambiguity, or other strains will occur between them but also the greater the possibility of creating alternative sources of positive identity. Inasmuch as a person feels him- or herself to be part of two or more ethnic/cultural groups, one single ethnic self-identification is inaccurate. Such persons identify themselves as partly ethnic and partly mainstream. Often this bicultural/bilingual alternative (or integration) is the most satisfactory one for the individual.

Bilingual Communication

Bilingual communication, in which two languages or dialects are used, usually involve members of different ethnolinguistic groups. One of the most common phenomena in bilingual communication is code switching, defined generally as the alternate use of two or more languages in the same utterance or conversation. Code switching is determined by a variety of different factors. Some of these characterize the situation, others the individual communicators, and yet others the social positions of the language groups represented by the interlocutors. Social psychology tends to focus on the individuals involved and their motives, perceptions, and identities. But the social context of the interlocutors, particularly the power and status relationships between the language groups represented by the interlocutors, has a decisive influence on code switching.

In bilingual contexts, languages (codes) often serve as powerful cues for categorizing people into social/ethnolinguistic groups. This categorization often triggers efforts to achieve positive distinctiveness, as discussed previously. But as the notion of ethnolinguistic vitality implies, sociostructural characteristics of the language groups involved have a strong impact on ethnolinguistic identity. Group numbers and power and status differentials have strong effects on intergroup behavior. Members of dominant and high-status groups tend to favor their own group members more than members of subordinate and low-status groups do. In fact, the latter sometimes favor members of other groups more than their own. Being in a numerical majority in a particular social context offers a kind of "security in numbers" and diminishes the probability of out-group discrimination.

However, both majority and minority groups can be either psychologically secure or insecure, and these psychological states elicit different behavior in minority than in majority members. Insecure majorities feel threatened in their majority position, and, as a consequence, discriminate against out-groups. Insecure minorities, in turn, are not convinced of the intrinsic value of their own culture and language and therefore tend to favor the out-group rather than the in-group. In contrast, psychologically secure minorities feel more free to reject the majority language and culture and assert their own distinctiveness, whereas secure majorities are tolerant of minorities.

This is why dominant high-status group members tend to be more discriminatory when they are in a minority than when they are in a majority position and vice versa; subordinate low-status group members tend to favor out-group members more when in a numerical minority than when in a numerical majority position. For example, Bourhis and Sachdev (1984) found that English Canadians were more tolerant of Italian usage when they composed a numerical majority rather than a numerically equal group in their local school setting. Similarly, anglophones in Montreal are an example of a dominant high-status group in a minority position, and feelings of insecurity associated with that position may explain the in-group favoritism in language evaluation displayed by this group in many studies.

Second-Language Acquisition

Acquiring native-like proficiency in a second language is said to differ from most other learning tasks because it involves adopting an alien cultural perspective and therefore becomes a question of identity. However, this depends on the learner's attitude toward the second language in question. If the attitude is a purely instrumental one, the second language is viewed only as a tool for communication and does not affect identity. In contrast, an integrative attitude toward the second language means that this language has a symbolic value and implies identification with speakers of that language. Only in the latter case is acquisition of the language in question a matter of identity.

Speech-accommodation and ethnolinguistic-identity theories have exciting consequences for the study of second-language acquisition. The motivation to learn a second language is far more decisive of the end result than is any aptitude for learning languages. Motivation is a product of different features of the social context in which the learning process takes place.

In the so-called intergroup model of second-language acquisition, the focus is on how members of subordinate groups can acquire native-like mastery of the language of a dominant group. The basic hypothesis here is that native-like proficiency in a dominant group's language would be "subtractive" to the ethnic identity of members of the subordinate group if

- They identify strongly with their (subordinate) in-group
- Language is a central feature of their own group
- There are few other or only lower-status groups with which to identify
- Subjective ethnolinguistic vitality is high.

The model thus predicts that native-like proficiency in a dominant group's language would, under these conditions, attract hostility from other members of the subordinate group, even accusations of ethnic betrayal, and that it would create fear of assimilation. In these conditions, the model suggests, only classroom proficiency in the dominant language would be accepted. In contrast, native-like proficiency in the dominant group's language is seen as being "additive" under conditions opposite to those listed. This means that native-like proficiency under such opposite conditions would foster integration into mainstream society and facilitate access to social and material rewards.

However, this intergroup model of second-language acquisition has also been severely criticized. It has also been difficult to verify the model in empirical research; in some studies, the stronger the in-group identification, the more tolerance there is for out-group members and the greater the competence in the out-group language. In other studies, the opposite is true. If weak in-group identification and/or low perceived in-group vitality will most likely lead to native-like proficiency in the dominant group's language, this would imply that, for example, one cannot be a proud Indian, a proficient bilingual, and a legitimate member of the mainstream society all at the same time. In other words, the acculturation strategy of integration would be more or less impossible.

The problem with the intergroup model of second-language acquisition is that it fails to distinguish between long-term identity processes and situational shifts, between more stable language identity and language use. Native-like proficiency in a dominant out-group's language does not necessarily mean rejection of one's own cultural or linguistic identity. It could mean only an instrumental attitude toward the dominant language, which is seen as useful for acquiring social and material rewards. Even if bilingualism is lost, even if proficiency in one's own language declines as a result of the shift to a dominant language, this does not necessarily mean loss of linguistic identity (cf. the example of English and Irish in Ireland, referred to previously).

The Effects of the Ethnic Revival

In people's minds, as in the physical world, there seems to appear for every action an equal and opposite reaction. The development of the relations between large-scale social groups (e.g., language groups and ethnic groups) since World

War II has been characterized by two continuous processes which seem to pull in opposite directions and yet complement each other. These are the simultaneous growth of interdependence among and differentiation between social groups. Although international political and economic interdependence is clearly present and visible everywhere, many societies are shaken by internal claims for increased decentralization or even internal splits into smaller independent units.

This development is not too hard to understand if one considers that there are thousands of ethnic and linguistic groups in the world but only around 200 nation-states, very few of which can be called ethnically or linguistically homogeneous. The ethnic revival, starting in the late 1960s, resulted in a worldwide push toward differentiation among minority groups. This push was called the "new ethnicity." Many of the movements toward differentiation have common claims based on the right of minorities to be different and to preserve their distinctiveness as defined in their own terms and not in terms implicitly or explicitly dictated by the majorities.

The ethnic revival gave a veritable vitamin injection to the social psychology of language. Since the mid-1970s, there has been an outpouring of research that gave rise to a definable social psychology of language. In the beginning, however, this research area was a mainstream reaction to the ethnic revival. The research was carried out by mainstream researchers who adhered to mainstream theories of and attitudes toward minorities. In the mainstream perspective, language is not an essential component of identity. Both language and ethnicity are seen as negotiable commodities to the extent that they hinder a person's security and well-being. Only from the early 1980s onward has this mainstream social psychology of language been challenged by a steady and growing stream of studies showing the importance of language for many ethnic minorities. These studies emphasize the possibility and desirability of active bilingualism and the right of minorities to remain linguistically distinct.

Questions for Further Thought and Discussion

1. Can one consider oneself to be, for instance, a Greek/Polish/German-American without understanding the Greek/Polish/German language? Why? Why not?

2. Why is a "cost-benefit" model of ethnicity not satisfactory?

3. Can ethnic identity survive without a distinct language?

4. What distinguishes groups with high from those with low ethnolinguistic vitality?

5. When and why do people accentuate speech and nonverbal differences between themselves and others?

6. What different options are available for linguistic minorities in terms of their relationship to the linguistic majority?

7. How does a language group's status and power influence its attitudes toward other linguistic groups?

8. What is the difference between secure and insecure linguistic minorities?

Selected Bibliography

Berry, J. W. (1990). Psychology of acculturation. In *Nebraska Symposium on Motivation: Vol. 37*. 201–235. *Cross-Cultural Perspectives*, J. J. Bremen (ed.) Lincoln: University of Nebraska Press.

Bourhis, R. Y., and I. Sachdev (1984). Vitality perceptions and language attitudes: Some Canadian data. *Journal of Language and Social Psychology* 3: 97–126.

Fishman, J. (1989). *Language and Ethnicity in Minority Sociolinguistic Perspective*. Clevedon, England: Multilingual Matters.

Giles, H., and P. Johnson (1987). Ethnolinguistic identity theory: A social psychological approach to language maintenance. *International Journal of the Sociology of Language* 68: 256–269.

Giles, H., and W. E. Robinson (eds.)

(1990). *Handbook of Language and Social Psychology*. Chichester: Wiley.

Gudykunst, W. B., and L. I. Gumbs (1989). Social cognition and intergroup communication. In *Handbook of International and Intercultural Communication*, M. K. Asante and W. B. Gudykunst (eds.), 204–224. Newbury Park, Cal.: Sage.

Liebkind, K. (1996). Contact linguistics and social psychology. In *Kontaktlinguistik. Contact Linguistics. Linguistique de Contact. An International Handbook of Contemporary Research*, H. Goebl, P. H. Nelde, S. Denek, and W. Wölck (eds.), 41–48. Berlin: Walter de Gruyter.

Tajfel, H. (ed.) (1978). *Differentiation Between Social Groups: Studies in the Social Psychology of Intergroup Relations*, London: Academic Press.

Sociolinguistics

JOSHUA A. FISHMAN

Sociolinguistic Perspective

Many of the chapters in this book start by defining the terms *ethnicity*, *identity*, and even *language*. In this chapter I assume that those terms are roughly understood by now; as necessary, I will define them only implicitly, in the context of examples and more general discussion. Nevertheless, the term *sociolinguistic* may benefit from definition at the very outset, because it refers to a rather new area of specialization and because it is used here as an adjective rather than as a noun. I use this adjective to embrace both the sociology of language and sociolinguistic. These two specializations constitute, respectively, the more sociological and the more linguistic aspects of a growing awareness that language use and language behaviors (including both language structure and a variety of behaviors toward languages) vary in accord with the social contexts in which they transpire. The total awareness, in all of its richness, is what I refer to when I speak of "sociolinguistic perspective." Because neither traditional sociology nor traditional linguistics has paid much attention to the potential boundary area between them, sociolinguistic perspective has developed to fill this gap. Ultimately, like social psychology, it may find a real home in one or both of its parent disciplines.

Sociolinguistic perspective has enabled researchers to document and to measure a hitherto overlooked type of variation in language use and language behavior. Instead of referring to "the French language," as though it were always one and the same in any given period of time, sociolinguistic perspective has revealed the existence of different kinds of French (differing grammatically, phonetically, and lexically), often being used by the very same speakers but on different occasions (e.g., informal, semiformal, and formal), both in speech and in writing. In addition, of course, there are the different kinds of French utilized by different segments of francophone society: the urban and the rural, the educated and the relatively uneducated, and the various professional, gender-related, and interest related varieties. Naturally, many of the foregoing types or categories of French speakers also demonstrate a repertoire of usages, sometimes speaking one way and sometimes another, in accord with what suits their fluctuating purposes and intentions. Who among us has not had that experience? We are approached differently (and approach others differently) when the agenda is an intimate, non-status-stressing one than when it is quite the opposite. And if this "repertoiral" virtuosity is true even within the monolingual use of one language, then it is all the more true when bi- or multilinguals interact with one another. Many speakers of French are bilingual (just as are many speakers of English or of almost any other language on the face of the earth). Their use of French with other similar bilinguals will vary from certain topics and relationships in which French is most common to others in which another language (e.g., Dutch or even Flemish in Brussels; German or even Alsatian in Strassburg) is most common.

Bilingual or multilingual settings are very commonly studied in order to gauge sociolinguistic variation (and to relate such variation to the identity and purpose of speakers on different occasions and in different contexts), because the variation between languages is easier to monitor (particularly by sociologists) than is the variation within one and the same language. And it is because the degree of variation between languages is often related to variation in ethnic identity, ethnic attitudes, and ethnic behaviors that the language and ethnicity link has so frequently been explored by those interested in sociolinguistic variation. There is hardly a major researcher devoted to sociolinguistic inquiry who has not devoted attention to some aspect of the language and ethnicity link at some time or other; some have devoted a substantial part of their careers to research and theory dealing with such contexts, whether intragroup (e.g., how Alsatians of different social classes interact with one another) or intergroup (how Alsatians interact with Frenchmen on the one hand and with Germans on the other within any given social class).

Variation in Ethnolinguistic Saliency

One of the truisms that derives from a sociolinguistic perspective on language and ethnicity is that "ethnolinguistic identity is not a unit trait." Our own awareness and implementation of our ethnic identity is not invariant but changes from one occasion to another. When I am at Yeshiva University, I am usually not very aware of being an Orthodox Jew; but when I am at Stanford University, I am usually more aware of that identity, perhaps because I am more contrastively recognizable as such in that context, always wearing a yarmulke (an orthodox male headcover) as I do. However, at neither university am I as aware of also being an American as when I am attending a conference in Uppsala or in Santiago de Compostela. At Yeshiva University, there are many people with whom I can interact in Yiddish, so that I do not particularly need to seek them out. At Stanford, I am delighted when I bump into any one of the handful of people there who enjoy speaking it as much as I do. However, in Santiago de Compostela it is English speakers that I tend to sit next to and eat with, because I speak no Gallego and my Spanish is not as good as is that of the Galicians.

Examples such as the foregoing indicate that group membership may be multiple (even ethnicity may be hyphenated, all claims to the contrary notwithstanding) and that the saliency of the particular component that is highlighted on any given occasion will vary. Another way of saying this is that ethnic identity is contextually constructed. Given the common link (N.B.: "link," not "equivalence") between language and ethnicity, the saliency of specific language use (where a repertoire of languages or varieties is shared by the interlocutors) is also contextually constructed. What are some of the contextual characteristics that tend to elicit or prompt one language to be used rather than the other in settings in which either one could potentially be utilized? Just as ethnic identity is fostered by intergroup grievances, so the language use corresponding to such identity is fostered. Thus when use of one's ethnically associated language is restricted or denigrated, the users who identify with it are more likely to use it among themselves (and to organize in order to have it accepted and recognized by others) than if no such grievance existed. This is a sociolinguistic perspective that "English-only" advocates in the United States might do well to keep in mind, for their campaign—however disguised by patriotic slogans and by limited functional targets—may actually strengthen the very languages which they oppose.

It is difficult to oppose languages without opposing their speakers and their community interests. As might be expected, communities that are opposed frequently organize ("mobilize"), consciously, openly, unconsciously, covertly, to resist such opposition and to advance their own interests. They may very well use their second language (and, in some cases, even learn it better than they did before) in order to influence the majority public and its authorities, but the latter will become even more conscious of and identified with their traditionally associated "ethnic mother tongue" than before and, in some cases, learn it better than heretofore as well. Giving up a traditionally associated ethnic mother tongue is both a result of and a cause of ethnocultural dislocation. Although some dislocated ethnic groups have been able to weather such dislocation with their identities intact, most have not been able to do so. Also, an intact identity is not the same as an intact tradition. Although many people recover from cancer, no one looks forward to having cancer in order to see if one can do so.

However, the heightening of ethnolinguistic saliency occurs not only on conflictual or potentially conflictual grounds. "Figure-ground" contrast may be sufficient (as it is for me as one of the rare Yiddish speakers at Stanford), or specific ethnic occasions (in which both grievances and contrastivity may be lacking but mutuality is stressed) may also temporarily heighten such saliency. But the saliency of ethnolinguistic preferences also corresponds to certain large-scale sociopolitical/socioeconomic developments, two of which are discussed in the following section because they have both been frequently examined from a sociolinguistic perspective.

Variation in Language Attitudes and Language Functions

Ethnic identity is a sociopsychological variable which may not be at all conscious but one of which minorities are more often conscious than are majorities. Once developed and aroused by historical and cultural "saliency-raising experiences," it can be called into consciousness on a contextual basis. If one compares "English-only" attitudes toward English with the attitudes toward English that are reflected in Shakespeare's *Two Gentlemen of Verona*, it is clear that the attitudes toward the language among most of its own speakers have greatly changed during the past 500 years. From a language which generally had an inferiority complex among its own speakers and was held in little esteem among cultured circles in Europe (e.g., vis-à-vis Latin, French, or even Italian), a language that was viewed, both internally and externally, as "uncouth" and as having "no compass for ground or authority.... No rare cunning.... No hope of greatness," English has become the most widely used and the most highly regarded language in the world.[1]

The improvement in attitude vis-à-vis English and its functional expansion are circularly linked in a mutual feedback sense. Clearly, however, there were some few who dared to defend and to advocate the virtues of English far before its functions really expanded significantly, either at home or abroad. But England's fortunate role in the industrial and commercial revolutions, the conquest of empire, and the Anglo-American triumphs in two world wars, not to mention America's superpower position and its attendant econotechnical superiority, have all contributed even more decisively to the position English has attained by the dawn of the twenty-first century. Thus both insider and outsider attitudes have fed on and strengthened each other but have, nevertheless, been unable to satisfy a gnawing fear among "English-only" advocates that English is not sufficiently safe and respected in its own home and that native English speakers are losing control to outsiders. Both contrast and grievance are obviously involved in the greater saliency of English in the American mainstream sense of identity today than was the case half a century ago—greater saliency, in fact, than any rational analysis of the obvious benefits that English provides for many of those who master it, on the one hand, and the continued high attrition rate of all other languages in our country, on the other, would seem to justify. Thus although functionality and attitudes may be linked, they are not always so, since other considerations can come to the fore (symbolic, demographic, ideological, and historical), particularly in the short run, which tend to make them become out of synch with each other.

Other examples of the lack of full symmetry between functionality and attitudes abound. The functionality of French in Quebec is now at an all-time high, yet the fears and trepidations of francophone politicians and ideologues (and their respective constituencies there) seem not to have been at all assuaged thereby. Because the power of English worldwide, as we have seen, is also at an all-time high, these francophones' sense of being the lone French-speaking people on the American continent evokes in them a sense of duty and an anxiety as to their ability to remain "masters of their own house." Other language communities, too, exemplify the lack of complete correspondence between functionality and attitudes.

At the same time that English is the world's superlanguage (if not "killer language," as some would have it), more small languages are being read and written today than ever before. In Europe alone, there were no more than thirty-one standardized languages of literacy at the beginning of the century, whereas there are more than 100 such today, if we count all those that are utilized at least in elementary education and initial adult literacy programs. In the world at large, an even more startling growth has occurred, with literacy being supported at some level or other in roughly one-fourth of all languages. Of course, literacy is not all of one piece. There is both higher-level and lower-level literacy, and many of those who are literate in their ethnic mother tongues are actually bi- or multiliterate. While more and more Frisians are becoming literate in their own language, Frisian, they are also all literate in Dutch and becoming increasingly literate in English. Each language is generally utilized for specific types of reading matter, so that the complexity of the literacy repertoire in many parts of the world may be as great as or even greater than the complexity of the local oral repertoire. In the long run, it may be primarily native English speakers who remain monoliterate and, as such, familiar only with their own culture, rather than with any others, in a constantly shrinking and more intercommunicating world.

The ability of many societies to maintain two languages, each for its own distinctive purpose, has been referred to as *diglossia* (bilingualism is a characteristic of individuals rather than of societies). Diglossia is a long-term and widespread complementary distribution of functions between the languages of a speech-and-writing community. Of course, the languages are rarely hermetically sealed off from one another, so that they may influence each other somewhat, both orally and in writing, even though on the whole their functions tend to differ. Functional boundaries are also socially constructed, and they may vary in compartmentalization. As a result of a millennium of Yiddish-Hebrew diglossia, Hebrew has "leaked" into the Yiddish lexicon and grammar (particularly in learned discourse and writing) and Yiddish has "leaked" into Hebrew (particularly in informal names and in other informal secular contexts, as well as in Orthodox learned contexts) as well. Interlocutors can relax, even in a formal study context, and it is in such functional crossovers that the greatest amount of "leakage" occurs from one language into the other. Thus, although English may be a danger to many small and weak languages around the world, diglossic arrangements may ultimately be achievable in many of these threatened contexts, so that complementarity rather than conflict of functions is possible. However, diglossia is neither an easy nor an acceptable goal everywhere (as Quebec itself illustrates). Where it is achievable, we may also find additional examples of a mismatch between attitudes and functions, functional restrictions often going hand in hand with attitudinal acceptance and even indiginization of both languages.

Variation in Language Policies

Thus far we have reviewed sociolinguisitic perspective in terms of three major things it reveals about language and ethnic identity: the importance of contextual

variation (grievance and contrast heighten ethnolinguistic saliency once consciousness has been aroused); functionality (advantageous functions heighten ethnolinguistic saliency); and the possibility of attitudinal-functional mismatch (a re-
minder that attitudes are merely predispositions to behavior and, therefore, are
not the same as overt language use, the acquisition and implementation of which
is quite separately governed). Sociolinguistic perspective also helps us to realize
that language planning occurs, both with respect to the functional utility of languages and with respect to the corpus of languages per se. Societies and networks
organize their members to intervene in the fortunes and in the paths of change of
the languages that are of significant interest to them, whether positively or negatively. As a result of language planning, policies are adopted and implemented in
order to foster (or hamper) and to modernize (or, more rarely, to archaicize) one
or more languages of a community's repertoire.

There have been several instances of language planning on behalf of English
in the United States. "English-only" itself is one such effort, but language planning on behalf of American English goes back to Revolutionary days and to Noah
Webster's lexicographic efforts to develop a Federal English that would be more
distinctively American and less like British English. Similarly, French has benefited from language planning, not only in Quebec but also on the European continent and throughout French-speaking areas the world over. The French government is involved in and supports many different agencies whose purpose is to
foster the use of French around the world and, directly or indirectly, to stem the
avalanche of English in entertainment, diplomacy, commerce, science, and technology. But today government agencies and quasi-government academies are the
major practitioners of language planning on behalf of late-modernizing languages
on the one hand and of minority languages on the other. Late modernization and
minoritization may thus be viewed as another set of variables which tend to
heighten ethnolinguistic saliency. Of course, both are also strongly colored by
grievance and by contrast processes in a world in which the most powerful economies and their associated languages are all supported by powerful interests that
work directly or indirectly on their behalf. Such planned supports, whether fostered by early modernizers or late modernizers, are intended either to influence
the languages per se (their lexicons, orthographies, even grammars and phonolo-
gies), in which case they are referred to as *corpus planning*, or to broaden the
functional range of the languages involved (particularly in the direction of acquiring more power-related functions), in which case they are termed *status planning*.
Both types of planning normally occur together and in close tandem with one
another.

But the little languages of the world have not thrown in the towel. In the Basque
Country and in Catalunya, in Israel and in Friesland, among the New Zealand
Maoris and among the Arizona Navajo, through the Romansh League in Switzer-
land and the League for Yiddish in New York (with no governmental base what-
soever), via the Committee for the Standardization of Romani and the Pilipino
Language Office, through the mentor-apprentice program on behalf of vanishing
Amerindian languages in California and the American Indian Language Develop-
ment Institute, via organizations such as Terralingua and the Endangered Language

Fund, through the European Bureau for Lesser Used Languages (an affiliate of the European Union) and the Universal Esperanto Association, both status planning and corpus planning are being attempted, often with considerable success. There is serious danger that two-thirds or more of all of the languages spoken in the world today will disappear from societal usage during the twenty-first century, but if this is so, then many of them plan to go down fighting and are putting up a considerable resistance. This resistance may make it possible for some of them to avoid going entirely into museums or into data banks and enable them to remain languages of everyday life, at least for dedicated devotees and exceptional communities.

Variations in Language Policy

With respect to status planning, policies may be supportive or permissive on the positive side and restrictive or prohibitive on the negative side. A policy of "no policy" (such as that which has characterized the United States vis à vis minority languages during most of its history) is technically "permissive." However, by exposing minority languages to the overwhelmingly powerful competition of the English-dominated marketplace, media, school system, youth culture, entertainment industry, government, and society, the result is devastation to the point of ultimate annihilation. In a monolingually oriented, Anglo-controlled environment that has also largely been "language unconscious," only nonparticipatory minorities such as the Old Order Amish, the Khasidim, the Hutterites, and certain isolated Amerindian and rural Hispanic groups can maintain intergenerational non-English mother-tongue transmission on a stable basis. It should be noted that even the above-mentioned nonparticipatory groups are bilingual, most of their members being able to speak (and many being able also to read and write) English, at least for purposes of economic interaction with their Anglo neighbors.

On the other hand, none of the above groups can engage in corpus planning sufficiently to enable their members to communicate with one another in their home languages about all of the topics and all of the objects that they experience in their interactions with the Anglo-American world, limited though the latter may be. As a result, the economic sphere, willy-nilly, becomes the entering wedge for diglossia at the very best and for disruptive language shift at the very worst in each of the above speech communities. For diglossia to obtain under these circumstances, a sharp compartmentalization between "inside" and "outside" values and norms is necessary. The outside language may be admitted for well-defined internal purposes, but outside values and norms must be vigilantly guarded against.

It is precisely because this is a difficult balancing act to achieve that Basque authorities have really not opted for Basque-Spanish diglossia as their preferred solution to the problem of "Basquifying" their autonomous community (Euskadi). Their goal, on the contrary, is to achieve universal bilingualism for all residents of the community, such that Spanish is used with the "outside" (Spain and its representatives and authorities) and Basque is used with the "inside" (defined as including all permanent residents of the Autonomous Basque Community) in all realms of interaction. This goal cannot be achieved without ample corpus planning as well, touching on all fields of modern life, including technology and the sciences. However, it is precisely in such functions that impulses toward language purity and authenticity are most severely tested and most often compromised.

A historical sense of grievance and contrast taken together is still not enough for such an enterprise to succeed. It is not sufficient to be grappling with late modernization or to be attitudinally well disposed toward such an enterprise nor even to be actually implementing it by establishing the requisite authoritative academy and government agencies in order to provide the new lexicons, teachers, and textbooks that are required. All of the moral and political power of local law is required in order to provide funding for, to map out, and to keep pushing ahead on the Basquization programs that have been adopted. There is political will and, ultimately, the readiness to use all of the sanctions against recalcitrants that societies traditionally utilize against those who disobey the law. Basque society is not only passively permissive in regard to furthering the Basque language in the autonomous community, it is also actively and imaginatively supportive of the language at every turn. And for those who oppose this drive toward full bilingualism, it may yet become not only restrictive but also prohibitive. Just how prohibitive will the Secretariat of Language Policy in Vitoria-Gastéiz ultimately become? As prohibitive as the general political culture is in all matters of public policy (e.g., in commerce, industry, education, etc.). Language policy is always enforced in accordance with the values and conventions of the culture within which it exists. Other aspects of enforcement are simply numerical (in demographic and economic terms). The values and conventions of the culture are common and widespread prerequisites of enforcement.

Democratic political cultures will, quite naturally, also implement their language policies democratically and, hopefully, with an even higher regard for pluralism and diversity than that which they have evinced in the past. Language policy and its implementation is the sixth and final variable derived from a sociolinguistic perspective. It is merely an extension of our earlier realization that language attitudes are not the same as language behaviors. Language behaviors that are authoritatively implemented via the legal system of a speech community constitute its language policy. Sociolinguistic perspective has shed a strong and steady light on the successes, excesses, and failures of such policies in various parts of the world and throughout different periods of human history. In doing so, it has contributed to greater appreciation of the social construction of the language and ethnicity link, while at the same time faithfully reporting the primordial passions and interpretations of this link that are still current in many parts of the globe and in not a few disciplines as well.

"Outside"-"Inside"

All six of the aforementioned saliency-highlighting variables with respect to the language and ethnicity link have one trait in common: They pertain to "outsider" perspectives on this matter. Social scientists (those with sociolinguistic perspective not excepted) are usually, and by conscious choice, outsiders to the behaviors and sentiments which they observe, describe, and analyze. However, the explanatory variables that they propose on this basis, powerful though they may sometimes be, often fail to convey the real flavor and forcefulness of the experiences and perspectives of "insiders" who are engaged in the very behavior under study. Thus, although research may gain much in terms of objectivity by adopting the dispassionate "outsider" stance, it unfortunately also loses something crucial thereby. Without adequately taking into consideration the "insider" views, convictions, and interpretations, no full or richly nuanced understanding of the behaviors being researched is possible.

There can be little doubt that intraculturally, that is, among "insiders," the language and ethnicity link is generally experienced positively, particularly when collective consciousness and mobilization have been attained. From that point on the linkage is often wrapped up in notions and assumptions of kinship, history, responsibility to one's people and to its linguistically encoded heritage, and the aesthetics of the "beloved language" (its beauty, precision, exhaustiveness, and uniqueness), as well as the eternity and the utter appropriatenesss of the language's association with the collectivity. Although social scientists usually claim that the linkage is socially conditioned, the insider-"true believer" often considers it to be an everlasting (therefore "primordial") and essential or inborn (therefore "essentialist") characteristic of "the people." Such views have also been espoused by noted philosophers and historians, particularly during the period of the European romantic age and most particularly among Germans, Slavs, and late-modernizing ethnic protest and liberation movements (Irish, Basque, Frisian, Jewish [whether pro-Yiddish or pro-Hebrew], Romansh, etc.). Subsequently, these views spread throughout the world, so that today they may be encountered among those for whom language and ethnicity are now salient almost anywhere. Recent advocates of Guarani, Quechua, Sindhi, Manyjilyjarra, and Maori have all accepted and identified with most of these romantic and essentialist European notions and, in doing so, have experienced the language and ethnicity link with new and powerful intensity. The tremendous reserves of ethnolinguistic devotion, self-sacrifice, and creativity which such views have released give ample testimony to the importance of tapping "insider" assumptions, beliefs, and convictions (or "linguistic culture," in Schiffman's terms; see Chapter 28, this volume) whenever the language and ethnicity link is being examined in sociolinguistic perspective.

However, the other side of the same coin should not be overlooked. The exhilaration, devotion, and newly found energy that positive ethnolinguistic consciousness releases can also be turned in negative, extrapunitive, and even genocidal directions. This is particularly so because the very grievances that foster ethnolinguistic saliency are also likely to be mutual and intergenerational. Negative consequences may flow from any human dimension that becomes a basis of collective behavior, be it class, gender, age, religion, race, or ethnicity. Rather than deny the legitimacy of any of the above because of the excesses to which one or another may have contributed, individuals, societies, and states must all learn to accept one another for their common humanity while accommodating to and respecting their unique differences. Our communalities and differences occur simultaneously, the one leading to the acquisition of lingua francas and the other leading to language loyalty within particular ethnolinguistic traditions. Both tendencies represent worthy characteristics of human social behavior and correspond to deeply ingrained human needs. Any frictions they cause must be arbitrated.

Conclusions

Sociolinguistic perspective helps us recognize the contribution of six interrelated variables to the socially constructed saliency of language in ethnic identity: (1) grievances of one language group against another, (2) contextual contrast of one language group vis-à-vis another, (3) attitudes toward a given language and ethnic identity, (4) the overt functionality or rational-reward basis of the language and ethnicity link, particularly in contexts of (5) late modernization, when early modernizing competitors are already entrenched and (6) the intensity of community sanctions with respect to the enforcement of language policy (at least for intracommunal purposes). The language and ethnicity link is strongest where it is energized by collective grievances between apparently contrasted collectivities, particularly when the linkage is fostered by leaders who can arouse language convictions in connection with the mobilization of potential followers. The link is rendered even more salient when it strategically rewards competitive late modernizers and when it is explicitly fostered by language policies that pursue either status or corpus planning. Ethnic revivals in general and the revival of the late 1960s to the late 1970s in Western Europe and North America (as well as subsequently elsewhere) are characterized by some or all of the above phenomena.

As modernization pressures differentially and incrementally reach various parts of the globe, the language and ethnicity link will repeatedly become more salient in some areas just as it is becoming less evident in others. In an increasingly interactive world, it would seem to be increasingly unlikely that one could withhold vernacular recognition—whether functional or symbolic—to some languages while (or after) permitting or granting them to others. Nevertheless, late and still later modernizers may find that multilingualism and multiliteracy are actually their best options for more quickly attaining both symbolic vernacular recognition on the one hand and the greater material advantages that are associated with languages of wider communication on the other. These two goals, when pursued simultaneously, go far toward explaining why, at the same time that English and a few other megalanguages (French, Spanish, German, Japanese, Chinese, and Arabic) continue to spread throughout the world, more and more local languages have become vehicles of local literacy, government, media, and economic development.

Because the social sciences, like languages, are not separated by natural boundaries but merely by conventional ones (university catalogues and departments are socially constructed to an even larger degree than is the language and ethnicity link), it should not surprise us that many of the above-mentioned sociolinguistic variables and points of view are also shared with and even further elaborated by various other areas of specialization included in this volume. However, in the brief one-third of a century that modern sociolinguistic perspective on language and ethnic identity has been developed, it has added a much-needed sensitivity to our total outlook on this topic by bringing the aforementioned six major variables together and by focusing on both their individual and their cumulative and interactive impact.

Questions for Further Thought and Discussion

1. How does the sociolinguistic perspective on language and ethnic identity differ from the applied linguistic perspective on the one hand and from the sociological perspective on the other?

2. Of the six variables that are suggested as being crucial for a sociolinguistic perspective on language and ethnic identity, is there one that you think is the most important and another that you think is least important overall?

3. Why (in terms of the six variables discussed in this chapter) might Yiddish have been more central to Jewish ethnolinguistic identity in interwar Poland than in the United States at the same time (or subsequently)?

4. How did Soviet policy toward languages other than Russian differ from U.S. policy toward languages other than English during the period 1945–1990?

5. Russyn is very similar to Ukrainian. Urdu is very similar to Hindi. Why does Russyn have so many additional problems in maintaining its saliency in ethnic identity than Urdu has?

6. Tamil has maintained a diglossic relationship between the spoken vernacular and the classical language for millennia. In contrast, the diglossic relationship between Swiss-German and High German has tended to weaken during the past fifty years, as has that between the dialects and the standard in Germany proper. What might be some of the reasons for the differences between the Tamil and the German cases?

7. Many believe that economic circumstances are not sufficiently represented in the sociolinguistic perspective. What do you think? Which of the six variables best reflects the economic contributions to sociolinguistic saliency?

8. The United States and Australia are both immigrant-based English-dominant countries. What might be some of the reasons why languages other than English are so highly prized in Australia but yet so undervalued in the United States?

Note

1. R. Mulcaster, sixteenth-century English "clark," in his *The First Part of the Elementarie* (1582), reprinted in Fishman (1997: 205–206).

Selected Bibliography

Britto, Francis (1986). *Diglossia: A Study of the Theory with Application to Tamil*. Washington, D.C.: Georgetown University Press.

Edwards, John (1994). *Multilingualism*. London: Routledge.

Ferguson, Charles A. (1996). *Sociolinguistic Perspective: Papers on Language in Society*. New York: Oxford University Press.

Fishman, Joshua A., Andrew W. Conrad, and Alma Robal-Lopez (eds.) (1996). *Post-Imperial English*. Berlin: Mouton de Gruyter.

Fishman, Joshua A. (1997). *In Praise of the Beloved Language: A Comparative View of Positive Ethnolinguistic Consciousness*. Berlin: Mouton de Gruyter.

García, Ofelia, and Joshua A. Fishman (eds.) (1997). *The Multilingual Apple: Languages in New York*. Berlin: Mouton de Gruyter.

Graddol, David (1997). *The Future of English: A Guide to Forecasting the Popularity of the English Language in the 21st Century*. London: The British Council.

Hamel, Rainer Enrique (ed.) (1997). Linguistic human rights from a sociolinguistic perspective. *International Journal of the Sociology of Language* 127. Berlin: Mouton de Gruyter.

Khubchandani, Lachman M. (1997). *Revisualizing Boundaries: A Pluralingual Ethos*. Thousand Oaks, Cal.: Sage.

McKay, Sandra Lee, and Sau-ling Cynthia Wong (eds.) (1988). *Language Diversity: Problem or Resource?* Boston: Heinle and Heinle.

Newton, Gerald (ed.) (1996). *Luxembourg and Letzebuergesch: Language and Communication at the Crossroads of Europe*. Oxford, Clarendon.

Zentella, Anna Celia (1997). *Growing Up Bilingual: Puerto Rican Children in New York City*. Oxford, Blackwell.

Sociology

GLYN WILLIAMS

It is important to recognize that sociology began as a political science and that the current shape and concerns of the discipline derived from the preoccupation with founding the modern state which was the cornerstone of eighteenth-century philosophy. The classical Greek concept of *ethnos* contrasts with *demos* in the opposition between the romantic sense of the word *people* and the social sense of the same word. It is exemplified in the difference between how the French Jacobins defined nation in terms of *jui soli*, or right of the soil, and how the German romantics defined it as a *jus sanguis*, or right of blood.[1] The modern state rests on a particular form of relationship between ethnos and demos, and it is not possible to understand the sociological concept of ethnicity without reference to the relationship between the state and its population.

Below I show how ethnicity derives from the need to incorporate people from different cultural backgrounds into the same political state, how its meaning is conditioned by the peculiar concept of a state which represents the will of these people, and how it relates to a biased understanding of culture within which one culture is favored over another. Given that the state represents the will of the people, some means must be found whereby that will is uniform and is expressed as a uniform identity with the state. Thus the problem of the relationship between a people formed out of a diversity of cultures and a uniform identity is highlighted in the concern with ethnic identity. Sociology resolves this dilemma by means of a specific argument concerning the relationship between peoples and cultures. I claim that this argument represents a statist bias and the associated denigration of those labeled as ethnic and that the concept should be abandoned.

Primordiality, Modernity, and Evolution

Three central ideas around which sociology has been constructed are evolution, normativity, and social order. Together they condition the manner in which the concept of ethnicity is formulated. It is appropriate to begin with an account of how these ideas, which were so important in the emerging political philosophy of the eighteenth century, fed into sociology.

Evolution

Western ontology, or the philosophy of being, has rested on the idea of evolution. During the eighteenth century, at a time when we find protosociology emerging, the idea of a scientific endeavor based on the importance of reason was firmly established. It was argued that a specific form of rationalism was the cornerstone whereby the laws of nature were discovered. This process of discovery was cumulative in the sense that new knowledge encountered through discovery was fed into the storehouse of knowledge, which was epitomized as "progress." This form of argument relied on the emergence of humankind as firmly in control of its own destiny. Sociology became the science that discovered the laws of human progress. In this respect it relied upon a shift in thinking from one in which God is the source of being by which everything is—God is the Word—to one in which humankind is held to be in charge of its destiny through the gift of reason and its relationship to language as an expression of that reason.

At least from the time of Bacon in the seventeenth century, the progressive development of knowledge was viewed as natural and normal. By the time of Kant in the following century, it was claimed that progress was inevitable and would ultimately lead to a condition of perfection. Thus progress was linked with the idea of the good life which could be achieved cumulatively through progress toward perfection. Two ideas become central to this claim: first, as I have indicated, that knowledge was cumulative, and second, that knowledge was equivalent to ability—that is, the more we know, the more able we are. It is this relationship that is at the heart of the weakness of evolutionism and of sociology as a discipline.

A recent television advertisement for cigars showed two Stone Age men dressed in animal skins trying to light a fire by rubbing sticks together. Enter an aristocrat dressed in a fur coat. He looks at the two Stone Age men, smirks, pulls out his cigar and proceeds to light it with a lighter. The two Stone Age men, seeing this, seek to imitate the aristocrat, treating their sticks as lighters. This ad only succeeds in conveying the desired meaning if we accept the relationship between cumulative knowledge and ability. The aristocrat is of now, and therefore has far more knowledge accumulated over the ages than Stone Age men do and is therefore more able than they are. Break this relationship between cumulative knowledge and ability and the ad falls flat on its face. The two Stone Age men may simply know different things and may be more able in a different way than the aristocrat—for instance, being able to light a fire with sticks. However, the relationship between cumulative knowledge and ability is so embedded in our conceptions of the difference between the past and the present that such an argument is unlikely to strike us; or, if it does, it fails to lead to recognition of the extent to which our assumptions about the world are conditioned by this relationship.

Of course, there is another anomaly here, one I shall return to momentarily. The aristocrat and the Stone Age man exist in the same place at the same moment in time. If we believe in the idea of progress over time, how is it that we do not conceive of the protagonists in terms of the same frame of reference rather than by reference to dichotomies such as primitive/civilized or traditional/modern? Something other than time is involved. This is the centrality of the idea of Western superiority that is the cornerstone of social and cultural evolutionism.

It was Leibniz, writing at the end of the seventeenth century, who argued that change did not occur in stages but was a gradual and cumulative affair. He also claimed that the future was predictable from a knowledge of the present, the kind of conjectural history that constitutes the central idea of planning. However, such a conception of progress was linked with the claim that any institutions and beliefs which stood in the way of progress were swept aside by it. This idea of the simultaneous existence of both the forces of progress and of institutions and value systems that hindered its development was translated into various dichotomies, including civilization/barbarism and modern/traditional, and ultimately into a range of different social forms that were held to be characteristic of each element of the dichotomy. Indeed, once the idea of the existence of such dichotomies was accepted, it became a matter of developing the characteristic features of the respective types of existence. Thus we have a typology of society, of civilization, of barbarism, and so forth. Inevitably it is here that we encounter Eurocentrism in that the latest point of development was held to be Europe, and therefore the typologies were premised on this idea so that the characteristics of European society became one set of types, and the non-European the converse type.

This was the beginning of comparative sociology. By the second half of the eighteenth century, it was argued that progress was a global process involving the "development" of one type of society out of another. Clearly, if Europe was the pinnacle of this process or civilization, then, if this process did not proceed everywhere at the same pace, locations outside of Europe would contain the kind of society which was at a different stage in this development, one which European society had already passed through. This was the principle of multilineal evolution.

Social Order

Since the time of Locke and Machiavelli, there has emerged an argument about a new basis for social order. In line with what we have discussed above about the centrality of reason, it was claimed that natural laws would replace irrational domination whereby royalty ruled as a consequence of divine intervention. Thus what we see in the social philosophy that preceded the emergence of sociology is a prolonged political struggle that sought to replace one order by a new order. The new order claimed to replace the violent by the state of law and the market and drew on science in order to direct social life toward individual and collective needs. Within this context, modernism came to be understood as the diffusion of the products of rational, scientific, and technological administrative activity.

Prior to the French Revolution, power was exercised by the royal household and involved a stabilized relationship both between the royal line and the people and between royalty and the territory to which it pertained. However, the territorial dimension was tempered by the tendency to establish a European dimension through kinship allegiances constructed around the exchange of women. The royal household was defined by reference not merely to the royal line but also to the bourgeoisie and nobility of the robe who had been drawn into the household. The king was the symbol of the unity of his subjects, a unity which was defined as a collective "we." In many respects, despite an awareness that each "people" was distinct from any other, any conception of nation gave way to a European political space.

At the end of the eighteenth century, this conception was replaced by one that involved the creation of a new active role for a people by reference to their government. It involved creating a sense of nationhood that, regardless of any prior basis of difference, had to conform with the territory by creating common characteristics. The earlier conception of community as that in which social order was developed as a primordial quality gave way to the state as a community of citizens. The state became the sum of all of the communities within its territory, but with the difference that social order and social control now pertained to the state and not to the moral regulating force of community. The individual had to be transformed into a citizen with a conscious identity; the "good of the state" transformed the individual into a moral citizen. This transformation demanded political unity. Hobbes stated, ". . . if the general will is to be able to express itself, then there should be no partial society within the state. . . ."

Normativity

The centrality of evolutionism is focused on this conception of the moral citizen. It saw civilizing forces, and particularly Christianity, as moral forces, as those that drew humankind out of a state of nature in which the emotional prevailed. These emotions had to be controlled and channelled into reason, the very basis of development and civilization. If this could be achieved through reason as the force of modernity, then a modern state could be established. This modernity was evidently the converse of "tradition," which was conceived of as an allegiance to sentiments, customs, and beliefs that did not conform with reason. Thus the modern/traditional dichotomy that has been so central to sociology as a discipline and that has been so damaging to the interests of minorities was established. History came to be seen as that which has a reason-driven and -governed rationality in displacing tradition and particular allegiances in favor of the state. It is no coincidence that the concept of culture emerged in the eighteenth century, linked to civilization as a superior lifestyle and as a peaceful and orderly society. It was a force which strove to advance reason at the expense of the emotional in each individual. In association with education as the means of achieving this goal, culture became a tool in achieving social order and harmony. The triumph of progress was achieved by opposing modern and traditional cultures or societies. We thus find one sense of culture that pertains to the danger of a prevailing emotional condition and another that operates as a civilizing force. These cultures, in turn, align with different forms of society—the traditional and the modern—the first being emotional and thereby irrational and the other entirely rational and progressive.

A model of what was required in order to develop a state was premised on the joint ideas of a nation consisting of the will of the citizenry and a rationalism which conditions that will. This model was the basis for developing a normativity, or a sense of the acceptable norm within the state. It conformed with the principles of modernity and thereby was seen as modern rather than as traditional, the latter being that which had to be expunged. Because rationalism was conditioned by culture, normativity must relate to the cultural. As a consequence, it is also necessary to distinguish between rational, or modern, culture and traditional, or emotional, culture. Language played a central role in the construction of the normative.

Constructing Language as an Object

It is in this context that language attains importance both as a unifying force and as the means whereby the civilizing goal is achieved. However, a specific shift in the conception of language had first of all to be achieved. Each language is allocated an autonomous grammatical space so that languages can be compared without having to refer to signification. Also, they can be analyzed according to their internal structures, allowing the comparison of languages. Onto this shift was grafted the claim that logic or reason clarifies the thought of the individual and that grammar existed in order to ensure the correct correspondence between words and ideas, with the sequence of words correctly representing the sequence of thought on which it is based. Good language leads to good thinking. It leads to a focus on communication through grammar and on the importance of normative consensus, or the agreement across all peoples who use a particular language.

Classical Greece was personified as the exemplar of civilization and the Greek language as the epitome of reason. Other languages had to be modeled on Greek. Thus we find distinction between "languages of reason" and "languages of emotion," which lay outside of reason. Languages of emotion name the objects which strike the senses, whereas the languages of reason are languages in which one first names the subject, then the verb, and finally the object. French syntax, for example, was changed in order to develop the essential clarity: "French, by a unique privilege, lies faithful to the direct order. . . . French syntax is incorruptible. It is from this that its admirable clarity derives, the eternal base of our language. That which is not clear is not French" (quoted in Calvet, 1987:74, my translation).

The political nature of language planning and standardization derives from this change. It was repeated across Europe, leading to the Indo-European typology of languages constructed out of a kinship analogy involving people as families. There is no linguistic reason why there should have been so many languages designated as European languages; they could well have been limited to three. The issue of what is and is not a language is a political rather than a linguistic issue. As such it involves people, nation, character, and language. In accordance with the above argument, each state had to have its own language, in standard form, in order that it could be the vehicle whereby the people could be transformed into citizens through the "reason" which standard forms exemplified.

It becomes clear how evolution, the state, reason, language, and morality are intertwined. More important from our viewpoint is the manner in which the assumptions that underlie this explicitly political argument become the same principles on which sociology was founded. As such, sociology carries a distinctive state bias that is very important when we consider concepts such as ethnicity. It is exemplified in the manner in which the converse of the normative was constructed. It relates to language and culture in that those languages and cultures which were not deemed to be rational and were therefore not standardized were held to be emotional. Because language pertained both to the individual and to the collectivity that spoke it, it was possible to label people as emotive, as nonrational; that is, as nonnormative. This position was exemplified in the manner in which numerous states excluded those citizens who did not speak the relevant language of reason from participation in the democratic process, the epitome of a political system premised on reason.

Another problem arises. This labeling may well be fine in reference to populations outside of the state or outside of Europe that could be labeled as "primitive" in accordance with this argument. It was something else to label as "primitive" those people who did not speak the language of reason but who lived within the state. It is estimated that at the time of the French Revolution fewer than half of the population living within the territory of the French state spoke French. Such people could not be classified as outside of the state by reference to space, even if they could by reference to reason. Somehow they had to be incorporated, even if that incorporation sees them as sinister, as "strangers within." Such incorporation was achieved by referring to them as "traditional," as outmoded remnants on their way to becoming modern. All that was required was to remove their cultural attributes and replace them with the attributes which generated reason. Education and the various apparati of the state were geared to this end of creating a uniform normativity.

Sociology and Ethnicity

Sociology grew out of this body of thought, assimilating this metadiscourse into its conception of itself as the means of uncovering the laws which governed the social order. Sociology itself was a form of reason. There is a sense in which it can be claimed that sociology has merely reinterpreted the same discourse by reference to a social-analytical rather than an explicitly political context. It is hardly surprising, therefore, that the early principles of sociology involved designating a single society for each state. The setting of boundaries which had been based on a distinction between "us" and "them" was partly defined by reference to state territory, but the issue of the "stranger" within that state was quite different. It involved a commonality within which the peasantry was transformed into a unitary citizenry constructed out of a common language and a normative consensus. There was little room for any tolerance of diversity.

Sociology assumed these ideas by reference to the conception of society as a modern society constructed out of reason. Linked to modernity was the idea of modernization and, as we have already implied, a historicism that emphasized the relevance of forms of production and industrialization. Social problems were conceived of in terms of the struggle of the future against the past, whereas the internal functioning of society is explained in terms of its relationship to modernity. An explicitly political argument is transformed into an argument wherein the focus shifts from the state to society, whereas the driving force of progress, still retaining an appeal to reason, focuses on the process of industrialization. Industrial society becomes an evolutionary type, linked to the argument that if society is progressive, the converse of industrial society is a nonprogressive preindustrial society.

Within this single society with its normative consensus, any deviation had to be accommodated without permitting the social form to lie outside of that society. It was claimed that there were social differences which derived from the division of labor associated with industrialization, itself a source of great concern in early sociology. Whereas Comte claimed that specialization constituted a threat to orderly progress, Durkheim maintained that the division of labor leads to an increase in a new and higher form of social cohesion which he called organic solidarity. This new element of social binding grew alongside the more archaic mechanical solidarity that was based on a cohesion of individuals and that derived from similarity of *consciences*. Comte, a student of St. Simon, who shared the latter's view of ideology and sociocultural change, spoke of order and progress. He drew on a biological analogy in conceiving of society as a system consisting of parts, each of which carried a functional interrelationship to other parts and to the whole body. He never attempted a detailed analysis of any social system but rather drew on Condorcet's evolutionary stages and on a faith in the development of intellect as the driving force of progress, and, in so doing, dismissed those who were regarded as atavistic. In many respects, Comte can be claimed to be drawing on St. Simon's claim that a social system is merely the application of a system of ideas or a system of thought. By the time of Durkheim, the emphasis was very much on social solidarity. Yet both Comte and Durkheim shared a concern about the breakdown of social cohesion and order, and Durkheim argued for an evolutionism within which the transformation from one form of solidarity to the other ran parallel to the expansion of the legal and administrative apparatus of the state. For Durkheim, the consciousness of any individual derived from the consciousness of the group to which he or she belonged, claiming that it is from this group that social beliefs and practices derive. Social facts are "collective representations," or ideas experienced by the group mind and expressed or "reincarnated" in the minds and behavior of the individual members of the social group. Thus, because collective consciousness, or the idea of a group mind, derived from the cultural order, a nonnormative order was incapable of achieving the progressive organic solidarity. This organic solidarity was akin to the "nation" based on reason which each state had to create. The notion of society designated a concrete collectivity, defined by frontiers of recognized sources of authority or organs of application of laws and a conscience of belongingness, effectively making society, nation, and state coterminous. In the name of liberation and the genesis of a new society, it animated a struggle against what is labeled a "traditional society."

Because of the preoccupation with evolution, normativity, and social order, this theme of different bases of solidarity associated with the difference between the progressive modernity and the retrogressive tradition reappears in the work of others, including Toeniess' *Gemeinschaft* and *Gesellschaft*, Weber's formative and substantive rationality, and Linton's ascription and achievement. For all of these authors, the basis for defining the "modern" part of the pair of ideas is vague, with only traditional society being organized around a positively defining principle. The problem is not that a duality of social systems is constructed but rather that the systems are treated not as simply different but as superior or inferior. This is achieved by emphasizing a normativity linked to a concern with social and political order, a polarization of reason and emotion, and a weak evolutionary argument that justifies one against the other. In many respects, it can be claimed that sociology has always been the defense of modernity and rationalization in the name of the state and its nationalism.

This is where the concept of ethnicity is grounded. It is conceived with reference to a specific form of solidarity associated with the traditional order, this solidarity being the basis of specific kind of community. As such it constitutes a part society in that it cannot lie outside of society without lying beyond the social and territorial space of the state; it is also a part culture in that the culture of the state must be accessible to everyone, even if their primary allegiance and solidarity is to another cultural order. It is premised on a nonrational culture which contrasts to the rationalism of the standard culture.

The evolutionary thrust and the inevitability of change meant the inevitable demise of what is posited as an earlier form, this demise being a feature of its own failure or weakness. Thus the primordiality of an ethnicity constructed out of cultural difference would eventually disappear through contact with the forces of reason. Where the single society that existed within the state was associated with a rationally based normative consensus, there persisted cultural forces which were claimed to derive from a premodern past. These were the languages which somehow lay outside of reason in not being those which defined the normativity. They were the social forms which, in being labeled traditional, were linked to such languages. These existed within the same state, that is, in the same place at the same moment in time as the languages and speakers of reason, yet the two were judged to be "tradition" and "modern," respectively. Evidently, the dichotomy rested on a judgment about the superiority and preference of coexisting social and cultural forms. If progress was to be achieved and if the sanctity of the state was to be protected, the traditional had to be expurgated. Whereas the "us" of the state was largely defined by difference from the "them" of the stranger that was defined on the basis of state territory, there was also a far more dangerous "stranger" that was part of the "us." Its danger lay in its ability to present a claim for a rival nationalism constructed out of the emotive nature of culture and thereby present to itself as a claim for the existence of a rival state-within-a-state through its relationship to an allegiance based on different forms of the same elements that state-nationalism was constructed out of. However, because it was premised on emotion, such nationalism was particularly dangerous, being outside of the control of rational political agency. A struggle ensued between the forces which sought to gel the entire population of the state into a nation on the one hand and those who sought to retain the social and cultural integrity of difference on the other. The forces were heavily loaded against the latter, because all of the resources of the state, including sociology, were pitted against them. The entire field of knowledge that leads to constructing concepts such as assimilation and acculturation derives from this erroneous premise. It includes the entire body of work on language contact and the associated concepts of language shift. It involves an inability to conceive of language by reference to the social and an associated tendency to reify language, thinking of it as something with its own life and death!

As part society, ethnicity pertained to the traditional element. As such, it was a primordial allegiance that involved outmoded emotive attachment to an order that would, in time, disappear, giving way to an ill-defined modernity. It was an allegiance defined not by reason but by the emotive context of culture and was therefore defined by reference to a culture which served to resist the promotion of reason. In this respect, this culture contrasted with the high culture that was standardized, promoted, and sponsored by the state, leading to universal forms of language, of music or dance, based upon the classical. Any other cultural form, including language, was relegated to a demonic world imbued with emotion and somehow outside of reason. The goal of the study of ethnicity was that of discovering the nature of this culture so that it could be expurgated and the forces of reason accelerated in the name of progress. Failure to achieve this goal could lead to the rise of a subversive nationalism that could threaten the integrity of the state. Given this line of reasoning it is tempting to view sociology as akin to a state ideology charged with removing the internal enemy.

This line of reasoning assumed a particular orientation in North America. Conquest and colonialism had succeeded in negating the threat of the Native Americans; their culture was desecrated and neutered and the population herded into reservations. Yet there remained the problem of creating a normativity out of diverse cultural backgrounds. Whereas in Europe this normativity tended to be that of the dominant autochthonous population within the state territory, it was not so clear-cut in North America because the autochthonous population had been conquered as "primitives." There was not only the problem of how to establish normativity but also that of how to generate conformity across the entire population. Sociology responded to the challenge through the assimilation/acculturation thesis and concepts such as nation building. Early American sociologists such as Lloyd Warner or Leo Srole assumed that in a matter of one or two generations immigrants would be assimilated into what was seen to be a plural society. This involved acculturation to a secular culture and then assimilation, which was presented as the end point of the acculturation process, with any features of cultural distinctiveness disappearing into the melting pot of the overarching society.

The associated normativity was meant to be a reflection of the melting pot of culture generated by the range of immigrations from different parts of the world. What emerged was in effect what has been termed WASP culture—a normativity based on white Anglo-Saxon Protestantism. The American Revolution was a means of creating a modern state based on the rational principles of modernity while simultaneously redressing the negative effects of colonialism. The manner in which all of the state's resources were mobilized in order to assert this normativity suggests that the state was never meant to be a multicultural paradise premised on a conception of freedom that lauded the deviant. Such had not been the case in Europe; why should it have been in a new world constructed from conquest and miscegenation? However, perhaps toleration was not the issue; if the claim is made that the primordiality of minority culture will inevitably succumb to the forces of modernity and reason, the issue is more one of failing to promote the survival of minority culture. Yet this normativity was challenged from within both by the polarity that led to the Civil War and subsequently by blacks, Native Americans, and Chicanos.

In many respects, it can be claimed that whereas sociology in the nineteenth century belonged to Europe and reflected European concerns, sociology in the twentieth century has been the concern of the Americas. The prominence of the Chicago School and the subsequent monopolization of mainstream sociology by Talcott Parsons and his associates, even though they drew on the European founders of sociology, has given the discipline a distinctive orientation. Yet we should not forget that Parsons owed a legacy to both Comte and Durkheim. It is from the same legacy that the modernization thesis that dominated Parsons's work and that I discuss below derives. It was a thesis which claimed that modern politics was based on individual achievement rather than ascription. It was articulated by reference to nation building in the work of Karl Deutsch, who saw modernization as a unilinear development toward a secular, industrial nation-state and the associated modern, participating society. True to its French roots, there was little room for diversity. As the early work of Clifford Geertz emphasized, primordiality was the essence of ethnicity and was doomed to disappearance with the modernization of society. The net result was a necessary ethnic purification.

Within this perspective, language and identity are linked in a specific way. Identity is premised on the idea of the rational being consciously expressing what he or she feels or he or she is. Of course, given that ethnicity was premised on the emotional, then such an identity was an expression of an emotional attachment to the irrational. It was dynamic in the sense that it was inevitably subject to change, forever merging increasingly with the rationalism of modernity. The relationship between language and identity involved the separation of language and thought, a separation which had existed at least since the time of Bacon. The individual person was the creator of his or her own thought, which he or she expressed through language. The relationship between the mind and language involved the kind of psychologism in which language merely serves as a conveyor of thought. However, language was also cultural and thereby related to ethnicity in the sense that it conditioned the thought of the individual while also expressing it. Speech became the expression of social convention or norms, and, as such, language exists outside of the social. Thus two things follow. First, an analysis of speech leads to discovering the nature of the identity that is being expressed; and second, the analysis also uncovers the cultural and social context of expression or the nature of both a social and a cultural identity. That is, language is representational and, as such, signifies the rational intention of the human subject.

The Ethnic Revival

What has been termed the "new ethnicity" was not new but rather involved a reassertion of a positive conception of what sociology had constructed as negative. It was a reaction to sociology's tendency to "blame the victim." It coincided with, and fed off, a parallel revolution that rejected the orthodox conception of the relationship between the First World and the Third World. What these two strands shared was a rejection of the orthodox understanding of the relationship between evolution, progress, and reason.

The modernization thesis which derived from Parsonian structural functionalism was premised on the inherent superiority of First World culture. It argued for the same diffusionism and homogenization expressed by states across the world. In order to "develop" through modernization, the Third World had to become the mirror image of the developed West. Latin American sociologists and economists such as Andre Gunnar Frank, Francisco Cardoso, and Oswaldo Sunkel resorted to the arguments of Leninist Marxism in developing what became known as "dependency theory," a perspective which refuted the modernization thesis. They argued that the underdevelopment of the Third World was not the consequence of cultural deficiency, as the modernization thesis claimed, but of a structural relationship between the West and the Third World which served to foster a particular form of dependent relationship. This claim broke with the orthodox paradigm of a unilinear, evolutionary relationship between modern and traditional.

This theme was taken up by Emanuel Wallerstein in his portrayal of the world by reference to a capitalist world system characterized by different regions—core, periphery, semiperiphery—which served different functions within the system in consolidating a series of dependent spatial relationships. Michael Hechter, a student of Wallerstein, applied dependency theory to Europe and in so doing focused on ethnicity. Again, he challenged sociological orthodoxies in arguing that ethnicity was not an atavistic entity in an inevitable process of recession in confronting modernity but was a variable capable of being rationally mobilized for specific purposes. This simple observation meant that it was no longer possible to treat ethnicity as an allegiance to the irrational. It allowed Hechter to reject diffusionism and to integrate social class divisions with culturally based differences in the influential concept of the cultural division of labor. His book *Internal Colonialism* (1975) outlined the nature of the division of labor in the Celtic nations. Together with Frantz Fanon's *The Wretched of the Earth*, it became a major seller in Wales and Ireland. It was also influential in Scotland and Catalonia, despite these places being viewed as overdeveloped rather than underdeveloped peripheral locations. It was a major influence on Tom Nairn's book *The Break of Britain*, which was also important for ethnic studies during the 1970s.

During the 1970s, a series of authors extended such arguments. The anthropologist Frederik Barth had already argued that ethnicity was not a primordial pregiven but was often a matter of self-selection and transference. It led him to discuss ethnic groups by reference to boundaries engendered by a subjective "we" which conditions objective delimiters. Working with immigrant groups in the United States, Edna Bonacich drew upon the concept of the split labor market in demonstrating how group identity premised on cultural differences enters the relations of production by segmenting the labor market and promoting class fragmentation. Williams (1992) argued that control over the means of production by an ethnic group was an important ingredient in sustaining the diacritica of ethnicity and that language prestige, or the value of a language for social mobility, was a central feature of language production and reproduction. Benedict Anderson (1983) claimed that nations were "imagined communities" because all members could not possibly know one another, even though the nation was premised on a sense of comradeship.

These two lines of argument, one emphasizing the material function of ethnicity and the other its subjective support, were part of a wider political climate. The arguments of the Black Power activists and general anticulturalism of the 1960s had considerable influence in articulating the way many people who were classified as "ethnic minorities" felt about how the orthodox arguments constructed them. In Europe, the relaxing of centrist authoritarian regimes such as Franco's Spain opened up political and economic space. The intellectual work associated with these developments owed a great deal to Marxism, which was seen as a problematic that lay on the margins of the prevailing sociological orthodoxies. Yet it is important to recognize that Marxism shares many of the assumptions that derive from eighteenth- and nineteenth-century political philosophy with other sociological perspectives. It is evolutionist, functionalist, and statist. Where it stands out is in its emphasis on the ideological basis of consciousness, and it was this thrust, together with the relationship between infrastructure and superstructure, which was most important in the developments discussed above. Particularly relevant in this respect was the translation of Antonio Gramsci's *Prison Notebooks* into English in 1971. Yet there is also a sense in which the Marxist concept of ideology claims that individuals are not free to form their own identity and thereby to rationally mobilize it as a resource. It also tends to prioritize social class relations which conform with the equation of state and society. Again we encounter the argument that ethnic identity gives way through evolution to class consciousness, an argument which conformed with the orthodox claim that individual action is normatively determined. These were the ideas inherited from the eighteenth and nineteenth centuries that sociologists were obliged to struggle with in reaching the conclusion that different facets of social inequality had to be dealt with simultaneously. Rarely did these ideas spill over into the sociology of language, but there were exceptions.

While the "new ethnicity" did challenge some of the assumptions of mainstream sociology, most notably the idea of primordiality, it also persisted in many of its questionable assumptions. Indeed, on reflection, the new ethnicity in some respects seems remarkably similar to the "old ethnicity." Most notably there remains the idea that there is a qualitative difference between social groups constituted out of different bases—social class and the economic order, gender and the biological order, ethnicity and the cultural order. This relates to two assumptions: first, that priority should be assigned to the economic order, and, second, that the economic activity is not, simultaneously, a social activity. This view is currently in retreat, as is the view that gender behavior is biologically constructed. Together with the demise of evolutionism and historical teleology, these developments are important for the study of ethnicity in that they challenge the distinction between subjective and objective categories. They lead sociologists to question why groups which they categorize as pertaining to the ethnic domain require a different orientation and, indeed, a different methodological approach than do groups which pertain to the domain of social class. It leads to questioning the assumption that ethnic groups are constituted by a cultural deviation from the norm, whether that deviation is a matter of self- or other categorization. It begs the question of why they cannot be treated as normative categories, albeit a normativity that challenges state normativity. Of course, this line of questioning eventually leads to an awareness of the relationship between normativity, ideology, and the state on the one hand and of the role of sociology on the other in this relationship. It begins to challenge the monolithic relationship between culture and society and even leads to reevaluating the importance of diversity. In turn, it leads to the demise of concepts such as ethnonationalism or cultural nationalism that suggest deviation from the rationality of normative or political nationalism.

The new ethnicity has persisted in assuming the nonnormative nature of ethnicity while rejecting the judgmental relationship between the normative and the nonnormative that derived from evolutionism. It has led to a range of approaches to the study of ethnicity that focused on the nature of subjectivity, studies which ranged from the symbolic to the constructivist. Within sociolinguistics, it fostered a range of simplistic orientations that persisted in linking reason and behavior, leading to different avenues of inquiry concerning the strategic use of language by rational subjects mobilizing different identities. The use of minority languages was seen as ethnic in the sense that it was an expression of a desire to remain nonnormative or deviant. There was a failure to view them as a manifestation of a different conception of normative. In this respect, studies of language and ethnicity tend to be reduced to a kind of psychologism that somehow seems detached from sociology, requiring distinctive methodologies. The ethnic is marginalized, not merely by reference to the normative of society but also by reference to the orthodox practices of sociology and sociolinguistics, where it is treated as a residual category. The extreme of this tendency is that the same social actors seem to be treated differently within these social sciences according to which language they use, being "ethnics" when using the minority language and "normal" when using the state language.

Sociology and sociolinguistics seem systematically incapable of treating a society constituted out of nonnormative diacritica as being of relevance to their customary practices because they begin from the assumption that it is a part society with a part culture. It is not ethnicity or the ethnic subject that is the problem, but sociology itself. The social is treated as outside of language or discourse and the sociological as something separate from language. It generates a strange relationship between the sociologist and both language and discourse. Language becomes no more than a tool for the expression of the concerns of sociology, and, as such, it is also a phenomenon that can be studied. However, the sociological discourse as a constructing discourse is not included in such a study except within its own terms. It is this exclusion that poststructuralism redresses. The new ethnicity is in demise as sociologists adopt a new approach.

Poststructuralism

Unfortunately, space precludes a thorough discussion of poststructuralism and its relevance for ethnicity and language.[2] Nonetheless, we would not be doing the subject justice without at least a cursory glance at the relevant issues. It should be clear from the preceding that sociology has always assumed that behavior is the product of rational subjects fully in control of their own actions. Sociology became the study of patterned behavior. The same line of thinking claimed that human subjects produce their own knowledge and act in accordance with it. Thus there is a truth and reality which exists independently of language, with people using language in order to encounter and discover this truth and knowledge. During the 1960s, French authors such as Jacques Derrida, Michel Foucault, Roland Barthes, and Jacques Lacan reversed this assumption, claiming that the human subject did not preexist knowledge and therefore was incapable of producing it. The individual is not capable of the self-knowledge that Enlightenment philosophy claims. Reality is something that is constructed in and through discourse. Thus the reflective individual, generating an identity which becomes an expression of ethnicity, also cannot exist. It leads to a distinctive approach to the social construction of meaning, with distinctive conceptions of both language and identity.

A distinction is made between language and discourse. Language is viewed as a form which carries infinite possibilities of meaning, whereas discourse is the point at which these possibilities are activated within social practice. If I say, "it is cold," and somebody closes the window, then my statement has had an effect as a consequence of a certain meaning for my statement having been constituted. There is the assumption that this is not the only meaning possible for that statement and that the objects, such as "Wales," which are used in discourse carry a number of possible meanings—as a region, as a nation, and so forth. Meaning is not the fixed quality of the dictionary. Thus the individual subject does not relate to "real" objects that exist in some world independent of the act of stating. Meanings can become stabilized, but even these stabilized meanings will be subject to contest because, essentially, meaning is always ambiguous.

Meaning is not only not fixed but it is also not assigned by preexisting subjects, as in the orthodox conception of semantics. This condition is true because the subjects are also created in and through discourse. In writing a paper for a publication that discusses the relationship between sociology and ethnicity, I have been constructed as a sociologist by the discourse, which simultaneously establishes other subjects— the student, the reader, the publisher, the editor, and so forth—and also other objects to which these subjects relate, such as other disciplines, the world, the university, and so forth. Thus the relationships between subjects and objects are always shifting and are always beyond the control of the rational human subject. Of course, the stabilizing of some of these relationships derives from prior discourses, from the past, and the subject relates to the traces of these prior discourses. Thus the relationship between the student and the university may have been quite different 400 years ago than it is today. Nonetheless, for the past 200 years it has tended to be stabilized, and this stability feeds into the way this relationship between the student as subject and the university as an associated object is constructed today.

Language now becomes something quite different from the way in which it is constructed within the modernist discourse. The distinction between language and the social collapses, the emphasis upon discourse as the point at which meaning is constituted, means that the language act is simultaneously a social act. The individual subject is no longer able to manipulate language for some preconceived goal. I will not enter into the manner in which this leads to a distinctive form of linguistics that focuses on the relationship between time, space, and person and an emphasis on signification but will merely state that sociolinguistic analysis takes a new direction that focuses on clarifying how different discourses relate to each other and how each discursive formation constitutes the subject-object relationship in different ways.

This direction of clarification does have profound implications for sociology and for language and ethnicity. Sociology now does not lie outside of discourse as some independent entity that can be drawn on in order to analyze what happens in some "real" world. Rather, it also must be subject to analysis and deconstruction. This is sometimes profoundly disturbing for those sociologists who think that their identity is constructed out of this independence. Ethnicity is now discussed by reference to how it is constructed by sociology and sociologists and how it, in turn, relates to the ethnic subjects which are similarly constructed and constituted. Language becomes central to the analysis of the discourses which are central to these constructions. It is no longer an object that somehow exists independently of discourse.

Conclusion

This chapter has sought to uncover the assumptions associated with the concept of ethnicity, assumptions which are stabilized in sociology as a discipline. It has claimed that the ethnocentrism of the state constructs an "Other" as deviant from the normative order. This is sustained by a series of assumptions and constructions which are an integral feature of sociology writ large. It leads to a suspicion of what is constructed as "the stranger within," and a state which presents itself as the guardian of a social order that is a manifestation of a normative consensus that finds difficulty in tolerating the stranger.

Current processes of political and economic restructuring in Europe highlight the problem. The deregulation of the economy in order to make Europe competitive as a geo-economic force diminishes the role and relevance of the state. The associated processes of European integration and the rolling back of the state within the prevailing neoliberal discourse reinforces this tendency. As a consequence, the region is being redefined, raising questions about the nature of the preconstructed— is it a state region or a European region? The sociological premise of a single society for each state is thrown into doubt by the drive to create a European society. It leads to questions about the normativity associated with this protosociety and of the deviations from it that constitute the ethnic. Such issues highlight the dilemma of a sociology constructed out of eighteenth-century political principles.

Questions for Further Thought and Discussion

1. To what extent is it possible to claim that the concept of ethnicity is offensive to the people to whom it pertains?

2. If ethnicity is constructed by sociology, and if it is constructed in such a way that it is detrimental to those to whom the term applies, to what extent can it be claimed that sociology is implicated in the political?

3. Consider the implications of the manner in which "language" was conceived in the eighteenth century for subsequent developments of linguistics as a discipline. To what extent can we claim that linguistics is value-free and objective?

4. If we are correct in suggesting that it is the process of language standardization that has been responsible for constructing languages, what are the consequences for linguistic science? Should it be rethought as a political science?

5. To what extent can it be claimed that the difficulty of accommodating the new ethnicity into sociology lies with the manner in which sociology has been constructed and that the new ethnicity constitutes little more than a reconstitution of the old ethnicity?

6. Consider the extent to which studies of ethnic identity rest on a misplaced understanding of the nature of identity.

7. Seek out the sociological definitions of normativity and social order and consider the nature of the relationship between them before considering the implications for ethnicity and nationalism.

8. If there is no truth or reality outside of discourse or the way in which we talk about people (subjects) and things (objects), what are the implications for sociolinguistics?

9. If ethnicity is conceived of as difference from the normative, why should members of ethnic groups be concerned about relinquishing that which makes them different?

10. Given that there is only one society for each state and that ethnicity is defined by reference to the normativity of the state, if the current state structure in Europe is yielding to a proto-European sociopolitical order, what are the implications for ethnicity in Europe?

Notes

1. The difference between the French and German conceptions is important in that it conditions the different ways in which "nation" is understood. Nonetheless, it is the French conception that has been the mainstay of sociology.

2. For a further discussion, see Williams, 1998.

Selected Bibliography

Anderson, B. (1983). *Imagined Communities: Reflections on the Origin and Spread of Nationalism.* London: Verso.

Barth, F. (ed.) (1969). *Ethnic Groups and Boundaries: The Social Organisation of Cultural Difference.* Boston: Little Brown.

Calvet, L. J. (1987). *La guerre de la Langue.* Paris: Payot.

Deutsch, K. (1966). *Nationalism and Social Communication.* Cambridge: MIT Press.

Glazer, N., and D. P. Moynihan (eds.) (1975). *Ethnicity: Theory and Experience.* Cambridge: Harvard University Press.

Hechter, M. (1975). *Internal Colonialism: The Celtic Fringe in British National Development, 1536–1966.* London: Routledge and Kegan Paul.

Tiryakin, E., and R. Rogowski (eds.) (1985). *New Nationalisms of the Developed West.* London: Allen and Unwin.

Touraine. A., et al. (1981). *Le Pays Contre l'Etat.* Paris: Seuil.

Williams, G. (1992). *The State and the Ethnic Community.* Cardiff: University of Wales Press.

Williams, G. (1998). *French Discourse Analysis: The Method of Poststructuralism.* London: Routledge.

Second-Language Learning

BERNARD SPOLSKY

Second-language learning is the process by which an individual who has, during the first few years of life, acquired one language (or, often, more than one language) from his or her caretakers or peers goes on to add one or more new languages to his or her repertoire. The context of learning might be informal intercourse with people using a different language, or the organized instruction of an educational system, or a program of self-instruction, or a combination of these. From the point of view of such a broadly defined field of second-language learning, language and ethnicity can be looked at in two ways. First, we can ask how those asserting ethnicity (in revival movements, for instance) have needed to become involved in language teaching. Second, we can look at the influence that the ethnic revival and heightened understanding of language and ethnicity have had on the field of second-language learning.

Because language is fundamental in defining identity, it is inevitable that ethnic revivals become involved in language matters. The renewed debate over Black English (or Ebonics, if you prefer the term) is a continuation, in another context, of the struggle for definitions of identity. Among the Crusaders, the national groups were called "langues," so that the German-speaking Templar Knights lived separately from the French-speaking majority. The Talmud remarks that one of the ways that the children of Israel maintained their identity during their period of slavery in Egypt was by not giving up their language. Language is a central feature of human identity. When we hear someone speak, we immediately make guesses about gender, educational level, age, profession, and place of origin. Beyond this individual matter, a language is a powerful symbol of national and ethnic identity.

Language maintenance or revival, therefore, is commonly a central component of an ethnic movement. Very often, the worry about language arises because external and internal social, political, economic, and cultural pressures have forced or drawn members of the ethnic community away from their traditional language (Fishman 1989). The task of reversing, halting, or even slowing the shift away from a traditional ethnic language calls for active language teaching (Fishman 1991). The ethnic movement has to make up for language loss that occurs when young people do not acquire full competence in the ethnic language. Thus the first obvious point of intersection between the ethnic revival and second-language learning is in the elaboration of programs intended to teach the threatened ethnic language to members of the ethnic community.

In the nineteenth century, nationalist movements were regularly plunged into campaigns to revive or standardize national vernaculars. In much the same way, more recent ethnic revival movements are often obligated to try to restore the place and use of language varieties that are becoming obsolete (Haugen 1966. Language loss is a fact of life (and death) for modern ethnic groups. Linguists are convinced that the large majority of languages spoken in the world today should be classified as endangered and fear that half of them will be extinct within 100 years (Krauss 1991). Thirty years ago, we estimated that 95% of five-year-old Navajo children knew their language. Now, we suspect that 30% of this age group do not know Navajo and that this proportion is increasing rapidly. Stories like this can be repeated about many languages. To reverse this trend, supporters of ethnic revival movements are forced to develop a core of language teaching expertise. To illustrate this point, the next section of this chapter will look at some typical examples.

There is a second side to the story. Those of us concerned with the field of second-language learning have been forced by the ethnic revival and by our new appreciation of language and ethnicity to extend our concerns to embrace the social context in which the teaching takes place. We do this reluctantly, for we naturally prefer the neatness of parsimonious explanations. It is much simpler to restrict a model of language learning to linguistics (which should tell us all about language) and psychology (which should complement this by telling us all about learning) and not have to add all the complexity of the social world. But, as we will see in the final section of this chapter, language teaching activities associated with ethnic movements have started to add a new socially relevant dimension to their previously apolitical second-language-learning theory and practice. Foreign- and second-language teachers have been challenged to recognize the political effects of their customary work. Whereas they had thought they were neutral and academically objective, they found their professional occupation supporting the spread of imperial and world languages and contributing to the demise of powerless languages (Skutnabb-Kangas 1996). By observing how social context, identity, and attitudes influenced second-language learning, they were led to develop richer theories and better practices. In the long run, it may well be that these ethnically inspired sociolinguistic influences on language learning and teaching theory and practice last longer and have a deeper effect than the generally more highly honored influence of changes in linguistic theory that went on at the same time, for they deal not just with the *what* and the *how*, but the very *why* of language learning.

Second-Language Learning
and Teaching in the Ethnic Revival

Other chapters of this book have given many examples of ethnically motivated efforts to maintain the strength of languages associated with ethnic revival movements. Here, I will simply touch on three cases to give some notion of the kind of language teaching and learning involved in ethnic revival and of its successes and failures. The first is the Zionist program at the end of the nineteenth century to revitalize Hebrew as a national language for the Jewish people and for a new state. The second is the twentieth-century Irish program to revive knowledge of Irish outside of the *Gaeltacht*, where it was still spoken. The third is the recent movement in New Zealand in favor of the revival of the Maori language. In each of these cases, the revival or maintenance of an extinct or dying language became a central feature of a policy of reestablishing identity. In each case, the revivers had to add programs for teaching the language to their work. Interestingly, in order to meet their goals, all seem to have been led to similar programmatic choices.

In the Zionist case, the policy of revitalizing and revernacularizing Hebrew, a language that had been generally restricted to formal and written use for some 1500 years, became a key component of the restoration of national Jewish identity. "You're Hebrew, speak Hebrew" was the slogan of the movement (Spolsky 1996). The ideologists were soon forced to add to their enterprise the demanding task of teaching young children to speak a written literary language. The teachers in the pioneering Hebrew teaching schools in the Jewish agricultural settlements in the late nineteenth century had no model for their assignment. They themselves had learned to read Hebrew in traditional ways, from teachers who continued to speak with them in their mother tongue, Yiddish. It is easy to imagine their difficulties in starting to speak Hebrew themselves and in then trying to develop similar skills in young children.

Two programmatic innovations seem to have been of great benefit. The first was finding a way to increase the time available for teaching the language. This they did by starting school a year earlier than normal, adding a kindergarten year to the curriculum. At this younger age, children are often more open to being spoken to in a new language. The second innovation was to adopt an idea that was becoming accepted among teachers of modern languages at the end of the nineteenth century. This idea was to use the target language, Hebrew, as the language of instruction in the classroom. Traditional foreign-language teaching, drawing on the methods by which literary languages like Latin, Greek, and Hebrew had long been taught, assumed that the teacher would use his or her and the pupil's own mother tongue to teach the vocabulary and grammar of the target language. This achieved quite good success in developing reading ability, but once the aim was to develop ability to use the language in speech, it was necessary for the teacher and pupils to speak the target language from the beginning. This new approach, called the "direct method" in the second-language professional literature, was probably learned by the early Zionist teachers from Berlitz schools in which it was practiced.

Besides these two new methods, the revitalization of Hebrew depended on the strength of ideological commitment on the part of teachers and parents. Their fervor was transmitted rapidly to the young pupils, who came to feel themselves to be pioneers in their use of the revitalized language outside school. In twenty years or so, starting in 1890, the "miracle" was accomplished. The status of Hebrew as the public language of the Jewish community of Palestine was firmly entrenched by the start of the British mandate in 1920. The earliest textbooks and curricula may have been naive and limited, with short lists of words to be learned, but the insistence on using only Hebrew in the classroom, the extra year provided by an early start, and the unwavering commitment to the ideological significance of learning Hebrew were critical elements leading to an unusual success.

The Irish efforts at restoring Irish language use in the large sections of the country where people had switched to English were largely focused on formal education (O Laoire 1996). The school system had come under the authority of the Irish republican government after independence from British rule. Many different language teaching approaches were tried, ranging from the formal teaching of the language using the methods that were regularly used for foreign languages to serious efforts at offering bilingual education with instruction offered in both Irish and English. For the large proportion of students, Irish seems to have remained a school subject, something to be studied. It was compulsory for annoying, although important, examinations, but it failed to become a language to be used outside school. In those schools which actually taught Irish in Irish, results were much better, but there was a marked lack of public enthusiasm for such schools. The very existence of an Irish-speaking remnant in the poorer parts of Ireland certainly did not help. In recent years, there has been a new interest in preschool immersion programs, teaching the language to young children in school-created Irish environments. Where there is ideological commitment, the combination of early start and using the target language as language of instruction seems to promise success.

A third case is the indigenous language of New Zealand, Maori (Spolsky 1996). The Maori language held on moderately well for the first years after white settlement of New Zealand in 1840, boosted by the growth of a high standard of literacy in the language that was encouraged by missionaries. Starting in the 1860s, however, the government started to impose strong pressure to use English. A period of resulting English-Maori bilingualism gave way to a rapid shift to English in the mid-1930s. By 1960, the proportion of Maori children growing up speaking the language began to decline rapidly; there were few native speakers under the age of thirty. The only existing school programs were formal classes taught at the secondary level.

In the 1980s, some Maoris who were alarmed by their loss of linguistic identity initiated a preschool program for language revival. Conducted in local community and church halls by grandparents who still spoke the language, these *kohanga reo*, or "language nests," provided day care and informal Maori language practice for children whose parents did not themselves speak the language. The movement grew rapidly, so that very soon most communities had at least one language nest in operation. As a result of the success of the program, many parents wanted their children to continue acquiring Maori when they transferred to regular elementary school.. With some encouragement from the Ministry of Education, bilingual or immersion programs were opened in a number of schools. The teachers were usually older experienced teachers who had themselves spoken Maori as children but who had not had occasion to use it throughout their teaching careers. Again, the pattern that seems to have most to offer involves intensive programs that start very early and provide the children with immersion in the ethnic language.

For some supporters of the Maori ethnic revival movement, even these immersion programs, operating more or less autonomously within a state school, have not gone far enough. In a number of regions, taking advantage of the government's concern to bolster Maori rights and to make up for years of neglect and also of a policy to decentralize education, these supporters have set up independent schools, *kura kaupapa*, that are attempting to recreate Maori knowledge and content for the curriculum, as well as to present the educational program in Maori. Although it is true that the large bulk of efforts concerned with Maori ethnic revival has been put into political and economic concerns, it is also true that a good deal of work is going into attempting to reestablish the vitality of the Maori language.

As different as the three cases are, they have in common that they are attempts to find formal and informal solutions to the problem of increasing the ability of group members to know and to use an endangered ethnic language. They also make clear how hard the task is: Programs that do not make the same commitment of ideology and time and effort are unlikely to achieve success.

Language revival movements have generally faced one or both of two tasks. The first is the intricate operation of attempting to restore lost normal intergenerational transmission, working to reestablish the language as a home language or mother tongue, passed naturally from parents to children. This task we may label either *vernacularization*, taking a formal literary language and making it a spoken vernacular, or *revitalization*, restoring vitality or the status of being a mother tongue. The second task is to take a vital, spoken vernacular and transform it into a standard language that can be used for a wide range of literacy and higher functions. This task involves both *modernization* and *standardization*. For most vernacular languages introduced into education, this involves the development of a vast new set of words to handle all the concepts of modern life. For others, like Maori, it also involves answering the question of which dialect to favor in school programs.

Along with these needs to modify the language, there is the equally daunting problem of teaching it. Commonly, ethnic revival language programs start by teaching the writing system and the formal grammar and the vocabulary of the ethnic language in traditional formal ways. The possible but limited success of such an approach was demonstrated by the Irish revival program, which produced more and more people who knew Irish. Its weakness, though, was shown by the fact that increased knowledge of Irish did not result in greater use of it. As a result, more and more ethnic revival language programs have found it necessary to alter the method of teaching and to adopt (at the very least) a direct method or immersion approach, teaching the language in the language, and adding to this as conditions permit the kind of intensity of instruction that may claim the label of immersion teaching.

Beyond the issue of teaching, as numerous studies have shown, the support of the educational system is a necessary condition for language maintenance, but it is not a sufficient condition. Success requires at the least ideological and institutional support from the wider community. Here, especially, identity issues are paramount, for the value of ethnic membership plays a large role in determining what effort people will make to learn, teach, and use the ethnic language.

Effects of the Ethnic Revival on Second-language Learning

Our concern in this section is with the effects that the ethnic revival has had on the field of second-language learning. The simplest and most obvious answer is the way that it has forced scholars interested in second-language teaching and learning to visualize the field in its complex social settings and to recognize the critical human and social values that identity in general and ethnic identity in particular impart to all second-language learning (Spolsky 1989). This new contextualization shows up in a number of different ways, which will be considered now in turn.

Second- and Foreign-language Learning

One important modification has been to blur the once simple distinction between teaching a *foreign* language and teaching a *second* language. Traditionally, *foreign*-language teaching and learning referred to the approach developed when a select few major European languages of high culture were allowed in the schools as a replacement for the teaching of classical languages such as Latin. *Second*-language teaching and learning, on the other hand, was the development of functional competence in a language used within the same community or country. Although this distinction is sometimes still useful, it is often now the case that elements of both types of teaching and learning are involved.

The blurring of the distinctions is one effect of the enormous increase in immigration over the past half century. How can Spanish be considered a foreign language in the United States when it is so widely used by so many Hispanic immigrants and citizens? How can the teaching of Arabic in Israel ignore the Arabic-speaking minority or the extensive use of Arabic in the region? How can English be considered a foreign language in countries in which it has become established as the language for commerce and higher education?

Putting aside the older simple differentiation between foreign-language learning and second-language learning, the ethnic revival and the associated multilingual and multicultural patterns have challenged second-language pedagogy to acknowledge the relevance of elaborate functional profiles of linguistic skills and knowledge. In complex modern multilingual societies (and almost all societies nowadays fit this description), we use a number of different languages and varieties to a range of different purposes. When we learn another language, it is to use it for some of these purposes, whether it may be for social interaction or for educationally and economically valuable skills in accessing information or for presenting information orally or in writing. The simple dichotomy between second and foreign languages does not let us capture the necessary richness of these dimensions. The ethnic revival, then, encouraged us to see and to teach language in its social context.

Additive and Replacive Teaching

There has been another related effect. To the extent that foreign languages in schools were a substitute for classical languages, the teaching was usually premised on the assumption that the language was an addition to a home language already known and used by the students. In the traditional approach, one added Latin or Hebrew or Sanskrit or classical Arabic to a student's linguistic repertoire with the intention that it be used in specific formal situations and for defined purposes. True, the classical or foreign language had a higher status, the status accorded to languages of culture and civilization. But there was rarely the assumption that the newly taught language should completely replace the learner's home or regular vernacular, spoken at home and in normal social life.

In *second*-language teaching, however, the much higher status of the language being taught and the accordingly lower status of the home language encouraged a replacive approach. This was particular true when the target language was a colonial or imperial language that was believed to be a "correct" and better language than the home language (Phillipson 1992). Just as the standard variety is often taught as though it were intended to replace the local dialect, so an imperial or international second language is commonly taught as if it were intended to replace the home language. This outlook has clearly played a major role in the annihilation of hundreds of languages.

A more sensitive appreciation of language and ethnicity encourages an additive rather than a replacive approach. Just as a person normally has multiple allegiances that form a complex personal identity, so a rich linguistic repertoire includes linguistic reflexes of these various networks. Until the ethnic revival, the field of second- or foreign-language learning and teaching took the issue of additive or replacive language learning for granted. Foreign-language teaching was normally agreed to be additive. One learned a foreign language in order to add to one's skills of communication or to provide additional access to other cultures or bodies of knowledge or people. Knowing a foreign language was an supplementary qualification, and no one was expected to shift linguistic identity.

In second-language teaching situations, in contrast, there was commonly an automatic assumption that a valued standard language, associated with a dominant culture, should replace the use of the less prestigious mother tongue. This pattern has developed in many areas of the world: Native Mexican Indian languages have been replaced by Spanish; Russian replaced national languages during the period of Soviet domination; English was learned as a replacement for the various Indian languages among highly educated upwardly mobile Indians; French was seen as a desirable replacement for Arabic in North Africa. The effect of the ethnic revival has been to open up this question again, not only in cases where there is now government action to reverse the shift away from the ethnic language (as in the former Soviet republics) but even where the ethnic movements lack political power.

The Canon (Repertoire)

The ethnic revival movement has also made a contribution to the choice of what languages should be taught, resulting in an expanding canon or repertoire of languages taught in schools. The original set of languages to be taught was quite limited. In countries under imperial rule, the first choice was set—English in the British Empire, Russian in the Soviet Union, French in their colonies. In officially bilingual countries, there was also a forced choice: Swedish or Finnish in Finland, English or Afrikaans in South Africa, French or German in Switzerland. But beyond this, foreign-language teaching was commonly restricted to a handful of Western European languages of high culture, usually English, French, Spanish, or German. Occasionally, as in the United States in conditions created by the Second World War and the cold war that followed, government interest led to the creation of a wider range of language programs, such as those developed for Asian, African, and Middle Eastern languages (Lambert 1994).

The ethnic revival boosted these programs and added many others. The growth of Spanish into the major "foreign" language taught in schools in the United States was induced by the rapid growth of Spanish-speaking communities. The teaching of Arabic and Chinese was encouraged by swelling immigrant and ethnic communities. Hebrew and Greek owed much to the strong support of community groups. The teaching of Swahili was perhaps as much to be attributed to Afro-American ethnic movements as to an interest in African languages per se.

One of the important effects of the ethnic revival on language teaching, then, was the increase in the number of languages taught and the addition to the foreign-language repertoire of languages that had previously been of very minor interest to the academy. Because most of these languages were new, the teachers and their methodologies tended to be new, and the emphasis commonly moved from the written to the spoken language. All this led to changes in approaches to second- and foreign-language learning and teaching.

Cultural and Practical Goals

In spite of these changes at the periphery of the curriculum, the bulk of school formal foreign-language programs has nonetheless continued to be dominated by a few languages and by the traditional cultural goals beloved of the literature departments that in most countries still control language teaching. The drop in enrollment in these traditional literature-related programs in the United States and England is often blamed on the insensitivity of established departments to the growing demands for more practically focused, instrumentally motivated programs often designed for some special purpose, whether it be reading of academic material or business activities or some other professionally designated use (language for engineers, lawyers, and so forth). Similarly, the language teaching profession has failed to exploit the potential interest of the ethnic and community language speakers, rejecting the home-language knowledge that many pupils bring as being of an "inferior" spoken variety. In this way, the potential to add the home-language knowledge of new immigrants to the national linguistic capacity of a country has been frittered away .

Integrative Motivation
and Second-language Learning

For a long time, language learning theory has accepted the importance of motivation, seen practically as the effort a person will make to learn another language (Gardner and Lambert 1972). The ethnic revival and consequent understanding of the relation between language and identity have been instrumental in appreciating the nature of integrative motivation, simply defined as learning a language in order to become a member of the group that speaks it.

This is clearly close to the interests of the ethnic revival, particularly for members of the ethnic group. The goals of ethnic revival language teaching are identity and integration. By learning the appropriate language, the ethnic group member is making a close connection with the ethnic group, reaffirming identity with the past and with the present community.

This of course raises intriguing conflicts in the case of nonmembers of the ethnic group who study an ethnic language. Should the pakeha (white) child in New Zealand be encouraged to join Maori language revitalization classes? What happens to the many non-Catalans living in Catalonia? Should Arabs in Israel learn Hebrew for instrumental or integrative purposes? The ethnic revival, by raising these questions about motivations for second-language learning, has at the same time set new challenges for theory, forcing it to question the goals of instruction and to recognize the political significance of the language teaching enterprise.

Goals and Methods

In Western European language teaching (and in the many other educational systems throughout the world that were influenced by the Western European model), the teaching of modern foreign languages tended to be a modification and continuation of the older teaching of classical languages, Latin and Greek. Teachers of modern foreign languages carried on many of the approaches of the teacher of a classical language. They taught the standard written form of the language, its grammar, and its best literature, with practical concern for the spoken language reserved for occasional lessons or left for commercial programs. There was room in these programs for only a small number of languages. In the United States, the bulk of teaching was in French and German, with Spanish starting late but growing, especially after German declined. The initiative for the teaching of the less commonly taught languages came from the exigencies of the Second World War and continued for cold war purposes. Although at its height, this initiative included many languages, its main contribution was programs in Russian, Chinese, and Japanese.

Cultural Awareness and Political Conscience

By its understanding of language and ethnicity, the field of second-language teaching and learning was forced out of its traditional nonpolitical languor into a new awareness. It came to realize that it was deeply implicated in what was at best the growth of the hegemony of world languages or at worst a carefully designed policy to achieve power through linguistic imperialism. Whereas all writing in the pre-ethnic-revival days was about the value of learning whatever language was being taught, a sizable body of writing now decries the effects on minority languages and groups of being encouraged or forced to learn a world language (Skutnabb-Kangas 1981). Whether this is seen as a direct working out of a national policy (as in the Stalinist efforts to spread Russian in spite of the formal protection for other languages in the Soviet constitution, or in the German-language diffusion policies of Bismarck, or in the continued French drive to spread *la francophonie*) or as a combination of political, economic, and scientific pressures, as in the growing hegemony of English, it is more and more considered to be a problem that language teachers much face. The ethnic revival has created or forced a social and political conscience on the field of language teaching .

Looking at published material on language learning and teaching before and after the ethnic revival, the most striking feature is the addition of what is sometimes called cultural awareness. Language teaching before was divided between two main emphases. In the universities, the main emphasis was in the teaching of the high culture. In the commercial language teaching enterprises, the main emphasis was on practical competence. The high schools wavered between these two purposes. In the postrevival writing, the dominant theme is multiculturalism, with the addition of issues of race and ethnic group, class and gender to the traditional curriculum. Although often bitterly debated, the change has effected key documents, such as the recently published Standards for Foreign Language Learning (National Standards in Foreign Language Education Project 1996) with its references to "multilingual communities at home and around the world" and the ongoing changes in the canon of literatures studied in the university (Mullen 1992).

Conclusion

Adding all these facts together, it is clear that the student of second-language learning must nowadays be aware of and sophisticated in the field of language and ethnic identity. At the same time, those concerned with language and ethnic identity can be fairly expected to appreciate the relevance of second-language learning to their interests. Such an interdisciplinary approach, consistent with the approaches of sociolinguists, can contribute to better theory and practice for both areas.

Questions for Further Thought and Discussion

1. What are the reasons for regretting or opposing the loss of languages? Is there a parallel to be made between the loss of a species of animal and the loss of a language?

2. Find in one of the other chapters in this book a case other than Hebrew, Irish, and Maori in which ethnic revival has required language teaching. How does it compare with the three examples described in this chapter?

3. What are the main languages taught in the educational system of your country? What are the reasons each language is on the list? Is there a language omitted which you think is very important?

4. Do you agree with those who argue that there is a political bias in second- and foreign-language teaching?

Selected Bibliography

Cooper, Robert L. (1989). *Language Planning and Social Change*. Cambridge: Cambridge University Press.

Fishman, Joshua A. (1989). *Language and Ethnicity in Minority Sociolinguistic Perspective*, D. Sharp (ed.) Clevedon, England: Multilingual Matters.

Fishman, Joshua A. (1991). *Reversing Language Shift: Theoretical and Empirical Foundations of Assistance to Threatened Languages*. Clevedon, England: Multilingual Matters.

Gardner, Robert C., and Wallace W. Lambert (1972). *Attitudes and Motivation in Second Language Learning*. Rowley, Mass.: Newbury House.

Gumperz, John J. (1983). *Language and Social Identity*. Cambridge: Cambridge University Press.

Haugen, Einar (1966). *Language Conflict and Language Planning: The Case of Modern Norwegian*. Cambridge: Harvard University Press.

Krauss, Michael (1991). The world's languages in crisis. *Language* 68(1): 4–10.

Lambert, Richard D. (ed.) (1994). *Language Planning around the World: Contexts and Systematic Change*. NFLC Monograph Series. Washington, DC: Natioinal Foreign Language Center.

Mullen, Edward J. (1992). Foreign language departments and the new multiculturalism. *Profession* 15: 54–58.

National Standards in Foreign Language Education Project (1996). *Standards for Foreign Language Learning: Preparing for the 21st Century*. Lawrence, Ks: Allen.

O Laoire, Muiris (1996). An historical perspective of the revival of Irish outside the Gaeltacht, 1880–1930, with reference to the revitalization of Hebrew. In *Language and State: Revitalization and Revival in Israel and Eire*, Sue Wright (ed.), 51–75. Clevedon, England: Multilingual Matters.

Pennycock, Alastair (1990). Critical pedagogy and second language education. *System* 18(3): 303–314.

Phillipson, Robert (1992). *Linguistic Imperialism*. Oxford: Oxford University Press.

Skutnabb-Kangas, Tove (1981). *Bilingualism or Not: The Education of Minorities*. Lars Malmberg and David Crane (trans.) Clevedon, England: Multilingual Matters.

Skutnabb-Kangas, Tove (1996). The colonial legacy in educational language planning in Scandinavia: From migrant labor to national ethnic minority? *International Journal of the Sociology of Language* 118:81–106.

Spolsky, Bernard (1989). *Conditions for Second Language Learning: Introduction to a General Theory*. Oxford: Oxford University Press.

Spolsky, Bernard (1996). Conditions for language revitalization: A comparison of the cases of Hebrew and Maori. In *Language and the State: Revitalization and Revival in Israel and Eire*, Sue Wright (ed.), 5–50. Clevedon, England: Multilingual Matters.

PART II

REGION & LANGUAGE PERSPECTIVES

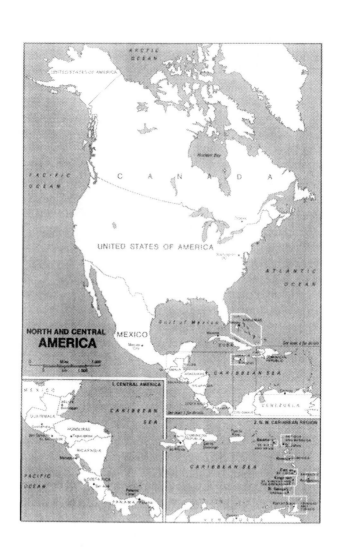

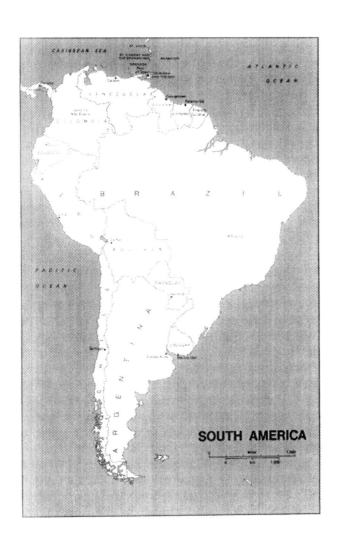

SOUTH AMERICA

Amerindians

TERESA L. McCARTY
OFELIA ZEPEDA

> My mother and father came upon this land so many years ago. I don't remember
> much of it. I think I was about five years old. Here we stay on our land that we
> have had for so many years. Here we have our homes. Our sheep, horses, and
> cows—these came here with us. We made life here. My parents said that there
> will be life here and the people will live here. My father and mother have passed
> on. Now there are only those of us who are the children, so this is how we live.

In her seventies when she gave this account, this elder of Rough Rock, Arizona,
speaks of the abiding attachment that Navajo people, Diné, feel for the land. The
past "lies embedded in features of the earth," anthropologist Keith Basso writes:
"Knowledge of places is therefore closely linked to knowledge of the self, to grasp-
ing one's position in the larger scheme of things, . . . and to securing a confident
sense of who one is as a person" (1996: 34). Kiowa author N. Scott Momaday con-
curs: "None of us lives apart from the land . . . such an isolation is unimaginable"
(1997: 33).

The fundamental and inescapable connection of people to land, of personhood
to place, frames and textures the oral traditions of groups indigenous to North
America. Stories, songs, prayers—for millennia these have carried the histories
of indigenous peoples, rooting them within the landscape and the network of social
relations it supports. Acoma writer Simon Ortiz (1993: 29) describes his childhood as "the oral tradition of the Acoma Pueblo people." He continues:

> It was the stories and songs which provided the knowledge that I was woven
> into the intricate web that was my Acoma life. In our garden and our cornfields
> I learned about the seasons, growth cycles of cultivated plants, and what one
> had to think and feel about the land; and at home I became aware of how we
> must care for each other: all of this was encompassed in an intricate relation-
> ship which had to be maintained in order that life continue (1993: 38).

It is language, of course, that orders, carries, and expresses this experience and, as Ortiz so eloquently describes, transmits it to future generations. But this implies more than simply language capacity or language as speech. The meanings, symbolism, shared history, and experience of a people within a landscape all reside within individual languages. Navajo prayers, for example, begin with *shimá nahasdzáán*. "By this," Navajo educator Galena Dick writes, "we mean that we have the same relation to mother earth, *shimá nahasdzáán*, as we have to the person who gave birth to us" (Dick & McCarty 1997: 71). And, speaking of his mother tongue, Ortiz (1993: 38) reflects, "We have always had this language, and it is the language, spoken and unspoken, that determines our existence, that brought our grandmothers and grandfathers and ourselves into being in order that there be a continuing life."

In this chapter, we examine the relationships among land, language, and identity in indigenous North American communities. Referring to the stories and songs that compose her heritage, Navajo poet Luci Tapahonso (1987: 53–54) writes:

> Because I was born into and come out of an oral culture, I learned early that the use of words involves responsibility and respect for oneself. A person is known primarily by his use of language and song. . . . and my sense of language, my awareness of words, becomes entangled with songs, memories, history and the land.

"My sense of poetics," she concludes, "becomes a sense of myself" (1987: 54).

We preface our discussion with a few words about our own senses of self. Ofelia Zepeda is a native speaker of Tohono 'O'odham, a tribe of 18,000 whose name, Desert People, reflects their Sonoran homelands. Growing up in a landscape which industry and capital have transformed into irrigated fields, Zepeda's early years were spent with her extended family in and around the cotton fields of Stanfield, Arizona. A linguist and poet who writes in O'odham and English, she currently teaches very near her birthplace, at the University of Arizona in Tucson. Teresa McCarty is a non-Indian anthropologist and educator, a native speaker of English who grew up in a working class neighborhood of pavement and postage-stamp-size yards in Columbus, Ohio. Graduate studies brought her to the Southwest and, eventually, to reside and work in the Navajo community of Rough Rock. She currently teaches at the University of Arizona and continues to conduct research on indigenous literacies with bilingual teachers from the Rough Rock Community School.

Together, we have collaborated for many years as faculty members and co-directors of the American Indian Language Development Institute, an international university-based program concerned with indigenous North American languages, bilingual education, and language rights. This work, our research, and our other life experiences have developed a deep appreciation for the embeddedness, within indigenous communities, of sense of self in sense of place. For Zepeda, that appreciation is personal, contained in lived experience, memories of growing up in a family of farm laborers, and the "ever-abiding fear and respect" for rain nurtured in a land of little rain (Zepeda 1995: 3). For McCarty, these understandings are less direct but nonetheless personal, acquired through long-term participation in indigenous communities and especially through listening to and recording the life histories of Rough Rock community members as part of an extensive ethnographic project there.

Here, we bring together the perspectives developed in these shared and different places. We begin with some demographics and a critique of the terms *American Indian* and *Native American*. Explicating those terms, we argue that understandings of indigenous identity must be pluralized and multilayered; as Elinor Ochs (1993: 298) points out, our identities are manifold, shifting, multiple, blended, even "blurred." Gender, ethnicity, social class, urbanity, rurality, age, sexual orientation, ability, and region of birth are only a few of the axes of identity construction.

Nonetheless, for indigenous groups in North America, place remains one of the most salient and resilient factors in identity formation. We focus, therefore, on place sense and self-sense, showing how these are represented in tribally specific oral tellings and written texts. Our examples derive from the place we know best: the Greater Southwest, one of the most culturally and geographically diverse regions in North America. We conclude with a reflection on the role of indigenous languages in constructing and reconstructing sense of place and sense of self and with a final question: If a language dies, are place sense and self-sense sacrificed as well?

Names and Misnomers

"Native people know that the term 'Indian' is a misnomer," Nez Perce author Inés Hernandez (1993: 8) states, "but we have made it our own, just as we have made 'American Indian' and 'Native American' our own. . . ." The terms American Indian, Alaska Native, and Native Hawaiian refer less to any subjective categories than to federal acknowledgment of the unique status of indigenous people in the United States as "sovereign but dependent" domestic nations. Nearly two million indigenous people so categorized reside in the United States, representing over 500 federally recognized tribes and 175 distinct languages. Beyond their remarkable diversity, what they share in common is a history as the first occupants of the Americas—an "identification with this hemisphere as our original land base," Hernandez (1993: 9) states, "articulated through the oral tradition." They also share a history of colonization that, especially in the United States and Canada, was carried out through the dual and deadly strategies of military force and compulsory schooling. One consequence of that history has been language loss, a symptom of the even more profound historical facts of territorial usurpation, dislocation, assimilation, and genocide.

Indigenous people in the United States jokingly refer to the term "Indian" as a name conjured up by someone who was lost. "We refer to each other by the tribe or nation that we are from—that is one of the first questions we ask each other," Hernandez (1993: 8) says. Despite multiple accidents of naming by outsiders, the names indigenous people call themselves generally translate as a word meaning "people"—as in Yoeme (Yaqui) and Diné (Navajo)—and/or they make reference to the place of the people, as in the case of Tohono 'O'odham. The name Akimel 'O'odham, Riverine People, refers to the linguistic and cultural relatives of the

Tohono 'O'odham and their aboriginal territory along desert rivers now dry. Similarly, Havasuw Baaj, People of the Blue Water or Havasupai, refers to the people who reside in a side canyon of the Grand Canyon watered by a turquoise stream and its waterfalls. Their linguistic relatives living above the canyon on the Coconino Plateau refer to themselves as Hwal Bay (Hualapai), People of the Tall Pines.

Such naming traditions exist throughout North America, and it is these names rather than any externally imposed labels that serve to reference indigenous identities. Self-naming is perhaps the simplest yet most profound act of human autonomy; the fact that tribal names have been ignored, appropriated, and distorted by outsiders speaks volumes about the history of the people so named. But the original names have persisted, carried both by oral tradition and the written word. "[W]e were and . . . are still . . . all related in our relationship to this particular land base," Hernandez (1993: 9–10) maintains; each distinct people "learned (and learns) its form and expression from the particular sacred places or land base that its people are from."

We turn now to five accounts which illustrate these forms and expressions. Four derive from oral histories collected by McCarty in her seventeen years of ethnographic work on the Navajo Nation. All of these were recorded first in Navajo and subsequently translated into English by a Native speaker. The fifth account is part of Zepeda's family history. In presenting these accounts, we attempt to retain the narrative quality of the original telling. We begin with a story of the events precipitating the founding of modern Rough Rock.

Hwééldí

On a warm June day in 1981, Bit'aanii Yéé Be'azaan sat on a narrow bed under a juniper-covered shade house adjacent to her home, or *hooghan*, a gray kitten curled alongside her. She was perhaps ninety years old at the time. Bit'aanii Yéé Be'azaan had lived all her life near the place called Tsé Ch'ízhí, Rough Rock. Rough Rock is named for the springs in a canyon at the base of Black Mesa, which rises darkly above the springs, stretching for some sixty miles before tapering off into the badlands at the westernmost edge of the Navajo Nation. Below the mesa, red rock buttes punctuate a high desert landscape of pinyon, juniper, prickly pear, and sage.

On that June day, Bit'aanii Yéé Be'azaan was being asked by the visitors from the local school to recall how people settled this land. Her words summoned up both hope and despair. Bit'aanii Yéé Be'azaan's mother had been born in captivity at a place Navajos call Hwééldí and which the U.S. government named Fort Sumner, New Mexico. In the autumn of 1863, Colonel Kit Carson led a scorched earth campaign through the Chinle Valley just east of Rough Rock, burning fields and homes and slaughtering hundreds of sheep. That winter, Bit'aanii Yéé Be'azaan's grandmother and thousands of other Navajos surrendered to U.S. forces at Fort Defiance, Arizona. From there they were marched at gunpoint to Hwééldí across 300 miles of wintry plains. The Long Walk to Hwééldí claimed many lives, some at the hands of soldiers. Over 2,000 more people died at Fort Sumner of rampant disease and hunger.

"My mother's name was K'é Hoonibah," Bit'aanii Yéé Be'azaan began. "She was born at Fort Sumner"—

> When my mother was being born, a group of soldiers came up over the hill carrying swords. My mother's grandmother was afraid. "What are they going to do to us this time?" my grandmother thought. But all this time, the soldiers had only come to discuss peace with the *ná'át'áánii* [Navajo leaders] at Fort Sumner. Then all of a sudden, there were a lot of people talking up there over the hill. There was peace [*k'é*].

K'é Hoonibah means "Peace Finally Found You," or "Peace Caught Up With You." "After my mother was born," Bit'aanii Yéé Be'azaan said, "they moved back near Rough Rock. My grandmother used to tell me this story."

A Foretelling

On the northern face of Black Mesa is a V-shaped talus slope several hundred feet high. It marks the remnants of a rock slide, an event people say foretold the tragedy of the Long Walk and Hwééldí. "It happened a little before the people were taken to Hwééldí," one man recalled. "The rock slide was a foretelling that something big was going to happen, something that would really change people's lives. . . . That slide, and the event it forecasted, mean a lot to Navajos. They shed tears even to think of it today, and what happened afterward—the anguish and turmoil they went through."

More than 100 years later, on a sunny January day in 1996, World War II veteran Blair Tsosie sat in the living room of his small frame house about ten miles from Rough Rock Springs. Around him were gathered the Anglo ethnographer and several staff members and students from the Rough Rock School. They had composed several interview questions; the high school students would videotape Blair Tsosie's stories for an oral history project commemorating the thirtieth anniversary of their school.

Blair Tsosie recalled what his grandmother had told him years ago about the rock slide:

> This is what I heard my grandma say. She said it took four days for the rock slide to happen. When the rocks started sliding, the horses began to neigh and the sheep began to cry. About four years later, . . . all the animals we used to have were taken away. People went hungry; they began to starve. All the people had nothing to live on, but they moved on to Fort Sumner. . . .

For four years, Blair Tsosie's grandmother and two of her sons were held captive at Fort Sumner. They saw their relatives die. Then, in 1868, twenty-nine Navajo leaders signed *Naaltsoos Sání*, the Old Paper, a treaty with the U.S. government, which returned to the people a portion of their lands. Blair Tsosie continued:

> My great-grandmother said she had no horses left because the soldiers took them away. When the people were released, she was given two goats and her sons were given two goats each. So there were six livestock they brought back from Fort Sumner. This is how we began life here again.

Personhood and Land

The children and grandchildren of Hwéeldí survivors speak of a time in early childhood when they "became aware"—*hání hazlíí*—or "self-aware"—*adáá' ahozhniidíí*. This is the time when personal histories begin. "I became aware of things when I turned six years old," an elderly man from Black Mesa recalls. His first memories are of the land: "The land is what used to help people survive. Planting, the animals—these are what used to help the people."

Dorothy Begay has lived much of her life below the mesa. In the winter of 1996, she was interviewed as part of the Rough Rock School's oral history project. Sitting at her kitchen table, the late afternoon sun casting white light across her face, she held her young grandson as she told this story of the place where she grew up:

> At that time, we had a lot of rain. *Yíltsá nidi ba'áté áden iidáá*—female [gentle, penetrating] rain. There were plants everywhere. During the spring, there would be all different flowers making up the earth. When it would get dark, you could see a highlight of plants against the sky. There were yucca plants all over. That is how different flowers made up the place. And that is how we lived with them.

Margaret Dalton, in her seventies when she was interviewed in 1996, grew up on top of Black Mesa. Her first memories are of the seasons and of earth, water, and sun:

> When it rained, it did not rain with lightning. I became aware of it when there were rainbows across the skies. It would rain like this. During the winter, the earth would freeze. . . . And when spring came around, when it first rained at that time, the land would puff up and rise like bread dough around the plants. That is how I became aware of it here.

Other stories describe family movements across the land. "We used to plant corn and squash, watermelon and canteloupes," Thomas James, a seventeen-year member of the Rough Rock School Board, said. "During the summer, we would go to the valley below and bring back things when they ripened. Then we lived on them, the corn, during the winter. That is how it was."

Embedded in such stories are life lessons about the importance of kinship, cooperation, respect, responsibility, endurance, and peacefulness. These values are all implied by the term *k'é*. Hasbah Charley, a great-grandmother when she was interviewed in 1996, gave this example of *k'é*: "When it snowed, when food was scarce, we would hear that someone had butchered a horse. We would go over there. The meat would be cut up for us, and we would bring it back." And Blair Tsosie recalled these lessons from his parents and grandparents:

> "You take care of yourself, you teach yourself. . . . You help whenever, and keep yourself strong. . . . If you are sincere you will lend your horse to someone. You will help them survive." Those are the teachings that have been passed down.

Going to School

In most indigenous North American communities, there is another kind of story—a special genre that is characterized by conflict between home and alien places. These are stories of going to school.

In 1887, the United States government instituted a new Indian policy of compulsory schooling and coercive assimilation. A primary means for implementing this policy was the removal of children to distant boarding schools, many located at the forts which had served as military staging areas against the tribes only a few years before. Stories abound of young children being kidnapped from the fields or while out herding sheep and being taken by government-deputized Indian agents to the boarding schools. There, children faced a system of militaristic discipline, manual labor, instruction in a trade, and abusive treatment for "reverting" to the mother tongue. Many children fled these conditions only to be rounded up by Indian agents (called "school police" in Navajo) and returned to school.

Thomas James described the resistance he and his young friends mustered to these practices and the tragedy that befell one boy who failed to escape:

I was sixteen years old when I left for school in 1925. That was when the school police came to visit us. I left with my maternal grandfather, Tsinaahjinii Hastiin. . . . I sat behind him on a horse, and he took me to Chinle. I had a hair bun. They cut off my hair bun there. That is when I started going to school. . . .

I spent about two weeks at Chinle Boarding School when some boys told me to run back home with them at night. It was me, a boy named Mush, one from here named Ashkii Litsoii [Yellow Boy] and his brother. So there were four of us. We ran alongside the road to a place called Ma'ii To'í [Coyote Wash], in between the rocks. Just when we started to cross it a horse came up behind us. There was a man riding his horse. His name was Kenneth; it was him. He had a belt with a switch attached to it. Just when the horse starting going down into the wash, there was a cliff down by us, and Mush and I ran down there. We ran and crawled into a cave. We were standing there when he rode by on his horse. The other boys ran on toward a side hill. They were running so fast. Just before they could reach the hill the horse caught up with them.

That's when we finally came back out and went on. We ran beside a hill and from there, we sat watching the boys run around grabbing rocks and hitting the man. . . . We ran as fast as we could to school at night. . . . We really got scared. I guess while the man was trying to get the boys together, he ran over one with his horse. The boy died.

A month later, Thomas and his friend Mush again ran away from school. This time they made it to Mush's home several miles away. Mush's father chided the boys: "Why do you run away? There is a horse outside; I am going to take you both back [to school] sitting behind each other."

"That is what he said," Thomas remembered. "I thought, I am not going to sit behind no one again." He finished his story:

We slept there and the next morning I went out for awhile, but I just started running again this way [toward Rough Rock]. I ran to a place called Tó Ak'eeyalí [Little Spring Coming Down a Tiny Hill]. There were houses in the cave area there. When I got back home, it was almost noon the next day. I spent a week there when [the school policeman] came again on horseback. I was herding sheep, and when I came back home, I saw the horse there. He was riding a dirty horse, and here that horse was there again. I almost ran off again. But my mother told me to go back inside the hooghan. I went back inside then. I ate, and he told me we were going to go now. I did not say no again.

Going Home

Our final account takes place in the Sonoran desert to the south of Navajo country, within the traditional territory of the Tohono 'O'odham. It is a story of one family's homecoming.

Her last request was that she be buried "back home." But home meant a village and a cemetery that had been abandoned years ago. As the generations passed on, fewer descendants were left who would go back, even to the cemetery. In time, mud adobe buildings melted back into the desert floor. The meager graves did the same.

With much trepidation, the woman's adult children began the arrangements for her passing. To take their mother "back home," they had to negotiate with the government of the Tohono 'O'odham Nation and their reservation. This place, the reservation, is indeed a home to many 'O'odham people, but not all. Additionally, her children had to negotiate an international border, an artificial boundary for the 'O'odham that signified only two countries, the United States and Mexico.

For this woman, none of these nations was home. Instead, the place she was going was a small space in a vast desert, the place considered home by her parents and grandparents. To anyone else this piece of desert would appear to be an unwelcome site—certainly not a place one would readily consider "home." Indeed, the extreme aridity of this place had led to its abandonment nearly two generations before. But for her it was home. She had vague childhood memories of this place, enhanced by stories told by her parents and grandparents. They had spoken of it fondly as *t-kiidag*, "our dwelling place."

For the people who were from this place, their primary reference was a range of mountains. "The village was right here," they would say, each pointing to the exact same spot. Then, as if watching a TelePrompTer, they would wave their arms in each of several directions, pointing out the lay of the village, who lived where, and where the well used to be. At such moments, for these people, this place was still very real. It was home.

Language and Indigenous Identities

> A piece of land is like a book. A wise person can look at the stones and mountains and read stories older than the first living thing . . . and since the first people first made homes on the land, many people and many tribes have come and gone. The land still remembers them, however, and keeps . . . the things they left behind (Bingham & Bingham 1984: 1).

Each of the five accounts here describes the home places of their narrators. The stories from Rough Rock speak especially of the creation of community; they name the sacred sites, collective struggles, and communal values that connect people to land and to place. The 'O'odham account describes a place indistinguishable to outsiders but identified as home by those whose memories it holds. That identification is made through signage—the landmarks that help people remember—but also through oral tellings in 'O'odham about those landmarks.

In these and other indigenous oral accounts, it is the language rather than the identifying landmarks that is portable. It is the language that represents experience with and knowledge of a place. It is the language that conveys a sense of places considered home. In its versatility and complexity, it is the language that is most capable of portraying events and places to children and grandchildren who have never experienced them. And, as the last account reveals, it is the language that paints an image so strong that it flames the desire to return there as a final resting place.

The inextricable connection of land, language, and people is embodied in these narratives. They remind their listeners that this is where they come from; these are their relatives; this is who they are. The stories do not merely label physical structures or geographical features, but rather tell of the mountains, the water, the secret or sacred places, and the events, both recent and ancient, that are the shared history of a people.

Such collective memory from traditional oral accounts has recently been developed into forms of written literature. For example, in this song, Havasupai medicine man Dan Hanna (1995: 27–28) portrays the beauty and significant features of his homeland:

> The land we were given
> the land we were given
> It is right here
> It is right here
> Red Rock
> Red Rock. . . .
> Down at the source
> A spring will always be there
> It is ours
> It is ours
> Since a long time ago
> Since a long time ago . . . .

And in this song history, George Blueeyes (1995: 9–10) describes sacred landmarks and his own sense of Navajo-ness:

> Blanca Peak
> Mount Taylor
> San Francisco Peaks
> Hesperus Peak
> Huerfano Mountain
> Gubernador Knob
> They were placed here for us.

We think of them as our home.
Blanca Peak is adorned with white shell.
Mount Taylor is adorned with turquoise.
San Francisco Peaks are adorned with abalone.
Hesperus Peak is adorned with jet.
Huerfano Mountain is dressed in precious fabric,
While Gobernador Knob is clothed in sacred jewels.
This is how they sit for us.
We adorn ourselves just as they do,
With bracelets of turquoise,
And precious jewels about our necks . . . .

For Zepeda, her poetry is influenced not only by a contemporary home in a rural 'O'odham community but by an unbroken continuum of knowledge about the places her family calls home. This includes the small village in what is now Mexico. Describing the act of rain in the desert, she evokes living images of this home place:

> The odor of wet dirt precedes the rain. It is an aroma so strong for some that it wakes them from sleep. People like to breathe deeply of this wet dirt smell. It is the smell not only of dirt but of the dry bark of mesquite and other acacias. It is the smell of the fine dust that must settle on all the needles and spines of saguaro and all manner of cactus. . . . It is all those things that give off an aroma only when mixed by rain. It is all breathed in deeply. (Zepeda 1995: 2)

In these narratives and in oral texts, land and place hold the mnemonic devices to assist collective memory. They prod the storing and transmission of memory, coloring the words with distinctive images. And in the tellings about land and place—in the social transactions surrounding these texts—identities are constructed, reconstructed, and affirmed.

What is interesting here, however, is the fact that, in many cases, the places identified in the texts have been appropriated by others, disfigured, and even destroyed. Red Rock—the site to which Dan Hanna refers—is not included within the modern Havasupai reservation and is planned as the location of a uranium mine. Yet Hanna repeats, "It is ours, it is ours, since a long time ago, it is ours." Huerfano Mountain, Gobernador Knob, and the four sacred mountains that anchor Navajo country in George Blueeyes' account all lie outside the Navajo Nation. Paved with roads and cross-cut by ski runs, the San Francisco Peaks today overlook a small city. Still, Blueeyes says, "They were placed here for us. We think of them as our home." And an international border slices across traditional 'O'odham territory, politically separating Zepeda's family from their homeland. It is the stories, the poetry, the prayers, and the songs that continue to fix these places in collective memory, recalling their images, commanding respect, and helping those for whom the narratives are intended to define who they are. Landscape or place sense is no more, or no less, important than language in this process. It is within the places in the stories that the "sense of ourselves" resides.

"If a Child Learns Only the Non-Indian Way of Life, You Have Lost Your Child"

We turn now to the "identity crisis" under way in indigenous communities today—a crisis suggested by the words of the Navajo elder that head this section. If it is indeed the stories, songs, and daily interactions in the Native language that convey and transmit sense of place and sense of self, what happens when the language falls out of use?

This is the situation Native American communities now face. Of 175 indigenous languages still spoken in the United States, perhaps twenty are being transmitted to children. Languages in the U.S. Southwest are among the most vital—especially Navajo, Tohono 'O'odham, Havasupai, Hopi, and Hualapai—with a significant, though declining, number of child speakers. But by far the largest numbers of indigenous languages are spoken only by the middle-aged or grandparent generations.

Contemporary Native writers such as Ortiz, Momaday, Tapahonso, and others demonstrate that indigenous traditions *can* be represented in English. But Native speakers, particularly those immersed in the oral literature of their people, are quick to say, "Yes, but the text is not the same. There is something missing." In some cases, it is easy to point to words that lack even an approximate English equivalent. The 'O'odham word *himdag*, for example, is often translated as "culture." But 'O'odham speakers say his is only a distant approximation; speakers understand this word to have various levels of complexity. As a consequence, they have taken up the practice of using the 'O'odham word when speaking about it in English.

This example highlights the fact that human cultures are not interchangeable; the loss of even one language and the cultural knowledge it encodes diminishes us all. Recognizing this, many tribes are actively engaged in language restoration efforts. In California, where fifty indigenous languages are spoken—none as a mother tongue by children—a bold language revitalization movement is under way. "No one feels this impending loss more strongly than the Native Californians themselves," linguist Leanne Hinton (1994: 14) maintains. "Many are making enormous efforts to keep the language and cultural practices alive . . . even as they participate in the cultures and intercultures more recently derived from Europe and elsewhere" (Hinton, 1994: 14).

One such effort is the California Master-Apprentice Language Learning Program, in which Native speakers and younger apprentices live and work together over months or years, doing everyday things but communicating through the heritage language. Speakers from ten language groups have thus far been trained, and several apprentices have achieved conversational proficiency. In Hawaii, language immersion programs have successfully revived Hawaiian in dozens of homes. Language immersion programs also have been instituted on the Navajo Nation, among the Mohawks in New York, Ontario, and Quebec, and in numerous other indigenous communities throughout the United States.

The development of indigenous literacies has accompanied many of these efforts. As in many tribes, among the Hualapai of northwestern Arizona the development of a practical writing system grew out of local initiatives in bilingual education. There is now a significant body of Hualapai literature, including a grammar and dictionary, children's and adolescents' storybooks, poetry, teachers' guides, and anthologies of traditional stories and songs. All of this has raised support for larger, community-wide language maintenance efforts, including tribal sanctions for conducting tribal business in English, and the involvement of children, parents, and grandparents in language revitalization projects.

Literacy in indigenous languages, however, remains primarily restricted to schools, buttressing rather than replacing home- and community-based language transmission. Yet literacy is a powerful symbol of indigenous identity; it valorizes the community and publicly demonstrates the ways in which it is using its language in active and creative ways. By providing new forms for the preservation and transmission of traditional knowledge, indigenous literacy tangibly connects the language with the culture and history of its speakers. Finally, as the Hualapai example shows, indigenous literacy can stimulate other, more diffuse forces for language and culture maintenance. In all of these ways, literacy in indigenous languages is an asset and ally in the struggle to resist linguistic assimilation.

But the fact remains that there is an ever-decreasing pool of Native language speakers. This situation is a direct consequence of the history of colonialism and language repression that indigenous people have, for centuries, endured. Nonetheless, as Darrell Kipp of the Piegan Language Institute pointed out at a recent meeting of indigenous language activists, without their tribal languages, many indigenous communities "will cease to be." The loss of language, he states, "is like throwing away your universe."

We are heartened by the awakening of tribal peoples to this language crisis and by efforts such as those in California and the U.S. Southwest that can rightfully be called a language renaissance. There is recognition, widely shared, that indigenous languages are imperiled. There is shared talk about the urgency of the situation, considerable sharing of ideas and strategies, and, most important, action on behalf of threatened languages and their communities. Speakers of endangered languages throughout the world are in communication. We are hopeful that, in combination with local grassroots initiatives, these global efforts will ensure that indigenous North American languages survive.

Much work remains to be done to shore up threatened indigenous languages. The responses to this crisis will have a huge influence on the "sense of ourselves" that indigenous people are able to construct and transmit for generations to come.

Questions for Further Thought and Discussion

1. Review the narrative accounts presented here. How, specifically, do they represent a sense of place? A sense of self?

2. In the case of early European immigrants and recent immigrants to the United States, how does the notion of place or homeland manifest itself? Is

this comparable to the Native North American senses of place and identity discussed here? Why or why not?

3. Consider the fact that many Native Americans are learning their heritage language as a second language. What are the implications of this for the development of their senses of place and self?

4. Do you believe a sense of place plays a strong role in contemporary American life? Why or why not?

5. Should the "accuracy" of traditional American Indian oral literature published in English be questioned—even it it is written by a Native writer?

6. The California Master-Apprentice and Hawaiian Immersion Programs are only two of many successful efforts to revitalize imperiled indigenous languages. What issues might arise in attempting to undertake such revitalization activities? What suggestions would you make for indigenous communities who seek to implement these or similar programs?

7. Many have argued that schools are proper sites for language revitalization. Others claim that schools only transfer responsibility for mother tongue transmission from its natural and necessary domain—the home and family—to a secondary or tertiary institution. Do schools have a role to play in indigenous language revitalization? Why or why not?

8. The English-only movement has a strong constituency in the United States. Given what you have read here, what arguments might you use to resist this movement?

9. When the question is asked, "Why bother to save a language spoken by a small number of people," how would you respond? Is language only a tool or does it serve other functions as well?

Selected Bibliography

Basso, K. (1996). *Wisdom Sits in Places: Landscape and Language among the Western Apache.* Albuquerque: University of New Mexico Press.

Bingham, S., and J. Bingham (1984). *Between Sacred Mountains: Stories and Lessons from the Land.* Tucson: University of Arizona Press.

Blueeyes, George (1995). Sacred mountains. In *Home Places: Contemporary Native American Writing from* *SunTracks*, L. Evers and O. Zepeda (eds.), 7–11. Tucson: University of Arizona Press.

Dick, G. S., and T. L. McCarty (1997). Reclaiming Navajo: Language renewal in an American Indian community school. In *Indigenous Literacies in the Americas: Language Planning from the Bottom Up*, N. H. Hornberger (ed.), 69–94. Berlin: Mouton de Gruyter.

Hanna, Dan (1995). Havasupai medicine

song. In *Home Places: Contemporary Native American Writing from SunTracks*, L. Evers and O. Zepeda (eds.), 19–27. Tucson: University of Arizona Press.

Hernandez, I. (1993). Foreword: Reflections on identity and culture. In *Growing Up Native American: An Anthology*, P. Riley (ed.), 7–16. New York: Morrow.

Hinton, L. (1994). *Flutes of Fire: Essays on California Indian Languages*. Berkeley, Cal.: Heyday Books.

Momaday, N. S. (1997). *The Man Made of Words*. New York: St. Martin's Press.

Ochs, E. (1993). Constructing social identity: A language socialization perspective. *Research on Language and Social Interaction* 26(3): 287–306.

Ortiz, S. (1993). The language we know. In *Growing Up Native American: An Anthology*, P. Riley (ed.), 29–38. New York: Morrow.

Tapahonso, L. (1987). A sense of myself. *Diné Be'ííná', Journal of Navajo Life* 1(1): 53–54.

Zepeda (1995). *Ocean Power: Poems from the Desert*. Tucson: University of Arizona Press.

African American Vernacular English

SONJA L. LANEHART

Darlene trying to teach me how to talk. She say us not so hot. A dead country give-away. You say *us* where most folks say *we,* she say, and peoples think you dumb. Colored peoples think you a hick and white folks be amuse. What I care? I ast. I'm happy. But she say I feel more happier talking like she talk. . . . Every time I say something the way I say it, she correct me until I say it some other way. Pretty soon it feel like I can't think. My mind run up on a thought, git confuse, run back and sort of lay down. You sure this worth it? I ast. She say Yeah. Bring me a bunch of books. Whitefolks all over them, talking bout apples and dogs. What I care bout dogs? I think. Darlene keep trying. Think how much better Shug feel with you educated, she say. She won't be shame to take you anywhere. Shug not shame no how, I say. But she don't believe this the truth. Sugar, she say one day when Shug home, don't you think it be nice if Celie could talk proper. Shug say, She can talk in sign language for all I care. . . . But I let Darlene worry on. Sometimes I think bout the apples and the dogs, sometimes I don't. Look like to me only a fool would want you to talk in a way that feel peculiar to your mind.

—Alice Walker, *The Color Purple*

Although language consists of arbitrary signs, symbols, and/or sounds constructed to make meaning, it is not meant simply to communicate, nor is communication necessarily essential to the purpose of language. According to Freire and Macedo, "Language should never be understood as a mere tool of communication" (1987: 28). "Language arises from man's need to express himself, to objectify himself. . . . And if language also serves as a means of communication, this is a secondary function that has nothing to do with its essence," according to Bakhtin (1986: 67–68).

Language can be a means of solidarity, resistance, and identity within a culture or social group. The language a person speaks is the language that person identifies with and is therefore very important to the individual. Language is a part of one's culture and identity. To try to dictate and to purge one's language is to try to change the individual; you thereby change his or her identity and make unnecessary and possibly detrimental demands on his or her culture and person. At present, two constructs explicate the link between language and identity: Lesley Milroy's *social networks* and Robert Le Page's *acts of identity*.

Lesley Milroy's social networks construct proposes that "varieties of language are subject to maintenance through pressure exerted by informal ties of kin and friendship" (Milroy and Milroy 1991: 58). It provides insight into why low-status local and regional varieties of language have such a strong capacity to persist despite the institutional pressures that favor prescribed English. "Any attempt to eliminate or stigmatize a nonstandard variety will not work, and will be seen as a direct attack on the values and social identity of the speaker" (Milroy and Milroy 1991: 108). The extent of this identity depends on the strength and density of the social network(s).

Although Milroy focuses more strongly on language and community, Le Page accentuates language and the individual:

> People create their linguistic systems (and we all have more than one) so as to resemble those of the groups with which from time to time they wish to identify. Both the groups, and their linguistic attributes, exist solely in the mind of each individual. When we talk we project the universe as we see it on to others as on to a cinema screen in our own images, expressed in the language we consider appropriate at that moment, and we invite others by these acts to share our universe. This does not necessarily mean that we accommodate our behaviour to resemble that of our audience, though we may do so. Rather, we behave in the way that—unconsciously or consciously—we think appropriate to the group with which at that moment we wish to identify. This may be quite distinct from the group we are talking to. (1986: 23)

Little can be done to erase language choice as long as we are social beings with individual and community identities. Our identities emerge from our transactions. We develop within a culture or cultures in which language is an important aspect. Our experiences within our cultures, our communities, and families and with schools, the media, and our jobs help shape the people we are continually becoming. These relationships with other people and institutions are constructed within the realm in which identity emerges—our sociocultural and historical contexts. As such, the social networks we form and our acts of identity are essential to the individuals we choose to be—or not to be. We create such networks and form such identities based on our experiences, our desires, and our inevitable right to choose—a right that has been and continues to be tested regardless of our race, ethnicity, gender, or regional affiliation. However, some language varieties get tested more often than others.

African American Vernacular English (AAVE) is one example of a language variety spoken by those whose right to choose how to speak is sorely tested. AAVE is not a high-prestige language in the view of mainstream society. Many view AAVE as a bastardized form of English that is spoken because the speakers do not know any better. However, AAVE survives because there is a population of speakers who use it in their daily lives and know that it is the appropriate style of speaking for their personal needs (Baugh 1983). Like most language varieties that are considered nonstandard, it developed and continues to persist, in part, because the communities who speak it often do not have much contact with other ways of speaking or because such communities define themselves partly by their speech. Smitherman says:

> As far as historians, linguists, and other scholars go, during the first half of this century it was widely believed that enslavement had wiped out all traces of African languages and cultures, and that Black 'differences' resulted from imperfect and inadequate imitations of European American language and culture. George Philip Krapp, writing in the 1920's, is one linguist who held this view about the speech of Africans in America. (1994: 4)

There are many in the African American community who share these beliefs. They either do not believe in such a thing as African American Vernacular English (or Black English, BE, or Black English Vernacular, BEV) or they do not believe that AAVE is something to be proud of and, therefore, preserved. Alexander says:

> I will not accept the legitimacy of Black English or any other kind of non-prescribed English—no matter what many of my colleagues may say. . . . My parents' words came back to me when I read of the recent ruling by U.S. District Judge Charles W. Joiner in Ann Arbor, Michigan. His ruling, which calls for implicit recognition of Black English, is nothing more than blatant plantation mentality. I cannot support it. . . . If people cannot communicate in Standard English and have not developed their talents and skills—then who wants them? . . . I consider it a cheap insult to see educational standards lowered in Ann Arbor schools—solely for black students. How can we justify recognition of their non-prescribed broken English and then ask teachers to learn it? (1979: 437–438)

Many have these perceptions about varieties of a language that are not "prescribed"—regardless of how misinformed their views are. However, Alexander does make an important point about how this language is referred to. Alexander says:

> Many blacks in America deeply resent the fact that the non-Standard English that is spoken by the students in Ann Arbor, Michigan, is called Black English. These blacks feel the term is racist, since the non-Standard English spoken by the white immigrants, earlier, was not called White English.
> Moreover, they are aware, particularly the educated blacks, that whenever society wants to take a perfectly good word or noun and make it negative, it too often only has to add the word black as an adjective. For example, the good word

mail plus black becomes blackmail, list becomes blacklist, hand becomes black hand, flag becomes black flag, art becomes black art, market becomes black market, and, of course, English becomes Black English.

The above is one of the main reasons so many blacks prefer the name Afro-American over black, particularly the young college black. (1979: 438)

There are those who do not like the name "Black English" for the very reason he mentions. However, that AAVE exists cannot be dismissed because of a problem with what it is called nor because some see it as romanticized instead of as a valuable cultural and social artifact.

Although there is a bit of discussion about what the language used in the African American community should be called within the community itself, there is not as much discussion about the existence of such a language. By that I mean that those of the African American community may currently be disputing whether AAVE is a separate language or a variety of the English language, but few can dispute the existence of a linguistic system used by many African Americans that is distinct from that of other language varieties used in the United States. What is distressing in this name and language battle is that AAVE is often equated with or called "bad" English—even by those who strongly identify with AAVE. The point is that there are obviously many who identify with AAVE by their actual use of it despite the name or its language status.

Three participants in a research study I did were AAVE speakers and strongly identified with the language but differed in their perspectives of it. "Maya" believes she speaks both AAVE and "bad" English and that she will continue to do so. Because she thinks she speaks both, it may not be a stretch to say that she believes the two are the same, but it is still likely that she does not equate the two. She believes she speaks AAVE, but she does not find that to be particularly problematic as a possible self. She demonstrates more of an affiliation with AAVE than with "standard" English, even though she would like to be able to speak "standard" English. Nevertheless, she chooses to maintain her identity with AAVE.

Maya does not hold her speech in high regard compared to her perception of standard English as the benchmark for American English, but she is quite unflappable in her resolve that over the course of her life she has done all she can under the circumstances and that is all she can do or expect unless someone or something intervenes. Below is Maya's dual perspective in her own words.

[People who speak good English] use and spell words properly. They does. They uses their language very well. I be trying to help myself. Now I don't be saying everything right either, but I do be trying to help myself. It's important. It's very educated to me. At least, you know, some education anyway. But like somebody I know, I gets a li'l slacker with them. You know how you get comfortable with somebody you know. [But I talk the way I do because] sometime I don't know how to use the word, the real right word in the real language.

"Grace" has a little different perspective of AAVE, even though it is the language she grew up using and is the language she continues to use. She certainly identifies with the language, but she is torn—as can be seen in Grace's own words (written and spoken).

Black English is a beautiful language among blacks and that is as far as I would take it. I believe black english started doing slavery time. Blacks were not able or aloud to learn how to read or write the Caucasian english. I feel the blacks who got a chance to live or work in the white house as maids or buttlers got a chance to hear and pick up on some words of the Caucasian english. When they talked the blacks would try and listen and try to pronounce the words but, not knowing how to spell the word they would half pronounced the word and when talking to the other blacks who worked in the fields trying to help them learn the english, the word was pronounced wrong. Like they would say 'dhis' for this and 'dhat' for that and that was past on from generations to generations because of not knowing how to read, write or spell the Caucasion english. I believe if you can't spell a word it is hard to pronounce the word correctly because you don't know the sound of the letters.

[Speaking Black English is important] when you are talking to other black people who can only speak black english and if you are an actress or actor and is playing a part of speaking black english or just being yourself as a black person around other blacks that you feel comfortable with.

Grace indicates she does not like the way she talks, but that occurs only when she feels there are others around her who speak standard English and expect to engage in conversation using standard English. She is perfectly fine talking with others who speak the way she does. Le Page's acts of identity construct is relevant to her situation because she wants to be able to use various modes of discourse to adapt to her current circumstances and to the speakers she wants to identify with at any given time. The problem is that she is not currently able to do so.

"Deidra" has the strongest identification with AAVE of the three. Though she, like Maya and Grace, would like to be able to use standard English effectively but cannot, she is the least likely to want to give up what she considers a viable part of her identity. In Deidra's own words (both written and spoken) she believes:

[Bad English and Black English are] two different things. [Speaking Black English is] knowing what your Black culture is about. And how they uses their English. What type of words they uses. And understand the Black world. I'm not sure [if speaking Black English is important]. Unless your speaking to a Black Brother or Sister. [I value Black English more than I value standard English] because I can understand Black English better than I can understand standard English and not that I feel as if I'm Black and I suppose to. But if I were Black and can speak standard English, and there are Black people who speak good English, then I wouldn't see a problem with that. I'm not saying that I don't understand the standard English, I do understand it because when someone is talking to me now, I mean back then I prob'ly wouldn't have understand anything. But now I understand when people are talking to me because half of the people here don't speak good English at all.

I feel like Black know their English and they know what they can comprehend and understand what each other is talking about compared to someone who speak proper English or good English. They might not understand what they are saying but in some ways they do understand because I heard people say something like, "Well, explain to me what you're talking about, you know, from a Black point of view, tell me what you mean by what you're saying?" Even though they speak correct English they also learn that there are different cultures and they learn their languages somewhat because everybody doesn't talk the same.

Deidra identifies with the AAVE speech community above any other. She has the most salient AAVE linguistic features which would coincide with her choice to identify with the community that uses AAVE.

So despite efforts to degrade AAVE and to deny its existence, it persists because it does exist and because its speakers choose to identify with it as a viable language of the African American community.

The 4-1-1

African American Vernacular English is a variety of language. Many in society may dispute its existence, but there really is no getting around the legitimacy of its reality. Scanning the television or radio reveals not only African Americans but other racial and ethnic groups touting aspects of African American language and culture. It has become a big business with the growing popularity of rap and hip-hop. Smitherman says:

> Through various processes such as "Semantic Inversion" (taking words and turning them into their opposites), African Americans stake our claim to the English language, and at the same time, reflect distinct Black values that are often at odds with Eurocentric standards. "Fat," spelled *phat* in Hip Hop, refers to a person or thing that is excellent and desirable, reflecting the traditional African value that human body weight is a good thing, and implicitly rejecting the Euro-American mainstream, where skinny, not fat, is valued and everybody is on a diet. Senior Blacks convey the same value with the expression, "Don't nobody want no BONE." (1994: 18)

It is not uncommon to hear an African American say "What up?" or "He be trippin'." In fact, it is often used stereotypically by white speakers who are trying to mimic AAVE speakers. However, it is not taken into account that not all African Americans use the copula, or the verb "to be," in these ways, nor do these mockers realize that white speakers use the verb "to be" in these ways as a legitimate facet of their speech. An irony in the situation is that white speakers who try to mock AAVE speakers often use these salient characteristics incorrectly, thereby speaking nonstandard or incorrect African American Vernacular English. This is interesting because AAVE is considered a nonstandard or even substandard language variety of American English by many nonlinguists.

In the last ten years, a growing number of white establishments are using nonstandard forms of the verb "to be," as declared by prescriptive grammarians—those authorities who say that speakers are only to communicate in a particular way, which also happens to be the correct way. These prescriptions are made without respect to how people actually speak; hence, the rift between spoken English and prescribed English. Such a rift instigated by prescriptivists might not exist if they—and we—all kept in mind that language is a species-specific, controllable, conscious, arbitrary, abstract, conventional, complex, local, and productive system of signs, transmitted through the auditory channel or a substitute, with which human beings communicate to each other their thoughts, feelings, experiences, desires, perceptions, etc.; preserve and transmit their culture; store their knowledge; establish an atmosphere of sociability; establish, maintain, and signal social structures; project individual personalities. In other words, language is arbitrary; hence, there is no language that can be described as inherently correct or incorrect in comparison to another language. Likewise, the aesthetics of language are relative to the individual, but the function is arbitrary.

Over the years, I have collected several instances of AAVE usage by white establishments. One was used in a 1988 national advertising campaign for a major sports shoe company. Later, the slogan was adopted at a major university town in the southwest (if not by other universities or colleges around the country) as a slogan on T-shirts. The slogan was "U.B.U." As a takeoff on this, several other slogans were put on T-shirts and other articles, such as "I.B.A." with a picture of a longhorn, and "U.B. where U.B." Other nonstandard usages of the copula by white speakers or establishments are, "If you ain't, you be wishin' you was," "I be jammin'," "Willie B. Wright," and "I. B. Fixin'."

The copula can be used in several different ways in AAVE that would be incorrect for prescribed English. For instance, there are distinctions in AAVE among the following sentences: (1) She married; (2) She been married; (3) She *been* married; (4) She be tired.

The first sentence indicates that this person is currently married. The copula is not used because in AAVE, the forms of the verb "to be" can be deleted wherever they can be contracted in prescribed English. Hence, in prescribed English, this sentence would be, "She is married" or "She's married." Although many linguists (and nonlinguists) until the mid-1970s thought this was an example of the "lazy" speech of African Americans, it was actually a rule in AAVE. The second sentence indicates that this person was married before but is no longer married. The rule in AAVE of deletion where contraction occurs in prescribed English applies in this sentence as well. In prescribed English, the sentence would be, "She has been married before," or "She's been married before." The third sentence indicates that this person has been married for quite some time. This is an example of *aspect*. Aspect means the verb is inflected (i.e., an affix is added) to indicate the duration, repetition, completion, or quality of the action or state denoted by the verb. This exists in other languages, such as Russian and Latin. The second and third sentences also illustrate a comparable distinction between the perfect and pluperfect tenses (i.e., they represent points on a continuum for past time). The fourth sentence indicates this person is constantly tired. It is an example of *invariant be* used in a *habitual* manner, since the action extends over a period of time. *Invariant be* is probably the most salient characteristic of AAVE.

I have four examples of usage by African Americans. The interesting thing was the diversity in education level. One was by a young female who was receiving federal aid to help care for herself and her young child. In an interview, her response to the question of her feelings about being a single parent at such a young age was, "If it wasn't for her I wouldn't be having the things I have now." In this sentence, she responded with *invariant be*.

The second speaker was a professional baseball player who completed high school but did not go to college. Because of his athletic ability, he is paid very well. In an interview in which he was asked about the strategy of the competing baseball team in trying to keep him from stealing bases, he responded, "I know they go'n' drive me." He responded with the AAVE rule of deletion where contraction occurs in prescribed English.

The third speaker was a young female college student. She normally speaks AAVE in informal situations with her family. While conversing with her mother about the disposition of a mutual friend, she asked, "What be wrong with her?" She used *habitual be* to express her uncertainty about the mental health of a person.

The fourth was by a well-known minister in the Dallas area who has a Ph.D. He is the head of a nationwide program called the Urban Alternative. While giving a message, he said, "I [God] left you on earth for seventy years and you goin' through culture shock." He uses the AAVE rule of deletion where contraction occurs in prescribed English.

This lends support to the phenomenon that a large number of African Americans, regardless of geographical location or educational level, share syntactic features in their speech. This is a phenomenon because regardless of the accent or language-variety region—Southern, New England, or Inland Northern—the sentence structure of many African Americans remains somewhat of a constant. Hence, lexical items may vary, but the construction of the utterances varies little. I would venture to say that such a constant has to do with the issues of identity, culture, community, and the effects of racism.

Let the Revolution Begin

African American Vernacular English has been studied for decades, although, before the mid-1970s, mostly by white scholars. It has also been studied from different perspectives: linguistic, sociolinguistic, creolist, anthropological, and ethnographic. Smitherman says:

> Today scholars generally agree that the African heritage was not totally wiped out, and that both African-American Language and African-American Culture have roots in African patterns. . . . Over time, and after prolonged contact with European Americans, Africans in America adopted some Eurocentric patterns, and their African patterns of language and culture were modified—but they were not erased. (1994: 4–5)

The paucity of African Americans studying AAVE before the mid-1970s was unfortunate because of the loss of an invaluable perspective and because of the hint of inauthenticity or the possibility of fraud. However, an increase in the number of African American scholars who are conducting sociolinguistic research in the African American community has helped to close the gap. Instead of some white scholars studying AAVE to make further claims about the inferiority of African Americans, or some with good intentions but a lack of access, more researchers have come to better deal with the variable role and implications of the fieldworker. Because many African American communities view whites with suspicion, and because it is difficult for outsiders to elicit the vernacular, it is hardly surprising that the data collected by some earlier white scholars could be suspect.

Because of the growth in this area of study, it is more likely that researchers can access not only what is called AAVE but also the variation in a language that belongs to a group of people that has many similarities and differences. Research in AAVE and other language varieties has been important because it has helped make some people more aware of the efficacy, viability, and naturalness of linguistic variation and less fixated on establishing the dominion of a particular variety of the English language. Nevertheless, it continues to be important because there are still too many people who are willing to believe in the myth of a prescribed language and demanding that others do the same—or else.

The intolerance for language variation as a product of racism is real. Language diversity provides a means for justifying discrimination based on differences. I am very concerned with the socioeconomic restraints placed especially on minorities who do not speak this prescribed English. This language farce is merely an easy target for a greater problem. Sledd says:

> In the U.S.A., we are being told, everybody wants approval—not approval for doing anything worth approving, but approval for doing whatever happens to be approved. Because approval goes to upward mobility, everybody should be upwardly mobile; and because upward mobility is impossible for underdogs who have not learned middle-dog barking, we must teach it to them for use in their excursions into the middle-dog world. There is no possibility either that the present middle class can be brought to tolerate lower-class English or that upward mobility, as a national aspiration, will be questioned. Those are the pillars on which the state is built, and the compassionate teacher, knowing the ways of his society, will change the color of his students' vowels although he cannot change the color of their skins. (1972: 325)

In the early 1960s, there was a political instrument invented called *bidialectalism*. Sledd (1972: 321) says, "The basic assumption of bi-dialectalism is that the prejudices of middle-class whites cannot be changed but must be accepted and indeed enforced on lesser breeds. Upward mobility, it is assumed, is the end of education, but white power will deny upward mobility to speakers of black English, who must therefore be made to talk white English in their contacts with the white world." According to Sledd (1972: 322), "No language variety is better than any other, yet poor and ignorant children must change theirs unless they want to stay poor and ignorant." However, realistically, if all African Americans spoke prescribed English, society would find some other reason to use minorities as scapegoats for poverty, crime, and all the other negative aspects of living in a world where people do not get along with one another because they are different. The fact is that employers dislike black faces but use AAVE as an excuse. African American Vernacular English, though it has no intrinsic evils, has become an automatic shibboleth for the social, educational, and economic advancement of African Americans.

Edwin Newman (1974) further supports this bias by his view of the reasons for the decline in language: "It stems in part from large causes. One of those causes is the great and rapid change this country went through in the 1960s. . . . Another aspect of that change was that people who felt oppressed by society organized to enforce their demands either for the first time or with greater success than ever before—blacks, Indians, Chicanos, women, homosexuals, lesbians, prison inmates, welfare recipients" (1974: 9).

It is not so much that the 1960s brought about tremendous social changes but that a great many people were being heard—possibly for the first time in recent history. It was not that blacks, Indians, Chicanos, and women *felt* oppressed; they *were* oppressed. With their outcries, the diversity of a nation in decline was being heard, but these people had been here all along. They were not new—they were overlooked or ignored. African Americans have spoken AAVE for almost as long as they have been in America. The notoriety of their culture and language did not cause a decline in language but rather a greater awareness of real and valid language diversity. It made the concept that one language variety was just as good as another more real. It brought the underlying fears of an establishment to the light. Sledd says:

> The person who talks right, as we do, is one of us. The person who talks wrong is an outsider, strange and suspicious, and we must make him feel inferior if we can. That is one purpose of education. In a school system run like ours by white businessmen, instruction in the mother tongue includes formal initiation into the linguistic prejudices of the middle class. (1972: 319)

However, the educational system has failed in its job to eradicate diversity in language. We all have the choice to speak as we choose and we continue to make that choice.

According to Sledd, "formal education could possibly produce real bidialectals in a vast system of state nurseries and boarding schools to which the children of the poor and ignorant would be consigned at an early age; but such establishments would be prohibitively expensive, intolerable to the people, and still not absolutely certain of success, because the most essential of all conditions might not be met—namely, the desire of African American children to talk like the white middle class" (1972: 327).

At this point, language diversity is discouraged to the extent that many are made to feel insecure, inferior, and unintelligent about their language variety. We must keep in mind that no matter how many times teachers tell students their language is beautiful or quite acceptable at home or with friends, it all goes for naught when it is paired with "but in school we must use standard English" as a rebuke. Despite how indirect or polite the rebuke, the message is still the same: "Your language is not good enough for the language required in school." Translation: "You are not good enough."

Ironically, one who does not know at least two languages may be considered unenlightened or uninformed, since it would be intelligent to know more than one language in this day and age, as those in earlier centuries did. At one time, Latin, Greek, Italian, and French were common languages of the educated. The operative word here is *educated*. Given this, maybe the bidialectalists were not far off base. Maybe it would make better sense to require whites to speak AAVE in their dealings with African Americans since whites tend to have more educational and economic advantages than African Americans and since some whites have historically considered themselves more intelligent than African Americans. In any event, only requiring AAVE speakers to become bidialectal is not acceptable.

There is so much interaction between countries of differing cultures and languages that it would only be reasonable to speak a language besides one's native language. As a consequence of the ingrained ethnocentrism of Americans and the negativism that is integrated with it, many in turn project those pernicious feelings onto others of differing language varieties. Hence, a cycle of intolerance is created. According to Sledd (1972), at best bidialectal students will get somewhat better jobs and will move up a few places in the rat race of the underlings; at worst, they will be cut off from other African Americans, still not accepted among whites, and economically no better off than they were before.

Sledd (1972: 320) says, "The object of life in the U.S.A. is for everybody to get ahead of everybody else, and since linguistic prejudice can keep one from moving up, it is taught that people who want to be decision-makers had better talk and write like the people who make decisions." Life does not work that way. The rules would only change and the players would still be the same.

Our perceptions of our language are integrated with our perceptions of ourselves. Because of that, when we talk about language, we should also talk about identity, because it is at stake—or at risk. However, in discussions about AAVE, bidialectalism, or the more recent discussions about Ebonics, this issue of identity is ignored and not recognized. Identity is a key issue in discussions about language use, especially usage that is not highly esteemed. African American Vernacular English certainly fits that bill. Those who use less prestigious ways of speaking or who choose to identify with cultures that are not part of the mainstream are punished. They are punished by society, by the educational system, by pedagogical methods, and by the ideologies held in American culture. We must keep in mind that language is part of one's culture, one's heritage, and one's being. To punish one's language is to punish the individual—and the community of those speakers.

Summary

In the second grade, I remember Mrs. Polly drilling me on how to speak "good" English. I could not use "ain't" and double negatives or use "be" in the "wrong" place. I used my precious grammar book to conduct classes out of my garage for neighborhood children. By teaching others, I was able to practice using "good" English. I still have this book stored in a box at home.

My teacher had a profound effect on my desire to learn all that I could about "correct" pronunciation and "correct" English. I would go with my mother through stores reciting a variety of paradigms to instill this correct English. I would constantly correct the way my parents or others in my family spoke. This fervor for speaking correct English lasted for several years. I even entered college as a speech pathology major (as if varieties of a language are pathologies to be cured) in order to further my progress in speaking correct English as well as teaching others to do the same. My family still expects this of me.

In the midst of my "correct English" crusade as an undergraduate student at the University of Texas, I began studying varieties of English. I became deeply interested in different dialects and accents of English because they showed the diversity in language. Now, I do not go around stores practicing paradigms in order to instill "good" English. I realize the English language consists of many varieties and no one variety is inherently inferior or superior to any other—each is just different.

Often lost, ignored, or buried in the quest for admiration and acceptance outside of one's (cultural) community are the trials, tribulations, and consequences of that quest. In a paper I coauthored for a gender and literacy class I took in 1992, I related a story of an incident that happened to me during elementary school and my reaction to that story at the time of the class.

> I was in the fifth grade. It was my second year in a magnet school where I was being bused from my home in a working-class neighborhood in Houston, Texas. The school was Henry Wadsworth Longfellow Elementary School in the middle of a white, middle-class neighborhood that didn't resemble mine at all. All of the teachers there were white as I recall. The students of color that attended the school were all bused in from my part of town. We took long bus rides in the morning and afternoon to get there. It was a big change for me, but I liked the school. I got along wonderfully with my teachers. My fifth-grade teacher was Mr. Reeves. I thought he was wonderful. He liked me too. Sometimes I would sit next to him at lunch and we would talk about all kinds of stuff. Once he had me guess his age during lunch and I guessed it correctly. To this day I'm not sure that was a good thing to do. One day in class we were doing an activity. Students were all over the room. Troy, one of the kids being bused to the school like me, was fiddling with something and Mr. Reeves yelled to him, "Get your *black* hands off of that." He had never told anyone to get their "white" hands off of anything. Why did he have to say "black"? Why did he have to say it so loud and so hurtful? I don't know how I changed at that time, but I must have because we all do. I still had white friends at school and special friendships, but I always remember that day and it always hurts me deeply.
>
> I am a black woman and I am proud of it. . . . I don't wonder what it's like to be white. I wonder what it's like to be black and respected, or to be black and equal in the eyes of society.

Not long after that paper, I read an essay by David Mura entitled "Strangers in the Village" (1992). In it, he expresses what I had been feeling for quite some time. It was a feeling that had been growing anonymously but which was beginning to take a coherent and speakable form. The feeling has not gone away or been cured—that may never happen. But being able to speak it and write it makes it easier to cope with. Mura says:

> What I am trying to do in both my writing and my life is to replace self-hatred and self-negation with anger and grief over my lost selves, over the ways my

cultural heritage has been denied to me, over the ways that people in America would assume either that I am not American, or conversely, that I am just like them; over the ways my education and the values of European culture have denied that other cultures exist. I know more about Europe at the time when my grandfather came to America than I know about Meiji Japan. I know Shakespeare and Donne, Sophocles and Homer better than I know Zeami, Basho or Lady Murasaki. This is not to say I regret what I know, but I do regret what I don't know. And the argument that the culture of America is derived from Europe will not wipe away this regret. (1992:17)

I have long since moved beyond my prescriptivist views of language into one more appreciative of differences. I came to realize that earlier in my life I had chosen what was peculiar to my mind.

Like most people, I believed the rhetoric that prescribed English is good and everything else is bad. Because I grew up speaking AAVE, I heard that message constantly and with conviction. I was ashamed of my language. Williams (1970) says:

As we ask a person to learn and use a way of speech, we are at the same time asking him to function (if sometimes only to a small degree) in that society. One of the problems associated with such candidacy is the strain put upon a person who, because he is trying to assume a role in a new social structure, feels regret at leaving behind his parent structure and also feels uncertainty about being accepted in the new structure. (1970: 396)

I am told I speak "proper" English. I share features of AAVE, but it is not a mode I often communicate in nor one that is often associated with me—even by my husband. He teases me when I talk to a family member because he says I "try" to sound black—but I do not. He does not associate my speech with others in my family just as others in my family do not associate my speech with theirs. Yet I do possess several features of AAVE in my speech. They are most likely operative when I am talking to my family (or sometimes other African Americans).

I do not remember when or how my language changed, but I know my schooling was influential, as well as my acceptance of the indoctrination of schooling. I went to an integrated school when I was in the fourth grade because my parents had me bused to a magnet school in Houston. Most of the students were white. The African American students were bused in just as I was.

We moved when I was in the sixth grade to a more integrated neighborhood, but the school I transferred to was no longer predominantly white. By the time I reached high school, the school I went to was predominantly African American. When I decided to go to college, I went to a predominantly white university. My mother often tells me how she would not have sent me to that university had she known how things were going to turn out. She says that at the same time that she says how proud of me she is.

According to O'Barr, "each of us could write a linguistic autobiography, and our divergent stories would be united by tales of early awareness that provoked us to seek ways of comprehending language as we have known it" (1993: 320). In the process of (re)discovering what is peculiar to our minds, we perhaps get a better view of how our experiences and cultures shape our views of ourselves and our world and where both can and cannot (or maybe should and should not) go.

Questions for Further Thought and Discussion

1. What is the relationship between language and identity? Provide examples from your own life experiences.

2. Compare and contrast Milroy's social networks construct with Le Page's acts of identity construct. Which construct better conforms to your own experiences with language and identity?

3. Given the debate about the Oakland School Board's December 1996 decision to incorporate "Ebonics" into their curriculum and the prominence of the term "Ebonics" as a result of the debate, why do you suppose the author never uses that term?

4. What images or impressions do the terms "African American Vernacular English," "Black English," and "Black English Vernacular" create for you? Do you agree or disagree with the impressions Alexander mentions for the terms? Please explain your answer.

5. What are denotations and connotations of "black/Black?" African American? How do they differ? How are they the same? Does it really matter which you use?

6. What is bidialectalism and how can it or should it be incorporated into the educational system? Please explain your answer.

7. What effects did the changing face of research in the 1970s have on the study of African American Vernacular English? What is a parallel example of this "revolution?"

8. What would your linguistic autobiography look like? Would it include incidences of language use that were "peculiar" to your mind?

Selected Bibliography

Alexander, Benjamin H. (1979). *Standard English: To Hell with Anything Else.* South Bend, Ind.: American Council on Education Fellows.

Bakhtin, M. M. (1986). The problem of speech genres. In *Speech Genres and Other Late Essays*, Caryl Emerson and Michael Holquist (eds.), 60–102. V. W. McGee (trans.). Austin: University of Texas Press.

Baugh, John. (1983). *Black Street Speech: Its History, Structure and*

Survival. Austin: University of Texas Press.

Freire, Paulo, and Donaldo Macedo (1987). *Literacy: Reading the Word and the World.* South Hadley, MA: Bergin and Garvey.

Le Page, Robert B. (1986). Acts of identity. *English Today* 8: 21–24.

Milroy, James, and Lesley Milroy (1991). *Authority in Language: Investigating Language Prescription and Standardization* (2nd ed.). London: Routledge & Kegan Paul.

Mura, David. (1992). Strangers in the village. In *Race, Class, and Gender: An Anthology*, Margaret L. Andersen and Patricia Hill Collins (eds.), 11–20. Belmont, Cal.: Wadsworth.

Newman, Edwin. (1974). *Strictly Speaking: Will America Be the Death of English?* Indianapolis: Bobbs-Merrill.

O'Barr, William M. (1993). Professional varieties: The case of language and law. In *American Dialect Research*, Dennis Preston (ed.), 319–330. Philadelphia: Benjamins.

Sledd, James H. (1972). Bi-dialectalism: The linguistics of white supremacy. In *Contemporary English*, David L. Shores (ed.), 319–330. Philadelphia: Lippincott.

Smitherman, Geneva (1994). *Black Talk: Words and Phrases from the Hood to the Amen Corner.* Boston: Houghton Mifflin.

Williams, Frederick (1970). Language, attitude, and social change. In *Language and Poverty: Perspectives on a Theme*, Frederick Williams (ed.), 380–399. Chicago: Markham.

Latin America

OFELIA GARCÍA

Somos un agujero	We're a hole
en medio del mar y el cielo	in the middle of sea and sky
500 años después,	500 years afterwards,
una raza encendida	a gleaming race
negra, blanca y taína	black, white and indian
pero, ¿quién descubrió a quién?	but, who discovered whom?
!Ay! y el costo de la vida,	Oh! and the cost of life
pa'rriba tu ves,	goes up, you see,
y el peso que baja	and the peso goes down,
pobre, ni se ve,	poor thing, hardly seen,
y la medicina,	and medicine
camina al revés,	goes backwards,
aquí no se cura	here one can't cure
ni un callo en el pie,	not even a foot corn,
y ahora el desempleo	and now unemployment
me mordió también;	has also bitten me;
a nadie le importa,	no one cares
pues no hablamos inglés,	because we don't speak English,
ni a la mitsubischi	not to Mitsubishi
ni a la chevrole'	nor to Chevrolet.

Juan Luis Guerra, "El costo de la vida," *Areíto*

The Sound of a Merengue

The well-known merengue just quoted eloquently expresses the sentiments of today's Latin Americans toward their cultural and linguistic identity. Although he

226

is speaking of Dominicans, the popular poet Juan Luis Guerra and his famous music group transcend national identity, as Latin Americans everywhere vote with their dancing feet their approval of Guerra's critical vision of Latin American identity.

The popular poetry of this merengue confirms concepts that were clearly defined by Latin American thinkers and essayists of the early twentieth century. Instructive in this regard is Guerra's allusion to the 1492 encounter between Europeans and Native Americans and his definition of today's Latin Americans as "a gleaming race/black, white and *taína* but, who discovered whom?" Guerra's verse is reminiscent of Mexican essayist José Vasconcelos's 1925 essay entitled "La Raza Cósmica." The recognition of *mestizaje*, of the mixture of races, is essential in defining Latin America in the twentieth century, as is the *transculturación* that has molded its identity and is exemplified in the question, "but, who discovered whom?" The concept of transculturation was first defined by Cuban ethnologist Fernando Ortiz in his 1940 book, *El contrapunteo cubano del tabaco y el azúcar*. By opposing his transculturation to the Anglo-American concept of acculturation, Ortiz identifies a symbiotic Latin American identity, the product and recreation of the many cultures of those who have been in and come to Latin America.

But this *mestizaje* and transculturation that are such integral parts of a Latin American identity have not produced the "cosmic race" that Vasconcelos had optimistically predicted. The continent that was to encompass the vastness of the cosmos has turned, sings Guerra, into "un agujero," a hole in the ground. The optimistic identity once defined by the presence of a dominant messianism has yielded to a pessimistic perception increasingly dominated by absences, as poor and indigenous Latin Americans have raised their multilingual voices to claim recognition for their differences and their social problems.

The merengue expresses this smothering negativity: Everything "goes down," "walks backwards," becomes almost invisible, "ni se ve." And it turns out that no one cares, no one listens, because even when said beautifully in the crystalline diction of Guerra's Caribbean Spanish and to the seductive tune of a noisy merengue, there remains the trouble that "no hablamos inglés"—that we lack the language that is not just the language of the "Coloso del Norte" but now, too, of the multinational corporations like Mitsubishi and Chevrolet.

The sense of spiritual superiority of Spanish- and Portuguese-speaking Latin Americans over the utilitarian English-speaking Anglo culture, best expressed by the Uruguayan José Enrique Rodó in his 1900 essay "Ariel," has been nearly lost today. In the early 1960s, *el hombre nuevo*—dreamed of in the early optimism of the Cuban revolution and sung in the ballads of Pablo Milanés and Silvio Rodríguez —was to give voice to the poor and oppressed in Latin America, as Indians and blacks, the poor and uneducated, stood shoulder to shoulder next to the mostly white Latin American intelligentsia. But then came the 1970s and 1980s, and this "new man," who, in different languages and different varieties of Spanish, was to realize the ideals of the early decades of the century, was silenced by repressive regimes. As the twenty-first century approaches, many areas have seen at least a dampening of the most brutal forms of repression and a return of some of the electoral trappings of a tentative and timid democracy. Although indigenous groups have progressively demanded that their native languages and cultures be recognized as national languages and communities, the pluralistic and multilingual reality of Latin America remains officially unrecognized.

Toward a Definition of Latin American Ethnolinguistic Culture

Guillermo Bonfil Batalla, a noted Mexican anthropologist, explains the situation in which Latin America finds itself:

> En América Latina hay muchos más pueblos que estados nacionales. La inmensa mayoría de las llamadas sociedades nacionales contienen en su interior, no uno, sino una diversidad de pueblos distintos. Son, por eso, sociedades plurales. El problema es que esa condición plural no ha sido reconocida por los estados con todas sus consecuencias. . . . Una sola lengua, una sola raza, una misma historia, una cultura común: tales eran los requisitos para consolidar un verdadero estado (napoleónico). Y la realidad iba por otros cauces, lo que exigió que el Estado se pretendiera constituir en forjador de la nación unificada, uniforme culturalmente, *inexistente*. La terca realidad seguía siendo plural: había indios, ante todo; pero también negros y ciertas regiones que desarrollaban su propia identidad (1992: 19, emphasis added).

> [In Latin America there are many more nations than nation states. The immense majority of the so-called nation states contain in their interior, not one but many different nations. They are, therefore, plural societies. The problem is that the plural condition has not been recognized by the states, thus having many consequences. . . . Only one language, one race, one same history, a common culture: those were the requirements to consolidate a true (Napoleonic) state. And reality went a different way, making it a requirement for the state to try to constitute itself into the creator of the unified nation, culturally uniform, *nonexistent.* The stubborn reality continued being plural: There were, beyond everything, Indians; but there were also blacks and some regions that had their own identity.] (1992: 19, emphasis added)

This nonexistent Latin America, promoted by the official governments, usually encompasses the countries of South, Central, and North America and the Caribbean islands that officially speak Spanish, Portuguese, or French. In an incisive analysis of the ethnolinguistic diversity of the Americas, Darcy Ribeiro (1977) identifies three different types of national societies in the region:

1. The "witness nations" (*los pueblos testimonios*) include Mexico, Central America, and the Andean countries of Ecuador, Peru, and Bolivia. These nations had advanced precolonial civilizations: Incas, Aztecs, and Mayas. These groups had extensively populated the region prior to the arrival of Europeans. Darcy claims that in these countries there has been, and continues to be, a continuous process of ethnic reconstitution.
2. The "new nations" (*los pueblos nuevos*) are Brazil, Colombia, Venezuela, Chile, and the nations of the Caribbean. These countries were formed

through the miscegenation of peoples of very different ethnic origins, Europeans, Africans, and indigenous groups, under a tyrannical colonial regime.

3. The "transplanted nations" (*los pueblos trasplantados*) include the countries of the River Plate (Argentina and Uruguay), as well as Anglo America. These nations were formed when Europeans arrived in scarcely populated regions and displaced the indigenous population, many times through violence.

The European colonizers in Latin America were mostly Spaniards and Portuguese. But there were also French, Dutch, and British, especially in the area of the Caribbean. And the immigrant wave of the early twentieth century included, besides Spaniards and Portuguese, Italians, Germans, and French.

African slaves were brought to the New World on a large scale, especially to Brazil and Cuba, until 1886. Approximately 2 million slaves from the western coast of Africa made their way to the Caribbean and 4 million to Brazil, where they worked on sugar plantations and completely altered the ethnoracial composition of the region.

The indigenous groups of Latin America number more than 400, totaling more than 30 million people. The most numerous group speaks Quechua, the former language of the Incas. Quechua is spoken extensively today in Peru, western Bolivia, and Ecuador. Approximately one-fifth of Peruvians (5 million), living mostly in the southern states, speak Quechua as their first language (Godenzzi 1996: 240). Quechua is also spoken by over one-fourth of Bolivians (2.8 million). The variety of Quechua spoken in Ecuador is known as Quichua and is spoken by 1.5 million people.

There are at least four other Indian language groups that have more than 1 million speakers: Nahuatl, Maya, Aymara, and Guaraní. Nahuatl, once the language of the great empire of the Aztecs, is still the most important Indian language in Mexico, spoken by 1.5 million Mexicans. Maya, the language of the great Maya civilizations, exists today in different forms that can be grouped into about eight languages in Mexico and about twenty in Guatemala. Approximately one-third of Guatemala's 10 million people are Maya Indians who speak Mayan languages, the most important of which is Quiché (Richards and Richards 1996). In Mexico, around 1 million people speak Yucatec, the most important Mayan language. Aymara is spoken by more than 1.5 million people in Bolivia and another one-half million in Peru. Finally, Guaraní is spoken by approximately 75% of the 5 million Paraguayans.

Table 16-1 summarizes for the reader the situation of the major indigenous languages in Latin America.

Part of the difficulty in defining a Latin American ethnolinguistic identity stems from the contradiction between the real, mostly oral, pluralism of Latin America and the official, mostly written, posture, which states that all Latin Americans share a common origin, history, and culture. The Latin American emphasis on a legal written corpus maintained since colonial times has created what Angel Rama (1984) has called "la ciudad letrada." This lettered and learned city's sole pur-

Table 16-1. Major Indigenous Languages of Latin America

Country	Total Population (in Millions)	Language	No. of Speakers (in Millions)	% of Total	Language	No. of Speakers (in Millions)	% of Total
Bolivia	7.5	Quechua	2.8	37	Aymara	1.8	24
Ecuador	11	Quechua	1.5	5			
Guatemala	10	Maya	3.3	33			
Mexico	90	Nahuatl	1.5	2	Maya	1	1
Paraguay	5	Guaraní	3.8	75			
Peru	25	Quechua	5	20	Aymara	.5	2

pose has been to defend a written Spanish language that was and often continues to be a minority and almost secret language and to separate it from the speech of unschooled people, often a different language that is generally spoken in more rural regions or in poorer urban areas. The Latin American "linguistic culture," in the sense defined by Harold Schiffman, is derived from the distance created between the written official position advanced by government policy, legislation, literature, and essays and the daily speech of millions of Latin Americans. Despite the difficulties in defining a Latin American ethnolinguistic culture, the following traits characterize it:

1. A pluralistic cultural identity based on the concepts of *mestizaje* and *transculturación*.
2. A recognition of the region's multilingualism, despite official claims of a monolingual identity.
3. A recognition of the region's distinct linguistic identity from that of Spain or Portugal, despite an official attitude of *purismo* in the use of the European languages. In practice, Spanish and Portuguese are transplanted languages that are realized in many places as contact dialects sprung from the interaction through the centuries with Native, African, and other European languages and more recently with English. There are also significant minorities in both rural and urban Latin America for whom Spanish and Portuguese are second languages.
4. An insistence on using Spanish and Portuguese as markers of ethnolinguistic identity and in opposition to Anglo America.

In essence, however, it is only the colonial history of 500 years of *dependence*, mainly on Spain, more recently on the United States, and the resistance to it that gives cohesion to the region and is at the core of its ethnolinguistic identity (see Zea 1991). Limiting itself to Hispanoamérica, this chapter starts with a brief recounting of the encounter between the Old and the New World and identifies the different movements in identity that have been the product of sociohistorical forces in the twentieth century.

From the Spanish of the Empire
to that of Hispanoamérica

Europeans found three important civilizations when they reached present-day Latin America: the Mayan, the Aztec, and the Inca. The Mayans occupied the Yucatan peninsula, southern Mexico, and most of present-day Guatemala. The Aztecs were in the central valley of Mexico. The Inca empire stretched along the Andes from northern Ecuador through Peru to southern Chile. There were also many other Indian nations.[1]

Spanish was the language officially sanctioned by the Spanish Empire to convert the Indians during the first two centuries of Spain's rule. But Spanish missionaries, frustrated by the difficulty of teaching Spanish to the many Indians, started instead to spread among the Indian population those languages that were more universal. These Indian languages, called then *lenguas generales*, included Quechua, Náhuatl, Chibcha, and Tupí-guaraní.

Spanish was not generally taught until the eighteenth century. In 1770, Carlos III ordered that the Indian languages be extinguished and that only Spanish be used, a difficult task, when, for example, in Mexico City there were 8,000 Spanish residents and more than 2 million Indians.

This situation of a powerful numerical minority speaking the language of the empire and a numerical majority with little power speaking other languages characterized the beginning of the nineteenth century, when most countries in South and Central America became independent. As the eighteenth century closed, 78% of the population of New Spain were Indians (Cifuentes and Ros 1993: 135). Yet the independence movement in Spanish America that took place between 1910 and 1924 included mostly Spanish-speaking elite *criollos* (Latin Americans born of Spanish parents), led notably by Simón Bolivar, José Antonio de Sucre, and José de San Martín. Only in Mexico did the masses of Indians and others of mixed blood, encouraged by a local priest, Hidalgo, participate in a revolution that was both for independence and social improvement. Yet independence in Mexico was only achieved when Hidalgo was shot, the popular movement squelched, and an elite *criollo*, Iturbide, declared himself emperor of Mexico and of the Capitanía de Guatemala, which included most of present-day Central America.

The cultivation and spread of Spanish for its homogenizing nationalist effects became an important agenda of the first independent governments. In 1835, Mexico founded its first Language Academy, followed in 1875 by a Mexican Academy of Language that corresponded to the Real Academia Española in Spain. As early as 1847, Andrés Bello, born in Caracas before independence, wrote *Gramática de la lengua castellana* to avoid the degeneration of the Spanish of Spanish America into "dialectos irregulares" and to maintain "unidad nacional" (Ripoll 1966: 56). When, in 1877, José Pedro Varela declared that education in Uruguay was to be free, required, and under secular control, he stipulated that Spanish, as the national language, had to be used in all schools of the country. Spanish spread quickly, although not entirely. By 1898, when Spain lost its last colonies, including Cuba and Puerto Rico in the Caribbean, only 17% of the entire population were monolingual speakers of indigenous languages. In 100 years, Spanish had gone from being the minority language of the powerful elite to the vehicular language for much of the Latin American population and the officially sanctioned language of Spanish American identity.

During this entire period, native non-European elements of Spanish American culture were recognized and sometimes even idealized during the romanticism of the late nineteenth century. In fact, a budding Spanish American literature started distinguishing itself from the peninsular one by introducing native groups such as the "gaucho" (*Facundo*, 1845, by Domingo Faustino Sarmiento; *Martín Fierro*, 1872, by José Hernández) and the "Indian" (*Tabaré*, 1886, by Zorilla de San Martín; *Enriquillo*, 1879, by Manuel de Jesús Galván). But despite this pluralistic recognition, the official cultural identity of Spanish America remained mostly European. In an important essay called "Conflicto y armonías de las razas en América" the Argentinean Sarmiento, author of *Facundo*, expresses the reigning attitude toward those whom he calls "the savages":

> La masa indígena absorbe al fin al conquistador y le comunica sus cualidades e ineptitudes, si aquél no cuida de transmitirle, como los romanos a galos y españoles, a más de su lengua, sus leyes, sus códigos, sus costumbres.

> [The indigenous mass finally absorbs the conqueror and communicates to him its qualities and ineptitude, if the conqueror is not careful to transmit to him, as the Romans did with the Gauls and the Spaniards, besides its language, its laws, its codes, its customs.] (Sarmiento 1883, cited in Ripoll 1966: 99)

The year 1898 is important not only because it represents political independence from Spain and the accompanying fear that the Spanish of Latin America would further degenerate but also because it marks the second successful attempt by the English-speaking United States to officially take over the Latin American world. In 1848, through the treaty of Guadalupe Hidalgo, the United States had taken half of Mexico's territory, from present-day Texas to California. In 1898, the previous Spanish possessions of Puerto Rico and Cuba became U.S. possessions. The ethnolinguistic identity of Spanish America was now threatened on two fronts, not only because of its further political and emotional distance from Spain, "La Madre Patria" [The Motherland], but also because of new contact with another powerful language, that of the United States.

In the late nineteenth century, the political and literary contributions of the Puerto Rican Eugenio María de Hostos and the Cuban José Martí did much to promote Latin American unity and nationalism. In the essay that was to become the ideal of that era, "Nuestra América," José Martí declares with pride: "El vino, de plátano; y si sale agrio, ¡es nuestro vino!" [Wine, of banana; and if it comes out bitter, it's our wine!]. In search for an identity different from that of Spain, the first truly independent literary movement of Spanish America, the *modernismo*, had taken refuge in the exotic and French climates of the Nicaraguan Rubén Dario´s *Azul* (1888). José Martí brings back the "preciosismo modernista" to the reality of peasants, of the "Guántamera," popularly sung today to Martí's "Versos sencillos."

The end of the nineteenth century is marked with the publication of José Enrique Rodó's "Ariel," in which the Uruguayan praises Spanish America for its idealism in the face of Anglo America's utilitarianism. Spanish America's ethnolinguistic identity now seems firmly set, openly claiming Spanish, in the face of Theodore Roosevelt's "big stick" policy, as the differentiating element from the English-speaking "Colossus of the North."

Twentieth-Century Indigenismo and Afro-Antillanismo in Spanish

The late nineteenth century work of the *caribeños* Eugenio María Hostos and José Martí had already acknowledged the *mestizaje* of Latin America. In an essay titled "El Cholo," Hostos had said: "América deberá su porvenir a la fusión de razas. . . . El mestizo es la esperanza del futuro" [America will owe its future to the fusion of races. . . . The mestizo is the hope of the future] (Hostos 1870, quoted in Ripoll 1966: 164). And Martí in "Mi raza" had said: "El hombre no tiene ningún derecho especial porque pertenezca a una raza o a otra: dígase hombre, y ya se dicen todos los derechos" [Man doesn't have any special right because he belongs to one race or the other: call it Man, and all rights have already been mentioned] (Martí 1893, quoted in Ripoll 1966: 250).

While Hostos and Martí preached racial fusion and harmony in the Caribbean, the rest of the continent, which often considered racial differences equivalent to linguistic differences, held a white and Spanish-only supremacy racist attitude toward its identity. For example, in an essay published in 1910, the Argentinean José Ingenieros wrote about the Latin American "malady," "the preponderance of 'inferior' non-European races in our midst." And he proposed the cure: "European immigration, absorption of the colored races, education, and utilization of the nonwhite within the restricted limits of his abilities" (quoted in Stabb 1967: 32).

The struggle for a definition of ethnolinguistic identity that included the indigenous population of the Americas came to the forefront during the Mexican Revolution (1910–1920), portrayed in what was to become the first novel of social protest in Latin America, Mariano Azuela's *Los de Abajo* (1915). As a result, a national Mexican ideology came into being, grounded in the symbiosis of two races and cultures, those of Spain and of the New World Indian, and its ensuing *mestizaje*. This ideology of inclusion of all races in a Latin American identity now became prevalent throughout the continent. And this pride in a Latin American *mestizaje* expressed in Spanish became the differentiating symbol from an Anglo America that watched over Cuba through the Platt Amendment and had taken over Puerto Rico.

In Puerto Rico, English and Spanish had been declared official languages in 1902, and English became the preferred language of instruction until 1948. As a reaction, Spanish and a Hispanic culture became the symbol of Puerto Rican identity. Antonio Pedreira, in his 1931 essay "Insularismo," says: "Nosotros fuimos y seguimos siendo culturalmente una colonia hispánica" [We were and continue to be culturally a Hispanic colony].

During this period of intense opposition to an English-speaking Anglo America, the Latin American identity, affirmed in Spanish, started expressing a sympathetic awareness of native Americans and an increased consciousness of African elements, especially in the Caribbean, where the African slave trade had proliferated.

The maximum exponent of the sympathetic view of the Indians in the movement that became known as *Indigenismo* was José Vasconcelos, who, in his two monumental works *La Raza Cósmica* (1925) and *Indología* (1929), expressed his hope for Latin America in opposition again to Anglo America:

> Solamente la parte ibérica del continente dispone de los factores espirituales, la raza y el territorio que son necesarios para la gran empresa de iniciar la era universal de la humanidad.
>
> [Only the Iberian part of the continent has the spiritual factors, the race, and the territory that are necessary for the great enterprise of initiating the universal era of humanity.] (quoted in Ripoll 1966 336)

The Latin American left also espoused this new optimism. This was the case, for example, of the father of the Peruvian social reform party, the APRA (Alianza Popular Revolucionaria Americana), Manuel González Prada, and of José Mariátegui, author of "Siete ensayos de interpretación de la realidad peruana" (1928), in which the economic exploitation of Peruvian Indians is denounced. And in literature, the Ecuadorian Jorge Icaza wrote *Huasipungo* (1934), a novel portraying Indians not as silent partners in a romantic vision of Latin America but as peasants voicing their social protest in a white European Latin American world. In 1940, the First Inter-American Indigenista Congress took place in Pátzucaro, Mexico.

In the Caribbean, the ethnologist Fernando Ortiz worked on identifying the ethnocultural formation of Cuba around this time. In 1906, he had published *Los Negros Brujos*, in which for the first time he made reference to "lo afro-cubano" (p. xviii). By 1940, in his *Contrapunteo cubano del tabaco y el azúcar*, Ortiz acknowledged the "tranculturación" of Cuban culture, the synthesis of the complex cultural transmutations that were present in Cuba. The Cuban Nicolás Guillén and the Puerto Rican Luis Palés Matos filled their Spanish-language poetry with African sounds in expressions of "lo afro-antillano" during this period.

But despite the acknowledgment of the Indian and African cultures and languages in the forging of the Latin American ethnolinguistic identity, a voice was not given to those who did not speak or write anything but formal Spanish. In 1928, the Dominican Pedro Henríquez Ureña, in his "Seis ensayos en busca de nuestra expresión," identified Spanish as the only valid language identity of a Latin American writer. He referred to the few works written in Indian languages as lacking "propósitos lúcidos" (clear proposals). And he concluded:

> No hemos renunciado a escribir en español, nuestro problema de la expresión original y propia comienza ahí. Cada idioma es una cristalización de modos de pensar y de sentir, y cuanto en él se escribe se baña en el color de su cristal.
>
> [We haven't renounced writing in Spanish, our problem of expression that is original and autochthonous starts there. Each language is a crystallization of ways

of thinking and feeling, and whatever is written in it is bathed in the color of its glass.] (1928: 382).

Only Spanish was valid, but the European language molded the Latin American identity, repressing and silencing that of those who were not Europeans and who spoke other languages.

Henríquez Ureña (1940) was also responsible for first identifying the five dialect areas of Latin American Spanish, based on common history and substrata of indigenous languages:

1. The Caribbean, including not only Cuba, Puerto Rico, and the Dominican Republic but also much of Venezuela and the Atlantic coast of Colombia.
2. The Andes (Peru, Ecuador, Bolivia, northwest Argentina, most of Colombia, and part of Venezuela)
3. The River Plate (Argentina, Uruguay, and Paraguay)
4. Mexico (Mexico and Central America)
5. Chile

The silencing of the "other" Latin America—that of the countryside rather than the city, that of the Indian rather than the white European, that of speakers of languages other than Spanish—became the subject of essayists searching for identity as the twentieth century unfolded. In a 1952 essay, the Colombian Germán Arciniegas said:

There are two (Latin) Americas: the visible and the invisible. The visible (Latin) America ... of presidents and embassies, expresses itself through official organs, through a controlled press. ... And there is the mute, repressed America, which is a vast reservoir of revolution. ... Nobody knows exactly what these 150,000,000 silent men and women think, feel, dream, or await in the depths of their being. (quoted in Shapiro 1963: 1)

The Chilean Nobel Prize-winning poet, Pablo Neruda, wrote his *Canto General* (1950) as an elegy to Latin America, and in the act of naming its geography, history, and heroes, he gave voice to the poor and the suffering. In his essay titled, significantly, "Nosotros los indios" [We the Indians], Neruda referred to the contradiction between idealizing the indigenous Araucano warriors portrayed in *La Araucana*, the first Latin American epic poem written by the Spaniard Alonso de Ercilla in the mid-sixteenth century, and silencing the Araucano heritage of all Chileans:

Nuestros recién llegados gobernantes se propusieron decretar que no somos un país de indios. Este decreto perfumado no ha tenido expresión parlamentaria, pero la verdad es que circula tácitamente en ciertos sitios de representación nacional. *La Araucana* está bien, huele bien. Los araucanos están mal, huelen mal. Huelen a raza vencida. Y los usurpadores están ansiosos de olvidar o de olvidarse. En el hecho, la mayoría de los chilenos cumplimos con las disposiciones y decretos señoriales: como frenéticos arribistas nos avergonzamos de los araucanos. Contribuimos, los unos, a extirparlos y, los otros, a sepultarlos en el abandono y en el olvido.

[Our recently arrived governors decided to decree that we are not a country of Indians. This perfumed decree has not had parliamentary expression, but the truth is that it circulates tacitly in various places of national representation. *The Araucana* is fine, smells fine. The Araucanos are rotten, smell rotten. They smell as a conquered race. And the usurpers are anxious to forget or to forget themselves. In fact, the majority of Chileans are faithful to the ruling dispositions and decrees: As frenetic upwardly mobile people we're ashamed of the Araucanos. We contribute, some to remove them, others to bury them in abandonment and forgetfulness.] (quoted in Skirius 1994: 259)

The 1960s and Beyond: Multilingual Attempts

The demand for a voice for the Araucanos, the poor, and the silent America was answered by the Cuban Revolution of the early 1960s. Fidel Castro´s revolution reconnected with the nationalist identity that had been espoused much earlier by José Martí. And this socialist reality for an "hombre nuevo" created a different definition of ethnolinguistic identity as Latin Americans. Che Guevara explained it thus:

> En este continente se habla prácticamente una lengua. . . . Hay una identidad tan grande entre las clases de estos países que logran una identificación de tipo "internacional americano," mucho más completa que en otros continentes. Lengua, costumbres, religión, amo común, los unen. El grado y las formas de explotación son similares en sus efectos para explotadores y explotados de una buena parte de los países de nuestra América.

> [In this continent practically only one language is spoken. . . . There is such a great identity between classes in these countries that they realize an identity of an "international American" type, much fuller than in other continents. Language, costumes, religion, common master, unite them. The degree and the form of exploitation are similar in their effects for exploiters and those who are exploited in a good part of the countries of our America.] (1971: 136)

The new ethnolinguistic identity of Latin America is now based on its exploitation by a common master, the United States. And this sense of being exploited, first by the Europeans, then by the United States, is the core of the reinterpretation of a bleeding Latin American identity made by Eduardo Galeano in his famous *Las Venas abiertas de América Latina* (1971).

The *hispanidad* (the turning toward Spain and the Spanish language) of a Latin American identity was transcended and attacked during this period. The Cuban novelist Alejo Carpentier, noted for creating, in opposition to the European artificial "surrealism," the "real maravilloso" that already existed in Latin American reality, attacked the concept of *hispanidad* in a 1961 essay:

> Tras de la hispanidad se oculta un racismo solapado; se acepta que el negro, el indio, aquí, allá, hayan añadido su acento, su genio rítmico, al romancero de los conquistadores. Pero lo universal americano, lo ecuménico, sigue siendo lo que

trajeron los conquistadores. . . . Ni el 'nuestramericanismo' . . . ni el mito de una latinidad, de una hispanidad . . . vendrán a resolver nuestros problemas agrarios, políticos, sociales. . . . La Revolución Cubana, con los medios de expresión que pone y pondrá en nuestras manos . . . ha dado un sentido nuevo a nuestros destinos.

[Behind the *hispanidad* there is a hidden racism; it is accepted that blacks, Indians, here, there, have contributed their accent, their rhythmic genius, to the *romancero* of the conquerors. But what is universally American, what is ecumenical, is still what the conquerors brought. . . . Neither the "nuestramericanismo" nor the myth of a Latinness, of an *Hispanidad* . . . will solve our agricultural, political and social problems. . . . The Cuban revolution, with the modes of expression that it has put and will put in our hands . . . has given our destinies a new sense.] (1966: 84, 88)

This faith in the new Latin American society based on a socialist revolution and the need to transcend *la hispanidad* and the Spanish language that expressed it was responsible for the "boom" of the Latin American novel of the 1960s. In language and images that were playful and risky, the Argentinean Julio Cortázar, the Colombian Gabriel García Márquez, the Peruvian Mario Vargas Llosa, and the Mexican Carlos Fuentes exported a vision of a vigorous, fresh, and modern Latin America, no longer "underdeveloped," but the future just society. But the boom, the noise, and the energy were short-lived. By the mid-1970s, most Latin American countries were immersed in the silence of dictatorships.

The process in Peru is indicative in this regard. From 1968 to 1975, Peru was ruled by a progressive military regime under Velasco Alvarado. Besides the social reform program that included the expropriation of land and estates, a voice was claimed for the indigenous population of Peru. In 1972, Quechua was officialized, and bilingual education was encouraged. But there was a violent reaction from the white and mestizo Spanish-speaking bourgeoisie. In 1980, under the regime of Morales Bermudez, Quechua once again lost official status, and bilingual education was deemphasized. Today Quechua and Aymara are recognized as national languages, with coofficial status in certain territories and sectors, although only Spanish is official.

This process was repeated throughout Latin America. As military dictatorships became entrenched, the gains made by the indigenous populations in the 1960s and 1970s were repressed. This silencing of the indigenous population was promoted as a struggle against anarchist guerrillas and for democracy.

For example, in Bolivia there were three symposiums on "lenguas nacionales" in Cochabamba between 1973 and 1979. However, after the coup d'état in 1980, teaching in Aymara was prohibited. The government issued a statement indicating that insistence on doing so would be taken as evidence of leftist sympathies.

Nevertheless, since the 1960s, there has been a progressive awareness in Latin America of the role that the cultures and languages of indigenous groups have had in the gestation of a Latin American identity. And this greater consciousness has been accompanied at times by efforts to obtain official recognition for these languages and cultures. The indigenous groups themselves have been responsible for many brave attempts at what Hornberger (1996) has called (in the title of her book) "language planning from the bottom up." Indigenous communities have developed projects to support their *etnodesarrollo*—the development of their identity as different social, cultural, and historical units that have been dominated by the nation states—and their struggle for official recognition by those nation states.

The efforts for *etnodesarrollo*, a concept promoted by UNESCO, has been accompanied by the development of many bilingual education programs. A specific example has been the development and teaching of the Zapoteco alphabet (widely spoken in the state of Oaxaca, Mexico) as a symbol of linguistic and social resistance. Javier Castellanos explains:

> Impulsamos y fomentamos la escritura del zapoteco porque si no, se muere. . . . Escribimos para ganarle espacios al español, . . . para arrebatarle aquellos espacios que día con día se va adueñando.

> [We push and promote writing in Zapoteco because otherwise it would die. . . . We write to gain spaces from Spanish, . . . to take away from it those spaces that day by day it gains.] (quoted in Pardo 1993: 122)

Writing a language other than Spanish in the "ciudad letrada" is in itself a way of making inroads into an identity that has been constructed mostly through the written Spanish word.

In Mexico throughout the 1980s, the indigenous population had a recognized voice. For example, from 1982 to 1988 there was a Dirección General de Educación Indígena, and in 1983 the Consejo Nacional de Defensa de Idiomas Originarios de Mexico was established. The wording of the Mexican Constitution of 1991 granted formal equality to the indigenous communities for the first time:

> The Mexican nation has a multicultural composition, stemming originally from its indigenous communities. The law will protect and promote the development of their languages, cultures, usage, customs, resources and specific forms of social organization and will guarantee to the members of those communities effective access to the jurisdiction of the state. (quoted in Salinas Pedraza, 1996: 171)

Yet even in Mexico, the teaching of literacy by using the students' first language has been questioned since 1990. Increasingly, the state has used the argument that the modernization required under the North American Free Trade Agreement can only be achieved through education in Spanish. Hamel comments on the situation of bilingual education programs in Mexico in the present: "In 1991 alphabetization in vernacular languages is not the real policy in public Indian education, and in probably more than 90% of the schools in the bilingual system it does not take place" (1994: 286).

By the late 1980s, there had been a return to discussion of the integration of Indians into "civilized life" and a growing defense of the Spanish legacy. As early as 1980, there was a Symposium of the Academias de la Lengua Española in Lima, Peru, at which Latin American countries were asked to defend the Spanish language legally (Lara 1993: 164). From 1981 to 1983 Mexico established a "Comisión para la Defensa del Idioma español," with the explicit purpose of collaborating with Spain to defend the Spanish language. Using the avalanche of English as an excuse, Mexico reacted against its own indigenous languages. Representative of this attitude is the one expressed in *Novedades* (September 15, 1981): "El español de México está asediado por el inglés. Algo tiene que hacerse . . ." [The Spanish of Mexico is threatened by English. Something has to be done . . .]. In 1997, Mexico hosted the First International Congress on the Spanish Language, with the dual purpose of improving the status of the Spanish language while at the same time claiming linguistic independence from Spain.

Pardo (1993) explains this affirmation of the Spanish legacy in studying the situation in Oaxaca, the Mexican state that has the greatest number of Indians and the most linguistic and cultural diversity and in which one-half of the population speaks indigenous languages and inhabits three-fourths of the territory. Pardo states: "From the integrationist perspective and the neoliberal current of development that is sustained by the hegemonic sectors of the state society, the indigenous presence in Oaxaca is assumed as one of the causes of the backwardness and socioeconomic margination of that entity" (1993: 114).

The ethnolinguistic identity of Argentina and Uruguay, countries of the River Plate that had a small indigenous population, is instructive in understanding the forging of a Latin American ethnolinguistic identity. Both countries had huge migratory waves made up of Italian speakers, as well as Spanish speakers. And although both countries are fiercely proud of the distinguishing characteristics of their Spanish, standardized through the efforts of the Argentinean Spanish Language Academy, there is a strong national conscience of Spanish monolingualism. As a result, for example, the language situation of the border region between Uruguay and Brazil was officially ignored until recently, when the work on the sociolinguistic situation of the Dialectos Portugueses del Uruguay and the impact of the long-standing educational policy of Spanish-only in the border region has been extensively studied (see, for example, Elizaincín, Behares, and Barrios, 1987).

Today, some limited recognition of the indigenous languages of Latin America remains. Peru, Ecuador, and Nicaragua have established Spanish as the only official language, although they have granted specific status to the indigenous languages. In Ecuador, Quechua and Aymara have been recognized as belonging to the national culture. And in Paraguay, where 40% of the population are monolingual Guaraní speakers, Guaraní has been granted status as a national, although not official, language (Hamel 1994: 291).

While Latin America has been slowly silencing the indigenous voices that have sprung up, Puerto Rico, where Spanish for the first time became official in 1981, once more claimed Spanish and English as official in the 1990s. As in the rest of Latin America, the official ethnolinguistic position in Puerto Rico is clearly out of synch with its linguistic reality (that of being Spanish speaking) and with its attitudinal culture (the desire to speak Spanish).

Lara's words regarding the situation in Mexico explain that, although there have been changes in social values in Latin America, little has been altered in ethnolinguistic identity:

En el campo de lengua, por el contrario, no hay cambios de valores apreciable; los valores puristas siguen siendo los únicos inteligibles para la mayor parte de los mexicanos. El valor central de la lengua, que reúne la española y las amerindias en el campo de la legitimación identitaria, no admite, en realidad, el plurilingüismo de la nación (1993: 171).

[In the field of language, however, no real changes in value have taken place; the purist values continue to be the only ones understood by most Mexicans. The central value of language, which encompasses both the Spanish one and the Indian ones in terms of a legitimate identity, does not truly admit the nation's multilingualism.] (1993: 171)

Recently, in 1994, the rebellion among the indigenous people of Chiapas in Mexico sparked the renewal of ethnic and indigenous movements. Yet it is instructive to remember that the person who emerged as the leader of the Chiapas resistance, General Marcos, was not from Chiapas; his Spanish-speaking ability was certainly helpful in his leadership role. And Rigoberta Menchú, a recent winner of the Nobel Peace Prize because of her resistance to an oppressive Guatemalan regime and her work on behalf of Indian languages and cultures, only acquired a voice after her own language and culture were silenced.

The Mexican Nobel Prize Winner, Octavio Paz, has been an incisive thinker about Latin American ethnolinguistic identity. His famous 1950 essay titled *El Laberinto de la Soledad* reviews Mexico´s cultural history and psychology and identifies the *máscara* (mask) which the Mexican wears because "no quiere o no se atreve a ser él mismo" [(he) doesn't want to or doesn't dare be himself] (Paz 1959: 66).

In 1950, Paz wrote: "Escribir, equivale a deshacer el español y a recrearlo para que se vuelva mexicano, sin dejar de ser español" [To write is equivalent to undo Spanish and recreate it so that it turns Mexican, without letting it be anything else but Spanish] (1950: 148).

In 1991, in "La Búsqueda del Presente," he repeated:

Arrancadas de su suelo natal y de su tradición propia, plantadas en un mundo desconocido y por nombrar, las lenguas europeas arraigaron en las tierras nuevas, crecieron con las sociedades americanas y se transformaron. Son la misma planta y son una planta distinta. . . . Mis clásicos son los de mi lengua y me siento descendiente de Lope y de Quevedo como cualquier escritor español . . . pero no soy español. El México precolombino, nos habla en el lenguaje de mitos y leyendas. Ser escritor mexicano significa oir lo que nos dice ese presente—esa presencia (quoted in Skirius 1994: 432).

Torn from their birthplace and their own tradition, planted in an unknown world yet to be named, the European languages took root in the new lands, grew with the American societies and were transformed. They are the same plant and they are a different plant. . . . My classics are those of my language and I feel a descendent of Lope and Quevedo just as any other Spanish writer . . . but I´m not a Spaniard. . . . Pre-Colombian Mexico speaks to us the language of myths and legends. To be a Mexican writer means to hear what that present tells us—that presence.] (Skirius 1994: 432)

Despite the multilingual and pluralistic rumblings, little has changed in the official position of Latin American nation states in the last fifty years, as expressed by Paz. The myths, legends, and history of pre-Colombian civilizations and of African slaves are present in Latin American consciousness, much more so than in the early part of the century, and all Latin Americans claim them as their "ethnolinguistic culture." But pride in past glorious civilizations has little to do with giving voice to poor and marginalized indigenous groups, who remain, despite constant efforts, mostly excluded from participating in this Latin American identity.

Summary

As before the ethnic boom of the 1960s, Latin American ethnolinguistic identity continues to cluster around two poles that remain distant:

1. Its identification with the Spanish language and *hispanidad* as the contrastive marker with Anglo America.
2. Its differentiation from Spain through its identification with the autochthonous languages of the Americas, the languages of African slaves, and those spoken by colonizers and, more recently, immigrants who speak languages other than Spanish.

Depending on sociohistorical conditions, attitudes cluster around one or the other pole. In between the two identity poles, however, lies reality, a linguistic reality which in its oral manifestation is less Spanish speaking than the attitudes clustered around the first pole and in its written manifestations is more purist than the attitudes represented by the second pole. It is this lack of fit between attitudes and reality, between the oral and the written word, that creates the hole, the sense of "agujero," which Juan Luis Guerra triumphantly fills with the sounds of his merengue.

Questions for Further Thought and Discussion

1. Why could this chapter be entitled "Latin American Ethnolinguistic Identity: Between the Written and Oral Word"?

2. Define the term "transculturation" and trace its historical origins. How is the Latin American concept of transculturation different from Anglo American acculturation?

3. Trace the evolution of Latin American ethnolinguistic identity from the formation of nation states to today.

4. Explain the situation and the role of indigenous languages in Latin America today.

5. What characterizes a Latin American ethnolinguistic identity?

6. Trace the role of Spanish from conquest to Latin American national formation.

7. What has been the impact of the United States and English on Latin American ethnolinguistic identity?

8. Trace the development of Indigenismo and Afro-Antillanismo in twentieth-century Latin American essay and literature.

9. Explain the impact of the Cuban Revolution on Latin American ethnolinguistic identity.

10. Define the concept of *etnodesarrollo* (ethnodevelopment) and explain the impact it has had in Latin American indigenous communities.

11. Explain how Latin America has used language both to differentiate itself from Spain and from the United States. What have been the linguistic consequences of this differentiation?

12. Select a country in Latin America. Explain in depth its sociolinguistic reality. How does that reality differ from the official linguistic position?

Note

I am grateful to Ricardo Otheguy for his comments on this paper.
1. The term "Indian" has been vindicated by the Latin American indigenous minorities. It is used in this article interchangeably with "indigenous."

Selected Bibliography

Albo, Xavier (1988). El futuro de los idiomas oprimidos. In Orlandi, pp. 75–104.

Bonfil Batalla, Guillermo (1992). *Identidad y pluralismo cultural en América Latina.* San Juan: Editorial de la Universidad de Puerto Rico.

Carpenter, Alejo (1966). *Tientos y diferencias.* Montevideo: Arca.

Che Guevara, Ernesto (1971). *El socialismo y el hombre en Cuba.* Mexico City: Editorial Grijalbo.

Cifuentes, Barbara, and María del Consuelo Ros (1993). Oficialidad y planificación del español: Dos aspectos de la política del lenguaje en México en el siglo XIV. *Iztapalapa* 13(29): 135–146.

Elizaincín, Adolfo, Luis Behares, and Graciela Barrios (1987). *Nos falemo brasilero: Dialectos portugueses en Uruguay.* Montevideo: Amesur.

Godenzzi, Juan Carlos (1996). Literacy and modernization among the Quechua speaking population of Peru. In Hornberger, 237–250.

Hamel, Rainer Enrique (1994). Indigenous education in Latin America: Policies and legal frameworks. In *Linguistic Human Rights: Overcoming Linguistic Discrimination*, Tove Skutnabb-Kangas and Robert Phillipson (eds.), 271–287. Berlin: Mouton de Gruyter.

Henríquez Ureña, Pedro (1926). El descontento y la promesa. In Ripoll, 376–390.

Henríquez Ureña, Pedro (1940). *El español en Santo Domingo.* Buenos Aires: La Universidad de Buenos Aires.

Hornberger, Nancy (ed.) (1996). *Indigenous Literacies in the Americas: Language Planning from the Bottom up*. Berlin: Mouton de Gruyter.

Hostos, Eugenio María de (1870). El cholo. In Ripoll, 163–165.

Lara, Luis Fernando (1993). Crónica de una política del lenguaje abortada: La Comisión para la Defensa del Idioma Español. *Iztapalapa* 13(29): 147–176.

Martí, José (1893). Mi raza. In Ripoll, 250–252.

Orlandi, Eni Pulcinelli, ed. (1988). *Política linguística na America Latina*. Campinas: Pontes Editores.

Ortiz, Fernando (1973 [1906]). *Los negros brujos*. Miami: Ediciones Universal.

Ortiz, Fernando (1978 [1940]). *Contrapunteo cubano del tabaco y el azúcar*. Caracas: Biblioteca Ayacucho.

Pardo, María Teresa (1993). El desarrollo de la escritura de las lenguas indígenas en Oaxaca. *Iztapalapa* 13(29): 109–134.

Paz, Octavio (1959). *El Laberinto de la soledad*. Mexico City: Fondo de Cultura Económica.

Paz, Octavio (1991). *La búsqueda del presente*. In Skirius, 431–442.

Rama, Angel (1984). *La ciudad letrada*. Hanover, N.H.: Edición del Norte.

Ribeiro, Darcy (1977). *Las Américas y la civilización*. Mexico City: Colección Latinoamericana.

Richards, Julia Becker, and Michael Richards (1996). Mayan language literacy in Guatemala: A socio-historical overview. In Hornberger, 189–212.

Ripoll, Carlos (ed.) (1966). *Conciencia intelectual de América: Antología del ensayo hispanoamericano (1836–1959)*. New York: Las Américas.

Salinas Pedraza, Jesús (1996). Saving and strengthening indigenous Mexican languages: The Celiac experience. In Hornberger, 171–185.

Sarmiento, Domingo F. (1883). Conflicto y armoníos de las razas en América. In Ripoll, 94–100.

Shapiro, Samuel (1963). *Invisible Latin America*. Boston: Beacon Press.

Skirius, John (ed.) (1994). *El ensayo hispanoamericano del Siglo XX*. Mexico City: Fondo de cultura.

Stabb, Martin (1967). *In Quest of Identity. Patterns in the Spanish American Essay of Ideas, 1890–1960*. Chapel Hill: University of North Carolina Press.

Vasconcelos, José (1925). *La Raza Cósmica*. In Ripoll, 321–327.

Vasconcelos, José (1927). *Indología*. In Ripoll, 337–345.

Zea, Leopoldo (1991). La identidad cultural e histórica de América Latina y la universidad. *Cuadernos Americanos* 6(24): 181–191.

Zuniga, Madeleine, Ines Pozzi-Escot, and Luis Enrique Lopez, eds. (1991). *Educación bilingue intercultural*. Lima: Fomciencias.

Zuniga, Madeleine, Juan Ansión, and Luis Cueva, eds. (1987). *Educación en poblaciones indígenas: Políticas y estrateqias en América Latina*. Santiago de Chile: UNESCO.

The United States and Canada

RICHARD Y. BOURHIS
DAVID E. MARSHALL

The United States and Canada have many similarities: Both were the products of British Empire expansion; both contain conquered language minorities (Spanish and French, respectively) that seek maintenance of their languages and cultures as "national minorities"; both are known as "immigrant countries" of the New World that have depended on international immigration to build their respective multiethnic and multicultural societies; and, continentally, both developed westward, displacing aboriginal peoples (First Nations) who were conquered militarily and marginalized in their respective cultures and governments. English is used as the majority language in both countries, a language that symbolizes the powerful hegemony of two consecutive capitalist world empires: the British and then the American. Despite the unrelenting spread of English worldwide, internally both Canada and the United States face political turmoil that surrounds issues of language choice, ethnic identity, equality, and justice, and both are experiencing crises of national identity and the process of "renationalization" through the changing of their respective concepts of who they are and what they are about as nation states.

Although they share the longest undefended border in the world and are increasingly uniting within a common free-trade marketplace, both nations have marked differences. Today, Canada has a population of 30 million in slightly more territory than the United States, whereas the United States has more than 250 million inhabitants, almost ten times the population of Canada. Politically, there is a sharp contrast between the parliamentary (Canada) and congressional (United States) systems of representation, with different means of changing governments and thus policies. The ten Canadian provinces have more political autonomy than do American states, whose powers are subject to the more centralized national government in Washington. Historically, Canada chose to remain part of the British Empire, whereas the United States opted for the struggle of independence from

Britain; in Canada, the French were conquered in the mid-1700s, whereas in the United States the Hispanics were conquered in the mid-1800s. The francophone minority in Canada had more opportunities to develop political resistance to anglophone ascendancy than did Hispanics in the United States. Canada has officially (de jure) recognized English-French bilingualism, whereas the United States still wrestles with the question of recognizing its bilingual realities. Canadian language issues are more closely matched to provincial boundaries, with the French-majority province of Québec being a case in point, whereas in the United States, the question of linguistic minorities is not as readily focused geographically, although language minorities are concentrated in the Boston-Washington megalopolis, in other major metropolitan areas, in Florida, and primarily in the southwestern states from Texas to California.

Today, one of the critical differences between Canada and the United States is the "visibility" of ethnic and linguistic minorities; this crucial cross-national distinction can be readily appreciated in the 1990 and 1991 census figures presented Table 17-1.

More than nine out of ten Canadians but only three out of four people in the United States are white, and less than 10% of Canada's population but 25% of the U.S. population is made up of "visible minorities." The largest ethnolinguistic minority in Canada, the francophones (23%), are white, a nonvisible minority, whereas in the United States visible minorities comprise African Americans (12%), Latin Americans (9%), and Asian Americans (3%). Thus, in the United States, there is a significant differentiation brought about by the "visibility" of most of its linguistic minorities, providing a racial undercurrent to the question of language choice and acceptance of linguistic and ethnic pluralism. Canada's challenge is how to accommodate a large French mother-tongue "national minority" of 23%

Table 17-1. Visible and Nonvisible Ethnic Populations in the United States and Canada

Ethnic and Racial Groups	U.S. Census 1990		Canada Census 1991	
	No.	%	No.	%
Nonvisible Caucasian total:	189,000,000	75	24,493,000	91
British background				29
French background				23
other European				39
Visible minorities total:	62,000,000	25	2,507,000	9
African	31,000,000	12	251,000	1
Latin American	22,000,000	9	178,000	0.7
Asian[1]	7,000,000	3	1,608,000	6
Aboriginal, First Nations	2,000,000	<1	471,000	2
Total population	251,000,000	100	27,000,000	100

Adapted with permission from Driedger (1996), Table 10.2. Copyright 1996 by Oxford University Press.

1. For this table, Asian includes the following groups: Chinese, Indo-Pakistani, Filipino, Arab, and Indo-Chinese.

of the population, along with a growing minority of allophones (17%) whose mother tongue is neither English nor French and of whom a growing number are visible minorities (Driedger, 1996). Although not the topic of this chapter, the greatest moral challenge to the Canadian state is its uneasy relationship with "First Nation" aboriginal peoples who constitute 2% of the Canadian population. Differences and similarities between the situations of Canada and the United States are highlighted when one considers recent demographic projections for the United States made by the U.S. Census office:

> Figures on the demographic shifts in American population from 1980 to 1990 underscore how rapidly the demographic profiles of the American population are changing. During the past decade, Asian and Pacific Islanders experienced the largest growth—108 percent, a group that had more than doubled in the previous decade (1970–1980); the Black or Afro-American population increased 13 percent; the American Indian, Inuit, and Aleut population gained 38 percent, while the White population increased only 6 percent. In 1990, "the White population's share of the U.S. total population reached its lowest level ever— 80.3 percent." The Hispanic population (listed under the White category) grew 53 percent. Projections for the future show a "rising proportion of racial and ethnic minority groups"; a "decreasing proportion of a non-Hispanic White majority"; and ". . . continuing, if changing, disparities between racial and ethnic minority groups and a White majority group." (Marshall 1996: 78; quotations are from *Review of Federal Measurements of Race and Ethnicity* (1994))

The U.S. Census projections indicate that racial and ethnic minorities will compose one-half of the total population by 2050; the Hispanic population will triple and become larger than the African American population, which itself will double along with those of American Indians and Native Alaskans; Asian Pacific populations in the United States will quadruple, whereas the non-Hispanic white population will increase only 5% (*Review of Federal Measurements of Race and Ethnicity* 1994: 39). Thus the challenge for the United States is how to incorporate growing "visible minorities" that are not only linguistic minorities but that are also often perceived as racially different from the Anglo-American mainstream. More fundamentally, current and projected demographic changes are affecting the core identity of the American nationality and forcing many to consider transforming its content from a traditional Eurocentric Anglo-American "melting pot" to a more complex multicultural, multiethnic national identity.

Thus, in both the United States and Canada, the challenge of the twenty-first century is the question of restructuring each nation's imagining of itself, its *ethnie* (Smith 1991: 39), and its sense of a national agenda, its *mythomoteur* (Armstrong 1982: 9). Canada has sought to create language equity between the French and the English through constitutional provisions and bilingualism laws while also being the first country in the world to adopt a multiculturalism law in 1988 that was designed to preserve and promote the distinctive languages and cultures of its immigrant minorities (Driedger 1996). In contrast, the United States faces its current challenge of incorporating primarily national and visible minorities whose demographic base is growing toward majority status by relying less on legislation than on "free-market forces," which, for much of this century, have worked in favor of assimilation to the Anglo-American mainstream.

The way questions of ethnic and linguistic pluralism came about illustrates how distinctive each nation's "renationalization" efforts have become (Smith 1991). The recent histories of both countries provide insights into these processes and deserve examination at a more detailed level. The first part of this chapter deals with language and ethnicity issues in the United States; the second part is devoted to an analysis of language issues in Canada and Québec. The chapter closes with a brief analysis of language pluralism issues pertinent to both the United States and Canada.

The United States: Undissolved Lumps in the Melting Pot

Fundamentally, the contemporary conflict over language policy in the United States is not about "language" at all; it is rather, an *ethnic conflict* in which language has become implicated in several ways.

(Schmidt 1993: 73)

Historically, United States policies toward linguistic and cultural diversity have been influenced by two classic approaches to such issues: the assimilation ideology and the civic ideology. The assimilation ideology is exemplified by policies adopted in France, where the central government is involved in defining and regulating the national culture, seeking to enshrine the French language as the only language of the state and protecting it from foreign influence. Within France, the equal treatment of all citizens is granted on the condition that linguistic and cultural minorities, both national and immigrant, assimilate to the dominant French language and culture.

The civic ideology is exemplified by Great Britain, where the state is "seen as neither the representative nor the guardian of an official culture." Rather, the cultural order utilizes but is not symbolized by its language, which serves as an instrument but perhaps not the only one aiding governance. The United States inherited from Britain not just its language, but its understanding of the relation between language and national identity" (Nunberg 1992: 481). In the earliest years of the United States, it was felt that the new constitution would, in time, create the development of a new language: American. "The founders viewed American political institutions not as resting on a national language or a national culture, but as giving rise to them" (Nunberg 1992: 485). The new political institutions would create a new culture, symbolized by a new language, as different from any other as its political opportunities were different from those of the Old World.

Although some people, such as John Adams and Benjamin Franklin, argued that English might need some protection, their views did not carry, and the universal and pragmatic attitude toward language use lasted as long as did the sense of the newness of the nation. With increasing immigration, particularly non-

Northern European and non-Protestant, there came a new attitude, a differentiation between the older and the newer immigrants. Some of the older immigrants fostered a movement toward nativism, empowering the "haves" over those who did not have so much. One means of doing this was demanding the use of English. Under the older consensus, which sought increased immigration, other languages were readily accepted, so much so that some states published their laws in several languages besides English. Pennsylvania published its statutes in German from 1805 to 1850 and Louisiana in French from 1804 to 1867 (Heath 1977). With the rise of nativism, states began to repeal these laws and to enact legislation that favored literacy in English, specifically to control the political power of non-English speakers (Leibowitz 1976).

During and after World War I, laws were passed that demanded the sole use of English, but these were struck down by the United States Supreme Court as unconstitutional and a denial of personal freedom of speech (Leibowitz 1976). The effect of American participation in World War I was to wipe out a widely spread German-language school system. German speakers were the largest ethnolinguistic minority in eight of the ten largest U.S. cities and in twenty-six of the forty-eight states, constituting a self-consciously united power block, replete with newspapers, social centers, and thousands of schools, all of which were quickly dissolved by the political fervor of war against Germany. World War II (1941–1945) finished what had begun earlier in 1917–1918, leaving few remnants of German-language use in the United States outside of small groups such as the Old Order Amish and the Mennonites. The prevailing attitude was that patriotism demanded assimilation, and assimilation was signaled by the sole use of English. Americanization programs during the 1920s and early 1930s strove for assimilation and complete transition to English use. It was no longer sufficient for the immigrants to acculturate; to be "good Americans," they had to assimilate.

With this shift in relationship between political institutions, culture, and language, the United States moved from the British toward the French idea of language as the main carrier of national identity and culture. It was argued that English was the "glue" that held the nation together, and thereby the movement to make English the official language received its impetus (Marshall 1986). The first proposed English Language Amendment to the U.S. Constitution was introduced April 27, 1981, by Senator Hayakawa (R-California). In his initiating speech, Senator Hayakawa gave the following reasons for wanting to make English the de jure instead of just the de facto official language: a) "a common language can unify, separate languages can fracture and fragment a society"; b) "learning English is the major task of each immigrant"; c) "only by learning English can an immigrant participate in our democracy" (*Congressional Record*, S. 3998–99).

Since that speech, there has been an amendment proposed in each Congress in both the House of Representatives and the Senate. So far, none have passed, although one did pass the House of Representatives during the last Congress but failed in the Senate. What is causing this rush to de jure authorization of English is a perception by some people in the United States that English is endangered. Far from being at any time at risk, English is rapidly gaining speakers around the world and also in the United States. Immigrants are now required to read and write

English and must pass their examinations in English. The perception comes from the increase in Hispanic presence and their rise in socioeconomic status. Spanish is more widely used today in the United States than it has been in the past, but at no time has it threatened or even challenged English as the dominant language, any more than German did in the first decades of this century (Marshall 1986, 1996; Marshall and Gonzalez 1990).

Tom McArthur, editor of *English Today*, described how the misperception of Hispanic immigration and culture, not language, was central to the political fight over the English Language Amendment:

> The languages in question are just one kind of badge; it is the heartland or core assumptions that matter. Such "heartlanders" (physically in Indiana, psychologically in California) have never felt the need to make English the official language of the United States in response to the agitation of the French in Maine, angry Injuns at Wounded Knee, aggrieved Hawaiians, or any other tiny minority. They only defend the tool called English (about which they are otherwise entirely pragmatic) when it is threatened by the one other linguistic tool that signifies in the Americas, the tool used in Puerto Rico, Mexico, Cuba, Dominica, Honduras, Nicaragua, El Salvador, Guatemala, Costa Rica, Panama, Ecuador, Venezuela, Peru, Bolivia, Columbia, Uruguay, Paraguay, Chile and Argentina.
>
> The border is porous to the south. Its equal porosity to the north is irrelevant; there is not threat from the north, where Canada's few millions, even if some speak French, are manageable. But the millions of Hispanics down there are not manageable. The concern that Anglo-America could be swamped by Hispanic-Americans is comparable to the fear that French America (Québec) could be swamped by English America (the rest of Canada plus the States) and is not unlike the perennial fears in "white Australia" that one day the Yellow Peril will come (now called "Asianization"). The Hispanic issue is complicated by the fact that Latin America is largely part of the "Third World" while many Americans see themselves as the great bastion of the never-stated "First World." It happens that Spanish is the language of masses perceived variously as illiterate, impoverished, dirty, backward, criminally inclined, residually Roman Catholic, prone to Communist infiltration, dark-complexioned, and now pushing cocaine and marijuana north for all they are worth. (McArthur 1986: 91).

Basically then, the English Language Amendment movement was a means of preventing Hispanic immigration; however, there already was a Hispanic "national minority" in the United States. Just as the British conquered the French in Canada, so did the United States conquer Mexico, gaining one-third of its western continental holdings. The states of New Mexico, Arizona, Nevada, Colorado, and Utah make up most of the conquered territory, and in 1850, when the Treaty of Guadalupe-Hildago was signed, most of the inhabitants were Hispanic or Native American. Texas won its independence from Mexico through revolution. Today, along with Florida and California, these states hold the majority of the Hispanic population in the United States. However, "language shift" to English is systematic by the second and third generation within the Hispanic population (Veltman 1983) and therefore these minorities constitute no threat to the overall linguistic hegemony of English within the United States (Marshall 1996). Sociolinguists agree that it is recent immigration rather than language maintenance among second- and third-generation immigrants that continues to "feed" non-English language communities in the United States (Fishman 1989).

Even as members of the largest linguistic minority in the United States, Spanish speakers are caught in a dilemma: To appear to be "good Americans," they feel pressured to shift to English as quickly as possible; but they also recognize that in the long run this shift may be achieved at the cost of losing their mother tongue and their Hispanic cultural and ethnic identity. Thus "subtractive bilingualism" may be the rule rather than the exception for Hispanic minorities in the United States. However, could "additive bilingualism," in which English is acquired without losing competence in and identification with Spanish, be a viable option for Hispanic national and immigrant minorities in the United States? Most bilingual programs in the United States are "transitional" rather than "maintenance" in orientation (Fishman 1989). *Maintenance bilingual* programs aim to preserve and value the native tongue of the minority group while teaching the language of the majority group. Under optimal circumstances for the linguistic minority group, maintenance bilingual programs are more likely to foster additive than subtractive bilingualism. In contrast, *transitional bilingual* programs are aimed at teaching the native tongue only in the early grades so as to establish the cognitive anchor needed to replace it with the learning of the dominant language of the majority group. Consequently, transitional bilingual programs are more likely to contribute to the subtractive bilingualism of Hispanics than to foster additive Spanish-English bilingualism. In the long run, viewing stable additive bilingualism as generating linguistic and cultural capital to be used for international exchange rather than as a threat to the unity of the Anglo-American nation offers a useful framework for reassessing traditional approaches to bilingual education in the United States (Fishman 1989).

With the failure to adopt a federal constitutional amendment, the backers of the English Language Amendment shifted their efforts to states in which Hispanics constituted sizeable ethnolinguistic minorities. Although various forms of "English-only" legislation have been passed so far in eighteen states, the laws in eleven of these states—Alabama, Arkansas, Colorado, Florida, Georgia, Illinois, Indiana, Kentucky, Mississippi, North Carolina, and North Dakota—"are virtually identical and wholly symbolic," having little if any effect on language use other than to make English the equivalent of the state bird, tree, flower, or mineral. Only the laws in California, Hawaii, Nebraska, South Carolina, Tennessee, and Virginia "go beyond symbolism since they imply or stipulate some kind of enforcement" (Tatalovich 1995: 22–23). Arizona's law also went beyond the symbolic, but the state supreme court rejected it as an unconstitutional denial of the freedom of speech. Attempts at passing an "English-only" law in Texas have repeatedly failed, partially because of its politically well-organized Hispanic community. Illinois had an "American-language" law for decades, which it changed to English in 1969. Hawaii is officially bilingual, recognizing both English and Hawaiian, so it is not by any means "English-only." The movement seems to be declining nationwide as multilingualism is seen as a tool for improving international trade within the "global village" and as perceptions that English is threatened subside (Marshall 1996).

Two major factors reduce the rate of language shift from Spanish to English among Hispanic minorities in the United States: one is the proximity of Spanish-speaking nations to the U.S. border and the other is cyclical migrations to and from those Latin American nations to the United States (Cafferty, 1982). Spanish speakers are aware that knowledge of English is crucial for their economic survival in the United States while also being concerned with the maintenance of their Hispanic linguistic and cultural identity. With the increase in Hispanic population forecast for the next half century, the concomitant increase in political and economic power of this ethnolinguistic minority may create a parallel to the Québécois French sovereignist movement. However, it is extremely doubtful that Spanish speakers will ever advocate separation or that secession will ever become a political issue unless "English-only" federal legislation, laws which would completely forbid the use of Spanish, is passed and enforced nationally. Given the jurisprudence against "English-only" constitutional amendments within the U.S. Supreme Court, such legislation would most likely be declared unconstitutional. Thus the advocates of the English Language Amendment face an impasse: They do not have the necessary two-thirds of the states ready to ratify a federal constitutional amendment (most state laws are only symbolic), and the growing political power of hispanophones and voters of Hispanic background in the United States poses serious questions about whether such an amendment could ever win the consent of Congress. As a local, perhaps statewide, movement, "English-only" may still have some political life, but as a national issue, its fate is sealed, for neither the Democratic nor Republican party would wish to alienate its Spanish-speaking adherents by advocating such national legislation. The English Language Amendment issue has moved to a new, less inflammatory level in U.S. politics and will pose less of a problem on the federal level as U.S. demographics continue to change.

Linguistic Diversity in Canada

For historical reasons, English Canadians and French Canadians have been known as Canada's "two founding people." France was among the first colonial powers to occupy parts of North America in the eighteenth century. Consequently, descendants of French settlers in New France are known as one of the two "founding nations" of Canada. French-English rivalries for control of the North American continent culminated in the Seven Years' War, which was settled in 1759 with the victory of the British in an epic battle fought on the outskirts of Québec City. With the signing of the Treaty of Paris in 1763, France ceded New France to Great Britain. The British established the Common Law system and the Protestant church while consolidating its British settlement policy. Thus as descendants of British immigrants, English Canadians also became known as members of one of the "two founding people." Given its status as a former British colony, it is inevitable that the majority of the population of Canada would emerge as English speakers of

British background, with the exception of the Province of Québec, where French speakers originating from France remained in the majority.

As of the most recent Canadian census (1996), English is the mother tongue of the majority of the Canadian population (60%; 17 million speakers), followed by French (23%; 6.7 million) speakers and by allophones, others whose mother tongue is neither French nor English (17%; 6.3 million speakers). Census results also show that the percentage of French mother-tongue speakers has been steadily declining, from 27% in 1931 to 23% in 1996, while the proportion of English mother-tongue speakers has increased from 57% in 1931 to 60% in 1996. This increase is not the result of sustained immigration from the British Isles but is mainly due to the linguistic shift to English of French Canadians and immigrant Canadians during this century. The proportion of "other" mother-tongue speakers has remained relatively constant this century (16% in 1931; 17% in 1996) as a result of succeeding generations of immigrants settling in Canada.

Figure 17-1 shows a map of Canada with the language composition of each province as recorded in the 1996 census. Québec is the only province in which French mother-tongue speakers constitute the majority of the population (81%; 5.7 million) and English mother-tongue speakers are the minority (622,000 anglophones). The election of the prosovereignist Parti Québécois in 1976 and the passage of language laws designed to increase the status of French relative to English contributed to the loss of close to 140,000 anglophones, who emigrated to English Canada, resulting in a decline in the proportion of Québec anglophones from 12% in 1971 to 9% in 1996. In contrast, English mother-tongue speakers are the majority in all the other provinces and make up the majority of the Canadian popula-

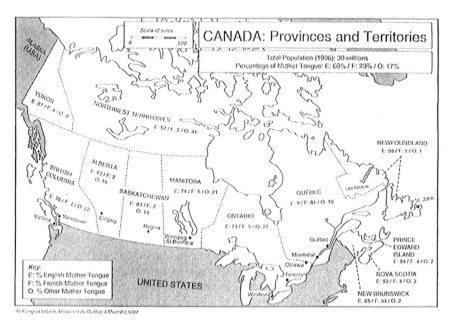

Figure 17.1 Language Composition of the Canadian Provinces

tion. However, 1 million French mother-tongue speakers do live outside of Québec and are concentrated in two Canadian provinces: Ontario and New Brunswick. In Ontario, one-half million Franco-Ontarians make up 5% of the population, whereas in New Brunswick, the Acadian minority of 245,000 French mother-tongue speakers make up 33% of the population.

According to the 1996 census, 17% of Canadians declared themselves to be bilingual in French and English. It is within Québec (38%), followed by New Brunswick (33%) and Ontario (11%), that the greatest number of bilinguals can be found in Canada, and it is within this "bilingual belt" that the fate of Canada's linguistic duality will be determined in the decades to come (Bourhis 1994a). The vast majority of French mother-tongue speakers living outside of Québec are bilingual (78% in 1971; 84% in 1996); for them the necessity to know English is imperative economically and socially. This is further confirmed by language shift data that show that English use at home is increasing among the French mother-tongue population that lives outside of Québec. Whereas 29% of such francophones had adopted English as their home language as of the 1971 census, this proportion increased to 39% in 1996. In contrast, despite Canada's official bilingualism policy, anglophones in the rest of Canada do not feel the need to learn French, and bilingualism remains the exception (3% in 1971; 7% in 1996) in the nine provinces where anglophones constitute the dominant majority.

In Québec, where language laws in favor of French have been in effect for more than 30 years (Bourhis 1984, 1994b), the proportion of English mother-tongue speakers who are bilingual rose from 37% in 1971 to 62% in 1996. This increase is not only due to the number of anglophones who learned French as a result of pro-French language laws but is also explained by the fact that many unilingual anglophones left Québec during this period dissatisfied with Québec's language and fiscal policies. French-English bilingualism among allophones, who form 10% of the Québec population, has also risen from 33% in 1971 to 47% in 1996. This increase in bilingualism can be attributed to the 1977 language law (Bill 101) which obligated recent immigrants arriving in Québec to send their children to French schools. Thus 47% of Québec allophones are in fact trilingual: They maintain knowledge of their mother tongue, learn French at school, and adopt English as the language of Anglo-American culture and upward mobility in North America. Bilingualism is also rising among Québec francophones: The proportion of French mother-tongue speakers who know English rose from 27% in 1971 to 34% in 1996. The growing internationalization of the Québec economy through greater trade with the United States, along with the drawing power of Anglo-American culture, accounts for this increase in bilingualism, especially among the younger generation of Québécois francophones.

Franco-Ontarians constitute the largest francophone minority outside of Québec. However, individual bilingualism has contributed to language shift in favor of English among a substantial proportion of the Franco-Ontarian population, despite the fact that this minority is concentrated in the eastern and northeastern regions of the province. Mostly of working class background, as many as 84% of Franco-Ontarians are bilingual, of whom 20% claim dual French-English mother tongue. As of the 1981 census, as many as 33% of Franco-Ontarians reported

English as their main language of communication at home, a language shift pattern which increased to 39% in 1996. Among the many factors that account for the linguistic assimilation of Franco-Ontarians, French-English mixed marriages have been shown to have a near total negative impact on French language maintenance at home.

Of historical importance for Franco-Ontarians was Regulation 17, which in 1912 banned the teaching of French from all public schools while government efforts were also made to curb the development of French Catholic private schools, hospitals, and parishes. At that time, Franco-Ontarians constituted 20% of the Ontario population, and though repealed in 1927, the law achieved its intended effect of reducing the number of francophones in the province. In the 1980s, Franco-Ontarians were more successful in their efforts to improve the provision of French-language teaching in primary and secondary schooling and in the delivery of French-language services at the provincial level. However, in the mid-1990s, massive Ontario government cuts in education, social welfare, and health care undermined earlier gains achieved for French-language services. For instance, despite widespread protest by the Franco-Ontarian minority, Ontario's only French-language hospital was demoted to 40% of its working capacity in 1997, a measure nevertheless denounced as "pro-French favoritism" by anglophone elements in the province. Continuing sociolinguistic pressures that contribute to English assimilation, combined with government cuts in French-language services and a measure of intolerance toward the French among vocal anglophones, may undermine the capacity of present and future generations of Franco-Ontarians to reverse language shift.

The Acadians of New Brunswick constitute Canada's second largest francophone minority outside Québec. The French language and the Catholic religion remain cornerstones of Acadian identity in a province controlled economically and politically by the anglophone majority. Traditionally of farming and fishing occupational background, Acadians are the descendants of French settlers who, under British rule in the eighteenth century, refused to swear allegiance to the British crown. As a result, more than 90% of Acadians were dispossessed of their farms and deported to various colonies by the British army between 1755 and 1763. In 1764, after the Treaty of Paris, Acadians were allowed to return on the condition that they swear allegiance to the crown of England and that they disperse in small groups on lands not occupied by the British settlers who had replaced Acadians on vacated homesteads.

Today, New Brunswick is the only Canadian province that has declared itself officially bilingual (in 1969). At first, this status did not resolve the linguistic, economic, and social disadvantages of Acadians relative to the anglophone majority. Only after sustained struggles during the last thirty years have Acadians gained from the majority the right to have their own French primary and secondary schooling, a French university, French hospitals, and bilingual government services in eastern regions of the province, where francophones were in the majority or constituted substantial minorities. Despite gains in the educational field, francophones in New Brunswick remain disadvantaged economically and socially, although the ethnic revival movement contributed to the Acadian cultural achievements of the last two decades. Language shift in favor of English at home remains lower (10%) for Acadians than for other francophone minorities outside of Québec. However, lack of population density, exogamy, and urbanization remain the major factors that account for linguistic assimilation among francophones in New Brunswick. Although not numerous as a minority, Acadians are considered to enjoy better overall prospects of surviving as a distinctive linguistic collectivity than most francophone minorities across Canada.

What are the survival prospects of francophone minorities beyond New Brunswick and Ontario? Canadian experts are very pessimistic concerning the fate of demographically weak francophone minorities such as those found in Newfoundland, British Columbia, the Yukon, and the Northwest Territories. As can been seen in Figure 17-1, the proportion of French mother-tongue speakers in the prairie provinces of Alberta, Saskatchewan, and Manitoba are also very weak. Language shift through the adoption of English as the language of the home continues to increase among francophones in Alberta (68%), Manitoba (53%) and Saskatchewan (71%; 1996 census). Though many francophones in these provinces have survived by living within concentrated communities in specific regions, linguistic intolerance, enshrined in a long string of municipal and provincial laws, has undermined the linguistic vitality of these communities (Bourhis, 1994a). The francophone minorities of Nova Scotia and Prince Edward Island have also met with such difficulties in Atlantic Canada. However, it is the determination of francophone minorities to maintain their language and culture during this century that "justified" Canadian government efforts to reverse language shift through the adoption of its official bilingual policy.

Canadian and Québécois Language Policies

As part of the ethnic revival movement of the late 1960s, Québécois nationalists expressed their dissatisfaction with Anglo-Canadian control of the political and economic national agenda. The rise of nationalism in Québec disrupted the federal-provincial status quo and threatened Canadian unity. Québec nationalists advocated the creation of a sovereign Québec state as a means of regaining control of their own collective destiny and preserving the fate of the last viable enclave of French language and culture on the continent. In an effort to neutralize these threats, the federal government appointed the Royal Commission on Bilingualism and Biculturalism in 1963. In its final report, the commission confirmed the equal status of Canada's "two founding people" and proposed a series of measures to improve the status of French in the federal administration. Measures proposed to equalize the status of French and English as Canada's two official languages culminated in the 1969 Official Languages Act. This law adopted a "personality" approach by providing schooling and federal government services in the preferred language of individuals whose mother tongue was either English or French across regions of Canada where the concentration of these "official language minorities" was considered sufficient (greater than 8%). The law also increased the number of French-speaking federal employees so that francophones were equitably represented relative to their proportion in the Canadian population. Canada's Official Languages Act, including its 1988 update, was seen by many as a progressive language policy which ensured that French minorities outside of Québec and the English minority inside Québec were provided with the institutional support they needed to maintain their respective linguistic and cultural vitality as members of Canada's two founding people.

Although Canada's Official Languages Act contributed to slowing down the territorial segregation of the French in Québec and the English in the rest of Canada, politically it came "too little too late" as a measure to limit the growth of Québec's independence movement (Bourhis 1994b). The bilingualism policy was also criticized on other fronts as further polarizing French-English rivalries in Canada; failing to stem the tide of linguistic assimilation among francophones outside Québec; failing to stop the decline of the English minority in Québec; and belittling the contribution of ethnic groups other than the English and the French within Canadian society.

While the Canadian government moved toward the personality approach through the Official Languages Act, Québec moved from a personality approach to a "territorial approach" in its language policies (Bourhis 1984). The territorial approach is based on the notion that it is individuals who accommodate to the language of the region or province in which they reside. The policy of giving virtually complete control of a territory to a single language group can help defuse linguistic tensions because it stabilizes language boundaries and the demolinguistic position of the language communities who inhabit the territory. However, the territorial approach poses difficulties for minority individuals, whose linguistic rights and privileges may be eroded by those of the territorial majority.

A premise of Québec language planners was that francophone minorities outside Québec were doomed demographically and that Québec remained the last region in which a distinctive French society could survive within North America. Numerous factors prompted provincial governments to adopt language laws designed to improve the status of French in Québec during the 1970s (Bourhis 1984, 1994b). Demolinguistic changes within Québec confirmed the decline in the birthrate of francophones from one of the highest to one of the lowest in the Western world. Without a sustained francophone birthrate, reliance on immigration and the assimilation of immigrants to the French majority became crucial for maintaining the stability of the French-speaking majority in the province. However, freedom of language choice in Québec schools meant that the majority of immigrants chose English-medium rather than French-medium schools for their children. The cumulative impact of such choices meant that a majority of second-generation immigrants assimilated to the English rather than the French milieu, thus undermining the long-term growth of the French community. There was also growing awareness among francophones that Québec's anglophone elite did dominate most of the business and economic activity in the province. The report of the Royal Commission on Bilingualism and Biculturalism showed that even with equal education and qualifications, francophones were discriminated against in regard to salary and promotion within English-controlled industries and business firms established in the province. Results of the Gendron Commission (1972) showed that English, not French, was the language of work and upward mobility, whereas even as clients francophones had difficulty obtaining services in their own language from anglophone clerks in Montréal stores. Taken together, these factors did not bode well for the future of French in Québec.

The first legislative act of the prosovereignist Parti Québécois government, elected in 1976, was the adoption of the Charter of the French Language (Bill 101, 1977), which declared French as the only official language of Québec (Bourhis 1984). The law enshrined the right of francophones to receive communications in French when dealing with the provincial administration, health and social services, semipublic agencies, and business and retail firms. Similar rights were also guaranteed for Québec anglophones, especially regarding the delivery of provincial services in English to individuals who wanted them. Bill 101 also established the right of francophones to work in French and not to be dismissed for the sole reason that they were unilingual French. "Francization" programs were adopted to prompt business firms and industries of more than fifty employees to adopt French as the language of work and to obtain a "francization" certificate, while guaranteeing English schooling to all present and future Québec anglophone pupils and to all immigrant children already in English schools in 1977. However, the law stipulated that all future immigrants to Québec must send their children to French schools. Freedom of language choice remained for postsecondary education, which included state-funded French and English colleges, three English-language universities, and four French-language universities. Regarding the "linguistic landscape," outside public signs and commercial advertising were required to be in French only, although languages other than French were allowed on signs related to public safety and humanitarian, religious, and cultural services and products.

Québec francophone reactions to Bill 101 were quite positive, as the law was seen as effective in securing the future of French in the province (Bourhis 1984, 1994b). After twenty years of implementation, the law has been successful in increasing the status and use of French as the language of work within business and industry and as the language of retail activity. However, given that English remains the language of business in North America, many francophones recognize that economic and social mobility within and beyond the Québec border still depends on individual bilingualism. Despite numerous changes to the law in the last twenty years, the Québec linguistic landscape became predominantly French, not only on government road signs but also in domains such as store signs and advertising billboards. However, francophone nationalists were frustrated that aspects of Bill 101 were declared unconstitutional by the Canadian Supreme Court, which, for example, ruled that all laws passed in French since Bill 101 had to be translated into English and declared official in both languages.

Despite considerable guarantees that their language rights would be preserved, anglophone opposition to Bill 101 was vehement, as the law was seen as a direct attack on the traditional elite status of the English minority in Québec (Bourhis 1994b). "English rights" associations and parties funded in part by the Canadian government were formed to combat specific features of Bill 101, such as French-only commercial signs and restrictions on English schooling imposed on immigrant children. Two decades after the adoption of Bill 101, more than 80% of immigrant children were enrolled in French rather than English primary and secondary schools. This shift in favor of enrollment in the French school system had a negative impact on the English school system, whose student population dropped by as much as 60%. Bill 101, added to the emigration of Québec anglophones to English Canada, did erode the demographic base of the English minority. However, to this day, the strong degree of institutional control enjoyed by Québec anglophones in education, health care, religion, the mass media, and all aspects of the economy distinguishes this linguistic minority from the less advantaged francophone minorities in English Canada. Québec anglophones can receive most federal, provincial, municipal, commercial, and financial services in English, and given their demographic concentration within the western regions of the province and in Montréal, it remains quite possible for English Québecers to live much of their daily life solely through the medium of English.

Can strong institutional control be enough to sustain the vitality of English Québec despite recent losses on the demographic front? English-rights activists warn that if anglophones themselves do not take measures to maintain their demographic base in Québec, they might lose vital components of the institutional support they presently have due to lack of demand resulting from the demographic decline of their community. Québec anglophones may need to develop cultural strategies which foster sufficiently strong loyalties within Québec society to offset their tendencies to emigrate to Anglo Canada.

However, the "partitionist movement," which emerged following the 1995 Québec sovereignty referendum, suggests that an opposite trend is developing. Gaining strength among anglophones, the "partitionist movement" advocates that English-majority municipalities separate from Québec and join Canada in the event that the majority of Québec citizens vote in favor of independence in the next referendum. Forty Québec anglophone-majority municipalities representing close to one-half million citizens have voted in favor of partitionist resolutions in the past two years in Montreal and western regions of the province.

Canada and the Rivalry
between National Identities

In October 1995, Québec held a referendum that proposed that Québec become a sovereign nation with the option of negotiating an economic association with the rest of Canada. Following a heated political debate on the advantages and disadvantages of separating or staying within Canada, Québec citizens voted in favor of the status quo by a margin of 50.5% to 49.5%, with a participation rate of 93%; voters chose to remain within Canada by a margin of only 50,000 votes, the equivalent of a large audience at a baseball game. Although the vote in favor of Canada was overwhelming among anglophones and ethnocultural minorities, the majority of francophones (60%) did vote in favor of Québec sovereignty.

The polarization of voting behavior along language boundaries in the Québec referendum is yet another testimony of the enduring rivalry between two national identities in Canada, the Anglo-Canadian and the Québécois French. In 1980, a Québec referendum on "sovereignty association" was rejected on the promise that the federal government would launch a constitutional renewal granting Québec greater self-government within the Canadian Confederation. As a result of controversial negotiations among the ten provinces in 1982, the federal government repatriated from the United Kingdom the British North America Act (BNA Act), which in 1867 had established the "Dominion of Canada" as a self-governing part of the British Empire. The Constitution Act of 1982 incorporated the BNA Act, as well as its amendments, thus providing Canada with a renewed constitution. The Constitution Act was endorsed by the nine English-majority provinces but not by Québec, whose government refused to sign the agreement but was nevertheless subject to its provisions. Until then, Canada's federal system was built on the notion of two founding peoples, one English, the other French. This historical arrangement granted Québec a traditional veto power on constitutional change, which helped safeguard the interests of the French minority in Canada. However, the Constitution Act demanded unanimous agreement by *all* provinces to enforce constitutional changes, thus reducing Québec's status to only one of ten voices in the federation. Furthermore, the Constitution Act, included a bill of rights, entitled the Canadian Charter of Rights and Freedoms, which enshrined individual rights at the expense of collective rights, including those of French Canadians and First Nation peoples who requested special protection as minority groups in Canada (Bourhis 1994a).

Without the endorsement from Québec, which represented one-fourth of the Canadian population, the 1982 Constitution Act created an impasse which increased rather than decreased tensions regarding the role of Québec in the Canadian Federation. In 1990, a proposed "Meech Lake Agreement" was not ratified by two of ten provinces (Manitoba and Newfoundland), thus killing an attempt to solve the impasse by recognizing in the constitution that Québec was a "distinct society" with special collective needs. Numerous polls had shown that the vast majority of English Canadians opposed the agreement, believing that Québec must *not* be recognized as a distinct society within the Canadian constitution. Thus Québec was isolated politically as Canada's only French-majority province whose linguistic, cultural, and legal identity could not be recognized constitutionally.

As a collectivity, the Québécois remain acutely aware that their province is the last territorial enclave in which a distinctively French society can survive within North America, where the French of Québec number less than 2% of the continental population. In contrast, mainstream English Canadian nationalism is developing according to the notion of individual rights as enshrined in the 1982 Canadian constitution, which limits the possibility that a province or ethnolinguistic minority could be granted special status other than the existing right to be educated in either one of Canada's two official languages "where numbers warrant." Other special legal or constitutional treatment for a particular group or province is seen as a form of privilege, implying that not all citizens have equal status as individuals or collectivities across Canada. Thus Anglo-Canadian nationalism has difficulty accommodating the collective aspirations of not only the Québécois but also those of the First Nation peoples. After decades of political debates, constitutional negotiations, and failed accords, it is doubtful that Canada's three rival nationalisms can be reconciled constitutionally within the foreseeable future.

The Future of Language and Ethnicity Issues
in Canada and the United States

In a recent comparative analysis, Schmidt (1998) has shown how recent language policies in the United States and Canada have differed greatly in regard to the treatment of their respective linguistic minorities: the hispanophones in the United States and the francophones in Canada. The historical, demolinguistic, economic, and political position of Spanish-speaking minorities in the United States is somewhat similar to the position of Canadian francophone minorities outside of Québec, but is much weaker than that of the francophone majority within Québec. Schmidt argues that the structural weakness of Hispanic minorities in the United States makes it difficult for them to mobilize politically in the way that Québec francophones have done in order to increase their share of power and linguistic recognition. Even if such mobilization were to grow, it would be confronted by the strength of the Anglo-American assimilationist tradition, which has curtailed the recognition of linguistic and ethnocultural diversity in the United States during this century. Despite the current moribund stalemate that resulted from the waning influence of English-only advocates, there is little chance that what the English-only advocates fear—Spanish-speaking enclaves advocating Spanish-only laws or moving toward independence—will ever happen. Spanish speakers in the United States have too much to gain from their rising political and economic power to endanger this status by advocating sovereignty in a region in which they form a substantial minority or an emerging majority.

The solution to preserving language rights and ethnic identity in the United States will probably be found in the personality approach rather than in any territorial approach to bilingualism. Given the strength of the assimilationist legacy in the United States, the provision of maintenance bilingual education and the expansion of multilingual services at the local level, including voting rights, may represent the most far-reaching policies likely to emerge as adaptations to the changing American demographic situation. However, state-endorsed social exclusion and lack of linguistic and cultural accommodation toward sizeable visible and nonvisible minorities may sow the seeds of separatist options that may be difficult to control as the demographic balance shifts in favor of such minorities in the generations to come.

Why the reluctance in the United States to recognize official English-Spanish bilingualism at the state or national level, as Canada recognized official English-French bilingualism? Recently, Schmidt (1993) proposed that this recognition would imply such a fundamental transformation of the "American nationality" that the policy is too difficult for many Americans to even consider. It is useful to quote Schmidt's analysis of the issue:

> Public acknowledgement of language diversity as fully *American* symbolizes acceptance of "cultural" diversity and therefore of a broader range of the full identities of non-European Americans. This "reconstruction" of American national identity means that European-origin Americans are themselves being constructed anew as "ethnics" (for example, as "Anglos" or "Euro-Americans") rather than as "just Americans." A truly multi-cultural and multi-racial under-

standing of American national identity, in short, would mean that European-origin Americans would be "reduced" from being the standard, the prototype, against which all *Others* are to judge their own "Americanness" to being one ethnic group among many in a "decentered" multi-cultural polity (JanMohamed & Lloyd 1990). (1993: 88–89)

The Canadian case study illustrates how language policies developed at different levels of government (federal and provincial) can be used to manage tensions between competing language groups. More often contradictory than complementary, the Canadian Official Language Act and the Québec Charter of the French Language nevertheless share a concern which is fundamental within democratic states. In both cases, the language policies were adopted following both scientific research and sustained public consultations with the language communities most affected by the proposed laws. The laws were adopted by democratically elected governments with the aim of balancing the rights of minorities with those of the majority in a context in which the ethnocultural identity of the language groups was respected and valued. Though the original goals of the policies have not yet been achieved and may never be attained as originally intended, it is the democratic process of adopting the laws and of implementing them more than the achieved results that may in the long run best establish the legitimacy of the language planning effort in Québec and Canada.

Although Québécois and Canadian language policies have conflicting goals, they are inspired by a common demolinguistic reality: the increasing territorial segregation of the French and English communities in Canada. While Canadian federalists use language policies to limit the growing territorial segregation of Canada's "two linguistic solitudes," Québécois patriots wish to consolidate these trends through the institutionalization of Québec's status as a distinct French society within North America.

The Canadian case also shows how various demographic, economic, and political factors may shift immigrant integration policies from a mainly xenophobic orientation to a predominantly pluralistic vision as enshrined in the Canadian Multiculturalism Law, which gives diverse ethnic groups the right to cultural survival (Drieger 1996). This policy is credited for the relatively harmonious relations which exist between Canadian host communities and first- and second-generation immigrant groups. However, as in countries which have *not* adopted official pluralism policies, it remains true that visible minority immigrants who have low entrance status in the workforce are the groups most likely to encounter discrimination within the host society.

The North American Free Trade Agreement (NAFTA) has already been credited as a factor in accounting for the erosion of Canadian social policies such as universal health care, social welfare, and state-funded secondary and university education. Reduction of government support for these "social net" programs is advocated by American, Canadian, and Mexican corporate interests, who wish to establish a "level playing field" designed to reduce corporate taxes and facilitate the free movement of capital, goods, services, and labor across the continent. With the U.S. population and economy being ten times the size of those of Canada, it is possible that U.S. assimilationist orientations toward linguistic and ethnocultural minorities will also have an eroding impact on Canadian bilingual and multi-culturalism policies in the future. As the recent debate concerning universal health care in the United States has demonstrated, it is unlikely that the "Canadian way" can be used effectively as a precedent or justification for modifying mainstream orientations toward linguistic and ethnocultural diversity in the United States.

Questions for Further Thought and Discussion

1. If the territorial approach in language planning is workable on the local and state/provincial levels, why does it *not* seem workable on the national level in Canada and/or the United States?

2. Why do the anglophones of Québec enjoy more language rights than the francophone minorities in most other Canadian provinces? What factors help explain the rise of the "partitionist" movement among Québec anglophones following the 1995 Québec referendum?

3. Why is the difference between the francophone *nonvisible* minority of Canada and the *visible* minorities of the United States so crucial in the methods of handling the question of language and ethnicity in the two countries? Does visibility of a minority through color or other means cause problems that cannot be solved only through language planning?

4. Is the territorial approach as opposed to the personality approach (individual rights) possible in the United States? Why or why not? Which forces mitigate against its application in the United States? In Canada?

5. Why did "English-only" take hold as a movement in the United States? How do you account for the success of this movement in the states that adopted its resolutions? Compare and contrast the profile of the groups or individuals who are most likely to support "English-only" with those who are most likely to oppose this movement in the United States.

6. Discuss why and under what circumstances maintenance bilingual programs are more likely to foster additive bilingualism whereas transitional bilingual programs are more likely to foster subtractive bilingualism among linguistic-minority-group speakers in Canada and the United States.

7. Why did the Québec sovereignist movement succeed in gaining majority support among Québécois francophones in the last decade? Identify a linguistic or ethnocultural group in the United States which could be tempted to adopt an autonomist position akin to that of the Québécois and identify the factors most likely to foster such sentiments in the U.S. context.

8. What factors led successive Québec governments to adopt language laws in favor of French during the last decades? Were the measures contained in Bill 101 to defend the French language justified and were they effective in improving the status of French relative to English in Quebec?

Selected Bibliography

Armstrong, J. A. (1982). *Nations before Nationalism.* Chapel Hill: University of North Carolina Press.

Bourhis, R. Y. (1984). *Conflict and Language Planning in Québec.* Clevedon, England: Multilingual Matters.

Bourhis, R. Y. (1994a). Introduction and overview of language events in Canada. Special issue. *International Journal of the Sociology of Language* 105–106: 5–36.

Bourhis, R. Y. (1994b). Ethnicity and culture in Québec. In *Ethnicity and Culture in Canada*, J. W. Berry and J. A. Laponce (eds.), 322–360. Toronto: University of Toronto Press.

Cafferty, P. S. J. (1982). The language question: The dilemma of bilingual education for Hispanics in America. In *Ethnic Relations in America*, L. Liebman (ed.), 101–127. Englewood Cliffs, N.J.: Prentice-Hall.

Driedger, L. (1996). *Multi-Ethnic Canada: Identities and Inequalities.* Toronto: Oxford University Press.

Fishman, J. A. (1989). *Language and Ethnicity in Minority Sociolinguistic Perspective.* Clevedon, England: Multilingual Matters.

Heath, S. B. (1977). Language and politics in the United States. In *Linguistics and Anthropology: Georgetown University Round Table on Languages and Linguistics*, M. Saville-Troike (ed.), 267–296. Washington, D.C.: Georgetown University Press.

Leibowitz, A. H. (1976). Language and the law: The exercise of political power through official designation of language. In *Language and Politics*, W. M. and J. F. O'Barr (eds.), 449–466. The Hague: Mouton.

McArthur, T. (1986). Comment: Worried about something else. *International Journal of the Sociology of Language* 60:87–91.

Marshall, D. F. (1986). The question of an official language: Language rights and the English Language Amendment. *International Journal of the Sociology of Language* 60: 7–75, 201–211.

Marshall, D. F. (1996). The politics of language in America: Attempts to prevent an emerging renationalization in the United States. In *What Became of the Great Society? Comparative Perspectives on the U.S.A. in the 1960s and 1990s*, W. Herget (ed.), 67–80. Trier: Wissenschaftlicher Verlag.

Marshall, D. F., and R. D. Gonzalez (1990). Una lingua, una patria? Is monolingualism beneficial or harmful to a nation's unity? In *Perspectives on Official English: The Campaign for English as the Official Language of the USA*, K. L. Adams and D. T. Brink (eds.), 29–51. Berlin: Mouton de Gruyter.

Nunberg, G. (1992). Afterword: The official language movement: Reimagining America. In *Language Loyalties: A Source Book on the Official English Controversy*, J. Crawford (ed.), 481–490. Chicago: University of Chicago Press.

Review of Federal Measurements of Race and Ethnicity (1994). Hearings before the Subcommittee on Census, Statistics and Postal Personnel of the Committee on Post Office and Civil Service, House of Representatives, 103 Congress (First Session), Serial no. 103–7. Washington, DC: U.S. Government Printing Office.

Schmidt, R. (1993). Language policy conflict in the United States. In *The Rising Tide of Cultural Pluralism: The Nation-State at Bay?* C. Young (ed.), 73–92. Madison: University of Wisconsin Press.

Schmidt, R. (1998). The politics of language in Canada and the United States: Explaining the difference. In *Language and Politics in the United States and Canada: Myths and Realities*, T. Ricento and B. Burnaby (eds.), 37–70. Philadelphia: Erlbaum.

Smith, A. D. (1991). *National Identity*. London: Penguin Books.

Tatalovich, R. (1995). *Nativism Reborn? The Official English Language Movement and the American States*. Lexington, KY: University Press of Kentucky.

Veltman, C. (1983). *Language Shift in the United States*. Berlin: Mouton.

EUROPE

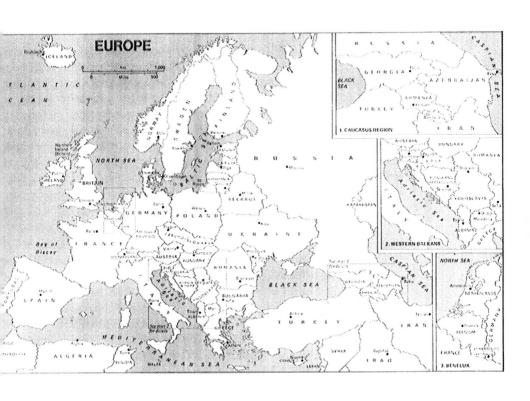

The Celtic World

COLIN H. WILLIAMS

The Ethnic Revival

The so-called ethnic revival of Western Europe involves the reassertion of the rights and obligations of long-submerged identities in an increasingly uniform world order. From a Celtic perspective, it is perverse that both language and ethnic identity are subject to intense debate. All Celtic languages are spoken by a minority in their respective territories. Many inhabitants of the six nations involved—namely, Brittany, Cornwall, Ireland, the Isle of Man, Scotland, and Wales—would object to having an "ethnic identity" ascribed to them and would deny that they inhabited a Celtic world. There is a contested reality here which needs careful interpretation.

Four explanations may be offered for this revival in the postwar period. First is the ethnic continuity model, which holds that ethnic regional awareness in advanced industrial states is part of a global resurgence in ethnic identification that is challenging social class and other bases for group membership and political behavior. Second, the salience of ethnicity is a reaction against the increasing scale of human organization and anomie felt by those socially excluded from mainstream economic and technological developments. Third, the internal colonial thesis posits that core-periphery interaction and the uneven development of capitalism operates through a cultural division of labor to disadvantage the ethnic periphery. Subject peoples can liberate themselves from structural discrimination by adopting nationalist programs to overthrow their hegemonic "colonial" masters. Fourth, great play is made of the role of the ethnic intelligentsia. Through their unique vision of history and their self-defined mission-destiny, they are well placed to mobilize the populace on issues such as relative deprivation, unfulfilled aspirations, and opportunism, hoping thereby to renegotiate the terms of their ethnic region's relationship with the international community.

The nationalist intelligentsia sought to explain the current plight of the masses by reference to the absence of indigenous political institutions which could wield real power. Radical appeals to issues of social justice within civil society replaced the previous preoccupation with the protection of ethnic homelands and the conservative imagery of rural communitarian politics. The key issue of such radicalism in Corsica, Euskadi, and Northern Ireland was whether violence could be deployed as a successful tactic for ethnolinguistic recognition and political reform.

Elsewhere, it was the turn toward an increasingly federal Europe which animated activists as they sought to harness overlapping multiple identities through the forging of political alliances with various green movements, anti-Fascist organizations, advocates of a nonnuclear economy, women's groups, and representatives of the "rainbow coalition." In several states, such pressure has forced more established political parties to advocate various decentralist reforms while increasing attempts by governments to manage tension and conflict through regional development programs, through establishing regional and national assemblies, and through recognizing the inherent pluralism of European society in social and economic policy formulation.

In Celtic societies, the collective defense of land, language, and resources have dominated the relationship between the indigenous elite and the incursive, hegemonic state power. Recently, the standardization and normalization of certain Celtic languages, together with their struggle to resist the incursions of English and French, have heightened the tension between attempts to protect a threatened language and to reproduce its historically conjoined culture. Consequently, one can quite readily maintain an ethnic identity without any reference to fluency in the indigenous language, as is the case in Cornwall, Scottish Gaeldom, and Ireland. In the case of Brittany and Wales, the maintenance of a separate language is judged to be crucial to the reproduction of an autonomous culture, though it is highly debatable as a foundation principle for Celtic identification elsewhere.

This ambiguity is precisely what makes the relationship between language and ethnic identity such a lively and uncomfortable issue. A question often asked is, Can one *really* be Breton or Welsh without speaking the language? The answer, of course, is that identity can be related to many other forms of cultural expression, and an insistence on the primacy of a linguistic definition of ethnicity can lead to troubled waters in terms of the debate between authentic and imagined communities.

However, there is a profound need for an indigenous language as a means of communicating shared ideas, values, significant experiences, and literature, and this is why so much of the effort of the Celtic revivalists has concerned language and linguistics. It is quite another question to ask to what extent such efforts have been repaid in terms of the actual increase in the daily use of a particular Celtic language. Two other trends deserve special attention: namely, European interdependence and globalization. Ethnolinguistic minorities have reacted to these twin impulses by searching for European-wide economies of scale in broadcasting, information networking, education, and public administration, by establishing their own European Union institutions and bureaus, and by entering new alliances to influence European Union decision-making bodies.

Other processes of social transformation, such as the erosion of conventional communication networks and the disintegration of traditional homelands, suggest that culture is becoming decoupled from territory and place and recoupled to new agencies and domains in predominantly urban environments. Consequently, threatened cultures are tied ever closer to a new state dependency by being institutionalized in spheres such as education, public administration, and the legal system.

Attempts to resist the "folklorization" of places, the "museumization" of communities, and the commodification and gentrification of ethnolinguistic regions through tourism and the heritage industry focus on the opportunities to empower selected communities. The sources of this power include new telecommunication networks, the mass media, and linguistic intervention. Increasingly, cultural and economic concerns are being integrated within comprehensive infrastructures which seek to increase the opportunities for bilingual provision and for working within a lesser-used language. Elements within this new infrastructure might include language enterprise agencies, linguistic *animateurs*, local authority resource centers, and sustainable local economic development agencies with a language promotion mandate. The latter focus on relevant sustainable indigenous economic activity is a long-overdue counterbalance to the overconcern with cultural affairs. In combination, both economic initiative and strategic planning intervention should provide the necessary infrastructural support to encourage language reproduction within most domains in the community.

Before the Ethnic Revival

A central feature of the Irish Gaelic revival that led to national independence was the need to differentiate Irish culture and values from British mores and interests. Catholicism, the land, and language were prominent in the nationalist struggle. Which land, which peoples, and which dynasties were to be elevated to national prominence as the prototype "Irish" was a matter of political choice, not objective scholarship. Erin McNeill's myth of Irish descent, rooted in the golden age from the sixth to the eighth centuries when Ireland became the European center of religious and secular learning, was a powerful basis for later regenerative efforts. (McNeill was a leader of the Gaelic League before the Civil War, speaker of the *Dáil* in 1921, later Minister of Education.) Up to the sixteenth century, Irish was the predominant language, but the political changes which began in the next century dispossessed the Irish aristocratic families and introduced relatively large numbers of native-born English, forming a new landlord class together with a burgeoning urban, commercial sector. In 1801 Ireland was formally united with the British state, and its population of about 8 million in 1841 contained some 2.5 million Irish speakers. However, the great famine of 1845–1849 devastated the western Irish-speaking areas in particular, with about 1 million perishing and about 1.5 million emigrating. A movement for the preservation of Irish emerged in 1893 with the founding of the Gaelic League. Only 19% of the population of the area which now comprises the Republic of Ireland was Irish speaking, some

664,387 at the 1891 Census, whereas 90% of Irish speakers resided in the two provinces of Munster and Connacht.

McNeill's insistence on the primacy of Irish was nonsectarian but had profound religio-political implications. By reinforcing the rural, Gaelic basis of national identity, he implicitly subverted the Protestant contribution. Nationalists fired by the desire for economic, as well as cultural, independence from Britain overemphasized Catholicism, the land, and Gaelic culture as the defining elements of Irish identity and underemphasized economic reality as a means of realizing these components of national mythmaking.

After independence in 1922, the government committed itself to the legitimization of Gaelic through a comprehensive strategy to restore Irish as the national language. Cultural nationalists turned once again to the rural west, to the "primal center of the nation," and, in rejecting the "visionary world of heroic warriors" as portrayed by Yeats and Pearse, they found solitude and strength in the vision of the honest peasant, struggling against both nature and powerful human interests in order to survive. The western *Gaeltacht*, a designated Irish-speaking heartland, was to be the putative bastion of Irishness and the inspiration for Fianna Fáil's attack on an English-influenced, Dublin-rooted *étatist* oligarchy.

In the middle of the 1932 Depression, Fianna Fáil and Eamon De Valera were returned to power and set about the establishment of a regenerate Irish nation. One of Fianna Fáil's central aims was to improve the status of Irish by institutionalizing it in the everyday affairs of the young state. Within the educational system more time was given to Irish, which was an obligatory subject in primary and secondary schools. Passing an examination in Irish was necessary to receive the Certificate of Education and for entrance into one of the Republic's two universities. Recruitment to the civil service was changed so as to accelerate the entry of Irish speakers over and above the university-educated children of the established Catholic middle classes.

In promoting the education system as the single most important agency, the government ignored the real question of weakened demolinguistic vitality in the remaining heartland areas of the *Gaeltacht*. Indeed, it was not until 1972 that the Comhairle na Gaeilge (a government Irish-language advisory body) recognized the need to conceive of the *Gaeltacht* in holistic, social, and economic terms and recommended the establishment of a central agency, Udarás na Gaeltachta (founded in 1979), to take over responsibility for previously fragmented government functions.

British rule had created the infrastructure of a dependent economy and a subservient political culture. Processes of industrialization and urbanization, late as they were to Ireland, eroded the rural, agrarian social order that sustained the culture. Group self-esteem was diminished by the labeling of Gaelic as primordial and antiquarian, of limited use in a modern world. The universality of English militated against the establishment of autonomous speech domains within which Irish could be nurtured. Occupational mobility and migration patterns, whether to the United Kingdom or to North America, underscored the global relevance of achieving fluency in English. No wonder then that Irish cultural nationalists often despaired that the people had forsaken their language and culture and engendered a crisis of identity.

Underlying these contextual factors was the continued decline of the Irish-speaking community, from 29% in 1851 to a low of 18% in 1911, followed by a gradual revival as a result of government efforts for the rest of the century.

Contemporary Ireland

There is a remarkable paradox today in that the number of people who claim a knowledge of Irish is increasing, while its use as a community language is decreasing. This is because the constitutional position of Irish and its prominence in the rhetoric and mythmaking of political parties gives a misleading picture of its everyday strength. The 1991 census data indicated a marked increase in the total number of reported Irish speakers over the past decades, up from 789,429 in 1971 to 1,095,830 in 1991. Irish speakers constituted 31.6% of the total Irish population aged three and over. Within the *Gaeltacht*, the Irish-speaking heartland, the number of Irish speakers rose from 55,440 in 1971 to 58,026 in 1981. However, the number of non-Irish-speakers also rose, from 11,400 in 1971 to 16,974 in 1981. In 1991 the *Gaeltacht* contained only 2.3% of the national population but 45% of Irish-speaking families.

Public support for Irish has been overwhelmingly positive, and it is often cited as a defining element of Irish national identity. Commenting on major survey data, O Riagáin reports that the public consistently supports "policies to maintain Irish in the Gaeltacht, to provide Irish language services on the national television channels, to use Irish on public notices, to provide state services in Irish and officials who can speak Irish and to support voluntary Irish organisations" (1997: 279). There was an increase in public support between the major surveys he conducted in 1973 and 1993, and on this basis he concludes that "the general population is willing to accept a considerable commitment of state resources to ensuring the language's continuance and even to support a considerable imposition of legal requirements to know or use Irish on certain groups within society, such as teachers and civil servants" (1997: 279).

However, the majority of the population would not support a more active promotional policy in favor of Irish, despite the pleas of a minority of language activists who press for a new Irish Language Act and urge pragmatic support for the voluntary sector to reenergize Irish as a community language. The promotional work of Comhdháil Náisiúnta Na Gaeilge (the Central Steering Council of Irish Language Communities) and its 21 member organizations is vital in this respect. Through planning, policy recommendations, education and training, lobbying, and initiating new partnerships with community-based projects such as Glór na nGael, Gaillimh le Gaelige and Comhluadar, it strives to serve the Irish-speaking population and attract the majority English-speaking population to its activities and events.

Evidently, the majority are satisfied to restrict Irish to artistic and cultural life. Although the educational system incorporates the teaching and use of Irish, it does not produce large numbers of competent bilinguals who wish to use their language skills in the economy. Consequently, the current emphasis is on survival rather

than revival. Successive governments have supported the all-Irish schools movement but have been unable to halt the erosion of the place of Irish within the
mainstream curriculum. Unstable sociolinguistic networks and the atrophying of
Gaeltacht communities create the distinct possibility that, having sought to master Irish in school, a whole new generation is unable to find appropriate places in
society in which it can exercise its school-based proficiency.

Ireland has so far failed to translate the potential goodwill of its citizenship
into an out-and-out revival of spoken Irish in an optimum range of social domains.
There is no question but that Irish identity is very strong. In cultural terms, it is
rooted in English-medium popular literature and mass entertainment, particularly
Celtic and Anglo-American fusions of traditional and rock music. Ireland's self-
confidence is growing, based as it is on the maintenance of responsible government, full participation within the European Union, and a remarkably successful
economy.

So successful is this amalgam that attempts to further strengthen Irish through
a substantial increase in state funding are likely to be resisted. Despite a great deal
of state and community investment, the majority of its citizens chose not to engage in daily life through the medium of Irish. It may be that the reality reflects
the political ambition of the people. For so long Irish was the symbol of resistance
to an occupying force. Having achieved independence, the language of dissent
was not adopted as the language of responsible citizenship, a sobering thought
indeed for all engaged in language revitalization efforts.

Scotland

Scottish national identity is based upon historical and institutional distinctiveness with little more than a passing symbolic regard to the maintenance of Gaelic—
a fact that reflects the limited geographical strength and relative national insig-
nificance of Gaelic, not surprising perhaps when one considers that the 65,978
Gaelic speakers represent only 1.4% of the Scottish population. Within the structures of the nation, the language has limited public recognition and use, despite
the maintenance of a virulent institutional system based on distinctive educational,
legal, and religious domains. There is little real association between the promotion of Gaelic and particular political parties. Paralleling the Irish and Welsh
experience, there has been an historical concern demonstrated by the Scottish National Party to champion the language issue. But given the small electorate who
are Gaelic speaking, it is fair to say that the greatest concern has been demonstrated
within the Highlands and Island region rather than at the national political level.

Only two local authority areas have a Gaelic-speaking population in excess of
40% of the total population. These are the Western Isles (a unitary authority where
19,546 people, 68% of the population, speak Gaelic) and Skye and Lochalsh District, where 4,715 people speak Gaelic (41% of the population). These authorities
have a combined population of 39,865 representing 0.8% of the population of
Scotland and a combined Gaelic-speaking population of 24,261, 37% of the Gaelic-
speaking population of Scotland. None of the other 49 districts or island council

areas has a Gaelic-speaking population in excess of 5%. Only Aberdeen, Edinburgh, Glasgow, and Renfrew, together with the residual Gaelic area of Perth and Kinross, have in excess of 1,000 Gaelic speakers. Whereas the historic Gaelic-speaking area of Scotland (broadly, the Highland region minus Caithness district, together with the Western Isles Argyll and Bute) makes up 43% of the Scottish land area and 5% of the Scottish population, 59.2% of the Gaelic speakers live in this area.

After centuries of political discrimination, forced exile through Highland land clearances, the destruction of the clan system, and massive emigration at successive periods, particularly to Canada, the United States, and Australia, it is remarkable that Gaelic is still spoken at all in parts of Scotland. The traditional economy that supports the maintenance of some Gaelic communities has been based on crofting, which is a unique type of land holding, comparable to the historical Welsh *tyddyn*, in central Highlands and Islands society. Areas with the highest proportion of registered crofters (17.5% or more), with the exception of north and west Sutherland, are also areas where Gaelic is strongest—the Outer Hebrides, Skye, Applecross, and Tiree. Naturally, attempts at revitalizing crofting have important consequences for Gaelic communities. The Western Isles Integrated Development Program (1982–1987, partly EC-funded), the North West Development Program (1983–1993), and the Skye Development Programs (both Highland and Islands Development Board [HIDB] funded) helped revitalize crofting. The Crofters Commission's new entry scheme seeks such revitalization through new local tenancies. Interestingly for a Scottish body, four of the seven commissioners are Gaelic speakers.

The popular attitude toward Gaelic is that it should be preserved within traditional areas and integrated into regional development plans and tourism, but there is little support for its introduction as a mainstream subject within the school curriculum outside the Highland region. The existence of a successful Gaelic-medium play-group association may presage an extension of Gaelic-medium education into primary and secondary education, but it is not a priority for educational planners. The overwhelming majority of citizens is uninterested in the promotion of Gaelic at a personal level and does not show any inclination to adopt it as a marker of personal Scottish identity.

The HIDB adopted a "think big" strategy in the growth years after its establishment in 1965, fueled by the "oil boom," but since 1976 its "look small" strategy has supported community enterprises, decentralization of its offices and decision making, and greater attention to remote areas. The HIDB commissioned its Gaelic Report *Cor Na Gaidhlig*—Language, Community, and Development in 1982, and consequently Comunn na Gaidhlig (CnaG) was established in September 1984 to develop a national policy for Gaelic. Its current "Strategy for Gaelic Development in the 21st Century," published in 1994, details how CnaG, in partnership with the Highland and Island Enterprise network, intends to use Gaelic as a motor for economic development by exploiting opportunities for new Gaelic-based businesses, including media, leisure, and cultural tourism. Gaelic presence in existing businesses will be furthered by area-based development officers. A parallel program calls for converting the much-publicized advantages of Gaelic tourism into reality, with CnaG working with Highland and Island Enterprise, the Local

Enterprise Councils, the National Trust for Scotland, Scottish National Heritage, and Historic Scotland. Gaelic tourism is seen to comprise:

- an association with a beautiful, dramatic, and clean landscape
- traditional and contemporary Gaelic arts that are vibrant and distinctive
- interest in minority cultures and languages
- a view of Gaelic culture as an increasingly appreciated part of the pan-European culture

It is estimated that Gaelic tourism should be capable of generating an industry with an annual turnover of £20 million and employing 2,000 people.

In an attempt both to popularize Gaelic and to raise levels of awareness as to its integral role within the region, the Highlands and Islands Enterprise, as successor to HIDB, has prioritized specific policies for implementation. It seeks to:

- assist in the development of a new Gaelic broadcasting industry (especially training and development)
- improve employment opportunities through targeted training programs (e.g., the media, teaching Gaelic language, the arts, and management)
- provide a versatile delivery service free for Gaelic development, including training and business growth (including utilizing new technology)
- initiate a series of pilot and research projects to exploit and demonstrate the possibilities of development through Gaelic (including cultural tourism, Gaelic producers, Gaelic as a development tool, study of the effects of development potential on emigration and immigration)

Three reasons are given to justify direct involvement in support for Gaelic development: (1) improving economic performance through growing self-confidence among individuals and communities; (2) developing social and tourism benefits from the culture; and (3) specific business development and training. Throughout the Highlands and Islands, almost 350 community action grant projects have been assisted at a cost of £1,100,000.

Elsewhere, newer initiatives promise to increase the opportunities nationwide to speak Gaelic, and supporters hope to encourage young people in particular to seize on the opportunities denied to their parents. Gaelic broadcasting and folk and rock music in Gaelic are burgeoning, as is the attempt by the current Labor Government to boost Gaelic as an element of Scottish identity on the eve of the establishment of a national assembly. Attitudes toward Gaelic should improve significantly when policies are decided within Scotland rather than at Westminster, though given the meager size of the Gaelic-speaking population, it will always be a difficult task to impress on the majority the acute needs of the minority.

Wales

Following the Edwardian conquest of Wales after 1282 A.D., English colonial control turned to a form of shared power with the accession of the Welsh nobleman, Henry VII, in 1485. His heir, Henry VIII, enacted the Acts of Union of 1536 and

1542, which formally incorporated Wales into the legal and political realm of England. The Acts' most significant clause in terms of the future of the Welsh language was to exclude Welsh from official life and to require all public official-dom that was transacted in the "principality" to be in English. Having forbidden Welsh, the Tudor state in 1588 authorized a Welsh translation of the Holy Bible and the Book of Common Prayer so as to secure a Protestant base against Catholic incursions at home and from Ireland. The Welsh Bible was critical, for it provided a modern, standardized, elegant version of Welsh, encouraged wider scholarship and publication of related literature, and stimulated a national network of church-sponsored agencies that nurtured a largely literate and involved population at an early stage compared with developments elsewhere in Europe. In the succeeding centuries, despite discrimination and persecution, dissenting religious groups flourished and encouraged a trans-Atlantic, Welsh-medium network of correspon-dents, journalists, teachers, and social and spiritual interpreters that culminated in a period of late-nineteenth-century liberal radicalism during which the lasting values of modern Wales were formed.

Wales's huge population growth in the mid-nineteenth century following indus-trialization, a growth based on the mineral exploitation of iron and coal together with steel and engineering production, meant that bilingualism became a mass phenomenon. It was reflected in new codes of worship, of work, leisure, and po-litical beliefs which were transmitted to an increasingly literate workforce by a mass media created by print capitalism. The Welsh language was undoubtedly saved by this redistribution of a growing population—for the Welsh, unlike the Scots or the Irish, did not have to abandon their language and homeland for em-ployment abroad, particularly in the New World.

This may be the principal reason why modern Welsh identity is more closely linked to the maintenance of language than any other Celtic case. Welsh culture is less reliant on institutions and is reflected more through popular involvement in chapel-based social activities; choral festivals; *Eisteddfodau* competitions in music, drama, and poetry; a brass band tradition; miners' libraries; and early na-tional sporting federations. These manifestations were as much a redefinition of indigenous Welsh culture as they were the sharpening of a distinctly Anglo-Welsh identity and tradition, best represented in the literary work of Dylan Thomas, Gwyn Thomas, and R. S.Thomas.

However, this mutually dependent Welsh and Anglo-Welsh popular culture has heavily influenced the nature of urban Welsh-medium culture, for, unlike in rural Wales, such changes were operative within a set of formal, English-medium public sector and commercial domains.

Imperial economic advances and state intervention following the Education Act of 1870 and the Welsh Intermediate Education Act of 1889 bred a new aware-ness of English values, culture, and employment prospects and gave a powerful institutional fillip to anglicization, which encouraged the normality of transmit-ting Welsh identity through the medium of English.

Within the space of two generations, 1930–1960, the population of industrial Wales had abandoned Welsh as a first language, as both natives and migrants turned to English as the only official language of commerce and industry, thereby diminishing the separateness of an autonomous Welsh culture. During this period it was commonplace to argue that Welsh was a dying language and an impediment to full participation in an increasingly Anglo-American-dominated world economy. The familiar cliché, "if you want to get ahead get an English head," was far too poignant to be dismissed lightly, for nearly all aspects of formal Welsh life were transmitted through English.

A minority resisted anglicization and developed countermovements dedicated to the promotion of Welsh, inspired by intellectuals such as the Reverend Michael D. Jones, who led the small exodus to Patagonia (in Argentina) to establish a wholly Welsh migrant community. The Reverend Emrys ap Iwan was the first minister of religion to appear before a court of law and insist on the primacy of the Welsh language in legal proceedings in Wales. Dan Issac Davies, the Head Master for Schools, advocated a greater use of Welsh-medium education. Thomas Gee, the publisher of such ambitious multivolume encyclopaedias as *Gwyddoniadur*, was an advocate of mass circulation periodicals in Welsh. The most influential family of all was headed by O. M. Edwards, the university teacher, writer, publisher, and first Chief HMI [Her Majesty's Inspector] for schools in Wales, who tried to establish a more tolerant approach to bilingualism by attacking the injustice associated with the Welsh outside of the school system (the practice, common in the nineteenth century, whereby teachers, at the request of parents and governors, punished pupils for using Welsh within the school). Edwards's son, Sir Ifan ab Owen Edwards, established Urdd Gobaith Cymru (The Welsh League of Youth) in 1922; it has become the largest mass movement in Wales, encouraging children and young adults to develop skills, competence, and leadership qualities in community work, *Eisteddfodau* (the largest cultural youth festival in Europe), and sporting achievements.

In the liberal heyday, Wales established a set of national institutions that paralleled those in Scotland and Ireland. These include the federal University of Wales (established 1883); the National Library of Wales; Aberystwyth and the National Museum of Wales at Cardiff, which were established in 1907; and the church in Wales, which was created following the Act of Disestablishment in 1920. A variety of cultural movements flourished, such as Undeb Cenedlaethol Y Cymdeithasau Cymraeg (the National Union of Welsh Societies, formed in 1913) and Urdd Gobaith Cymru in 1922. Within cultural circles, academics, such as John Morris Jones, were revising Welsh orthography, and the self-confidence of the period was reflected in a significant increase in the range and reach of literature such that linguistic normalization and literary rejuvenation went hand in hand. This had a huge impact on the popularity of local *Eisteddfodau*, the establishment of new literary journals, and weekly newspapers.

This political-cultural infrastructure was dependent on British-wide external factors and finance. The dominant ideologies were British conservatism and international socialism; liberalism was on the wane, and the specter of nationalism was anathema to the overwhelming majority of the population, who saw it as either dangerous or irrelevant.

A minority concluded that the reproduction of indigenous Welsh culture necessitated a form of genuine self-government or home rule. Thus, in 1925, Plaid Genedlaethol Cymru (the Welsh Nationalist Party) was formed by a group of bourgeois intellectuals which included Saunders Lewis, a university lecturer and playwright; the Reverend Lewis Valentine, a Baptist minister; and D. J. Davies, an economist. Their initial concerns were the preservation of Welsh cultural and spiritual values, the maintenance of a small-scale, primarily rural, communitarian lifestyle, and a concern with taking the moral high ground to distance themselves from the twin evils of imperialism and social class antagonism. The Welsh Nationalist Party developed an image as the only political movement preoccupied with language promotion and cultural defense, and although this won the hearts and minds of dedicated cultural nationalists, it antagonized the vast majority of the population, who began to perceive the promotion of Welsh as an extension of nationalist policies and convictions.

The most significant popular manifestation of the ethnic revival was the formation of Cymdeithas yr Iaith Gymraeg (the Welsh Language Society) in 1963. Initially concerned with single-issue campaigning in favor of such reforms as bilingual forms, tax, and television licenses, a separate Welsh-medium television channel, and greater equality between Welsh and English in judicial affairs, the Cymdeithas has developed into a real force for change in Wales. Over a thirty-year period its members have engaged in a series of direct-action campaigns which have involved violence to property but never to persons.

Contemporary Wales

The attitude of the majority toward Welsh has changed remarkably. In the early postwar years, the language issue was closely identified with Plaid Cymru (the Welsh Nationalist Party), and talk of the imminent death of Welsh and its irrelevance in a modern society was commonplace. Today the majority accept that bilingualism is an integral element within society.They applaud the availability of bilingual provision, especially in terms of advancing their children's education and social prospects. This is a remarkable turn around in the general attitude towards the role of Welsh and English. A minority of parents agitated for Welsh-medium education, which the Labor Party developed through its pioneering bilingual educational policies in anglicized Wales, especially Flint and Glamorgan. Today the majority accept that bilingualism is an integral element within society. They applaud the availability of bilingual provisions, especially in terms of advancing their children's education and social prospects. This is a remarkable turnaround in the general attitude toward the roles of Welsh and English.

The first language census in Wales in 1891 had recorded 898,914 Welsh speakers (54.4%). At its census peak in 1911, the Welsh-speaking population numbered 977,366 (43.5%), of whom 190,300 were monoglot Welsh. A summary of the most recent census findings (1991) suggests that the Welsh-speaking population of 510,920 (18.7%) continues to decline, albeit at a modified rate; that it is predominantly aging; that it is concentrated in proportional terms in the north and west; that it shows encouraging signs of growth among the younger age groups, particularly in the industrial south and east; and that this growth can be largely attributed to the development of Welsh-medium education in such areas, in combination with the wider scale revival of interest in the language and its institu-tionalization in many aspects of public life. Following the passage of the Welsh Language Act (1993) and the establishment of the statutory Welsh Language Board, Welsh has become increasingly identified with government support and targeted for an increase in use as a working language, especially for the heartland region. However, many Welsh speakers find it difficult to secure adequate employment within predominantly Welsh-speaking regions, which atrophy because of the emigration of the young, fecund, and well educated and the immigration of non-Welsh-speaking residents who are attracted by a variety of factors. Thus a cen-tral issue is whether or not a viable Welsh culture can survive without its own heartland communities serving as a resource base for language transmission.

The dynamic Welsh-medium school system has done more than any other agency to promote the language and introduce it to hitherto non-Welsh speaking families. There is now a very positive attitude toward bilingual education, based on three convictions: (1) that such education encourages a sense of national pride in the language, literature, history, and geography of Wales; (2) that the high quality of education offered is a distinct advantage over many other forms of state educa-tion; and (3) that in an increasingly competitive job market, the additional skill of knowing Welsh has high added value and is therefore prized for reasons of in-strumental achievement.

The 1991 census reported that 16.1% of three- to four-year-olds spoke Welsh compared with 13.3% in 1981 and 11.3% in 1971. However, other data sources suggest that the mother-tongue figure is closer to 4.6%. Higher percentages of Welsh speakers among five- to nine-year-olds (24.7%) and ten- to fourteen-year-olds (26.9%) as compared to a three- to four-year-old cohort in 1981 (13.3%) sug-gests a value-added effect of primary and secondary education, as schools are the primary extrafamilial agency for language transmission. A partial explanation for this discrepancy is that the public's interpretation of the census questions has changed, because Welsh has been included in the national curriculum since 1988.

Although the 1991 census suggests that 24.7% of five- to nine-year-olds spoke Welsh, head teachers' educational returns for January 1994 suggest that only 14.9% of five- to nine-year-olds were fluent. These comprised two groups: 6.5% were fluent and spoke Welsh at home, and 8.4% were fluent but did not speak Welsh at home. At state supported rather than voluntary or church secondary schools in 1996, 11.5% were being taught Welsh as a first language, 56.8% were being taught Welsh as a second language, and 31.7% were not taught Welsh at all. The school's role is likely to increase following the reforms of the 1988 Education Act, which stipulates that Welsh be a core subject in the national curriculum. It is now pos-sible to teach a wide range of subjects, including mathematics, science, design, and computing, through the medium of Welsh. There is also a growing recogni-tion of the need for a change of emphasis from bilingual education in Wales to education for a bilingual Wales if the more positive attitudes and state-directed language promotion are to be inclusive facets of an increasingly self-confident culturally plural nation.

In higher education circles also, there is a wide range of vocational and non-vocational courses available to full- and part-time students, and although small in total numbers, this change in direction is significant. This nationwide network of primary, secondary, and tertiary Welsh-medium institutions is actively socializing a younger generation into anticipating living in a fully functional bilingual society.

The greatest boost to the popular and technical use of Welsh was the inauguration of Sianel Pedwar Cymru (S4C, a Welsh-language television channel) on November 1, 1982. For thirty years there had been a gradually expanding television output in Welsh, such that by 1982 some 10% of programs were broadcast in Welsh. The 1974 Crawford Committee suggested the establishment of a Welsh-medium channel, as did the conservative manifesto pledge of 1979. However, within a few months of taking office, the new administration withdrew its commitment, preferring to improve the existing broadcasting arrangements. This policy change engendered the largest mass protests witnessed in postwar Wales. The pivotal act of this campaign was the May 5, 1980, decision of Gwynfor Evans, a former leader of Plaid Cymru, to fast to death unless the government announced the creation of S4C (Sianel Pedwar Cymru). On September 17, 1980, the government reversed its decision, and today some 30 out of 145 hours per week are broadcast in Welsh, mainly at peak times. The programs reach a relatively high percentage of their target audience. Because S4C is a commissioning rather than a production body, it has spawned a network of independent filmmakers, animators, creative designers, and writers who often turn their original Welsh-language programs into English or "foreign" languages to sell in the international media marketplace. Cardiff ranks second to London as a media-production center in the United Kingdom, with all the technical, economic, and postproduction implications of a growing infrastructure in such a specialist industry.

At a voluntary level, there is an active network of *Eisteddfodau* (competitive cultural festivals) which nurture school and community performances of Welsh plays or plays in translation and of musical items and poetry and production of craftwork, art and design, and scientific projects. More recently, the Urdd (the Welsh League of Youth) has reinterpreted traditional Welsh mass culture by adding go-carting, tenpin bowling, discos, and surfing "in Welsh." An additional voluntaristic element is the adult learning of Welsh through Wlpan (intensive language-teaching courses) and related schemes, which are geographically widespread and well attended. These in turn often feed Welsh clubs and social centers, which may have sports, folk dancing, or music as their focus but offer a wider entry into the indigenous culture. Capping all this is the healthy and vibrant Welsh popular music scene, which has emerged since the 1970s. It reflects a fusion of three trends: indigenous Welsh music, a revitalized Celtic music industry, and the international popularity of Welsh bands, who perform in both Welsh and English. For the first time in living memory, major British newspapers are hailing the Welsh youth scene and most of its associated activities as "energized," "sexy," and "cool."

Much of the financing for this burgeoning cultural revival has come from consistent Welsh Office support for Welsh language education, together with many social activities, for example, Mudiad Ysgolion Meithrin (the Welsh Nursery Schools Movement), Eisteddfod Genedlaethol Cymru (the National Eisteddfod of

Wales), Cyngor Llyfrau Cymraeg (the Welsh Books Council), and some economic activities such as Menter a Busnes (Business and Enterprise), which promotes enterprise in rural Welsh-speaking Communities.

Having fought to obtain a semblance of equality for both Welsh and English in the postwar period, it is likely that the next generation's concerns will have far more to do with questions of economic development, environmental protection and conservation and holistic planning. This is particularly true for the heartland region, for despite its relative decline as the source for initiative and social change, it is still the base and bedrock of a relatively autonomous Welsh culture. No amount of formal language planning geared toward the gaining of new speakers in anglicized towns can substitute for the popular will to reproduce a language and culture.

The mere fact that at least 18.9% (508,098) of the population is Welsh speaking gives the language issue a significance that is absent in Scotland. Also the iconography of the landscape reflects an increasingly bilingual society, with far greater use of Welsh in public signs, advertisements, place-names, the media, and general conversation. The language and its associated culture is very much alive, vibrant, and ever-present, particularly at a symbolic level. Compared with the 1950s and 1960s, it is fair to say that Wales is a far more bilingual society now. However, this development has been at the expense of the traditional predominantly Welsh-speaking communities, which have been in decline. The dominant theme in the geolinguistics of Irish, Welsh, and Gaelic has been the collapse of the territorial strength of the north and west, which raises the question as to whether a virulent Irish, Welsh, or Gaelic culture can survive without their own autochthonous core areas as a resource base. A critical concern of sensitive planning is how to establish an infrastructure whereby the rights and obligations of Welsh/ English, Gaelic/ English, and Breton/French speakers can be realized in tandem within a changing geographical context. Such a context must take account of substantial Welsh- and Breton-speaking communities outside the national territory in historically significant cities such as Liverpool, Manchester, London, and Paris.

In Wales, concepts derived from "cydymdreiddiad tir ac iaith" (the interpenetration of land and language) have very recently been given practical shape in planning policies which aim to bolster Welsh-speaking communities through environmental improvement and rural-economic diversification. The language movement has rediscovered its "ecological" heritage and has repackaged what were deemed in the 1920s and 1930s to be rural community issues as issues of "cultural species" survival and as a local response to globalization.

Many individuals are more autonomous, exercising language community without geographical contiguity. Processes such as the immigration of non-Celtic language speakers, mixed marriages, language shift, the revolution in telecommunications, and commuting to work patterns have all contributed to the fragmentation of the traditional strongholds.

In consequence, Welsh has entered a new phase of legitimacy following the passage of the Welsh Language Act in 1993. Support for Welsh can no longer be interpreted as essentially a symbol of resistance to anglicization, for the language is itself deeply imbued in the process of state socialization. Welsh has become a contested instrument both of reform and of governance, of opposition and of authority. Welsh is increasingly incorporated into the machinery of government, of justice, of public administration, and of civic control.

Developments in Welsh Language Policy

The current challenge is to strengthen sympathetic attitudes by creating new opportunities for language choice. The statutory Welsh Language Board, established in 1993, has a mandate to promote bilingualism in the public sector, to oversee the provision of Welsh-medium education and the language policy of major media institutions such as the BBC and S4C (Sianel Pedwar Cymru), to audit the financing and subscription levels of Welsh journals, and to require local authorities to submit language plans which detail their policy and bilingual provisions.

Within the private sector the Welsh Language Board seeks to encourage the voluntaristic adoption of bilingual practices through joint ventures and initiatives such as marketing the language, devising language courses for employees, and preparing commercial documents and terminology to smooth the transition from English-only to bilingual working practices. The Welsh Language Board adopts a holistic perspective on language in society and, given its statutory powers, it will be able to influence social behavior and in some measure redress some of the grievances that have accumulated as a result of centuries of denial of language legitimacy and all its associated discriminatory implications for Welsh life.

The Welsh Language Board has set itself four priorities. The first is to increase the number of Welsh speakers. The second is to increase opportunities for the public to use the Welsh language with organizations that deal with the public in Wales. The third is to ensure that Welsh-speaking communities be given the facilities and opportunities and the encouragement needed to maintain and extend the use of Welsh in all aspects of communal life. The fourth is to increase the habitual use of Welsh by speakers of the language. The challenge over the next five years will be to harmonize Welsh Language Board–approved language schemes so that that they are effective in serving the public while being careful not to overburden public sector personnel or to instill further resentment toward the use of Welsh as a working language.

The most underdeveloped topic as far as language policy is concerned is the relationship between regional development, enterprise, and cultural reproduction. Comparative European research has focused on the role of language policy in regional economic development and community regeneration and on questions of accessibility in accommodating immigrants and in relating questions of community leadership, social cohesion, and confidence in language use to the formal framework of bilingual public services, the operation of the voluntary sector, and the increased penetration of the private sector. Understandably, many hesitant citizens ask what they can do with the bilingual skills they acquire through the school system. How practical is their knowledge of Welsh going to be, and how may they use it in the job market, if at all?

The context of Welsh employment is critical to give material effect to the bilingual skills the education system claims are prized in society. In rural heartland areas, employment has been heavily dependent on farming and extractive industries which are cutting back on labor. Elsewhere, the atrophying of heavy industries such as coal mining, iron and steel, and tin-plate working has not only caused a transformation of conventional patterns of economic activity but has also isolated women as the main breadwinners in many families because of the relatively high rates of male unemployment in these areas. New gender-related roles have an impact both on parenting and on language transmission processes. Little is known in detail as to what effect this has on community involvement, the viability of scattered rural settlements, labor training, and skill acquisition. Also, the size of companies in predominantly Welsh-speaking areas is limited, leading to narrow regional economic diversity and an undeveloped urban network wherein alternative sources of employment in the service sectors could be provided along the lines suggested by the experience of local economic development agencies.

Class differences are also pertinent in influencing public attitudes toward the language, for middle-class Welsh-speakers are differentially concentrated in the bilingual public sector, particularly in Gwynedd, whereas English immigrants are overrepresented in the private sector managerial classes. This reflects a dependency culture, which ties Welsh speakers into the local state; interventionist employment-generation agencies such as Menter a Busnes (Enterprise and Business) seek to counter this disparity. It has also been argued that the Welsh express collectivist community values rather than individualistic ones, reflecting the ideological basis of Welsh culture. Little is known how messages relating to business, enterprise, political representation, regional development, and planning are constructed and diffused.

Community Fragmentation and Linguistic Regeneration

Is fragmentation and collapse the inevitable future for the Irish, Gaelic, and Welsh heartland? Should we be less concerned with territorial control and resistance to externally induced change? If territorial heartlands are passé, we are led to depend on the mass media to play a role in integrating Celtic-language speakers within a communication network that makes up a postmodern community. As the relationship between the mass media and the reproduction of language and culture is unclear, Celtic-language speakers will still need to have places wherein their languages, at the very least, are coequal with English. The key issues are to assess how language planning intervention will affect the behavior of individuals and how the relative cultural autonomy of the group will be affected by the increasing dependence of the language on state provision and control.

In discussing digital technology and interactive media networks, we may ask how far the Celtic languages can benefit from this global telecommunication trend. Can bilingual public services be so technologically ordered as to compensate for the loss of territorial/communal dominance? Or does the increased internationalization of English and French inevitably threaten the ability of Gaelic, Irish, Welsh, and Breton to compete and survive well into the next century?

In the postwar period, attempts to institutionalize Irish, Gaelic, Welsh, and Breton within education, public administration, and the media have met with varying degrees of success. In part, this reflects the redefinition of the relationship between the individual, the indigenous language community, and society. It also reflects the expanding nature of state involvement in all aspects of social and economic life. Consequently, the relative autonomy enjoyed by Celtic culture is increasingly dependent on state legitimization and financing. A critical change in the linguistic arguments of late has been a switch in emphasis from urgent promotional work within individual domains, such as education, to a realization that cultural reproduction can be sustained only if holistic solutions, including local economic development, are adopted.

At the national level, the chief challenge facing those involved in formulating language policy is providing an appropriate infrastructure wherein questions of language choice may be exercised. A second challenge is normalizing any of the Celtic languages so that they are used as a vehicle for normal communication in a wider set of domains. But this involves much more than popular expressions of goodwill or the provision of opportunities and an ancillary right to language choice. It involves investment, training, encouragement, and conviction, for the development of a thoroughly bilingual employment market is still a novel idea. We should not be unduly optimistic about changing patterns of behavior over the short term nor unduly pessimistic that most will continue to favor using English or French as the effective means of communication in most cases. Unitary authorities and national language coordinating bodies have a critical role as legitimizing agencies in constructing new forms of partnership through statutory obligations and pump-priming initiatives. But the long-term infrastructural support will be nongovernmental and grounded within local economies and communities. Hence the critical need to tackle the indigenous economic and cultural development questions if the Celtic languages are ever to recover their role as community languages. The message from the Celtic world is that the majority of people are favorable to the maintenance of Celtic languages for others, but only a minority in each case are convinced that bilingualism is a worthwhile personal goal. Times are changing, and the expansion of the infrastructure to allow citizens to exercise a language choice in many new domains may prove critical. The majority have concluded that there is no necessary relationship between the maintenance of a distinct national identity and fluency in the national language. For a minority, however, the complete opposite is the case, and they will continue to swim against the tide so that their interests and viewpoints are represented within the state system and public domain. The Welsh case provides some hope that revival, not merely survival, is a distinct possibility for some Celtic languages. In order to realize this goal, one would have to go beyond the well-meaning palliatives of sympathetic attitudes. Community action and political commitment are the watchwords of language revival if we are to realize the the good wishes and laissez-faire assumptions of liberal individuals as social fact.

Questions for Further Thought and Discussion

1. Is fragmentation and collapse the inevitable future for the Celtic heartland regions?

2. If so, should we be far less concerned with notions of domination, of hegemony, of territorial control, and of resistance to externally induced change?

3. What are the perceptions held by consumers, agencies, and educators as to what constitutes an appropriate place for proficiency in a Celtic language in contemporary society?

4. Can linguistic minorities achieve sufficient relative sociocultural autonomy through the adoption of mass technology and internal communicative competence?

5. Will ethnicity as a base for social mobilization and group development increase or decrease with greater European political-economic integration?

6. What effect will the enlargement of the European Union have on the internal management of its constituent ethnolinguistic and regional groups?

7. Will the proposed national assemblies for Scotland and Wales necessarily strengthen a new definition of national identity? And with what consequences for the promotion of the national language?

8. Do many Irish/Gaelic/Welsh speakers work in the public sector primarily because it is one of the limited employment domains in which they may function in a bilingual environment? If so, does this weaken the relationship between the lesser-used languages and the commercial and voluntary sectors?

Selected Bibliography

Aitchison, John, and Harold Carter (1993). The Welsh language in 1991. *Planet* (97): 3–11.

Davies, Janet (1993). *The Welsh Language*. Cardiff: University of Wales Press.

James, C., and C. H. Williams (1996). Language and planning in Scotland and Wales. In *Planning in Scotland and Wales*, H. Thomas and R. Macdonald (eds.), 264–302. Cardiff: University of Wales Press.

MacKinnon, K. (1994). *Gaelic in 1994: Report to E.U. Euromosaic Project.* Black Isle: Surveys of Gaelic Research Unit and Database.

Menter a Busnes (1994). *A Quiet Revolution: The Framework of the Academic Report*, Aberystwyth: Menter a Busnes.

O Riagáin, P. (1997). *Language Policy and Social Reproduction: Ireland 1893–1993*. Oxford: Clarendon Press.

Sproull, A. (1996). Regional economic development and minority language use: The case of Gaelic in Scotland. *International Journal of the Sociology of Language*, 12: 93–118.

Williams, Colin H. (ed.) (1991). *Linguistic Minorities, Society and Territory*. Clevedon, England: Multilingual Matters.

Williams, Colin H. (1994). *Called Unto Liberty: On Language and Nationalism*. Clevedon, England: Multilingual Matters.

Williams, Glyn (ed.) (1987). The sociology of Welsh. *International Journal of the Sociology of Language*, 66.

Williams, Gwyn Alfred (1985). *When was Wales?* London: Black Raven Press.

Germany

JAMES R. DOW

> It distinguishes the Germans, that they never get tired of asking
> who they are.
>
> Friedrich Nietzsche, *Jenseits von Gut und Böse*, 1886

In 1938, Adolf Bach wrote a statement which he continued until 1971 to publish in subsequent editions of his *Geschichte der deutschen Sprache*:

> In Germany it is generally assumed that the *Germanen* [Germanic tribesmen] (of all the Indo-Germanic [Indo-European] individual groups) were the only ones to remain in the old Indo-Germanic homeland, even if they slowly spread their settlements far beyond. This interpretation is supported by Tacitus (*Germania* II): "The Germans themselves I should regard as aboriginal, and not mixed at all with other races through immigration and intercourse." (1971: 39)

A century earlier, in 1856, Wilhelm Grimm wrote in the introduction to the final edition of the *Household Tales*:

> We shall be asked where the outermost lines of common property in stories begin, and how the degrees of affinity are gradated. The outermost lines are coterminous with those of the great race which is commonly called Indo-Germanic, and the relationship draws itself in constantly narrowing circles round the settlements of the Germans. . . . (1856: 427–428)

Three hundred years prior to the Grimms, in 1541, in his *Chronica vom vrsprung, herkommen und Thaten der vralten Teutschen*, Johannes Aventinus made pointed reference to the *Germanen* as the ancestors of the Germans, effectively leaving out all of the other Germanic peoples who also trace their lineage back to these early tribes. And more than 1,400 years prior to Aventinus, in the year 98, Tacitus produced in his *Germania* an ethnography which was long considered by many to be *the* source of information on Germans (not *Germanen*), including details of their divine descent and their uniqueness among their neighbors in both language and customs. After this small work was found in the middle of the fifteenth century and then published in Italy in 1470, it was frequently cited in the German-speaking world to document that the Germans were native born, an untainted race, and a unique breed: *tantum sui similis gens*, that is, "like none but themselves." As Adolf Bach quotes above, they were "aboriginal, and not mixed at all with other races." We now know that such characterizations were prime examples of "transference," that is, terminology that was frequently used to describe other peoples, including other major European groups such as the Celts and the Scythians, by writers like Herodotus and Poseidonios. There is in fact no evidence that Tacitus was ever in Germany, and his reasons for writing the *Germania* probably reflect his personal objections to the moral and political decadence of Rome. Nevertheless, his words have been cited for more than five centuries by speakers of German to justify ethnic purity and continuity.

As we can see, German ethnic identity has a long and well-documented history. There is also considerable comment by reputable scholars that suggests that the homeland of the Indo-European peoples was Germany, that the *Germanen* are the direct descendants of the original Indo-European peoples, and that German ancestry can be traced in an unbroken line to these same tribesmen. Through time, this identity has also been specifically associated with the German language.

In order to understand this topic better, it is important to be aware of a romantic strain of writing about the German language which has, as we have seen above, always been present. Such writings contain, in Fishman's terms, elements of both nostalgia and nationalism. On occasion some of the writings, especially when they are nostalgic, can be dismissed as little more than *Deutschtümelei* [jingoistic emphasis on things German]. In other cases, however, the mindset leads directly toward and eventually into a *völkisch* [folkish; pure German] attitude. These concepts, romantic, *Deutschtümelei*, and *völkisch*, are then often nationalistic; there are virtually always latent racial aspects, and the subtext is that of German uniqueness and superiority. This attitude developed into unbridled and brutal racism during the National Socialist era, and German linguistic scholarship did not remain above the fray.

There is, of course, always the potential for ethnic identity to take on racist thought and biases, but Germany remains a special case because the happenings of 1933–1945 gave a unique impetus to German *Sprachwissenschaft* [language scholarship]. Like all other scholarship, this was subjected to the irrational forces of the National Socialist totalitarian state, so much so that the scholarship of the period that concerns other races still requires special critical viewing. We might disregard this strain of writing as insignificant, or, as some have done with the *völkisch* elements, as an aberration, if it were not for the fact that in the three countries which arose out of the ashes of the German Reich, the Federal Republic of Germany, the German Democratic Republic, and the Republic of Austria, many *völkisch* elements survived intact through several decades after the war, both in the scholarly arena and in the public sector. New scholarly agendas were pursued in the postwar years in each of the new political states, but for each a treatment of "language and ethnic identity," and later the concept of an "ethnic revival," bore a special onus. Briefly stated, an "ethnic revival" was viewed with great skepticism in the German-speaking world, and its manifestation does not look like that of the United States. Language and ethnic identity in Germany is thus a study in how good *Sprachwissenschaft* is constantly shadowed by an irrational element.

In eighteenth-century Germany, it was Johann Gottfried Herder who would utilize elements of the French Enlightenment to build his own philosophy of history. Herder spoke of a *Volksgeist* [folk spirit], which he viewed as an intellectual foundation. Language incorporated this spirit, for it represented a link with the past, the mythological roots of a nation. Herder's biological and organic worldview compared the growth of humanity to that of plants, and it would not be long before he applied this same thinking to the development of language. Just as humans progressed from childhood to youth, then to adulthood and old age, language also moved through these various stages. It is ironic that Herder, himself a clergyman, wrote his treatise *Abhandlung über den Ursprung der Sprache* (1770) to counter another clergyman's "proof" that God created language with twenty-four sounds! Herder clearly suggested a human origin for language, making a historical perspective on language development possible. Throughout the nineteenth century, scholars would build on this historical basis for their understanding of language evolution, but it would not be long before some would pick up ideas from Herder's organic concept and use them for nationalistic and German identity purposes. During the Napoleonic Wars, for example, in his *Reden an die deutsche Nation* (1808), Johann Gottlieb Fichte referred to Germans as the *Urvolk* [the original (primeval) folk] and sought to establish his thesis by associating language, the nation, and the state. Only Germans, Fichte (following Tacitus) reasoned, as "aboriginal, and not mixed at all with other races," continued to use a language that was also "not mixed" and was thus capable of pure learning; that is, German is *Übersinnlich* [supersensual]. In contrast, Fichte saw that the romanized *Germanen*, also the speakers of Romance languages, spoke a language that was "mixed" and which had thus become what he referred to as torpid and abstract.

By the early nineteenth century, the brothers Grimm, most notably Jacob, built on Herder's historical perspectives of language, including recent advances in scholarship concerning Indo-European. German was clearly part of a larger grouping of languages which reached back into prehistoric times, to protolanguage forms and to reconstructed [*erschlossen*] words. Within this new and more reliable philological scholarship, German still occupied a special place for the Grimms. Their philology, historical study of the language, was without equal in the early nineteenth century. Still today we ascribe our understanding of the intricacies of the two sound shifts, that is, the development of High German, to Jacob Grimm— "Grimm's Law." However, romantic notions are found alongside this scholarship: "No folk on earth has such a history for its language as does German. The sources reach back over 2000 years into its past" (1819: 38). German was conceived of by the Grimms as young and vigorous at a time when the Mediterranean languages were, in Herder's terms, reaching adulthood and old age. It is specifically their understanding and usage of the word *deutsch* which reveals that the Grimms conceived of Germans as the heirs of the Indo-Europeans. In his *Deutsche Grammatik*

(1819), Jacob Grimm treats all Germanic languages; but in his *Deutsche Mythologie* (1835) and his *Geschichte der deutschen Sprache* (1848), he refers to the *Germanen* of Tacitus as "our ancestors." It was, however, the monumental *Deutsches Wörterbuch* which seemed to combine the Grimms' best philological scholarship with their own private dedication to a romanticized and continuing German *Volksseele* [folk soul]. The dictionary, whose first entries were published in 1854 and which was not completed until a century later in 1960, does not read like a dictionary that was designed for scholars or for school use but rather for the everyday household. It also suggests a patriarchal approach to German language uniqueness: ". . . the dictionary could be used for household purposes . . . why shouldn't the father pick out a few words and go through them with his boys, while testing their language ability and refreshing his own? Mother would happily listen to this."

During most of the nineteenth century, Germany remained politically divided. As the Holy Roman Empire of the German Nation disappeared, many of the nation-states of modern Europe were emerging, but Germany would take three-fourths of the century to overcome the personal allegiances of its citizenry to the feudal social structure and create the first German nation. It is important to note that language allegiance also grew throughout the period and finally made a political allegiance easier in 1871 simply because the one common cultural heritage for all of the German-speaking world was its language. Thus a *Kulturnation* [culture nation] was possible where a *Staatsnation* [state nation] had been difficult. The nineteenth century would, however, continue to reflect the Grimms' romantic notions of a German folk soul as reflected in its language. Even the school system offered examples of a romantic approach to language. In the study of German, feeling and mood were emphasized over intellect, so much so that finally a polemic developed. Karl Lachmann, whose scholarship encompassed both German and classical philology, emphasized strict philological study, but, as is so often the case, the scholarly controversy was being carried out in an academic setting, whereas the romantic and emotional aspects reached into the broader populace. To Lachmann's opponents it was clear that their romantic notions of language and the *Volk* were losing ground to a pure academic interest in the language. *Deutschtümelei* intensified, but with the appearance of Darwin's *Origin of the Species* in 1859, the division between rigorous philology on the one hand and the romantic notions of a *Volksseele* on the other were complicated by a new thrust, the introduction of the Aryan question.

The Indo-Germanist August Friedrich Pott utilized the work of the Frenchman Gobineau to introduce the so-called Aryan theory into discussion in Germany. Joseph Arthur Compte de Gobineau adhered to a deterministic, fatalistic historical construction concerning race or racial mixing. Following research which had established the genetic relationship of Indo-European languages, Gobineau transformed these ideas into a racial theory and maintained that the Aryans were racially the purest and thus the most noble members of the white race. The theory degenerated quickly into discussions about an "Aryan race," with pure "blood" lines and was supported by distinctions that could ostensibly be seen and documented through "craniology." With the door now open, through Darwin and Gobineau, German-language scholars like August Schleicher could develop a

Stammbaumtheorie [family tree theory], and his student Johannes Schmidt could refine this further into a *Wellentheorie* [wave theory]. These new theories effectively replace Grimm's romanticized philology with a taxonomical classification of languages and a notion of language change that develops through successive waves of language growth over linguistic boundaries; but romantic notions of German uniqueness, continuity, and purity did not disappear.

Toward the turn of the century there was once again a battle to keep German unmixed with other languages. Under fire at this time were foreign words and phrases, while the *Erbwort* [native term] expressed that which was the very essence of German. Dialects were promoted, language societies formed, and attacks leveled against the Berlin Academy of Sciences, which had viewed the rich array of foreign words as expressive of a highly developed culture language. The Academy, however, was also viewed as promoting Gypsy languages, "nigger English," and Yiddish as "culture languages." Soon there were contentions that mixing of language is the first stage of *Rassenschande* [racial shame].

In the early decades of this century, there was indication that language scholarship was ready to move beyond the earlier bilateral split, that is, between language as some kind of organic essence and the romantic notions of a language as expressive of a *Volksseele*. A focus on language as intellectual history became apparent. Virtually every history of the German language arguably contends that standard German developed under the influence of the chancelleries of the Holy Roman Empire of the German Nation; for example, from Prague. When Hans Naumann published his *Primitive Gemeinschaftskultur* (1922) and put forth his ideas on *gesunkenes Kulturgut* [sunken cultural goods], he advanced a theoretical construct that language, just like "cultural goods" is developed in upper strata of society such as the chancelleries and inmcorporates borrowings from neighboring cultures before it descends to the lower strata. Folk speech and dialect are not just deviations but descended [*gesunken*] forms of speech from higher strata. The result is that the *Volk* and their speech are conceived to be noncreative. Naumann was following the lead of his fellow folklorist, Eduard Hoffmann-Krayer, who had maintained that the "folk does not produce, it reproduces" (1903: 60). Little could Naumann know how much difficulty his theory of the *Volk* would cause him. Although he was a member of the Nationalsozialistische Deutsche Arbeiter Partei, participated in book burnings, and presented birthday paeans to Hitler, he was removed from his professorship and psychologically terrorized for reducing the German *Volk* to a level of receptivity and noncreativity. All of the romantic notions and the *Deutschtümelei* of the nineteenth and the early decades of the twentieth century now supplied the basis for a political usurpation of German-language scholarship for party purposes. Not only did the war years change German scholarship, but the postwar years also proved immeasurably difficult ones for continuing research on German, as well as on the languages of other peoples. In order to more completely understand the impact of this period in German *Sprachwissenschaft*, it is important to remember that the National Socialist regime cannot be limited to twelve years. Two postwar literary figures express it best. Christa Wolff (1983: 268) asks in one of her novels, "But when does the prewar begin?" and the Nobel Prize-winning author Heinrich Böll states that in 1945, "Zero hour was not really zero hour." Both tendencies and individuals in German-language research preceded the regime and continued to function for extended periods after the war.

Of particular interest during the prewar years are ideas that came from scholars at the universities of Bonn and Marburg. Theodor Frings of the Universität Bonn set forth what we now refer to as the "Bonner method." He was most interested in the so-called *Kulturraum* [cultural region] and viewed language study as associated with the dynamics of language within this area. Closely associated were ideas by Fritz Maurer, who refined Frings' thinking by viewing language study as *Volk* history. Language reflects not individual expression but intellectual developments within a cultural region. Such ideas would be innocuous enough if they had not been misused by scholars of the Marburg *Deutscher Sprachatlas*. For example, the raw data on dialects for the atlas included the Eastern and Western cultural regions in which some form of German had been spoken in the past. Of special note is the controversy that ensued around the Franconian settlements of the Carolinian period (ninth century). The controversy sought to deal with Franconian versus French place names in what is now Wallonia (Belgium) and, particularly, in the region between the Seine and the Loire river valleys of France. Were the place names part of a forward, frontier settlement of the Franconians? Had the French re-Romanized or de-Germanized these place-names? Were the names remnants of Franconian *Volk* settlements? Again, the controversy would be of limited significance if such theories had not been used by the Third Reich during the occupation of France as propaganda and justification for the military seizure of this region. In the east, the controversy concerned the development of the standard language, High German. Hans Naumann's theory of *gesunken* language was countered by the contention that standard German was made up of the many *Volk* elements that were part of the Eastern cultural region. Some of this thinking (was it linguistic nationalism?) survived the Third Reich virtually intact.

One of the most interesting figures of the period is Leo Weisgerber, who was also interested in the boundary regions. His interests were not in formal or structural studies but rather in what he referred to as the *inhaltliche Leistung* [content accomplishments] of a language which he would later see as the intellectual self-fulfillment of a folk nation. He did not view language primarily as a means of communication but rather as the creative force of a folk society. By 1941 he would use the party jargon and publish an *Arteigene Sprachlehre* [Racially Pure Language Teaching], suggesting that the *Muttersprache* was closed to others whose worldview was different. Language in the boundary areas was also of interest to Weisgerber, so much so that he would soon offer a new interpretation of the word *deutsch*. According to Weisgerber, the word was developed in a world where folk values were appreciated, and he makes reference to the German/Romance language boundary area for his interpretation of the word. For Weisgerber the word was developed as a *Heimatruf* [calling home] for the Franconians who were in the midst of Romanization, that is, becoming French. He saw it as a "proud word" in the battle for ethnic identity of the German *Volk*. Weisgerber stated that modern French had developed from a vulgar version of a *lingua sacra*. German too had its vulgar tongue, indeed two such languages: one also was from a *lingua sacra*, but another was the vulgar (folk) language, and this language was, according to Weisgerber, referred to as *theodisk*. Although much of this reasoning is based on good evidence, there is unfortunately once again the underlying romantic and nationalistic notion, now a political suggestion, that seems to dominate Weisgerber's thinking. In the postwar years, there were many who held to his romantic and nationalistic interpretation of the word for German.

Language scholarship never rose to the level of a central discipline for the National Socialists for the simple reason that language can be acquired, whereas race cannot. In contrast, in the discipline of *Volkskunde* [folklore], racial studies *were* central, and worldview lectures were held in every university. Here German identity is clearly not based on language but rather on race. During the twelve years of Hitler's Thousand Year Reich there were many abuses of language scholarship for blatant racial purposes. Only one case will be mentioned, since most of this kind of writing can easily be dismissed as *völkisch*—that is, politically coordinated nonscholarship, sometimes by reputable scholars. For example, the rector of the Universität München, Walter Wüst, was a scholar of Indo-Germanic who today is best remembered for his *völkisch* pronouncements that the German language came from indigenous peasants. He contrasted these people, whom he referred to as a kind of Nordic nobility, with nomadic Semites, whom he clearly felt to be inferior. As a side note, Walter Wüst was the rector of the university when two students, Hans and his sister Sophie Scholl, were arrested for their participation in a protest movement (which they called the "White Rose") against the Hitler regime. Together with a folklorist, Kurt Huber, who assisted them in their well-known protest, they were executed by a *Volk* court.

Invectives against one specific ethnic/racial group were targeted against Jews. It is perhaps appropriate to offer the following brief summary (of such views):

> German linguistic scholars have helped with the removal of the German-Jewish citizens from the German state and from among the German folk. Arntz hoped that the racial laws would reestablish the basic unity of race, language and culture. One of the main arguments was: "Using the German language, even as a mother tongue, does not make Jews into Germans" [1937]. Geißler wrote: "Not everyone who speaks it, participates equally [in the language]!" [1937]. Glässer maintains: the folk community is formed by racial-political powers and forces, not by the language community [1939]. Banniza von Bazan: "Not everyone is able to awaken the ancient memory of the birth and the development of his language community in himself, only he whose racial inheritance reaches back to the language-creating forefathers of the grey past" (1933). The Jews do not belong to the racially based German language community. Heinz Kloss, after the war the director of a Research Office for Nationalities and Linguistic Questions, wrote in 1933: the German-Jews we no longer intend to count as part of the German folk-nation. Hermann Güntert in 1938: participation in a language is not at all participating in the folk. "Language alone never makes one a true folk comrade. . . . A stranger to the folk and the race will not become a folk comrade because he speaks a language which is originally foreign to him, even if his ancestors are supposed to have used the language that was originally foreign [to them]." (Römer 1989: 177)

Several allusions have been made to the survival of romantic (*völkisch?*) sentiments into the postwar years. One such example will be offered in some detail. Adolf Bach, whose *Geschichte der deutschen Sprache* was first published in 1938 and was issued in a total of nine editions through the 1970s, wrote the following statement:

> German Language—German Destiny. If we look back on the path we have traveled, it becomes clear to us that the German language is a reflection and an expression of German destiny. We still sense today the indelible and firm foundations of Indo-Germanic language unity, as well as the Germanic which grew out of it. These foundations have been preserved for millennia, during which time there was a continuing and endless productive confrontation with that which was foreign. One can still sense today the close contact which German has with other living Indo-Germanic sister languages. Even so, the formative force of German destiny is unique in the German language; it is reflected therein—unaffected by all European and Occidental relationships—with all the clarity and uniqueness which the Indo-Germanic and the Germanic heritage was to acquire in our folk. Moreover, the German language lets us perceive the accomplishments and the individuality of the German spirit, including its occasional failures, and [lets us also perceive] German history in its glory and at its low points, as well as its destiny. The depths and the heights of the living language are all part of this, dialect as well as the High language, which have continued to exist in an unbroken mutual relationship.
>
> Thus, the German language is shown to be a truly pure German edifice in whose expansion and preservation all the historical forces have worked throughout the centuries, all folk groups, all individuals, the rulers in the realm of intellect and the masses of the unknown. It appears to us to be the fateful development of the fruit of pure German life, a reflection of the German spirit in its uniqueness. As Schiller says: "Language is the mirror of a nation. When we look into this mirror, a large and fitting image of our selves comes forth."
>
> The German language is a reflection of the world view and the essence of German man. It lets us see the spirit of the Nordic people in a special way: Germans experienced the historical and spatial world differently than the other Nordic people; in this way they gained their own uniqueness within the Nordic world. History and space in unison with biological forces have created in the German language that which is exclusively German, which other Nordic people have no part of, or it is different. In this way, however, it creates the strongest connection that holds the German folk together as a unit. Thus, the German language guarantees the continuation of our folk-nation [*Volkstum*]. . . . Every new generation of young Germans—from the very beginning, through inheritance and environment, acquires in this relationship a special ability to receive—thus growing into the world of the German language and becoming a part of the world which has become German, directly partaking of the German folk relationship; it gains in this way the ultimate possibility of bearing the inheritance of the German folk-nation on into the future. The battle for the existence and the purity of the German language is thus a fight for the existence, the unity and the spirit of the German folk in the future. "The German language thereby becomes a destiny—today more than ever before. 'The power of language binds people and holds them together; without such a bond, they would disintegrate.' " This is what Jacob Grimm thought. (1971: 376–377)

Although this romanticized view of the German language continued in post-war language scholarship, new research would also emerge. By 1949, when both of the new German political states had their beginnings, the matter of ethnic identity was made more difficult for the simple reason that there were now two countries, not just one. If Austria is added, as well as those areas of Switzerland, South Tyrol, Alsace, Belgium, and Luxembourg in which German represents a major component of the linguistic geography, the view is broadened, but the task is even more formidable. In the two new German states in particular, two major problems would develop in the postwar years. The first of these would continue to the present; the second would disappear only when the former German Democratic Republic (East Germany) fell and Germany was reunited in 1989–1990. The first problem was in fact the language of fascism, which later came to be associated with the larger movement of *Vergangenheitsbewältigung* [overcoming the past]. The second was the matter of the linguistic consequences of a divided Germany, which led to a claim in the Federal Republic of Germany (West Germany) of an *Alleinvertretungsanspruch* [claim of sole representation]. A related point of interest is the fact that in the German Democratic Republic, the language of those in control would be based on an ideology that had been developed in the German language during the nineteenth century. Thus when the new ideology was expressed, no new linguistic expression was needed, nor was the terminology radically new or revolutionary. In West Germany, both before and after the unification in 1990, it seems that the populace did not have a clear understanding of the terminology with which to verbalize some of the very questions it was now dealing with, terms like *nation, statehood, patriotism*, and, yes, *ethnicity*. These terms had been usurped by the Nazi regime, and thus German speakers were left with a difficulty in conceptualizing just what the words meant. For the most part, however, there was little new in the world of language scholarship during the first two postwar decades. Scholarship reflected the slogan of the conservative party in power and its chancellor, Konrad Adenauer: *"Keine Experimente"* [No Experiments]. By the mid-1960s the scene would change radically, reflecting to a degree the perceived ethnic revival in the United States.

Some basic factual information will help to clarify later happenings. Both Germany and Austria would devote much of their postwar energy to structural studies, but each in different ways. By 1964 a new research institute was founded in West Germany, the *Institut für deutsche Sprache* (IDS) in Mannheim. The stated goal of the institute was for the study of the German *Standartsprache* since 1945, from which an authoritative grammar of German was to be compiled. The IDS, by its position in West Germany, has always been open to various theoretical perspectives. In East Germany, a counterpart to the IDS would be established, first referred to as the *Arbeitsstelle für strukturelle Grammatik*, where *strukturell* was understood to mean "transformational-generative" grammar. Later this institute was renamed the *Zentralinstitut für Sprachwissenschaft* of the Berlin Academy of Sciences. In the early years, scholars in the *Zentralinstitut* most often concentrated their research interests on their own native languages, but their goal was the development of universal linguistic theory. In time they would include other languages, especially languages of the countries in which they had political and economic interests, for example, Albanian, Russian, and Spanish. During its entire history, the *Zentralinstitut* remained committed to transformational theory.

These research institutes show that linguistic research in the German-speaking countries was devoted to scholarly agendas that intended to be less German-national and elitist than they had been in the past. The IDS, for example, in conducting its research for a complete German grammar, utilized a corpus of words from running texts that represent several cultural levels and from recorded continuous discourse. By the mid- to late 1960s, however, the years that we associate with the ethnic revival in the United States, social changes were also taking place which would have a direct effect on the universities and the research institutes of all three German-speaking states. East Germany continued to isolate itself following the construction of the Berlin Wall in August of 1961, but in West Germany student revolts, particularly in the late 1960s, resulted in what was called the "long march through the institutions." In fact, students soon learned that modern revolutions do not require occupying buildings so much as taking possession of the terminology by which a government rules. Austria would not be far behind West Germany, but it remained more conservative in the beginning in refocusing its interest in language research. In the two western countries, levels of teaching and research responsibility were reformed for faculty, and all scholarship would be required to be more socially responsible. In East Germany, the universities and research institutes felt that they had always been required to be socially responsible, and thus were not as interested in the kinds of reforms that took place in the West.

Because of the abuses of the past, all three countries were and still are hesitant to view their refocusing of research toward some of the ethnic groups with which they deal on a regular basis as any kind of ethnic revival. In fact, each country behaved differently in this regard. For example, in the world of German studies little attention is paid to the "'official minority" of East Germany, the Sorbians, who live mostly in or in the vicinity of the city of Bautzen. These Sorbians, also called Wends, received considerable attention from the East German government, including some support for a research center and publications in their Slavic language. The underlying political purpose was apparent to all who knew of these promotions: the socialist need to disestablish ethnic barriers in their called-for multiethnic people's republic. East German linguistic scholarship that dealt with speakers of other languages, that is, those outside the political boundaries of the German Democratic Republic, included countries with whom they conducted economic trade—for example, the Soviet Union and most of the countries within its sphere of influence, Cuba, and Albania, as well as a variety of African and Middle Eastern countries.

Austria has, for the most part, remained faithful to language research devoted to German, but here too there is a minority, Austria's only recognized minority, the Slovenians, a Slavic-language-speaking group along Austria's southeastern boundary, in and around the city of Bad Radkersburg. Because of its position as something of a gateway to the Balkans, considerable research in Austria has always been devoted to the many languages of this region, some of which, such as Hungary, have in the past been politically a part of Austria. In addition, there has been significant research devoted to other Western languages, such as English, French, and Spanish.

By the 1960s, new ethnic forces would come into play and would affect the entire German-speaking world, but West Germany more intensely. Here both scholars and the broad populace found themselves in the position of having to deal with many other languages because of Germany's commitment to the European Union. The arrival of virtually millions of *Gastarbeiter* [guest workers], many with their families, established Germany as a multiethnic society where Turks, Italians, Greeks, and North Africans, as well as what were generically referred to as Yugoslavians, were found not only in the workplace and all commercial establishments but also in the schools and universities. In addition to the *Gastarbeiter* who would come to Germany as part of European Union developmental contracts, there would also be a flood of immigrants into Germany who were seeking political asylum. During the 1980s, the country's welfare system would be nearly overwhelmed by hundreds of thousands of asylum seekers who knew that German law required it to accept anyone who claimed political persecution. Asylum seekers from the Eastern bloc would also make their way to East Berlin and then cross over into West Berlin, where they immediately asked for and received political asylum. In time these people moved from refugee camps into the workforce, and their children went to German schools. This means that Germany experienced an ethnic revival that had as its first impetus the economic betterment of people from the southern European and northern African regions and as its second impetus the arrival in Germany of large numbers of people, often of color, who were leaving their home countries for political reasons. Language scholarship was not quick to respond to this new situation, but in time bilingual textbooks would be developed, language planning would become a part of the process in the educational ministry, and the concepts of a multicultural and multiethnic society would emerge, even in public discourse. And finally, during the two years 1990–1992, more than 850,000 German *Aussiedler* [emigrants of German heritage] came to Germany, many from the Eastern bloc countries but others from as far away as Sri Lanka. There were Volga Germans from Russia, Transylvanian Saxons from Rumania, Danube Swabians from Hungary, others from the Banat and from Gottschee, and many from the former German regions that are now part of Poland. These new settlers would join the multitude of *Gastarbeiter* and asylum seekers, along with the existing ethnic minorities in the former German Democratic Republic (Sorbians) and Austria (Slovenians) to such an extent that the linguistic makeup of the German-speaking area underwent sudden and dramatic change.

Such an increase in foreign populations in Germany and Austria has also brought about a political and popular backlash: *Überfremdung der deutschen Sprache und Kultur* [overwhelming of German language and culture (by foreigners)]. All of the *Ausländer* [foreigners] have brought out terminology that is found in the publications of or through media interviews with the leaders of the right-wing political parties—the best known being the *Republikaner*. Not only are these "foreigners" viewed as "too many" [*Wir sind Fremde im eigenen Land* ("We are strangers in our own country")] and "too difficult," but they also have "different customs"; they cause a "housing shortage" and a "rise in unemployment";

and they came in "illegally" [*unkontrolliertes Einströmen* (uncontrolled influx)]; and even though racism is denied, the term *Volk* is once again being used in an exclusionary way—that is, referring only to those of German heritage. Popular expressions such as *Ausländer raus* [foreigners get out] and *Türken raus* [Turks get out] have drawn the countercry *Nazis raus* [Nazis get out] and expressions of *Europluralismus*.

Of equal interest, and indeed the one topic which directly addresses the question of language identity *and* the ethnic revival, are developments in all German-speaking countries in the matter of dialects. Here can be seen parallels that reach outside of the political boundaries of Germany and Austria into those regions in which the German language still has a degree of autonomy. Since the 1970s, there has been a remarkable resurgence of ethnic and regional awareness, which is best seen through a few comments about the revival of interest in dialects. Although there is some strong indication that local dialects are disappearing, there is equally strong indication that regional dialects are strengthening. Dialect is now most often learned not from parents but from peers and may also reflect an increase in informality in the language, such as the increased usage of the informal *Du* as opposed to the more formal *Sie*. Nowhere is this latter statement more dramatically documented than in the student movement of the late 1960s, when all students switched to the use of *Du* in their communications with other students. Both dialect usage and the increasing informality in the language were certainly part of a language of protest, what one scholar (Clyne 1995) refers to as an "emancipatory strategy." In the past, young people had viewed dialect usage as conservative or fascist (cf. *Blut und Boden* [blood and soil]), but now educated and socialist-minded young people tended to use dialect to show their solidarity with the working class. There is also an amazing array of documentation of this change not just in Germany but also in those countries in which there has traditionally been a German-speaking population. In Austria, the thirty-fifth edition of the *Österreichisches Wörterbuch* (1979) seeks to show the distinctiveness of Austrian German as a standard language separate from standard German. In Switzerland, the address given by the president on National Day is in dialect, an unusual case of informal speech making its way into a formal setting. Over 55% of the Swiss prefer that the president's message on New Year's day be given in dialect. In South Tyrol, the Autonomy Statute (1972) assures language rights to German and Italian speakers, but school policy was written in such a way as to give advantage to speakers of German. And as recently as January 1993, it was guaranteed by law in the Alsace that German could be used as a language of instruction in elementary school.

As was the case with both East Germany and Austria, West German scholars also found interest in other languages. No central thrust is discernable, but as an example, a few individual scholars have devoted their entire careers to scholarship on a variety of German spoken primarily in North America, Pennsylvania German. Although there are no speakers of this dialect in Europe, a significant body of research in Germany is devoted to these Amish and Mennonites. There is also a significant body of research on the Gypsies as one of the best known ethnic and linguistic minorities of Europe. Scholars in East Germany have also published numerous detailed and excellent studies of many African languages and of Spanish, together with those of other Eastern European languages and dialects.

Speakers of German have a long history of identifying themselves with their language. Throughout much of their history, this identification was little more than a romanticized view of themselves, occasionally becoming what has been referred to as *Deutschtümelei*. The National Socialist era drew on some of these sentiments and vigorously supported what came to be called a *völkisch* approach to the German language and culture, an approach that finally culminated in an inflated image of a German master race and a misogamistic approach to people of other ethnic—that is, racial—origins. Some of this same thinking continued in the first postwar decades, but the German-speaking world progressively opened its borders first to *Gastarbeiter*, then to asylum seekers, and finally to immigrants of German heritage. While this was happening, personal and regional identity were supported by the promotion of dialects, and at the end of the twentieth century the land where German is spoken found itself in the midst of a new multicultural and multiracial existence.

Questions for Further Thought and Discussion

1. How do speakers of German trace their origins back over 2,000 years?

2. Why do scholars in so many disciplines consider Johann Gottfried Herder to be such an original thinker?

3. What are some of the elements which have contributed to the long-standing "romantic" view of German language and culture?

4. Is there a definable German linguistic thrust throughout German language scholarship?

5. Did German speakers participate in the ethnic revival?

6. What aspect of German scholarship would most interest you if you were to continue your reading in the area?

Selected Bibliography

Bach, Adolf (1961 [1938]). *Geschichte der deutschen Sprache*. Heidelberg: Quelle & Meyer.

Clyne, Michael G. (1995). *The German Language in a Changing Europe*. Cambridge: Cambridge University Press.

Gobineau, Joseph Arthur Compte de (1853–1855). *Essai sur l'inégalité des Races Humaines*. Paris. English translation: *The Inequality of Human Races* (New York: Fertig, 1967).

Grimm, Jacob, 1819. *Deutsche Grammatik*. n.c., n.p.

Grimm, Jacob and Wilhelm. 1856. *Kinder- und Hausmärchen*. Leipzig: Reklam.

Hoffmann-Krayer, Eduard. (1903). Naturgesetz im Volksleben. *Hassische Blatter für Volkskunde* 2: 57–64.

Jones, Randall L. (1970). German language research in East and West Germany. *Die Unterrichtspraxis* 3(2): 96–100.

Klemperer, Viktor (1987 [1946]). *LTI (Lingua Tertii Imperii) Die unbewältigte Sprache. Aus dem Notizbuch eines Philologen*. Cologne: Röderberg-Taschenbuch Bd. 35.

Lockwood, W.B. (1965). *An Informal History of the German Language*. Cambridge: W. Heffer and Sons.

Polenz, Peter von (1970). *Geschichte der deutschen Sprache*. Berlin: de Gruyter.

Römer, Ruth (1989 [1985]). *Sprachwissenschaft und Rassenideologie in Deutschland*. Munich: Wilhelm Fink Verlag.

See, Klaus von (1984). Politisch-soziale Interessen in der Sprachgeschichts-forschung des 19. und 20. Jahrhunderts. In *Sprachgeschichte. Ein Handbuch zur Geschichte der deutschen Sprache und-ihrer Erforschung*, Werner Besch, Oskar Reichmann & Stefan Sonderegger (eds.), 242–257. Berlin: de Gruyter.

Stevenson, Patrick (1995). *The German Language and the Real World. Sociolinguistic, Cultural, and Pragmatic Perspectives on Contemporary German*. Oxford: Clarendon Press.

Townson, Michael (1992). *Mother-Tongue and Fatherland. Language and Politics in German*. Manchester: Manchester University Press.

Waterman, John T. (1991). *A History of the German Language* (Rev. ed.). Prospect Heights, IL: Waveland Press.

Weisgerber, J. L. (1935). *Deutsches Volk und deutsche Sprache*. Frankfurt am Main: Verlag Moritz Diesterweg.

Wolff, Christa. (1983). *Kassandra*. Berlin: Aufbau-Verlag.

Scandinavia

LEENA HUSS
ANNA-RIITTA LINDGREN

The Languages of the Nordic Countries

The Nordic countries include Denmark, Finland, Iceland, Norway, and Sweden. Moreover, the Faroes and Greenland belong to Denmark, and the Åland Islands to Finland, as regions with considerable self-government. Majority languages of independent states in the area are: Danish in Denmark, Finnish in Finland, Icelandic in Iceland, Norwegian in Norway, and Swedish in Sweden. The language of the Åland Islands is Swedish; the main language in the Faroes is Faroese, and, in Greenland, Inuit.

Of the present official languages, Swedish, Danish, and Finnish also appear in a numerical minority position in some places: Swedish in Finland, Danish in the Faroe Islands and Greenland, and Finnish in Sweden and Norway. There are also two indigenous peoples living in the area: the Inuit, who mainly live in Greenland, and the Sámi, whose traditional territory has been split into four parts by national borders, resulting in Sámi minorities in Norway, Sweden, Finland, and Russia. The Finnish-speaking populations in Norway and Sweden comprise two groups of quite different nature. The first is an old regional minority living in the Arctic area, known in Sweden as the Tornedalians and in Norway as the Kven. The second is an immigrant population that has moved to Norway and Sweden since the 1950s and is now scattered in different parts of these countries.

Apart from the historical main languages, other languages are also spoken in the area. There are, for instance, old German, Jewish, Rom, Russian, and Tatar populations in the Nordic area. Moreover, every Nordic country now has a new, growing, and very heterogenous group of immigrants. Sweden has the highest percentage of immigrants, approximately 10% of the total population, and Finland has the fewest, approximately 1.4%.

The Nordic language minorities have quite different characters. Even though only 6% of Finland's population is Swedish speaking, Swedish is constitutionally one of the two national languages of Finland, and therefore has a relatively strong position. Similarly, Faroese and Inuit are the main languages of the Faroes and Greenland, respectively, but the state language, Danish, although numerically in a minority position, also has a strong position there. In consequence, both Faroese and Inuit face, to a certain extent, the same kind of problems usually faced by minority languages. Finnish in Sweden and Norway, as well as Sámi in all countries, occupy more conventional minority positions in these areas, as do the languages of the remaining ethnic minority groups.

Ethnic Revival

Ethnic revival and linguistic and cultural revitalization in the Nordic countries have been most apparent among the minorities in the Arctic region, especially among the Sámi. The Sámi movement started in the 1950s within a small circle of people and spread gradually during the 1960s (Eidheim 1997). The breakthrough came in the 1970s: The status of the Sámi, and indeed the status of all minorities, was discussed in the Nordic countries. The Sámi organizations and pan-Nordic Sámi activities were greatly invigorated, and a very fruitful and creative era (which still continues in the 1990s) began in Sámi cultural life. Sámi literature, theatre, film, music, and visual arts have developed significantly during the last few decades. The societal and cultural activities have created a new Sámi symbolic world that reflects the ethnic awakening and Sámi identity. Since the 1970s, the status of the Sámi language has also risen in schools, universities, and the mass media.

It was also in the 1970s that the first signs of an ethnic revival among the Tornedalians and the Kven were seen. The Finnish language gained a foothold as a school and university subject, and attitudes began to change. Organizational activities first began in the 1980s, coinciding with a discussion about the relationship between the variety of Finnish spoken by these minorities and the Finnish language in Finland. The Sámi have achieved more reforms that strengthen the position of minorities than have the Tornedalian and the Kven—probably due to the fact that the Sámi have engaged in much more minority political work than the other two groups. This means also that they, more than any other minority group, taught a quite new form of minority politics and minority way of thinking to the Nordic majority populations. The most radical phase in recent Nordic minority politics was the conflict at the River Alta,[1] Norway, in the late 1970s and the early 1980s, in which the Sámi fought side by side with environmentalists from the Nordic countries. The struggle included, among other events, a long-term resistance camp in the area of the planned dam, two hunger strikes in the Norwegian capital, Oslo, and several mass marches and protest assemblies in different parts of the country. Some of the Sámi who participated in the struggle have maintained that even though they lost their case, they did win many other things. The majority in Norway learned to take the Sámi seriously and, to a greater degree than before at least, to respect their legitimate aspirations. Many reforms were enacted: particularly important was a Sámi legislation which included provisions about the status of the Sámi language. Today, there are elected Sámi parliaments that act as state advisory bodies in Norway, Sweden, and Finland. Since 1992, the Sámi language has been an official language in the Sámi core area in Norway and Finland.

Even though the ethnic revival initially began among the ethnic minorities of the Arctic area, it now more or less concerns all minorities. The ethnic revival is, so to say, contagious, and it forces the majorities to reassess their thoughts and actions.

Minority Movements as Emancipation Politics

The interaction between humans is often characterized and regulated by some kind of power hierarchy—"pecking order"—both at the individual and collective levels. By *emancipation politics* is meant the changing of this hierarchical power structure, so that a new, democratic (or at least more democratic than before) structure emerges. Emancipation movements in the Nordic countries have generally brought about gradual reformations rather than precipitous revolutions. The labor movement and the women's liberation movement, for example, have, in ever-changing forms, been influential from the nineteenth century to the present.

Reflecting collective power relations, languages have varying positions of importance and constitute a linguistic hierarchy. Power relations are always in a state of flux, and so the positions of languages in a given area are also constantly changing. The nationalism of the nineteenth century led to a remarkable emancipation of some languages in the Nordic countries: Faroese, Finnish, and Norwegian. These languages had had the status of more or less unofficial vernaculars during the preceding centuries, whereas the literary, public, and elite languages had been Swedish in Finland and Danish in Norway and the Faroes. As a result of the emancipatory process, which took several decades, these languages came to be employed in both oral and written forms in all aspects of the official, public, and cultural sectors, as well as in the schooling system and universities.

The ideology of nationalism was epitomized by the concept "one people—one state—one language." The "Janus face of nationalism" means that, although the national awakening in the nineteenth century benefited certain formerly repressed peoples, languages, and cultures, remaining minorities were often persecuted and forced to assimilate in nation-states. Thus the flip side of nationalism was the birth of calculated assimilation politics that targeted several minorities at the end of the nineteenth century. This tendency was very strong in the Nordic countries until the middle of the twentieth century. Nationalism created a very strong collective way of thinking that comprised a range of emotional attitudes that still remain today.

The ethnic awakening in the 1960s started a new wave in the emancipation of the languages in the Nordic countries: the revitalization of minority languages.

In contrast to nationalism, the ethnic activists did not strive for either state building or monolingualism; rather, they aimed at multilingualism and the acceptance and support of multiculturalism. They struggled for the right to identify with their own ethnic groups without being stigmatized and for the possibility of developing their own cultures and their own linguistic human rights in full. Thus the Nordic minority movement challenges the deep-rooted nationalistic attitudes and forces the majority to reconsider things, because, according to the pluralistic approach, multilingualism and multiculturalism are natural resources of mankind. Both locally and globally, they represent a heritage and resource that must not be destroyed. The aim is a pluralistic state, tolerance, and internationalism.

Since the 1970s, ethnic movements have gained understanding and support from part of the majority, and the number of positively inclined individuals seems to have grown in the course of the last few decades. It has been perceived that the results of ethnic emancipation are good and useful for everyone, including the majority, because reforms are socially "therapeutic." Nevertheless, ethnic movements remain in a state of struggle. Minority issues are constantly debated, both publicly and privately. Attitudes favoring assimilation, as well as the old ethnocentric and racist attitudes, still persist and appear in new forms as the social dialogue about minorities continues. An ongoing struggle is ensuing between the assimilationist and pluralist ideologies at the same time as a race is going on among minorities between assimilation and revitalization. In each case, rapid changes take place in both directions.

Some places have experienced the backlash phenomenon of active resistance to emancipation. Quite recently, anti-Sámi circles in northern Norway and Finland have established associations and developed new strategies.

Language and Identity in the Nordic Countries

In this chapter we focus on the language-ethnicity link among the minorities that, so far, have experienced the most pronounced ethnic revival: the Arctic minorities in Norway, Sweden, and Finland on the one hand and the Sweden Finns, an immigrant population in Sweden, on the other hand. The Sweden Finns, primarily an urban minority, outnumber all other immigrant groups, their number being estimated at some 400,000. The largest of the Arctic minorities are the Sámi in Norway and the Tornedalians (both approximately 40,000), and the smallest are the Kven (10,000) and the Sámi in Finland (6,500). The number of the Sámi in Sweden is approximately 20,000. The figures may appear small, but the population density in the Arctic areas tends to be very low and, as a consequence, the Sámi share of the whole population in large northern peripheries is considerable. The Sámi form a majority in one municipality in Finland and in four municipalities in Norway, and in other places these groups form majorities or large minorities in many villages.

Ethnic Minorities in the Arctic Areas: The Sámi, the Tornedalians, and the Kven

Modernization, Identity, and Language

Industrialization and modernization[2] started in the Nordic countries in the late nineteenth century, first in the south, and later gradually in the north. Consequently, at the beginning of the twentieth century, life was still premodern in the Arctic areas, whereas in the southern parts of these countries, modernization was well established. The timing of modernization seems to have had an impact on minority identity and on the problematics of its revitalization process.

Before the beginning and in the early stages of modernization, many of the ethnic minorities in the Nordic countries lived close to nature. Multifaceted working skills were learned from the extended family, and one's livelihood was gained using one's own language. Knowing only the mother tongue or, in addition, another minority language did not prevent people from being successful in their lives.

The mother tongue was, thus, a natural part of the culture, and people had relatively clearly defined roles as members of ethnic and local communities. In spite of this, individuals and groups could identify with several languages and ethnicities. In some areas, multiculturalism and multilingualism were more common; in other areas, less so; but these differences were only relative. Multiculturalism was typical of the Arctic parts of the countries involved, and very many people were descended from several ethnic groups. Individuals, as well as groups, could shift language, culture, and identity. These kinds of processes took different directions: from minority to majority, from majority to minority, and from one minority to another.

Then came the phase that was characterized by both nationalism and incipient modernization. In the spirit of nationalism, a conscious assimilationist policy was adopted by the countries in the late nineteenth century. From the beginning of the present century, the impact of modernization grew little by little, but did not fully penetrate everywhere until after World War II. Modernization implied that the role of school education grew in importance and came to have a central influence on the lives of children and young people. The states developed an efficient school system dominated by the majority language. This system was also used to promote assimilation. In sparsely populated regions, many children had to live in boarding schools that had been built in a conscious effort to promote assimilation. Modernization brought the mass media, efficient transportation and administration, and an economic life that more than ever before integrated the Arctic regions into the nation-states; the capitals and the southern regions populated by majorities gradually came nearer to the periphery.

The first phase of nationalism and modernization elicited a resistance among the northern minorities. It was partly channeled into a religious movement known as Laestadianism, which has had great influence among the minority populations. This movement was characterized by a practical multiethnicity and multilingualism, as well as by an antimodern value system. Through Laestadianism, the northern people voiced their protests against majority rule, modernization, the value systems of the church and the school, and assimilation politics. Laestadian culture became a fortress of both the premodern culture and the minorities of the Arctic area, and it promoted considerably the maintenance of the northern minority languages during the assimilationist era.

In the next stage, which began at different times in different areas during the twentieth century, the construction of a modern and democratic welfare state became the joint goal in large circles, crossing ethnic borders. In Norway and Sweden, this goal was greatly influenced by the success of the labor movement and the coming to power of the Social Democratic parties, which also gained support in the northern regions. Under these circumstances, many minority members and local communities accepted assimilation, assuming that the new way of life required it. Minority culture appeared to them to be associated with an outdated way of life, with poverty and the inequality of the class society, whereas the building of the welfare state was seen as belonging to majority culture. Assimilation was at this stage seen as emancipation, because the "Nordic democracy" was implemented in such a way that the assimilation of ethnic groups was seen as making all members of "primitive" cultures equal. Part of this assimilation was the letting go of minority languages and cultures and the shifting of identity: Multilingualism was considered harmful; monolingualism of state and people was idealized. Thus the nationalism of the nation-states and the development optimism of modernization became intertwined, so that many people, as their lifestyles gradually became more modern, shifted both language and ethnic identity.

The timing of modernization differs by several decades within the Arctic areas that form a very large and multifaceted entity. Where modernization started early, the tendency among the minorities to shift language and identity was usually strong. This was the case with the Kven, the Tornedalians, and the Norwegian coastal Sámi. In areas where modernization set in later, as in the Sámi core area, the assimilation period was short before the ethnic revival started to change the situation. The connection between the timing of modernization and the impact of assimilation is also shown by the fact that the Kven and the Tornedalians were more thoroughly assimilated in central than in peripheral areas. There are also regions in which people shifted language but maintained a strong ethnic identity. Good examples of this are the southernmost "buffer zones" of the Sámi in Middle Scandinavia and in a corresponding region in Finland.

The ethnic revival in the 1960s began when the minorities started to develop the "Nordic democracy" according to a new idea: that a minority should have the right to its own ethnic identity together with full citizenship. From this point of view, assimilation is persecution, whereas true democracy requires pluralism, multilingualism, and affirmative action. Affirmative action is regarded as essential for overcoming the negative results of former persecution and assimilation.

Apart from emancipatory politics, another factor that influenced the transformation of values has also heightened the appreciation of ethnic cultures in the 1970s. The optimistic-development stage of modernism ended with the realization that nature was being destroyed and that, as a consequence, modernization has resulted in globalized risks. Criticism of modernization was now being heard not only from Laestadians and their peers but also from modern, highly educated intellectuals. Cultural forms in which a balance has developed between nature and the actions of humans found new respect based on new arguments. This development facilitated the promotion of cultural relativism and pluralism into the value system of Nordic democracy and the Nordic welfare state.

The start of the ethnic revival and the revitalization of minority languages was further influenced by the new results from Anglo-Saxon bilingualism research in the 1950s and 1960s that indicated the positive impact of bilingualism on the linguistic and identity development of the minority child. This will be discussed more thoroughly in a later section.

On Identity Strategies and Language

In the premodern world, life was close to nature and local ethnic identity and the language of the individual were givens. Today, when a battle rages between assimilation and revitalization, ethnic identity and the use of the minority language become matters of choice. For instance, the choice of the minority language as the language of communication between parents and children presupposes an independent decision—it is no longer a given, as it was in the premodern world. The advancement of revitalization means that a growing number of parents choose their own language. In both the areas where the Sámi and the Tornedalians live, there are villages where parents speak the majority language to elder children while speaking the minority language to the younger ones (see Aikio 1994).

Since the 1960s, some of the Kven, the Sámi, and the Tornedalians have moved to towns and cities; the capitals and the northernmost towns in particular are populated by these minorities. Of the Finnish Sámi, for instance, a third live outside the traditional Sámi regions. There are no statistics for the other groups, but the figures are probably similar. Those who moved away are no longer a marginal group; rather, they make up a considerable proportion of these minorities. Even though many individuals were assimilated after moving to the towns, there is a strong revitalization of identity, culture, and language going on in urban minority circles. Particularly in university towns, vigorous, renovative organizational and cultural activities have emerged. Among the urban Sámi, there are growing numbers of parents who speak their own language to their children, and in some places Sámi-medium kindergartens have been established.

Revitalization has clearly started, but it remains only a beginning. Sámi-medium school instruction is today available in some areas in all three countries, and most of the minority children in traditional minority regions have at least the opportunity of getting some instruction in the minority language; however, children living outside these areas have fewer chances along these lines.

The language choice within the family is, in many ways, dependent on the surrounding society. When the progress of the minority language within the public sector and the schools and kindergartens is slow, the choice of minority language as the family language presupposes a relatively strong identity or, at least, a strong motivation to revitalize one's identity. The choice of language today is more and more dependent on the individual identity strategy. Among those who have left the traditional areas, the impact of identity on language choice is emphasized even more than among those who stay behind. Considering the circumstances, the revitalization of language and identity shown by the urban Sámi is an astonishing proof of ethnic vitality.

In the present situation, individual identity strategies can differ greatly. At the opposite pole from ethnic activists are individuals who have suffered from racism, linguicism, or ethnocentrism targeted at the minority group and who have absorbed the values promoted during the assimilative period. They have tried to cover up their ethnic background and consciously blend into the majority. There are many alternatives between ethnic activism and conscious assimilation. The differences in identity strategies seem biggest among middle-aged and elder people, who were children and youths during the assimilative period and who then experienced the rise of ethnic awakening in the 1960s and 1970s. Among young people, ethnic identity is often positive but not as confrontational as among the pioneer generation of ethnic activists born in the 1930s, 1940s, and 1950s. When revitalization of ethnic identity is already a fact, thanks to the efforts of the preceding generation, the new generation does not need to be as radical as the previous one (Stordahl 1997).

In the age of ethnic revitalization, identity strategies can also change over the course of the individual's life, slightly or sometimes very dramatically. Among today's middle-aged and elder people, there are individuals who were raised to become members of their own minority group. Then they were put into a school that was marked by assimilation politics, where they painfully experienced the oppression of their own group and for this reason decided to do anything to blend into the majority. At a certain point, this road led either to a dead end or to a turning point at which the outwardly assimilated individual embarked on a quest for an authentic identity and embraced ethnic revival (see Marainen 1988).

The connection between identity strategy and multilingualism is manifested in the level of literacy in the minority language. Unofficial minority languages have usually attained only oral uses. The rise in the use and significance of written language in modern times led to an increase in the use and command of the written form, but for many Sámi, Kven, and Tornedalians the written language is primarily the majority language, not the mother tongue. Recently, the beginning of revitalization has begun to change the situation somewhat, but it is still quite unbalanced. The kind of reading and writing proficiency in one's own language which is today taken for granted among Nordic majorities and strong minorities (for instance, Finland Swedes), is, among the weaker minorities, nothing more than a luxury of ethnically active individuals, who acquired it by studying on their own initiative. Thus, reading/writing ability and practice among middle-aged and older people is to a considerable degree dependent on individual identity strategies. For young people, in contrast, the beginning of revitalization has somewhat balanced this disparity, a result of the fact that they have had better opportunities than the generations before to study their own language in school.

We have already mentioned that timing of modernization seems to have an impact on minority identity and the problematics of the revitalization process. When modernization changes the minority culture, it breeds such opinions as that only premodern minority culture is authentic or real and that the modern culture of the minority is not, because modernization is seen as belonging to the majority culture or as a derivative thereof. Thus, in northern Norway, modernization has been seen as "Norwegianization," and the culture of the grandparents' time is seen as authentic Kven and Sámi culture. In northern Sweden, correspondingly, the modern is Swedishness and the premodern, Sáminess and Tornedalianness; in northern Finland, the modern is southern Finnish. A situation has been reached in which the stereotypic views of the minority cultures, among the minority and especially the majority, do not correspond to the minority's present reality. This situation creates identity problems among minority members, causing them to doubt that they are "real" or "authentic" representatives of the group. Particularly among Norway's Sámi, there have recently been discussions about what it means to be a Sámi in the modern world (Stordahl 1997). The situation is shared generally by all northern minorities, but it has a special relevance for the young. Ethnic activists have, on the one hand, fought for the old cultural legacy, to free it from being stigmatized as "primitive." On the other hand, they have rebuffed the view that only the premodern is "real" minority culture. Any other view would mean that the representatives of the minority and the minority as a whole would not have the right to modernize without losing their identity. Many minority representatives are today of the opinion that their culture can change and does change, just as the cultures of all other peoples do.

On the Identity of the Group and the Language

The ethnic awakening presupposes that the minority redefine and reevaluate itself, its culture, and its relationship with other groups, both the majority and other minorities. One manifestation of reevaluation is the change in ethnonym selection. As far as the Kven are concerned, the old ethnonym used by outsiders as an insult during the assimilation period has been rehabilitated and is now used in a positive sense.[3] The alternative would be the ethnonym "Finn," but because many Kven people do not presently want to identify with the Finland Finns, they have rehabilitated the ethnonym "Kven." The attitude, "I am a Kven and proud of it" has, in fact, rehabilitated the ethnonym. Similarly, the ethnonym "Tornedalian"[4] is nowadays preferred to "Tornedal Finn,"[5] a term frequently used before the revitalization started. As regards the Sámi, the ethnonym based on the Sámi language has, both among the minority and the majority, replaced "Lapp" and the other former majority-language words. The change in ethnonym use reflects the revitalization of identity among minoritites and the respect for minority revitalization among the majority.

The development of the written language is very central in the revitalization of minority languages, because in a society like that of the present-day Nordic countries, a language which is only in oral use is not likely to have any continuity. Neglecting to develop the written language would ultimately mean extinction of the language, it is believed. The development of the written language and bringing of the oral language into the public sphere requires adopting language planning measures: development of orthography, standardization, and modernization of the vocabulary.

Linguistic emancipation processes are sometimes connected with autonomization processes of dialect groups. The dialects of the Kven and the Tornedalians have traditionally been considered to be Finnish dialects; dialectologically, they have been seen as belonging to the same dialect group as the dialects of Finland's northernmost provinces. In the 1980s and 1990s, the Tornedalians and the Kven have had heated discussions about the possibility of acknowledging the Tornedalian and Kven varieties as languages in their own right. The publication of literature, especially in the Tornedalian, has accelerated since the 1980s, comprising teaching materials for schools, fiction, newspaper articles, and parts of the Bible. The language has been given the name "Meän kieli" ("our language"), which manifests its relationship with identity. It has been studied as a subject in many schools in the Tornedal but as of yet in only one school among the Kven.

The two minorities have so far not been in agreement about whether it would be advantageous to become linguistically independent from standard Finnish or not. Those who advocate independence say that they cannot identify with the Finnish that is spoken in Finland. When the state of Finland became independent in 1917, it did not include the whole area in which Finnish dialects were spoken; the Kven and the Tornedalians had always lived outside of it. These minorities are not well acquainted with the standard language created in Finland, and if it is taken as the norm, then their language will always be thought of as "worse." With standard Finnish as the norm, the advocates of independence say that they will lose their language altogether, for as long as it is in the position of a minority language, they will never learn standard Finnish as well as the Finns; this frustration will lead to language shift and "Norwegianization" and "Swedicization." The Finnish standard language is also emotionally foreign. When the Tornedalians heard the Bible in Meän kieli for the first time, it was an overwhelming experience—people cried.

The Sweden Finns—From Immigrants to a Linguistic Minority

Minority Languages in the School

From early on, a strong focus on language came to characterize the ethnic awakening and cultural revitalization of the Nordic minorities. The ethnic activists were highly influenced by the Anglo-Saxon research on bilingualism in the 1950s and later. New theories—according to which the cultivation of bi- and multilingualism, especially among minority children, was exceedingly important both for the children's linguistic development and for their identity—reached the Nordic countries primarily thanks to a small number of linguists. The discussion in Sweden was started by Nils-Erik Hansegård, whose book "Bilingualism or Semilingualism?" was published in 1968. In his book, Hansegård severely criticized the assimilation policy of the Swedish school system toward the Tornedalians and the Sámi. Tove Skutnabb-Kangas, a former student of Einar Haugen in the United States, was a leading figure in the debate that followed. Skutnabb-Kangas was working with Pertti Toukomaa, whose studies of Finnish children in Sweden gave empirical support to the new theories. In the 1970s, Skutnabb-Kangas was also communicating directly with the minorities and spoke in favor of bilingualism and mother-tongue education in many forums at the very time when the intense debate was going on in Sweden about immigrant children and language teaching. This so-called home language debate was eventually won by the side that believed that immigrant children should be given the chance to study their own language in school. For the sake of revitalization, it was imperative that bilingualism researchers communicate with minorities, because even in the early 1970s many parents of minority children were told by both teachers and health personnel that it was best to avoid teaching two languages to a child. In practice, this meant that parents were encouraged to speak the majority language to their children even when they did not really speak it themselves. The linguist Els Oksaar, who had escaped from Estonia when young, traveled around Sweden in the 1970s and thereafter, speaking about the benefits of bilingualism. Several later researchers on bilingualism have strived to act in the same way.

However, research findings did not settle the dispute once and for all. Sweden is a good example of how quickly the so-called general opinion can change. As was shown previously, during the late 1960s and the early 1970s, there was a gradual shift from open assimilation politics to a more pluralistic way of thinking. The discussion about the education of immigrant children became urgent in the wake of a huge immigration from Finland to Sweden in the 1960s and 1970s, when a large group of Finnish immigrant children appeared in the Swedish schools. The teachers felt that they were facing insurmountable difficulties when the non-Swedish-speaking pupils could not follow instruction at all. In the discussion that arose about immigrant children in school, the significance of the children's own mother tongue and the possibilities of making them permanently bilingual came to be stressed. The spreading of a pluralistic way of thinking in Sweden resulted in the 1976 Home Language Reform, according to which the municipalities were obliged to offer instruction in the mother tongue (home language) to immigrant and minority children if the language was "a living part of the home environment" as it was expressed. People no longer spoke about the assimilation of immigrants but of cooperation between groups and freedom of choice, which was understood in the sense that immigrants should be able to participate in Swedish society without having to sacrifice their own ethnicity or language.

In the schools, the practical significance of this new policy was that home-language support was offered to immigrant children. It was frequently given as home-language instruction, which the children received one to two hours weekly in the form of "pull out" classes. For some large language groups, such as Finnish, Spanish, and Arabic speakers, so-called home-language classes were sometimes organized, where part of the instruction was given in the children's mother tongue. The third alternative was integrated classes, in which one-half of the children were native Swedish speakers and one-half were speakers of some other language. Typical of the two last forms of teaching was that the fraction of mother-tongue instruction was largest in the lower grades and decreased, eventually disappearing altogether, as the students advanced to higher grades. It has been remarked that all these forms of teaching can in practice be considered as transitional programs, even though the official aim of home-language teaching was preserving and developing the children's mother tongue. In the last few years, however, it has become easier than before in Sweden to set up so-called free schools, private schools of a kind which can be specialized in different ways. Some language groups, especially Finns, have set up schools that aim at language maintenance and in which the amount of mother-tongue-medium instruction is much greater than in the home-language classes. Another new phenomenon in Sweden is the special language maintenance programs that the Centre for Research in Bilingualism at Stockholm University has assisted in developing in Sámi schools.

Conversely, the social atmosphere in Sweden has undergone major changes in the last ten years. While the minority groups have become active and started working toward language maintenance, the groups who resist pluralism have also become more vocal. Since the middle of the 1980s, home-language teaching and bilingualism have once again been questioned in mass media and other public forums. Home-language classes and instruction have been cut down dramatically, and the home-language lessons have been moved outside the regular curriculum. The formal right to receive home-language instruction has also been reduced. The change in atmosphere has led to a situation in which speaking languages other than Swedish, both inside and outside the classroom, may be forbidden in schools and kindergartens because it is considered to hamper the acquisition of Swedish by immigrant children. Kenneth Hyltenstam of the Centre for Research in Bilingualism and many others in the field have remarked that the results of bilingualism research are not taken into consideration when decisions are made about the education of immigrant children; the politicians and officials act according to their own opinions and with reference to "common sense." This has led during the past few years in Sweden to a polarization of the minority language debate and to the spreading of a kind of unofficial "Swedish-only" ideology.

Development of the Sweden Finnish
Minority Identity

At the same time, Sweden's Finnish-origin immigrant minority, the Sweden Finns, have become more and more language conscious. Many of those who nowadays identify themselves as Finnish-speaking or Sweden Finns are a rather recent result of the age-old movement between the two countries. Like the earlier groups who moved from what is now Finland to Sweden—for instance, Middle Sweden's "Forest Finns"[6] and the Finnish population that has lived in Stockholm since the late Middle Ages—the later Sweden Finns have also lived under heavy assimilation pressure, and it has been extremely hard for them to preserve their own language and culture. Only since the end of the 1970s and the beginning of the 1980s has the situation changed somewhat, Finnish-language instruction having become more widespread and Finnish-language services having been improved in many respects. However, virtually all Finnish-medium activities have been subject to heavy budgetary cuts during the recession of the 1990s in Sweden.

The Sweden Finnish minority identity of the Finnish speakers who moved into Sweden in the 1960s and 1970s has emerged little by little, and only in the 1990s can it be considered clearly established. In their former home country, Finnish speakers belonged to the linguistic majority, and many of them came to Sweden with the typical majority attitude of "when in Rome. . . ." Under such circumstances, it was easy to accept the assimilation politics employed by the majority. Only later, when the "Swedicization" of the second and third generations was progressing rapidly, did worries about the loss of the Finnish language and culture and the alienation of the children surface. At the same time, it was commonly realized among the Sweden Finns that Finnishness and the Finnish language had roots in Sweden as old as those that Swedish had in Finland.

The national organization for Sweden Finns, the RSKL (Ruotsinsuomalaisten Keskusliitto), has traditionally had the task of safeguarding the social and political interests of the Sweden Finns. In its circles, faith was long put in Sweden's labor-union activities and in the program of the Social Democrat Party, which granted immigrants the same rights as Swedes. Later, when they wanted to really further Sweden Finnish causes, RSKL found that these rights were not enough. Since the 1980s, RSKL has been pursuing clearer and more independent minority politics and has supported, for instance, Finnish-medium school education, considering language maintenance to be a key factor for the future of the minority group.

The position of the Sweden Finns has traditionally been bolstered by the fact that they are the Nordic countries' largest minority group and that cooperation between Sweden and Finland has been close throughout history. Nevertheless, Finnish in Sweden has traditionally been associated with shame and stigma, and its status has been much lower than the status of the Scandinavian languages. Many Finnish speakers have been conditioned to believe that even knowing Finnish is an affliction, the sign of low status and lesser opportunities. Many Finnish speakers have thus, in the course of time, adopted the negative Swedish attitudes toward Finnishness, and it has been difficult to purge these attitudes, even when conditions have changed and revitalization has started. It has been said that the integration of Sweden Finns into the majority society and their finding a voice of their own has taken three to four generations. Language has traditionally been a cultural core value for Finns, but they have been expected by the Swedish majority to rapidly shift to Swedish. Language shift was taking place on a large scale until the 1970s, but since that time Finnish speakers have gained a slightly better chance of maintaining their language, and at the same time the interest in their own language has increased. Since the 1980s, young Sweden Finns have become more bilingual and biliteral than before, and their language attitudes are more positive (Lainio 1997).

The minority political organization of Sweden Finns has been branded by some critics as Finnish nationalism or even militant ethnicity, and it has been stated that the movement has mainly been led by a well-educated Finnish elite. One of the most active groups to work for the Finnish language, however, has been the parents of school-age children, who have at different times and in different places even gone on strike and organized demonstrations on behalf of the Finnish language. These efforts have been rendered more difficult by the fact that Sweden has wished to conform to the so-called unity principle, according to which special treatment of some groups in a society is not desirable. For instance, Sweden was not willing to draw a distinction between immigrants and historical minorities until the 1990s. The position of the Sámi and the Tornedalians was for a long time weaker than that of the immigrants, and they gained the right to home-language support only at the same time as the immigrants. Sweden still has not officially acknowledged the existence of historical minority languages in the country. In contrast, the European Bureau for Lesser Used Languages has since 1995 (when Sweden joined the European Union) considered Sámi, Finnish, and Meän kieli as "regional and minority languages" in Sweden.

During the last few decades, the Sweden Finns have also been receiving support from their mirror image on the Finnish side of the border: the Finland Swedes. One reason for this is the general increase in cooperation between minorities; another is that the asymmetry between Sweden and Finland regarding policies toward the neighboring language is becoming too apparent in the present-day world. The weak position of the Finnish language in Sweden creates resentment on the Finnish side and provides arguments to those who wish to weaken the position of Swedish in Finland. The centuries-long shared history of the two countries has been referred to in Finland by those who support the position of the Finland Swedish. In Sweden, the shared history has had little effect; Finnish has largely been considered as just one of the many immigrant languages in Sweden.

During the last few years, the activities of the Sweden Finns have taken on entirely new forms. The Finnish organizations now have yearly discussion days, when all kinds of common concerns are discussed. During the 1992 discussion days, the organizations signed a proclamation that the Sweden Finns are a domestic minority in Sweden. The proclamation is, however, unilateral, and the state of Sweden has not affirmed it as of yet. At this moment, the subject under discussion is the formation of a Sweden Finnish parliament, which would function in the same way as the Finland Swedish parliament or the Sámi parliaments in Finland, Sweden, and Norway.

The strengthening of the Sweden Finnish identity has become visible via the fact that the ethnonym "Sweden Finn"[7] has come more and more into use, replacing "Finn" or "Swede." Finns mix easily with Swedes with regard to appearance and customs, so the adoption of the ethnonym Sweden Finn is quite voluntary, at least for the second and third generations, who speak Swedish without an accent. The status of Finns among Swedes has probably risen because the portion of visible minorities has increased notably and because there is a tendency when speaking of immigrants to mean groups that are clearly distinguishable from Swedes. Moreover, the Finnish group has become so heterogenous in the last few decades that they and their descendants can now be found at every level of society; they are no longer largely blue-collar workers, as they were a couple of decades ago. Finnishness, then, has lost some of its stigma and become "normalized" in Swedish society, facilitating the birth of a more positive Sweden Finnish identity. However, it is feared that the normalization is in fact a two-edged sword: it certainly bolsters a positive identity, but it also facilitates the assimilation process. The crucial question is whether the Finnish language, virtually the only element that distinguishes a Swede from a Finn, will survive among the coming generations.

In this connection, both the RSKL and language-conscious Sweden Finnish parents have put their faith in the school. Apart from the weekly home-language lesson, Finnish-speaking pupils have had the opportunity to attend home-language classes or integrated language groups. Nevertheless, all these supporting activities have been greatly reduced in the last years, as was mentioned earlier. For this reason, Sweden Finnish parents have started no less than fourteen private bilingual schools in the 1990s in which Finnish-medium instruction plays a prominent role. However, the issue of ethnic and language schools is controversial in Sweden, and many municipalities oppose the establishment of such schools. For many Finnish and other minority pupils, the only mother-tongue support remains the weekly home-language class, but even such classes have diminished dramatically. The opposition toward home-language instruction and language-oriented private schools has become the main concern of the language-conscious group of Sweden Finns. It has even triggered negative attention and official statements in favor of Finnish-medium education and other Finnish-medium infrastructure in Sweden from politicians in Finland, as well as from the president of Finland.

During the past couple of years, a new feature in the minority discussion has emerged: the question of whether the Sweden Finns should accept a certain amount of change in their own language or whether Sweden Finnish should be subject to rigorous language cultivation efforts and follow the Finland Finnish language norm. It has been argued that the changes that are triggered by the minority position and the ever-present language contact are a distinct feature of Sweden Finnish and thus part of the Sweden Finnish identity. According to this view, a local norm should be allowed to develop, even at the risk of creating a totally new language in Sweden. The opposite and currently dominant view is that the local Finnish variety should be consciously purified so as to keep the written form as close to Finland Finnish as possible. This is also the aim of the Sweden Finnish Language Board, founded in 1975.

The Ethnicity-Language Link and the Majority Populations: Pan-Nordic Communication in Transition

As has been shown before, ethnic revival implies that the minority starts redefining and valuing itself and its own culture more positively. However, in the course of the continuing ethnopolitical discussions, even the Nordic majorities have come to reassess some aspects of themselves and their cultural heritages. In the last few years, these reassessments have had a tendency to focus on language.

The inter-Nordic language unity has for decades been considered as the backbone of Nordic cooperation. It has meant that Scandinavians proper (Swedes, Danes, and Norwegians) especially have been able to communicate with each other in their own languages. In the course of years, however, it has been shown that this language unity is partly illusory, although still adhered to. The others who participate in Nordic cooperation, the so-called non-Scandinavian language speakers, have always been in a linguistically weaker position. Icelanders, the

Faroese, and the Finns have had to communicate in the former power languages of their regions, Danish and Swedish, instead of their mother tongues (except for Finland Swedes, who have been able to use their mother tongue). The Faroese Tori Joensen (1989: 15) has written: "We who live in the non-Scandinavian Nordic countries often feel as if the Scandinavians look upon themselves as being the real Nordic people—we others can play with them as well when conditions allow it, but we can also be ignored at will." The situation is even more difficult for the Sámi and the Inuit, whose languages played practically no role whatsoever in inter-Nordic cooperation until the last few years. It has long been discussed how this inequality among the languages could be remedied. Suggestions have been offered ranging from translation and interpretation to adopting English as the language of communication in the Nordic countries to urging Scandinavians "to speak their languages as clearly as possible."

Finns especially have chosen translation and interpretation in order to be able to use their own language in Nordic contexts, but the Faroese and the Icelanders have usually been expected to be able to use Danish at conventions and conferences. Greenlanders are also expected to understand Danish and even other Nordic languages.[8]

The adoption of English as the language of Nordic cooperation has been resisted most steadfastly. It has been feared that this would destroy the very base of the Nordic feeling of unity. On the other hand, young people especially, who are not used to hearing other Nordic languages, routinely use English in inter-Nordic communication. More general fears about the diminishing role of the Nordic state languages in favor of English due to European integration and globalization have recently been expressed by language cultivators and linguists in several Nordic countries.

Summary

As a result of internal immigration and global mobility, many new minorities have appeared since the 1960s. During these decades, several old and new minorities have waged political battles for their rights. This situation has broken the assimilative trend which began with nationalism in the nineteenth century and changed the situation into a race between assimilation and revitalization. Some of the minority groups have achieved a more visible and respected position than they had earlier, and some have managed to create a new minority identity after having belonged to a former majority population. The rise of minorities and indigenous peoples is a movement in the direction of cultural and political independence. On the other hand, economy and culture are becoming more globalized, and international cooperation increases on many levels.

The Arctic minorities in the Nordic countries have, during the course of some generations, experienced considerable changes in their value systems and lifestyles —changes that have greatly influenced their identities and language choices. Nationalism and modernization, intertwined and occurring simultaneously, have resulted in strong assimilation pressures. These pressures have been somewhat uneven and have influenced minorities and groups among the minorities in different ways. Thus the results have varied greatly. Linguistic assimilation has taken place in numerous areas, whereas many local communities have nevertheless maintained their languages. Some of the groups that shifted language shifted identity as well; others retained their identity while shifting language.

The aim of the ethnic revival among the minorities of the Nordic countries is a pluralistic, multilingual society, as opposed to the ideal of nationalism: "one nation—one people—one language." The ethnic revival that started during the 1960s has resulted in linguistic and cultural revitalization that is constantly starting in new places. The revitalization of language presupposes the revitalization of identity, whereas the revitalization of identity does not necessarily encompass linguistic revitalization.

Individual identity strategies vary, ranging from ethnic activists to those who consciously choose to be assimilated. Identity strategies are crucial when choosing one's family language or the medium of education for the children. However, only a few of the minorities discussed in this article have a choice in regard to education. This means that choosing a minority language to be used at home presupposes a strong identity.

One effect of modernization has been that some linguosocial domains, which were previously less significant, have grown to become very important. These are the state-run school system on all levels, mass communication, and public life. In our times, hardly any population group in the Nordic countries can stay completely outside of modernization. If a minority language is not being used in the domains that are important today, it means that the continuity of minority language use is not being given a real chance. The linguistic domains whose significance have increased notably in connection to modernization are in the hands of the majorities in the Nordic national states. The minorities are dependent on how much the majority allows the minority to be seen and heard in the schools, in mass media, and in public life. The Nordic majorities are facing a societal choice: Should linguosociological modernization be extended to the minority languages by taking them into use in all areas of life, or would it be preferable to let them be extinguished?

Most of those minority languages in the world that are transmitted from parents to children stay in the home and immediate circles and never spread into other domains. Many of these languages may be very strong, although their speakers use other languages in all official contexts. In the Nordic countries, however, the tendency seems to be for the public sector to take on a central role in language maintenance. With modernization, the official state language has entered everyone's communicative environment in a more forceful way, and the mastery of the official state language has become more important among all groups. Because of this situation in the Nordic countries, the entry and use of a minority language in the public sector (for example, in mass media and schools) is a matter of life and death for that language and a key concern for those who pursue its revitalization.

The linguistic attitudes born during nationalism remain deep-rooted, though challenged by the pluralistic ideology. At present, there is an ideological and political battle going on between assimilationist ideology and pluralistic ideas.

There are individuals, families, villages, and groups who shift language and identity and others who stick to their language and fight for their linguistic human rights. Furthermore, there are those who had already more or less assimilated but then returned to their previous ethnic identity, their culture, and their language. Where does revitalization lead? As we have seen, rapid changes in both directions have taken place during the last few decades. It is a very difficult or even impossible task to give prognoses about the future of minority languages. The task for a scholar, or indeed for every fellow human being, is rather to observe what is happening and to support all efforts to create a world tolerant of linguistic and ethnic diversity.

Questions for Further Thought and Discussion

1. Which factors have promoted the assimilation of language and identity among the Arctic minorities in the Nordic countries?

2. Which factors seem to have supported the revitalization efforts among the aforementioned minorities?

3. What kind of change is seen to have taken place in the relationship between language and identity during the 1900s?

4. What are the most important differences between the situation of the Sweden Finns and that of the Arctic minorities in the Nordic countries?

5. In Sweden, there has traditionally been a great reluctance to distinguish between historical and immigrant minorities and to make special arrangements for each group. Is there, in your opinion, a need to distinguish between them, and if so, why?

6. There is often a discrepancy between the findings and recommendations of modern bilingualism research and the de facto education policy directed toward linguistic minorities. Discuss the reasons for this discrepancy and the possibilities of remedying the situation.

Notes

1. The construction of a dam was planned for a power plant, and opponents tried to prevent it. The struggle ended in favor of the government rather than the Sámi and the environmentalists.

2. Modernization is here understood as consisting of urbanization, wider access to mass media, economic integration, changing values, secularization, and so forth.

3. "Kvääni"/"kveeni"; in Norwegian, "kven."

4. "Tornionlaaksolainen"; in Swedish, "tornedaling."

5. "Tornionlaakson suomalainen"; in Swedish, "tornedalsfinne."

6. "Forest Finns" or "Värmland Finns" were Finnish farmers welcomed by the Swedish Crown during the sixteenth century because of their special land-clearing method, burn-beating, which speeded up the colonization of lands near the Norwegian border. The last of them who spoke Finnish as his mother tongue is said to have died in 1965.

7. "Ruotsinsuomalainen"; in Swedish, "sverigefinne."

8. Jakob Lyberth (1989) illuminates the position of Inuit by describing a Nordic women's conference at which the Greenlandic participants were unable to get anything out of the event but smiles and laughter because they could not understand what the others said. No interpretation had been arranged.

Selected Bibliography

Aikio, Marjut (1994). The Sami Language Act and the case of Lisma. In *Finnish Essays on Arctic Issues*, Olli-Pekka Jalonen (ed.), Occasional Papers No. 54, 9–19. Tampere, Finland: Tampere Peace Research Institute.

Eidheim, Harald (1997). Ethno-political development among the Sami after World War II: The invention of selfhood. In *Sami Culture in a New Era: The Norwegian Sami Experience.* Harald Gaski (ed.), 29–61. Karasjok, Norway: Davvi Girji OS.

Hansegård, Nils-Erik (1968). *Tvåspråkighet eller halvspråkighet?* Stockholm: Aldus/Bonniers.

Joensen, Torið S. (1989). Sproglige vanskeligheter i det nordiske samarbejdet for færinger. In *De ikke-skandinaviske språkene i Norden. Rapport fra en konferanse i Bergen 2.-4. desember 1988*, 13–15. Oslo: Nordisk språksekretariat.

Lainio, Jarmo (1997). Swedish minority language treatment and language policy—positive public rhetoric vs. grassroot struggle. In *Sociolinguistica* 11: 29–42.

Lyberth, Jakob (1989). Det gronlandske sprogs stilling i det nordiske samarbejde, in *De ikke-skandinaviske språkene i Norden: Rapport fra en* *konferanse i Bergen 2.–4. desember 1988.* Nordisk språksekretariats rapporter 13, pp. 67–72. Oslo: Nordisk Språksekretariat.

Marainen, Johannes (1988). Returning to Sami identity. In *Minority Education: From Shame to Struggle*, Jim Cummins and Tove Skutnabb-Kangas (eds.), 179–185. Clevedon, England: Multilingual Matters.

Skutnabb-Kangas, Tove (1998). Bilingual education for Finnish minority students in Sweden. In *The Encyclopedia of Language and Education*, J. Cummins and David Corson (eds.), 217–227. (Volume on *Bilingual Education*). Dortrecht: Kluwer.

Stordahl, Vigdis (1997). Sami generations. In *Sami Culture in a New Era. The Norwegian Sami Experience.* Harald Gaski (ed.), 143–154. Karasjok, Norway: Davvi Girji OS.

Vikør, Lars S. (1993). *The Nordic Languages. Their Status and Interrelations.* Oslo: Nordic Language Secretariat and Novus Press.

Wingstedt, Maria (1996). *Language Ideology and Minority Policies: A History of Sweden's Educational Policies towards the Saami, including a Comparison to the Tornedalians.* Stockholm University: Centre for Research on Bilingualism.

The Slavic World

MIROSLAV HROCH

What is referred to in this chapter as the "Slavic World" is a hetero-geneous sample of several nations having two principal features in common: First, their languages belong to a single Slavic linguistic "family"; second, they have inhabited since the sixth century the almost compact territory of east central and eastern Europe.

From a linguistic point of view, it is possible to distinguish three subgroups of Slavic nations: the Western Slavs (Poles, Czechs, Slovaks, and the Sorbs in Lusatia); the Eastern Slavs (Russians, Ukrainians, Byelorussians); and the Southern Slavs (Slovenes, Croatians, Serbs, Macedonians). But Slavic nations also differ in their religious traditions, the borders of which run sometimes parallel to and sometimes across the linguistic differences. Western Slavs are mostly Catholic, with some important remnants of Protestant tradition traceable among the Slovacs and the Czechs. Eastern Slavs are mostly Orthodox, except for a strong minority of West Ukrainians (Ruthens) who accepted the union with the Catholic Church (Greek Catholics). Southern Slavs are by religion divided into the Orthodox (Serbs, Bulgarians, Macedonians) and the Catholic (Croats, Slovenes) traditions. There is also a small Slavic-speaking Muslim community in Bosnia which has declared itself to be a nation within recent decades.

Slavic nations have not been the only inhabitants of east central and south-eastern Europe, and mention must also be made of Lithuanians and Latvians who belong to the Baltoslavic linguistic group, Magyars and Estonians who belong to the linguistic group of Finno-Ugrians, and Rumanians and Albanians as well.

With the exception of the Russians, all Slavic nations passed through a period of national revival, although at different times and in different political conditions. When their national movement were at first beginning, Slavic ethnic groups inhabited the territory of three multiethnic empires, each of which had an oppressive, late-absolutist political system: the Russian Tsarist Empire, the Ottoman Empire, and the Habsburg (since 1806 the Austrian) Empire. The language of administration and of higher education in Austria was German, in Tsarist Russia it was Russian, and in the Ottoman Empire it was Ottoman Turkish.

At the beginning of the nineteenth century, some Slavic languages were codified and were able to link themselves to an older linguistic tradition, albeit an interrupted or weakened one, as languages of literature and administration (Polish, Czech, and to some extent Croatian). Others existed only as examples of dialects (Slovac, Slovene, Ukrainian, and Bulgarian).

From a sociological point of view, members of almost all Slavic ethnic groups (except for Russians and Poles) belonged to the lower and lower-middle classes. They had no share in political power and only in exceptional cases obtained access to higher education and to better paid professions, initially and above all the clergy.

Case studies of the major Slavic groups follow.

Czechs

Ethnic Czechs inhabited the territory of three historical administrative units: the Kingdom of Bohemia, the Margraviate of Moravia, and Austrian Silesia. In the late Middle Ages, they were united in one state, known as the Lands of the Czech Crown. Czech written literature, both religious and secular, began to emerge in the fourteenth century, and in the fifteenth century Czech became the language of state administation. However, during the second half of the seventeenth century, Czech was replaced by German as the language of central and later, local administration. It was during this time that Czech written literature became limited to the subject matter of religion topics (prayers, sermons, poems, songs) and popular educational tales.

The Germanization of the upper classes, along with a total subordination to Habsburg rule, modified identities in Bohemia and Moravia. Although the ruling classes maintained an identity only with the political unit (*Landespatriotismus*), the Czech ethnic identity survived among the Czech-speaking lower and lower-middle classes. Only some educated individuals, most of whom belonged to the Catholic clergy, combined the state identity with the ethnic one.

In the last decades of the eighteenth century, a small group of enlightened patriots began to study and modernize the Czech language, partly for the practical purpose of education and partly as an expression of their emotional attitude toward the country, its people, and its vernacular. Scientific grammars of the Czech language were written, as were several passionate "defenses" of the Czech language.

All of these patriots were bilingual, and the majority of them had no faith in the possibility of Czech replacing the ruling language of German. Nevertheless, with the appearance of a new generation of patriots in the first two decades of the nineteenth century, this attitude changed. This generation, represented above all by Josef Jungmann, stressed that the Czech nation-to-be was, like all other nations, defined by its language, and it demanded an equal standing alongside German for the Czech language. Hence they developed an ambitious linguistic program which included as a first step the introduction of Czech into high schools as a language of educational instruction and as a second step the demand for equal rights for Czech in administration. At the same time, an effort was made to intellectualize the language by translating literature from more highly developed languages into Czech and by encouraging Czech authors to write secular literature.

During the decades that followed these activists managed, step by step, to persuade the Czech-speaking population to understand its ethnic identity as a national one, or, in other words, to become aware that all Czech speakers belong to one and the same nation. In the revolution of 1848, the enthusiastic participation of the masses on the side of the Czech patriots represented the first success of this link between a linguistically defined national identity and political demands.

As a result of this mass support, Czech leaders, during the second half of the nineteenth century, achieved several important successes in introducing the Czech language as a language of education in the schools and as a language of administration in the Czech-speaking territories of Bohemia and Moravia. Even though the Czech population was by no means threatened with assimilation, a demand for full equality for the Czech language in all spheres of administration and public life continued as a part of Czech political claims until the formation of independent Czechoslovakia in 1918.

Slovaks

Ethnic Slovacs were a relic of the Slavic population of the Great Moravian Empire, which was destroyed by the invasion of the Magyars around 900. The Magyars exterminated or assimilated the population in the core territory of the kingdom that they created during the tenth century, although in the north the Slavs survived. During the Middle Ages, the majority of the Slovak gentry was Magyarized, and the upper class in the newly founded towns was German and Magyar. There are known to be some sources written in Slovak dialects that date from the fourteenth century, but during the sixteenth and seventeenth centuries the Lutheran Reformation penetrated into northern Hungary using "national" languages, German among the German speakers in town, and Czech among the Slovak speakers, both in towns and in the countryside. From this time, Czech remained the language of liturgy and of education for the Lutheran Slovak minority in Hungary.

Even though the Kingdom of Hungary was a multiethnic state, linguistic differences did not play any important role, because Latin was, until the 1780s, the official language used in administration and political life. The first attempt to create a Slovak literary language was made by the Catholic clergy in the 1780s, at the very same time that the Hungarian Estates protested against the decision to introduce German as the language of administration throughout the Habsburg Empire. The Slovak linguistic norm was based on West Slovak dialects, which were somewhat similar to the Czech; but this new language was accepted only by the Catholics, whereas the Lutherans and some of the intellectuals retained Czech as their literary language.

This linguistic division caused some serious problems for Slovak speakers in Hungary in defining their ethnic and national identity. As inhabitants of the kingdom for almost 1000 years, they all shared a Hungarian state identity. As for ethnic identity, the Protestants regarded themselves as a part of the culturally defined Czech nation (more and more frequently referred to as Czecho-Slavic or Czecho-Slovak). The Catholic clergy supported the Slovak ethnic identity based on the everyday experience of being different from both Magyars and Germans.

In the 1840s, a group of young patriotic intellectuals, both Catholics and Protestants, under the leadership of Ludovit Stur, decided to address the problem of ambiguity and to create a new literary language based on the dialects of Central Slovakia. After several decades of dispute, the new linguistic norm was generally accepted among Slovaks, while the majority of Czechs (and a small number of Slovaks) regarded it as a written dialect belonging to the Czech language. During the last one-third of the nineteenth century, there emerged a rich selection of Slovak literature, even though the Slovak language was not permitted into the sphere of public life in Hungary, where the government strictly attempted to Magyarize all non-Magyar ethnic groups in the kingdom, such as the Serbs, Rumanians, Ukrainians, and Jews.

The Slovak language was permitted only at the elementary school level (and always alongside Magyar), but it was excluded from all spheres of public and economic life. Consequently, patriotic intellectuals were only able to obtain their education abroad, in Vienna or more often in Prague. Although this strengthened their links to Czech culture and to the Czech nation, the only basis for Slovak national identity which could be (with some limitations) publicly expressed was the Catholic Church.

The newly independent state of Czechoslovakia, which was founded after the decline of the Austro-Hungarian Empire, was based on the official "Czechoslovakist" ideology, which regarded Slovaks as a part of the Czechoslovak nation. There was, however, one specification: They were allowed to use the Slovak language on Slovak territory but had to accept the equal standing of Czech in schools and in administration. A strong minority of Slovak politicians opposed the concept of Czechoslovakism and demanded an autonomous status for Slovakia. This demand was fulfilled with the support of Nazi Germany in 1939, when a fascist Slovak state was created as a German satellite.

After World War II, the reestablished Czechoslovakia was declared a state of two equal nations: the Czechs and the Slovaks. The Slovak language was acknowledged as a fully independent one, and its further development was officially supported and became, among Slovaks, a symbol of their demand for more autonomy. This demand was fulfilled in 1968 by the new constitution, which declared Czechoslovakia to be a federation. For this reason, Slovak scholars and political authorities supported endeavors to make the Slovak language even more different from the Czech. This trend continued even after the declaration of an independent Slovakia.

The Sorbs in Lusatia

Several hundred thousand Sorbs lived in nineteenth-century Lusatia, a small remnant of the Slavic tribes who in the Middle Ages had inhabited the territory of present-day Germany. Their territory was divided between Saxonia and Prussia, and they were also divided by religion into Catholic and Lutheran regions. Linguistically they had two main dialects: Upper and Lower Sorbian. The strongest ethnic identity could be observed among the Catholic minority in Upper Lusatia, whose priests were educated in Prague.

It is therefore understandable that, under the influence of the Czech national movement, some educated Sorbs initiated national agitation in the 1840s, primarily in Upper Lusatia, and formulated linguistic demands. No difficulty faced the acceptance of linguistic norms: In accordance with the two main dialects, two written languages were constructed—Upper and Lower Sorbian. Although they gained some support, especially among Catholics, their movement had no chance of success. They were too weak to resist systematic Germanization, especially after the founding of the Second Empire in 1871, and the Sorb ethnic group lived almost exclusively in villages, whereas the urban population was German.

Germanization continued even during the twentieth century, so that all Sorbs, even if they kept their ethnic "national" identity, are bilingual, and the remnants of any specificity are mainly of ethnographic interest.

Croatians

The early medieval kingdom of Croatia consisted of three parts—Croatia proper, Dalmatia, and Slovenia—and was inhabited by a predominantly Slavic population. From the twelfth century on, the kingdom was joined to Hungary but retained its own diet and self-administration. Later on, Dalmatia fell partially under Venetian rule and partially under the dominance of the City Republic of Ragusa (Dubrovnik). In Hungary, the common language of administration was Latin; in Dalmatia, Latin was later replaced by Italian. Under the influence of Italian humanism, the first literary works in Croatian were printed in Dalmatia during the sixteenth and seventeenth centuries.

Linguistically, the inhabitants of Croatia were divided into two basic groups of dialects: in the north of Croatia proper there was the Kaikavian dialect, and in other areas the Stokavian dialect dominated. This Stokavian dialect was also in use outside the territory of the kingdom, in Bosnia (inhabited by Catholic, Greek-Orthodox, and Muslim Slavic speakers) and in Serbia, both territories falling under Ottoman rule. For this reason, the ethnic identity of the Croatian population at the outset of the period of modern nation formation could be defined by linguistic criteria only in Dalmatia and at the Magyar border, whereas in relation to the Serbian and Muslim populations, religious difference established the decisive criterion. To complete the picture, the Istrian peninsula, which politically never belonged to Croatia, was inhabited by a Slavic population, which spoke dialects more similar to Croatian.

For this reason, the initial national movement had some difficulty with self-definition. The leading group of Croatian intellectuals, led by Ludovid Gaj, was convinced that language was the main criterion for defining a nation, and thus the concept of *illyrism* was developed. This concept suggested that not only the inhabitants of Croatia but also the Slavic speakers of Bosnia and Serbia belonged to one and the same nation because most of them used the same dialects. The Kaikavian and even Slovenian dialects were included in this idea of one "illyric nation." This concept nonetheless failed during the revolution of 1848, where Serbs and Croatians formulated political goals which were mutually incompatible.

Even though national identity differed, the idea of a common language remained as a matter for negotiation. After some discussion, the patriots from Serbia and Croatia signed a compromise in the 1850s on a common and unified Serbo-Croatian language, with two written variants—one in Latin and the other in the Cyrillic script. The Slovenes refused to participate in this concept of illyrism; the Muslims were not invited; and some Croatian patriotic intellectuals refused or modified this unified language. This situation, however, proved to be no source of obstruction to the emergence of modern Croatian literature.

The Croatian national movement was later divided into two camps: One camp prioritized the principle of linguistic unity and Slavism and maintained the idea of a close collaboration with other Southern Slavs, above all Serbians; the other camp stressed the historical argument of a preexisting Croatian state and its "historical rights" and rejected unity with the Serbs. The radicals in this camp regarded the Slavic-speaking Muslims in Bosnia as a "Muslimized" part of the Croatian nation and claimed that all Bosnian territory should be included in "Greater Croatia."

As the concept of Yugoslavism gained primacy during World War I, a new state, Yugoslavia, was created as a kingdom of three nations: Serbs, Croatians, and Slovenes. However, Serbian dominance very soon provoked a strong Croatian movement which rejected the concept of linguistic unity with the Serbs and claimed political autonomy. Even though this claim was fulfilled in Communist Yugoslavia, in which Croatia with its historical borders was one of the federative republics, the national movement was revived, especially in the 1980s, and achieved the status of an independent state with its own Crotian language in which the differences from the Serbian are strongly overemphasized.

Serbs

The strong Serbian medieval kingdom fell within the sphere of influence of the Greek Orthodox Church but at least obtained full independence from the Patriarchate of Constantinople. In addition, after the Ottoman conquest at the end of the fourteenth century, the Serbian church remained independent and claimed itself to be the keeper of Serbian identity. Its language was originally Church Slavic, later influenced by spoken Serbian and sometimes called Slovene-Serbian, and used by a very limited strata of educated clergy. Nevertheless, under the conditions of Otoman rule, the secular literary tradition was, until the end of the eighteenth century, primarily represented in an oral tradition: epic folk songs and tales.

Defined above all by Orthodoxy, a number of Serbian groups migrated, especially after 1700, into the southern part of Hungary (a territory newly reconquered by the Habsburgs and until today known as Vojvodina), where during the following century they created a cultural center for all Serbs. The first Serbian gymnasium was founded here, as well as the first institution for the encouragement of the writing and publishing of secular books in Serbian. From here the discussion on the codified form of the Serbian language was decided in favor of the modern spoken Stokavian dialect.

Under the influence of the successful Serbian upheavals against Ottoman rule, which enabled the establishment of an independent Serbia during the first half of the nineteenth century, the reflection on Serbian identity was initiated. It was primarily defined by political and religious criteria, but later on some intellectuals, under the leadership of Vuk Karadžič, who accepted the concept of a nation defined by common language, renounced the priority of religious confession and developed the idea of a "Greater Serbia." They argued that all people who spoke the Stokavian dialect belonged to the Serbian nation. This idea implicitly and later also explicitly included Muslims in Bosnia and limited the Croatian nation to those who used the Kaikavian dialect. Even though this idea was not accepted by all Serbs, it provoked the "Greater Croatia" response and created the political unrest that continues to have a great impact up to the present.

Whereas the Croatian intellectuals regarded the construct of the Serbo-Croatian (or in their eyes, the Croato-Serbian) language as too far-reaching a concession and stressed the difference between the Latin and Greek Orthodox traditions as decisive for national differentiation, the Serbs made claims to strengthen this compromise in favor of their own language. The attempt to transform interwar Yugoslavia into a Greater Serbian-dominated state failed, but nonetheless it contributed to the development of prejudices and negative heterostereotypes, which played their tragic role during World War II and again in the present day.

Slovenes

Even though in contemporary history since 1918 the Slovenes have been joined with Yugoslavia, the formation of their national identity followed an entirely different pattern than that of all other southern Slavs. The name "Slovene" was invented at the outset of the nineteenth century as a means of expressing the fact that, in the territory of southeastern Austria and in the northeast part of the Venetian state, there lived a population which employed similar Slavic dialects. Later on, illyrists attempted to include these groups into the construct of one nation, but during the 1840s, Slovene (and Austrian) scholars proved that these dialects had linguistic features different enough from the Kaikavian and Stokavian dialects that they could form the basis for a separate literary language. After some discussion, a new, codified language was constructed, based on a combination of various dialects and placed at the focus of a modern Slovene identity.

Up until this time, Slovene speakers had defined their ethnic identity in terms of how they differed from their German and Italian neighbors. However, this identity was usually combined with a regional identity and limited to the valleys which they inhabited. This weak ethnic identity was also the reason for their rather strong assimilation, particularly in cases in which they had migrated to the towns. In

Austria, a favorable precondition for such assimilation was formed by the fact that most elementary schools on their territory used both Slovene dialects and German as languages of instruction.

Nevertheless, the national movement, above all stressing linguistic demands, delayed assimilation and almost brought it to an end. Linguistic demands included both the introduction of the Slovene language into high schools and the intellectualization of the language. By the end of the nineteenth century, the Slovene population became nationally mobilized, and its demands were also concerned with the equality of the Slovene language in local administration and with some degree of political autonomy. At the same time, modern Slovene literature emerged, as did differentiated political programs.

Bulgarians

The Christianization of medieval Bulgaria at the end of the ninth century was accompanied by the acceptance of the Slavic—originally Great Moravian—language of rite. This language, later known as Old Slavic or Old Bulgarian, became the basis for medieval literature, not only in Bulgaria but also in Serbia, Rumania, and Russia. Nevertheless, after the Ottoman conquest in the fourteenth century, very little of this culture remained on Bulgarian territory. The culture was entirely subordinated to the Greek Orthodox Church, and the Greek language became the only language of instruction and of liturgy. There were almost no remnants even of Bulgarian ethnic identity: The population defined itself as Christians, according to the Ottoman system of millets.

The first attempts to define a Bulgarian ethnicity started at the beginning of the nineteenth century. At the same time, the first attempts were made to develop modern Bulgarian as a printed language. Only a very small group of patriots, some of them clergymen and some of them merchants, began to furmulate the first linguistic demands: to substitute the Bulgarian language for Greek in the church and in the schools. Some progress was made after the 1830s, and success was achieved in the 1860s. The problem was that, having rejected the possibility of "modernizing" the Old Bulgarian language, Bulgarian patriots had to answer the question of which dialect would best be suited to become the written national language. For several decades, each author wrote in his own dialect, declaring it to be the most suitable for use among all Bulgarians. As a result of the increasing number and importance of intellectuals and writers who originated in the eastern part of Bulgaria, the eastern dialects were accepted as the basis for the linguistic norm.

From at least the 1860s, the Bulgarian language became a self-evident criterion for belonging to the new nation. National claims switched to the political sphere, and autonomy or even independence dominated the political program. It was only after having achieved partial independence in 1878 that political leaders stressed the importance of the Bulgarian language as the language of communication in the newly born state: it was codified, introduced into the newly established school system, and supported as a language of modern literature.

Nevertheless, language became a tool for political dispute. As in the case of the Serbs, a great number of Bulgarian speakers lived outside the territory of the independent homeland. It was difficult to distinguish bilingual Bulgarians (above all those in the towns) from Greeks, and there was the added irritation of the newly emerging Macedonian national movement. The territory between Skopje and Thessaloniki became a matter for dispute among Serbs, Greeks, and Bulgarians.

Macedonians

From the time that the Bulgarian wars for national liberation achieved their first successes and created a separate nation-state, a new national movement emerged in Bulgaria's western neighbor. A group of intellectuals, led by Krste Missirkov, declared that the dialects spoken on this territory were not east Bulgarian dialects but rather a separate national language—Macedonian. They declared themselves the successors of ancient Macedonians and initiated a national agitation in an effort to transform the local or regional identity into a national one. However, their attempt failed: The Ottoman army squelched their upheaval, and not one of their neighbors recognized them as a nation. Bulgarians regarded their vernacular as a west Bulgarian dialect, Serbs regarded them as Bulgarized Serbs, and Greeks refused even to accept their name, stressing that Macedonians are a part of the Greek nation. During the interwar period, Macedonians in Yugoslavia were declared to be Serbs, and during the war their territory was joined to Bulgaria (which was an ally of Nazi Germany). The continuity of national agitation was, however, never completely severed. With the establishment of socialist Yugoslavia, Macedonia was declared as one of the federal republics, with its own Macedonian language.

Poles

The Polish nation formation differed from all the other Slavic cases in that language demands and ethnicity originally played no relevant role. Poland-Lithuania survived from the late Middle Ages as an important and independent state in which from the sixteenth century on the Polish language, alongside Latin, was a language of high culture, the language of administration and politics. After the loss of independence (as a result of the division of its territory between Prussia, Russia, and Austria), Polish patriots focused their struggle on political aims: the reestablishment of their state.

Because this struggle did not achieve its goal, the ethnic Polish territory not only remained divided but also was gradually integrated into the administrative structure of the occupying powers. This meant that, especially in the case of Prussia, the government initiated a Germanization of all spheres of public life. Soon after, in the 1840s, the Poles felt even their ethnicity to be threatened and, as a means of defense, emphasized linguistic and cultural instead of political goals.

The same development may also be observed in the Russian part of the territory after the defeat of the revolutions in 1831 and, particularly, in 1863–1864, when the Russian tsar punished the rebellious Poles with a total Russification of schools, administration, and public life. Only in the Austrian territory were the politics of Germanization merely temporary (until 1860) and limited to state administration. From the 1860s on, not only high schools but also universities introduced Polish as the language of instruction. For this reason, Galicia (the Austrian part of old Poland) became the core territory for the development of Polish cultural and scientific life.

Another specific feature should also be mentionned. As a result of several persecutions, a large Polish emigration moved to and settled in Western Europe. These Poles were both educated and wealthy enough to develop their own cultural life and were always in contact with those who had remained at home. Thus the Polish culture also differed (and differs) from all other Slavic cultures in its close and organic contact with Western cultures.

Ukrainians

The Polish-Lithuanian state was a multiethnic empire. Its eastern part was inhabited by numerous non-Polish ethnic groups: Lithuanians, Ukrainians, Byelorussians, and Jews. At some point, but certainly following the decline of the old Polish state, the idea of being a distinct nation was raised by some educated members of these ethnic groups. This meant that everywhere these national movements were faced with both the old Polish ruling nation and culture and the culture and language of the new ruling state elites. In the Ukrainian case, the situation was even more complicated, because the territory, inhabited by people who are today called Ukrainians, was divided: the smaller part fell under Habsburg rule (the eastern part of Galicia) and the larger, under Tsarist Russia.

In both parts, the first attempts to start a national movement came under way in the 1840s, but the result was entirely different. Russian authorities never regarded the population that lived in what is the present-day Ukraine as a distinct nationality. According to them, this population used a Russian dialect and was referred to as "Little Russian." All patriotic activities were considered as anti-Tsarist and were persecuted. Until the end of the century, all attempts to initiate national activities were oppressed and persecuted. The opposite situation occurred in Austria, where Ruthens (the official name of later Ukrainians) were from 1860 allowed to develop their national agitation, to publish journals and newspapers, to create national organizations, and so forth.

Ukrainian demands in eastern Galicia were primarily concerned with linguistic matters: to introduce their language into schools and the administration, which was then Polish. At the beginning of the twentieth century, most Ukrainian children could attend elementary school and be taught in their own vernacular; there existed several high schools with Ukrainian as the language of instruction; and even some departments at the University of Lviv were allowed to use Ukrainian.

The problem was how to construct a literary language which would be understandable throughout the vast territory between Lviv and Charkiv. Originally, the writers in Galicia primarily used and cultivated their own dialect, but they were aware that this dialect was hardly comprehensible to East Ukrainian peasants. In addition to this, a growing number of intellectuals, emigrés from Russia, participated in Ukrainian national activities in Galicia, and it was also generally accepted that the historical metropolis of Kiev would be the center of the future awakened nation. For all these reasons, during the decades before World War II, a growing number of intellectuals accepted central Ukrainian as the basis for linguistic unification. Despite this, a strong tendency to include Galician elements into this written language still survived. At the same time, a growing number of intellectuals and politicians regarded the language not merely as a means of communication within all strata of the population but also and primarily as a symbol of Ukrainian cultural tradition and identity.

The tragic events during the Russian Revolution ended with a new division of Ukrainians. The majority were included in the newly founded Ukrainian Soviet Republic, in which Ukrainian was officially accepted as the language of administration alongside—and in the shadow of—Russian. But the language became "sovietized," or, in other words, the Galician influences were suppressed and the Russian supported. The majority of the population were not mobilized and were therefore open to this "sovietization," and the remaining national activists were imprisoned or frightened off by the Stalinist persecutions.

The western territory was joined to reestablished Poland, and Ukrainian activists were regarded as enemies of the state. After the occupation of this territory by the Union of Soviet Socialist Republics, a mass persecution of nationalists came under way. The language remained the only symbol of national identity for the remaining Ukrainians, who maintained their national awareness and based it, above all, on the national language.

Russians

The Russian case differs entirely from that of all other Slavic nations. Since the Middle Ages, the Russian language had been a written language, and when the strong Russian state was reconstituted in the fifteenth century, Russian became the language of court and administration. From the seventeenth century on, many books were printed in Russian, focusing above all on religious matters; but the first Russian grammar did not appear before 1757. As Russia developed under Peter the Great and his successors into a multiethnic empire, the Russian language emerged as the state language of the ruling elites, originally without any relation to the ethnic identity of the uneducated masses.

Even though the elites temporarily preferred French as their language of conversation and letters, modern Russian literature nonetheless continued to develop from the end of the eighteenth century. The link to ethnicity followed in the specific conditions of the doctrine on "official Russian nationality," which was declared in the 1840s. This official nationality was based on three principles—autocracy, Orthodoxy, and nationality—and language was the common denominator of all three of these principles.

Language emerged as an important argument in the nationalist movement of "slavophiles," who regarded Russian culture as autochthonous and rejected the westernization of Russia. Under their influence, the tsar accepted, at the end of the nineteenth century, the idea of the Russification of non-Russian ethnic groups living on the territory of his empire. Efforts in this direction failed, but the Russian language remained the language of communication for all ethnic groups and nationalities, not only during the last decades of the monarchy but also after the establishment of the Soviet Union in 1922. In the eyes of non-Russians, the Russian language occupied an ambiguous position: It was the medium of a high developed literature and science but at the same time a hated symbol of political oppression and assimilation.

Summary

The link between language and ethnic identity differed according to the traditions of a given ethnic group and according to the political and cultural conditions in the empire in which it lived. The case of Russian was completely different, being above all the language of the empire and at the same time the language of the state elites before it became a tool for the national mobilization of the masses. A somewhat analogical role was played by Polish, alongside Latin, in the Polish-Lithuanian commonwealth up until its dissolution during the second half of the eighteenth century.

According to the general political conditions, the linguistic situations of ethnic groups in the above-mentioned three multiethnic empires differed rather distinctively.

Until 1860, the Habsburg Empire guaranteed a privileged position for the German language but accepted ethnic differences and ethnic identities. From the 1860s on, national movements were able to achieve some improvements in the status of their languages, especially in the western part of the empire; whereas in the eastern Hungarian section after the Compromise of 1867, an assimilation of non-Magyar ethnic groups was introduced.

In the Ottoman Empire, the non-Muslims were regarded as one community in accordance with their religion; language played an unimportant role. In those cases in which the linguistic difference coincided with religious organization, the development toward ethnic identity proceeded rather quickly (as in the cases of the Greeks and the Serbs). Nevertheless, the linguistic program did not play a relevant role. Moreover, the oppressive character of Ottoman rule, together with a general backwardness in cultural matters, hindered the move toward language planning and toward the intellectualization of the language.

In Russia, the position of non-Russian Slavic languages was extremely difficult: Ukrainian and Byelorussian were merely regarded as dialects, and Polish was suppressed for political reasons after the defeat of the revolution in 1863–1864.

At the same time, Russian slavophiles supported Slavic national movements abroad, both in Austro-Hungary and in the Balkans.

Another differentiation emerged as a result of different previous cultural developments. Language played an important role as a powerful tool for ethnic and national identity in those areas in which it had existed as a written and printed language since the Middle Ages and could be codified without relative difficulties (as in the cases of the Czechs and Poles). In most cases, however, a modern literary language had to be constructed on the basis of one or more dialects.

With the exception of the Russian case, national movements sooner or later included linguistic demands as a part of their programs. Linguistic demands involved several stages, differing in their timing and also in their capacity to strengthen ethnic and national identity. At the first stage, the language was celebrated and defended against the threat of assimilation. At the second stage, the language was planned and codified, which involved a simultaneous process of linguistic organization and standardization, including unified orthography and distinct language borders. The third stage was aimed at an intellectualization of the national language, the writing of poetry, short stories, and novels, and the development of the language of scientific literature. The fourth stage was represented in the demands for the introduction of this codified and intellectualized language into the high schools. The fifth stage demanded full equality for the language in all spheres of public life.

Of these stages, only the first three have to do with language in the proper sense of the word. All Slavic national movements tried to purify their languages of loanwords, but they also worked on morphology, syntax, and orthography in order to accentuate their differences from the ruling state language or from the old church Slavic. At the same time, they needed to modernize the lexicology through neologisms and by making use of loanwords from other Slavic languages, primarily from the developed ones—Russian and Polish. Generally, the feeling of a Slavic linguistic similarity (community) was strong in all Slavic national movements without necessarily developing into pan-Slavism. The success of national demands depended both on the general political conditions and on the support which could be received from members of the ethnic group. This support was stronger in cases in which the population was literate and mobile and in which the linguistic diference simultaneously corresponded to some kind of social or political tension. The general success of introducing the language into schools, administration, and public life established one of the most important preconditions for the success of nation formation among all Slavic national movements. During the period when national movements were developing their political programs, linguistic demands entered the field of politics, and the language aquired, in addition to its communicative functions, some "nonlinguistic," noncommunicative functions. Language became a myth, a symbol for national existence, a matter of prestige, and a tool for "disciplination," and anyone who intended to become a successful politician had to support linguistic demands.

In this connection, it is worth mentioning that the English term "nation" has different connotations from its equivalent in most Slavic languages: The English "nation" is defined by its relation to the state, whereas, for example, the Czech "národ" is defined by its relation to the ethnicity. For this reason, the transformation of an ethnic identity to a national one is, in Slavic languages (with perhaps the exception of Polish), understood as a change, a "process" inside one and the same entity, whereas in English it means two different qualities. This semantic difference also explains why language (i.e., ethnically defined identity) played such an important role in Eastern Europe in comparison to the national movements in the English-speaking world—Ireland and Scotland.

This is, however, only one of the preconditions which need to be mentionned when attempting to understand the close connection between language and national identity. In other words, Why did the linguistic program receive such strong mass support?

Decisive preconditions proceeded from the social sphere. There existed a distinct correlation between an incomplete social structure and the charisma of language. The more difficulties that the members of a nondominant ethnic group had in moving from the lower to the higher classes, the more significant was the association between their language and the social position they occupied. An incomplete social structure also had an impact on political culture: National movements always involved social groups who possessed neither political experience nor political education and could, therefore, better understand ethnolinguistic arguments than abstract political theories. Linguistic demands were, from this point of view, not intellectual games of frustrated philologists but rather an expression of the transformation of concrete interests and of painful experiences.

Questions for Further Thought and Discussion

1. Discuss differences in the situations of various Slavic national movements under Ottoman, Habsburg, and Russian rule.

2. Why was it important to have an older tradition both of written language and of "national" literature?

3. What was the basis for the codification of various Slavic languages in the nineteenth century?

4. In the relation between language and politics, why did language enter the sphere of political demands?

5. Did the religious, confessional difference influence the role of language in the nation formation process?

6. Why could linguistic demands achieve such strong mass support?

7. Try to imagine the different linguistic connotations of the Slavic equivalents for the English term "nation."

Selected Bibliography

Auty, R. (1958). The linguistic revival among the Slavs and the Austrian Empire, 1780–1850: The role of individuals in the codification and acceptance of new literary languages. *Modern Language Review* 53: 392–404.

Auty, R. (1979). Language and nationality in East-Central Europe 1750–1950. *Oxford Slavonic Papers, New Series,* 12: 52–83.

Brang, P., and M. Züllig (eds.) (1981). *Kommentierte Bibliographie zur slavischen Sociolinguistic* (vols. 1–3). Bern: P. Lang.

Fishman, J. A. (1974). *Language and nationalism: Two interative essays.* Rowley: Newbury House.

Hroch, M. (1995). The social interpretation of linguistic demands in European national movements. *European University Institute Working Papers* 94-1.

Lencek, R. (1983). The role of sociolinguistics in the evolution of Slavic linguistic nationalism. *Canadian Review of Studies in Nationalism* 16: 99–115.

Thomas, G. (1991). *Linguistic purism.* London: Longman.

Vočadlo, O. (1926). Slavic linguistic purity and the use of foreign words. *Slavonic Review* 5: 352–364.

Western Europe

ANDRÉE TABOURET-KELLER

The Present Concept of Western Europe

This book contains chapters about different parts of Western Europe—Germany and the Celtic world—as well as other parts of Europe, Scandinavia and the Slavic world, each possessing specific language features. Therefore this chapter might deal with any of the rest of Western Europe—Britain, Holland, Belgium, Luxemburg, France, Spain, Portugal, Switzerland, and Italy. Only four of these countries, France, Britain, Spain, and Belgium, will be mentioned at some length here, and none of them will be treated exhaustively. I prefer to illustrate the complexity and the great variety of situations in Western Europe by detailed examples, taken from one or another of these four countries, rather than to build some kind of larger and therefore more artificial representation.

Today Western Europe is a weak concept. Its geographical limits to the west, the north, and the south are easy enough to define—the Atlantic Ocean, the Northern and Baltic Seas, the Mediterranean—but its eastern borders are harder to draw. As long as the Communist bloc existed, *Mitteleuropa* (Central Europe) was said to be the limit, but this is no longer the case.

Politically, things are even more problematic. Self-proclaimed democracy and the open-market economy are ill defined, and specialists do not agree on precise definitions. The creation of the European Union does not help, either: Although its main institutions are located in Western Europe (Luxemburg, Brussels, Strasbourg), the Union's limits are gradually expanding eastward and may before long coincide with the old geographic boundary of the Urals.

It will not be possible to avoid outside considerations entirely, either. In Western Europe, the language-ethnicity perspective cannot be isolated from that of other parts of Europe. One example may suffice: It could not and still cannot avoid the effects of the turmoil generated by the ethnic war in the former Republic of Yugoslavia. It was during this war, in the present decade, that the Western public discovered ethnic cleansing: the murder of numbers of civilians, including women and children, because of their nationality and/or religion. Serbo-Croatian, a common language in the former Republic of Yugoslavia, showed only slight dialectal and regional differences in pronunciation and in the lexicon. These former varieties are now in the process of becoming separate languages, Croatian, Serbian, and Bosnian, by cleansing each variety of foreign features and by imposing on it specific features which become ethnic markers, particularly through education and administration.

It must also be stressed that though it is possible to speak of some large language areas such as the Slavic world (see chapter 21), in the case of Western Europe this is hardly possible. There, it is impossible to speak of a one-language world, for what we see is a multicolored language puzzle made up both of long established minorities and of recently established immigrants (sometimes in "pockets," sometimes not). As a consequence, we must consider that in our languages and the cultures they embody, the use of the word *ethnic* and the definition of the notion to which it refers varies in significant ways.

That is why we must start with questions of method before going on to describe the realities of what some people might label *ethnicism* and others *nationalism*, *regionalism*, or *minoritism*.

Questions of Method: The Use of *Ethnicity* and Other Ethnic Terms

We cannot understand the meaning of *ethnicity* and other ethnic terms in Western Europe without contrasting them with one of the main concepts of the social sciences in the nineteenth century, the concept of *race*. In itself, this concept covers a large and complex set of notions which may or not contradict the concept of ethnicity, including or excluding it. The present difficulties of language politics and policies linked to ethnicity derive in some respect from overlappings and confusion between the concepts of racism and ethnicity. The concept of race covers at least three sets of meanings: (1) family, considered to be the succession of generations and the continuity of characteristics; (2) biological species, made up of animals bearing common hereditary caracteristics; (3) human groups, each differentiated by a set of hereditary physical characteristics: color of skin, form of the head, proportion of blood groups, and so forth.

Toward the end of the nineteenth century, ethnography, a vigorous new field, discovered populations that could be described as "natural" groupings of people with similar features (physical, mental, cultural, etc.) rooted in a common past; a collection of such groups could be considered to be of the same race. Each such natural group was called an *ethnie* in French and the other Romance languages, from which the term was borrowed by English and other languages. This gave *ethnic* terms a first application in the restricted field of ethnography.

Today, for obvious ideological reasons due to the impact of racism in contemporary history, the use of *race* tends to be avoided, and the notion of ethnicity (or *ethnie*) tends to be preferred, particularly by educated people. But it must be observed that the avoidance of a term is not sufficient to prevent xenophobic and racist movements from gaining ground once again throughout Western Europe. More recently, the concomitant development of biologically based criticism of the existence of a hierarchy of distinct human races on the one hand and of political racist ideologies on the other have reinforced the avoidance of the term *race*. But *ethnie* and ethnicity are not salient notions for many, and the general public would hardly use such learned terms, speaking rather of *foreigners* or in a more simplistic way of *immigrants.*

Broadly speaking, the term *ethnic* is not commonly used when referring to traditional Western European minorities except by educated people or within a nationalistic context. But for any human group, whether cultural, religious, linguistic, or other, that live in or comes from other continents, particularly from Third World countries, the term ethnic tends to be used in the press, both in English and in the Romance languages. One salient example is the ethnic war in Africa between Tutsi and Hutu in Rwanda. However, the term would not be used by the general public and might even not understood by large parts of it in the Romance parts of Europe.

This chapter is concerned with the fact that whatever the differences in the meanings of ethnic terms, processes of ethnicization are always at work. What are they and what is their relationship to language? One approach might be to choose a single point of view—for example, to retain only cases in which language and ethnicity are strictly bound to one another. Instead, I will take a dynamic view and try to discover the complexities of the relationship in its ongoing contemporary form.

First, we must look at the transnational language policies adopted by the European institution (the European Union [EU], formerly the European Economic Community [EEC]) to which all Western European countries with which we are dealing belong with the exception of Swizerland. In order to best illustrate the manifold facets of the Western European language-ethnicity situations, I will consider four different settings, restricting the discussion to specific salient aspects in each case: education, ethnicity, and language in immigrant populations in Britain and France; aspects of regional language policies in France; and examples of ethnicization in the Autonomous Basque region of Spain and in the Flemish autonomous region of Belgium.

European Union Language Policies

No child should have to discard the language of the home on entering school, but no basic principle is less observed! Education is among the main factors which split the language-ethnicity link.

Most European nations have developed on the assumption that a common language was the condition whereby all the people of a state could communicate; hence the condition of democracy (Baggioni 1997). The main result of such a policy is that it breeds the philosophy that monolingualism is the norm and multilingualism the exception. This is reflected both in the national state-language policies and in the European institutions' policies. Regarding the latter, I will briefly discuss the European Charter on Regional or Minority Languages and the *Council*

Directive on Education of Migrant Workers; both relate to what in an American context would be referred to in language-ethnicity terms but what in an European context is defined in terms of "regional language" or "minority language" or even "lesser-spoken language."

The European Charter on Regional
or Minority Languages

On November 5, 1992, the council of ministers of the European Parliament submitted the European Charter on Regional or Minority Languages to be signed by member states. As an indication of its political importance, note that most members signed it at once, some have since signed, but others such as France still have not. A signature, however, simply indicates adoption of the charter's general principles and does not, as we will see later, implement legal measures for their application.

The aim of the charter is cultural: to protect regional or minority languages, not to formulate political rights for them. The functions of language are considered cultural and social facts above all. Regional or minority languages must fill three criteria: They must be part of the European cultural heritage; they must have a territorial base; and they must be identifiable as separate languages. A regional language is supposed to have a fairly large territory and strong cultural attributes; a minority language has a small territory, uncertain prospects for survival, and limited potential for development. The distinction between the national languages and regional or minority languages is loose, since the national language of one state might be a regional language in a neighboring state (see the cases of Alsatian and Corsican, p. 343).

Thus the aim of the charter is to protect regional or minority languages as such, which is a matter both of nondiscrimination and of promotion. Based on the idea of equality between speakers rather than between languages, nondiscrimination is an attitude rather than a precise rule. Promotion, on the other hand, means a series of concrete measures to help a language survive, measures which may involve a wide range of domains such as education, public services, media, administration, legal authorities and the law, cultural facilities and activities, economic and social activities, and transfrontier exchanges.

All these measures are liable to restriction: member states are free to list the languages to which they agree the measures should be applied; for each language to which they believe the charter should apply, they can choose the provision(s) to which they subscribe.

An important difficulty, still unresolved, lies in the task of elaborating a common juridical frame to control the application of the charter in the member states which have adopted parts or all of it.

The Council Directive on Education
of Migrant Workers

The 1977 Council Directive on Education of Migrant Workers (77/486, Brussels) was preceded by a set of recommendations (European Charter for Minority and

Regional Languages: The Children of Migrant Workers, EEC, Brussels). Gardner-Chloros stresses the considerable gulf between the experts' recommendations and the "watered down" directive (1997: 195). The prior recommendations consistently referred to migrant workers from nonmember states of the European Union, as well as to those who had migrated within it, whereas the directive restricts its aim to making it possible for the 6 million children from other European Economic Community countries to be reintegrated in due course in the school system of their country of origin. In the original recommendations, the need for education of the migrant workers was not reduced, as it is in the directive, to the sole motive of facilitating their reintegration in a school in their country of origin but also called for "the full development of the personality of children situated between two cultures." The *Directive*'s recommendations "wanted the member states to make arrangements for the mother-tongue and culture of the country of origin to be taught in the school curriculum, gratis and throughout the period of compulsory education, in accordance with the educational standards normally applicable in the host country, as well as for appropriate teacher-training" (Gardner-Chloros 1997: 195). None of these aspects was reflected in the directive in its final form. The directive gave rise to intense debate and to the iniation of various pilot and research programs, but the support of actual teaching programs in accordance with the directive was left to the member states. The European Charter for Minority and Regional Languages of Maastricht (1992) makes no mention of the languages spoken by the established immigrants in Europe but deals only with indigenous regional or minority languages.

Only Foreigners Are Ethnic

In a recent book on vernacular literacy (Tabouret-Keller, Le Page, Gardner-Chloros, and Varro 1997), Gardner-Chloros adopts the following definition:

> *Linguistic minorities* [are] communities whose languages have been indigenous to the State at issue over a considerable period of its history (Welsh, Breton, Friulians, etc.) or whose minority status is the result of the redrawing of political frontiers (Alsacian, Macedonian). *Ethnic minorities* usually refers to the groups of more recent migrant origin. (Gardner-Chloros 1997: 189–221)

Modern urbanization and industrialization rests on intensive migration and on mass transfer of entire populations throughout the entire nineteenth and twentieth centuries. Just as xenophobic reactions have been common in the United States since the end of the nineteenth century, so have they become common in Western Europe since the 1950s. After the First World War, shortages of manpower gave rise to large influxes of immigrants, particularly to the coal and iron fields, who came mainly from the south of Italy and from Poland. After the Second World War, for the same reason, new waves of immigrants arrived to the nonanglophone northwestern parts of Europe from all southern countries of Europe (Italy, Spain, Portugal, Greece, and Turkey), from the former French colonies in North and Central Africa, from Southwest Asia, and from the Commonwealth countries of Britain.

Language policies that concern immigrant populations differ largely from one country to another, as do those that concern traditional language minority populations. Take the contrasting cases of Britain and France. Their global approaches to language policy in general differ in major aspects; moreover, Britain is characterized by a highly decentralized administration largely based on local management, whereas in France administration is highly centralized. In France, for over two centuries, the French language has been both the instrument and the symbol of national unity building; but the United Kingdom has never declared English its official language. There are, therefore, two very different ways of tackling language in general and ethnicity and language in particular. I have already stressed that in the first case ethnic terms are not used at all, and in the second they refer only to immigrant groups. I must nevertheless emphasize that, despite the differences, a common trend exists: during the past fifty years, legislation in both countries has changed an open- to a closed-door policy, particularly toward immigrants from the former colonies.

Ethnicity and Language in Britain

In academic usage, the term *ethnicity* tends to become detached from its original racial connotations, though they may still linger in such designations as "ethnic food" or "ethnic music." Race, ethnicity, and minorities remain closely connected concepts. In 1985, the Commission for Racial Equality published *Ethnic Minorities in Britain: Statistical Information on the Pattern of Settlement* (London); in 1986, the same commission published *Black Teachers, the Challenge of Increasing the Supply* (London).

In Britain, the 1948 Nationality Act established a distinction between the citizens of the United Kingdom and the colonies on the one hand and citizens of the independent Commonwealth on the other, but allowed all groups to enter Britain. The 1981 Nationality Act, which went into force in 1983, created different classes of British citizens: those resident or born in the United Kingdom before 1983 and those who lived in British protectorates or colonies. The act also abolished the long-established right of those born in British territories to British citizenship.

The post–World War II period (the 50 years since the first Nationality Act) witnessed a considerable change in the views taken concerning ethnic minorities and education in Britain (for detailed accounts, see Gardner-Chloros 1997 and Joly 1994, from which I have taken much of this passage). In the 1950s and 1960s, the prevalent view reflected the assimilation ideology; in education this meant giving priority to English and recommending that no more than 30% of a school's student body should be made up of immigrant children. From the mid-1960s on, these views were abandoned, and subsequent legislation incorporated the notions of social disadvantage and urban deprivation, applied to all the "poor." Ethnic minorities were not particularly mentioned as the beneficiaries of these measures. The recession of the 1970s hit the poorest parts of the population, especially ethnic minorities (successive riots took place in British inner cities, in 1980–1981 and again in 1985). But whereas in 1975 the Bullock Report (issued by the Department of Education and Science Committee of Inquiry) stressed that no child should have to discard the language of home on entering school, in 1985 the Swann Report (issued by the same Committee) declared that research evidence was inconclusive in this area and that mother-tongue maintenance was best achieved by the ethnic minorities themselves. Indeed, since the 1980s, new developments in policies for ethnic minorities have been largely initiated by the minorities themselves. The minorities had become organized into associations, committees, and campaigns and knew that their votes had to be taken into account, at least on a local level.

What are the present trends in the language-ethnicity issue? The answer is complex. On the one hand, the present third generation is much more integrated and more concerned with education and work than with maintaining their grandparents' language of origin. On the other hand, ethnic feelings might be easily revived precisely on the basis of general unhappiness and lack of economic intergration. These feelings, however, are now shared by young people who are not of immigrant origin.

Ethnicity and Language in France

The term *ethnie* is still not much in use in France. In their studies of stereotypes, sociolinguists of the school of Robert Lafont (of Montpellier) define two kinds of stereotypes: *sociotype* and *ethnotype*. The former applies to any social division such as white collar worker or policeman, whereas the latter refers to divisions based on physical appearance, on having the "look" of an Arab or an African (Lafont 1972). This is a scholarly description of how ethnicization develops as a result of social prejudice.

For many years, French public opinion has constantly been stirred by the presence of immigrants (statistics are utterly unreliable, but out of 57 million people living in metropolitan France, 3 million are said to be of immigrant origin). The rise of such social consciousness rests mainly on four developments.

1. Increasing unemployment has been explained by an oversimplified discourse on the presence of immigrants, who are said to be "stealing" jobs from native French citizens.
2. As a consequence of youth unemployment, groups of "idle" youngsters in the suburbs misbehave. These areas are predominantly populated by immigrants and the poorest proportion of the native population. According to the dominant stereotype, these people have lost control over their children, who are accused of bad behavior.
3. Almost permanent constitutional and legal hassling continues in Parliament over the rights of immigrants and foreigners in general. Over the past twenty years, the public has been kept aware of such discussions because political leaders have turned immigration into a major issue (for example, whether immigrants' children born in France should automatically have French citizenship or not, or whether homeowners should have

to declare the comings and goings of their immigrant visitors or tenants to the administration.

4. The consolidation of an extreme right-wing political party, whose anti-foreigner discourse is its main strategy, has been quite successful in some parts of the country where the immigration rate is high and in other parts where the population is very conservative. However, the stereotype of the immigrant is marked by physical features, not by linguistic ones.

From the point of view of the immigrant groups themselves, it is not their language behavior as such which is an important feature of identity but rather the symbolic value given to language. In a survey on proclaimed identities of young people in the suburbs of Grenoble, one young man declared: "Arabic is my language but I cannot speak it." It is a token of renewed ethnic pride. Most immigrants want integration for themselves and their children; this requires the mastery of French. They also want their chidren to know their home language and culture, but for this they have to rely mainly on themselves.

Between 1973 and 1982, the European Economic Community (EEC) scheme was implemented in France under a series of bilateral agreements with eight other governments (Portugal, 1973; Italy and Tunisia, 1974; Spain and Morocco, 1975; Yugoslavia, 1977; Turkey, 1978; and Algeria, 1982) under which instructors were hired and paid by those governments to teach immigrant children their respective official language. Through the mid-1980s, the idea that immigrants and their children would return to their home countries was shared by the public, by institutions, and by the immigrants. More recently, it came to be realized that large numbers were going to stay in France. Official policies began to shift their aim toward "integration." Satisfactory acquisition of French became the target, and maintaining language of origin became the excusive affair of the above-described EEC scheme, financed by the various states and by a large but not always cohesive network of voluntary associations (Varro 1992). On another level, the economic status of English is such that about 80% of state school pupils choose it as their first foreign language in secondary school.

Legal Difficulties in Naming
the Regional Languages

Since 1951, a series of legal measures have been taken in favor of the teaching of indigenous regional languages. These measures never became mandatory; however, indigenous languages may be taught in primary schools at the request of a sufficient number of pupils' parents, and they may be part of the school curriculum in secondary schools.

Table 22-1 shows the terms chosen to designate both the status of the languages and their proper names, arranged in chronological order. I have solved the difficulty that in French a difference exists between *langage* (any kind of language variety) and *langue* (a language embodied in some kind of institution), a difference for which English does not have distinct terms, by putting both French terms in italics.

Table 22-1. Proper Names and Status of Languages

Status of the *Langages*	Proper Names of *Langues* and Regions
1951	
Unifying term: local	
Local *langages* and dialects	
Local manner, form of speech	Breton, Basque, Catalan, *langue* Occitane
Local *langue*	Celtic *langue* and literature
Local *langues* and dialects	Basque *langue* and literature
Local *langues* and literature	Catalan *langue* and literature
1966	
Regional *langues* and regional studies	
1969	
Unifying term: regional	
The region itself	For Brittany: Celtic, Welsh, Cornish, Irish, Scotch Gaelic
Langue	
Regional *langues*	For *Pays d'Oc:* Catalan
The regional *langue*	For *Roussillon:* Occitan
Regional *langues* and cultures	For *Pays basque:* peninsular Basque
Regional civilizations	
Regional/national history	Celtic country
Regional life (considered in itself)	Basque country
Local and regional facts	Occitan-Catalan ensemble
Some interregional zones	
Regional diversity	
Cultural ensemble to which the region belongs	
The autonomous linguistic system/French	Regional French
1971	
Regional *langues* and cultures	
1974	
Local *langues* and cultures	Zone of influence of Corsican
1975	
Regional *langues* and cultures	
Local or regional cultures	
Regional *langue*: in some districts	
Regional cultures: in all districts	
1976	
New terms: national, French heritage	
Linguistic and cultural French heritage	
Region in its administrative meaning	
Local *langue*/national reality	
Local culture, local *langues* and dialects	

Table 22-1. (*continued*)

Status of the *Langages*	Proper Names of *Langues* and Regions
Regional organisms (administrative meaning) Recognized *langues*	Breton, Basque, Catalan, *langue d'Oc*, Corsican
1981	
Local *langues* and dialects	Zone of influence of Tahitian
1982	
Regional *langues* and cultures	
1983 **New term: identity**	
Regional identity	
1994 **New term: bilingual**	
Candidates for a bilingual French-regional *Langue* class (in school) *Langue* *Langues* and dialects of regional extension	Alsatian, Basque, Breton, Catalan, Corsican, Creole, Flamish, Gallo, *langue d'Cc*, Norman, Picard, *Poitevin*
1995 **New term: bilingualism**	
Bilingual education Bilingualism	

The change in terms for designating these languages is symptomatic of the re-luctance shown by the French state administration to encourage the formation of specific groups by naming them, a measure which could become a springboard for nationalistically colored ambitions (in American terms, ethnically colored ambitions). Table 22-1 shows the development from a very cautious vocabulary, around a neutral term like *local language* (1951), to a politically marked term like *regional language* in 1966 and to even more marked terms like *regional identity* (1983) and *bilingualism* (1994). Hence, the reluctance to shift from the term *local* to *regional* lasted fifteen years (from 1951 to 1966) and the reluctance to name regions lasted three more years (from 1951 to 1969). The notion of a regional iden-tity appears even later, in 1981, thirty years after the first law that introduced the teaching of regional languages. At that time, only four regional languages appeared in the text of the law: There was no reason to mention Alsatian or Corsican, as they were considered mere dialects of German and Italian, respectively, the offi-cial languages of neighboring countries. Forty years later (1994), eight more lan-guages were mentioned. Notice also that the notion of bilingual education and bilingualism (in this context, French and a regional language) appeared in a legal text as late as 1995. Securing the relative freedom to teach regional languages has taken such a long time that regional languages that were still spoken in everyday life in the early 1950s are now threatened with extinction.

From Hidden Processes to Overt Processes of Ethnicization

Ethnicization and Language: An Old Story

The language a person speaks and his/her identity as a speaker of this language are inseparable, a fact surely as old as human speech itself. *Shibboleth* is a Hebrew word used by Jephthah as a test word to distinguish the Ephraimites, who were unable to pronounce the *sh*, from the men of Gilead at the passage of the Jordan (42,000 are said to have perished; Judges 12). Many shibboleths have been known to historians ever since, and this was certainly not the first. A speaker of a language is never alone; he is a member of the group of speakers of this language. Is this group a race, a nation, an *ethnie*, a minority? The terminology depends largely on the period and on the ideology, which make it appear preferable to use certain terms and avoid others.

Ethnicization and Language: New Dimensions and New Dangers

The Case of Basque and the Basques

In recent times, the Basques of northwestern Spain (there is a small Basque pocket in southwestern France) are well known for their economic success and for their intense and seemingly successful struggle to reassert their identity, partly by reviving their language and making it a symbol of that identity (Le Page 1997). The third article of the new Spanish Constitution of 1978 recognized Catalan, Basque (or Euskara), and Galician as official languages in their respective autonomous regions and made those languages mandatory in their schools. A good deal of the revival and the development of these languages stems from their role during the Franco regime, particularly through underground language schools such as the *ikastolas* in the Basque region, which promoted Basque linguistic, cultural, and national identity.

A pseudoscience of race and of race-language correlations has cropped up recently in the context of this success. J. Bertranpetit and L. L Cavalli-Sforza (1991) have based their race-language correlation hypothesis on genetic work (the application of principal component analysis to the distribution of variation of 54 alleles of blood groups, proteins, and enzymes in 635 sample populations in the Iberian Peninsula): "the Basque identity has been ascertained in a geographical perspective and with a large number of genes. ... There are many signs that characterise the Basque area since Upper Paleolithic times: a delay in absorbing most cultural innovations and the maintenance of special cultural aspects, mainly the language, of unquestionable antiquity" (Bertranpetit and Cavalli-Sforza 1991: 57). Cavalli-Sforza (1991) proposed matching the hypothetical "family tree" of mankind, starting with its dispersal from Africa perhaps 100,000 years ago, with the historical linguists' family tree of the world's languages. As Le Page observes "he neglects the gross disparity in the period of time covered by the two trees, and also the considerable modifications which have had to be made by linguists to the concept of linguistic 'relatedness' in the light of the findings of socio-linguistics and creole language studies" (1997: 35).

The Case of Belgium: Flemish and the Flemings

In Belgium, language does not function as a symbol of national unity. In 1962–1963, linguistic legislation precisely defined linguistic territories by administratively establishing linguistic borders for the country's three languages: Dutch, German, and French (Nelde 1997). Until then, the "personality principle" was in force: French speakers, for example, who, for a complex set of reasons, were felt to be dominant, were allowed to use their first language freely in most daily situations. As a consequence, the people of Flanders felt that their language was threatened. The implementation of the new legislation took several years: Four of Belgium's seven government crises between 1979 and 1990 were triggered by language issues. By way of applying its principle of territoriality and linguistic planning, it introduced a rigorous partitioning of linguistic territories. Whereas in Switzerland this principle is mainly limited to administration and education, in Belgium it also applies to communication in the workplace: language use between employers and employees has to obey linguistic regulations in accordance with the type of territory in which it takes place. The definition of the different types of territories is quite complex (Figure 22-1). It comprises (1) two large monolingual territories, Flanders and Wallonia; (2) the bilingual territory of Brussels, the capital, an increasingly cosmopolitan city in which Dutch and French have equal linguistic rights which must be upheld, particularly in all administrative settings. As a result, the domains of education, administration and work have become organized in two unilingual networks, one for each of the two languages of the city; (3) territories that are defined as monolingual but that provide linguistic facilities for the minority. Nelde points out that since "the establishment of a strict linguistic boundary cannot perfectly take into account the minorities located on one side or the other of this boundary, Belgian linguistic policy includes protective measures for the Dutch, French, and German border minorities" (1997: 295); and (4) monolingual territories without specific rights for the native speakers. This is notably the case for the German linguistic territories in Belgian Luxemburg (near the town of Arlon/Arel) and central Old Belgium (north of the Grand Duchy). As a result, Belgium has no fewer than eight different kinds of constitutional entities, each defined by a specific language policy (see Figure 22-1).

It must be stressed that although individual multilingualism is desirable, it is not prescribed by linguistic legislation with respect to linguistic practices. This means that throughout the country separate monolingual educational and administrative institutions exist. The Belgian army has separate units for the three lan-

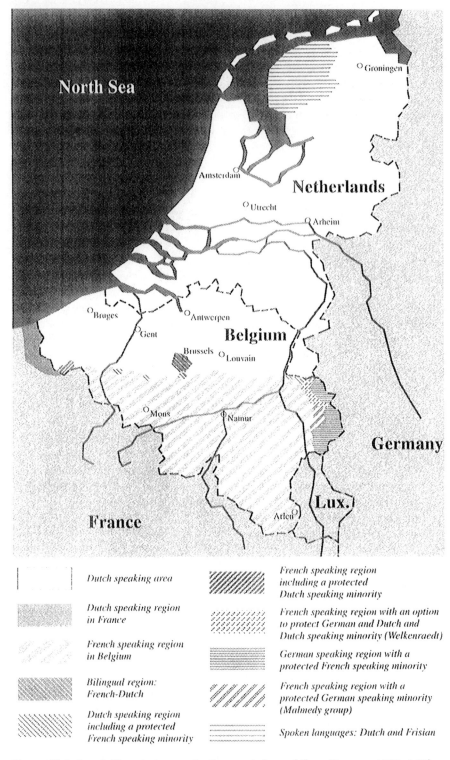

Figure 22-1 Dutch linguistic area in Europe (adapted from Deprez, 1995, 212)

guages of the country. This is an example of how a systematic application of the territoriality principle produced a kind of language jigsaw puzzle that invites some comparison with the ethnic picture of former Yugoslavia and even more with that country after the Dayton Treaty (1995). Could it be the source of new conflicts? Authors such as Nelde believe that today Belgium "owes a certain sociopolitical and economic stability to the principle of territoriality" (1997: 296). Others such as Deprez (1995) stress another negative consequence of the territoriality principle: Its application brought about a strengthening of the use of Dutch as opposed to Flemish, of the Dutch dialect generally spoken in everyday life until recently and today still spoken by the middle-aged and older generations. The speakers of Flemish developed a certain linguistic insecurity toward a linguistic center that embodied the standard but was located outside of their own political frontiers. Under the influence of school and the pressure to use Dutch in the work sector, the younger generation tends to shift from the use of their parental idiolect to a standardized form of Dutch. What is more, francophones and migrants learn school Dutch on the one hand and dialectal terms on the other, as well as a kind of in-between language which is the linguistic form of their social integration (Deprez 1995: 206). This is one consequence of the fact that the European Charter did not take into consideration the regional variations in the standard norm of a different country. The same holds true for the Alsatian dialect as opposed to standard German, which is the sole medium considered in schools.

Ethnic Revival in Western Europe

There is no need for an ethnic revival in Western Europe because the history of this century seems to be designed in such a way as to permanently revive nationalism and ethnicism. The motto, "one language, one nation," be it German, French, or any other language, can be traced well back into the nineteenth century. For two centuries, constant series of wars, some local, some reaching far out of Europe, have rested on a mixture of false and true declarations. For example, the provinces of Alsace and Lorraine, which became part of the emerging German Empire after the war of 1870–1871, had to be regained by France in the First World War. But it is also well known that the real stake was the redistribution of the colonial territories, mainly in Africa, but also elsewhere. At the end of the war, President Woodrow Wilson defended the nationality principle (one point on which Lenin agreed), the application of which, even partially, has up to now produced an endless history of war.

More generally, the building of nation-states has, with a few exceptions, been backed by monolingual "national" language policies, which meant that regional and lesser-spoken languages were ignored, if not discriminated against. The existence and survival of these languages was more a matter of nationalistic ideologies than of any "reethnicizing" discourse. The problem of this century's immigrants is different: Torn between the desire to integrate and the need to keep up features of their original identity, they have always had to struggle. But today their life is threatened by the hardships of the unyielding European context of unemployment and the resulting unhappiness and unrest in which racial harassment can be an element. In this, various markers of ethnic pride (hairstyles, dress, songs, accents, etc.) can be an anchor, but in this case language is far from being the main marker of ethnicity.

Questions for Further Thought and Discussion

1. Although Western Europe, as it is defined in this chapter, represents a small part of the world, it illustrates a more general point. Nations, states, and people have kept a series of specific features, especially where language and ethnicity are concerned, although history has interwoven their destinies. These features are influenced by historical, economic, and cultural factors. How do they interrelate? Are some more powerful then others? Why do people start killing their neighbors on grounds of ethnicity? Why do they accept the partitioning of a language into two or more languages? Who are the masters of language: speakers, politicians, sociologists, linguists?

2. Comparative studies provide further insight into the issues under discussion when we move from the West European context to a broader one. What are the differences between, for instance, Europe and the United States of America insofar as language and ethnicity are concerned? What are the causes or factors involved? Can such differences be explained?

3. A description of facts, as is attempted in this chapter, is basic. But it must not prevent us from trying to explain the facts and to define where each of us stands on the issue. What is the relative power of facts and feelings when considering language and ethnicity? Here, again, the answer points to complexity. The link between language and ethnicity may be focused here and diffuse there: diffuse where the price for social and economic integration provides enough freedom to keep up specific behavioral features, linguistic and otherwise; focused as soon as religious and nationalistic concerns become a political keynote that promises an answer to poverty and lack of freedom.

Selected Bibliography

Baggioni, Daniel (1997). *Langues et nations en Europe.* Paris: Payot (Bibliothèque scientifique).

Bertrandpetit, J., and Cavalli-Sforza, L. L. (1991). "A genetic reconstruction of the history of the population in the Iberian Peninsula," *Annals of Human Genetics* (London) 55: 51–67.

Cavalli-Sforza, L. L. (1991). "Genes, peoples, languages," *Scientific American* 72–78.

Coulmas, Florian (ed.) (1991). *A Language Policy for the European Community. Prospects and Quandaries.* Berlin: Mouton de Gruyter.

———— (ed.) (1997). *The Handbook of Sociolinguistics*. Oxford: Blackwell.

Deprez, Kas (1995). Soldats du néerlandais. In *Badume-Standard-Norme: Le double jeu de la langue*, Jean Le Dû and Yves le Berre (eds.), 189–215. Breste: Centre de Recherche Bretonne et Celtique.

Gardner-Chloros, Penelope (1997). Vernacular literacy in new minority settings in Europe. In *Vernacular Literacy: A Reevaluation*, Tabouret-Keller et al., 67–92.

Joly, Danièle (1994). Is "multiculturalism" the answer? Policies on ethnic minorities in Britain. In *Questions de minorités en Europe*, P. Grigoriou (ed.), 5–54. Brussels: Presses interuniversitaires européennes.

Lafont, Robert (1972). Deux types ethniques. In *Le Nord et le Sud. Dialectique de la France*, R. Lafont (ed.), 101–136. Toulouse: Privat.

Le Page, Robert (1997). Political and economic aspects of vernacular literacy. In Tabouret-Keller et al., 23–81.

Nelde, Peter Hans (1997). Language conflict. In *The Handbook of Sociolinguistics*, F. Coulmas (ed.), 285–300. Oxford: Blackwell.

Tabouret-Keller, Andrée (1997). Les langues régionales comme objet d'écriture dans les textes législatifs français, entre 1951 et 1995. Issue on "Etudes récentes en linguistique de contact," *Plurilingua* 20: 376–384.

Tabouret-Keller, Andrée, Robert Le Page, Penelope Gardner-Chloros, and Gabrielle Varro (eds.) (1997). *Vernacular Literacy: A Re-evaluation*, Oxford Studies in Anthropological Linguistics (Vol. 13). Oxford: Clarendon Press.

Varro, Gabrielle (1992). Les "langues immigrées" face à l'école française. *Language Problems and Language Planning* 16(2): 137–162.

AFRICA

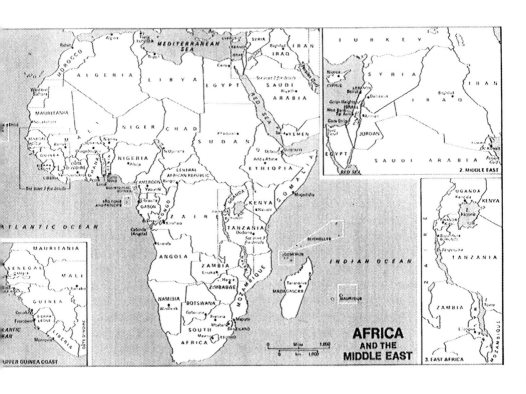

Sub-Saharan Africa

SAMUEL GYASI OBENG
EFUROSIBINA ADEGBIJA

This chapter examines the nature of the relationship between language and ethnic identity in sub-Saharan Africa. First, we examine the correlation between language and ethnic identity before colonial rule. Second, we investigate the interplay between language and ethnic identity during colonial rule. Third, we examine the period after colonial rule, paying attention to such issues as language in education, prejudices and stereotypes, language in the mass media and in religion, and how language and ethnic identity are pertinent to the important question of the selection of national languages in densely multilingual sub-Saharan African countries.

The issue of language and ethnic identity relationships provides considerable insights into the link between language and culture. Close and systematic attention to the relationship between language and ethnicity illuminates processes of cultural change and continuity (Fishman et al. 1984). Every language carries a distinct and weighty ethnic baggage.

In sub-Saharan Africa, there is a strong emotional attachment to language and ethnicity. Language is seen as the storehouse of ethnicity: Each ethnic group expresses and identifies itself by the language it speaks, and its cultural paraphernalia is shaped by its language. Sameness of language and ethnicity creates a bond of acceptance and provides a basis for togetherness, for identity, for separateness, for solidarity, and for brotherhood and kinship. It is not unusual to hear a Ghanaian, Nigerian, Ugandan, Sierra Leonian, Cameroonian, or Togolese refer to somebody as "my brother" simply because they share the same language and ethnic group background. This feeling of solidarity is much stronger when members of the same group meet one another in a strange land (e.g., in a different country or in a different part of the world, such as in Europe or North America). Such ethnically and language-conditioned friendship and solidarity is commonplace in sub-Saharan Africa. Language and ethnic enclaves are commonly created in big towns in Africa because members of the same ethnic and language group tend to flock together, like "birds of a feather." Nevertheless, language and ethnic affiliation are not necessarily always coterminous. There are people who speak a particular language but do not necessarily identify with the ethnic group that the language represents. On the other hand, there are others who love to identify with a particular ethnic group but cannot speak their language.

Language and Ethnic Identity before the Ethnic Revival

Before Colonial Rule

Africans lived predominantly in distinct ethnic and linguistic groups prior to their coming into contact with the outside world—particularly with Europeans. Thus, before the modern political map of Africa was drawn in the late nineteenth century, the various ethnic groups lived in a state of autonomy vis-à-vis each other. Each ethnic group had its own government (political and administrative institutions), its unique language, and often its unique cultural values. The various ethnic groups constituted "states," with members speaking the same language. The Akan of Ghana, for example, saw themselves as a state, and the Akan language performed a dual function—it both brought the Akan people together and set them apart from other peoples. Each African language thus acted as an instrument of self-manifestation and of intraethnic communication. Each language, in effect, constituted a binding force that linked families (nuclear and extended), lineages, clans, and the entire ethnic group together. Thus language constituted the storehouse of ethnicity, with each ethnic group expressing and identifying itself by the language it spoke.

Within the large linguistic group, individual dialects of the language, to a similar extent, led to the creation of smaller, often more cohesive, small units. Generally speaking, therefore, within ethnic groups, language acted as a symbol of the group's uniqueness, as well as of the group's cultural heritage.

In sub-Saharan Africa, it was almost impossible to talk about language without talking about ethnicity. They were intricately bound together and almost always pulled in the same direction. Language was often a passport to ethnic origin, just as ethnic background was indexical of language. Ethnic roots were usually deep and were weighty in the bestowing of favors in interpersonal relations and the according of privileges at the individual and group levels. At the group level, membership in a big language and ethnic group almost always connoted power and potential for dominance of those who belonged to smaller ethnolinguistic groups.

Ethnicity and linguistic affinity thus strengthened the groups and consolidated their walls against invasion by outsiders. Specifically, speakers of the same language who belonged to the same ethnic group had a feeling of solidarity or 'we-ness' (i.e., belonging) and therefore stuck together in times of strife and happiness. This is not to say that unity of language automatically engendered an allover unity. The Akan of Ghana, for example, fought among themselves more than they did with the other ethnic groups in Ghana.

An unfortunate sociopolitical and ethnolinguistic situation which developed from sharing a language was exclusionism. Specifically, the togetherness of the in-groups who had identical linguistic habits and ethnicity led to the exclusion of people who were linguistically and ethnically different. The exclusionism often led to various degrees of indifference and xenophobia (reinforced by ethnic prejudices), as well as shades of reaction ranging from mild amusement to indifference and, in extreme cases, to hostility toward other ethnic and linguistic groups. Such prejudices resulted in stereotypes of other ethnic groups and, on occasion, of languages. Thus, in some parts of Africa, there was an inclination to form ethnic rather than linguistic bonds (Bamgbose 1991). Despite the fact that the language of the nomadic Fulani of Nigeria and Cameroon is endangered, they have continued to exist and to identify themselves as an ethnic entity, united and different from other ethnic groups.

The immense political and economic importance of some African languages of wider communication (e.g., Douala and Fulfulde in the Cameroon, Hausa in Nigeria and Niger, Akan in Ghana and Côte d'Ivoire, Bambara in northwestern Africa, Wolof in Senegal, Sango in the Central African Republic, Lingala in the Congo, Swahili in Tanzania, Kenya, and Uganda, Zulu and Xhosa in southern Africa) meant that such languages were used beyond their original boundaries or spoken areas. With the "contact" situation, such languages of wider communication became instruments for overcoming the boundaries of ethnicity, especially for individuals who, in addition to their own languages, could function in any of the languages of wider communication. Access to the culture of speakers of the languages of wider communication was thus gained by members of other ethnic groups, who through trade, conquest, demographic submersion, and so forth, learned another language.

In view of the fact that such attributes as power, superiority, prestige, and dominance were associated with such languages of wider communication, several attitudes (favorable and unfavorable) toward the languages and the speakers of such languages developed. Such attributes as weakness and inferiority, associated with the smaller languages and the speakers of such languages, also fostered several attitudes. Speakers of small languages who felt threatened or intimidated responded with either resentment (which led to divergence from the language of wider communication and its speakers) or convergence.

During Colonial Rule

With the arrival of the European traders, explorers, missionaries, educators, colonial officers, and, in certain areas, settlers, new and larger communities made up of people of different ethnic and linguistic backgrounds were created. New political frontiers cut through ethnic groups and led to situations in which the inhabitants were torn between ethnic and linguistic allegiances and allegiance to the state. The Ewe in Ghana, for example, were torn between allegiance to Ghana and to Ewes in the neighboring state of Togo. So also the Nzema and the Brong

(Akan groups) in Ghana were torn between Ghana and other Nzema and Brong (Abron) in Côte d'Ivoire. This situation obviously led to political problems. The European languages (especially English, French, and Portuguese), as well as Arabic and major indigenous African languages such as Swahili, Hausa, and Lingala, however, transcended and still transcend ethnic barriers.

The colonialists' unwillingness to learn the languages of Africa led to the imposition of European languages as official languages. The educational policies of the colonialists, as well as the policies of their religious institutions (Christian missions), led to the propagation of foreign languages like English, French, Portuguese, and so forth and to the marginalization of the African languages. Apart from the native courts, in which the African languages were used by chiefs and other customary leaders who presided over customary litigation matters, European languages were used in the law courts. Ultimately, even local African political institutions conducted most of their deliberations in the European languages.

Boadi (1971: 49) rightly points out that another circumstance that may have led to the imposition of European languages on sub-Saharan Africans was the practical aim of establishing cohesion in political units that the colonialists had won either by conquest or treaty. The governments saw European languages as instruments of unity and of nation building. Specifically, each colonial administration thought of its language as a unifying element for the distinct ethnic and linguistic groups it had colonized and was administering. Given the fact that very few people in the colonies went to school at that time, one can also argue that if the colonial languages did unify the people at all, they could only have unified those who had formal education and were literate in those languages. In a country like Cameroon, in which two European languages—French and English—existed, the relationship between language and ethnic identity, as well as between language and national identity, was extremely visible. The dichotomy between French and English Cameroonians seems stronger than that between the local African native and national languages. The majority status of French allowed for its dominance over English, and this resulted in animosity in the domains of politics, economics, and even education (Beatrice Wamey, personal communication).

The language policy of the Germans in Tanzania can be seen as the complete opposite of that of the British, because, unlike the British, the Germans were quick to recognize the importance of Swahili, the local lingua franca, in the lives of the people and therefore encouraged its usage. What is interesting, though, is that the German policy is often criticized as being ethnocentric. Specifically, it is often asserted that the Germans' ethnocentric values prevented them from sharing knowledge of German with the Africans (see Hoben 1991 for some details).

Prior to the ethnic revival in sub-Saharan Africa and in particular during the colonial period, competence in spoken and written English was a passport to prestigious and relatively well-paid employment (Obeng 1997). English helped to promote personal careers and acted as a social status marker. In view of the tremendous prestige the European languages enjoyed before the ethnic revival, they became very popular among those with Western education, as well as among those without Western or formal education. The European languages were viewed favorably, whereas the African languages were looked down on as inferior. Even people without any formal education often mixed their local languages with a few European words to show that they were not as "illiterate" as those with Western education might think.

In most anglophone sub-Saharan African countries such as Botswana, Malawi, Ghana, and Nigeria, much prestige was attached to English before the ethnic revival, and this facilitated the consolidation of the position of English in the academic curriculum. In Ghana, for example, the Methodist mission schools, which provided education almost entirely in English, looked down on the Basel mission (now the Presbyterian Church) schools as unprogressive because of the comparatively high value the Basel mission placed on the vernaculars. In most parts of West Africa, students who spoke West African languages on the school compounds were punished. In Ghana, for example, students who spoke a Ghanaian language on a school's premises were disgraced by having a board with the inscription "I'm stupid, I spoke a vernacular on the school's premises today" placed on their chests. Other forms of punishment, including being asked to cut grass or fetch water to water the school's garden, were meted out to "offenders" against the language "policy."

The situation was worse in French-speaking African countries, because in those countries virtually no African language was taught in schools. The African languages were treated as though they did not exist. Unlike in the British colonies, in which some African languages were reduced to writing, in the francophone African countries, little attempt was made to write these languages, let alone include them in the educational curriculum. The factors mentioned above go a long way to show why the European languages remained and still remain the dominant languages in most African educational institutions.

Language and Ethnic Identity
after the Ethnic Revival

The 1960s and 1970s were marked by a blossoming of ethnic revival movements in sub-Saharan Africa. Politically, this era was marked by the struggle (peaceful as well as armed) for independence.

The ethnic revival brought with it several changes in the attitude of Africans toward the linguistic, political, socioeconomic, and cultural legacies they received from their colonial masters. In Zaire (now the Democratic Republic of Congo) and Togo, citizens with European names were forced to replace them with African names. There was also "Africanization" in the naming of some countries. Congo Kinshasa became Zaire, Gold Coast became Ghana, and Upper Volta became Burkina Faso.

Among African Catholics, Latin was replaced by African languages during Mass, as encouraged by the Vatican. In the former British colonies, a heightened awareness of African languages was evidenced by the policies on language in education and on language use in politics. In most of francophone Africa, the ethnic revival did not result in any effort beyond raising ethnic consciousness about ethnic languages.

We will now examine the correlation between language and ethnic identity in sub-Saharan Africa after the ethnic revival under six subheadings—education, politics, prejudices and stereotypes, mass media, religious life, and the selection of national languages.

Education

In most anglophone African countries, African languages were used in the first three years of primary education in the public schools. However, it was expected that they would be replaced by English from fourth grade through university level. However, in reality, the African languages were used side by side with English up to the end of elementary school. Here are some of the reasons for this state of affairs. Some teachers were not very proficient in English and therefore felt more at home with the African languages than with English. Also, most of the pupils in the upper primary grades and even in the junior high schools still had a weak command of spoken and written English. The only reasonable option left for the teachers was to teach in the African languages. In the privately owned or mission primary schools, the medium of instruction from the beginning was often a European language. In schools meant for expatriate personnel and for well-to-do Africans, the medium of instruction was solely English, because in countries like Ghana, Nigeria, and Sierra Leone, such children mainly sat for international examinations (Obeng 1997). In view of the above-mentioned problems, the ministries in charge of education in some African countries officially encouraged the use of African languages for the first six years of primary education when deemed appropriate. In Ghana, for example, language policy EP. 439/II/221 of February 1, 1971, stated, "It is now Government policy that the main Ghanaian Languages at present provided for in the curricula of primary and middle schools should be used as the medium of instruction in the first three years of the primary school and where the subject makes it possible, in the next three years as well."

In the secondary schools (particularly the junior high schools), the official language policy in most of the anglophone countries suggested that English was to be used except during African-language lessons. Even at this level, however, it was not uncommon to see teachers explain certain salient points in a Ghanaian language, since some of the teachers' competence in the English language could be called into question and the pupils or students knew very little English.

The Ile-Ife project in Nigeria is a good example of the many important achievements brought about by the ethnic revival as far as language in education was concerned. In that project, students of St. Stephen's "A" School were taught in Yoruba at various levels of their education. The students performed better both in Yoruba and in English than did their fellow students who studied only in English. Although this project was later discontinued, it created a sociolinguistic awareness among politicians and educators; for once they realized the advantage of mother-tongue education over studying in a foreign language. The Tanzanian experience, although motivated primarily by the "communalist" ideology of President Julius Nyerere rather than by ethnic revival per se, is also worth mentioning. The predominant use of Swahili as a medium of instruction at most levels of primary and some secondary schools led to massive increase in the literacy rate. In fact, it made Tanzania one of the most (if not the most) literate countries in sub-Saharan Africa.

The medium of instruction in most universities in sub-Saharan Africa even after the ethnic revival was still a European language. In Ghana, however, it was a requirement of the university that every first-year student should take a course in African studies. A Ghanaian language (other than the student's mother tongue) had to be studied. In Tanzania, Nigeria, Ghana, South Africa, Zimbabwe, and some other sub-Saharan African countries, several universities established departments of African languages and literatures. It is also worth pointing out that immediately after the ethnic revival, some African countries, including Ghana, established tertiary institutions in which only African languages were taught. In the School of Ghanaian Languages at Adjumako (Ghana), for example, six Ghanaian languages were taught in the languages themselves.

In francophone sub-Saharan African countries, however, the picture was quite different from what obtained in the anglophone countries. The colonial French policy of "total assimilation" led to the superimposition of the French language and several aspects of French culture on the peoples of the colonies (particularly the educated), even after the ethnic revival. In Côte d'Ivoire, for example, it was not until 1972 that the idea of adapting the curriculum to include indigenous languages began. Even after the discussion began, Ivoirians had to wait for five more years (until 1977) for a law—the Educational Reform Law—to be passed that brought the policy into effect (see Kwofie 1977 for details). To date, apart from Dyula, Bété, and Baoulé, most indigenous Ivoirian languages do not have established orthographies. A variety of French called *popular French* or *Francais du Treichville*[1] gained popularity at the expense of African languages after the ethnic revival. Many politicians, business people, and ordinary Ivoirians identify with this variety of French rather than with the indigenous Ivoirian languages. The Ivoirian situation was similar to what obtains in quite a number of francophone sub-Saharan African countries. In most such countries, even after the ethnic revival, French continued to be the language of work, trade, and school, whereas the indigenous African languages were reserved for use in the home, particularly in the village. In fact, as Kwofie notes, most parents insisted that their children use French even while conversing with their friends. Some parents even insisted on their children learning French prior to learning their native language, as a guarantee of a prosperous future. A number of francophone sub-Saharan Africans even identify French as their first language (Kwofie 1977). In conclusion, French (both standard French and popular French) continued to play a significant role in the lives of sub-Saharan Africans even after the ethnic revival.

Politics—The Judiciary, the Executive, and the Legislature

In most sub-Saharan African countries, European languages continued to be used at all levels of the Western-based judiciary even after the ethnic revival, although there existed interpreting facilities where necessary. However, in Tanzania, Swahili was used alongside English in the lower courts. In countries like Zimbabwe and Ghana, in which Native Authority Courts existed side by side with the Western-based courts, the Native Authority Courts used African languages.

With regard to the executive function, most sub-Saharan presidents continued to speak to their people on national radio and television in the European languages which were recognized as official languages in such countries. Only a few presidents, notably President Julius Nyerere of Tanzania and Jomo Kenyatta of Kenya, are known to have used Swahili and Kikuyu, respectively, on a few occasions. Even those who preached against Western imperialism, such as Kwame Nkrumah of Ghana, addressed their people not just in English but in complex and often difficult-to-understand English. It is a common joke in Ghana that a member of President Nkrumah's Convention People's Party is alleged to have told a politician in the opposition United Party that although Nkrumah spoke long and incomprehensible words, they preferred to listen to him than to that politician who spoke simple and easily comprehensible English. In effect, linguistic incomprehensibility was preferable and politically more suitable and acceptable. In francophone African countries, as well as in former Portuguese colonies such as Mozambique and Angola, European languages were used by the executives in addressing the people. The Organization of African Unity (OAU), an association of independent African countries, did not adopt any sub-Saharan African language. Rather, such European languages as French and English became the medium through which the association's business was conducted.

As far as the legislature is concerned, apart from Tanzania (which is known officially to have encouraged the use of Swahili), sub-Saharan African countries continued to use European languages in their parliaments, constituent assemblies, legislative assemblies, and district assemblies. In fact, use of a European language in the above-mentioned branches of government was stipulated in the constitutions of most sub-Saharan countries. In Ghana's 1969 constitution, for example, Article 71(d) stated that a Member of Parliament must be "able to speak and, unless incapacitated by blindness or other physical cause, to read the English Language with a degree of proficiency sufficient to enable him to take an active part in the proceedings of the assembly." This by implication suggests that people who were nonliterate in English were excluded from any meaningful political activities. In fact, in most sub-Saharan African countries, politicians whose level of competence in the European language (recognized as an official language and hence the language of administration) was low became the object of ridicule by their fellow politicians and sometimes even by others who were themselves nonliterate in such European languages. Although in some countries competence in a European language is no longer a requirement for active participation in high levels of government, government business continues to be done primarily in the European languages. This by implication suggests that politicians or potential politicians without communicative competence in an official European language are unofficially still excluded from holding political office.

In some countries, attempts made by some members of the legislature to pass motions on the possible use of African languages as official languages have in past met great opposition, because such motions were seen as an attempt to elevate one ethnic group above the others.[2]

Prejudices and Stereotypes

After the ethnic revival there was the feeling in some sub-Saharan African countries, particularly Ghana, Tanzania, Kenya, and the Republic of Guinea, that ethnicity was not a major problem or a hindrance to development in view of attempts by political leaders to encourage their members to put national interests over and above ethnic feelings and interests. In fact, there was even talk (particularly from Ghana's first president, Kwame Nkrumah, and the then Guinean president, Sekou Tourre) of unifying all the independent sub-Saharan African nations into one political unit (to be called the United States of Africa), along similar lines as the United States of America, and adopting an African language, possibly Swahili, as an official language. To play down ethnic feelings and to encourage Kenyan nationalism, President Jomo Kenyatta of Kenya took note of the relevance of language and culture in nationalism. In 1974, he took a decision to make Swahili the national language of Kenya. Not only did he, by his decision, preempt the growing dominance of English over the local Kenyan languages, such as Kikuyu and Luo, but he was also initiating a bond which he felt would hold the newly independent Kenyan nation together. In neighboring Tanzania, President Julius Nyerere, in an attempt to foster national unity over ethnic diversity and to bolster his African model of communism (Ujamaa or communalism as he called it), encouraged the use of Swahili at the official, national, and educational levels. Use of native African languages of wider communication in Kenya and Tanzania may have helped unify people of different ethnic origins only to a very limited extent, since local people continued to view themselves as different from those in other localities.

What these politicians failed to see was the fact that the almost irrevocable bond between language and ethnicity resulted in the development of enduring stereotypes of those who share a language and an ethnic identity. In Nigeria, for instance, some commonplace stereotypes are of the Ebiras as noisy; the Hausas as self-loving, domineering, and carefree and hating Western education; the Yorubas as gullible, unreliable, and betraying; the Idomas as promiscuous; and the Igbo as lovers of money. The situation is not different in any other African country. In Ghana, Fiscian (1972) found such stereotypical images as of the Ewe as hardworking, the Ga as aggressive, and the Asante as loyal. Amonoo (1989) notes that the scrawls and graffiti in the Balme Library copy of *Universitas* identify the Ewe as tribalistic and inward-looking, the Ga as barbarous, and the Asante as "Kalabuleic" (corrupt).

The ethnic consciousness had thus brought with it a reawakening of resentful feelings; some members of some ethnic groups thought of themselves as superior to all other peoples and hence looked down on languages other than their own and on the people who speak such languages. The ethnic revival did little to discourage resentment of members of other ethnic groups; it did little to promote interethnic understanding and friendliness beyond the official level. In most cases, some ethnic groups became associated with a large number of discriminatory, prejudicial, and stereotypical images, and people discouraged members of their ethnic groups from having anything to do with such stereotyped groups. In South Africa, for instance, owing to a sordid apartheid and racist past, ethnic and language identities are socially marked, racially sensitive, and often powerfully loaded. In spite of the official end of apartheid, ethnic and language loyalties and identities remain solid, potentially divisive, and socially rancorous. Consequently, a white person who belongs to the Afrikaner ethnic group, and who therefore speaks Afrikaans, still perceives himself as master over the black Xhosa. For the white person, identity with Afrikaans and membership in the Afrikaner racial group is emblematic of being in charge, being in control, and being naturally qualified for the best of the best in South Africa. To a very large extent, the same is true of the white English-speaking South African. For the black South African however, in spite of Nelson Mandela's presidency, belonging to an ethnic and language group that is racially black connotes possessing the identity of the oppressed, the downtrodden, the belittled, and the marginalized. Although the sociopolitical landscape is gradually beginning to change, perhaps at a snail's pace, membership in one ethnic and language group rather than another is still heavily loaded, racially sensitive, and politically charged. Although it is largely true that race is at the root of such cleavages, the fact remains that they have been perpetuated, sustained, and maintained by the distinctiveness of language and ethnic identity.

In effect, although several different ethnic groups may be "clumped" together in one polity, the sub-Saharan African situation points to the fact that there may not be a strong sense of political belonging. In countries in which little or no emphasis was put on the African languages and the intent was to "unify" the people through one or another European language, the consequences were disastrous. The continued use of the European languages created a form of dejection in the masses, who by default were excluded from participation in public activities, from the labor market, and from decisions affecting their own lives. Such people had no choice but to intensify their links with their ethnic groups, which were linguistically and culturally accommodating.

The strong ethnic feelings and hatred toward members of other ethnic groups often resulted in civil strife. In some cases, there were secessionist attempts (e.g., the case of Biafra in Nigeria) or scares (e.g., the Antor secessionist scare in Ghana in the late 1950s). In other cases, strong ethnic feelings led to "ethnic cleansing" (Rwanda and Burundi) and civil war (Liberia). Although people could, with some difficulty, live together as members of one nation, they were unable to feel as one. After all, each ethnic group had specific characteristics, such as language, food, origins, religion, and so forth, that distinguished them and set them apart from other ethnic groups. They continued to see themselves as distinct ethnic groups living together under the same broad political institution or unit. Thus, although politicization may help change ethnicity into nationalism, in sub-Saharan Africa, the situation has sometimes been slightly different. The sometimes overly strong ethnic bonds exhibited before and after the ethnic revival oftentimes threatened the unity of many a nation.

The ethnic revival and the accompanying strong ethnic feelings also brought with it political exclusionism and unique voting patterns during political elections. In most independent sub-Saharan African countries, politicians could count on the votes of members of their ethnolinguistic groups even if they (the politicians) were professionally incompetent.

Mass Media

The ethnic revival made an important contribution to language use in the mass media in general and in the fields of radio and television broadcasting in particular. In quite a number of countries, attempts were made to decentralize radio and television broadcasting through the establishment of smaller radio stations in order to broadcast in African languages. In Ghana, for example, there were radio broadcasts in such Ghanaian languages as Akan (Twi and Fante), Ewe, Ga, Dagbani, and Nzema. Other languages which were later added to the aforementioned languages in radio broadcasting are Dagare, Kusaal, and Gurenne. There was also a radio broadcast in Hausa, a Nigerian language of wider communication in northern Ghana and in the inner cities in southern Ghana. In Nigeria, the ethnic revival brought tremendous linguistic awareness. This resulted not only in the use of Nigerian languages on radio and television but also in the giving of lessons in various Nigerian languages to adults who were absolute beginners. This practice, in principle, was aimed at helping to break the numerous ethnic and cultural barriers and thereby help to resolve the prejudices, stereotypes, fears, and resentments of one ethnic group toward the other. Whether or not the desired aim was achieved is a question which there is insufficient information to answer. It ought to be pointed out, though, that this linguistic enterprise did very little to diminish the use of the English language. In fact, English continues to play an important role in the socioeconomic and political lives of Nigerians.

The ethnic revival also brought with it the establishment of newspapers in the African languages for the propagation of political, social, and religious ideas. In Ghana, for example, the Akan language paper *Nkwantabisa* was launched. The *Catholic Standard* also devoted space to such Ghanaian languages as Akan, Ewe, and Ga. In Nigeria, the Hausa language paper *Gaskiya Ta Fi Kwabo* has existed for well over a quarter of a century.

In francophone African countries, the picture was quite different, since very little emphasis was put on African languages as far as the mass media were concerned. French continued to be used extensively. In the print media, the propagation of political agendas, political education, trade, and commerce all continued to be written in French. Little attempt was made at reaching those nonliterate in French, and this obviously led to the exclusion of the mass of the people from the day-to-day information flow in their respective countries. However, both Cameroon and Niger broadcast radio programs in some local languages.

Religious Life

Another area in the lives of sub-Saharan Africans in which one could see the interplay between language and ethnic identity after the ethnic revival was religion. In the Republic of Congo, Nigeria, and Ghana, there was a high degree of "Africanization" of Christianity, and aspects of African culture, including language, began to be incorporated into Christianity. The Africanization led to the use of African languages in church sermons (including the replacement of Latin in the Catholic Mass by African languages). In some Africanized churches (e.g., the Africania Mission in Ghana), libation prayer (an act which was considered demonic before the ethnic revival) was performed in Ghanaian languages during church services.

In addition to the incorporation of African languages and cultures into Christianity, the ethnic revival helped to encourage the translation of religious literature into African languages, especially in anglophone sub-Saharan African countries. Obeng (1997) notes that in Ghana, for example, over twenty Ghanaian languages (including Akan—Akuapem, Asante and Fante—Ga, Dangme, Ewe, Nzema, Dagbani, Frafra [Gurenne], Sisala, Dagaare, and others) have been used for Bible translations. The Jehovah's Witness group began to publish its religious pamphlets *Awake* and *Watchtower* in some African languages, and the Presbyterian Church devoted some space in its monthly newspaper, *The Christian Messenger*, to Ghanaian languages like Akan, Ga, and Ewe. Similarly, in Nigeria, the Bible (especially the New Testament) has been translated into numerous local languages, and the Koran has been translated into Hausa.

However, it must be noted that most of the churches, especially those in the urban centers, continued to use European languages in their services even after the ethnic revival.

Language, Ethnic Identity, and the Selection of National Languages

A national language is the language used for national identity. It is a source of pride for citizens of a nation. It is a symbol of national identity and a mobilization and rallying point. Every bona fide national language is emblematic of the spirit of a nation and is seen as a unifying force. Fasold (1984: 77) views a national language as:

1. The emblem of national oneness and identity
2. Widely used for some everyday purposes
3. Widely and fluently spoken within the country
4. The major candidate for such a role, since there is no alternative, equally qualified language within the country
5. Acceptable as a symbol of authenticity
6. Having a link with the glorious past

Many believe that a national language should be a language indigenous to a particular nation.

In sub-Saharan Africa, generally, the issue of language and ethnic identity has made the selection of a national language a very sensitive one. Many circumstances may be responsible for this. Multilingualism and mother-tongue loyalty are attributes for which Africa is so distinctively noted. The fact that in most African countries no one major language is generally understood and loved by all is another major impediment for the selection of a national language. Many people are emotionally attached to their mother tongues and are unwilling to countenance any impression that another language is being imposed upon them, no matter the guise in which such imposition may occur. The fact that many people have a strong attachment to their language and their ethnic group origin has made it difficult for national languages to emerge. Many of the indigenous languages that should have qualified for such a role are not considered to be ethnically neutral. Instead, the ethnic partiality of most languages and the fact that they show the identity of particular language groups by their traditional ethnic association makes it difficult for languages that could symbolize national identity for sub-Saharan African countries to emerge. East African countries, such as Tanzania in particular but also Uganda and Kenya, to a lesser extent, have adopted Swahili as a national language, even though its use has been somewhat hampered by ethnolinguistic politics.

Infighting and sociopolitical rancor among major language groups have stifled the emergence of bona fide national languages that could be symbols of identity in most African countries. In Nigeria, for instance, although the constitution recognizes Hausa, Yoruba, and Igbo as coofficial with English, it is very obvious that the English language performs most official and quasi-national roles. However, being bereft of any Nigerian cultural or ethnic flavoring has made it difficult for English to effectively perform the role of a national language.

Given the strong attachment to mother tongues, it seems likely that in most sub-Saharan African countries, European languages will continue to function in the dual capacity of official languages and quasi-national languages. In fact, as Adegbija (1994) rightly points out, attitudes continue to be positively skewed in favor of European languages, even in national affairs.

The argument has sometimes been proffered in some quarters that in view of the fact that local varieties of European languages in Africa have developed, the European languages can indeed be taken to have an African aura around them and so may not be as ethnically neutral as one may think. In many anglophone countries, for instance, local varieties of English have developed. Thus one frequently hears of Ghanaian English, Nigerian English, Kenyan English, Ugandan English, Gambian English, and so forth. Each of these varieties has a distinct local vocabulary, which may not be understood in other countries. Some people have therefore argued that these European languages have become nativized and so could be used for expressing national identity. However, no matter the degree to which they have been indigenized or nativized, many Africans would still have difficulty in accepting European languages as a symbol of their identity as a nation.

An alternative suggestion that has sometimes been made as a solution to the problem of selecting a language that can serve as a symbol of national identity is that pidgin varieties of European languages should be selected as national languages in Africa, as is the case with Tok Pisin in Papua New Guinea and Bazaar Malay in Indonesia. As Bamgbose (1991: 29) argues, pidgin is an attractive candidate for national-language status because it does not suffer from the elitism associated with English. For this reason, it is considered as satisfying the requirement of "authenticity and vertical integration." The apparent neutrality of pidgin varieties has also been used to argue for their acceptance as national languages or symbols of national identity. However, the fact that a pidgin's cultural characteristics are difficult to specify makes it difficult for it to be a symbol of identity in Africa. Pidgin varieties of languages in Africa are easy to acquire, even at the grassroots level. Nevertheless, in most African countries, pidgin varieties are seen as low, unimportant languages and so have been given no place in national life. To be considered as a symbol of ethnic or national identity, pidgin varieties would have to be seen as possessing deeply native roots within Africa and would have to possess indigenous rather than imported "raw materials." It is precisely because pidgin varieties lack the "son of the soil" quality that they cannot serve as a symbol of identity. Moreover, most pidgin varieties in Africa are stigmatized, have a low status, and are associated with non-Western-educated people. Consequently, they lack prestige and cannot be the emblems of ethnonational identity, as most African languages are.

Summary

In most parts of sub-Saharan Africa, there is a considerable close connection between language and ethnicity. The sense of ethnic self is created and perpetuated by language. Ethnic and linguistic identification were at the forefront of the sociopolitical and cultural lives of sub-Saharan Africans before and immediately after the ethnic revival. This state of affairs will most likely continue as long as ethnolinguistic minorities continue to feel marginalized, belittled, suppressed, and trodden on. There is no doubt that the bond of ethnicity will continue to be created by language and vice versa.

On the whole, it might be observed that sociocultural life in sub-Saharan Africa has a predominant, hard-core ethnic and language overload that many a time overarches life and, in some instances, determines privileges, positions, achievable heights, goals, and aspirations. Willy-nilly, ethnic identity is preserved through language, and ethnicity has been one of the many tools and strategies for the assertion of superiority and the denial of, or protest against, being labeled ethnolinguistically inferior. In opposing a motion on the selection of an indigenous Ghanaian language as a national language by a member of Ghana's Second Republican Parliament, A. G. De Souza said, "Mr Speaker, language is a solemn thing. It grows out of life, out of its agonies and ecstacies, its wants and weariness. Every language is a temple in which the soul of those who speak it is enshrined" (quoted by Amonoo, 1989: 42). Amonoo quotes another member of Parliament who also opposed the motion as saying "To attempt to adopt one particular language as a national language is trying to elevate one tribal group above the others" (1989: 42). The above quotations not only show the emotional attachment people have to language and ethnicity but also show people's preparedness to oppose the imposition of one language or ethnic group over the other. Based on the close connection between language and ethnicity, we would want to agree with Solé's (1995) assertion that the language of a people is often endowed with the highest and innermost expression of their identity cores.

SUB-SAHARAN AFRICA **367**

Questions for Further Thought and Discussion

1. To what extent did the ethnic revival influence the use of African languages in sub-Saharan African educational institutions?

2. It is sometimes said that language and ethnic identity are inseparable in sub-Saharan Africa. How true is this statement?

3. Discuss the role played by African languages in the various branches of government before and after the ethnic revival.

4. If you were asked to advise a sub-Saharan African government on the selection of a national language, would you recommend an African language of wider communication or a European language? Give reasons for your choice.

5. Given the advantages of mother-tongue education, why do you think some parents in some sub-Saharan African countries still want their children to be educated in a European language?

6. "Strong attachment to one's ethnic group or one's language leads to the development of prejudices and stereotypes." Discuss the above statement.

7. Discuss any two language and ethnic identity issues in sub-Saharan Africa before and during colonial rule.

8. Did the ethnic revival play any significant role in the use of African languages in religion and in the mass media?

Notes

1. A variety of French, the phonology and syntax of which are markedly influenced by Ivoirian languages.
2. See Ghana National Assembly Debates, 1961, 25: 210–234 and Ghana Parliamentary Debates, 1971. 6(35–37): 1514–1606.

Selected Bibliography

Adegbija, Efurosibina (1994). *Language Attitudes in Sub-Saharan Africa: A Sociolinguistic Overview*. Clevedon, England: Multilingual Matters.

Amonoo, Reginald F. (1989). *Language and Nationhood: Reflections on Language Situations with Particular Reference to Ghana*. Accra: Ghana Academy of Arts and Sciences.

Bamgbose, Ayo (1991). *Language and the Nation: The Language Question in Sub-Saharan Africa*. Edinburgh: Edinburgh University Press.

Boadi, Lawrence A. (1971). Education

and the role of English in Ghana. In *English Language Series. The English Language in West Africa*, John Spencer (ed.), 49–65. London: Longman.

Fishman, Joshua A., Michael H. Gertner, Esther G. Lowy, and William G. Milán (1984). *The Rise and Fall of the Ethnic Revival: Perspectives on Language and Ethnicity.* Berlin: Mouton.

Fiscian, Charles E. (1972). The psychological bases of tribalism. *Universitas* 3:29–37.

Ghana National Assembly Debates (1961) 25: 210–234.

Ghana Parliamentary Debates (1971) 6 (35–37): 1514–1606.

Hoben, Susan J. (1991). *Language Use and Literacy: Lessons from Eastern Africa.* (Working Paper No. 101). Boston: Boston University.

Kwofie, Emmanuel N. (1977). *Le Langue Francaise en Afrique Occidentale Francophone.* Québec: Centre Internationale de Recherche sur le Bilingualisme.

Obeng, Samuel G. (1997). An analysis of the linguistic situation in Ghana. *African Languages and Cultures* 10(1): 63–81.

Sole, Yolanda R. (1995). Language, nationalism and ethnicity in the Americas. *International Journal of the Sociology of Language* 116: 111–137.

Afro-Asian Rural Border Areas

TOPE OMONIYI

Rural communities are often treated as completely distinct entities from urban ones. The inhabitants of both community types are presumed to have stereotypical characteristics that contrast almost perfectly. For instance, rural life is simple, whereas urban life is complex; rural environments lack the infrastructure that adorn urban spaces; rural folks lack the sophistication of urban folks; crime is a reality of urban life, but it is supposedly almost totally absent in rural areas. The contrasts can go on and on. However, in reality, some rural communities have an urban dimension to them, and the social context thus set up becomes unconventionally complex. Rural towns and villages that have international boundaries running through them exemplify such communities.

Naturally, notions of identity will differ between rural and international domains. On the surface, rural identity seems to be anchored primarily to ethnicity, whereas border identity, like urban identity, may be debatably described as primarily anchored to nationality. The relationships and differences between these identities and language have not been sufficiently addressed by researchers, especially with regard to African borderlands. Although this concern engages our interest in this essay, the focus is more general than particular in nature.

Several variables may be used in identifying individuals and groups in society. Some of these include region, social class, gender, language, race, ethnicity, and nationality. It is possible, for instance, to distinguish southerners from midwesterners, middle class from working class people, male from female, African American from Native American, and so on, based on cultural and behavioral characteristics such as speech, occupation, dress mode, and attitudes. Each of these variables can form a barrier and delimit membership, but some variables are less definitive than others are, and their distinctive capacity may vary with context and location. Some of these social distinctions are less obvious in the cities and more elaborate in the rural areas. My objective in this chapter is to determine the implications of rurality and boundaries for language and ethnicity and to draw

attention to the relative importance of language, ethnicity, and nationality in defining people's identity in nonmainstream communities such as borderlands and
rural areas.

Because societies differ one from another, language and ethnicity often vary
in their relevance to people's identity. By this I mean that ethnicity may be considered the most important identity by the citizens of Country A, whereas in
Country B it may be nationality that is so considered. Similarly, border, rural
and hinterland communities are differently structured and thus constitute different contexts of identity. The part of a country in which a community is located may become a significant factor in determining the link between identity
and language, ethnicity and nationality. To make our examination of these relationships less cumbersome, the discussion is organized into four sections which
examine the impact of colonialism, religion, education, and economy, respectively, on the relationship between language, ethnicity, and identity in relation
to rural communities across international boundaries. I draw on findings from
my studies of Idiroko-Igolo (Nigeria-Benin) in 1991–1992 and of Woodlands/
Johor Bahru (Singapore-Malaysia) between 1996–1997, as well as on available
information in the literature pertaining to the United States-Mexico border
(Hidalgo 1986) and other border areas of the world. Before continuing, however,
it is necessary to explain or define the operative words *ethnicity*, *nationality*,
and *rural borderlands*.

Understanding Ethnicity and Nationality

Both of these terms are subject to some degree of change in consonance with human
development, and quite a bit of controversy surrounds their usage. For convenience, the terms will be examined separately and without intricate debate. However, we must be careful not to suggest that they are completely separate and independent entities. They are interconnected in many ways. Some schools of
thought regard nationality as a more modern identity, a progression from ethnicity
(Fishman et. al. 1984) and the distinction between the developed and developing
worlds. This position has been criticized as Eurocentric and imperialistic by some.

Ethnicity

In popular culture, the term *ethnic* is used to describe fashion items of an exotic
nature that express the culture and tradition of particular peoples and places, often
non-Western and "premodern." It is sometimes used interchangeably with "racial"
in politics. The complex and transitory nature of ethnicity underlies the problem
of proffering a definition. Ethnicity is the embodiment of race, religion, language,
politics, and occupation shared by a group of people which distinguishes them
from other groups. All members of an ethnic group are paternally linked, thus
setting up a system of patrimony (Marshall 1994, Fishman 1989). Ethnicity may
in addition be considered a spatially located social and cultural entity as suggested,
albeit derogatorily sometimes, by such media references as "mountain tribes,"

"swamp dwellers," and "creek folks." The appropriateness or inappropriateness of these definitions is not centrally relevant to us now. However, our examination of the impact of colonialism, religion, and so forth on identity will improve our understanding of the concept.

Nationality

Nationality describes an identity that links people to a home country. Following Anderson's (1983) definition of nations as "imagined communities" confined by territorial boundaries, nationality may be defined as a mental identity shared by people who reside within the same statutorily defined territory. It is thus a more political term than ethnicity in the sense that membership in the latter is not earned by legal treaty but by blood. Nationality is the identity that is indicated on travel documents such as passports and visas, which people are expected to carry when they cross international boundaries.

Nationality may change if people leave their home country permanently to settle in another country. For example, National Basketball Association star Hakeem Olajuwon of the Houston Rockets became a citizen of the United States by emigration and naturalization in 1994 after leaving his former home country, Nigeria. He remains ethnically Yoruba with reference to his status as an immigrant and "former Nigerian," but he is classified racially as African American in the United States. The same process applies to many other people around the world who have changed nationality by adopting a new home country.

It is obvious from this that nationality changes in a different manner than does ethnicity. Nationality may change due to relocation, but ethnicity changes in a slightly different way. Ethnic mixing may alter the texture of ethnicity in the long run, but it may not affect nationality. The intensity of nationality and ethnicity as alternative or complementary identities varies from place to place, and the discussion in the following sections corroborate this claim with reference to border communities.

Rural Borders and Marginal Communities

It is generally accepted that rural areas often suffer neglect in development planning relative to the urban centers. This factor is responsible for the rising rates of rural-urban drift around the world. In colonial times, the same factor implied that the impact of colonial administration was felt less in the rural than in the urban areas. The alien cultural and political values that accompanied colonization were more apparent in the cities, whereas indigenous cultures and languages were preserved in the villages and small towns. National identity remains an abstract concept to some inhabitants of very remote rural settlements even to this day. Metaphorically speaking, these people exist on the margins of the national community, and to them, the ethnic group is paramount.

Border communities are located on the margins of nations, and their inhabitants' share of economic and political power indicates their marginality. In this sense, borderland is synonymous with rurality. The more ambitious among border inhabitants have a tendency to set up businesses or seek employment in the city and visit home during vacations and festival seasons. However, borderlands may not be completely synonymous with traditional rural communities. The sensitive nature of international boundaries and the need to safeguard national integrity together necessitate the deployment of military and paramilitary personnel to the border, thus to some extent reducing remoteness from the center.

Because different social and cultural contexts have different impact on language and ethnicity, differences between models of border situations may have interesting consequences. Strassoldo (1989: 389) identified three models of border situations. They include the nation-building model, the coexistence model, and the integration model. In the first model, divergent paths of development nurture different loyalties, languages, and values and lead to intercommunity tensions and conflicts. He associated this model with 'nation-states of more recent origin' like Singapore-Malaysia and Nigeria-Benin. The coexistence model exemplified by the United States-Mexico border permits regulated cross-border interaction. A bilateral relationship exists between the two governments. The integration model ultimately erases boundaries through merging that follows extensive mutual interpenetration. This is the situation in communities along post-Maastricht European Union borders. In this model, border communities have the potential to "develop into the core area of new civilizations." It is obvious how these three may affect language, ethnicity, and identity differently. For example, the integration model can better support cultural continuity than the nation-building model.

Almost matching Strassoldo's models are Momoh's (1989) zero, minimum, and maximum borderland models, and they similarly affect language and ethnicity. Obviously, border monitoring will influence the relationship between communities separated by boundaries and determine the continuity or otherwise of language, ethnicity, and nationality. The nation-building models, or zero borderlands, impose nationality on ethnicity and treat cross-border interaction as an act of sabotage to some political cause.

Ideological differences between countries that are separated by a boundary correlate with the amount of cross-border traffic and interaction. The higher the volume of traffic and sustained interaction, the closer the systems. In turn, these affect the texture and continuity of ethnicity. Interestingly, the Malay in Johor Bahru (Malaysian border town) speak more English than their compatriots in more mainland areas like Kuala Lumpur, the Malaysian capital, and are thus closer to the Malay of Singapore in language behavior. This is in opposition to the Idiroko-Igolo situation in which the Yoruba minority in Igolo converges toward the Yoruba majority in Idiroko.

There is an inherent potential for conflict of identities if the administrations emphasize division while the rural community proclaims its homogeneity as an ethnic group. However, border inhabitants are aware of the implications of multiple identities and different social contexts. They base their choices on the perceived "benefit" of a particular identity in a particular situation. Their preferences are reflected in language attitudes and behavior. For instance, foregrounding border identity reduces their distance from the power base and, consequently, their marginality index when they are negotiating in the public domain. However, this may on occasion place them outside the network of communal obligations, goods, and services. Knowing which to choose, when, and where is what I describe as understanding the politics of identity in rural and border communities that bestride international boundaries.

Colonialism

Before colonialism, kingdoms such as Zulu, Shona, Yoruba, Berber, Hausa, Igbo, and Fante stretched across Africa's political landscape as mostly monolingual ethnic polities. Kingdoms and languages commonly shared the same names because the former evolved from organized aggregates of speakers of particular languages. However, when the continent was partitioned in the nineteenth century, the political structure of component states ceased to be based on ethnicity. The partitioning was more or less arbitrarily done (Asiwaju 1990), the consequence of which is the multiethnicity and multilingualism visible in many countries today.

But what is the relevance of colonialism to a discussion of identity, language, and ethnicity? The link is quite apparent. Parts of Europe, Africa, North and South America, Australia, and Asia have all been "colonized" at one time or another. However, the consequences of colonization in the twentieth century have attained a greater dimension than they ever did at any other time in history. The presence of Spanish, English, and French languages and cultures in places outside of Europe attests to this fact. Essentially, colonization weakened the previously strong language-ethnicity relationship and created the contact situations in which people have to make language choices and learn two or more languages and in which language change can occur through coexistence. The different varieties of English identified as non-native English (Kachru 1992) have resulted directly or indirectly from colonialism, and they reflect the alteration to the genetic character of ethnic groups in the societies in which they sprung up.

Colonization created the special "ethnic" identity "British subject," whose political anchorage was to the British Empire. This identity was largely regarded as a bureaucratic identity, especially among rural Africans who kept the colonialists outside the indigenous social networks, a situation found in several of Chinua Achebe's novels. In some sense, colonialism is also one of the determinants of the directions of international migration and therefore of the nature of new immigrant and diasporic identities. Citizens of former French colonies more easily head for France, and those from former British colonies set out for Britain and other English-speaking countries. It should be noted that international migration, other than that which is a consequence of natural disasters, is not part of rural culture, and so the "new" immigrant identities do not derive from rural communities. By implication, modifications to ethnicity that result from migration are arguably urban-induced.

The French policy of assimilation in the colonies sought to "Frenchify" Africans, and therefore indigenous cultures were extensively replaced, as is evident in people's names, food culture, and language use in Benin Republic and other francophone nations in sub-Saharan Africa. This is the concept of negritude in postcolonial literature. Today, there are children of elite families in Nigeria who have been brought up as monolinguals in English. This is a consequence of colonialism, as well as of postcolonial language policies that continue to promote the hegemony of English. In rural areas, the use of English is, relatively speaking, restricted to the education domain, unlike in the urban areas in which such use is pervasive, with English playing the role of a lingua franca among ethnically diverse populations.

At the level of empire, the competition was squarely between colonial authorities such as Britain and France. Evidence that the competition still rages is to be found in the activities of the Commonwealth of Britain and La Francophonie, its French counterpart. The indigenous populations were natives of colonized territories by statute even though, as the former claim, the boundaries only separated the English and the French. There are indications, however, that the decades of colonization took their toll on African societies in several ways besides political restructuring.

Religion

Religion is considered to be a strong component of people's identity, and ethnic groups identify with particular religious practices. In precolonial Africa, fraternities developed around several traditional deities, including Sango, Ogun, Okun, and Osa. For a long time after the arrival of Christianity, these practices continued, and they still remain among pockets of people in rural parts of the continent. Even where Christianity or Islam has displaced traditional religions, cross-border ethnic bonding is still apparent in the religious sphere. For instance, Christian and Muslim society memberships in Idiroko-Igolo defy the boundary. Mutual participation in the celebration of traditional annual religious festivals has also been observed. Thus to some extent religion helps to preserve ethnic groups, cultures, and traditions.

Evidence of the link between language and ethnicity abounds in religious expression, too. For instance, traditionally people's names are quite often linked to religious myths and beliefs, as illustrated by the Yoruba names Ogunsanya (the God of Iron rewards my suffering), Oshunbiyi (the Goddess of the Sea created this child), and Opalana (the Divine Staff of creation provides opportunities). These names may not be common at christenings any more, but they still constitute the majority of surnames among the Yoruba due to the group's paternity-patrimony culture, which means that family names are passed down (cf. Fishman 1989). This explains the similarity in religious practice and names between the Yoruba of southwestern Nigeria and Brazilians of African descent. The latter's ancestors were shipped out from West Africa as slaves to the cane plantations of South America in the sixteenth and seventeenth centuries. Conversely, religious practices distinguish the Yoruba from the Igbo or Hausa ethnic groups. The modes of worship and the deities worshiped are different. The question to ask then is, Does religion mark nationality in the same way as it does ethnicity?

Both Islam and Christianity have become part of the political culture in some countries. Malaysia and Ireland illustrate this point. Most of the citizens of these two nations are born into Islam and Catholicism, respectively, and the constitutions and government policies of the countries are strongly influenced by religious doctrine. As a matter of fact, religion almost becomes the basis of ethnic differentiation, as is the case between Protestants and Catholics in the Northern Ireland conflict and between Malays, Chinese, and Indians in Malaysia.

Are these observations the same for both urban and rural border areas? The situation differs from one border context to another, depending on the type of border in question. Idiroko-Igolo on the Nigeria-Benin boundary is different from the Woodlands-Johor Bahru border communities on the Singapore-Malaysia boundary in a number of ways. In Singapore and Malaysia, there is a high degree of correlation between ethnicity and religion, thus ethnic groups are easily stereotyped based on religious practice. Most of the Malay people, irrespective of the side of border they live in, are Muslims, and the majority of the Chinese are Taoists, Buddhists, or Christians. This kind of correlation is nonexistent in Nigeria and Benin because of the secular policies of the governments.

The language policy of the Malaysian government has promoted Malay over English for decades, whereas in Singapore, the government has promoted English over the indigenous languages as a step toward racial or ethnic harmonization. English is a colonial inheritance in both border communities, but its status varies, and so does the effect on ethnic and national identity. Although I am not aware of any hard evidence, it is possible that the dialects of Malay diverge as a result of the difference in the linguistic geography and language politics of both countries. In such a situation as this, border communities are unlikely to diverge at urban rates. Attempts to standardize Malay on a supraregional level will check such a development and homogenize the ethnic group.

Furthermore, links between religion, language, and ethnicity are evident in the changes that Christianity and Islam have imposed on societal values. I elaborate on this in the part section, which discusses the impact of education on language and ethnicity. Suffice it to say that names from the Bible and the Koran are now considered more appropriate than those linked to the old Yoruba deities. With this change, the pragmatic and semantic properties of the cultural contexts of naming have also changed.

Education

Education as it is known in large parts of Africa and Asia today may be described as a colonial legacy. Consequently, it has the same general effects on identity, language, and ethnicity as did colonialism and to a partial extent religion. Most of the earliest formal schools were established and run either by Christian or Islamic missionaries; the former worked closely with the colonial office. However, the specific applicability of the observations raised in the preceding sections is tempered by the nature of the borderland and rural area in point.

The existence of integration/maximum or coexistence/minimum borderland models (see the previous discussion) allows border inhabitants to choose between the education policies of the two contiguous states. In Idiroko-Igolo, I found that large numbers of children crossed the border daily to attend English-medium primary and secondary schools in Idiroko, thus narrowing the social and cultural distance between them and their kinsfolk across the border. The situation in the Woodlands-Johor Bahru communities is similar to the extent that several Malaysians are enrolled, especially Chinese Malaysians, who have a minority status in Malaysia but enjoy majority status in Singapore.

Functional and affective reasons may be adduced for this pattern. It may be an indication of people's desire for paternal association across the border, in which case it is affective. On the other hand, it could be the result of a pragmatic consideration of the potentials of the chosen medium of education. When respondents in the Idiroko-Igolo study were hypothetically empowered to select a language for the role of medium of instruction, the Igolo respondents preferred the indigenous language or English to French, even though the latter had been the medium of their own education. A majority of the Idiroko respondents preferred the official educational policy and chose English.

Whereas Singapore's education policy describes English as first language and the indigenous languages Mandarin, Tamil, and Malay as Second Languages, Malay is the national, official, and first language of Malaysia. Theoretically speaking, the implication of this is that Chinese Singaporeans require competence in English and have little or no need for Malay, whereas Malaysian Chinese require competence in Malay and may not need a knowledge of English if they are limited to a local network of association within Malaysia. The texture of Chinese ethnicity thus differs based on what side of the border they reside in. In reality, however, as a result of the greater economic success of Singapore in the region, there is evidence of slight convergence toward Singaporean language behavior patterns among Johor Bahru youths, irrespective of ethnicity.

The direction of convergence in conventional sociolinguistic literature is toward the mainstream—"mainstream" implying the empowered majority group. The attitude tests administered in my Idiroko-Igolo study corroborated this claim. The respondents from Igolo (Benin) displayed greater positive attitudes toward the indigenous languages than their Idiroko (Nigeria) counterparts did. Of course, the main Yoruba ethnic base is in Nigeria. Automatically, there is an implication that ethnic identity is preferred to national identity. Actual language use, however, showed that Igolo respondents used the former colonial languages more often and sometimes in domains that are traditionally regarded as domestic and conventionally set aside for indigenous languages. This is similar to De Marchi's conclusion from his study of the Friuli-Venetia Julia border:

> Language use and linguistic attitudes are indeed two separate dimensions, not always parallel, and sometimes contradictory. Although a connection undoubtedly exists between the two, the latter cannot be taken as a valid predictor of the former. Indeed, diffused preference for a local variety, interest for its maintenance, favour for its tutelage etc. do not necessarily correspond to widespread use. (1982; 204)

This is especially true of the relationship that exists between the attitudes of members of minority groups toward the dominant languages of their environment and the frequency of their use of these languages. I already explained that my finding in Idiroko-Igolo is a possible consequence of the policy of assimilation that the French colonial administration pursued in its African colonies.

In comparison, the situation in Woodlands-Johor Bahru is that Malay convergence toward Singapore language behavior is actually a divergence from the Malay mainstream behavior in Malaysia. This is the basis for suggesting that an economic consideration may be responsible. As a result of this, it becomes debatable whether Chinese convergence is genuinely an escape from minority status in Malaysia or a preference for the economic opportunities that Singapore promises.

Another issue of interest is the role that education plays in language development. Western education has displaced preexisting education systems and affected language and ethnicity by influencing indigenous social organization. For example, people's recognition of and obligation to the extended family as a social unit in African societies are being transferred to the individual and the nuclear family. In this regard, border and rural inhabitants are different from urban dwellers in keeping school and home separate and giving to Caesar what is Caesar's. The social values that Western education imparts are treated more as theoretical principles and confined to the school environment. This makes it possible to visualize some kind of split-identity complex in which people possess and display two different sets of social attitudes and behavior: one reserved for the home and the other for the school. In the cities, these values are more likely to be integrated, and therefore rural Yoruba may become distinct from urban Yoruba even in language behavior. For instance, I observed in Idiroko and Igolo that in informal interaction contexts, some public servants spoke the more "respectable" and "urban" Eko (Lagos) dialect of Yoruba as a marker of elitism, modernity, and "class" in contrast to the local inhabitants, who spoke the Anago dialect. Bidialectalism is a probable consequence of such a situation, and subsequently a speech community with a complex link between language and ethnicity may develop.

Let us consider another illustration from the Singapore-Malaysia border. In terms of population and diplomatic clout and in spite of economic supremacy, Singapore remains a minority state within the Southeast Asian political framework. Malay, which is the main language of Malaysia, Indonesia, and Brunei, is the most widely spoken language in the region. This situation grants the minority Malay in Singapore some respite and reduces the need to forcibly learn Mandarin Chinese, which is the language of 70% of the national population of 3 million. Malay bilingualism is therefore mostly characterized by the attainment of competence in English and Malay. Chinese bilingualism in Malaysia in contrast involves competence in Chinese and Malay. The reality is that many Malaysian Chinese borderland inhabitants are trilingual in Chinese, Malay and English due to considerations of residency in Malaysia and proximity to Singapore.

As I explained in the preceding discussion, the location of rural African communities outside the centers of action compared to urban communities is of great relevance to language, ethnicity, and identity. One obvious characteristic of rurality is the relative absence of multiethnicity. This is not to suggest total rural homogeneity, however. Nonindigenous settlers are welcomed, hosted, and gradually assimilated over several generations. In this circumstance, language and culture contact is not as intensive as in the urban area. The implication of this is that there is little or no need for the majority of the rural population to acquire bilingual skills. The urban contact situation creates competition among languages, and the complex demands of urban life dictate the character of individual and societal bilingualism. Consequently, the ethnic character of these two settings will vary slightly, with the chance that ethnic identity is broader in the urban community.

However, traditional rural communities differ from rural communities across international boundaries. The population of settlers in the latter is often more diverse, both in terms of source and sociocultural category. By this I mean that whereas the border community may attract people from different regions and different social groups, rural villages are less diverse.

The primary purpose for migrating to a border town may be to seek, explore, and exploit the secondary and "international" context of the boundary rather than the primary context of the country's local rural community. Government officials attached to the army, police, and immigration, customs, and excise departments can be classified as such. In a way, they have a potential to have an impact on the ethnic character of the indigenous population over time. For instance, the use of English among the rural population may grow as a result of constant interaction with people in the public domain whose employment requires that they use the language in defined contexts. In contrast, people who are attracted to a rural border community by its primary qualities are open to assimilation and are less likely to affect ethnicity. This was the case among Igbo motor-vehicle spare-part dealers and Hausa traders and transporters who have settled in Idiroko and Igolo.

Economy

Rural economies around the world are different from those economies that are linked to Wall Street and the stock exchange. They are often agriculture-based and mainly subsistent. The relevance of this distinction to our discussion of language, ethnicity, and identity lies in the fact that stock exchange economies are expressed in the powerful languages of the World Bank and the United Nations, such as English and French. The only languages of subsistence agriculture in Africa are the indigenous languages. However, in borderlands like Idiroko-Igolo, the nature of the economy is tempered by the presence of the Nigeria-Benin international boundary. A sizable proportion of the population is involved in smuggling and currency laundering, both of which are features of urbanism and internationalism. In this sense, rural and international cultures become interconnected, and this has a potential to influence society's values and consequently alter ethnicity, especially if this alternative economy is a booming one.

Closely related to this point is the problem of immigration that arises when the economies of the contiguous states are as sharply contrasted as those of the United States and the Mexican economies. The United States–Mexico border is the only border that separates a first world economy from a third world economy, and quite naturally, the perceived promise of an improved quality of life is a strong temptation for Mexicans to emigrate to the United States. The relevant point here is that the notions and passions of ethnic and national identities in the United States are different from those in Mexico.

Mazrui (1973: 67) assessed the English language as being "emotionally more neutral than French," which, in fact, according to him, made it "less of a hindrance to the emergence of national consciousness in British Africa." The same comparison may be extended to Spanish, which is the official and main language of Mexico. This emotional neutrality may have been beneficial to the survival and rejuvenation of indigenous traditions and values and, consequently, of primary ethnic group identity. In spite of this observation, the ethnic characteristics of immigrants to the United States from Mexico who settle into minority Mexicano communities are altered as they absorb America and are assimilated into mainstream American culture. Not even sustained contact between immigrants and their kinsmen across the border to whom they may regularly send fractions of the "American Dream" can prevent this from happening. It may, however, prolong the process of change.

Although a similar but less sharp contrast exists between the economies of Nigeria-Benin and Singapore-Malaysia, the ethnic compositions of these contiguous nations are different, and so too is the impact of immigration on ethnicity. In contrast, the boundary between North and South Korea separates people of the same ethnicity, but, as I pointed out earlier, the ideological difference between the two has created a nation-building or zero borderland. That is, there is no private domain interaction, in spite of the fact that blood relatives are split by the boundary. The choice of capitalism and democracy by South Korea in contrast to the communism of the North explains the emergence of the former as an "Asian Tiger" economy. This is closely associated with the embrace of Western ways of life and the presence of Korean-English bilingualism throughout South Korea. These are bound to affect the ethnic character of South Korean citizens and distinguish them from their North Korean kinsmen. These examples show that there is a link between economy, politics, and notions of ethnicity.

Summary

A number of conclusions about the relationship between language, ethnicity, rural communities, and international boundaries can be reached from the foregoing discussion. Border/rural communities set up different contexts of social interaction and identity from those of urban and hinterland communities. Border communities may not necessarily be as simple and remote as the rural stereotype in the literature depicts. Boundaries may or may not affect the relationship between language and ethnicity, depending on the nature of the "divide." Factors such as colonialism, religion, education, and economy mediate these relationships.

Although observations from specific studies of language-ethnicity relationships may be generalized, certain characteristics may be peculiar to a border community or ethnic group and may therefore limit the extent to which generalization can be reasonably done. Partitioned ethnic groups may reflect a convergence toward their ethnic core through language attitudes, language use, and other social behavior patterns. The exception to the rule may result from pragmatic considerations of the potential benefits of divergence. These benefits are usually of an economic or political nature. Finally, the inhabitants of rural communities across international boundaries appropriately manipulate their linguistic resources either to strengthen or to weaken their ethnic affiliation in line with the social contexts in which they are operating at any point in time.

Questions for Further Thought and Discussion

1. Is there a concept of ethnicity in the United States? If so, how does language help to distinguish it from race and nationality? How might this be different from language and nationality in other parts of the world?

2. In what ways is the rural United States likely to present a different context for the examination of language and ethnicity from the United States–Mexico border communities? Are there similar examples elsewhere in the world?

3. How can the relationship between language and ethnicity be of assistance to the management of border communities and the promotion of bilateral relations?

4. To what extent is the emerging global culture a threat to ethnic identity in different parts of the world? Why is there likely to be a variation in the intensity of such threats between regions?

5. In the first part of this chapter, some other social variables for identity were listed. Are there ways in which some of these may be linked to language and ethnicity? For example, sex/gender relationships may distinguish one ethnic group from another. Can you substantiate this with illustrations from your readings?

Selected Bibliography

Anderson, B. (1983). *Imagined Communities*. London: Verso

Asiwaju, Anthony I. (ed.) (1984). *Partitioned Africans: Ethnic Relations across Africa's International Boundaries, 1884–1984*. London: Hurst.

Asiwaju, Anthony I. (1990). *Artificial Boundaries*. Civiletis International.

De Marchi, B. (1982). A sociology of language research in Friuli-Venetia Julia, a multilingual border area. In *Boundaries and Minorities in Western Europe*, B. De Marchi and A. M. Boileau (eds.), 183–210. Milan: Franco Angeli Editore.

Fishman, Joshua A. (1989). *Language and Ethnicity in Minority Sociolinguistic Perspective*. Clevedon, England: Multilingual Matters.

Fishman, Joshua A., Michael H. Gertner, Esther G. Lowy, and William G. Milan (1984). *The Rise and Fall of the Ethnic Revival: Perspectives on Language and Ethnicity*. Berlin: Mouton.

Hidalgo, Margarita (1986). Language contact, language loyalty, and language prejudice on the Mexican border. *Language in Society* 15: 193–220.

Kachru, Braj (1992). *The Other Tongue: English across Cultures* (2nd ed.). Urbana: University of Illinois Press.

Marshall, Gordon (ed.) (1994). *The Concise Oxford Dictionary of Sociology*. Oxford: Oxford University Press.

Mazrui, A. (1973). The English language and the origins of African nationalism. In *Varieties of Present-day English*, R. Bailey and J. Robinson (eds.), 56–70. New York: Macmillan.

Momoh, C. S. (1989). A critique of borderland theories. In *Borderlands in Africa: A Multidisciplinary and Comparative Focus on Nigeria and West Africa*, A. Asiwaju and P. O. Adeniyi (eds.), 51–61. Lagos: University of Lagos.

Strassoldo, Raimondo (1989). Border studies: The state of the art. In *Borderlands in Africa: A Multidisciplinary and Comparative Focus onNigeria and West Africa*, Anthony A.Asiwaju and Peter Adeniyi (eds.), 383– 395. Lagos: University of Lagos Press.

The Arab World
(Maghreb and Near East)

MOHA ENNAJI

This chapter deals with the relationship between language and ethnic identity set against the historical and linguistic background of the Arab world. It looks at the changes that have occurred there in the domain of language and ethnicity since the 1960s and presents the reasons for this change. The extent to which the languages and varieties used in the Arab context are affected by the worldwide ethnic revival are examined. The chapter attempts to shed light on the Arab world, focusing particularly on the area of northern Africa called the Maghreb (Algeria, Morocco, Tunisia, and Mauritania), which is both Arab and Muslim.

Before I discuss the issue of language and ethnic identity, it is necessary to define some concepts such as nation and ethnic group on the one hand and nationalism and nationism on the other.

There is no clear-cut distinction between the ideas of *nation*, *state*, and *country*; they are all used to refer to political forms characterized by unity and independence, whereas *ethnic group* refers to a community which may be politically and socioeconomically dependent on a dominant group. The term *nationalism* refers to the movement for political and socioeconomic independence, and *nationism* indicates efforts focused on establishing a modern and efficient administration. For more details on this distinction, see Fishman (1968, 1971, 1977).

Language and Ethnic Identity

The topic of language and ethnicity is a controversial one. Two fundamental trends in scholarship exist. The first denies any direct or necessary link between language and ethnic identity, claiming that the relation between language and identity is accidental. Appel and Muysken (1987:15) think that race, political affiliation, and social class are more important factors in the determination of ethnicity. The second trend stresses that language is the vehicle of ethnic identity, the essential criterion, along with cultural heritage, assumptions, values, and beliefs. According to Fishman (1977), language and ethnic identity are intimately related as long as the members of a linguistic community hold a positive attitude toward their own ethnic group.

According to the second view, language has often been a criterion by which we define or determine ethnicity. Each ethnic group associates with a language, and, conversely, a language is a means of identifying an ethnic group. For example, a person who does not speak the language of a group or country is considered to be an alien because he or she does not belong to that speech community. Going back to ancient history, we note that the Greeks used the term "barbarous" to refer to anyone who did not speak Greek. Arabs used the words *Al £arab* (Arabs) and *al £ajam* (foreigners) to distinguish Arabic from non-Arabic speakers or nationals. In Morocco, Berbers use the words *Imazighen* (Berbers) and *agnawn* (non-Berbers) to refer to speakers and nonspeakers of Tamazight (Berber).

In the past, it was easy to differentiate Arabs from Berbers in the Maghreb because each community or group spoke only its own language; there were very few Arabic-Berber bilinguals. Today, most Berbers are bilingual (they also speak Arabic) because of social mobility, intermarriages, and socioeconomic interactions. Race, political affiliation, and social class are not so crucial as language in determining ethnic groups in the Maghreb; it is impossible to distinguish a Berber from an Arab on the basis of race. Furthermore, Berbers belong to various political parties and social classes, just as do Arabs. The sociocultural context does not help one to accurately distinguish one ethnic group from the other. In fact, many Arabic-speaking tribes were Berberized, and many Berber ones were Arabized over the centuries. The linguistic factor is, nonetheless, an important ingredient in the formation of an ethnic group. It is possible to state, therefore, that Berber speakers form an ethnic group in their own right, since non-Berbers very rarely speak Berber (cf. Ennaji 1991, 1997; Boukous 1995; Sadiqi 1997).

An ethnic group may, then, be defined as a group of people who share the same language, culture, history, religion, and values. Each ethnic group adopts a certain language and lifestyle to distinguish itself from other ethnic groups.

In the Maghreb, there are two major ethnic groups, Arabic speakers and Berber speakers. Historically, the latter were the first inhabitants of the Maghreb, whereas the former came from the Arabian Peninsula in the eighth century and brought with them the Arabic language and Islam. Because classical Arabic is associated with Islam and has a great literary tradition, it has been proclaimed the official language throughout the Arab world.

Historical and Linguistic Background

Historical Background

The Arab world was colonized by different European powers in the nineteenth and twentieth centuries. More precisely, the Maghreb countries, Lebanon, and Syria were colonized by France, whereas Egypt, Iraq, Jordan, Kuwait, Sudan, Yemen, and the United Arab Emirates were colonized by Great Britain and Libya by Italy.

After these countries achieved independence from the Western powers in the 1950s and the 1960s, various changes occurred on the linguistic and cultural levels—namely, the ethnic revival and the revitalization of the Arabic language and Islamic culture.

During the colonial period, the British and Italian colonizers in the Middle East and, especially, the French in the Maghreb made great efforts to dissociate the Arab societies from their languages and cultures. In the Maghreb, the French endeavored to divide the region into ethnic groups to facilitate the colonization process. This act was not arbitrarily implemented; rather, it was carefully planned, because the colonizers were aware of the strong ethnic feelings in the Arab world as a whole. As a case in point, in Morocco, the French passed the segregatory law known as the "Berber Decree" (*le dahir berbère*) in 1930. This decision was, however, strongly criticized by Berberophone and Arabophone scholars, political leaders, and ordinary people, all of whom opted for loyalty to their language and culture, national identity, and territorial integrity. For example, the leader of the National Popular Movement Party, Mahjoubi Aherdan, who is well known in Morocco for his struggle for the revival of Berber, has never been against Arabization nor for the separation of the Berber and Arab ethnic groups in Morocco.

Linguistic Background

The Arab world, and particularly the Maghreb, are characterized by multilingualism in the sense that many languages and varieties are used in different domains, namely, classical Arabic, standard Arabic, the regional varieties of spoken Arabic, Kurdish, Berber, English, French, Spanish, and Italian. The sociolinguistic situation in the Arab world differs from one country to another depending on the different varieties of spoken Arabic in use, the different colonial languages adopted, and the existing indigenous ethnic groups. The multilingual dimension of the Arab world has a direct impact on ethnicity and cultural life in this region of the world and brings about sociocultural problems that must not be overlooked in language planning and in education.

The most salient sociolinguistic feature of the Arab world is the emergence of a triglossic situation in which at least three Arabic varieties can be distinguished: classical Arabic, standard Arabic, and dialectal Arabic (cf. Ennaji 1991).

Classical Arabic is the language of Islam, which is the vehicle of a great literary tradition and enjoys immense prestige among the Arabo-Islamic population. Classical Arabic is a sacred language because it is the language in which the Muslim holy book, the Qur'an, was revealed and because it is a written code, unlike the dialects. It was used by the nationalist movements during the colonial era, together with religion, to rekindle feelings of nationalism and Arab patriotism in the fight for independence.

Like classical Arabic, standard Arabic is a written variety of Arabic that has no native speakers. Classical and standard Arabic are both learned at school only, as they are not spoken languages. Standard Arabic is both codified and standardized; the policy of Arabization has led to its modernization and to its use both as the lingua franca of the Arab world and as a vehicle of modern culture. It is made wide use of in education, administration, and the media. The expansion of free education in the Arab world has led to the spread of standard Arabic and to favorable attitudes toward it.

Dialectal (or spoken) Arabic is the most important mother tongue in the Arab world. Unlike classical and standard Arabic, dialectal Arabic is not written but spoken. It is generally acquired by Arabs as a native language and learned as a second language by non-Arabs such as Berbers in the Maghreb and Kurds in the Middle East. Dialectal Arabic can be divided into several regional varieties: Egyptian Arabic, Lebanese Arabic, Palestinian Arabic, Syrian Arabic, Iraqi Arabic, Saudi Arabic, Sudanese Arabic, Moroccan Arabic, Algerian Arabic, and so forth, each of which can be further subdivided into rural and urban dialects. These regional dialects are often intelligible to speakers of other dialects unless they are geographically distant from each other. For instance, a Syrian Arabic speaker can easily communicate with a Lebanese or a Palestinian Arabic speaker but cannot do so with a Mauritanian Arabic speaker. All across the Arab world, dialectal Arabic is usually stigmatized and treated as a corrupt form of Arabic (cf. Ennaji 1991).

The other major mother tongues spoken in the Arab world are Berber in the Maghreb and Kurdish in Iraq. These mother tongues are minority languages. They are looked upon as debased "dialects," essentially because they are uncodified and nonstandardized, have no religious connotations, and belong to ethnic minorities in the region.

Of the foreign languages in use in the Arab world, it is worth mentioning English, French, Spanish, and Italian. English is used as a second language in the Middle Eastern Arab countries that were previously colonized by Great Britain. It is widespread in education, international trade, and diplomacy. In the Maghreb, English has the status of a foreign language; it is widely taught in high schools and universities. It is indeed the most popular foreign language in the Maghreb because it has no colonial overtones in the region.

French is also widely used as a second language in the Maghreb and in Lebanon. Despite its being a colonial language, it is still prestigious, particularly in Morocco, Algeria, Tunisia, and Lebanon. Its chief domains of use are education, administration, government, media, and the private sector. It is employed to achieve efficiency, wider communication, and socioeconomic development.

Spanish and Italian are used to a lesser extent in Morocco and Libya, respectively. Spanish is especially popular in northern and southern Morocco. Both languages are taught as optional foreign languages in the above-mentioned countries.

Now I turn to the various changes that have occurred with respect to languages and ethnicity in the Arab world.

Changes Regarding Language and Ethnic Identity

The most prominent change that has occurred during the last generation is the implementation of the Arabization policy with the aim of revitalizing and modernizing standard Arabic. The overall goal is to generalize the use of standard Arabic to all domains as a language of wider communication, replacing English and French, which are considered by conservatives to be a threat to the linguistic and cultural identity of the region.

The process of Arabization was meant to modernize and standardize this language in order to meet the needs of the modern Arab states. It also aimed to replace English and French in many fields, particularly in education and mass media. Given the connection between standard Arabic, Islam, and national identity, Arabization may be considered to be a revival of the Arabic language and ethnicity in the societies concerned.

There are two types of Arabization: corpus and ethnic Arabization. The first is concerned with renovating and modernizing standard Arabic by introducing and coining new words; the second focuses on the spread of standard Arabic in all walks of life. It aims to assimilate non-Arab groups into the Arab society by helping them to learn Arabic and to adopt the Arab culture.

One of the purposes of Arabization is the assimilation of the minority ethnic groups, namely Berber and Kurdish, into Arab cultural identity. The result of this policy is the decline of these minority languages.

The unfair dichotomy between written (learned) languages—that is, classical Arabic, standard Arabic, English, and French—on the one hand, and dialectal Arabic, Berber, and Kurdish on the other—is sharpened by the policy of Arabization, whose aim is to introduce standard Arabic in all fields of activity as the symbol of cultural independence. Unlike in India, for instance, dialectal Arabic, Berber, and Kurdish are not given even the status of regional languages (see Fishman 1971). In the Maghreb, for example, policy makers did not take into account the great number of Berbers (45% of the population of Morocco, 25% of the Algerian population, and 1% of the Tunisian population). Because of this unnatural situation, Berber cultural demands have increased with the aim of doing justice to the Berber language and culture.

In the Maghreb, for instance, one major change is the evolution of the status of standard Arabic and Berber. The process of Arabization led to the modernization and revitalization of standard Arabic. The official recognition of Berber as part of the national heritage and cultural authenticity and the project of teaching it in Moroccan primary schools are good examples of the process of "ethnic revival." This revival is due mainly to the fact that both standard Arabic and Berber play a strong symbolic role in the national identity of the Maghreb and that both languages are somewhat threatened by foreign languages, chiefly French.

The attempts to revitalize Berber are motivated by the fact that Berber is the native language of about one-third of the Maghrebian population. This language has been in regression under the influence of French, standard Arabic, and Moroccan Arabic. As a means of alleviating this threat, Berber has recently been officially recognized as part and parcel of the national cultural identity. As a result of this move, authorities plan to introduce Berber into schools and have increased the number of hours allotted to it in the radio programs. Berber has also been introduced in television, particularly for news broadcasting. As a consequence of the revival of Berber, the number of Berber cultural movements and associations have multiplied (more than 20 exist in Morocco and about 100 throughout the world). Their objective is to codify and standardize the Berber language, revitalize its culture and literature, and sensitize people and governments to the cultural value of Berber as part of the national legacy.

Language Attitudes

The ethnic revival affected the attitudes of people toward languages and varieties before it affected the functions and domains of use of these languages and varieties.

Arab and Maghrebian people are generally proud of their mother tongues and national languages. Although attitudes toward the different mother tongues and languages have changed among the people, these attitudes have to a certain extent been ignored by Arab governments and decision makers. For instance, Arabization has still succeeded only partially after four decades of independence and struggle for the restoration of Arabic language and culture. The mother tongues, notably dialectal Arabic, Berber, and Kurdish, are neither codified nor standardized.

In the Maghreb, classical and standard Arabic are venerated by the population, as they have religious ramifications and symbolize national unity and Arab nationalism and solidarity. Berber and dialectal Arabic are considered means of communication only in intimate contexts and transactions, but they have become symbols of identity and authenticity nationwide and in intergroup relations.

The ethnic revival in the Arab world and in the Maghreb is shown through the process of Arabization, which has been implemented under the patronage of the Arab League since the 1960s.

At the academic level, conservative thinkers and purists who are mostly educated in Arabic claim the necessity to reinforce Arab nationalism and establish Arab unity, the purpose of which is to revive Arabo-Islamic values and beliefs and to gradually exclude the former colonial language and culture and Western values more generally. Aljabri (1995) and Almandjra (1996) are among the enthusiastic Arab academics who support Arab ethnicity.

Popular Thinking

At the popular level, good values are associated with the Arabo-Islamic culture. People wrongly associate Islamic beliefs with Arab ethnicity. They are unaware that there exist Christian Arabic-speaking populations in the Middle East (Lebanon, Syria, Egypt, Sudan, Iraq, etc.), as well as non-Arab Muslim populations such as the Berbers in the Maghreb, the Kurds in the Middle East, and the Pakistanis and Malaysians, for instance.

For many Berberophones, language maintenance is the only means to preserve and perpetuate their culture and system of beliefs. Others think that Berber is not really marginalized and that therefore it is a false problem. Berber-language activists argue that it is not sufficient just to undertake academic research on Berber. It is their aim to see their language restored and revitalized through its introduction into the school system and through its use in formal and informal settings. At any rate, the mother tongue must be revived and transmitted from generation to generation. Berber activists reject the idea of Berber becoming a memory language and fight to turn it into a language of active use and everyday communication.

For some conservative Arabophones, however, the promotion of Berber may be a danger to national unity and political stability. These views are by no means objective, as they are not based on any scientific research or reflection. They are, indeed, purely received ideas which aim to maintain a sociocultural status quo (cf. Ennaji 1997). For this reason, Muslim fundamentalists and other Arab purists think that only Arabic can guarantee economic progress and sociocultural development for the Arab world (see Boukous 1995). Nationalists, on the other hand, argue that only a pro-Arabic strategy will help to consolidate the political independence of the Arab countries and guarantee the Arabs their cultural dignity.

Scholars' View

Scholars and officials hold favorable attitudes to the Arabic language as it is associated with Islam. Classical Arabic is also considered the language of the "End of All Days" (*lughat al-hisab*). That is why it is highly venerated and respected. This attachment to Arabic is rather emotional and has nothing to do with the intrinsic superiority of Arabic.

According to Almandjra (1996), the Arab world cannot achieve socioeconomic development unless it attains linguistic and cultural independence. He argues that language loyalty and cultural identity are prerequisites for economic progress. The Arab world cannot reach total independence from the West unless it preserves and develops its own cultural heritage and authenticity. For Almandjra, the Westernization of the Arab world will only reinforce socioeconomic and cultural dependence; progress and modernization can be reached only if Arabs and Muslims hold positive attitudes toward their own language and identity. For him, development does not necessarily imply Westernization; development can be attained through the promotion of the Arabo-Islamic cultural identity.

From this perspective, progress can be achieved by the construction of an Arab identity, not through the Westernization of the Arab world. In other words, the gateway to development and progress is the adoption of the Arabo-Islamic system of values and beliefs, not the Western one; otherwise, the result will be the strengthening of sociocultural alienation (or acculturation) and loss of cultural identity. However, Almandjra (1996) recognizes that cultural independence is more difficult to achieve than economic independence and that it will take generations before it can be realized.

Total Arabization is strongly supported by religious groups and fundamentalists across the Arab world. Abdelaziz Benabdallah, former director of the permanent office of Arabization in the Arab world, highlighted the invaluable role of classical and standard Arabic in an interview that appeared in the Moroccan daily *Le Matin* of Sunday, November 2, 1997. He stated that "cette langue a certes un grand avenir qui contribuera à remonter le vrai visage de l'Islam," meaning that the Arabic language will contribute to showing the real face of Arabo-Islamic identity, one far from the image of fanaticism.

Furthermore, most scholars in the Arab world support bilingualism or mastery of foreign languages in addition to Arabic. The eminent Moroccan lexicographer, Lakhdar Ghazal (former director of the Institute of Arabization in Rabat, Morocco), argues that if Arabization is a duty, bilingualism is a necessity insofar as it serves the enrichment of standard Arabic. For him, Arabization is not only a technical problem but also a political and ideological matter. To succeed, it must be implemented gradually by revitalizing and modernizing the lexicon and structure of standard Arabic. This can only be achieved by constantly referring to English and French and borrowing concepts and terminology from those languages.

Nonetheless, the right-wing and conservative elite are for complete Arabization and the marginalization of dialects or mother tongues (cf. Aljabri 1995). Progressive and modern scholars advocate bilingualism and the revival of mother tongues (cf. Boukous 1995 and Ennaji 1997 and the references cited therein).

The situation in the Maghreb is somewhat different. The existence of two native languages, Arabic and Berber, reduces the enthusiasm for Arab unity and nationalism. Arabic is the majority language in the Maghreb, and Berber belongs to the minority speech community.

Thus the Arab world today experiences two sorts of ethnic revival: the revival of the Arabic language and Arabo-Islamic culture and the attempts to promote mother tongues such as Berber and Kurdish, which themselves are associated with ethnic minorities. The supporters of Berber language and culture claim that it is necessary to recognize Berber as a national official language side by side with Arabic (cf. Ennaji 1997).

The Effects of the Ethnic Revival on Languages in the Region

There is no doubt that ethnicity has a great impact on language attitudes and on language choice and use. The stronger the feelings of belonging to a certain group, the stronger the desire to promote the language of this group. Indeed, the "ethnic revival" has affected mother tongues, classical and standard Arabic, and the foreign languages in use. In Egypt, for example, educated people mix standard and dialectal Arabic; some writers, such as the Nobel Prize winner Najib Mahfoud, tend to use the mother tongue in their writings because it truly reveals the authentic aspects of their daily life and cultural identity.

The foreign languages are also subject to the influence of the ethnic variable. For instance, in Algeria, there is a call for using Arabic rather than French because the latter has colonial connotations. In Morocco, there is the puristic and conservative criticism of the use of French in education and media (see Ennaji, 1991). This criticism is justified by the fact that the nationalists prefer Arabic, which directly reflects the cultural roots of the population and mirrors their values, beliefs, and assumptions. Similarly, Berber has received much attention in recent years; Berber movements have increased in number, and there are attempts to revive the language through its codification, standardization, and introduction into the school system.

Arabization is the most noticeable change that indicates an "ethnic revival" since independence. It is mainly a political issue on which politicians and decision makers base their discourse. Right-wing political parties advocate total Arabization at the expense of mother tongues; however, total Arabization is difficult to achieve due to the specificities of every country. The relative success of Arabization has two major consequences: (1) it has contributed to the initiation of cultural decolonization in the Maghreb and the Arab world, and (2) it has led to the marginalization of the mother tongues—notably Berber, Kurdish, and dialectal Arabic.

The Arabization process has resulted in the promotion of modern standard Arabic, a variety that is used in government and all local administrative affairs. The standardization and modernization of standard Arabic were implemented to achieve a certain national identity. For this reason, Arabic has been modernized in that new terms have been coined and translation loans from other languages, chiefly English and French, are used (cf. Ennaji 1991, Boukous 1995, among others). The Arabization endeavors have led to the standardization and modernization of Arabic terminology all over the Arab world. Classical and standard Arabic have regained a prestigious status in that people in the Arab countries have become aware of the importance of Arabic as a means of unifying their struggle against colonialism and cultural imperialism and their efforts for socioeconomic development.

The Arabization policy was initially implemented by the authorities to attain national unity and political legitimacy; however, this policy has in a sense led to the birth and growth of the Islamic fundamentalist movement in the whole region. Thus the Arabization policy has in a way been turned against the public authorities, as it is exploited today in many Arab countries as a tool in the fight for power.

Arabization is still a controversial subject in the Maghreb. Total agreement on this policy has still not been achieved. Arabization is viewed differently by the government, the nationalists, and the Muslim fundamentalists. The government considers Arabization a means of preserving cultural identity, power legitimacy, and national unity. Nationalists see Arabization as a means of fighting for social justice and cultural independence. The use of standard Arabic at all levels of education may give lower-class children a better chance in public education and in social mobility. The fundamentalists see Arabization as essential in preserving and consolidating Islamic cultural identity, given that classical and standard Arabic are viewed as symbols of Islamic beliefs and precepts. They advocate total Arabization and the eradication of dialects and foreign languages. Only classical Arabic, they believe, should be reinforced because it is the language of Allah (God) (see Almandjra 1996).

Despite four decades of Arabization, French is still used in the Maghreb in education and administration and in the private sector. The efforts to Arabize the educational system have not fully succeeded for six main reasons.

1. Triglossia is an obstacle to Arabization. Besides being multilingual, the Arab and Maghreb societies are also triglossic—high and low varieties of Arabic coexist and influence each other. The high varieties (classical and

standard Arabic) are prestigious and standardized, whereas the low variety (dialectal Arabic) is considered debased. People are strongly attached to the high varieties for religious and cultural reasons, and they are naturally attached to the low variety (dialectal Arabic) because it is used daily and is the vehicle of popular thinking, beliefs, and values.

2. A lack of consistency and agreement exists among decision makers. The government position has been ambivalent: Arabization is total in primary and secondary schools but only partial in higher education. There seems to be no plan to Arabize higher education as yet. There are also contradictory attitudes toward Arabizing the different levels of administration.

3. The modern elite hold negative attitudes toward the idea of total Arabization and the way it has been politically used and implemented rather than toward Arabic itself.

4. Teachers are not sufficiently trained to teach in standard Arabic, which leads to their lack of competence in this language. Because many science teachers can barely read or write classical and standard Arabic, they often resort to dialectal Arabic in their classes.

5. French is still widely used in the private sector, in higher education, and in the ministries of finance, commerce, industry, transportation, and so forth. The most important socioeconomic professions and activities are not yet Arabized.

6. Standard Arabic-French bilingualism is still very strong and popular in the Maghreb, particularly in Morocco and Tunisia. This situation reinforces the dominance of French.

Another result of ethnic revival is that mother tongues are given much attention. There is even a tendency to codify and standardize unwritten languages such as Berber and dialectal Arabic. There are serious attempts to codify Berber in Morocco and Algeria. Egyptian, Lebanese, and Moroccan Arabic may undergo codification in the near future so that they may be used in folk literature and in the press. Mother tongues are no longer seen as debased, at least among educated people.

The revival of local dialects has been motivated by the fact that they are the symbols of the uniqueness of every Arabic country; each Arab country is proud of its own spoken variety of Arabic (see Ennaji 1991 and 1997 and the references cited therein). Mother tongues in general have become a symbol of the authenticity and identity of the population concerned. Globally, attitudes have changed in favor of mother tongues. In Morocco, for example, a few folk newspapers are written in Moroccan Arabic, namely, *suq al-akhbar* and *al-usbu' ad-daahik*.

As a lingua franca in Morocco and Algeria, dialectal Arabic has become a deep-rooted code in the minds of many Berberophones. They sometimes express their beliefs and feelings through it. Dialectal Arabic is used by both Arabophones and Berberophones as a means of expression of affective and cognitive experiences.

What applies to Berber in North Africa applies to Kurdish in Iraq. Generally, Arab people think of Berber and Kurdish as varieties which have a very limited range of functions in such specific domains as home, the street, work, and the market. These varieties have a low status and are not taught in schools. Nonetheless, Berbers and Kurds regard their languages as symbols of their identities and believe that they ought to be codified, standardized, and modernized in order to be useful in formal and informal situations.

Attitudes toward Berber have changed favorably since the royal speech of August 1994, when His Majesty King Hassan II of Morocco announced that Berber would be taught in primary schools in the future. Popular thinking and views about Berber have in general become favorable (see Ennaji 1997), and Berber academics and associations in both Algeria and Morocco are working on means to codify and unify their language.

The media reinforce the revival of interest in Berber. Moroccan and Algerian television recently began to transmit news in Berber as a sign of recognition of Berber as a national language variety. The number of broadcasting hours in Berber has been increased, and the number of newspapers and magazines in Berber is growing. *Tifawt*, *Tasafut*, and *Tifinagh* are cases in point.

On a scholarly level, university students and scholars enrich these mother tongues and national languages by their invaluable inquiries despite the absence of government funds to upgrade such research. The publications on Berber language and culture are flourishing. Many studies have been published on Berber in Arabic, French, Spanish, and English by Maghrebian academics (cf. Boukous 1995 and Ennaji 1997, among others).

On the other hand, foreign languages are still regarded as the languages of science and technology. However, although they are utilized as means of development and modernization, they have become less prestigious than they were a generation ago. In Morocco, for example, French has started to slowly give way to English (cf. Sadiqi 1991). There are two main reasons for this development: first, people see French as the language of the colonizer, and second, English is the first international language. At any rate, these European languages are not as predominant in education and administration as they were in the 1960s. Nevertheless, standard Arabic-French/English bilingualism is encouraged throughout the Arab world to achieve efficiency in international communication.

Reasons for the Changes

Different factors have contributed to the changes regarding language and identity in the Arab world. The struggle against colonialism has led to the "unification" of Arab countries through the enhancement of standard Arabic as the official language and the symbol of Arab patriotism.

The socioeconomic changes that took place after independence have affected the people's perception of how languages can be used. It is believed that Arabic in this respect should be developed to meet the needs of modern life. To keep pace with industrialized Western countries, foreign languages, namely English and French, are used as auxiliary languages. They are no longer seen chiefly as the languages of the colonizers but as means of communicating with developed countries for the purpose of acquiring new knowledge in science and technology.

Colonial languages have lost much of their importance especially in the Middle East, where most activities in administration, education, and government are now carried out in Arabic. In the Maghreb (particularly Morocco and Tunisia), the situation is different, because the ruling elite, the intelligentsia, and even the masses still hold a favorable attitude toward French. The majority of the population in this region think that standard Arabic-French bilingualism should be retained, as it is necessary for the development of the Maghreb (cf. Ennaji 1991).

The Arab world and the Maghreb are examples of how language shift and language maintenance are involved in the attainment of efficiency and international communication and in the promotion of the national languages and cultures. Language shift is attested when a language community decides to introduce a new language that may be practical and helpful for solving language (or ethnic) problems or for achieving progress and development. The Maghreb has adopted French as a second language for the sake of socioeconomic development and openness to the world, whereas the Middle East countries have chosen English as a second language for the same reasons.

Language maintenance exists when a speech community considers its language the best medium to serve in all formal and informal situations. The community concerned tries to preserve this language and generalize its use. Attempts are made to extend its functions and domains of use. This is the case with the revitalization and modernization of classical and standard Arabic sought by the proponents of the Arabization policy. The same process is under way concerning the maintenance of Berber through codification and standardization.

Summary

From the perspective of Arab and Maghrebian life and thought, language and ethnic identity are intimately related. The ethnic revival has led to a change in popular and scholarly thinking. It has brought about the rise of Arabo-Islamic culture and the rejection of the Western lifestyle. This is reflected in the growing emergence of Islamic fundamentalism and thought. Sociolinguistically, the ethnic revival has affected use of the mother tongues, classical and standard Arabic, and the foreign languages. The mother tongues, namely dialectal Arabic, Berber, and Kurdish, are now considered symbols of ethnic identity, intergroup relations, and cultural authenticity, as they reflect the typical cultural aspects of the region. Attempts are being made by scholars and cultural associations to codify, standardize, and promote these mother tongues to the level of recognized regional languages.

The Arabization policy has contributed to the strengthening of the positions of classical and standard Arabic and to the increase of Arab nationalism and ethnic identity. Standard Arabic has been modernized to the extent that it can be used all over the Arab world as a language of wider communication capable of meeting the needs of the modern Arab states and societies.

I, for one, think that language planning in the Arab world ought to be reconsidered, taking into account the multilingual situation and language attitudes in the region. An adequate policy must seek to attain three main objectives: (1) to further develop and spread standard Arabic; (2) to promote the mother tongues to the level of regional languages; and (3) to reinforce the teaching of foreign languages such as English, French, Spanish, and German. The first two objectives can achieve national unity and preserve cultural identity, whereas the third will contribute to establishing efficiency, modernity, and international communication.

Questions for Further Thought and Discussion

1. What are the languages used in the Middle Eastern Arab countries? Discuss the status of each language.

2. What languages are in contact in the Maghreb? Discuss the status of each language.

3. What are the most important mother tongues in the Arab world? In what way are they related to Arabic?

4. What are the main signs of ethnic revival in the Arab world? Discuss.

5. What are the main objectives of the Arabization policy in the Arab world? What are the hurdles that block Arabization in the Maghreb?

6. Discuss the different attitudes toward Arabization in the Arab world.

7. Discuss the role of Arab nationalism in the ethnic revival.

8. Discuss the domains of use of classical and standard Arabic. Why are they more prestigious than the mother tongues?

Selected Bibliography

Aljabri, M. A. (1995). *The Question of Identity* (in Arabic). Beirut: Publications of the Center for Arab Unity Studies.

Almandjra, M. (1996). *La Décolonisation Culturelle*. Marrakesh: Walili.

Appel, R., and P. Muysken (1987). *Language Contact and Bilingualism*. London: Arnold.

Boukous, A. (1995). *Société, Langues et Cultures au Maroc*. Rabat: Publications of the Faculty of Letters, Rabat.

Ennaji, M. (ed.) (1997). Berber Sociolinguistics. Special issue. *International Journal of the Sociology of Language* 123.

Ennaji, M. (ed.) (1995). Sociolinguistics in Morocco. Special issue. *International Journal of the Sociology of Language* 112.

Ennaji, M. (ed.) (1991). Sociolinguistics of the Maghreb. Special issue. *International Journal of the Sociology of Language* 87.

Ennaji, M. (1988). Language planning in Morocco and changes in Arabic. In *International Journal of the Sociology of Language* 74: 9–39.

Fishman, J. A. (1968). Nationality, nationalism and nation-nationism. In *Language Problems of Developing Nations*, J. A. Fishman et al. (eds.), 39–51. New York: Wiley.

Fishman, J. A. (1971). National languages and languages of wider communication. In *Language Use and Social Change*, W. H. Whiteley (ed.), 27–56. Oxford: Oxford University Press.

Fishman, J. A. (1977). Language and ethnicity in intergroup relations. In *Language and Ethnicity in Intergroup Relations*, H. Giles (ed.), 16–53. London: Academic Press.

Sadiqi, F. (1997). The place of Berber in Morocco. *International Journal of the Sociology of Language* 123: 7–21.

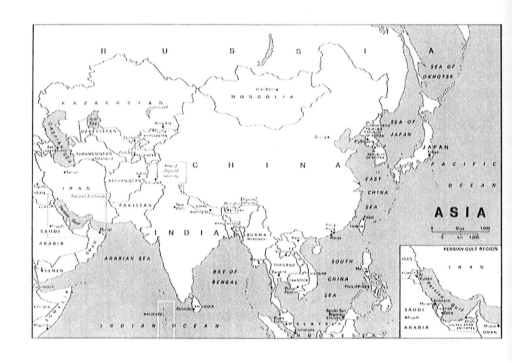

ASIA & THE PACIFIC

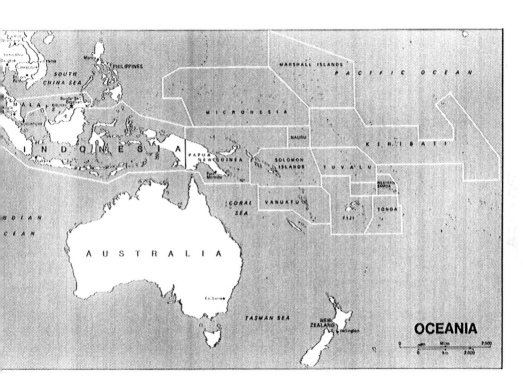

The Far East

FLORIAN COULMAS

The Far East has been defined as the domain of chopsticks and Chinese characters. The latter part of this rather loose definition is relevant to present purposes, for writing plays a major role in the linguistic culture all over East Asia. Popular notions of language strongly depend on writing to the extent that writing is often confused with language. Writing is at the core of Far Eastern cultures and dominates popular conceptions of language that regard the spoken word as an imperfect rendition of an ideal written norm. Such an attitude reflects the great emphasis put on education and the systematic study of written language. Although a variety of writing systems now exist in the countries of East Asia, the Chinese script, together with the classical Chinese written language, has spread throughout the region and thus become an essential part of the cultural heritage that unites the peoples who live between Singapore in the west and Japan in the east. Writing is critical in the development of bureaucratic states, and as a means of expressing government authority it ranks high in terms of binding loyalties. The long and deep-rooted tradition of classical Chinese literacy has furthermore softened the impact of European colonialism, limiting the hegemonic effects of cultural contact. In one way or another, Chinese writing has affected the complex structures of linguistic identities in East Asia. Although its functional importance has been reduced significantly in various areas in the course of this century, sentimental attachment to this tradition is still strong.

It must be noted that although Chinese was from antiquity until the nineteenth century the dominant written language of East Asia, it has always coexisted with local languages such as Vietnamese, Korean, and Japanese, which were reduced to writing much later than Chinese. These and other languages of the region were heavily influenced by Chinese but never in danger of being supplanted by it. The Chinese tradition, then, must be seen as an overarching reference plane of East Asian identity. Ethnic and national identities are tied to these languages, and although they have been overshadowed traditionally by the great prestige of Chinese, they have become a major focus of national identity. These languages in turn are the dominant but not exclusive languages of their respective states. A multitude of smaller speech communities exist in East Asia, interacting in various ways with the dominant groups by which they are accommodated, ignored, or repressed, as the case may be. This chapter will focus on the three major speech communities of East Asia: the Chinese, the Japanese, and the Korean.

China

Chinese is often cited as the language with the largest speech community in the world, a community which coincides to a very high degree with China's population. There are over 50 million Chinese scattered throughout the world, and China itself is home to fifty-five recognized indigenous nationalities that use more than ninety different languages. However, both of these groups are small in comparison with China's immense population of some 1.2 billion. More than 93% of these are Han Chinese, *Han* being the proper term that refers to the Chinese as an ethnic group. Although there is a certain distinction between northern and southern Han, the Chinese as a people are highly homogeneous and stable, settling in the Chinese homeland for thousands of years with little immigration.

Chinese Dialects

The Han speak Chinese, but this does not mean that they all speak the same language. How best to characterize the internal variation of Chinese is a matter of considerable controversy. Although it is common to speak of Chinese dialects, this term is somewhat misleading, dialect distinctions being more pronounced in the Chinese context than they are in Western languages. Some scholars have likened the Chinese language to the Romance language family. In this view, Chinese dialects correspond to separate languages such as Italian, French, Portuguese, Spanish, and so forth. However, it must be noted that unlike the Romance languages or other languages of the same stock, Chinese dialects are for their speakers not associated with ethnic, religious, national, or other divisions that could deepen the divide and lead to linguistic divergence. In this sense and despite mutual incomprehensibility between some of the dialects, it is appropriate to consider the Chinese a single speech community. The common written language does much to both justify and reinforce this perception, which is widely shared by the members of this community. To most Chinese, being Chinese implies speaking Chinese, where a broad range of variation is recognized as belonging to Chinese.

The Chinese term for dialect is *fāngyán* or "regional speech." Chinese scholars use this term for major regional speech forms and add another qualification for subvarieties, *dìdian fāngyán*, "local speech." To reflect this usage, it is convenient to make a distinction between dialect groups and dialects. The scores of dialects that exist within Chinese can then be classified into five major dialect groups.

Mandarin, by far the largest dialect group, is spoken by an estimated 73% of all Han Chinese. It also has the widest geographical extension, covering the northern provinces and the western parts of the coastal provinces of central China. It is also recognized as the standard variety of Chinese in Taiwan. *Mandarin* is the English term for what used to be called *Guānhuà*, "official language," and is now known as *Pŭtōnghuà*, "common language," in China and as *Guóyŭ*, "national language," in Taiwan. It is based on the dialect of Beijing.

Wu, the second largest dialect group is used by about 9% of the Han. Its center is the dialect of Shanghai, China's largest city. Other dialects that belong to this group are spoken along the lower Yangtze in the provinces of Anhui, Jiangsu, and Zhejiang.

Min, a dialect group of southern China, makes up 4.5% of the Han. Min is spoken in Fujian province; in Hainan, the large island in the Gulf of Tonkin; and in Taiwan. Northern Min and Southern Min are commonly distinguished, the latter being spoken in northeastern Fujian. The majority of Taiwanese are Southern Min speakers whose ancestors crossed the Taiwan Strait to colonize the island, which was formerly populated by speakers of Austro-Polynesian languages, now a tiny minority.

Yue, spoken by 5% of Han, is a dialect group centered in Guandong province. The speech of Hong Kong, Cantonese, also belongs to this dialect, which is spoken by many overseas Chinese communities. It is quite different from northern dialect groups, featuring, for example, nine as opposed to five different tones, as well as lexical and grammatical differences. Of late it has occasionally been used in writing in Hong Kong.

Hakka is spoken by 4% of Han. Having migrated from the north to the south, Hakka communities are scattered throughout a vast area in southeastern China and Taiwan. It is also spoken in Singapore. The name of this group is indicative of its history of migration: It means "guests." In spite of their division into separate communities, the dialects of this group exhibit relatively little variation.

The Written Language

Dialect distinctions are known to have existed in antiquity. Traditionally, they have not been associated with social stigma, perhaps because until a generation ago the overwhelming majority of China's population were rural and illiterate. Another factor is the written language, which, since it first appeared some 4,000 years ago, has enjoyed high prestige. In antiquity, it was associated with divination, and its mastery has always been the privilege of a small educated elite. The existing sources suggest that the Chinese have always had one written language. As the medium of what the Chinese consider the world's longest uninterrupted literary tradition, it is a matter of great pride. Literate Chinese from all parts of the country have been able to communicate with each other through writing. An enormous body of literature is accessible in Chinese, which for many centuries formed the bedrock of Far Eastern culture. In this sense, written Chinese was the most important instrument of cultural unification, which at the same time helped to secure China's cultural dominance over its neighbors.

Classical Chinese has always been a learned language restricted to the domains of higher culture. Yet the Chinese people, including the illiterate masses, have identified with this language as the proper form of Chinese. Language reform movements designed to narrow the gap between spoken and written language have been pursued with some measure of success since the Republic of China was first proclaimed in 1911. When the People's Republic of China was founded in 1949, illiteracy still was as high as 85%. To remedy this situation, the government proclaimed a policy to simplify the written language and to establish a common spoken language throughout China, which perhaps one day would be written in a simple Roman script. This language is *Pǔtōnghuà*, China's national language, which now coexists with the regional dialect groups. The language-spread policy has been quite successful, but although a Roman orthography for Chinese, called *Hànyǔ pīnyīn*, has been devised, the prospect that it will replace Chinese characters seems as remote as ever. Chinese characters continue to be a powerful symbol of Chinese ethnolinguistic identity.

Historically, the Chinese language has more than once proved its importance in safeguarding China's cultural integrity. Most significantly, it survived as China's predominant language in the face of political subjugation. The Mongol and the Manchu dynasties ruled over the Middle Kingdom, but they were unable to dislodge the Chinese language and put their own in its place, as happened so often in the history of conquest and colonization. Eventually, the conquerors adopted the language of the conquered, Chinese, allowing their own languages to be reduced to decoration. Although the Mongols in a bold move made the hP'ags-pa script the official script of the empire under the Yüan dynasty (1271–1368), this had little effect on the Chinese language and literary culture, whereas Mongolian drew extensively on Chinese for vocabulary. Mongolian is still spoken today by some 3 million speakers along the northern border of China, while Manchu has ceased to exist as a spoken language. During the Ch'ing dynasty (1644–1911) when they ruled China, the Manchu were thoroughly Sinicized. They became bilingual and eventually shifted to Chinese at the expense of their own language.

Similarly, the Chinese language has helped to deflect the impact of Western colonialism on China's culture. Embodying as it does a culture of learning and great distinction, it is revered by many Chinese as a superior language. Thus, even though the West for some time had better technology and weaponry and was hence able to encroach on China's sovereignty, China had an unmatched culture, which was most distinctly expressed through its language. Even highly regarded Chinese linguists such as Wang Li and Guo Shao-yu have praised the Chinese language for its alleged uniqueness, its correctness, its structural simplicity, and the succinctness of its monosyllabic words, each of which is elegantly represented by one Chinese character. These notions, as well as the idea that Chinese is more refined than other languages, are deeply ingrained in the public mind, notwithstanding the fact that they are hard to justify on scientific grounds. The Chinese define themselves through their language, being strongly committed to the idea that the Chinese language, in whatever form, is essential to Chinese ethnicity.

China's Minorities

Because of the great prestige and importance the Chinese language has tradition-ally been accorded, other languages spoken by peoples under Chinese dominion have never attracted much attention or been held in high regard by Chinese schol-ars. Until modern times, the sophisticated literate culture of Chinese left little room for the development of other languages. Yet fifty-five non-Chinese national minori-ties with a population of more than 60 million are recognized by the Chinese gov-ernment. These include, on the one hand, relatively large ethnic groups whose lan-guages are highly standardized, having been written in their own scripts for many centuries, such as Kazakh, Korean, Mongolian, Tibetan, and Uygur. On the other hand, there are many small speech communities, such as the Tuva with a few hun-dred speakers, whose languages have recently been reduced to writing or are not used in writing at all. Most of the minorities live in outlying provinces, especially Yunnan in the southwest, Xinjiang in central Asia, and in Inner Mongolia.

The constitution of the People's Republic states that "all of the nationalities of China are equal" and that "every ethnic minority is free to use and develop their language." The Chinese government has supported the cultivation of minority languages, but cultural autonomy was never allowed to take on political overtones that could challenge Chinese rule. Such aspirations, where they exist, are how-ever rarely focused on language alone. Both in Lamaist Tibet and among the Islamic communities of Xinjiang who speak Turkic languages, religion has been an addi-tional factor that feeds the desire for more political independence from Beijing.

There are more languages than ethnic groups in China, as some ethnicities have experienced linguistic divergence because of prolonged geographical isolation while preserving a sense of common ethnic affiliation. At the same time, a few minorities have adopted another language, such as the Manchu and the Hui, who use Chinese. At least fifteen of the fifty-five nationalities are split up into two or more language groups. The minorities are all to a greater or lesser extent bilin-gual. Chinese is the most widely used second language, but other patterns of bi- or multilingualism are also common. Elementary education is provided in many of the minority languages, but this in no way compromises the overall importance of Chinese as China's national language.

Hong Kong

Since July 1, 1997, Hong Kong is once again a part of China, but having been a British colony for 156 years, its cultural and linguistic identity differs markedly from the rest of the country. Until 1974, English was the sole official language, and both in public discourse and as a coofficial language it continues to play an important role. Chinese, that is, *Pŭtōnghuà*, is now the first official language of Hong Kong, but everyday life is dominated by Cantonese, the language 88.7% of the population claim as their usual language, according to a 1996 census. Because

Cantonese is not officially recognized as an independent language, there is some uncertainty as to what the shift in emphasis in the territory's language policy from English to Chinese will imply for the domains of education, administration, and law. The importance of *Pǔtōnghuà* is bound to increase, but at the present time there is nothing to suggest that the governments in Beijing or Hong Kong intend to pursue a rigid *Pǔtōnghuà* official language policy for Hong Kong.

Taiwan

Taiwan is a Chinese polity, but history has given it a distinct identity that finds expression, among other things, in language. The island was part of the Japanese empire for the half century preceding Japan's defeat in World War II. Japanese was then the national language and the language of instruction. It had a strong and lasting lexical influence on the Southern Min dialect spoken by the majority on the island. Nowadays, Mandarin (*Pǔtōnghuà*) is the medium of instruction at all educational levels throughout the country. However, it is the first language of only a minority of the population, having been brought to Taiwan by Chiang Kai-shek and his retreating Nationalist Chinese army in 1947. Because the national-ists treated the local population with contempt, Mandarin was not well received initially. The local Southern Min, often called "Taiwanese," continues to play an important role in everyday life. A diglossia situation persists, with Mandarin fulfill-ing the formal and written functions whereas Southern Min is prominent in oral communication.

Japan

Like the Chinese, the Japanese identify their ethnicity with their language. Minori-ties in Japan constitute less than 2% of the population, and Japanese minorities abroad are few. Thus there is a high degree of congruity of speech community and the inhabitants of Japan. There is a strong general interest in the language, which is often portrayed as incorporating the true spirit of the Japanese people. Such ideas are of modern origin and can be traced to European linguistic nation-alism. In a peculiar way, they reflect Japan's modernization during the Meiji pe-riod (1868–1911), a process set in motion in the mid-nineteenth century when Japan was forced at gunpoint by the United States to open its ports to interna-tional trade.

Language and Modernization

Until that time, the linguistic situation in Japan was characterized by the coexis-tence of many spoken and written varieties. Since the beginning of recorded his-tory the Japanese had been under the influence of Chinese culture. They learned the art of writing from the Chinese and for many centuries used Chinese as the major medium of written communication. Although a distinct script suitable for the Japanese language, which is unrelated to Chinese, had been developed more than 1,000 years before, literary Chinese continued to be used as the written language of high prestige until Japan's forced opening to the West. Recognizing the superiority of Western science and technology, the Japanese then made great efforts, during the final three decades of the last century, to absorb Western knowledge through translation. Because contact with the West came after 250 years of virtual seclusion, the Japanese scholars involved in this task experienced serious difficulties. Relative to Dutch, English, French, and German, the major languages they had to deal with, Japanese was underdeveloped. There was a marked deficit, especially in technical terminology. Both classical Chinese and Japanese were found wanting and unfit for modernity.

This experience of the translators, many of whom were prominent intellectuals, had a lasting effect on language attitudes. The Japanese turned away from the Chinese language as their major source of lexical innovation, as they turned away from Chinese culture, adopting many Western ways instead. Western languages became the yardstick of what was useful, modern, and good. To be sure, Japanese was very different from European languages; it was also cumbersome, old-fashioned, and hard to accommodate to the requirements of modern life. Because modernization was what many Japanese wanted at all costs, some went so far as to seriously consider replacing Japanese with a European language. Impractical as this proposal undoubtedly was, it is indicative of the language crisis many intellectuals sensed at the time.

However, couched in positive terms, the old-fashioned and awkward appearance of Japanese had to be seen as proof of its authenticity—notwithstanding that nearly half of the Japanese lexicon was of Chinese origin. The authenticity of the language, the Japanese intellectuals had learned from their European counterparts, was a valuable spiritual asset that could be exploited for the very purpose of modernization. Japanese was made Japan's national language, or *kokugo*. This term was coined in the Meiji period and is still used as the common designation of Japanese as a school subject. Through compulsory education, the Japanese government implemented a policy of linguistically unifying the country, making sure that standard Japanese based in the dialect of Tokyo came to be understood throughout the country. It also promoted the idea that Japan was a homogeneous country whose national identity "naturally" flowed out of its ethnic identity. In the north, the Ainu minority were forced to assimilate, leading to massive language shift, whereas in the south the Ryukyuan language was systematically downgraded to become perceived as a Japanese dialect. Japanese subjects were to be speakers of Japanese. The national-language ideology embraced by the government, following European models, fostered the idea of the identity of nation, state, and language.

Colonial Japanese

When the Japanese started to build their empire, which eventually included Taiwan, Manchuria, the Korean peninsula, and Micronesia, the government saw no contradiction between linguistic nationalism and a colonial language regimen of promoting Japanese at the expense of indigenous languages. Japanese was seen as a means of uplifting other races and offering them the opportunity to become good Japanese citizens. Early this century, Ueda Kazutoshi (1895, repr. 1903), a linguist who had studied in Germany, called the Japanese language "the spiritual blood of the nation" thus advancing a notion which was to reverberate in Japanese thought on language until well after the Second World War. Linking as it does the cultural with the racial aspect of perceived Japanese uniqueness, it encapsulates the essence of Japan's ethnonationalism. As a member of the National Language Research Committee, Ueda wielded considerable influence.

In hindsight, Japan's language-spread policy was not very successful. Unlike other colonial languages, such as English, Portuguese, and French, Japanese was not retained in any measure to speak of by sections of the populations that Japan once ruled in her overseas dominions. Rather, the experience of failed colonial expansion reinforced the idea that Japanese is the proper language of the Japanese only. Moreover, Japan's defeat in the war, combined with the strong ideological link between nation and language, once again rekindled the idea that Japanese was deficient, illogical, and inconvenient. In 1946 Shiga Naoya, a highly regarded novelist, publicly suggested that Japanese be abandoned and replaced by French, the most elaborate and beautiful language of the world. Such a suggestion was as outlandish as it was unrealistic and could never have met with public acceptance, but it was indicative of a strong commitment to linguistic determinism. According to this popular doctrine, a language shapes the ways of thinking of its speakers. To many Japanese it was, and still is, a matter of course that they think Japanese because they speak Japanese. The idea underlying Shiga's proposal was that by adopting a "better" language, the Japanese could improve their thinking and hence themselves.

From Postwar to Postmodern

Such expressions of linguistic self-deprecation notwithstanding, the Japanese share with the Chinese the perception that their ethnic and national identity is inextricably tied to their language. In contradistinction to the latter, however, they do not necessarily consider their language superior to others. Many Japanese believe in and cherish the idea that their language is unique, although this conviction is not based on any factual knowledge other than perhaps superficial exposure to English grammar at school. Having a unique language, in the public mind, can be a blessing as much as a curse. Whether it is one or the other depends not so much on cultural as on socioeconomic developments and on Japan's relationships with the rest of the world. The ideological linkage of language and ethnicity thus manifests itself in characteristically different beliefs about language in Japan and China. Whereas the superiority of Chinese is the eternal pivot of national pride untouched by historical ups and downs, the fate of the Japanese nation seems to rub off on its language. "I firmly believe," says renowned contemporary linguist Suzuki Takao, "that Japan's only hope of surviving as an economic superpower lies in maintaining its own values, cultural autonomy, and language in the international community" (1987: 134).

That their language not only possesses certain features that are unique or salient in comparison to other languages but also is unique in itself is a notion many Japanese embrace as part of a more comprehensive myth of their own insularity. Much emphasis is put on the fact that Japan is an island country. Standing alone in the world, the Japanese, not surprisingly, speak a language which is unlike any other human tongue. This conviction is undoubtedly a reflection of Japan's self-imposed seclusion policy from the seventeenth to the nineteenth centuries. It is, furthermore, fueled by the common confusion between language and script. Combining Chinese characters with two Japanese syllabaries, the Japanese writing system is both unusual and rather involved. As the most visible part of the language system, it manifests both Japan's indebtedness to China and her cultural independence. Accordingly, script reform discussions are invariably politically charged. Since the Meiji period, there has been a continuous tug of war between progressive intellectuals who advocate romanization or failing that the limitation of Chinese characters and conservative supporters of the traditional script, including an open-ended list of Chinese characters.

It is not uncommon that the written language is used as a means of social control, but in few cases is this more obvious than in Japan. This is largely due to the peculiar nature of the Japanese writing system, which lends itself to socially stratified literacy practices. In its present form, written Japanese makes use of two functionally and structurally quite distinct scripts, "kanji" or Chinese characters and kana syllabaries.

Japanese kanji differ from Chinese characters in the following way. In the Chinese context, a simple mapping relation holds: Each character stands for a Chinese syllable, which usually coincides with a Chinese morpheme. When Chinese characters were adapted to represent Japanese, this simple relationship was destroyed, as most characters came to be associated with both Chinese loanwords and Japanese words. As a result, kanji have multiple readings and often multiple meanings. Readings can be polysyllabic, because most Japanese words consist of more than one syllable. The official List of Characters for General Use of 1981, which is in force today, comprises 1,945 kanji with some 3,300 recognized readings.

Typologically, Japanese is very different from Chinese, which is an isolating language and relies on word order to indicate grammatical relationships. Japanese is an agglutinative language that expresses grammatical relationships by means of suffixes and other particles. Because these have no lexical content, they can be represented by means of Chinese characters only if the characters are used for the virtue of their sound value alone, disregarding their meaning. This usage, which was also applied to Japanese proper names, gave rise to a system of syllabic signs known as "kana." There are forty-six kana signs, which in combination with a small number of diacritics suffice to represent the Japanese language in an economical and elegant manner. However, this is not how they are used. Two graphically distinct sets of kana are in use; the rounded "hiragana" and the angular "katakana." Present-day written Japanese combines both with kanji. Content morphemes are typically written with kanji, whereas grammatical endings are indicated by means of hiragana. The latter are also used to annotate kanji that are not included in the official list or that for other reasons cannot be expected to be familiar to the reader. Katakana are used for emphasis, sound symbolism, and other ancilliary functions of writing.

In recent years, the appearance of roman letters, in addition to kanji and kana, in Japanese print material has become so frequent that the alphabet must now be regarded as an integral part of the overall system of Japan's written language. As this latest addition clearly indicates, the Japanese written language has undergone many changes over the centuries. Yet development toward a simpler system of writing has been slow. Whenever a simplification was effected, as during the education reform after the Second World War when the number of kanji in common use was substantially reduced, such moves were usually followed before long by countervailing policies. Thus, although character limitation after the war was conceived as a measure to facilitate the acquisition of literacy and reduce the importance of character knowledge as an indicator of social status, the slightly revised 1981 List of Characters for General Use was defined as a basic standard rather than an upper limit that should not be surpassed. In effect, therefore, the importance of kanji to written Japanese and that of kanji literacy to social advance had been reaffirmed. Appeals to tradition and to Japan's unique written language, which makes use of three different scripts, are very common. They camouflage, not always deliberately perhaps, the social control function of this written language which, by virtue of its complexity, continues to restrict upper-level literacy to the erudite elite.

Japan's literary culture clearly is distinctive and very elaborate, providing the notion of linguistic uniqueness with a measure of plausibility. It should be noted, however, that this idea is part of the general ideological baggage associated with language in Japan, an ideology which is not at all times equally prominent. Since the mid-1980s, a shift in emphasis has taken place as the notions of Japan's linguistic uniqueness and homogeneity have retreated somewhat into the background. An influx of foreign labor and the globalization of Japan's economy have exposed the Japanese to more variety in their everyday lives. Brazilian and Peruvian laborers of Japanese extraction who have come to Japan in considerable numbers have helped to sever the association in the public mind of race and language, because they are Japanese in appearance but do not speak Japanese. As a result, there is a growing awareness, especially among members of the young generation, of the presence of languages other than Japanese in Japanese society, as well as a growing readiness to make allowances for their speakers. This tendency is reflected in a number of publications of the 1990s that refer in their titles to a "multilingual Japan," which would have been quite improbable in the 1970s and '80s when the topics of uniqueness and homogeneity dominated the public discourse about the Japanese and their language.

Korea

For Koreans, peoplehood depends as much on language as it does for their powerful neighbors, the Chinese and the Japanese, and Koreans boast an even higher degree of congruity of speech community and nation. Whoever speaks Korean is a Korean. In the course of their long history, the Koreans often had to assert their ethnocultural identity against both China and Japan, and language has played a crucial role in this endeavor.

Pride in a Failed Reform

Under imperial suzerainty, Korea was exposed to the pervasive influence of China's rich culture. For many centuries it was a model Confucian state. Confucian ethics and scholarship were thoroughly absorbed by the educated classes, and Chinese political institutions were copied. Because the Chinese literary examinations were used in selecting bureaucrats, mastery of classical Chinese was an indispensable prerequisite to securing a place among the intellectual elite. The written language was cultivated much as it was in China. However, it was obvious early on that Chinese characters were ill suited for writing the Korean language. They were adapted for this purpose in the *Idu* clerical script, but this made for extremely cumbersome reading and writing.

In a remarkable attempt to open the world of letters to a greater number of his subjects and to make vernacular literacy possible, King Sejong undertook in the fifteenth century the ambitious project of writing reform. A group of scholars under his leadership designed an ingenious system of phonetic letters for writing the native language of the people. Known today as *han'gŭl*, "Korean letters," it is perhaps the most scientific system of writing ever invented and in use in any country. This is a matter of understandable pride for the Koreans. Shin Sang-Soon, a prominent contemporary Koreanist, has said that "Han'gŭl is the best asset which Korea has inherited from her past" (1990, xiii). It took many centuries for this view to gain acceptance.

King Sejong's new script was promulgated to the literate public in 1446 in a rescript entitled "The correct sounds for the instruction of the people." His motives were at least three: [1] to create a system with a good linguistic fit, [2] which would be uniquely Korean and [3] simple, so as to make literacy more accessible to the common people. Consisting of only 28 basic letters that represent the sounds of Korean in a straightforward and elegant manner, *han'gŭl* meets these requirements to a truly astounding extent. The king and his associates moreover created an ideological justification of the new script by tying it to the doctrines of the *Ijing*, the "Book of Changes," which the followers of Confucianism revered as the most important of the Five Classics. Providing highly sophisticated philosophical arguments, they tried to convince Confucian scholars that *han'gŭl* reflected the cosmic order and was destined to be the proper writing system for all Koreans. Yet the reform failed. It was several centuries ahead of its time. The idea of vernacular literacy ran counter to the communication practices of a highly stratified society in which elite literacy was a means of social control. The educated classes looked with disdain on the new system and continued to use Chinese writing until well into the present century. A vernacular literature has developed since the seventeenth century, but its prestige could never match that of Chinese.

Nowadays, however, the creation of *han'gŭl* is celebrated as the proudest moment in Korean cultural history. It was at the center of the commemorative events staged in Seoul in 1997 in honor of King Sejong's 600th anniversary. In North Korea, there is less inclination to credit royalty with Korea's most distinguished cultural achievement, but the script is used and held in high esteem nevertheless.

What caused the change? The single most important factor, it is fair to say, was Japanese colonial rule.

Near the end of the nineteenth century, Korea's conservative Confucianist elite proved to be unable to meet the political challenges that put Korea at the center of a power struggle between China, Russia, and Japan. Prevailing in two successive wars over the other two powers, Japan established itself as the dominant power on the Korean peninsula and, in 1910, made it part of its empire. The colonial administration first discouraged and later proscribed use of the Korean language, promoting Japanese instead. Their harsh language regime provided the conditions necessary to kindle the fire of linguistic nationalism, the first sparks of which had become visible before the turn of the century when progressive intellectuals who opposed the corrupt and impotent bureaucracy started to publish the all-*han'gŭl* newspaper *Tongnip Shinmun* ("The Independent"). Under the Japanese, using Korean became an act of insubordination and writing *han'gŭl* a visible symbol of opposition and self-esteem. During much of the colonial period (1910–1945), Korean in *han'gŭl* letters served as a vehicle for opposition to Japanization. Although in 1907, three years prior to the formal inauguration of Japan's rule over Korea, a mixed style of Chinese characters and *han'gŭl* was introduced for official documents by government decree, it was only when the Japanese had left that *han'gŭl* became the official script of Korean, five centuries after King Sejong's noble failure.

North and South

Korean is written in *han'gŭl* in both Korean states, but there are some differences, especially concerning the use of Chinese characters. It is possible and used to be common practice to write Sino-Korean words in *han'gŭl* texts with Chinese characters. Because close to half of the Korean lexicon is of Chinese origin, Korean texts can be densely packed with Chinese characters, making them inaccessible to less erudite readers. Shortly after their foundation in 1948, the Democratic People's Republic of (North) Korea and the Republic of (South) Korea adopted different policies on the standard form of the written language. North Korea abolished Chinese characters, which were associated with both Korea's Confucianist feudal past and the Japanese educational system. They were, moreover, seen as an impediment to implementing truly democratic vernacular literacy. School instruction in Chinese characters was, therefore, terminated, and Chinese characters were no longer used in newspapers, magazines, or books.

Contrary to this, successive governments in the South abolished and reintroduced the study of Chinese characters several times. At present, the study of some 1,800 Chinese characters is part of the secondary school curriculum, but the final decades of this century have seen a marked decline in the use of Chinese characters. The odd character on a newspaper page sticks out, and term papers by university students are commonly written without any Chinese characters. Street signs, posters, and other public displays are in *han'gŭl*, Chinese characters having all but disappeared from public places.

Ridding the written language of Chinese characters is linked to the so-called purification of Korean. This manifestation of linguistic xenophobia reflects a perceived need to assert ethnocultural identity. Again North and South pursue different approaches. In North Korea, the government plays an active role in advocating the use of newly coined Korean instead of Sino-Korean words, whereas in South Korea the cause of cleansing the language is pushed only by some individuals and private organizations without any official government support. It must be noted in this connection that many Sino-Korean words, especially those that refer to modern things, were borrowed, through the medium of the written language, from Japanese during the colonial years. Hence, to some language-conscious intellectuals, these words are a sign of Japanese dominance.

North Korea's language policy is not restricted to purification. Rather, it is an important instrument of indoctrination and of spreading party ideology. The spirit of this policy transpires from a 1966 speech by North Korea's former leader, Kim Il-sung:

> Firmly rooted in the rotten feudal, bourgeois life, the Korean language now spoken in Seoul still uses the type of nasal twangs favored by women to flirt with men. . . . On top of this, English, Japanese, and Chinese loan words, now swarming in Seoul speech, amounting to more than half of the Korean vocabulary, have turned it into a mixed language. Therefore, we should now take Pyongyang speech as the standard. (p. 71)

Owing to North Korea's seclusion during the past half century, its divisive language policy has had profound effects. A rival standard independent of the traditional prestige variety of Seoul has been enforced. Based on the dialect of Pyongyang, it is known as *Mwunhwae*, or "cultured language." In conjunction with the introduction of thousands of "purified" neologisms, this has clearly lead to linguistic divergence. Beyond regional dialect variation, Korean now has two different orthographies, two different phonetic norms, and two quite distinct lexical norms. As a result, although in a general sense the Korean language continues for its speakers to serve as an important marker of ethnic identity, its two diverging forms in the North and the South have become associated ever more strongly with the political identities of a divided nation.

Common Elements of Far Eastern Linguistic Culture

The Chinese, Japanese, and Koreans each have their own distinctive linguistic culture, but there are also some common elements, some of which echo a common tradition which, though considered obsolete by many, still in subtle ways influences their self-image and the way they conceive of language. All three cultures attach extraordinary importance to language, especially in its written form. This attitude can be traced back to the doctrines of Confucius of some two and one-half millennia ago.

Living at a time of political turmoil and moral decay, Confucius taught that it was necessary to return to the ancient Way. To this end nothing was more important than the "rectification of names" (*cheng ming*), a principle which has been variously interpreted as meaning that words should correspond to the things they designate or that the things of reality should live up to their names. Either way, the idea implies an essential relationship between words and things which can even be given a moral interpretation. This is accompanied by a strong commitment to the idea of linguistic correctness, which is tied to the literary standard. Mastering the written language through determined and scrupulous study leads to acquiring not just skill but virtue. Correct language use combines beauty, goodness, and rectitude and is a precondition for clear thinking.

In premodern times, these precepts were directed mostly at (the localized forms of) classical Chinese, but in the course of modernization they were redirected at the cultivated vernaculars, although filtered through the prism of linguistic nationalism. Although the feudal order of premodern times has given way to more egalitarian societies throughout East Asia, the idea that the learned class controls the language is still very strong. The vernacularization of literacy has done little to alter this perception. Thus, each in its distinctive form, the three Far Eastern linguistic cultures discussed in this chapter all combine a strong dose of ethnonationalism with an authoritarian attitude toward language.

Questions for Further Thought and Discussion

1. What form does the language-dialect distinction take in the Chinese context and how is it affected by the written language?

2. What does the notion of speaking a "unique language" imply in China and in Japan? Discuss the ideological differences.

3. How is the perceived identity of speech community and nation in Japan affected by socioeconomic developments?

4. Why did the writing reform attempted in Korea in the fifteenth century fail? What lessons can be learned from this example about literacy, bilingualism, power, and social stratification?

5. Which historical and political developments are reflected in linguistic purism in Korea?

6. In what sense can the Confucianist cultural tradition be said to be reflected in present-day language attitudes in East Asia?

Selected Bibliography

Befu, Harumi (ed.) (1993). *Cultural Nationalism in East Asia: Representation and Identity.* Berkeley: University of California Press.

DeFrancis, John (1984). *The Chinese Language. Fact and Fantasy.* Honolulu: University of Hawaii Press.

Kachru, Braj B., and Cecil L. Nelson (eds.) (1992). Language and identity. *Journal of Asian Pacific Communication* 3(1).

Lee Hyun-Bok (1990). Differences in language use between North and South Korea. *International Journal of the Sociology of Language* 82: 71–86.

Maher, John, and Kyoko Yashiro (eds.) (1995). *Multilingual Japan*. Clevedon, England: Multilingual Matters.

Ramsey, S. R. (1987). *The Languages of China*. Princeton: Princeton University Press.

Sang-Soon, Shin, Don-Ju Lee, and Hwan-Mook Lee. (1990). *Hunmin-jong um*. Seoul: Hanshin.

Sun, Hongkai, and Florian Coulmas (eds.) (1992). News from China: Minority languages in perspective. *International Journal of the Sociology of Language* 97.

Takao, Suzuki (1987). *Reflections on Japanese Language and Culture*. Tokyo: Keio University.

Twine, Nanette (1991). *Language and the Modern State. The Reform of Written Japanese*. London: Routledge.

Ueda, Kazutoshi (1903 [1895]). *Kokugo no tame* (For a Japanese Language) (2 vols.). Tokyo: Fuzambo.

Wang Li (1988). *A History of Chinese Linguistics*, James C. P. Liang (trans.). Providence: Foris.

The Pacific

HEATHER LOTHERINGTON

The nations of the Pacific can be divided into Pacific Rim and Island Pacific countries. The Pacific Rim includes continents bordering on the Pacific Ocean, such as Asia, Australia, and the Americas. The Island Pacific comprises a series of archipelagoes that support island states of relatively small populations and economies across a vast continent of water. Papua New Guinea is by far the largest island country in terms of both population (4 million) and area (462,840 square km.), with over 800 spoken languages. Tokelau, conversely, has a population of 1,600 people who live on three atolls which comprise 12.2 square kilometers of dry land.[1] The Island Pacific, together with Australia and New Zealand, make up Oceania.

This chapter focuses primarily on Island Pacific nations, specifically south of the equator on the islands of the South Pacific, and looks at competing political, social, economic, and cultural agendas for language use which have emerged particularly in response to the era of decolonization in the Pacific region.

The islands of the Pacific are typically grouped into three ethnogeographic regions: Melanesia ("black islands") in the southwest Pacific, Polynesia ("many islands") in the central and eastern regions of both the North and the South Pacific, and Micronesia ("small islands") in the central and western regions of the North Pacific with a few islands dipping into the southern hemisphere (see map of Oceania). This enormous area is home to more than a thousand languages which have developed from various exploratory migrations arriving from both sides of the Pacific over a span of tens of thousands of years.

A Brief History

Early Papuan-speaking settlers of parts of Melanesia are estimated to have found their way to the western islands of the South Pacific tens of thousands of years

414

ago. The next significant migration was of Austronesian-speaking peoples, whose superb navigation skills took them eastward, traveling in huge canoes, into Polynesia. The Polynesian migration was relatively recent in the history of the world's settlements, happening only a few thousand years ago. Last came the great ships of Europe, which over approximately the past 400 years have carried explorers who mapped the many islands of the South Pacific; missionaries who indelibly changed the social and cultural ways of the islands through their biblical practices; traders looking for exotic bêche-de-mer (a sea-slug prized by Chinese as a culinary delicacy) and precious sandalwood; and colonial settlers with imperialistic notions of territory. The most recent influx includes tourists, who fly into the Pacific from all corners of the earth or sail leisurely through the islands in cruise ships and private yachts, and the global business community, arriving en masse on the wings of technology. All of these people have brought their languages with them, and the linguistic demography of the islands today reflects the survival and development of the many languages to have reached shore.

Pacific islands also share a social history of colonialism, first at the hands of European missionaries—who arrived in eastern Polynesia just before the turn of the nineteenth century and moved westward across the Pacific in a tide of evangelism that has permanently altered the structure of Pacific societies and their practice of traditional customs—and subsequently by the political states of Western Europe and their colonized progeny, whose sway over most of these islands held until the latter half of the twentieth century, when Pacific islands began to acquire political independence. The majority of islands in the South Pacific are now independent.

Pacific Languages and Cultures

The linguistic and cultural demography, as well as the political traditions of the Pacific, are varied. The Melanesian countries host the greatest concentration of multilingualism on earth. For instance, in the tiny country of Vanuatu, 150,000 people speak more than 100 vernacular languages, as well as a pidgin and two colonial languages (Lynch 1996: 245). The linguistic demography of Polynesia and Micronesia is much less complex than that of Melanesia, varying from use of a single vernacular language, as in Western Samoa, to, at most, a small number of regionally distributed languages, as in the Cook Islands.

Melanesian social orders are typified by egalitarian, consensual governments in which leadership is achieved rather than ascribed. Polynesian societies, conversely, are characterized by rigid social hierarchies, differentiated by privilege and even by language. For example, in Tonga, the three social classes, royalty, nobility, and commoners, use different speech registers,[2] marking their status and dividing them socially (Lawson 1996: 87). Leadership is ascribed rather than achieved in Polynesia; eastern and western Polynesian societies are further differentiated as to the status women are accorded. In the eastern Polynesian societies of the Cook Islands, French Polynesia, Hawai'i, and Aotearoa, where traditional leadership roles are more ceremonial than powerful, women hold high titles. Interestingly, these are colonized territories with the exception of the Cook Islands, which is in sovereignty association with New Zealand. However, in western Polynesia, where chiefs are more politically powerful, women do not hold as many titles (Crocombe 1994: 189). Micronesian social orders include elements of both Polynesian and Melanesian societies.

Pacific Life: Myths and Realities

The islands of the South Pacific are home to many myths. Art and literature, even early anthropological accounts (not to mention travel brochures), have drawn images of azure, untroubled skies and crystal clear, abundant seas; of harmonious societies in which people live without fear of violence or abuse; of a sexually licentious existence under swaying palm trees; of bountiful fresh food; of smiles flashing healthy white teeth. Harsh realities away from the tourist resorts (where at least some of the above is created subject to the vagaries of local weather and, of course, for a price) paint a different picture of life.

Small island states are subject to natural disasters of national proportions incurred by hurricanes, tsunamis, and earthquakes, as well as floods and droughts. Low-lying atolls are at the mercy of contemporary global warming, which could raise sea levels sufficiently to inundate them. Pacific islands maintain delicately balanced ecosystems and sustain small economies, often reliant on a limited number of export crops which are subject to the aforementioned disasters. Resources are limited, and population growth in some islands is unsustainable. Unemployment is high; urban drift, attendant poverty, and crime are rising. "Brain drain" of educated professionals is another problem, one which is especially critical in Fiji, where, in response to the military coups of 1987, there has been a mass exodus of Indian professionals. In the late 1980s, the Pacific region received the highest per capita level of foreign aid in the world (Sanday 1988: 11), which has produced consumer societies dependent on foreign goods, money, and skills. As foreign aid declines in the 1990s, attendant problems of unemployment and trade imbalances become even starker. Finally, the diet is changing from traditional root crops and fresh fish to refined and canned products, contributing to a rise in lifestyle diseases: Obesity is a serious problem in many Polynesian countries, as is diabetes, and dental caries are on the increase.

Language is suffering in all this as well. In the climate of the late twentieth century, indigenous languages the world over are dying. The Island Pacific is home to a rich panorama of languages, some of which are fighting for survival in the increasingly global village of the world.

1962–1980: Political Independence and Decolonization in the Pacific

The Pacific of the 1990s is in visible political upheaval: Prodemocracy movements are emerging in various forms, particularly in Polynesian societies, and anticolonial and seccessionist movements are battling for self-determination in areas under foreign political and/or economic domination, sometimes fiercely, as in the Bougainville conflict in Papua New Guinea. Societies under pressure to simultaneously modernize and uphold traditional values are giving their citizens mixed messages about language, culture, and power.

I take as the fulcrum of change in this century the period between 1962 and 1980. During this eighteen-year period, the majority of island countries in the South Pacific achieved political independence in rapid succession. This was the beginning of mass decolonization in the Pacific—of psychological, as well as political, liberation. (See Table 27-1 for independent small island states and Table 27-2 for colonial powers in the South Pacific of the 1990s, together with their remaining territories.)

Postcolonial Social Trends

Although the formal government of a territory may be decolonized, economic, social and religious institutions do not necessarily follow.

(Uentabo 1992: 3)

The Pacific Way

The small island states listed in Table 27-1 have in common their relatively recent independence, which began with the establishment of Western Samoa in 1962 and followed in a chain of independence movements until 1980 with the dismantling of the British-French condominium government of New Hebrides and the birth of the nation of Vanuatu. This era of political emancipation inspired a revi-

Table 27-1. The postcolonial South Pacific

Independent postcolonial countries	
Fiji, Papua New Guinea, Solomon Islands, Vanuatu	(Melanesia)
Tuvalu, Western Samoa	(Polynesia)
Kiribati, Nauru	(Micronesia)
Independent countries of other status	
Cook Islands, Niue[1], Tonga[2]	(Polynesia)

1. Both the Cook Islands and Niue have a sovereignty association with New Zealand. Cook Islanders and Niueans carry New Zealand passports, but their countries have independent governments. However, the United Nations does not yet recognize these countries as fully independent states.

2. Tonga is a kingdom; it was never colonized by another power. Tonga did become a British protectorate in 1900, however, and it is a member of the British Commonwealth. Tonga also underwent significant political change in the era of decolonization following Queen Salote's death in 1965. Queen Salote's son and successor, King Taufa'ahau Tupou IV, the country's first university graduate (University of Sydney), has significantly modernized the Tongan monarchy (Lawson 1996: 95–98).

Table 27-2. Colonial territories in the South Pacific

Australia	Norfolk Island
Chile	Rapanui (Easter Island)
France	French Polynesia, New Caledonia (and the Loyalty Islands), Wallis, and Futuna
Indonesia	Irian Jaya (West New Guinea)
New Zealand	Tokelau
United Kingdom	Pitcairn
United States	American Samoa

sion of social, as well as political, identity, a refocusing and reinterpretation of Pacific life, which came to be known as *the Pacific Way.*

In 1970, Ratu Sir Kamisese Mara, high chief and prime minister of Fiji, presented the expression "the Pacific Way" in an address to the United Nations General Assembly (Lawson 1996: 2). The Pacific Way had been developing in Ratu Mara's Pacific oratory for a few years, taking shape as a political call for regional leaders to establish Pacific means of conflict resolution. The Pacific Way in Ratu Mara's rhetoric united the Pacific in a common destiny and underscored regional stability through a sense of cultural respect and tradition. It was a conservative vision, a politicization of traditional culture.

The Pacific Way spoke to the new Pacific by couching a romantic reconstruction of past tradition within borrowed British protocols, finding its voice in English, the regional artifact of British colonialism and the lingua franca of power, but its expression through the traditional Pacific vehicle of oracy rather than literacy. The Pacific Way revived past notions of culture that upheld hierarchical power structures as legitimate norms for present and future behavior and exhorted islanders to maintain a sense of "tradition," which was cultural and Pacific, construed in opposition to "development," which was modern and Western.

The message the Pacific Way sent to the masses was mixed: People were to preserve tradition, ensuring uncritical subservience to the traditional hierarchy and maintaining cultural ways and language. Yet the Pacific Way was communicated in English, the conduit to power, economic success, and status, even, manifestly, within the Pacific community.

Development

Development

Big Word
Lotsa meanings
Staka dollar
Magnetic circle
Entices me
Urban drift
Empty villages
Customs forgotten

Loose living
Lost identity
Rat race
Dollar talks
Values change
Wantoks[3] ignored
Every man for himself
I want to develop too!
Jully Sipolo
Solomon Islands
(1990: 8)

The economic backdrop of the past several decades is of island societies moving away from communal self-sufficiency toward a cash economy and undergoing considerable social restructuring in the process. Pacific island countries are following an increasingly industrialized vision of "development," which includes as models the Asian "four tigers" (Hong Kong, South Korea, Taiwan, and Singapore). Traditional cultures have had to accommodate market-driven priorities. The bonds of communalism have loosened and admitted a degree of individualism with this trend toward capitalism. Traditionally rural agrarian societies have become more urbanized. With increasing urbanization has come a reduction in traditional education and a linguistic reprioritization. The language of development is unquestionably English.

English as the Key to Development

The Pacific Islands have the distinction of being last in many historical developments—the last to be inhabited, to be "discovered" by Europeans, to be colonized, and to be decolonized. Decolonization provided the fulcrum for change in social, as well as political, systems, some of which had been instituted a century or more previously and woven firmly into the fabric of everyday cultural life. The Pacific Way attempted to light the way forward in postcolonial Pacific life through social and cultural revisionism, invoking a vision of precontact culture that was long on poetic license. However, many cultural institutions were absorbed into Pacific life through outside contact and are permanent, including, importantly, literacy, brought by the missionaries as a technological tool of (narrowly defined) development, and English, the lingua franca of the region, the cultural script of government and educational structures, and the voice of power.

Included in the many important decisions that had to be made after independence was the place of the colonial languages in the functioning of the newly independent states. The new postcolonial nations of the South Pacific continue to have need for a world language to link them with the rest of the world, particularly for economic purposes. Regional, as well as international, communication continues to be conducted principally in English. Indeed, in multiracial Fiji, which lies beyond the linguistic reaches of Melanesian Pidgin,[4] English has come to be used for intercultural communication as well.

English symbolizes political power and economic success across the post-colonial Pacific. Proficiency in English is needed for successful education, the attainment of prestigious white-collar jobs, and urban, regional, and international mobility. Australia and New Zealand, in particular, are beacons to the Island Pacific. Indeed, New Zealand is home to many more indigenous Pacific Islanders than are the islands of cultural origin of several Polynesian groups, including Cook Islanders, Niueans, and Tokelauans. Australia hosts Pacific Islanders, too, attracting Melanesians as well as Polynesians. The Micronesian republic of Nauru has very strong ties with the state of Victoria, and the nation has invested some if its substantial phosphate royalties in Australian real estate, including Nauru House in downtown Melbourne.

Furthermore, for Pacific Islanders, English may be more than simply a means to reuniting with Pacific Island community members in New Zealand; evidence of rapid language shift to English was reported in the early 1980s in a disturbing percentage of New Zealand-born Pacific Islanders, particularly those of Cook Island and Niuean origins (Benton 1981: 72).

In addition to white-collar job-seeking, urban education, and international family reunification, tourism and electronic communication have spurred the spread of English. Tourism is one of the most important industries in the Pacific. Better-known travel destinations such as Tahiti and Fiji depend heavily on their tourist dollars. English is the common lingua franca even in French territories in which English seems to have made headway in a sort of economic colonialism. Japanese has also begun to attract attention and has the dubious distinction of having preceded Fijian as a credit language course at the University of the South Pacific.

Urbanization and Consequences for Language Socialization

> But Fijian land is more than a resource; it is regarded as a homeland, and means of identity. The Fijian's land is part of his being, for not only does his land belong to him, it is also of him. This is why it is often said that the land is the people, the two are interwoven closely and cannot be separated completely.
> (Lasaqa 1984: 49)

Pacific Islanders have a very spiritual connection with their land—a connection that embraces the land and the people as one. This is a fundamental value, written into Pacific languages as "vanua" in Fijian, "fanua" in Samoan, "fonua" in Tongan, "fenua" in Tahitian, and "aina" in Hawaiian. The land unifies people; it houses the culture.

The Pacific still nourishes both rural and urban lifestyles, which are rapidly growing further apart. Life in outer islands continues in relative isolation, removed from the hustle and bustle of the towns by infrequent and unreliable transportation but increasingly accessible by electronic telecommunications. Subsistence farming and fishing still play a role in everyday existence. Life in towns is a world away, driven by the cash economy.

With socioeconomic change in Pacific life has come increasing urbanization, which beckons people from the *vanua*. Urbanization is changing the structure of Pacific families, thereby affecting opportunities for traditional socialization. In the village, people live in extended families. However, urban housing discourages extended family living through the space limitations of real estate. The emergence of nuclear family organization has implications for language and cultural transmission. In urban housing, there is not always room for the elders, who have traditionally had an important hand in the upbringing of children (Lasaqa 1984: 197–199). As such, urban children are increasingly cut off from traditional education. Indeed, for many urban children, it is television that tells most of the stories they learn from.

Most vernacular languages are still viable, being used in urban and rural communities alike. However, changing lifestyles are affecting opportunities for language maintenance on the home front. Increasing urban drift occurring in the Island Pacific is accompanied by increasing Westernization. In urban areas in particular indications of language shift to English are beginning to be seen.

Language and Literacy Education

Language Education

By the time of independence, English (and French in French territories) had been in educational use for over a century in some schools, particularly in postprimary education. To replace schoolbooks, retrain teachers, and undo decades of education and educational socialization in the colonial language was not feasible—and perhaps not even desirable in small struggling economies.

In Fiji, full government education was not provided for indigenous Fijians or for the progeny of indentured Indian laborers, who had been brought to Fiji by the British in the late nineteenth century to work the sugarcane fields, until well into the twentieth century. Schooling had been for the exclusive benefit of European children in early colonial days, and indigenous education was left largely to missionary and community groups. In 1916 the colonial government passed an Education Ordinance, which established a Grant-in-Aid scheme to support nongovernment schools. Strings were attached to the funding, including the provision that English be taught and that certified teachers whose training had been in English be hired (Tavola 1991). English was thus clearly a key to upward mobility in education. In the Fiji of today, in which racial differences are still written into the management of the 97% of schools that are nongovernment and run by community and religious bodies under the Grant-in-Aid scheme (Tavola 1991: 152), success in examinations conducted in English is still the measure of a good education.

In the 1990s, education in the Island Pacific is conducted largely in a world language: English in the majority of islands, French in past and present French colonial territories, and Spanish in Rapanui (Easter Island). Education in vernacular and community languages is largely transitional but includes a modicum of language maintenance education, with children in most countries beginning schooling in the vernacular, in which they acquire basic literacy and numeracy while learning English as a second language (ESL). A clear exception to the increasing trend in vernacular maintenance education is regional pidgins, particularly Melanesian Pidgin. Even in Vanuatu, where Bislama is the national language, Melanesian Pidgin does not have a role in formal education. In a few countries, education is still delivered in a world of English print with little concession, if any, to children's own languages.[5]

English is the main medium of education in postcolonial island nations across the South Pacific. French is also in use in Vanuatu's complicated "dual language" school system, which, sadly, maintains the dual infrastructure of the condominium English-French colonial system. Problems with the teaching of English in the Pacific abound: The curriculum-dictated changeover from use of the vernacular to English as classroom medium, which in most cases occurs in the fourth grade, is not mirrored in real classroom language use, where code-switching (switching from one language to another) is widely reported. Yet print resources, which are often in short supply, as well as formal assessment, are in English. Often, especially in the case of smaller, outer islands, English does not have currency outside the classroom, so children must learn to manipulate English for complex learning tasks on the basis of limited, non-native classroom exposure to the language. Finally, many teachers are quite insecure about their own English proficiency levels.

In Polynesian communities in New Zealand, however, the phenomenon of *language nests* is thriving. Begun in 1982 as part of the Maori revival movement, the *kohanga reos* (language nests) offered preschool English-speaking Maori children traditional language-in-culture socialization through immersion child care by Maori-speaking elders (Fishman 1991: 237–238). The *kohanga reos* have blossomed; furthermore, they have inspired language nests in other Pacific language communities intent on reversing language shift and maintaining culture.

Literacy Education

But the Pacific Way is spoken rather than written. Skills in written negotiation are not yet as polished as in verbal negotiation. With an increasing total amount of negotiating to do, and increasingly in written form, it will help The Pacific Way if written word skills can be developed to match the spoken, for personal contact costs time and travel money.

(Crocombe 1976: 16)

Literacy and formal education were introduced to the Island Pacific by European missionaries in the early nineteenth century. Prior to missionary contact, educational values were communicated through a strong oral tradition in daily community life. The oral tradition is still of manifest importance in Pacific Island life; oratory is highly valued and storytelling, a tradition. However, the introduction of literacy has permanently changed the social structure of the Pacific.

The place of literacy in contemporary cultural practice occupies a narrow range of activities, centering on ritual religious reading, general perusing of the newspaper (mostly in English), and attending to schoolwork. Recreational reading is not culturally valued or regularly practiced. Indeed, readers may be viewed as "lazy," because the solitary nature of reading does not conform to cultural expectations of communalism and orality. Vernacular reading materials are limited mostly to religious materials. Reading is not consciously introduced through preschool socialization as it is in metropolitan Anglo-centric nations where, for instance, reading a bedtime story is a classic routine. Islanders learn to read so they can read schoolbooks and write examinations in English. School literacy in Papua New Guinea has been referred to as "cargo reading" (Abare and Manukayasi 1996: 143)—reading not for meaningful life use but for academic performance.

In the nineteenth century, literacy created new social classes of Pacific Islanders: teacher-priests who spread the Word, using vernacular literacy and the translated Bible as tools. Authority was reassigned to literary sources and away from the traditional authority of oral narrative, devaluing indigenous tradition in the face of Western authority. Indeed, the narrative itself changed in shape, from the circular nature of Pacific oral tradition to a Westernized linear beginning-to-end structure (Topping 1992).

Although early literacy instruction was in the vernacular, increasing access to formal education has meant a shift to literacy in English. Attendant cultural values implicit in imported materials reflect Western ways of life. Concern over the inundation of culturally foreign curricula that characterized preindependence Pacific education found translation into locally written, mass-produced, vernacular medium materials only in the 1990s. Early attempts to provide education with a Pacific cultural background saw the implementation in the late 1960s of a pedagogically rigid English course written by Australian expatriate teacher Gloria Tate, based on her teaching experiences in Nauru, the Cook Islands, and the Northern Territory of Australia, and marketed by the South Pacific Commission (SPC), an umbrella group of Pacific Island nations and colonial governments based in Noumea, New Caledonia (Lotherington-Woloszyn 1992). This stilted and pedagogically outmoded English course and its companion readers were received by Pacific nations in the throes of decolonization as a pan-Pacific resource, despite flawed, composite Pacific characters with names like Ken and Alice who suffered an identity crisis in both visual and textual representation and who spoke the textbook English of 1950s readers. The SPC/Tate English course is still in limited use in parts of the Pacific today.

There are encouraging indications of increased attention having been paid to vernacular literacy and vernacular maintenance in schools since the mid-1990s with the eleven-country regional initiative, the Basic Education and Life Skills (BELS) program, launched by senior regional educators in tandem with foreign aid agencies in the early 1990s. One of the missions of BELS is to provide in-service education to primary teachers in literacy education. This teacher development gives fruition to the grassroots work begun by educators in the South Pacific in the 1970s and 1980s in projects such as the Oceania Literacy Development program, which sought to develop better literacy, both vernacular and ESL, through the creation and provision of good children's literature. The use of locally based stories, although written in English, was first piloted in 1978 by Peter De'Ath in the tiny Polynesian island state of Niue. The success of the Fiafia readers, as they were called, fueled the impetus for an experimental Book Flood project conducted in Fiji in 1980 by Warwick Elley and Francis Mangubhai that was aimed at improving literacy and educational achievement through the provision and use of storybooks (Elley and Mangubhai 1981).

Educators understand that vernacular literacy will facilitate both literacy acquisition and ESL proficiency through development of children's existing language resources. However, more time spent on vernacular education seems counterintuitive to parents who were not permitted to use their home language at school and who see English as the key to success. Despite the encouraging increase in vernacular literacy trends, there are still problems gathering community support for increased vernacular education, especially in Melanesian Pidgin.

Language Planning and Language Policy

The Commission believes it is essential for the survival of the language that a standardised written form be adopted by all those involved in the production of material in Maori, in order that a high quality literacy base may be built up as a resource for the Maori language learners of today and of the future.

(Te Taura Whiri i te Reo Maori [Maori Language Commission n.d.a: 1)

Colonial education in high-status world languages had socialized islanders to believe that English and French were somehow superior languages, better capable of expressing academic concepts. English was synonymous with economic success and political power; it was seen as the key to development. The parents and grandparents of schoolchildren today were dissuaded from speaking their vernacular languages in school, even to the point of being punished. This encouraged pidginized Englishes and, in multilingual Melanesia, where children came to school from different vernacular language backgrounds, increased use of Melanesian Pidgin on school playgrounds. Education officials debated the suitability of vernacular languages for communicating world knowledge in schools. This debate was particularly active for Melanesian Pidgin, which as a pidgin was seen to be an inadequate, inelegant vehicle of communication. Although the status of Melanesian Pidgin has continued to rise, it is still not used in mainstream education.

The issue of making vernacular languages capable of handling academic and technological discussion has given rise to debates about standardization; in postcolonial Pacific societies, this debate chiefly concerns orthographic convention, that is, standardizing spelling. Lack of agreement on spelling conventions means that materials are not printed in the vernacular. Without vernacular literature, vernacular literacy cannot be taught. There have been problems establishing orthographic standards in several Pacific languages, among them Nauruan and Tokelauan, as well as the dialects of Melanesian Pidgin, which at present do not share spelling conventions.

In Aotearoa, corpus planning to standardize and extend Maori is being promoted through the efforts of the Te Tauru Whiri i te Reo Maori (Maori Language Commission). This planning particularly concentrates on engineered lexical extension, which has raised a certain amount of controversy.

> It is our statutory obligation to promote the Maori language as a living language and as an ordinary means of communication. For any language to flourish in this, the information age, it is essential that the language has the necessary vocabulary to define, describe and denote the technological, social and political landscape of the late 20th century, and all its component parts. (Te Taura Whiri i te Reo Maori n.d.b.: 1)

Voices of Electronic Media

> One of the few continuing regional efforts to develop local programming has come from the United Nations Educational, Scientific and Cultural Organisation. It is currently supporting a Pacific women television producers' programme exchange and a fledgling news exchange project. But the efforts of UNESCO, the South Pacific Commission and small local producers are being overwhelmed by the flood of non-regional programming, mainly sold by Television New Zealand.
>
> (Waqa 1995: 17)

English is clearly the language of contemporary electronic media in the Pacific. The one exception to the reign of English is radio transmissions. However, visual media, on the dramatic increase with the recent arrival of television in the Pacific, broadcast predominantly in English.

Television is a relative newcomer in postcolonial Pacific societies. French and American colonial territories, on the other hand, have received broadcast television for over twenty-five years; Chilean (Rapanui), for twenty years. Tonga and Papua New Guinea started television services in the 1980s. Since the late 1980s, TVNZ (New Zealand) has been setting up and contributing to small networks across the Pacific, which are now functioning in the Cook Islands, Fiji, Niue, Nauru, Vanuatu, and Western Samoa (Royce 1993: 101–102).

Television is not the first visual medium in the Pacific. The use of videotapes preceded network television by many years, and, of course, cinemas are omnipresent. However, the limited literacy practices of Pacific Islanders coupled with traditional socialization not to question authority make Pacific Islanders a relatively uncritical television viewing audience. In addition, the material typically broadcast on television is chiefly American in origin, including cheap 1960s programs, and falls into a commercial funding paradigm that emphasizes advertising opportunities and deemphasizes quality programming. Therefore, Anglocentric, particularly American, television voices are being increasingly heard at home, where they have the potential to encroach on vernacular language use and usurp not only storytelling opportunities but also the stories told (Lotherington-Woloszyn 1995). Worse still, in light of the superficial acceptance of literacy practices that have nonetheless contributed to restructuring traditional authority, there is a very real question as to whether Pacific Islanders will slide into an image-centered culture without having fully incorporated a socially functioning and education-ally enriching print culture.

Voices of Dissent in the Colonial Pacific

The momentum for political independence was not completely built from within island societies. French Polynesia, which like many colonial possessions provided a safe Pacific harbor to a European administration, now finds contemporary aspi-rations of self-sufficiency and their audible voice enmeshed in the financial snare of submission.

The era of decolonization has not brought a renaissance in ethnic identity to everyone in the Pacific (see Table 27-2 for the remaining colonial powers and their Pacific Island possessions). Prodemocracy movements are erupting across the Pacific, voicing dissent against political, economic, and social orders in places such as Irian Jaya (West New Guinea), where Irian separatists are in continued guerrilla warfare with Jakarta; Papua New Guinea, where the Bougainville Revo-lutionary Army wages civil war; New Caledonia, with the Front de la Libération Nationale Kanak et Socialiste; Tahiti, where the position of the Independence party, Tavini-Huiraatira, is climbing in popularity in the electorate; and even in Tonga, where the Pro-Democracy Movement is addressing the Pacific's most du-rable social hierarchy. Even the leader in independence movements, Western Samoa, has only this decade moved to universal suffrage as opposed to the time-honored trend of matai-suffrage, in which only the chiefs spoke for the people.

These movements bring with them language issues. Interestingly, as the pres-sure for proficiency in English mounts in the postcolonial South Pacific, the omnipresence of francophony is attacked in French territories; and in Aotearoa, the Maori voice is being revived under well-planned linguistic reconstruction and standardization.

Colonial and postcolonial language pressures are in instructive counterbalance. Where the traditional has been devalued in education and literacy through con-tinued colonialism, movements towards linguistic and cultural revival are in evidence. Where economic development is influencing the social order in post-colonial societies, the balance is tipping toward English.

Summary: Cultural Maintenance or Economic Rationalism?

Postcolonial searches for identity have fractured language and culture in impor-tant ways between the traditional, which is socially directed and associated with vernacular language maintenance, and development, which is economic and associated with English. Pacific societies are in flux, supporting searches for a self-sustaining identity. The messages of the Pacific Way put people in the crossfire of somehow conserving tradition with its attendant ceremony and obligation while also working toward development for economic emancipation. Indeed, the Pacific Way has been criticized as an instrument of the indigenous elite to maintain their privileged, socially parasitic lifestyle (Lawson 1996: 4). Indeed, local culture with its social burdens is popularly seen as a virtual impediment to progress.

Pacific Islanders, like the rest of us, are trying to do the best they can to survive. Some of those survival tactics call for a more global, English-facilitated identity, although cultural identities and living languages are, for the most part, surviving. Fortunately, there are countercalls for vernacular revival as well in islands where the language of the people has already been all but silenced by the cultural politics of colonialism. At the dawning of the twenty-first century, both voices are heard.

Questions for Further Thought and Discussion

1. While on a short visit to the beautiful, remote Yasawa Islands (a chain of islands in the west of Fiji), staying in inexpensive backpackers' accommodation, I ask our host about his local Yasawa dialect, making some comparisons with the standard dialect (Bauan) in use on the main island. "Do children learn the Yasawa dialect in school?" I ask, hoping to hear that local teachers can bridge the many language needs of these children, given the vernacular domination of Bauan, the language of eastern high chiefs taught as standard Fijian in school and the overarching place of English in education. "No," he scoffs, "they can get that at home." I listen to the voices around me, tourist and host, speaking and being spoken to in English and wonder how long the local dialect will survive against the inevitable pressure of the dollar, given its exclusion from school learning. Do you think vernacular language maintenance should be important? What support for vernacular maintenance would you suggest for this population of rural, outer island, dialect-speaking Fijians?

2. How could small island states plan for education of elite professionals without jeopardizing mass education or encouraging "brain drain"?

3. One day as I was heading toward the staircase at work (in Suva, Fiji, which is a thriving urban center), I heard a child crying. As I turned into the stairwell, I saw Sala, one of the department secretaries, with a little girl of about four. Sala introduced me to her granddaughter, Mere. Poor Mere had just tripped on the stairs, knocking herself in the teeth and spilling some of her drink. Sala was cleaning her off, wiping up the spilled drink, and doing grandmotherly sorts of things—all in English. Sala is Fijian, as is her granddaughter. When I asked why they were speaking English together, Sala said that they always used English. It was a head start for school. What are the social influences of this behavior?

4. In what ways might urbanization affect language transmission?

5. One of my Samoan students, whose sister I had taught previously at the university, cheerfully pulled out a letter one day. "I've got a letter from Makalita," she said enthusiastically. Remembering Makalita as a delightful and dedicated teacher who had returned to Western Samoa to teach at a large secondary school, I asked her to please give me news of her. "You can read the letter and translate it to me," I said. "No need," she replied, showing me the letter. "We always write in English." How, in your opinion, might these sisters have begun the practice of writing to each other in English, although they speak Samoan together?

6. Suggest ways in which small island states could encourage a culture of print literacy without reinforcing language shift.

7. A taonga (sacred treasure) of Maori culture is the language. The sacredness of the Maori language to the Maori people is a key issue in the revival of Maori in Aotearoa. But along with the impetus to revive the language comes selective practice. Maori is primarily taught and maintained within the Maori community. How might cultural respect for Maori tradition be maintained in the process of mainstreaming the Maori language?

8. How has colonial suppression created renewed interest in language maintenance?

9. Here is the same sentence written in two different dialects of Melanesian Pidgin:

> Dispela haus em i bilong mi. (Tok Pisin)
> Desfala haos hem i blong mi. (Pijin)
> (This is my house.)

What issues have to be considered in language standardization? What benefits would result from the standardization of Melanesian Pidgin? Suggest ways in which orthographic standardization of Melanesian Pidgin could be attempted, bearing in mind that these dialects are spoken in different countries.

10. You have been charged with the responsibility of setting up a television station in a remote Pacific island state. You have a limited budget. The country is multilingual, but the population is largely educated in English. What do you propose to broadcast on your station and where will you get your programs?

Notes

1. However, about 5,000 Tokelauans also live in New Zealand.
2. Speech registers are specialized varieties of language used by a particular group of people which tend to center on a specific vocabulary.
3. A *wantok* is a person who speaks your language. This Melanesian Pidgin word evolves from: 'one talk'. In multilingual Melanesia where there are hundreds of languages, wantoks have a special rapport with each other. The word is metaphorically extended to indicate cultural inclusiveness and is used as a solidarity marker.
4. Melanesian Pidgin is spoken in several forms across much of Melanesia. Melanesian Pidgin came into being as a pidgin—a trade language—and it has become creolized in some urban areas now, that is, a more complex and stable form of the language is learned as a mother tongue. Melanesian Pidgin is spoken as Tok Pisin in Papua New Guinea, Pijin in the Solomon Islands, and Bislama in Vanuatu. It is used as a lingua franca between people who do not speak the same language and has come to be a badge of Melanesian solidarity. Melanesian Pidgin has a vocabulary which comes very largely from English, but it is grammatically structured as a Pacific language.
5. Education in Nauru is conducted in English following a curriculum from the state of Victoria in Australia; education in multilingual Vanuatu is in either English or French (but not both); education in the multilingual Solomon Islands is also largely in English, although there are indications of early provision of some vernacular base for children in the first couple of years of primary school. Bislama has the official status of national language in Vanuatu. However, public sentiment against use of Bislama in education continues to be strong.

Selected Bibliography

Abare, G. R., and V. B. Manukayasi (1996). The practice of the art of literacy in Papua New Guinea. In *Pacific Languages in Education*, F. Mugler and J. Lynch (eds.), 143–153. Suva: University of the South Pacific, Institute of Pacific Studies, Department of Literature and Language; Vanuatu: Pacific Languages Unit.

Benton, R. A. (1981). *The Flight of the Amokura: Oceanic Languages and Formal Education in the South Pacific.* Wellington: New Zealand Council for Educational Research.

Crocombe, M. T. (1994). Women and politics in Polynesia. In *New Politics in the South Pacific,* W. Vom Busch, M. T. Crocombe, R. Crocombe, L. Crowl, T. Deklin, P. Larmour and E. W. Williams (eds.), 185–210. Rarotonga/ Suva: University of the South Pacific, Institute of Pacific Studies; Pacific Islands Political Studies Association.

Crocombe, R. (1976). *The Pacific Way: An Emerging Identity.* Suva: Lotu Pasifika.

Elley, W. B., and F. Mangubhai (1981). *The Impact of a Book Flood in Fiji Primary Schools.* Wellington: New Zealand Council for Educational Research.

Fishman, J. A. (1991). *Reversing Language Shift.* Clevedon, England: Multilingual Matters.

Lasaqa, I. (1984). *The Fijian People: Before and After Independence.* Can-berra: Australian National University.

Lawson, S. (1996). *Tradition Versus Democracy in the South Pacific.* Cambridge: Cambridge University Press.

Lotherington-Woloszyn, H. (1995). Television's emergence as an English as a second language and literacy socializer in Fiji. *Pacific Asian Education,* 7 (1 & 2): 60–66.

―――― (1992). Confronting the ghost of colonialism: Progress and pitfalls in teaching primary ESL in Fiji. In *Teaching and Learning English in Challenging Situations*, B. Wijasuriya and H. Gaudart (eds.), 234–242. Selangor Darul Ehsan: Malaysian English Language Teaching Association.

Lynch, J. (1996). Banned national language: Bislama and formal education in Vanuatu. In *Pacific Languages in Education*, F. Mugler and J. Lynch (eds.), 245–257. Suva: University of the South Pacific, Institute of Pacific Studies, Department of Literature and Language; Vanuatu: Pacific Languages Unit.

Mediansky, F. A. (Ed.) (1995). *Strategic Cooperation and Competition in the Pacific Islands*. Sydney: University of New South Wales, Centre for South Pacific Studies; Pennsylvania State University, Australia-New Zealand Studies Center.

Mugler, F. (1996). 'Vernacular' language teaching in Fiji. In *Pacific Languages in Education*, F. Mugler and J. Lynch (eds.), 273–286. Suva: University of the South Pacific, Institute of Pacific Studies, Department of Literature and Language; Vanuatu: Pacific Languages Unit.

Royce, P. (1993). TVNZ's Pacific service: A new opportunity for broadcast television. *Pacific Islands Communication Journal*, 16 (1): 101–123.

Sanday, J. (1988). *South Pacific Culture and Politics: Notes on Current Issues*. (Working Paper No. 174, Strategic and Defence Studies Centre.)

Canberra: Australian National University, Research School of Pacific Studies.

Sipolo, J. (1990). Development. *Tok Blong Ol Meri Newsletter* 4: 8.

Tavola, H. (1991). *Secondary Education in Fiji: A Key to the Future*. Suva: University of the South Pacific, Institute of Pacific Studies.

Tepari'i, H. (1994). Culture: A product of colonialism in French Polynesia. In *New Politics in the South Pacific*, W. Vom Busch, M. T. Crocombe, R. Crocombe, L. Crowl, T. Deklin, P. Larmour and E. W. Williams (eds.), 55–62. Rarotonga/Suva: University of the South Pacific, Institute for Pacific Studies; Pacific Islands Political Studies Association.

Te Taura Whiri i te Reo Maori [Maori Language Commission] (n.d.a) 'Kia Ita!'. Mimeographed.

―――― (n.d.b) *Maori Language Development through the Ages*. Mimeographed. Wellington.

Topping, D. M. (1992). Literacy and cultural erosion in the Pacific Islands. In *Cross-Cultural Literacy: Global Perspectives on Reading and Writing*, F. Dubin and N. A. Kuhlman (eds.), 19–43. Englewood Cliffs, NJ: Regents/Prentice-Hall.

Uentabo, N. (1992). Decolonization and democracy in the South Pacific. In *Culture and Democracy in the South Pacific*, R. Crocombe, N. Uentabo, A. Ravuvu, and W. Vom Busch (eds.), 1–8. Suva: University of the South Pacific, Institute of Pacific Studies.

Waqa, V. (1995). What we see, where they get it. *Islands Business*, July, 17.

South and Southeast Asia

HAROLD F. SCHIFFMAN

Language and Ethnicity in South and Southeast Asia

In this chapter I take the approach that a study of language and ethnicity in South and Southeast Asia should be focused primarily on establishing some fundamental notions about the *linguistic culture* of the area by which I mean the sum totality of ideas, values, beliefs, attitudes, prejudices, myths, religious strictures, and all the other cultural ideas and expectations that South and Southeast Asians bring from their culture to their dealings with language. Because South and Southeast Asian linguistic culture has long been deeply concerned with the transmission and codification of language(s) used in the area, it is necessary to examine what notions about the value of literacy and the sanctity of texts are current in the area.

To establish notions of what constitutes a linguistic culture, I believe that we need to look not only at the overt manifestations of "high" linguistic culture—the explicit, the de jure, the codified, the written, and the official—but also at covert aspects of the linguistic culture: the implicit, de facto, unstated, unofficial, perhaps "folk-cultural" aspects of the linguistic culture.

For example, in Nagaland in northeast India (Sreedhar 1974), there exists a situation involving the overt use of English and covert use of Nagamese in the schools of the state as a kind of linguistic modus vivendi, a compromise, because Nagamese, although it is a pidgin language that all Naga children understand, lacks the prestige to be fitting as an official language of education for the state. Assamese, though known by many, is not acceptable for political reasons, so English, prestigious and neutral, makes a nice face-saving solution. In Nagaland, the covert use of Nagamese as the (unofficial, but de facto) language of explanation (whereas English functions as the official overt language of education), rather than being subversive, is supported at all levels by majority culture members and is only in conflict

431

with English when squabbles over the use of other languages (e.g., in the courts) arise. In other polities, there may be promotive use of a particular language although it is never identified as official, just as English, never officialized in the United States, is nevertheless perceived as official by almost everybody. Thus on the island of Madura in Indonesia, Madurese is typically used as the explanatory language of education, though Bahasa Indonesia is supposedly the only official language used in teaching. This is a kind of bilingual behavior that usually is not described in overt ways.

Although I have identified only two kinds of covert policies ("promotive/supportive" and "subversive"), one could conceive of other possibilities that might be applicable in other linguistic cultures. I want only to show that the area at one point in its history had a set of ideas about language that recognized multilingual diversity but that the advent of colonialism brought in ideas about appropriate language use ("monism") that were no longer in tune with its long-standing linguistic culture. The final result was overt policies that were dramatically out of line with the general linguistic cultures of the area.

Linguistic Culture and Ethnicity in South and Southeast Asia

It is no secret that South and Southeast Asian cultures are of extreme linguistic diversity, the parameters of which are on a scale and of a nature that are difficult for someone who is accustomed to conditions in a Western monolingual "egalitarian" society to imagine (Shapiro and Schiffman 1981). Not only is there great diversity and complexity, but also the cultures are highly concerned with language; they have been concerned with language, with the transmission of culture through language, and with the codification and regulation of language from earliest times. The very existence of the earliest texts as we know them today is dependent on this concern for language and its control. That is, the existence of these concerns, myths, attitudes, and elaborate cultural "baggage" about language are evidence for what I call not just linguistic culture but a highly developed, deeply seated, long-standing tradition of linguistic culture. We have these texts today because the culture found it important to preserve them and, in fact, to devote great resources to the task of preserving them.

In India, language is tied to religion; it is affiliated with caste and social structure; it differs from region to region and group to group; and it cannot be understood without reference to the long recorded history of the region. As far as this applies to Southeast Asia, we must note that Indic culture and religion was brought to the area before the arrival of Buddhism (in the early centuries of the Common Era) and that current expressions of, for example, Buddhism in Thailand and Islam in Indonesia are highly syncretic, incorporating pre-Buddhist and pre-Islamic elements of Indic culture (especially elements of folk Hinduism), as well as elements of Indic linguistic culture (including large numbers of loanwords), without batting an eyelash.

Language and Ethnicity
in the Ancient "Indies"

Scholars who study language and ethnicity in Europe and correlate it with the renaissance and the rise of nation-states seem to expect South and Southeast Asian language and ethnicity to have their roots in the same phenomena. Superficially, of course, this kind of development can be discerned. Yet there can be no ignoring the existence of classical languages such as Sanskrit, Pali, and Tamil, allegiance to some of which has strong bonds in the area and which cannot be overlooked in the study of their linguistic cultures. Modern linguistics, as developed and practiced in the West since the early nineteenth century, is inextricably linked both to the "discovery" of Sanskrit by Europeans in the late eighteenth century and to the discovery along with it of the Indian grammatical tradition that itself enabled the transmission of this culture. Nevertheless, modern linguists in the subcontinent have had to fight a thousand battles to get modern Indian students of language to disengage themselves from the classical grammarians Panini (ca. 500 B.C.E.) and Tolkappiyanar (ca. 300 C.E.) and look at the modern languages as independent from their classical precursors.

Perhaps the most salient feature of ancient Indic linguistic culture was the concern for the preservation of sacred texts and the purity of the language in which they were composed. This concern found support in the society not only for committing the resources (time, human resources, energy, and material resources) for this transmission but also for developing a technique that would guarantee the purity and constancy of the texts. The decision or strategy devised was to commit the sacred texts to memory and to transmit them orally but in a highly controlled way that was rightly felt to be the only way to avoid the introduction of error into the texts. As anyone who has witnessed a demonstration of this technique can attest, the outcome seems to be fairly foolproof, perhaps better than via literacy and handwritten transmission (particularly where books and literacy are rare), in which scribal error and individual additions and emendations can often be introduced.

The reliance on orality is motivated in part by the power of spoken words to invoke the intervention of the gods. In the Indic tradition, if the text has been learned in the proper way and by the proper person, then the power of the word, when spoken, is irrevocable—the gods must act and will act. Writing the word on paper (or stone, copper, etc.) is not a substitute for pronouncing it. The utterance of an invocation is thus automatically what modern speech-act theorists would call a *performative* speech act. In the saying of the word, something is also *done*, and it cannot be undone. (Indian literature is full of tales in which a word was misused, uttered capriciously or wrongly, with mischievous or even disastrous consequences.) The term "magic" comes to mind here, and in some ways the power of words can be seen as such; but this is not mere magic.

Cultural literacy in ancient India, although at first totally oral and focused on the magical power of language, became wrapped up in the issue of transmission and survival of the culture. This has been summarized quite succinctly by Madhav Deshpande:

The origin of the [grammarians'] conception that language is eternal lies in the Brahmanical concern for preservation of the Vedas which the [priesthood] shared with the Sanskrit grammarians. However, this conception of eternality of language is not a universal principle, but it applies only to Sanskrit. To be more specific, only the Sanskrit language is the eternal language, while all the *apabhramsa* "fallen, substandard" languages are noneternal (1979: 18).

One could give many more examples of this, but it is clear that the groundwork was laid at an early stage for all kinds of infrastructure to preserve the language and that attitudes about high and low language were extant from the earliest recorded history. What we must also assume was that although the Aryan overlords saw themselves at the top, with all other peoples and languages in an undifferentiated mass below them, those below them did not accept this lack of differentiation but in fact applied the same dichotomy to themselves and to people and languages that they felt were below *them*. That is, even *Mlecchas* ("barbarians") such as Tamils also imbibed these attitudes and hierarchized themselves in the same manner. Thus there were high Tamils, there was good Tamil (*centamir*), and there were lower Tamils and "broken" Tamil (*koduntamiR*). We can see that this kind of attitude was prevalent all the way down in the social system—even the tribal peoples of the Nilgiri Hills of South India hierarchize themselves: "In the local caste system of the Nilgiris, the Todas rank highest. Small as the community is, numbering approximately 600 people, it has a most complex social structure" (Emeneau 1964: 332). My point here is not so much to document exhaustively these aspects of Indic linguistic culture but to show that this linguistic culture, often thought of as only a thin veneer or a characteristic of only a tiny minority in the society, is deeply suffused throughout Indic culture, so intrinsically rooted that even illiterates of the lowest socioeconomic groups share the same value system about language, its preservation, perpetuation, and pivotal role in the transmission of the culture. Thus for the preliterate (or only orally literate) Todas, we can discern three distinct varieties of speech: spoken Toda, sung Toda (not automatically comprehensible to someone knowing only spoken Toda), and trance-language Toda (Emeneau 1964).

The preceding observations can be made about linguistic culture in South and Southeast Asia, but they are not the whole story. They have implications that fundamentally affect the symbolism, the instrumentality, and the perpetuation of anything having to do with language.

Diglossia

In this section I focus on one factor, diglossia, to illustrate one aspect of Indic linguistic culture that seems to persist at a covert level, defying all attempts to circumvent it. Diglossia is a sociolinguistic situation in which more than one form of a language interacts with other forms, such that one "high" form (H) is perceived as older, more prestigious, purer, more beautiful, and perhaps the only one deserving to be used for schooling, "high" literature, religion, and so forth. The other, "informal" language (L) is as different from the H variety as are Latin and French, but L has no prestige and is devalued and even despised, although it is the actual "mother tongue" of the population, being learned first and used by all members for colloquial (home, street, bazaar, humorous) purposes. Diglossia as a concept and as a feature of language has been well known since at least the appearance of Ferguson's seminal article (1959), and an extensive literature on the subject attests to its widespread manifestation in the languages of the world, not the least of which is India, classical and modern. To me it is clear that diglossia is so deeply rooted in Indian culture that it is not simply probable that we will find it no matter which language we look at; it is almost an inevitable feature of the Indian linguistic scene. It is not just a concern for purity but for purity of language(s) as a way of maintaining the purity of the channels for the transmission of culture. But the "flip side" of diglossia is that all sorts of things are allowed outside the arena of pure things, as long as they are not dignified by having any attention paid to them.

Diglossias of Various Types

Diglossia of the Ferguson (1959) type (involving the functional complementarity of genetically related language) also implies nongenetic diglossia of the Fishman (1967) type, which then licenses linguistic diversity at the grassroots level. Because diglossias typically reserve their concern for purity and uniformity at the H level but ignore linguistic habits at the L level, an illusion of uniformity and purity is maintained, whereas L-variety diversity can be tolerant of all kinds of things. This system thus unites the well-known diversity-within-unity paradox that Indic linguistic culture is famous for: unity at the top (H), overt level, diversity at the unofficial L-variety level.

Note that the regulation of language here is a kind of covert language policy. It falls within the realm of what is called "corpus planning"—structural control of the H variety in order to control its accuracy. It is also an example of "status" planning, in that it regulates the status of the H variety but not that of the L-variety. In my understanding of language policy, the regulation of the status and corpus of the H-variety is a prime example of overt policy, whereas the informal regulation of L-variety languages is an example of covert policy—it is not the case that there is *no* policy toward the L-varieties but simply that their de facto status is purposely unregulated. I would hold that both of these approaches, the overt and the covert, are deeply rooted in Indian linguistic culture. Both are part of the situation that persisted for centuries, perhaps millennia, as is clear from all the evidence we have from writing about language in the subcontinent.

Occasionally, however, the stability of this H/L dichotomy would be shaken by forces from within or from outside the society. An example of an "inside" force was Buddhism, which profited from the wide gap between the ritual forms of Sanskrit and the spoken vernacular by leaping into the breach and using the L-varieties as vehicles for the dissemination of Buddhism, first in India itself (beginning in the seventh century B.C.E.), then spreading throughout the lands of Southeast Asia (and elsewhere) in the next millennium. Buddhism, by choosing vernacular forms of language wherever it spread, thus empowered languages that previously would not have been written, and our earliest records of Southeast

Asian languages such as Burmese, Thai, Khmer, and Javanese (not to mention some of the Dravidian languages and Sinhala) appear with the spread of Buddhism.

This turn of events disturbed the system profoundly and led to a shakedown and abandonment of the exclusive dominance of Sanskrit but still allowed diversity to flourish—Buddhist Hybrid Sanskrit, Pali (the canonical language of Buddhism), and other linguistic traditions arose, such as the Dravidian languages (Tamil was already on the ascendant in the South)—but without displacing Sanskrit from its niche. Diversity was preserved.

An outside challenge to India's linguistic culture came with the arrival of Islam and the introduction of Persian as the "official" language of the Mugal Empire. Needless to say, Persian may have claimed a domain in government, law, and commerce in Mugal India, but it never displaced any other variety from its domains. It did have an effect on spoken Hindustani that resulted in the development of a literary variety written in Perso-Arabic script (Urdu); but again no exclusive domain was claimed by Urdu except perhaps eventually to replace Persian in the scheme of things, especially in postindependence Pakistan.

Even the arrival of European languages (chiefly Portuguese and then English) did not deeply disturb the equilibrium of Indian linguistic culture at first (although English replaced Persian), and even after the development of English-style education, English was not thought of as displacing others but as a variety that would allow the British to better govern India and bring it into the modern world. Most of the population of India was totally unaffected by English education, because they received no education at all in any language. As for Southeast Asia, colonial languages such as French and Dutch did have some effect on the linguistic cultures, but perhaps their greatest effect was to stimulate local elites to develop their own languages (such as Indonesian and Vietnamese) for use as postcolonial languages of education and administration. Today, forty or more years after the departure of the Dutch and French colonial powers, those colonial languages are now spoken by only a small number of very aged people.

Oriental Jones and the "Discovery" of Sanskrit

The discovery (in the late eighteenth century) by Sir William Jones and other Orientalists that Sanskrit was probably related to European languages in a genetic relationship that involved descent from a common source that "perhaps no longer exist[ed]" certainly changed the colonial perception of what was a language and what was not. Sanskrit became a language that was no longer inherently exotic or "Oriental" but a language with deep affinities with European classical and modern languages. It became a sister language, rather than a subaltern language, and its "discovery" had direct impetus for the development of historical and comparative linguistics and modern linguistics in general. It spurred inquiry into the genetic relationships of the daughter (and "granddaughter") languages of Sanskrit by scholars and missionary-grammarians of all sorts, which perhaps raised as many questions as it solved. It encouraged efforts to standardize and modernize Indian vernaculars for use in the administration of the East India Company (and post-1857 mutiny, of British India), and it legitimized the status and aspirations of certain languages and discouraged the hopes of others, as linguists were forced to make decisions of various sorts about what were "real" languages and what were "mere dialects."

But the "Orientalists" were not to prevail on the question of language and ethnicity in the area. Though Jones and others praised Sanskrit for its "wonderful structure, more perfect than the *Greek*, more copious than the *Latin*, and more exquisitely refined than either" (de Bary et al. 1958: 38), these sentiments were not shared by the Anglicists who came later and who lobbied for the exclusive use of English in the governance of India.

Missionary Activity on Behalf of Other Indian Languages

Missionary activity was discouraged in India until the Act of 1813, which allowed, in its thirteenth resolution, "such measures . . . as may tend to the introduction amongst them of useful knowledge, and of religious and moral improvement" (Spear 1958: 526). Almost immediately, we begin to see missionary activity focusing on language, since it is impossible to save souls and otherwise evangelize a population if their language is not known (especially in the Protestant approach.) Thus began the tradition of the missionary-grammarian, the English-educated divines whose classical education (in Greek, Latin, and often Hebrew) had prepared them to look at language within a particular paradigm. The list is too long to even begin to mention, but for each literary language and for many nonliterary ones as well the nineteenth-century production of grammars, dictionaries, guidebooks, textual editions, and so forth is impressive.

The Macaulay Minute and the Imposition of English

Simultaneous with this activity there developed another point of view, which eventually led to the momentous decision to place English education above education in Sanskrit, Arabic, or Persian: the famous (or infamous) "Minute on Education" of 1835, formulated by Thomas Babington Macaulay, according to which government funds would be used to support education in English in India and the curriculum would be based on one prevalent in schools in England. Macaulay felt that "the dialects commonly spoken among the natives of this part of India contain neither literary nor scientific information, and are, moreover, so poor and rude that . . . it will not be easy to translate any valuable work into them" (Macaulay, *Prose and Poetry*, quoted in de Bary 1958: 44). Macaulay and the Anglicists were, of course, strengthened in their resolve by the great interest in English education already evidenced among many educated Indians, such as Rammohun Roya Bengalis, who had founded his own English school. He had once written to the Governor General, Lord

Amherst, to protest the use of government funds to found and support (in 1823) a college for Sanskrit studies. Similarly, in Indonesia, educated elites campaigned vigorously to be allowed to receive a Dutch education, but the Netherlands East India Company opposed this beause it would have allowed Indonesians to occupy positions held by colonials.

The (Re)discovery of Other Roots of Tradition

The debate between the Anglicists and the Orientalists was not ended by the Minute of 1835, because their goals and their constituencies were different. The study of indigenous languages was not suspended with the advent of English education; it continued under the care of traditional pundits (teachers) and missionary-grammarians alike and led in fact to a polarization of language policy that then had to be resolved in postindependence India. In the case of some of languages of the area, it was the missionary-grammarians who helped establish the notion that their languages were separate genetically from Sanskrit. This idea then led to indigenous scholarship on these languages, scholarship that was thus both stimulated by and a reaction against the rise of foreign-language education and the work of "Orientalist" missionary-grammarians.

Language and Ethnicity
in the Postcolonial Period

Even before the various polities of the area began to gain their independence (the Philippines, India and Pakistan, Burma, Ceylon, and Indonesia in the late 1940s and the remainder in the 1950s), there were attempts to evolve policies that would be more suitable to the needs of self-governing nations than those in effect in the colonial period. In Indonesia, the development of a "standard" *Bahasa Indonesia* came about as a reaction to Dutch colonialism, to ensure that there would be some kind of lingua franca that Indonesians could use to even talk about independence. The experience of Japanese occupation helped solidify the instrumental functions of this language. For India, the following developments were factors that had to be taken into consideration.

The elites who had been allowed to function in lower-level administrative jobs during the colonial period all knew the colonial language(s), but knowing English (Dutch, French) was now perceived as a barrier that would prevent most citizens of the newly independent states from sharing rightfully in the rights and responsibilities of independence. The colonial languages were now seen as relics of imperialism and could be done away with, either gradually or abruptly, just as imperialism had been vanquished. In the case of French and Dutch, of course, this was true, and those languages disappeared very quickly in North Vietnam and Indonesia, respectively; in Laos, Cambodia, and South Vietnam, French persisted somewhat longer, but not to the extent that English did in the former British colonies. Policy planners in the former British (and American) colonies in the area seemed to think that, because Britain had been brought to its knees and was no longer a powerful world power, the English language would also suffer the same fate. In the Philippines, admittedly, hopes for supplanting English with a Philippine language such as Tagalog or Pilipino were not as widely shared as some hoped. In polity after polity (India, Pakistan, Malaysia, Singapore) attempts to eradicate English and replace it with some indigenous language seemed to stir up resentments that planners saw only as the complaints of disgruntled elites annoyed at the loss of their privileges.

The postindependence planners seemed to think that "foreign" languages could be eliminated, but they did not think that foreign language policy *models* were going to be a problem. The model that most wished to adopt, of course, was one or another variety of what is known as a *monistic* model, that is, a monolingual (with some minor exceptions) model that enshrined an indigenous language (Indonesian, Hindi, Vietnamese, Tagalog) in the place occupied formerly by a colonial language. In some cases this worked, such as in Indonesia, where consensus had already been reached that the majority language, Javanese, would not do as a national language. In Vietnam, Vietnamese was by far the majority language and had already been "modernized" and standardized under French rule. In India, Malaysia, and the Philippines, however, things were not so easy, and some linguistic minority groups in those polities did not see Hindi, Malay, or Tagalog (Filipino/Pilipino) as "their" language or as expressing their ethnicity, despite efforts to promote the languages in these functions.

The biggest mistake of postindependence language policy in India, to take one example, was not that planners sought a policy that would remove English and better suit Indian circumstances but that they chose another foreign model for their language policy, one that on the surface seemed egalitarian and multilingual but was otherwise ill equipped for Indian circumstances. In addition, they ignored the tremendous power of Indian linguistic culture and its built-in attitudes and assumptions about language, in particular the deep-rooted propensity toward diglossia.

The model chosen by India, of course, was a variant of Soviet language policy (one nationwide official language and many provincial official languages); I have discussed the ways that this was problematical elsewhere (Schiffman 1996: 162ff.). Essentially, what was needed was a flexible and modern language variety that could be easily adapted for education, mass literacy, and scientific and administrative uses, but what happened was that the traditional Indian *literati* took control of the Hindi language and subjected it to puristic strictures, closing the language to modern sources and opening it only to classical Sanskritic sources. This not only made the language useless for the aforementioned purposes but annoyed speakers of other languages, such as Tamil and Bengali. Contrast this with the experience of Indonesian, where loan vocabulary from Dutch, Portuguese, English, Indic languages, and Javanese combine to allow a flexibility and creativity that has made *Bahasa Indonesia* widely known among a multilingual population, of whom only a small percentage are actually mother-tongue speakers of the basic Malay/Indonesian linguistic base of *Bahasa*. Add to the latter the decision (taken during the colonial period) to write this language in a romanized script, and the formula for success indicates a model that other polities might well have emulated.

Three-Language Formula

What, then, is India's language policy today, and what is it an expression of? As Das Gupta (1970) points out, the issue of official language eventually became more than just a language issue; it became a regional issue, because the non-Hindi states were the strongest opponents of it. They attacked the policy promulgated by the national parliament (*lok sabha*) and organized regional opposition to it. As a counterweight to proposals made in the *lok sabha*, a conference of chief ministers of states developed a compromise formula known as the "three-language formula."

According to this proposal, three languages would be taught at the secondary-school level—English, the local language, and Hindi; in Hindi areas, another Indian or European language would be taught. In practice, of course, this proposal has been honored in the breach more than in reality, but it took widespread rioting and loss of life to force even this compromise. Meanwhile, support for Hindi that had previously been accorded to the Congress Party was transferred to other, often rabidly fundamentalist Hindu, parties, thus draining the congress of its traditional support. In actuality, then, in Hindi areas little attention is paid to English and even less to a third language; in non-Hindi areas, such as Tamil Nadu, Hindi is taught *sub rosa* if at all, whereas great support can be found for English (as well as literary Tamil). In other areas, such as Kerala, a more pragmatic outlook allows the teaching of as many languages as are deemed useful.

I would argue that the amorphous three-language formula is in fact consonant with the traditional multilingualism and linguistic diversity of the subcontinent. It fits the linguistic culture of the area, and it rejects the monism of policy planners who have tried to impose imported policies of the Soviet or other types. It does not make the Hindi areas happy, and it may fail to prevent the disintegration of India as we know it; but we have seen in the recent disintegration of the Soviet Union that their language policy did not succeed in making various linguistic groups happy. Therefore, we should not expect it to succeed in India, where it was perhaps doomed from the outset. However, a policy that recognizes historical multilingualism, linguistic diversity, and reverence for ancient classical languages is more likely to succeed than an imported model of any sort.

In the modern postpostcolonial era, in which language issues have been replaced by other allegiances, such as religious bonds, the modus vivendi involves finding a way to accommodate the language of wider communication, that is, the once-hated colonial languages. After experimentation with linguistic exclusivity, even Malaysia has had to admit that English must have a place in the educational system if Malaysians are to share in the fruits of economic development. In Vietnam, after forty disastrous years of following a Soviet model, including a Stalinist language-policy model, Russian is out and English is in, with French now the second foreign language.

In adopting more pragmatic policies toward international languages, some of the polities have lost track of the symbolic function that special languages often have in various polities. India lacks a candidate for the symbolic function, though Sanskrit used to suffice. Now individual languages such as Hindi and Tamil have taken on symbolic functions, and the instrumental value of either language is diminished; the tendency then is for English to take over as the instrumental language, to the detriment of all others. In Singapore, Malay is endowed with the symbolic function (it is the language in which the national anthem is sung), but English is rapidly becoming the lingua franca and even the mother tongue of former speakers of Chinese, Malay, and Tamil.

Guarantees for Linguistic Minorities

One other factor that ought to be mentioned in any discussion of overall linguistic culture is what happens to small linguistic groups that are not given control of a territory or linguistic state but still expect the same rights as larger groups. Many polities in the area contain linguistic minorities that have populations as large as those of such European nations as Denmark or the now-independent Baltic states; but many of these languages will never occupy anything but the L-variety niche in an overall diglossia in which English or another regional language dominates.

Summary: Antiquity, Ubiquity, Orality, Diversity

Students of language and ethnicity in South and Southeast Asia may be well motivated to ask what, if anything, is distinctive about their linguistic cultures and how they are different from those found in other parts of the world. It seems to me that there are basically four features of linguistic culture in the area that make them distinct. These are antiquity, ubiquity, the primacy of the oral tradition, and linguistic diversity.

Antiquity. There are many puristic linguistic traditions in the world, and many linguistic cultures have gone through periods of purism as a result of a perceived threat from some other language. Purism is also often related to a concern for the preservation of holy or magical texts and can be allied with religious fundamentalism of various sorts. What seems distinctive to me about the linguistic cultures of this area (exemplified most typically in the "Indic" tradition) is that they are so old; the language is the bedrock of the culture, not a response to something else. Thus the Sanskritization of Hindi (or Thai, Burmese, or Maithili) and the Pure Tamil Movement both wish to return to a former state, a linguistic ur-paradise, when there was no mixture of language and no strife between people.

Ubiquity. By this I mean the pervasiveness of Indic linguistic cultural norms —the fact that the Sanskrit tradition has a hierarchical view of language. Different versions of the language are specialized for different domains, and diglossia is deeply seated and deeply rooted in all its linguistic subcultures. Values concerning language and its preservation and tradition are shared throughout the area, and multilingualism is pervasive. The tremendous linguistic diversity of the area is therefore not accidental or exceptional; it is a product of the linguistic culture.

Orality. Another cornerstone of Indic-based linguistic culture is surely the reliance on orality and the elaboration of complicated methods of oral transmission of language. This continues to be one of the hardest facts about Indian linguistic culture for outsiders to the tradition to accept, because it contradicts their theoretical notions of what is possible and what is not possible. Were their theories grounded in empirical observation of the linguistic cultures, they might be less skeptical. To most observers who have studied the culture profoundly and to most native speakers of the tradition as well, orality and all it implies in the area's linguistic culture are fundamental and revelatory.

Diversity. I have presented the view that the great linguistic diversity of South and Southeast Asia has been seen as a source of conflict in the postindependence era, as the various polities have attempted to throw off vestiges of colonialism and find a language policy that suits their own conditions and that will help them modernize. But the linguistic diversity of the area can be viewed as not only a problem, not only an impediment to modernization or industrialization, but also as a resource. The linguistic diversity of the area, I contend, is deeply rooted in the linguistic cultures and is in fact a product of the culture, an outcome of cultural policy, rather than a vexatious hindrance. For India, the three-language formula, rather than being a stalemate or a failure of policy, is a negotiated outcome, a middle way between unfettered diversity and monolingualism. It recognizes the value of local linguistic resources and the need for a language of wider communication, indeed, of international communication. It allows different interpretations of the policy, depending on local sentiments and needs. In fact, if left to their own devices, many Indians will learn more than three languages and will expect the same of their children and their children's children.

Questions for Further Thought and Discussion

1. Given that the situation of diglossia adds pedagogical burdens to children who have to learn a written variety of their language that is different from the spoken variety, what is the prognosis for literacy in polities where diglossia is the norm?

2. Do you think that the success of Indonesian in displacing the colonial language (Dutch) and becoming the main vehicle of education and literacy would have been as great if the language it had had to displace had been English?

3. Even though Vietnamese was standardized before French colonialism ended, North and South Vietnam were separated politically for twenty years during the Vietnam War. After the "liberation" of South Vietnam, the North reimposed its control, including the Hanoi "standard" dialect, on the South. Do you think this has engendered any kind of problems for speakers of Saigon Vietnamese?

4. In the Philippines, we can see a diglossic relationship between English and Tagalog (a.k.a. Pilipino/Filipino), but as Tagalog has spread as the language of primary literacy and elementary education, what is likely to be the reaction of speakers of other major Philippine languages, such as Cebuano and Ilokano? Are they likely to see Filipino as a symbol of national unity and ethnic identity?

5. Why do you think that certain South and Southeast Asian nations voluntarily chose Soviet models of language policy at independence, and why have these borrowed models been less effective than a continuation of the colonial model?

6. What are the economic implications of language policies based on puristic nostalgia for an imagined pristine past? (Hint: What is the job market like for people with skills rooted in linguistic norms that have not been current for centuries or even millennia?)

Selected Bibliography

Das Gupta, Jyotirindra (1970). *Language Conflict and National Development: Group Politics and National Language Policy in India*. Berkeley: University of California Press.

De Bary, William T., et al. (eds.) (1958). *Sources of Indian Tradition*. New York: New York University Press.

Deshpande, Madhav M. (1979). *Sociolinguistic Attitudes in India: An Historical Reconstruction*. Ann Arbor: Karoma.

Emeneau, Murray B. (1964). Oral poets of South India—the Todas. In *Language in Culture and Society*, Dell Hymes (ed.), 330–343. New York: Harper & Row.

Ferguson, Charles F. (1959). Diglossia. *Word* 15(2): 325–340.

Fishman, Joshua A. (1967). Bilingualism with and without diglossia; diglossia with and without bilingualism. *Journal of Social Issues* 23(2): 29–38.

Schiffman, Harold F. (1996). *Linguistic Culture and Language Policy*. London: Routledge.

Shapiro, Michael C., and Harold F. Schiffman (1981). *Language and Society in South Asia*. Delhi: Motilal Banarsidass.

Spear, Percival (ed.) (1958). *The Oxford History of India* (3rd ed.). Oxford: Clarendon Press.

Sreedhar, M. V. (1974). *Naga Pidgin: A Sociolinguistic Study of Inter-lingual Communication Pattern in Nagaland*. Mysore: Central Institute for Indian Languages.

Concluding Comments

JOSHUA A. FISHMAN

There have been other books on the topic of language and ethnic identity (indeed, other books with that title; Gudykunst and Schmidt 1988), but none that have sampled the interdisciplinary and the regional perspectives as fully and as widely as has been done in this book. However, the very breadth and diversity of perspectives provided here makes it exceedingly difficult to summarize the views encountered, let alone to do so briefly and simply. Furthermore, the field of ethnicity-related research and theory is particularly alive at this time; the outpouring of scholarly and popular writings related to it is truly torrential and shows little sign of diminishing in the foreseeable future. Clearly, it would be unwise to try to "summarize" any field that is as large, as variegated, and as rapidly evolving as "language and ethnic identity," but a few comments on major points of agreement and disagreement may be in order.

Language

The definitional urge that marks the beginning of many chapters has largely been restrained in connection with "language." The difficulty of impartially making the dialect-versus-language distinction is alluded to in a few cases. ("A language is a dialect with an army and a navy" is a witticism that stems from the field of Yiddish linguistics, and one that neatly indicates the social rather than the linguistic basis of the distinction.) However, a thorough appreciation of the attachment of culture to languages—even world or international languages—is required if we are to do our subject justice. Languages do not just symbolize their associated cultures (as the major symbol system of our species, they obviously come to symbolize the peoples and the cultures that utilize them), and they are not just indexically better suited to their related cultures than are any other languages (indeed, having "grown up together," it would be odd if that were not the case).

What is most unique and basic about the link between language and culture is the fact that in huge areas of real life the language *is* the culture and that neither law nor education nor religion nor government nor politics nor social organization would be possible without it. As a result, even in parts of the world to which Europe's Romantic "love affair" with language has not penetrated (and such areas are becoming fewer and fewer), the association of "the language" with sanctity, with kinship, and with one's innermost feelings and aspirations is encountered (Fishman 1997). A sense of selfhood and society is not only expressed via a particular language but is also interwoven with that language and is part of the very warp and woof of the lay language experience and of the lay sense of language per se.

As with most social phenomena, therefore, a purely structural or "outsider" view of language or of a particular language is grossly insufficient for capturing the "insider" experience of that phenomenon. The fortunes and misfortunes of daily life, the camaraderie of shared challenges, the peak experiences of meaningfulness and the depths of despondency, the hunger for immortality that one's children and grandchildren represent, the recognition of the "sublime otherness" of sanctity—these all need to be accessible via a socially and emotionally realistic definition of language, that is, one that recognizes that language is both an abstract concept and much, since it makes abstract concepts possible, communicable, and recognizable as well. One of the fortunate by-products of studying a field as difficult as language and ethnicity is that it makes us more aware of the intellectual, affective, moral, and affiliative aspects of language per se, over and above what any formal linguistic analysis can discern. Our discussions in this volume make us more aware of how much more subtle and intricate most discussions of language still need to be.

Ethnicity

It may seem strange that so many authors felt called upon to devote definitional attention to the concept of "ethnicity." Undoubtedly that is because so little attention had been devoted to it, not to mention so little consensus being reached in connection with it, by the classic masters of social science inquiry and theory. Ethnicity was a peripheral phenomenon within the grand social theories constructed by Karl Marx (1818–1883), Emile Durkheim (1858–1917), Max Weber (1864–1920), and Talcott Parsons (1902–1979), probably because of their Western-Eurocentric philosophical certainty (born of uniformistic developments in commerce, industry, urban society, and mass communications) that what was basic—and would remain basic—in social life was supraethnic. No wonder then "that not one among the most perceptive thinkers of the 19th century . . . ever predicted" the importance that ethnicity would attain during the twentieth century (Berlin 1992), and no wonder that many of our authors are still struggling with the concept today.

Having long called for a social history of worldwide thought about "ethnicity" (Fishman 1977), I hope I may now be pardoned for insisting on the distinction between the term and the concept. The term *ethnic* (originally also *ethnik[e]* and even *ethnique*) is interesting in its own right. It is an old term in English, having first been attested—according to the *Oxford English Dictionary*—as far back as 1470 ("ethnicity": 1777) and glossed as "heathen, pagan, uncouth, neither Christian nor Jewish" (Fishman et al. 1985: 15). It derives from the Greek *ethnos*, which is first attested to in the Septuagint, the earliest (pre-Christian) Greek translation of the Old Testament, where it is used to translate the Hebrew term which generally represents the negative, morally disobedient, unregulated, and uncontrolled pole of "peopleness" (goy). Even the Latin counterpart term *natio* was used before the Middle Ages for "uncivilized" peoples, the Gentiles, whereas the "chosen people" were the *populus* (Huizinga 1959, Hertz 1994). *Natio* came to be semantically elevated by such cognates as *nation* and *nationality* (thereby leading to the lay reintroduction of "ethnicity" in a negative connotation), just as *ethnos* subsequently lost much of its originally negative aura in some social science usage (ethnography, ethnocognition, ethnosciences, etc.). Nevertheless, the utilization of *ethnicity* only for minority group phenomena, particularly intergroup hostility and incivility, is, in a sense, a continuation of its medieval nonmainstream and pejorative usage.

Although the terms *ethnicity/ethnic groups* may have become more mainstream in the English-speaking world than elsewhere (partially because of the poverty of English with respect to "peopleness" designations, the ambiguity of the terms *people* and *nation/national*, and the greatly diminished acceptability of the term *race*), its popularization elsewhere is probably only a matter of time, given the Anglo-American grip on the world's media. Whether it will ever achieve a more neutral semantic penumbra, roughly equivalent to *nationality* but less state- (i.e., polity-) associated (a distinction that goes back to Max Weber [1922] but which Calhoun [1993] has most recently reemphasized in differentiating ethnicity from nationalism), is more uncertain. Obviously, any scholarly definition that requires ethnicity to evaporate among the French in France and Quebec (where they are in the clear majority), only to emerge in Vermont and Ontario (where they are clearly minorities), leaves much to be desired in terms of identifying the underlying phenomenon to which it refers and the variations and transformations that it subsumes. The preceding is primarily a Western European and U.S. view (see, e.g., Phinney 1996) and is one of many indications that the field is still plagued by "intellectual uncertainty" and "the lack of any dominant paradigm" (Solomos and Black 1995: 403).

Primordial, Essentialist, Abstracted, Imagined, . . .

None of our authors has adopted the classic primordialist position that ethnicity is fixed once and for all and that it has an atavistic power—"the call of the blood"—that draws those characterized by it back to the fold should they attempt to stray. Indeed, none has even adopted the essentialist view that it is a given, like sex and bodily features, acquired by heredity and only mildly malleable thereafter. Actually, the "once and forever" view of ethnicity has had no serious champions among Western scholars since the times of Johann Gottfried Herder (1744–1803) and Ludwig Gumplewitz (1838–1909). Certainly Clifford Geertz, who introduced the term *primordiality* into the modern social science lexicon (1963), by no means subscribed to that position. It nevertheless remains a commonly held position in most cultures throughout the world, and we must all grant that if human beings define categories, whether for themselves or for others, as real, then they are real in their consequences.

Most of our authors have assumed "ethnicity" to be related to behavior and to identity that is generally "adopted and shed according to the requirements of different social situations" (Lal 1995: 421). They would agree with many other scholars that "the boundaries of an ethnic group expand . . . and contract . . . in response to new conditions, different leaders or changed stimuli" (421). In this respect, "ethnic collectivities have a base in reality as solid as that of any other type of social grouping, but from that base many variations can evolve" (Peterson 1997: 273). As for the saliency of ethnicity, whether that of the ethnic revival or of a more fleeting kind, many other investigators have concluded, as have most of our authors, that "individuals are persuaded of the need to confirm a collective sense of identity in the face of threatening economic, political or other social forces" (Wilmsen and McAllister 1996: ix). This, of course, is a phenomenon that is not particularly restricted to cultural minorities, nor does it necessarily make ethnic groups any more basically conflictual (another Weberian inheritance that has troubled this field) than are any of the manifold other memberships that may be affirmed in times of need, be these political party, gender, age, religious, class, or any other memberships.

It has taken the social sciences more than a dozen years to recover from Benedict Anderson's depiction of ethnonational groups as "imagined communities" ([1991] 1983). Just recently, however, Jenkins (1997) finally put it in a way that most of our authors would agree with, namely, that

> although it [ethnicity] is imagined [in the sense that most members will never interact with each other face to face and that, therefore, the group is an abstraction which they must conceive of and identify with], it is not imaginary. . . . Somewhere between irresistible emotion and utter cynicism, neither blindly primordial nor completely manipulable, ethnicity and its allotropes are principles of collective identification and social organization in terms of culture and history, similarity and difference, that show little sign of withering away. . . . It is hard to imagine the social world in their absence. (1997: 169–170)

Of course, other substantive designata have also been suggested, most commonly, purported kinship (yet another contribution of Max Weber) and thereby, the assumption of biological inheritance of widely shared cognitive, affective, and physical characteristics that purportedly make for unique differences between one group and another. Paul James observes that "a person can be institutionally *naturalized* as a national, whereas one still has to be born into ethnicity" (1997: 16), but it is worth remembering that "reethnization" does occur, both on a voluntary and on a forced basis. In any case, from an emphasis on culture, history, purported kinship, patrimony, and uniqueness it is but a short leap to language, the one behavior system that combines, expresses, and symbolizes all of these ideas. But the link to language is discussed more fully later.

Identity

Because of its narrower disciplinary base within social and developmental psychology (which is not to say that it has not been fruitfully illuminated from other perspectives as well), fewer of our authors have tried to cope with the ambiguities and fluidities of "identity." Of course, it is "social identity" that concerns us here, that is, that aspect of identity which Tajfel long ago described as "that part of an individual's self-concept which derives from his [or her] knowledge of his [or her] membership in a social group (or groups), together with the values and emotional significance attached to that membership" (1978: 63). To this Woodward has most recently added the observation that "[social] identities in the contemporary world derive from a multiplicity of sources—from nationality, ethnicity, social class, community, gender. . . . [It] gives us a location in the world and presents the link between us and the society in which we live. . . . Often [it] . . . is most clearly defined by differences, i.e., by what it is not" (1997: 1–2). The "multiplicity" that Woodward mentions must imply that we all have various social identities which we somehow fuse together, so the "what it is not" may vary, sometimes including more and sometimes excluding more than on other occasions.

Certainly several joint ethnicities are sometimes harmoniously combinable (e.g., Franco-Catalan, Swedo-Finn, Finno-Swede, Scotts-Irish, etc. [see Aspinal 1997]). This is because, as Hall has realized, "far from being grounded in a mere 'recovery' of the past, . . . identities are the different ways we are positioned by and position ourselves within the narratives of the past" (1990: 223). This is an extremely important realization, since it indicates that ethnicity need not be an all-or-none game, even though some combinations may be strategically impossible at any given time. Most important of all, in terms of the reiterated accusations that ethnic diversity inevitably leads to civil strife, are the findings to the contrary by many investigators. Park and Miller, as long ago as 1922, took pains to point out that most ethnic movements "represent an effort to increase participation in American life" (1969 [1922]: 43–44). Contemporaries of Park, such as Florian Znaniecki and Louis Wirth, also observed that "those immigrants fared best in the world outside their group, whose community supported them most. . . . Being a respected member of a functional community . . . is of advantage to the individual and to the . . . [larger] whole" (quoted in Lal 1995: 3). Kurt Lewin experimentally confirmed this very point in the 1940s (see, e.g., his 1948 discussion of this point). More recently, Lambert, Mermigis, and Taylor concluded that "the more secure and positive members of a group feel about their identity, the more tolerant they are of other groups" (1986: 50). My own statistical study of the relationship between ethnolinguistic diversity and social strife (Fishman 1989: 605–626) fully bolsters all of the above "paradoxical" interpretations and conclusions.

Nevertheless, all of this seems so counterintuitive to some Americans that they have labeled it the "ethnicity paradox." This is how Lal refers to the conclusion that "the celebration of difference and the assertion of a separate group identity may be valued in and of themselves, as well as being a strategy to improve the self-esteem of members . . . with regard to universal values sought by . . . society at large" (1995: 431). However, this does not seem at all paradoxical to a European scholar who recently observed that

> European identity includes cosmopolitan elements, but cosmopolitanism cannot serve as a simplistic substitute for traditional national identity. . . . The recipe for a member of a national community to become a self-confident European lies not in the denial or neglect of his national collective identity. . . . Somebody who considers him- or herself to be a cosmopolitan at the cost of national identity will hardly be in the position to appreciate the national components in other people's identity, and this can only weaken cooperation among Europeans. (Haarmann 1997, p. 151)

The Link to Language

How are ethnicity per se and ethnic identity more specifically linked to language? If neither ethnicity nor ethnic identity has been definitively defined nor exhaustively investigated, then their link to language must also suffer accordingly, both in theory and in practice. Indeed, the classic masters and founders of the social science disciplines generally ignored language altogether, considering it a constant (like breathing). They believed that it provided no variance to explain or that it was simply a redundancy with respect to ethnicity, both designata being expected to disappear in the more unified future that was presumably just over the horizon. However, several hypotheses have nevertheless been advanced that do relate these three constructs (language, ethnicity, and identity), and, as our authors have amply demonstrated, the relationship between them has recently been more widely attested in most social science disciplines, as well as having long been attested in most parts of the world.

Within the recent theoretical literature that deals with the orbit of ethnicity, Paul James in particular has staked out many positions that implicate language. When he claims that "as part of the 'nation of strangers,' we live its connectedness much more through the abstracting mediations of mass communications and the commodity market than we do at the level of face-to-face" (1997: xi), we must recognize the utter dependence of both of these modern integrative arenas on specific languages. Rather than language becoming less important, the local dubbing of CNN has made it more pervasive and less international-literacy dependent. This will not be the first time that a new means of cross-national integration has also led to greater specificity awareness. We no more experience CNN supralinguistically than we experience Europe supralinguistically. Indeed, even Latin, as James points out, the great supraethnic unifier of the intellectual, the clerical, and the secular elites, "became the means of . . . assert[ing] the richness and the relativity of the vernacular languages, and hence the [self-] marginalization of the old 'truth language'" (1997: 9). Even the Latin term *natio* itself, as Huizinga (1959: 110) points out, came to be used to "indicate an . . . interrelationship of tribe, tongue and region," just as, by the way, did the much earlier Hebrew term *lashon* (people group/language group, as in *romemanu mekol lashon* [thou has raised us above any other people/language]). How, then, should we understand the fact that both the supraethnic and the ethnic grow simultaneously, particularly given that we can all provide many examples of such disparate growth, to the point that neither one nor the other can be questioned? In James's view this is a result of "cultural management," or what has otherwise been called "culture planning," a task to which "language planning" is a vital contributor.

"Cultural management" is, of course, the province of the intelligentsia, language masters one and all. James reminds us that "the emotional evocation by the late medieval poet Petrarch of an abstract place [he] called Italia was expressed long before Italy was politically unified, . . . centuries before . . . industrialization, expansionist capitalism or post-patrimonial administrative apparatus" (1997: 188–189). Only language could evoke a sense of continuity in the midst of modernity's constant discontinuity, of community in the midst of its constant influx of strangers. It is our very time-and-place-bound languages which enable us to move ahead toward global social relations "in a way that does not reduce us to homeless minds . . . or to objects of abstract internationalism" (James 1997: 196). It is languages alone—particularly national and regional languages—that "offer the possibility of positively mediating the local and the global, . . . and meshing nationality and globality" (1997: 197). Clearly, it is no accident that the European Union has adopted a single common currency but has incorporated every national language into its operations and even found some way of recognizing and supporting subnational languages as well (Fishman 1994). This is because, as James underscores, "the processes of globalization have brought to bear new emphases on the local. . . . The fragility of identity has highlighted our relationship to [specific] place and people" (James 1997: xi), both of them being perceptibly specific-language-encumbered. The global and the specific are now more commonly found together, as partial (rather than as exclusive) identities, because they each contribute to different social, emotional, and cognitive needs that are copresent in the same individuals and societies and that are felt to require and to benefit from different languages in order to give them appropriate expression.

Very similar conclusions have been arrived at by several recent investigators of social identity. The most common comment about ethnic identity is to note its changeability in the direction of self-interest. This was commented on even by Cicero and has remained a political truism into modern times, although its constraints also need to be fully recognized. This, then, is the second "ethnic paradox," namely, that something that can be experienced so primordially can also be so modifiable for so many, particularly when change is permitted and rewarded. Nevertheless, James is right to point out that there is definitely a language link to whatever ethnic identity is subscribed to. "Ethnic identity," he stresses, "comprises a number of different components, including self-labeling," by means of which we grapple with "the subjectivities of contemporary social life" (James 1997: xv). McNamara makes this even more explicit when he documents how "changes in social identity are accompanied by changes in language attitudes" (1988: 70). Our forerunners, Gudykunst and Schmidt place the lability of social identity in experimental perspective when they note that "language and ethnic identity are related reciprocally, i.e., language . . . influences the formation of ethnic identity, but ethnic identity also influences language attitudes and language usage" (1988: 1), a view which is not only profoundly antiprimordial but also anti-Herderian (a perspective in which language is always the motor or prime cause). Fanon insightfully pointed out that ethnocultures must "describe, justify and praise the actions through which a people has created itself and keeps itself in existence" (1963: 233). Several authorities (e.g., Hall 1990 and Woodward 1997) have commented on the creative recovery of the past in which ethnic identity engages. Such recovery and creativity are inherently language-based. As Woodward summarizes it, "[ethnic] identities are given meaning through the language and symbolic systems through which they are represented" (1997: 8). Perhaps all that needs to be added to this chorus of awareness is that ethnic identity alone often sings the praises of and actively fosters the language which adds meaning to that identity. Meanwhile, the link to specific languages is something that governments, school systems, military establishments, literatures and the arts, and economic agencies of all kinds—all of them ethnically marked in the modern world—advance not only *by* their work but *in order to* work.

However, the ethnic revival ("return to roots," real, enriched, or fantasized) also calls for recognition of the possible continuity of identity under conditions of complete language shift. This has occurred most notably among American Jews, the Irish, and the Scots, in the Maghreb, among Amerindians and African Americans, and in indigenous Latin America, to name just a few widely scattered examples. What needs to be examined most painstakingly, however, is the question of exactly what "continuity of identity" means. Certainly, continuity of a label applied by groups to themselves or applied by others to a group is not the same, by any means, as continuity of the fine-grained feelings and enactments of identity that some of our authors have described. All should be free, of course, to choose and fashion their own continuity or discontinuity, but there should be no doubt whatsoever that changing the associated language means a drastic change in the content of ethnic identity and behavior, no matter how continuous the label that is attached thereto.

The Ethnic Revival

Most of our authors, whether writing from a disciplinary or from a regional perspective (a bit of both perspectives necessarily being jointly present in all cases), concur that the last third of the twentieth century has been marked by an ethnic revival. Some demur, but others point out that such revivals have occurred before, both regionally and even worldwide. Some claim that Western influences added to local ones in causing the most recent ethnic revival to come about. Others claim that the ethnic revival has already peaked and may now be past its greatest impact. All in all, one comes away with the impression that both globalization and its discontents are deeply implicated in these developments. It is also clear that they are not merely minority-based, since mainstream ethnicity (including mainstream language efforts) have also been given greater attention and more conscious cultivation (in Scandinavia and in the Maghreb, in Canada and in Latin America, in the United States and in Melanesia, in sub-Saharan Africa and in Central Asia) during this period, either as a counterreaction to the revivals or as an accommodative compromise with them.

In some parts of the world the ethnic revival should be related to another massive social trend during the same period, namely the growth of religious fundamentalism. Many religions are experienced locally as ethnoreligions, no matter how global their purview may be, and, like ethnicity, they are vernacular-language-dependent—even when vernaculars are not their scriptural or ritual languages. It would be a mistake, of course, to identify the ethnic revival with conservative religiosity alone (note, e.g., the religiosity-cum-leftism of many Latin American *indigenista* revivalist movements), the same mistake, indeed, that Marxism classically committed when it opposed ethnic awakenings and consolidations. Indeed, the scholars who have denounced the ethnic revival as chauvinist and who have attacked all ethnicity as "false consciousness" (see, e.g., Patterson 1977) have not only been mistaken about ethnicity but have themselves been guilty of the very phenomenon that they have attributed to others, namely, "false consciousness." As Ignatieff has recognized so poignantly, antiethnicity has become the last refuge of cosmopolitan authoritarians, whether of the left or of the right, who seek to force their ideological remedy on others (1994: 196). This attitude is no less reprehensible than forcing an ethnicity on those who do not identify with it, and, what is more, it also usually has a very specific language or cluster of languages associated with it at any particular time and in any particular region.

Another Change

Ethnicity and its link to language are always fully engaged in ongoing social change, notwithstanding the continuity and authenticity emphases that both display. One of the most notable recent changes is the fact that many more intellectuals, both within and without the halls of academia, have adopted a more positive stance toward the roles of language and ethnic identity in social, cultural, and political life. This volume itself is an indication of that, as is the very substantial and very substantive literature mentioned in these concluding comments. It is not that most of these intellectuals have become more ethnic in their own thinking, feeling, or overt behavior (although some have, as their biographical contributions here reveal), but rather that they have acknowledged that ethnicity per se and language and ethnicity in particular are worthy of study, that they will not wither away, and, indeed, that they have many positive manifestations in addition to the negative ones that have long been identified, notwithstanding (or even because of) the continued spread of supraethnic languages of wider communication and the identities associated with this spread. The repertoire range that characterizes more and more of human life includes a role repertoire, a linguisitic repertoire, and an identity repertoire, each in functional balance with the others.

In a century (and even in a decade) marked by ethnic excesses in various parts of the globe, the more evenhanded treatment of ethnicity and the greater awareness of its link to language, to identity, to cultural and intellectual creativity, and, even to globalization represents a change that is welcome indeed. The evils of ethnolinguistic violence will probably never totally disappear—no more than will the evils of science, of religion, of medicine, of the mass media, or of commerce and industry—but the ethnolinguistic link will also always be related to much of what is best and most treasured about humankind. The link between ethnicities and the specific languages that have been traditionally associated with them will always be associated with some of the most positive attributes and achievements of human life.

Selected Bibliography

Aspinal, Peter J. (1997). The conceptual basis of ethnic group terminology and classifications. *Social Science and Medicine* 45: 689–698.

Anderson, Benedict R. (1991 [1983]). *Imagined Communities: Reflections on the Origin and Spread of Nationalism.* London: Verso.

Berling, Isaiah (1972). The bent twig: A note on nationalism. *Foreign Affairs* 51: 11–30.

Calhoun, Craig (1993). Nationalism and ethnicity. *Annual Review of Sociology* 19: 211–239.

Fanon, Frantz (1963). *The Wretched of the Earth.* London: Paladin.

Fishman, Joshua A. (1977). Language, ethnicity and racism. In *Georgetown University Roundtable on Languages and Linguistics*, 297–309. Washington, D.C.: Georgetown University Press.

Fishman, Joshua A. (1989). *Language and Ethnicity in Minority Sociolinguistic Perspective.* Clevedon, England: Multilingual Matters.

Fishman, Joshua A. (1991). Interpolity perspective on the relationships between linguistic heterogeneity, civil strife and per capita gross national product. *Journal of Applied Linguistics* 1: 5–18.

Fishman, Joshua A. (1994). On the limits of ethnolinguistic democracy, in Tove Skutnabb-Kangas and Robert Phillipson (eds.) *Linguistic Human Rights.* Berlin: Mouton de Gruyter, 63–70.

Fishman, Joshua A. (1997). *In Praise of the Beloved Language: A Comparative View of Positive Ethnolinguistic Consciousness.* Berlin: Mouton de Gruyter.

Fishman, Joshua A., David E. Fishman, and Rena Mayerfeld. 1985. Am and goy in the Old Testament. In Joshua A. Fishman, et al. (eds.) *The Rise and Fall of the Ethnic Revival.* Berlin, Mouton, 15–38.

Geertz, Clifford (1963). The integrative revolution; primordial sentiments and civil politics in the new states. In *Old Societies and New States: The Quest for Modernity in Asia and Africa,* C. Geertz (ed.), 105–157. New York: Free Press.

Gudykunst, William B., and Karen L. Schmidt (eds.) (1988). *Language and Ethnic Identity.* Clevedon, England: Multilingual Matters.

Haarmann, Harald (1997). On European identity, fanciful cosmopolitanism and problems of modern nationalism. *Sociolinguistica* 11: 142–152.

Hall, Stuart (1990). Cultural identity and diaspora. In *Identity, Community, Culture, Difference*, J. Rutherford (ed.), 222–237. London: Lawrence and Wishart.

Hertz, Frederik (1944). *Nationality in History and Politics*. London: Kegan Paul.

Huizinga, Johan (1959). *Men and Ideas: History, the Middle Ages, the Renaissance*. New York: Meridian.

Ignatieff, Michael (1994). *Blood and Belonging*. London: Vintage.

James, Paul (1997). *Nation Formation: Towards a Theory of Abstract Community*. London: Sage.

Jenkins, Richard (1997). *Rethinking Ethnicity*. London: Sage.

Keefe, Susan E. (1992). Ethnic identity: The domain of perceptions of and attachment to ethnic groups and cultures. *Human Organization* 51: 35–43.

Lal, Barbara B. (1995). Symbolic interaction theories [of ethnicity]. *American Behavioral Scientist* 38: 421–441.

Lambert, Wallace, Lambros Mermigis, and Donald M. Taylor (1986). Greek Canadian's attitudes toward own group and other Canadian ethnic groups. *Canadian Journal of Behavioural Science* 18: 35–51.

Lewin, Kurt (1948). Self hatred among Jews. In *Resolving Social Conflicts*, G. W. Lewin (ed.), 219–232. New York: Harper.

McNamara, Thomas F. (1988). Language and social identity. In *Language and Ethnic Identity*, W. B. Gudykunst and K. L. Schmidt (eds.), 59–72. Clevedon, England: Multilingual Matters.

Park, Robert E., and H. A. Miller (1969 [1922]). *Old World Traits Transplanted*. New York: Arno.

Patterson, Orlando (1977). *Ethnic Chauvinism: The Reactionary Impulse*. New York: Stein and Day.

Petersen, William (1997). *Ethnicity Counts*. New Brunswick, N.J.: Transaction.

Phinney, Jean S. (1996). When we talk about American ethnic groups, what do we mean? *American Psychologist* 51: 918–927.

Solomos, John, and Les Black (1995). Marxism, racism and ethnicity. *American Behavioral Scientist* 38: 407–420.

Stone, John (1995). Race, ethnicity and the Weberian legacy. *American Behavioral Scientist* 38: 391–406.

Tajfel, Henri (1978). *Differentiation Between Social Groups*. London: Academic Press.

Wilmsen, Edwin N., and Patrick McAllister (eds.) (1996). *The Politics of Difference; Ethnic Premises in a World of Power*. Chicago: University of Chicago Press.

Woodward, Kathryn (ed.) (1997). *Identity and Difference*. London: Sage.

Index

Printed in the United States
72540LV00001B/3